IFIP Advances in Information and Communication Technology 770

IFIP Advances in Information and Communication Technology

The IFIP AICT series publishes state-of-the-art results in the sciences and technologies of information and communication. The scope of the series includes: foundations of computer science; software theory and practice; education; computer applications in technology; communication systems; systems modeling and optimization; information systems; ICT and society; computer systems technology; security and protection in information processing systems; artificial intelligence; and human-computer interaction.

Edited volumes and proceedings of refereed international conferences in computer science and interdisciplinary fields are featured. These results often precede journal publication and represent the most current research.

The principal aim of the IFIP AICT series is to encourage education and the dissemination and exchange of information about all aspects of computing.

More information about this series at https://link.springer.com/bookseries/6102

Luis M. Camarinha-Matos · Angel Ortiz ·
Xavier Boucher · Antonio Lucas Soares
Editors

Hybrid Human-AI Collaborative Networks

26th IFIP WG 5.5 SOCOLNET Working Conference on Virtual Enterprises, PRO-VE 2025
Porto, Portugal, October 27–29, 2025
Proceedings, Part I

Springer

Editors
Luis M. Camarinha-Matos
NOVA University Lisbon
Monte Caparica, Portugal

Xavier Boucher
Mines Saint-Etienne Univ Clermont
Saint-Etienne Cedex, France

Angel Ortiz
Polytechnic University of Valencia
Valencia, Spain

Antonio Lucas Soares
University of Porto
Porto, Portugal

ISSN 1868-4238 ISSN 1868-422X (electronic)
IFIP Advances in Information and Communication Technology
ISBN 978-3-032-05672-6 ISBN 978-3-032-05673-3 (eBook)
https://doi.org/10.1007/978-3-032-05673-3

This Springer imprint is published by the registered company Springer Nature Switzerland AG
The registered company address is: Gewerbestrasse 11, 6330 Cham, Switzerland

Preface

Artificial Intelligence (AI) is profoundly transforming work practices, enabling a wide range of operational tasks to be performed through the synergy of human expertise and machine intelligence. In a globally interconnected economy - where collaboration is increasingly reinforced as a key pillar of development - the design, support, management, and supervision of hybrid human-AI organizational networks present significant scientific challenges.

At the organizational level, hybrid intelligence demands: (i) the integration of artificial systems in the redefinition of goals, roles, and skill distribution; (ii) consistent alignment of AI capabilities with the values and objectives of human-centric organizations; and (iii) the effective management of new hybrid collaborative processes, including addressing human resistance to change.

At the technological level, such organizations require advanced interoperability at the cognitive level, facing critical challenges in data quality and availability, algorithm scalability and adaptability, as well as ensuring trust and transparency in decision-making processes.

Decades of scientific groundwork developed by PRO-VE in the design and management of collaborative networks provide a strong foundation for building hybrid collaborative intelligence. The multidisciplinary nature of the science of collaborative networks enables the tackling of a wide spectrum of organizational and technical challenges, each requiring thoughtful consideration and innovative solutions. On the technical side, key challenges include ensuring effective human-AI integration, scaling AI systems, and fostering trust and transparency. Organizationally, critical aspects involve addressing skill development, managing change, and establishing robust governance frameworks. Successfully balancing these challenges, while upholding ethical standards, is essential for achieving sustainable and impactful outcomes.

PRO-VE 2025 served as a forum for sharing and discussing current developments and experiences on the role of collaborative networks in the era of synergistic intelligence between humans and AI. Contributions were welcomed from a wide range of disciplines, including computer science, industrial and electrical engineering, manufacturing, organizational science, logistics, management, and social sciences, among others.

PRO-VE 2025 was the 26th event in the series of successful conferences, which includes: PRO-VE 1999 (Porto, Portugal), PRO-VE 2000 (Florianopolis, Brazil), PRO-VE 2002 (Sesimbra, Portugal), PRO-VE 2003 (Lugano, Switzerland), PRO-VE 2004 (Toulouse, France), PRO-VE 2005 (Valencia, Spain), PRO-VE 2006 (Helsinki, Finland), PRO-VE 2007 (Guimarães, Portugal), PRO-VE 2008 (Poznań, Poland), PRO-VE 2009 (Thessaloniki, Greece), PRO-VE 2010 (St.-Étienne, France), PRO-VE 2011 (São Paulo, Brazil), PRO-VE 2012 (Bournemouth, UK), PRO-VE 2013 (Dresden, Germany), PROVE 2014 (Amsterdam, The Netherlands), PRO-VE 2015 (Albi, France), PRO-VE 2016 (Porto, Portugal), PRO-VE 2017 (Vicenza, Italy), PRO-VE 2018 (Cardiff, UK),

PRO-VE 2019 (Turin, Italy), PRO-VE 2020 (Valencia, Spain), PRO-VE 2021 (Saint-Étienne, France), PRO-VE 2022 (Lisbon, Portugal), PRO-VE 2023 (Valencia, Spain), and PRO-VE 2024 (Albi, France).

These conference proceedings are organized in two volumes and include 61 selected papers from the 126 PRO-VE 2025 conference submissions. Each paper received an average of 3.4 double-blind reviews. These papers offer a comprehensive overview of the major challenges of Collaborative Networks in the area of AI, organized around the following main topics:

- Society 5.0
- AI as a Driver for Collaboration
- Collaborative Risk and Crisis Management
- AI for Logistics and Supply Chain
- Technologies for Adaptable Collaborative Networks
- People-Centered and AI-Driven Processes
- Multi-agent Systems for Hybrid Human-AI Collaboration
- Collaborative Healthcare Networks
- Human-Robot Collaboration
- Collaborative Workspaces
- Transition towards Collaborative Organizations 5.0
- Trust and Trustworthiness in Hybrid Human-AI Collaboration
- AI-Driven Manufacture-as-a-Service
- AI and Simulation-Supported Decision-Making
- Work Sharing in Human-AI Collaboration
- Collaboration in Sustainability

In line with the longstanding tradition of PRO-VE conferences, we expect this compilation of papers to serve as a valuable resource for those interested in research advancements and emerging applications in the field of collaborative networks. Furthermore, we hope it will assist in identifying future open challenges that merit continued research and development in this evolving domain.

On the occasion of the 26th anniversary of PRO-VE, we extend our deepest appreciation to the PRO-VE International Program Committee for their invaluable contributions. Their dedication, time, and effort were crucial in the careful selection of articles for this conference and in providing insightful and constructive feedback to help authors enhance the quality of their papers. Their support was indispensable in making this 26th anniversary a reality.

July 2025

Luis M. Camarinha-Matos
Angel Ortiz
Xavier Boucher
Antonio Lucas Soares

Organization

PRO-VE 2025 – 26th IFIP Working Conference on VIRTUAL ENTERPRISES
Porto, Portugal, 27–29 October 2025

Conference Chair

António Lucas Soares	University of Porto, Portugal

Program Committee Chair

Luis M. Camarinha-Matos	NOVA University Lisbon, Portugal

Program Committee Co-chairs

Angel Ortiz	Universitat Politècnica de València, Spain
Xavier Boucher	Mines Saint-Étienne, France

Program Committee

Antonio Abreu	Polytechnic Institute of Lisbon, Portugal
Kankam Adu-Kankam	University of Energy and Natural Resources, Ghana
María Del Mar Alemany-Díaz	Universitat Politècnica de València, Spain
Thecle Alix	Institut de Mécanique et d'Ingénierie de Bordeaux, France
Beatriz Andres	Universitat Politècnica de València, Spain
Dario Antonelli	Politecnico di Torino, Italy

Américo Azevedo	University of Porto, Portugal
Thais Baldissera	Instituto Federal Farroupilha, Brazil
Anne-Marie Barthe-Delanoe	IMT Mines Albi, France
Thomas Beach	Cardiff University, UK
Frédérick Bénaben	IMT Mines Albi, France
Peter Bernus	Griffith University, Australia
Marco Bertoni	Blekinge Institute of Technology, Sweden
Valérie Botta-Genoulaz	INSA-Lyon, France
Xavier Boucher	Mines Saint-Étienne, France
Luis M. Camarinha-Matos	NOVA University Lisbon, Portugal
Wojciech Cellary	Poznań University of Economics and Business, Poland
Nicolas Daclin	École des Mines d'Alès, France
Xavier Delorme	ENSM-SE, France
Rafael de La Guardia	Intel, USA
Maria di Mascolo	G-SCOP CNRS, France
Filipa Ferrada	NOVA University Lisbon, Portugal
Adriano Fiorese	UDESC, Brazil
Adrian Florea	'Lucian Blaga' University of Sibiu, Romania
Franck Fontanili	IMT Mines Albi, France
Rosanna Fornasiero	ITIA-CNR, Italy
Gary Fragidis	International Hellenic University, Greece
Cesar Garita	ITCR, Costa Rica
Luis Gomes	NOVA University Lisbon, Portugal
Carlos Gonçalves	Polytechnic Institute of Lisbon, Portugal
Ted Goranson	Sirius-Beta, USA
Juanqiong Gou	Beijing Jiaotong University, China
Paul Grefen	Eindhoven University of Technology, The Netherlands
Frederic Grimaud	Mines Saint-Étienne, France
Marius Huguet	École des Mines de Saint-Etienne, France
Dmitri Ivanov	Berlin School of Economics and Law, Germany
Tomasz Janowski	Gdańsk University of Technology, Poland
Arkadiusz Jurczuk	Bialystok University of Technology, Poland
Adamantios Koumpis	RWTH Aachen, Germany
Matthieu Lauras	IMT Mines Albi, France
Safa Layeb	University of Tunis El Manar, Tunisia
António Lucas Soares	University of Porto, Portugal
Patricia Macedo	Polytechnic Institute of Setúbal, Portugal
Guillaume Martin	IMT Mines Albi, France
Khaled Medini	Mines Saint-Étienne, France
Kyrill Meyer	Institut für Digitale Technologien, Germany

Paulo Miyagi	University of São Paulo, Brazil
Arturo Molina	Tecnológico de Monterrey, Mexico
Aurélie Montarnal	IMT Mines Albi, France
Sina Namaki Araghi	Tarbes University of Technology, France
Ovidiu Noran	Griffith University, Australia
Raphaël Oger	IMT Mines Albi, France
Ana Inês Oliveira	NOVA University Lisbon, Portugal
Martin Ollus	Socolnet, Finland
Angel Ortiz	Universitat Politècnica de València, Spain
A. Luis Osório	Polytechnic Institute of Lisbon, Portugal
Baris Ozkan	Eindhoven University of Technology, The Netherlands
Hervé Panetto	University of Lorraine, France
Iraklis Paraskakis	South-East European Research Centre, Greece
Adam Pawlak	Silesian University of Technology, Poland
Elena Pessot	University of Siena, Italy
Eva Petitdemange	IMT Mines Albi, France
Jorge Pinho Sousa	University of Porto, Portugal
Fabiana Pirola	University of Bergamo, Italy
Raul Poler	Universitat Politècnica de València, Spain
Ricardo Rabelo	Federal University of Santa Catarina, Brazil
André Rocha	NOVA University Lisbon, Portugal
Victor Romero	IMT Mines Albi, France
David Romero	Tecnológico de Monterrey, Mexico
João Rosas	NOVA University Lisbon, Portugal
Hans Schaffers	Radboud University, The Netherlands
Chrysostomos Stylios	University of Ioannina, Greece
Thomas Süße	Bielefeld University of Applied Sciences, Germany
Sergio Terzi	Politecnico di Milano, Italy
Slavisa Tomic	Lusofona University, Portugal
Mamadou Traoré	University of Bordeaux, France
Paula Urze	NOVA University Lisbon, Portugal
Wilfrid Utz	OMILAB gGmbH, Austria
Katri Valkokari	VTT, Finland
Rolando Vallejos	SENAI Goiás, Brazil
Agostino Villa	Politecnico di Torino, Italy
Bernd-Friedrich Voigt	South Westphalia University of Applied Sciences, Germany
Peter Weiß	Pforzheim University, Germany
Stefan Wiesner	Bremer Institut für Produktion und Logistik, Germany

Greg Zacharewicz	IMT Mines Albi, France
Andrea Zangiacomi	ITIA CNR, Italy

Special Session Organizers

Special Session on People-Centred and AI-Driven Processes and Environments of Tomorrow

Elena Pessot	University of Siena, Italy
Daniele Spoladore	National Research Council of Italy, Italy
Raksmey Phan	Mines Saint-Étienne, France

Special Session on Multi-Agent Systems for Hybrid Human-AI Collaboration in Industry

Davide Rua Carneiro	INESC TEC, Portugal
Henrique Diogo Silva	INESC TEC, Portugal

Special Sessions on Collaborative Healthcare Networks: (1) Design, (2) Decision Systems

Franck Fontanili	Mines Albi, France
Safa Layeb	Mines Albi, France
Marius Huguet	Mines Saint-Étienne, France
Sondes Hammami	EniCar, Tunisia

Special Session on Human-Robot Collaboration in Future Enterprises

Sanaz Nikghadam-Hojjati	CTS- UNINOVA, Portugal
Alexandre do Nascimento Silva	Universidade Estadual de Santa Cruz, Brazil
Eda Marchetti	ISTI "A. Faedo" CNR, Italy
Jose Barata	NOVA University Lisbon, Portugal

Special Session on Future Collaborative Workspaces in Organizations 5.0

Arkadiusz Jurczuk	Bialystok University of Technology, Poland
Thomas Süße	Bielefeld University of Applied Sciences, Germany
Adrian Florea	Lucian Blaga University of Sibiu, Romania
Fabiana Pirola	University of Bergamo, Italy

Special Sessions on Transition towards Collaborative Organizations 5.0: (1) Methods, (2) Case Studies

Arkadiusz Jurczuk	Bialystok University of Technology, Poland
Thomas Süße	Bielefeld University of Applied Sciences, Germany
Adrian Florea	Lucian Blaga University of Sibiu, Romania
Fabiana Pirola	University of Bergamo, Italy

Special Session on Trust and Trustworthiness in Hybrid Human-AI Collaborative Networks

Bernd-Friedrich Voigt	South Westphalia University of Applied Sciences, Germany
Wico Mulder	TNO The Netherlands
Thomas Süße	Bielefeld University of Applied Sciences, Germany

Special Session on AI-Driven Manufacturing-as-a-Service

Miguel Ángel Mateo Casali	Polytechnic University of Valencia, Spain
José Ferreira	NOVA University Lisbon, Portugal
Joan Lario Femenia	Polytechnic University of Valencia, Spain

Special Session on AI and Simulation-Supported Decision-Making in Collaborative VUCA Environments

Alessandro Bertoni	Blekinge Institute of Technology, Sweden
Marco Bertoni	Blekinge Institute of Technology, Sweden
Koteshwar Chirumalla	Mälardalen University, Sweden

Special Session on AI-Driven Sliding Work Sharing for Human-Robot / Human-AI Collaboration

Ana Correia	ATB, Germany
Sebastian Scholze	ATB, Germany

Organizing Committee

António Lucas Soares	University of Porto, Portugal (chair)
Filipa Rente Ramalho	INESC TEC, Portugal
Grasiela Almeida	INESC TEC, Portugal
Henrique Diogo Silva	INESC TEC, Portugal
Marta Oliveira	INESC TEC, Portugal
Sthefan Gabriel Berwanger	INESC TEC, Portugal

Technical Sponsors

ifip

IFIP WG 5.5 COVE
Co-Operation infrastructure for Virtual Enterprises and electronic business

SoCol net

Society of Collaborative Networks

Organizational Co-sponsors

U.PORTO
FEUP FACULDADE DE ENGENHARIA
UNIVERSIDADE DO PORTO

INESC TEC

NOVA
NOVA UNIVERSITY
LISBON

UNINOVA
CTS – Center of Technology and Systems

UNIVERSITAT
POLITÈCNICA
DE VALÈNCIA

MINES
Saint-Étienne
Une école de l'IMT

Contents – Part I

People-Centred & AI-Driven Processes and Environments of Tomorrow

Collaborative Healthcare Networks: Design

Collaborative Healthcare Networks: Decision Systems

Contents – Part II

Trust and Trustworthiness in Hybrid Human-AI Collaborative Networks

AI-Driven Manufacturing-as-a-Service

AI-driven Sliding Work Sharing for Human-Robot / Human-AI Collaboration

Impact of Collaboration in Sustainability

Society 5.0 and Collaborative Networks

Hybrid Human-AI Performance Evaluation System for Collaborative Business Ecosystems

Paula Graça[1,2(✉)] and Luis M. Camarinha-Matos[1(✉)]

[1] Faculty of Sciences and Technology and Uninova CTS, NOVA University of Lisbon, Campus de Caparica, 2829-516 Caparica, Portugal
cam@uninova.pt

[2] Instituto Superior de Engenharia de Lisboa, UnIRE - Unit for Innovation and Research in Engineering, 9 Instituto Politécnico de Lisboa, Lisbon, Portugal
paula.graca@isel.pt

Abstract. The growing adoption of artificial intelligence (AI) technologies has significantly transformed organizational behaviour and decision-making processes while simultaneously presenting notable societal challenges. Despite existing concerns, the benefits of AI are well-documented across various domains, including healthcare, manufacturing, and the creative industries. In the context of business ecosystems, this study introduces a simulation-based information system artefact designed to assess and influence inter-organisational collaboration, with the overarching goal of promoting ecosystem sustainability, particularly in environments with limited data availability. The proposed framework functions as a decision-support mechanism, enabling the CBE Manager to perform "what-if" analyses by adjusting the weights of selected performance indicators. AI plays a key role in this system by offering analytical insights through data analysis, pattern recognition, and predictive modelling. These capabilities facilitate evaluating individual and systemic collaborative behaviours across simulated scenarios, thereby informing strategic adjustments intended to foster enhanced performance and sustained collaboration within the ecosystem.

Keywords: Human-AI Collaboration · Collaborative Networks · Business Ecosystem · Performance Evaluation · Artificial Intelligence

1 Introduction

The rapid advancement and widespread adoption of artificial intelligence (AI) technologies have profoundly influenced organizational dynamics and decision-making processes, while also introducing significant societal challenges. Nonetheless, the advantages of AI are well recognized across diverse sectors, including healthcare [1, 2], manufacturing [3, 4], and the creative industry [5, 6], just to name a few.

Within this context—particularly in the domain of business ecosystems—the establishment of robust performance evaluation frameworks underscores the growing need for adaptive and intelligent performance management systems. To address this need, our

Published by Springer Nature Switzerland AG 2026
L. M. Camarinha-Matos et al. (Eds.): PRO-VE 2025, IFIP AICT 770, pp. 3–18, 2026.
https://doi.org/10.1007/978-3-032-05673-3_1

previous work introduced the Performance Assessment and Adjustment Model (PAAM) [7–10], which simulates a business ecosystem, incorporates key performance indicators (KPIs), and includes an influence mechanism that enables managers to guide organizations toward more effective collaboration. The ongoing work initiates the evolution of PAAM by integrating intelligent agents to support decision-makers in achieving more productive and effective management of collaborative business ecosystems (CBEs).

The remainder of the study is structured as follows: Sect. 2 provides a brief review of related literature. Section 3 outlines the research approach, details the PAAM model along with the decision support system, and introduces the key performance indicators and the influence mechanism. Section 4 presents various simulation scenarios and discusses the results. Lastly, Sect. 5 presents concluding remarks, highlighting the core contributions and identifying directions for continued investigation.

2 Related Work

Hybrid collaboration between humans and AI—aimed at enhancing decision-making, productivity, creativity, and problem-solving—has been gaining increasing relevance. By working together, humans and AI agents can improve productivity and decision-making accuracy. While humans contribute judgment, contextual understanding, and ethical reasoning, AI offers execution speed, pattern recognition, and data-driven insights [11].

Several authors have explored these capabilities. For instance, [12] explores the concept of collaborative intelligence, emphasizing how humans and AI can complement each other's strengths to improve decision-making, innovation, and productivity across organizations. In another example, [13] conducted a systematic review of empirical studies on AI-assisted decision-making. However, their findings reveal that current approaches often lack interactivity, emphasizing the need for more user-centred and collaborative designs in AI decision support systems.

On the other hand, agent-based modelling and simulation (ABMS) in innovation ecosystems has the potential to capture complex and dynamic interactions among heterogeneous actors [14]. Intelligent agents in networked environments, particularly in business ecosystems, can be assumed to simulate the behaviour of organisations based on defined roles or delegated responsibilities, functioning as a form of digital twins [15, 16]. As an example, [17] proposes a secure and trusted composite digital twin architecture to support collaborative manufacturing ecosystems by enabling real-time data sharing, decision-making, and resilience across distributed organizations.

3 Performance Evaluation for Collaborative Business Ecosystems

3.1 Research Approach

The aim of this research is to propose a simulation-based information system artefact to evaluate and influence inter-organisational collaboration within business ecosystems, aiming to enhance their sustainability, particularly in data-scarce environments.

This research adopts the Design Science Research (DSR) paradigm [18], which focuses on creating artefacts for practical application [19]. Simulation, involving human participants, computational agents, or hybrid approaches, is commonly used among the various evaluation methods for such artifacts. Notably, studies show that a significant portion of DSR research, about 37%, employs simulation, predominantly through computer-based methods [20].

3.2 The Artefact and Decision Support

The PAAM artefact [9, 10], is a simulation model of a CBE whose foundational logic is built upon: (i) a conceptual model of a business environment comprising organisations simulated by agents with distinct behaviours, based on their collaborative profiles, engaging in interactions and forming connections, i.e., collaborative opportunities, to seize market opportunities (Fig. 1), (ii) a set of performance indicators (Performance Assessment) aimed at measuring collaboration levels among ecosystem participants (Table 1), and (iii) an Influence Mechanism featuring different weights for the performance indicators. The approach supports a decision-making system providing the CBE Manager with a "what-if" mechanism by varying the weights of the adopted performance indicators, expecting to influence the organisations to change their behaviour towards improved performance and sustainability. The process of influence assumes a reaction similar to that of individuals when they are evaluated [10].

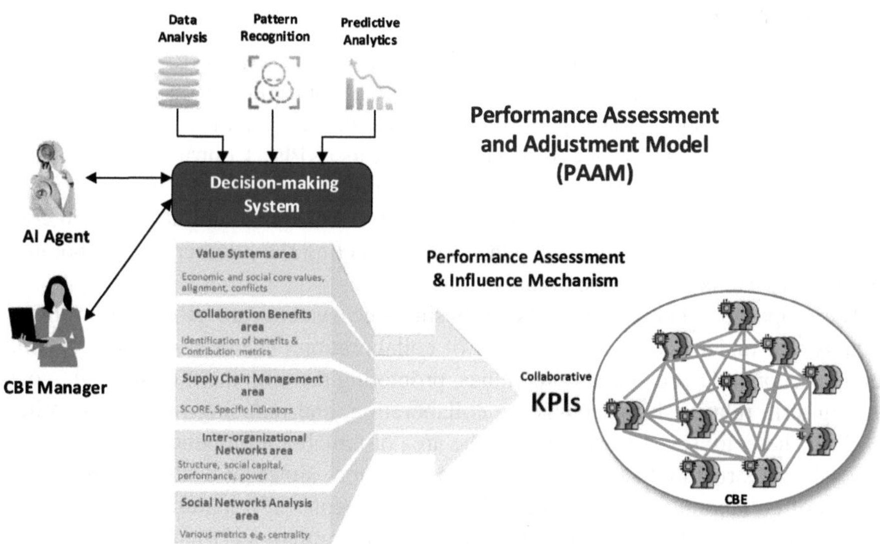

Fig. 1. Conceptual basis of PAAM.

Artificial intelligence can play a key role in supporting the decision-making system by providing the CBE Manager with insights derived from performance measurements of ecosystem collaboration across various simulation scenarios. According to [21], "*Human-AI collaboration (HAIC) in decision-making seeks to establish synergistic partnerships between human decision-makers and AI systems.*"

The AI agent can analyse the collaborative behaviour of individual organisations and the ecosystem as a whole by applying data analysis, pattern recognition, and predictive analytics. Guided by AI-derived insights, the CBE Manager can create various experimental setups by adjusting the weightings of selected performance indicators. These simulation scenarios support the identification of conditions that most effectively encourage organisations to improve their collaborative behaviour.

On the other hand, organisations can be modelled as intelligent agents, a kind of digital twins of organisations [16, 22], capable of making decisions based on predefined rules, market dynamics, or partners' behaviour. Depending on the level of autonomy delegated to the agents, they can pursue specific goals [17], such as improving performance or forming alliances, and adapt over time through induced feedback or self-learning.

To support these intelligent agents, agent-based modelling (ABM) is employed, allowing researchers to analyse collaboration, competition, and innovation dynamics within complex ecosystems. Moreover, agent-based modelling and simulation (ABMS) is particularly well-suited to capture the complex, dynamic, and nonlinear interactions among diverse actors, such as firms and universities, within ecosystems. By simulating local interactions among autonomous agents, ABMS can reveal emergent macro-level patterns such as innovation diffusion, collaboration dynamics, and system resilience [14].

3.3 Performance Assessment

The Performance Assessment of the CBE (Table 1), as proposed in prior studies [7–10], evaluates both the network structure and the strength of connections to assess the benefits of collaboration for individual organisations (O_i) and the ecosystem as a whole (CBE). It refines three collaborative key performance indicators (KPIs), Contribution (CI), Prestige (PI), and Innovation (II), to evaluate collaboration opportunities initiated (CI_{out}) or accepted (CI_{in}) by the organisations in the ecosystem. These collaborative interactions are represented by weighted connections, reflecting the number of collaboration opportunities exchanged by the organisations.

The proposed collaborative KPIs for business ecosystems are grounded in diverse domains that underscore the advantages of collaboration. The area of value systems identifies economic and social core values, promoting the alignment of strategic goals for long-term relationships, enhancing collaboration, and reducing potential conflicts [23–26]. There are several examples in the area of collaboration benefits, including: a proposal of a structured set of performance indicators aimed at evaluating the effectiveness of collaboration within networked environments [27]; a study addressing the contribution of collaborative networks to digital transformation [28]; a research exploring how collaborative networks can drive innovation in healthcare [29]; and real-world cases, illustrating the benefits of collaboration, the factors influencing successful network collaboration, and the value created through collaborative networks.

Concerning the area of supply chain management, SCOR provides standard KPIs organised into a set of performance attributes that enable organisations to benchmark themselves against peers and identify gaps, offering a common language to facilitate continuous improvement and digital transformation [30–33]. On the other hand, a number of specific metrics and indicators have also been proposed in studies focused on

Table 1. Formulation of the adopted collaborative KPIs within the context of the CBE.

Performance Assessment		
Collaborative KPIs for CBEs		
CI – Contribution Indicator	**Considering organisations as units**	
	$CI_i in$ $CI_i out$	Assesses the contribution of organisation O_i by counting the number of collaboration opportunities it has initiated or participated in (C_D – in/out degree centrality). $CI_i in/out = \frac{C_D(O_i)in/out}{C_D(O^*)in/out} = \frac{\sum_j O_{ij}\#CoOp_{ij}in/out}{\max \sum_j O_{ij}\#CoOp_{ij}in/out}$
	Considering the ecosystem as a whole	
	$CI_{CBE}in$ $CI_{CBE}out$	Quantifies the disparity in contributions by assessing the extent to which the organisation with the highest degree centrality (C_D) within the CBE surpasses the contribution levels of other organisations. $CI_{CBE}in/out = \frac{\sum_i [C_D(O^*)in/out - C_D(O_i)in/out]}{C_D(O^*)in/out * (\#O - 1)}$
	CI_{CBE}	Represents the ratio between the total number of collaboration opportunities established within the CBE and the total number of participating organisations. $CI_{CBE} = \frac{\sum_i \#CoOp_i}{\#O}$
PI – Prestige Indicator	**Considering organisations as units**	
	PI_i	Quantifies the prominence or influence of organisation O_i by analysing its involvement in collaboration opportunities, as measured through betweenness centrality (C_B). $PI_i = \frac{C_B(O_i)}{C_B(O^*)} = \frac{\sum_k \sum_j O_{kj}(O_i)}{\max \sum_k \sum_j O_{kj}(O_i)}$
	Considering the ecosystem as a whole	
	PI_{CBE}	Quantifies the disparity in influence by assessing the extent to which the organisation with the highest betweenness centrality (C_B) within the CBE surpasses the prominence levels of other organisations. $PI_{CBE} = \frac{\sum_i [C_B(O^*) - C_B(O_i)]}{C_B(O^*) * (\#O - 1)}$
II – Innovation Indicator	**Considering organisations as units**	
	II_i	Calculates the proportion of new products, services, or patents attributed to organisation O_i relative to the total innovation portfolio. $II_i = \frac{\#NewPd_i}{\#PortPd_i}$
	Considering the ecosystem as a whole	
	II_{CBE}	Assesses the innovation ratio of organisations within the CBE by considering the Spearman correlation coefficient (rS) derived from collaboration activity, including participation in virtual organisations and the resulting development of new products, services, or patents. $II_{CBE} = \frac{\sum \#NewPd_i}{\sum \#PortPd_i} * r_S(\#VO, \#NewPd)$

Note: KPI values are normalised on a scale from 0 to 1, relative to the maximum values observed within the current network.

supply chain collaboration [34–38]. Another important contributing area is that of inter-organisational networks, within which four main dimensions are identified [39]: "structure", which defines how actors are linked and coordinate; "social capital", reflecting the trust and shared norms that sustain collaboration; "performance", capturing the collective ability to generate value and innovate; and "power", which shapes influence, decision-making, and the balance of contributions across the network. Finally, from the area of social network, various metrics of centrality [40–42] can be used to explore the network structure of a business ecosystem [43]. The proposed KPIs, as summarized in Table 1, are based on these multiple contributions.

3.4 Influence Mechanism

The CBE Manager, informed by the KPIs of the Performance Assessment component, can modulate their associated weighting parameters to strategically influence organisational conduct in alignment with predefined objectives, such as the enhancement of collaborative practices, the augmentation of institutional prestige, or the promotion of innovation. These conceptual foundations constitute the core of the Influence Mechanism as proposed in previous publications [7–10], which is likewise integrated into the PAAM system.

Understanding the evolution of networked systems is essential for anticipating shifts in the distribution of benefits and limitations, thereby informing the sustainability of network-derived advantages. In fact, despite all known benefits of collaboration, most business ecosystems fail in the long run [44], which justifies further research on how to sustain collaboration. Network evolution, whether at the inter-organisational, intergroup, or interpersonal level, is shaped by micro-foundations, defined as the underlying drivers of *tie formation*, *persistence*, *dissolution*, and *content* [45]. These act through micro-dynamic mechanisms that modify network membership by altering the strength, nature, and multiplexity of ties [45]. The micro-foundations of dynamic capabilities are essential for scaling sustainability-oriented business models, as they explain how individual actions shape organisational outcomes [46]. This perspective offers insights into how firms develop the ability to sense, seize, and reconfigure in response to business opportunities. Specifically, it highlights how capabilities originate, evolve, and support organisational adaptation, innovation, and competitiveness in dynamic environments [46]. Building on this perspective, it can be argued that collaboration within a CBE evolves similarly, with the characteristics of organisations (micro-foundations) influencing tie dynamics (micro-dynamics) according to their collaborative profiles.

Furthermore, assuming that organisations respond to evaluation similarly to individuals, their collaborative behaviour can be influenced by adjusting the weights of performance indicators, where higher weights correspond to a greater degree of behavioural change. This approach allows the CBE administrator to strategically modulate collaboration in order to enhance the overall performance of the CBE in the desired direction. In this context, an AI-supported decision-making system can play a key role by exploring multiple simulation scenarios to identify the most effective outcomes.

Based on the previous considerations, the organisations in the ecosystem can be grouped according to their collaborative profile. These groups are designated as classes of collaboration willingness and are here generically named *Class A*, *Class B*, *Class C*, and so on. In the current implementation, each class is characterised by three attributes: *contact rate*, *accept rate,* and *new products rate*, as described in Table 2. Each attribute takes a factor between 0 and 1, representing a spectrum from minimal to maximal collaborative behaviour.

Table 2. Characterisation of four collaborative profiles in a hypothetical CBE.

Characterisation of four collaborative profiles in a CBE						
Collaborative Profiles			Class A	Class B	Class C	Class D
Classes of Collaboration Willingness	**Contact rate**	Inclination to propose collaborative initiatives	0,8	0,3	0,6	0,1
	Accept rate	Preparedness to participate in collaborative efforts	0,7	0,8	0,5	0,3
	New products rate	Tendency to adopt innovation-driven collaborative initiatives	0,7	0,3	0,5	0,1

Considering that the weights (*wCI*, *wPI*, *wII*) of each KPI (*CI*, *PI,* and *II*) range from 1 to 5, it is expected that, when the CBE manager adjusts the weights of the adopted indicators, organisations will react by realigning their collaborative profile. In other words, knowing how they are evaluated, organizations will try to "look good" in the picture. This adjustment results in an increase in the values of the affected factors within the collaborative profile, as calculated by formulas (1), (2), and (3) (see Table 3). It is assumed that the *CI*, which is related to ecosystem activity, influences the *contact rate*; the *PI*, associated with prominence or influence within the ecosystem, affects both the *acceptance rate* and the *contact rate*; and the *II*, linked to innovation, influences the *new product rate.*

Table 3. Description of the influence of the collaborative KPIs in the collaborative profile.

KPIs	Influences	Increment
CI wCI = [1..5]	Contact rate	$contact_{rate} += FI_{wCI}$ (1)
PI wPI = [1..5]	Accept rate Contact rate	$accept_{rate} += FI_{wPI}$ (2) $contact_{rate} += FI_{wPI}$
II wII = [1..5]	New products rate	$newprods_{rate} += FI_{wII}$ (3)

Formulas (1), (2), and (3), used to calculate the incremental influence on an organisation's collaborative profile, incorporate a factor of influence ($0 < \text{FI} < 1$), representing a percentage of overall improvement (e.g., 20%). An additional factor ($\pm Fe$) is also included to account for random positive or negative variations attributable to exogenous causes.

$$FI_{wCI} += contact_{rate} * (wCI + wPI) * \frac{FI}{wCI+wPI+wII} + F_e \tag{1}$$

$$FI_{wPI} += accept_{rate} * wPI * \frac{FI}{wCI+wPI+wII} + F_e \tag{2}$$

$$FI_{wII} += newprods_{rate} * wII * \frac{FI}{wCI+wPI+wII} + F_e \tag{3}$$

4 Experimental Evaluation

The experimental evaluation is conducted using hypothetical data, informed by real-world cases, to configure a set of simulation scenarios for the PAAM artefact. Implemented on the AnyLogic platform [47], PAAM integrates ABM to represent autonomous agents (i.e., representatives of organisations), and system dynamics to manage the human resources required for executing tasks associated with the collaboration opportunities created in the business ecosystem. These resources are quantified in person-days and allocated to three types of activities: research and development, consulting, and inner tasks. The collaborative behaviour of the agents in this experiment was simulated using stochastic functions, specifically the Bernoulli distribution [47], parameterised by the classes of willingness (A, B, C, D): *contact rate*, *accept rate*, and *new products rate*. In this context, higher parameter values correspond to a greater probability of yielding a "*yes*" outcome.

Table 4 presents the characterisation of four organisations with distinct collaborative profiles within a hypothetical CBE. An identical distribution of resources across the same activities is assumed for all organisations.

Table 4. Characterisation of organisations of four different collaborative profiles.

Characterisation of four collaborative profiles in a CBE						
Resources (person/days)		Profiles	Class A	Class B	Class C	Class D
Research & Development	220	Contact rate	0,8	0,3	0,6	0,1
Consulting	10 120	Accept rate	0,7	0,8	0,5	0,3
Inner Tasks	3 300	New products rate	0,7	0,3	0,5	0,1

Based on data presented in Table 4, the experiment was configured using the PAAM simulation model with 100 organisations, comprising 25 from each class of willingness. The model was then executed for one year of virtual time, considering 5,000 incoming business opportunities from the market, generated according to a Poisson distribution

[47], which resulted in the links (i.e., exchanged collaboration opportunities) shown in Fig. 2.

The partial outcomes of the experiment, namely, the KPIs measured for the organisations as a result of collaboration within the CBE, are presented in Tables 5 and 6. All values are normalised between 0 and 1. Table 5 shows the KPI outcomes derived from the links established through collaboration within the CBE, before any influence from the indicator weighting. Table 6 presents the results of a simulation experiment in which indicator weights were applied to influence the organisations. These weights can be adjusted to emphasise contribution or prestige indicators to varying degrees. In the experiments conducted, the level of innovation was held constant.

Figure 3 shows graphical representations of the experiments, highlighting the *CIout* indicator.

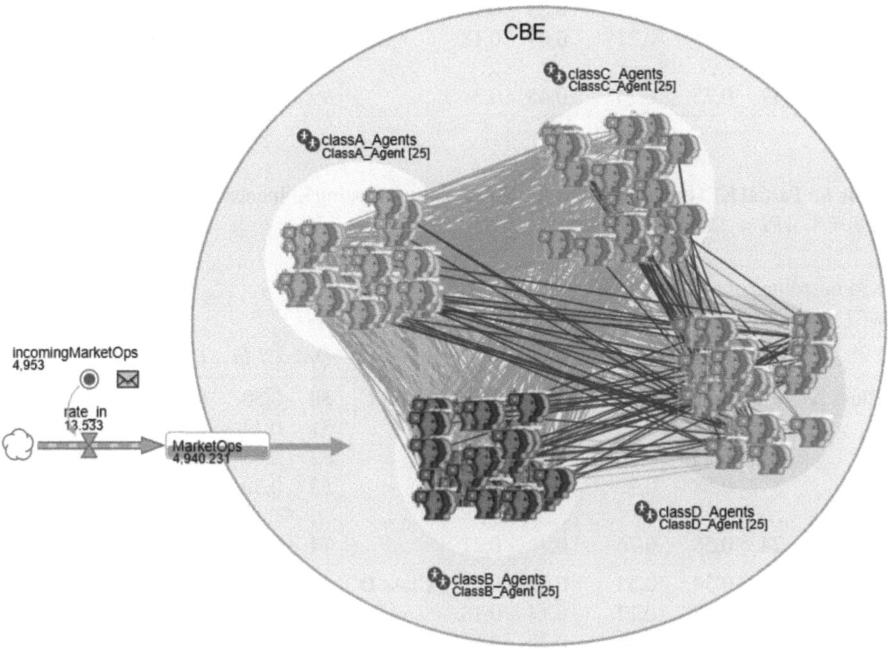

Fig. 2. Simulation scenario generated by the PAAM model, showing the collaboration (links) involving 100 organisations (25 agents of each class of willingness: A, B, C, D) after one year of virtual time.

Figure 3 provides graphical representations of the ecosystem corresponding to different simulation scenarios, showing the *CIout* indicator. Node size reflects $CI_i out$ magnitude (i.e., larger nodes represent higher levels of collaboration), and link strength is weighted by the frequency of exchanged collaboration opportunities.

Figure 3(b) and (d) show that placing a higher weight on the *CI* indicator leads more organisations to engage in collaboration (reflected by an increased number of blue nodes), which is also supported by the KPIs values in Table 7. On one hand, a higher

Table 5. Partial KPI outcomes of the organisations without influencing.

KPI outcomes of the Organisations (before de influence)											
	O_i	$CI_i in$	$CI_i out$	PI_i	II_i		O_i	$CI_i in$	$CI_i out$	PI_i	II_i
Class A	**0**	0,65	0,59	0,55	0,16	**Class C**	**50**	0,60	0,62	0,20	0,14
	1	0,55	0,66	0,45	0,24		**51**	0,60	0,45	0,69	0,21
	2	0,40	0,62	0,51	0,22		**52**	0.30	0,41	0,47	0,41
	3	0,85	0,52	0,55	0,30		**53**	0,70	0,38	0,15	0,32
	…	…	…	…	…		**…**	…	…	…	…
	24	0,60	0,76	0,62	0,15		**74**	0,30	0,62	0,26	0,18
Class B	**25**	0,75	0,10	0,08	0,16	**Class D**	**75**	0,10	0,10	0,00	0,38
	26	0,60	0,17	0,14	0,21		**76**	0,15	0,07	0,02	0,48
	27	1,00	0,17	0,23	0,22		**77**	0,35	0,07	0,01	0,38
	28	0,35	0,21	0,07	0,18		**78**	0,15	0,21	0,06	0,50
	…	…	…	…	…		**…**	…	…	…	…
	49	0,75	0,24	0,45	0,31		**99**	0,45	0,10	0,09	0,48

Table 6. Partial KPI outcomes of the organisations after being influenced by varying the weights: $wCI = 4$, $wPI = 1$ and $wII = 1$.

KPI outcomes of the Organisations $wCI = 4$, $wPI = 1$, $wII = 1$											
	O_i	$CI_i in$	$CI_i out$	PI_i	II_i		O_i	$CI_i in$	$CI_i out$	PI_i	II_i
Class A	**0**	0,75	0,86	0,91	0,26	**Class C**	**50**	0,50	0,76	0,40	0,39
	1	0,38	0,59	0,15	0,37		**51**	0,42	0,59	0,29	0,23
	2	0,83	0,76	0,47	0,19		**52**	0,83	0,52	0,49	0,30
	3	0,58	0,72	0,54	0,43		**53**	0,50	0,72	0,24	0,29
	…	…	…	…	…		**…**	…	…	…	…
	24	0,58	0,76	0,42	0,21		**74**	0,63	0,62	0,40	0,29
Class B	**25**	0,54	0,52	0,23	0,21	**Class D**	**75**	0,29	0,07	0,01	0,68
	26	0,67	0,17	0,14	0,18		**76**	0,38	0,03	0,00	1,12
	27	1,00	0,41	0,37	0,16		**77**	0,42	0,24	0,07	0,48
	28	0,67	0,14	0,05	0,19		**78**	0,50	0,14	0,09	0,57
	…	…	…	…	…		**…**	…	…	…	…
	49	0,79	0,24	0,21	0,39		**99**	0,50	0,07	0,05	0,83

CI_{CBE} (13,1) indicates that more collaboration opportunities were created; on the other hand, a lower $CI_{CBE}out$ (0,55) suggests a more uniform distribution of collaboration across the CBE.

The outcomes of the simulation scenarios, including KPI values and links resulting from collaboration of the organisations in the CBE, can be processed by the AI agent to inform the CBE manager and support a more intelligent and effective decision-making system (Fig. 4).

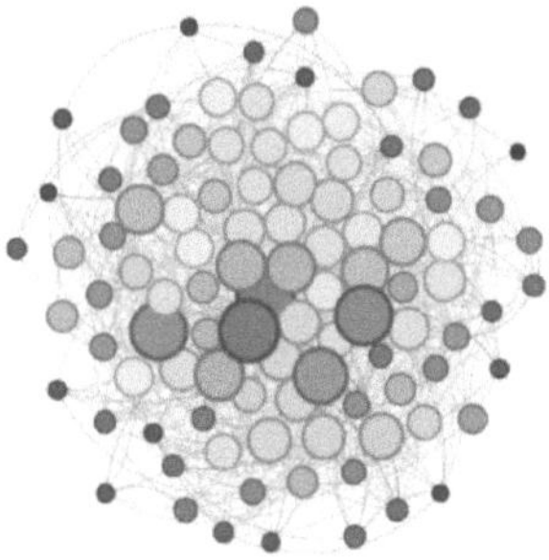

(a) CI_iout measures without influence.

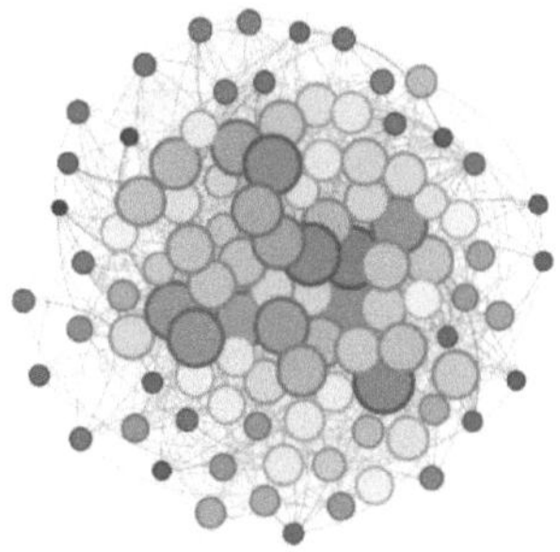

(b) CI_iout measures after the influence: wCI=4, wPI=1, wII=1

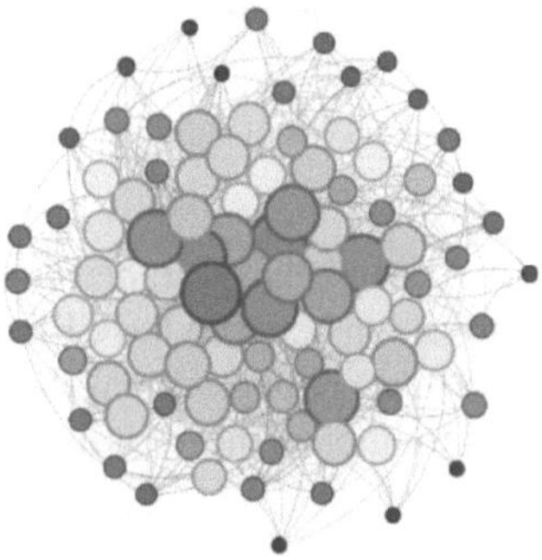

(c) CI_iout measures after the influence: wCI=1, wPI=4, wII=1

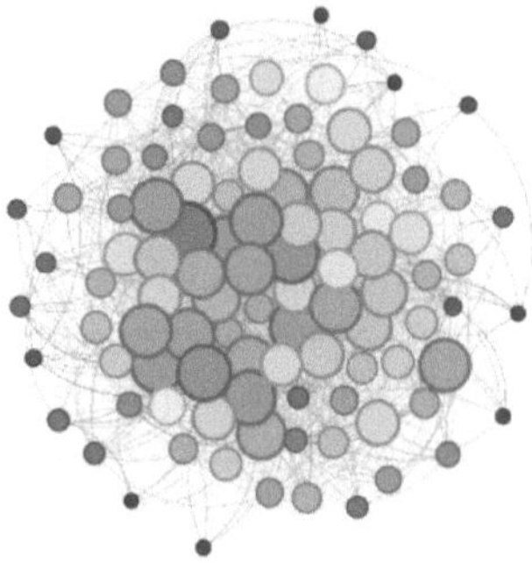

(d) CI_iout measures after the influence: wCI=4, wPI=2, wII=1

Fig. 3. CI_iout values measured before and after applying different KPI weightings.

Table 7. KPI outcomes observed in the CBE after a one-year virtual simulation period.

KPI outcomes of the CBE					
KPIs	CI_{CBE}	$CI_{CBE}in$	$CI_{CBE}out$	PI_{CBE}	II_{CBE}
Before influence	11,0	0,46	0,63	0,71	0,28
After influence $wCI = 4, wPI = 1, wII = 1$	13,1	0,46	0,55	0,72	0,30
After influence $wCI = 1, wPI = 4, wII = 1$	14,1	0,50	0,58	0,69	0,30
After influence $wCI = 4, wPI = 2, wII = 1$	13,1	0,55	0,55	0,75	0,29

The AI agent leverages three complementary techniques: data analysis to understand past and current states of the ecosystem; pattern recognition to identify clusters of organisations that frequently collaborate, underlying structures, trends, or behaviours;

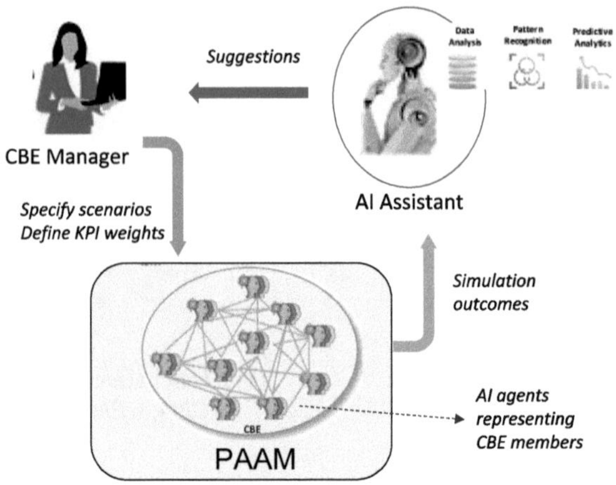

Fig. 4. Interaction CBE Manager – AI Assistant.

and predictive analytics for forecasting future collaboration behaviour, performance, or risks. Figure 5 presents a pipeline illustrating the interaction between the CBE Manager and the AI Assistant, proposing a dashboard to support management actions (both textual and graphical), as well as Business Intelligence tools to implement AI assistance.

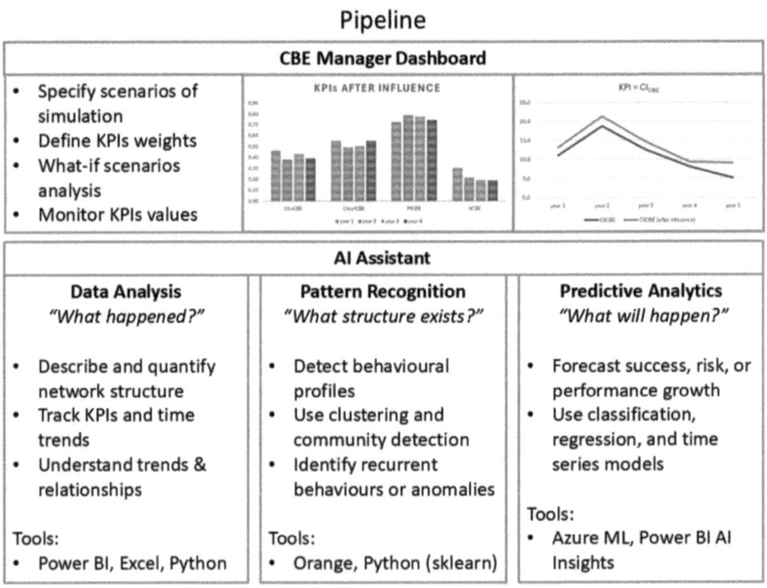

Fig. 5. Illustrative pipeline for the interaction CBE Manager – AI Assistant.

5 Conclusions

This work advances the ongoing development of the PAAM by studying how to integrate intelligent agents into a simulation-based artefact designed to evaluate and influence collaboration within CBEs. Grounded in the principles of hybrid human–AI collaboration, the proposed system enables ecosystem managers to explore "what-if" scenarios and dynamically adjust performance indicator weights to influence organisational behaviours toward improved collective outcomes.

While this study explores the potential integration of AI techniques, namely data analysis, pattern recognition, and predictive analytics, to enhance decision-making support through hybrid human-AI collaboration, the current implementation remains at the simulation and conceptual design stage. The simulation results demonstrate the system's ability to represent diverse organisational profiles and to model the effects of adjusting collaborative KPIs on both individual and ecosystem-wide performance. These findings highlight the promise of PAAM as a foundation for an AI-enabled decision-support tool aimed at promoting sustainable and adaptive collaboration in complex, data-scarce environments.

Future research will focus on effectively incorporating AI-driven components, refining agent behavioural models with real-world data, and enhancing the platform with learning mechanisms to increase responsiveness and decision-making realism.

Acknowledgement. This work was supported in part by the Portuguese FCT program UIDB/00066/2020 (Center of Technology and Systems – CTS).

References

1. Lai, Y., Kankanhalli, A., Ong, D.C.: Human-ai collaboration in healthcare: a review and research agenda. In: Proc. of the 54th Annual Hawaii International Conference on System Sciences, Hawaii International Conference on System Sciences, pp. 390–399, Dept IT Mgmt, Shidler College of Business, Univ Hawaii at Manoa 2404 Maile Way D307, Honolulu, Hawaii, USA (2021)
2. Bienefeld, N., Keller, E., Grote, G.: Human-ai teaming in critical care: a comparative analysis of data scientists' and clinicians' perspectives on ai augmentation and automation. J. Med. Internet Res. (2024). https://doi.org/10.2196/50130
3. Hartikainen, M., Spurava, G., Väänänen, K.: Human-AI collaboration in smart manufacturing: key concepts and framework for design. HHAI 2024: Hybrid Human AI Systems for the Social Good, pp. 162–172 (2024). https://doi.org/10.3233/FAIA240192
4. Wellsandt, S., et al.: Fostering human-AI collaboration with digital intelligent assistance in manufacturing smes. In: Advances in Production Management Systems. Production Management Systems for Responsible Manufacturing, Service, and Logistics Futures, APMS 2023, PT I, vol. 689 of IFIP AICT, pp. 649–661 (2023). https://doi.org/10.1007/978-3-031-43662-8_46
5. Kapoor, S.: Human-AI collaboration in creative industries: Exploring the role of generative models in art and design. Am. J. AI Innovation (2024). https://journals.theusinsight.com/index.php/AJAI/article/view/8
6. Haase, J., Pokutta, S.: Human-AI co-creativity: exploring synergies across levels of creative collaboration (2024). https://arxiv.org/html/2411.12527v1.

7. Graça, P., Camarinha-Matos, L.M.: Performance indicators of a collaborative business ecosystem – a simulation study. In: Technological Innovation for Life Improvement, pp. 3–17, Cham, Switzerland (2020). https://doi.org/10.1007/978-3-030-45124-0_1
8. Graça, P., Camarinha-Matos, L.M.: Evaluating and influencing the performance of a collaborative business ecosystem – a simulation study. In: Boosting Collaborative Networks 4.0, pp. 3–18, Cham, Switzerland (2020). https://doi.org/10.1007/978-3-030-62412-5_1
9. Graça, P., Camarinha-Matos, L.M.: Assessment of sustainable collaboration in collaborative business ecosystems. Computers (2021). https://doi.org/10.3390/computers10120167
10. Graca, P., Camarinha-Matos, L.M.: Influencing collaboration in sustainable business ecosystems. In: Collaborative networks in digitalization and society 5.0, PRO-VE 2023. Vol. 688 of IFIP Advances in Information and Communication Technology, pp. 3–20, Cham, Switzerland (2023). https://doi.org/10.1007/978-3-031-42622-3_1
11. Akinnagbe, O.B.: Human-AI collaboration: Enhancing productivity and decision-making. Int. J. Educ. Manage. Technol. **2**(3), 387–417 (2024). https://doi.org/10.58578/ijemt.v2i3.4209
12. Wilson, H.J., Daugherty, P.R.: Collaborative intelligence: humans and AI are joining forces. Harv. Bus. Rev. **96**(4), 114–123 (2018)
13. Gomez, C., Cho, S.M., Ke, S., Huang, C.-M., Unberath, M.: Human-AI collaboration is not very collaborative yet: a taxonomy of interaction patterns in ai-assisted decision making from a systematic review. Front. Comput. Sci. (2025). https://doi.org/10.3389/fcomp.2024.1521066
14. Luciani, F., Ferreira, W.P., Armellini, F., Eulalia, L.A.S.: An outlook on the contribution of agent-based modeling and simulation for innovation ecosystems. The International Society for Professional Innovation Management (ISPIM) 2021 (2021). https://www.proquest.com/conference-papers-proceedings/outlook-on-contribution-agent-based-modeling/docview/2617203303/se-2.
15. Tao, F., Zhang, H., Liu, A., Nee, A.Y.C.: Digital twin in industry: state-of-the-art. IEEE Trans. Industr. Inf. **15**(4), 2405–2415 (2019). https://doi.org/10.1109/TII.2018.2873186
16. Lim, K.Y.H., Zheng, P., Chen, C.-H.: A state-of-the-art survey of digital twin: techniques, engineering product lifecycle management and business innovation perspectives. J. Intell. Manuf. **31**(6), 1313–1337 (2020). https://doi.org/10.1007/s10845-019-01512-w
17. Kuruppuarachchi, P.M., Rea, S., McGibney, A.: Trusted and secure composite digital twin architecture for collaborative ecosystems. IET Collaborative Intell. Manuf. (2023). https://doi.org/10.1049/cim2.12070
18. Hevner, A.R., March, S.T., Park, J., Ram, S.: Design science in information systems research. MIS Q. **28**(1), 75–105 (2004). https://doi.org/10.2307/25148625
19. Hevner, A., Chatterjee, S.: Design Science Research in Information Systems, pp. 9–22. Springer US, Boston, MA, (2010). https://doi.org/10.1007/978-1-4419-5653-8_2
20. Nguyen, H.D., Eiring, O., Poo, D.: In-situ simulation in design science research: Evaluation of complex design artifacts. ICIS 2018 Proceedings (2018). https://aisel.aisnet.org/icis2018/design/Presentations/2.
21. Leitão, D., Saleiro, P., Figueiredo, M.A.T., Bizarro, P.: Human-ai collaboration in decision-making: beyond learning to defer (2022). https://doi.org/10.48550/arXiv.2206.13202
22. Rantala, T., Ukko, J., Nasiri, M., Saunila, M.: Shifting focus of value creation through industrial digital twins - from internal application to ecosystem-level utilization. Technovation **125**, 102795 (2023). https://doi.org/10.1016/j.technovation.2023.102795
23. Macedo, P., Camarinha-Matos, L.M.: A qualitative approach to assess the alignment of value systems in collaborative enterprises networks. Comput. Ind. Eng. **64**(1), 412–424 (2013). https://doi.org/10.1016/j.cie.2012.09.019

24. Camarinha-Matos, L.M., Macedo, P.: A conceptual model of value systems in collaborative networks. J. Intell. Manuf. **21**(3), 287–299 (2010). https://doi.org/10.1007/s10845-008-0180-7
25. Andres, B., Macedo, P., Camarinha-Matos, L.M., Poler, R.: Achieving coherence between strategies and value systems in collaborative networks. In: Collaborative Systems for Smart Networked Environments, pp. 261–272, Berlin, Heidelberg, (2014). https://doi.org/10.1007/978-3-662-44745-1_26
26. Camarinha-Matos, L.M., Afsarmanesh, H.: The Evolution Path to Collaborative Networks 4.0, pp. 170–193. Springer International Publishing, Cham, (2021). https://doi.org/10.1007/978-3-030-81701-5_7
27. Camarinha-Matos, L.M., Abreu, A.: A contribution to understand collaboration benefits. In: Emerging Solutions for Future Manufacturing Systems, pp. 287–298, Boston, MA, (2005). https://doi.org/10.1007/0-387-22829-2_30
28. Camarinha-Matos, L.M., Fornasiero, R., Ramezani, J., Ferrada, F.: Collaborative networks: a pillar of digital transformation. Appl. Sci. (2019). https://doi.org/10.3390/app9245431
29. Craven, B.C., et al.: Collaborative networks to achieve innovations in care. J. Spinal Cord Med. **44**(sup1), S5–S16 (2021). https://doi.org/10.1080/10790268.2021.1965449
30. Nguyen, T.T.H.: Measuring supply chain performance using the scor model. Oper. Res. Forum **5**(2), 37 (202). https://doi.org/10.1007/s43069-024-00314-y
31. Lemghari, R., Okar, C., Sarsri, D.: Supply chain performance measurement: a case study about applicability of scor model in automotive industry firm. MATEC Web Conf. **200**, 00016 (2018). https://doi.org/10.1051/matecconf/201820000016
32. Gopal, P.R.C., Thakkar, J.: A review on supply chain performance measures and metrics: 2000–2011. Int. J. Product. Perform. Manag. **61**(5), 518–547 (2012). https://doi.org/10.1108/17410401211232957
33. Mishra, D., Gunasekaran, A., Papadopoulos, T., Dubey, R.: Supply chain performance measures and metrics: a bibliometric study. Benchmarking Int. J. **25**(3), 932–967 (2018). https://doi.org/10.1108/BIJ-08-2017-0224
34. Ramanathan, U., Gunasekaran, A., Subramanian, N.: Supply chain collaboration performance metrics: a conceptual framework. Benchmarking Int. J. **18**(6), 856–872 (2011). https://doi.org/10.1108/14635771111180734
35. Ramanathan, U., Gunasekaran, A.: Supply chain collaboration: impact of success in long-term partnerships. Int. J. Prod. Econ. **147**, 252–259 (2014). https://doi.org/10.1016/j.ijpe.2012.06.002
36. Ramanathan, U.: Performance of supply chain collaboration - a simulation study. Expert Syst. Appl. **41**(1), 210–220 (2014). https://doi.org/10.1016/j.eswa.2013.07.022
37. Zhong, J., Jia, F., Chen, X., Hong, Y., Yu, Y.: Internal and external collaboration and supply chain performance: a fit approach. Int J Log Res Appl **26**(10), 1267–1284 (2023). https://doi.org/10.1080/13675567.2022.2042226
38. Ho, T., Kumar, A., Shiwakoti, N.: Supply chain collaboration and performance: an empirical study of maturity model. SN Appl. Sci. **2**(4), 726 (2020). https://doi.org/10.1007/s42452-020-2468-y
39. Ceesay, L.B.: Innovation and inter-organizational network: systematic review and bibliometric analysis. Bus. Perspect. Res. **12**(4), 505–522 (2024). https://doi.org/10.1177/22785337221148874
40. Freeman, L.C.: A set of measures of centrality based on betweenness. Sociometry **40**(1), 35–41 (1977). https://doi.org/10.2307/3033543
41. Freeman, L.C.: Centrality in social networks conceptual clarification. Soc. Netw. **1**(3), 215–239 (1978). https://doi.org/10.1016/0378-8733(78)90021-7

42. Opsahl, T., Agneessens, F., Skvoretz, J.: Node centrality in weighted networks: generalizing degree and shortest paths. Soc. Netw. **32**(3), 245–251 (2010). https://doi.org/10.1016/j.socnet.2010.03.006
43. Ribeiro, T.F., Nogueira, R., Chimenti, P.: Integrating business ecosystems and social networks: a case study on sustainable transitions. Sustainability (2024). https://doi.org/10.3390/su162411045
44. Reeves, M., Lotan, H., Legrand, J., Jacobides, M.G.: Chapter 3 how business ecosystems rise (and Often Fall), pp. 27–34. De Gruyter, Berlin, Boston (2022). https://doi.org/10.1515/9783110775167-003
45. Ahuja, G., Soda, G., Zaheer, A.: The genesis and dynamics of organizational networks. Organ. Sci. **23**(2), 434–448 (2012). https://doi.org/10.1287/orsc.1110.0695
46. Mehrabi, S., Mahdad, M., Bijman, J., Cholez, C., Perez Mesa, J.C., Giagnocavo, C.: Microfoundations of dynamic capabilities enabling scaling pathways of sustainability-oriented innovation business models. Bus. Strategy Environ. **34**(1), 849–871 (2025). https://doi.org/10.1002/bse.4004
47. Borshchev, A.: The big book of simulation modeling: multimethod modeling with AnyLogic 6. AnyLogic North America, Illinois, United States, 2013. isbn: 0989573176. https://books.google.pt/books?id=2c5FnwEACAAJ

Extending Personal Data Sovereignty by Enabling Governance of AI Training on Personal Data

Vijon Baraku[1](✉), Iraklis Paraskakis[2,3], Simeon Veloudis[2,3], and Poonam Yadav[1]

[1] Department of Computer Science, University of York, York, UK
vibaraku@seerc.org, poonam.yadav@york.ac.uk
[2] SEERC - South East European Research Centre, Thessaloniki, Greece
{iparaskakis,sveloudis}@seerc.org
[3] CITY College, University of York Europe Campus, Thessaloniki, Greece

Abstract. The practical exercise of personal data sovereignty remains limited, despite the rights established by existing data protection frameworks. Individuals often lack the ability to access and govern their personal data, particularly when it is distributed across organisational systems and used in contexts such as AI model training. This paper discusses the implementation of a data sovereignty framework designed to give individuals practical control over their distributed personal data, especially regarding AI training usage. The framework consists of two components: an Ontology-Based Data Federation (OBDF) system, which enables unified access to distributed data using Schema.org, and a Personal Data Policy Control (PDPC) service that supports detailed governance through extensions to the Open Digital Rights Language (ODRL). In addition to general policy controls, the framework introduces mechanisms to specify AI training restrictions, including prohibitions, algorithm- specific constraints, and purpose limitations expressed through privacy tiers. By combining data federation with enforceable, subject-defined policies, the implementation addresses practical gaps in personal data governance and supports more transparent and accountable data use in AI and beyond.

Keywords: Data Sovereignty · Policy Control · AI Training Restrictions · Data Federation · Trustworthy AI

1 Introduction

In the digital economy, data has become the lifeblood of innovation and technological advancement. A significant category within this data landscape is personal data, which plays an increasingly central role in modern technological systems. Contemporary artificial intelligence systems are trained on vast datasets often containing billions of personal records [1]. In parallel, collaborative networks function by exchanging personal information across organizational boundaries [2]. As AI systems increasingly shape critical

Published by Springer Nature Switzerland AG 2026
L. M. Camarinha-Matos et al. (Eds.): PRO-VE 2025, IFIP AICT 770, pp. 19–35, 2026.
https://doi.org/10.1007/978-3-032-05673-3_2

decisions in healthcare, finance, employment, and governance, the training data underlying these systems directly influences their fairness, accuracy, and trustworthiness [3]. In this context, individual sovereignty over personal data has emerged as a fundamental requirement for maintaining trust in human-AI collaborative networks [4]. Without meaningful control over how their personal information contributes to AI development and decision-making processes, individuals become passive subjects in systems that increasingly govern their lives.

Traditional data protection frameworks, while addressing basic privacy concerns, fall short of providing individuals with the granular control necessary for comprehensive data governance. The European Union's General Data Protection Regulation (GDPR) [5] and the AI Act [6] provide foundational protections but remain relatively coarse-grained for complex data processing scenarios [7]. This limitation becomes particularly evident when organisations seek to use personal data for AI training and development. AI training presents unique challenges that traditional data protection frameworks cannot adequately address: unlike conventional data processing with defined purposes and time limits, AI training transforms personal data into model parameters that persist indefinitely and influence decisions across unpredictable future contexts. Enhanced data protection frameworks specifically designed for AI contexts would enable individuals to express preferences about training methodologies, algorithmic approaches, and model usage constraints, thereby maintaining meaningful control over how their personal information shapes AI systems that increasingly govern critical life decisions.

Consider, for instance, a healthcare provider collecting patient data across multiple hospital systems. While the AI Act provides regulatory oversight for AI systems development and the GDPR establishes data protection principles, patients lack practical means to first identify where their scattered medical data resides across different organisational databases and then specify how this data may be used in AI model training. Even when individuals attempt to exercise their rights, they face significant challenges in understanding the full scope of data held about them and articulating precise restrictions on AI training usage.

This paper presents a discussion and implementation of a novel data sovereignty framework that attempts to address these challenges by enabling individuals to exercise fine-grained control over their personal data across heterogeneous systems. Our solution comprises two integrated components: an Ontology-Based Data Federation (OBDF) system that creates a unified view of personal data scattered across organisational boundaries, and a Personal Data Policy Control (PDPC) service that enables policy management through extensions to the Open Digital Rights Language (ODRL) standard. The framework allows individuals to discover, classify, and govern their personal data through privacy tier templates ranging from public sharing to highly restricted access. Within the context of AI training, individuals can specify constraints such as complete prohibition, algorithm-specific restrictions (federated learning, differential privacy), or purpose-limited usage. This granular control mechanism addresses the trust challenges in hybrid human-AI collaborative networks, where transparency and individual agency are essential prerequisites for effective cooperation. Achieving such transparency requires explainability, individuals must understand how their data governance policies translate into actual AI training restrictions and whether their specified constraints (such as algorithm-specific limitations) are being properly enforced across organisational boundaries.

The remainder of this paper is structured as follows: Sect. 2 provides background on data sovereignty, AI ethics, and trustworthy AI principles. Section 3 details the system architecture and implemented components. Section 4 focuses on the technical implementation of AI training restrictions. Section 5 evaluates our approach against existing frameworks. Section 6 discusses future work, and Sect. 7 concludes the paper.

2 Background

This section explores the key research domains underpinning our work on personal data sovereignty extended to AI training governance. We first examine data sovereignty concepts and existing architectural approaches, as these form the theoretical foundation of our framework. We then investigate ethics and privacy concerns for training AI models, which highlight the specific challenges our work addresses. Finally, we explore explainability and trust in AI systems, as these concepts are central to the acceptance and effectiveness of our proposed sovereignty mechanisms. Together, these three areas establish the context for our implementation and demonstrate the research gap our framework seeks to address.

2.1 Data Sovereignty in the Digital Era

Data sovereignty has emerged as a critical concept in our increasingly data-driven world. [4] define data sovereignty as relating to "meaningful control, ownership, and other claims to data articulated by a variety of agents ranging from individuals to countries". Their comprehensive review of 341 publications identifies how data sovereignty encompasses normative concepts including inclusive deliberation and recognition of fundamental rights of data subjects.

The increasing fragmentation of personal data across multiple systems creates significant challenges for achieving sovereignty. As personal information is distributed across numerous data controllers, individuals struggle to maintain comprehensive awareness and control over their data footprint [8].

Current research has developed two primary architectural approaches to address data sovereignty challenges. The first approach implements personal data stores that centralise an individual's information under their direct control. The Solid project, developed by [9], exemplifies this approach by storing personal data in "pods" that individuals control while granting selective access to applications. This decoupling of data from applications enables greater user control but requires organisations to migrate existing data into the pod ecosystem and applications to be redesigned around pod-based data access rather than direct database connections.

The second approach maintains data in its original location while establishing standardised protocols for secure exchange with usage control. One prominent example of this approach is The International Data Spaces Association (IDSA) with its reference architecture model [2]. This connector-based architecture enables data exchange while ensuring data owners maintain control by automatically enforcing their specified restrictions on how the data can be accessed, processed, and shared.

[10] have specifically addressed data sovereignty in the context of data sharing, proposing it as a normative reference point for responsible and ethically sound data-sharing mechanisms. Despite legislative advances such as the GDPR [5], practical implementation of data sovereignty remains challenging, with significant gaps between theoretical data rights and practical control mechanisms.

2.2 AI Training Ethics and Privacy Concerns

The ethical implications of training AI models on personal data have received increasing attention in research literature. [3] provide a comprehensive map of ethical concerns in data-driven systems, highlighting how AI introduces novel challenges beyond traditional data protection frameworks. These include issues of opacity, algorithmic bias, and challenges to individual autonomy that become particularly acute as AI systems increasingly influence high-stakes decisions.

Current approaches to AI ethics have focused primarily on organisational responsibility rather than individual control. [11] analysed 84 AI ethics guidelines, finding that while transparency and fairness are commonly emphasised principles, mechanisms for individual control over data contributions to AI systems receive limited attention. This creates a gap between aspirational values and practical sovereignty mechanisms.

Privacy-enhancing technologies (PETs) for AI training have emerged to address some of these concerns. Federated learning, as described by [12], enables model training across devices without centralising raw data. Differential privacy, formalised by [1], provides mathematical guarantees of privacy through controlled noise addition. Secure multi-party computation, as described by [13], enables computation over encrypted data.

However, these techniques are typically deployed at the discretion of organisations rather than according to individual preferences. As [14] note in their study of public sector algorithm use, deployment decisions rarely incorporate input from affected individuals. This creates a gap between technical capabilities and practical sovereignty requirements.

Regulatory approaches like the EU AI Act [6] establish important governance requirements but tend to focus on documentation and risk management rather than individual control mechanisms. This regulatory focus, while important, addresses only part of the data sovereignty challenge in AI contexts.

2.3 Trust and Explainability in AI Systems

Explainable AI (XAI) has emerged as a critical field addressing the lack of transparency in modern AI systems. [15] define XAI as techniques that "enable human users to understand, appropriately trust, and effectively manage AI systems". Their comprehensive review establishes how explainability directly contributes to the trustworthiness and adoption of AI technologies.

XAI approaches operate at multiple levels of granularity. [16] categorise these into global explanations that address overall model behaviour and local explanations focused on specific decisions. Local approaches include techniques like LIME (Local Interpretable Model-agnostic Explanations) developed by [17] and SHAP (SHapley Additive exPlanations) by [18].

Research increasingly emphasises the human factors in explainable AI. [19] demonstrates that effective explanations must align with human cognitive processes, being selective, contrastive, and social. This perspective suggests that explanations about data usage should be tailored to individual needs and contexts rather than provided as generic information.

Several studies establish direct connections between explainability and trust.

[20] demonstrates through empirical studies how explanation quality influences user trust in AI systems. However, [21] caution that poorly designed explanations may create false confidence, highlighting the need for rigorous explanation design.

The relationship between XAI and data sovereignty remains underdeveloped in current literature. While [7] propose counterfactual explanations as a mechanism for data subject empowerment, most XAI research focuses on model transparency rather than data usage transparency. This gap represents an important area for research, as comprehensive data sovereignty requires understanding not just how models make decisions but what data influences their development.

The growing literature on trustworthy AI consistently identifies transparency and accountability as core requirements. The European Commission's High-Level Expert Group on AI [22] positions transparency and human oversight as foundational requirements for trustworthy AI. However, achieving genuine human oversight requires both technical explanations and meaningful control over how personal data shapes AI systems.

3 Framework Design

This section presents the design of our data sovereignty framework, which responds directly to the limitations outlined in Sect. 2 and forms the basis for the system implementation described in Sect. 3.

Current approaches to personal data governance struggle to support individual control in environments where data is fragmented across organisational boundaries and used in complex processing scenarios such as AI training. Individuals often do not know where their personal data resides, how it is structured, or how it is being used. Even where regulatory frameworks such as the GDPR or the AI Act establish high-level rights, these are rarely supported by technical mechanisms that make them actionable in practice. Furthermore, the increasing use of personal data in AI model development introduces additional challenges of transparency and persistence, as data influence may remain embedded in model parameters long after the data itself is deleted or access is revoked.

Our framework addresses these challenges through two tightly integrated components: an Ontology-Based Data Federation (OBDF) system and a Personal Data Policy Control (PDPC) service. The OBDF system tackles the problem of fragmented data by enabling organisations to expose structured representations of their internal data using a shared vocabulary based on Schema.org. Rather than requiring data to be moved or centralised, the system creates a virtual, federated view that individuals can query to gain unified access to their personal data across multiple sources. This semantic alignment enables the discovery and interpretation of heterogeneous data while preserving the autonomy of data controllers.

The PDPC service builds on this foundation to enable personal control. Individuals can assign policies to specific data elements, either through predefined privacy tiers or custom rules, using an extended ODRL vocabulary. These policies specify permissions, constraints, and prohibitions that govern actions such as reading, sharing, or using data in automated processing. For AI-specific scenarios, users may allow or disallow training based on algorithm type (e.g., federated learning), purpose (e.g., medical research), or prohibit training entirely.

The framework contributes to explainable and trustworthy AI by making data governance itself transparent and accountable. Unlike conventional XAI techniques, which focus on making model outputs intelligible, our approach introduces a form of upstream explainability: individuals are able to understand how their data is being governed before it enters a model and what constraints apply to its use. This visibility into the training data pipeline complements model-level explanations by clarifying the provenance and policy context of the data used. In line with trustworthy AI principles, the design supports human oversight not by requiring individuals to audit algorithmic decisions after they have been made, but by allowing them to participate in shaping the data that influences those decisions in the first place.

4 System Architecture and Implementation

4.1 Framework Overview

This work presents the practical implementation of the personal data sovereignty framework theoretically established in our previous work [23, 24]. While the earlier paper conceptualised a data sovereignty model and defined research objectives, this implementation demonstrates how these concepts translate into functional systems capable of providing individuals with granular control over their distributed personal data.

The original framework identified four key research objectives: federation of heterogeneous personal data, efficient data annotation and classification, definition of data governance policies, and establishment of trust through transparency. The current implementation addresses the first three objectives, transforming theoretical models into executable systems that enable genuine data sovereignty (Fig. 1).

The system implements two interconnected components that respect existing data storage while creating a unified access layer for individual control. Rather than centralising personal data, the framework creates semantic connections that preserve organisational boundaries while empowering individuals with comprehensive visibility and control across distributed data sources.

The supporting infrastructure includes specialised databases: a System Database for user accounts and authentication, a Triple Store for semantic policies and categories, a Mapping Repository for OBDA files, and External Organisational Databases containing personal data. The Authentication Service provides security infrastructure with distinct roles for Generators (individuals) and Controllers (organisations), enforcing appropriate boundaries while facilitating necessary interactions.

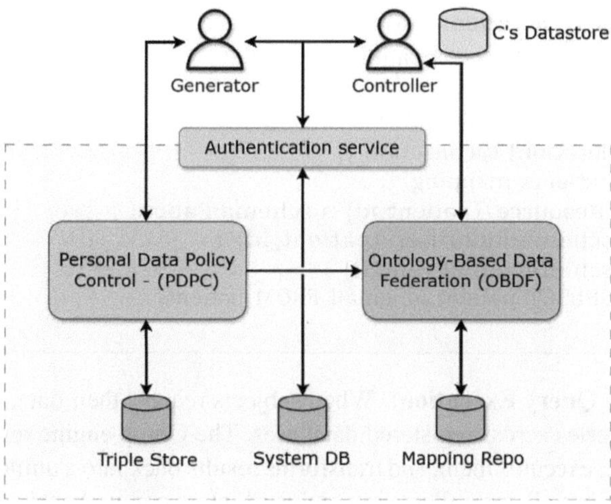

Fig. 1. High level system architecture

4.2 Ontology-Based Data Federation System

This component implements the first research objective, addressing the critical challenge of personal data heterogeneity across organisational boundaries. The necessity of federation stems from a fundamental requirement: individuals cannot exercise meaningful control over data they cannot access or comprehend in a unified manner. Without federation, policy application becomes impossible as subjects lack visibility into their complete data footprint.

The system employs virtual federation rather than data centralisation, preserving data sovereignty by keeping personal data under original organisational control while providing comprehensive visibility across digital footprints. This approach maintains regulatory compliance, avoids storage duplication, and eliminates centralised repository vulnerabilities. We selected Schema.org as our federation ontology due to its comprehensive coverage of personal data domains, widespread adoption in the industry for familiar integration, and machine readable specifications for automated processing.

Federation Workflow: The federation process follows this progression:

Controller Database Registration: Controllers select database types and provide connection parameters. The system tests connectivity, generates unique identifiers, and stores configurations in controller-specific directories.

Schema Discovery and Mapping: The system queries database metadata to extract tables, columns, and relationships. Controllers map these elements to Schema.org classes and properties through the mapping interface. For example, a healthcare provider might map:

- Table ‘patients’ → Schema.org Patient
- Column ‘email’ → Schema.org email

OBDA Mapping Generation: Based on controller mappings, the system generates formal OBDA mapping files compatible with Ontop:

Listing 1.1. OBDA Mapping Structure

```
[MappingDeclaration] @collection [[
mappingId  patients_mapping
target     :Resource/{patient_id} a schema:Patient ;
           schema:identifier {patient_id} ;
           schema:email {email} .
source     SELECT patient_id, email FROM patients
]]
```

Cross-Database Query Execution: When subjects request their data, the system executes parallel queries across registered databases. The Ontop engine rewrites SPARQL queries into SQL, executes them, and transforms results back into a unified RDF-aligned format. Results from all controllers are combined into a comprehensive view.

Data Presentation: The SubjectPage component receives combined results and organises data by source and property for coherent presentation. Each data element maintains provenance information, enabling subjects to understand data distribution across organisations.

4.3 Personal Data Policy Control Service

This component implements the second and third research objectives, enabling efficient data classification and governance policy definition. The PDPC service transforms data visibility into actionable sovereignty through fine-tuned policy management capabilities.

Policy Management Foundation. The system adopts Open Digital Rights Language (ODRL) as its foundation for policy representation, enabling unambiguous interpretation across organisational boundaries. The hierarchical policy organisation includes:

- **Policy Groups**: Collections of permissions, constraints, and consequences
- **Data Assignments**: Mappings connecting groups to specific data elements
- **Templates**: Pre-defined configurations for common scenarios

Policy components encompass permissions (read, use, share, modify, aggregate), constraints (purpose limitations, temporal restrictions), consequences (notifications, compensation), and specialised controls for AI training contexts.

Privacy Tier Templates. To address efficiency requirements, the system provides four progressive privacy tiers:

1. **Tier 1: Public Data** - Minimal restrictions for non-sensitive information
2. **Tier 2: Limited Sharing** - Internal processing only, prohibits external sharing
3. **Tier 3: Sensitive Data** - Restricted usage with privacy-preserving requirements
4. **Tier 4: Highly Restricted** - Minimal access for essential services only

Each tier provides predefined permission sets, constraints, and consequences appropriate for different data sensitivity levels, significantly reducing policy creation complexity while maintaining expressive power.

Policy Creation and Translation. Consider a patient in a healthcare system who wants to protect their medical records. Using the template system, they select Tier 3 (Sensitive Data) for their records. This preference translates into the following ODRL policy:

Listing 1.2. ODRL Policy Example

```
{
  "@context": "http://www.w3.org/ns/odrl.jsonld",
  "@type": "Policy",
  "uid": "http://ontosov.org/policy#policy-medical-records",
  "permission": [{
    "target":
    "http://ontosov.org/policy#data-123-hospital-medical-records",
    "assigner": "http://ontosov.org/policy#subject-123",
    "assignee": "http://ontosov.org/policy#controller-hospital",
    "action": "read",
    "constraint": [{
      "leftOperand": "purpose",
      "operator": "eq",
      "rightOperand": "Necessary Processing"

    }],
    "duty": [{
      "action": "notify",
      "target": "http://ontosov.org/policy#subject-123"
    }]
  }],
  "prohibition": [{
    "target":
    "http://ontosov.org/policy#data-123-hospital-medical-records",
    "assigner": "http://ontosov.org/policy#subject-123",
    "assignee": "http://ontosov.org/policy#allControllers",
    "action": "share"
  }]
}
```

This ODRL representation provides machine-readable policy enforcement while maintaining transparency for subject verification.

5 AI Training Restrictions Implementation

This section details our implementation of AI-specific policy controls, extending the general policy framework to address the growing concerns around AI training on personal data. While the PDPC service provides the foundation for data governance, we developed specialised extensions for AI training restrictions that enable individuals to exercise fine-grained control over how their data participates in machine learning processes.

5.1 Data Sovereignty in AI Training Contexts

AI systems increasingly rely on massive amounts of personal data for training, creating a critical need for individuals to retain sovereignty over how their information contributes to these systems. While traditional data protection focuses on direct usage of personal data, AI training presents unique sovereignty challenges that current frameworks inadequately address.

Personal data sovereignty faces several distinct challenges in AI training contexts:

- **Lack of Transparency**: Individuals rarely receive clear information about how their data influences AI models or what specific training techniques are applied.
- **Algorithmic Diversity**: Different AI training methods offer varying levels of privacy protection, from models that directly incorporate personal data to privacy-preserving techniques like federated learning or differential privacy.
- **Contextual Nuance**: Data appropriate for training in one domain (e.g., medical research) may be considered inappropriate in others (e.g., targeted advertising), yet current frameworks lack mechanisms for expressing contextspecific preferences.
- **Persistence of Influence**: Once personal data contributes to AI training, its impact remains embedded in model parameters indefinitely, even if the original data is deleted. This permanent influence extends beyond the lifespan of the data itself, creating long-term effects that traditional consent mechanisms fail to address.

Consider, for example, a patient who consents to their medical records being used for hospital operations. Under current frameworks, this general consent might permit using their sensitive health data to train clinical decision-support AI systems, insurance cost-prediction models, or even third-party commercial systems without specific knowledge regarding AI training purposes or methods. Without mechanisms for expressing AI training preferences, individuals become passive contributors to systems that increasingly govern important aspects of their lives. As algorithms shape decisions across domains from healthcare to finance, this lack of agency represents a fundamental challenge to personal autonomy and privacy.

Current legal frameworks provide general principles for data protection but offer limited practical mechanisms for individuals to express specific preferences regarding AI training. The GDPR establishes rights such as purpose limitation and data minimisation, while the AI Act introduces governance requirements for AI systems. However, these frameworks alone do not provide individuals with granular, technical means to control how their data participates in AI development.

Our ODRL extensions address this gap by translating legal rights into machine-readable policy expressions specifically designed for AI training contexts. By enabling individuals to specify preferences about algorithmic approaches and training purposes, the system transforms passive data subjects into active participants who can meaningfully shape how their information contributes to AI advancement.

5.2 ODRL Extensions for AI Policies

To implement AI-specific restrictions, we extended the standard ODRL vocabulary with custom terms enabling precise expression of AI training preferences. ODRL extension involves defining new vocabulary terms within a custom namespace that complements the standard specification while maintaining compatibility with existing implementations.

Our extension process followed these steps:

1. Definition of custom namespace for policy extensions
2. Creation of new action types and constraint operands specific to AI training
3. Integration with the standard ODRL processing pipeline
4. Validation to ensure compatibility with standard policy processors The specific extensions include:
   - **aiTraining**: A new action type specifically for machine learning training processes
   - **aiAlgorithm**: A constraint operand specifying permitted training approaches
   - **aiPurpose**: A constraint operand limiting training to specific purposes

These extensions are defined using RDF Schema, allowing them to be semantically linked to the core ODRL model. For example, the aiTraining action is defined as a subclass of the standard ODRL action class, inheriting its properties while adding AI-specific semantics:

Listing 1.3. ODRL Extension Definition

```
@prefix onto: <http://ontosov.org/policy#> .
@prefix odrl: <http://www.w3.org/ns/odrl/2/> .

onto:aiTraining rdf:type odrl:Action;
                rdfs:label "AI Training";
                rdfs:comment "Using data to train artificial
    intelligence models".

 onto:aiAlgorithm rdf:type odrl:LeftOperand;
                 rdfs:label "AI Algorithm";
                 rdfs:comment "Algorithm used in AI training process".
```

This extension mechanism ensures that our AI-specific policies remain compatible with standard ODRL processors while adding the needed expressiveness for AI governance.

5.3 AI Training Restriction Implementation

The system implements a spectrum of AI training restrictions that allow individuals to exercise fine-grained control while maintaining usability. These restrictions integrate with our privacy tier templates, while also supporting complete customization based on individual preferences.

Complete Prohibition. For the most sensitive personal data (Tier 4: Highly Restricted), the system enables complete prohibition of AI training. This creates explicit ODRL prohibitions that prevent any machine learning usage regardless of purpose or methodology.

This prohibition reflects the highest level of protection, appropriate for highly sensitive personal information such as biometric data, financial records, or intimate communications.

Algorithm-Specific Restrictions. For Tier 3 (Sensitive Data), the system implements algorithm-specific constraints that permit AI training only when using privacy-preserving techniques. This balanced approach allows beneficial uses while maintaining strong privacy protections. The implementation supports four predefined algorithm restrictions:

1. **Federated Learning**: Models train on distributed data without centralising raw personal information
2. **Differential Privacy**: Statistical noise protects individual privacy during training
3. **Secure Enclave Processing**: Training occurs within secure hardware environments
4. **Local Processing Only**: Restricts processing to local devices without data transfer

These constraints translate to ODRL policies with algorithm-specific limitations.

Purpose Limitations with Minimal Restrictions. For less sensitive information (Tier 2: Limited Sharing), the system implements purpose limitations without algorithm restrictions. This approach allows conventional AI training while restricting the contexts in which such training may occur.

For Tier 1 (Public Data), the system places no specific AI training restrictions beyond standard permissions, appropriate for non-sensitive information that individuals are comfortable sharing broadly.

Flexible Customisation Beyond Tiers. While privacy tiers provide convenient starting points, the framework is designed for complete flexibility. Individuals are not limited to predefined configurations:

- **Granular Data Control**: Apply different restriction levels to different data types based on contextual sensitivity (e.g., stronger protections for health data than for shopping preferences)
- **Policy Composition**: Combine elements from multiple tiers to create hybrid policies tailored to specific needs
- **Custom Restriction Logic**: Define custom constraints beyond the predefined options, such as limiting training to specific time periods or requiring additional notifications

This flexibility allows individuals to precisely calibrate their data sovereignty preferences while still benefiting from the structure provided by the tier system.

Multi-dimensional Controls. The system supports combining multiple restriction types to create tailored policies. For example, an individual might specify both algorithm type and purpose limitations.

This flexible approach with multi-dimensional controls ensures that individuals can apply appropriate protections tailored to their specific preferences. The integration with privacy tiers provides accessible starting points for those seeking simplicity, while the customization capabilities support tailored governance for those with specific requirements.

5.4 Trust Implications

The implementation of AI training restrictions directly addresses trust challenges in hybrid human-AI collaborative networks by enhancing transparency and control. By providing individuals with mechanisms to govern how their data contributes to AI development, the system enables meaningful participation in AI advancement while respecting personal privacy boundaries.

The AI training restrictions enable individuals to:

- Understand how their data may be used in AI development
- Specify boundaries appropriate to their comfort level and data sensitivity
- Maintain consistent control across organisations and data processors
- Participate selectively in AI advancement according to personal values

These capabilities transform abstract data rights into concrete mechanisms that build trust in collaborative AI systems through genuine individual agency. By addressing the opacity challenge through simplified templates, the transformation concern through pre-processing restrictions, downstream effects through selective participation, and algorithm selection through privacy-preserving constraints, the system provides a comprehensive approach to AI training governance that enhances trust in hybrid human-AI networks.

6 Evaluation and Comparison

6.1 Comparison with Data Sovereignty Frameworks

We compare our implementation with Solid and the International Data Spaces Association (IDSA), highlighting architectural contrasts, design priorities, and support for AI sovereignty (Tables 1 and 2).

Solid vs. IDSA. Solid, while empowering individuals via pod-based control, introduces high migration overhead and limits policy complexity. It is better suited for closed ecosystems rather than distributed, cross-organisational settings. IDSA focuses on secure B2B data exchange but provides only coarsegrained, organisation-centric controls. Neither framework supports algorithm- specific training restrictions or fine-grained individual governance.

Our Key Differentiators. Our framework overcomes these limitations with:

- **Virtual Federation:** Users access their data across organisations without relocating it.
- **Person-Centric Discovery:** Individuals gain end-to-end visibility into their full data footprint.
- **Granular Policies:** AI-specific ODRL extensions empower users to define training constraints with precision.
- **Low Disruption:** Organisations retain existing storage while layering sovereignty on top.

Table 1. Comparison with Existing Data Sovereignty Frameworks

Feature	Our Framework	Solid (Pods)	IDSA
Data Location	Original storage	Personal pods	With provider
Data Integration	Schema.org federation	Pod API	Connector-based
Governance	ODRL extensions	Web Access Control	Usage policies
Discovery	Cross-org federation	Limited to pods	Broker service
Integration Effort	Semantic mapping	Full migration	Connector setup
Individual Focus	Person-centric	Person-centric	Org-centric
AI Controls	Algorithm-specific	Not supported	Generic limitation

This combination supports scalable, real-world adoption with minimal technical friction.

6.2 AI Training Restriction Mechanisms

We assess our AI-specific policy features against platform-level controls and general legal frameworks to highlight how we move beyond passive rights toward enforceable user agency.

Table 2. Comparison of AI Training Control Mechanisms

Feature	Our Framework	Platform Settings	Legal Frameworks
Granularity	Per data element	Global opt-out	General principles
Algorithm Scope	Explicit constraints	None	Indirect risk focus
Mechanism	ODRL-based	Platform-defined	Textual policies
Data Linkage	Integrated federation	Disconnected	Separate

Most platforms provide basic opt-out options for data usage, rarely distinguishing between training algorithms or supporting data-specific preferences. Legal instruments like the GDPR and AI Act articulate high-level protections but stop short of offering technical enforcement pathways.

In contrast, our system provides:

- **Algorithm Specification:**
- Users select or prohibit training methods (e.g., federated learning, differential privacy).
- **Contextual Purpose Constraints:** Permissions can be linked to domains (e.g., healthcare only) to avoid misuse.
- **Integrated Enforcement:** Policies are machine-readable and tied directly to federated data representations.
- **Accessible Control:** Privacy tiers lower the barrier for non-technical users, while allowing full customisation for advanced needs.

By combining semantic data discovery with enforceable policy logic, we enable a practical foundation for trustworthy AI governance rooted in personal agency.

The framework directly addresses trust-building in hybrid human-AI collaborative networks through transparency enhancement, user agency empowerment, and accountability establishment. By enabling individuals to discover their complete data footprint and understand how their data contributes to AI training, the system transforms opaque processing into transparent, governed interactions. The privacy tier system and algorithm-specific constraints provide concrete mechanisms for individuals to express trust boundaries, moving beyond abstract consent to actionable control. This approach builds trust through proactive governance rather than post-hoc explanations.

7 Future Work and Conclusion

7.1 Future Work Directions

While our current implementation demonstrates the feasibility of personal data sovereignty with AI training restrictions, several areas remain for future development:

Policy Enforcement Mechanisms: The current implementation focuses on policy expression rather than enforcement. Future work will develop mechanisms to translate ODRL policies into enforceable controls within AI training environments. This includes integration with privacy-preserving frameworks to enforce algorithm constraints and developing verification procedures to ensure training compliance.

Blockchain Integration: As outlined in our original framework, incorporating blockchain technology for immutable policy records and transparent enforcement logs represents an important direction for enhancing trust. This would provide non-repudiation for data usage agreements and create auditable trails of AI training activities.

Extended AI Algorithm Support: The current implementation supports four predefined privacy-preserving algorithms. Future work will expand this vocabulary to include emerging techniques such as machine unlearning, homomorphic encryption, and secure multi-party computation, providing more nuanced control options.

8 Conclusion

This paper has presented the implementation of a personal data sovereignty framework that enables individuals to exercise fine-grained control over AI training on their personal data. By addressing the critical challenges of data heterogeneity and policy expression, our approach transforms abstract data rights into practical control mechanisms.

The framework's key contributions include:

1. An ontology-based data federation system that provides unified access to personal data scattered across organisational boundaries, creating the prerequisite visibility for meaningful sovereignty.
2. A policy control service with ODRL extensions specifically designed for AI training governance, enabling individuals to express nuanced preferences about algorithm selection and training limitations.

Our evaluation demonstrates that this approach addresses critical gaps in existing frameworks. Unlike pod-based approaches like Solid, our implementation avoids data migration requirements while providing more comprehensive discovery. Compared to connector-based approaches like IDSA, our framework offers person-centric sovereignty with AI-specific controls not present in organisational data exchange systems.

As AI systems become increasingly embedded in decision-making processes, giving individuals genuine control over how their personal data shapes these systems represents an essential step toward equitable and transparent AI development. This work demonstrates that such control is technically feasible while respecting existing data infrastructure and balancing expressiveness with usability.

Acknowledgements. This work is supported by the University of York and SEERC - South East European Research Centre. This work is also supported, in part, by EPSRC and DSIT TMF-uplift: CHEDDAR: Communications Hub For Empowering Distributed ClouD Computing Applications And Research (EP/X040518/1), (EP/Y037421/1), EPSRC IAA (EP/X525856/1), and EPSRC REMOTE (EP/Y019229/1).

References

1. Dwork, C., Roth, A.: The algorithmic foundations of differential privacy. Found. Trends Theor. Comput. Sci. **9**(3–4), 211–407 (2014)
2. Otto, B., Jarke, M.: Designing a multi-sided data platform: findings from the International data spaces case. Electron. Mark. **29**(4), 561–580 (2019)
3. Mittelstadt, B.D., Allo, P., Taddeo, M., et al.: The ethics of algorithms: mapping the debate. Big Data Soc. **3**(2), 1–21 (2016)
4. Hummel, P., Braun, M., Tretter, M., Dabrock, P.: Data sovereignty: a review. Big Data Soc. **8**(1), 1–17 (2021)
5. Voigt, P., Von dem Bussche, A.: The EU General Data Protection Regulation (GDPR): A Practical Guide. Springer, Cham (2017)
6. European Commission. Proposal for a Regulation laying down harmonised rules on artificial intelligence (Artificial Intelligence Act) (2021). https://eurlex.europa.eu/legal-content/EN/TXT/?uri=CELEX%3A52021PC0206. Last accessed 28 May 2024

7. Wachter, S., Mittelstadt, B., Russell, C.: Counterfactual explanations without opening the black box: automated decisions and the GDPR. Harvard J. Law Technol. **31**(2), 841–887 (2017)
8. Janssen, M., Brous, P., Estevez, E., et al.: Data governance: organizing data for trustworthy artificial intelligence. Gov. Inf. Q. **37**(3), 101493 (2020)
9. Sambra, A.V., Mansour, E., Hawke, S., et al.: Solid: a platform for decentralized social applications based on linked data. Techn. Rep. MIT CSAIL Qatar Comput. Res. Inst. (2016)
10. Hummel, P., Braun, M., Augsberg, S., Dabrock, P.: Sovereignty and data sharing. ITU J. ICT Discoveries **2**, 1–15 (2018)
11. Jobin, A., Ienca, M., Vayena, E.: The global landscape of AI ethics guidelines. Nat. Mach. Intell. **1**(9), 389–399 (2019)
12. McMahan, H.B., Moore, E., Ramage, D., et al.: Communication-efficient learning of deep networks from decentralized data. In: Proceedings of the 20th International Conference on Artificial Intelligence and Statistics, pp. 1273–1282 (2017)
13. Evans, D., Kolesnikov, V., Rosulek, M.: A pragmatic introduction to secure multiparty computation. Found. Trends Privacy Secur. **2**(2–3), 70–246 (2018)
14. Veale, M., Van Kleek, M., Binns, R.: Fairness and accountability design needs for algorithmic support in high-stakes public sector decision-making. In: Proceedings of the 2018 CHI Conference on Human Factors in Computing Systems, pp. 1–14 (2018)
15. Arrieta, A.B., D´ıaz-Rodr´ıguez, N., Del Ser, J., et al.: Explainable artificial intelligence (XAI): concepts, taxonomies, opportunities and challenges toward responsible AI. Inf. Fusion **58**, 82–115 (2020)
16. Guidotti, R., Monreale, A., Ruggieri, S., et al.: A survey of methods for explaining black box models. ACM Comput. Surv. **51**(5), 1–42 (2018)
17. Ribeiro, M.T., Singh, S., Guestrin, C.: Why should i trust you?: explaining the predictions of any classifier. In: Proceedings of the 22nd ACM SIGKDD International Conference on Knowledge Discovery and Data Mining, pp. 1135–1144 (2016)
18. Lundberg, S.M., Lee, S.I.: A unified approach to interpreting model predictions. Adv. Neural. Inf. Process. Syst. **30**, 4765–4774 (2017)
19. Miller, T.: Explanation in artificial intelligence: insights from the social sciences. Artif. Intell. **267**, 1–38 (2019)
20. Shin, D.: The effects of explainability and causability on perception, trust, and acceptance: Implications for explainable AI. Int. J. HumanComputer Stud. **146**, 102551 (2021)
21. Kaur, H., Nori, H., Jenkins, S., et al.: Interpreting interpretability: understanding data scientists' use of interpretability tools for machine learning. In: Proceedings of the 2020 CHI Conference on Human Factors in Computing Systems, pp. 1–14 (2020)
22. European Commission High-Level Expert Group on AI. Ethics Guidelines for Trustworthy AI (2019). https://digitalstrategy.ec.europa.eu/en/library/ethics-guidelines-trustworthy-ai. Last accessed 28 May 2024
23. Baraku, V., Paraskakis, I., Veloudis, S., Yadav, P.: Personal data sovereignty in virtual enterprises: implementing data capsules for enhanced privacy and compliance. In: Working Conference on Virtual Enterprises, pp. 447–461. Springer (2024)
24. Baraku, V., Paraskakis, I., Veloudis, S., Yadav, P.: Responsible information sharing in the era of big data analytics facilitating digital economy through the use of blockchain technology and observing GDPR. In: CLOSER, pp. 257–264 (2024)

Learning Factory 5.0: An Open Design Model for Human-Centric, Sustainable, and Flexible Technical Education

Rita Amaral[1], Hélio Castro[1,2(✉)], Filipe Pereira[1], João Bastos[1,2], Joaquim Moreira[1], Alzira Mota[1,2], and Paulo Ávila[1,2]

[1] ISEP, Polytechnic of Porto, Rua Dr. António Bernardino de Almeida, 431, 4249-015 Porto, Portugal
{1191005,hcc,fal,jab,jaq,atm,psa}@isep.ipp.pt
[2] INESC TEC, Rua Dr. Roberto Frias, 4200-465 Porto, Portugal

Abstract. This paper introduces a conceptual framework for Learning Factory 5.0 (LF 5.0), designed to address the evolving demands of Industry 5.0 in technical education. LF 5.0 emphasizes human-centricity, sustainability, and advanced technological integration, leveraging open design and open-source principles to foster accessibility and collaboration. The paper critically examines the limitations of traditional Industry 4.0 learning factories—such as limited flexibility, insufficient customization, and low emphasis on sustainability—and demonstrates how LF 5.0 overcomes these challenges through collaborative networks, immersive technologies, and circular economy practices. While the model is at a conceptual stage, it provides a strategic roadmap for aligning technical education with future industrial and societal needs. The discussion highlights implementation challenges, limitations, and directions for future research to ensure scalability and impact.

Keywords: Learning Factory 5.0 · Open Design · Industry 5.0 Collaborative · Networks

1 Introduction

The ongoing transformation toward Industry 5.0 demands a rethinking of technical education, prioritizing human-centricity, sustainability, and collaborative innovation. Learning Factory 5.0 (LF 5.0) is proposed as a model that integrates these principles, aiming to bridge the gap between theoretical knowledge and practical industrial skills through open design and open-source solutions. The core scientific objective of this work is to conceptualize and structure an LF 5.0 framework that addresses the shortcomings of Industry 4.0 learning factories—specifically, their limited flexibility, insufficient customization, and lack of focus on sustainability and collaborative networks. Differing from previous models, Industry 5.0 centers the human factor in operational activities, encouraging customization, resilience, and sustainability, alongside enhanced human-machine collaboration through Cyber-Physical Systems (CPS) and other advanced technological innovations [1].

Published by Springer Nature Switzerland AG 2026
L. M. Camarinha-Matos et al. (Eds.): PRO-VE 2025, IFIP AICT 770, pp. 36–51, 2026.
https://doi.org/10.1007/978-3-032-05673-3_3

Learning Factories (LF) have thus emerged as fundamental educational platforms, integrating theoretical instruction with applied industrial practice within regulated environments [2]. LF 5.0 is designed to create a training environment that meets the requirements of Industry 5.0, encouraging innovation through the application of Open Design principles and open-source tools, which support a collaborative, accessible, and sustainable approach [3].

This work aims to develop a learning factory model that empowers future professionals to address the challenges of Industry 5.0 by providing an immersive, sustainable, and accessible training environment. Central to this approach is the emphasis on technological solutions that foster collaboration and innovation. The LF 5.0 model is conceived as a benchmark for how education can adapt to rapid industrial transformation, preparing a new generation of workers to thrive in evolving contexts.

The primary objective of this work is to propose the implementation of LF 5.0, guided by the principles of Industry 5.0, Open Design, and Open Source. The central goal is to create an innovative training environment where students acquire practical and technical competencies aligned with the demands of the new industrial era. This environment is characterized by the integration of advanced technologies and the central role of humans in the production process. Furthermore, the project seeks to establish a replicable and accessible model through the use of low-cost solutions and open-source software, thereby promoting customization, resilience, and sustainability. LF 5.0 not only prepares students to operate advanced cyber-physical systems but also enables the exploration of novel methodologies for human-machine interaction, collaborative communication, and environmental management, consistent with the needs of Industry 5.0.

The main objective of this work is the proposal for the implementation of LF 5.0 guided by the principles of Industry 5.0, Open Design, and Open Source. The primary goal is to develop an innovative training environment that enables students to acquire practical and technical skills aligned with the requirements of the new industrial era, distinguished by the integration of emerging technologies and the centralization of humans in the production process. Additionally, the project aims to create a replicable and accessible model using low-cost solutions and open-source software, promoting customization, resilience, and sustainability. The LF 5.0 will not only equip students to work with advanced cyber-physical systems but will also allow the exploration of new methodologies for human-machine interaction, collaborative communication, and environmental management, in line with the needs of Industry 5.0.

Ultimately, the intention is for LF 5.0 to become a reference point for the application of Industry 5.0 concepts in educational settings, fostering a more interactive, sustainable, and collaborative approach to the training of future professionals.

The structure of this document is organized into five main sections, each designed to provide clear and logical progression of the research. Section 1 introduces the context and motivation for the work and defines the main objectives. Section 2 presents a comprehensive literature review, exploring key concepts such as Learning Factories, Open Design, Cyber-Physical Systems, and Industry 5.0, and discusses their definitions, characteristics, challenges, and future perspectives, establishing a theoretical foundation for the project.

Section 3 details the methodological approach and the application of reference models to analyze existing Learning Factories, highlighting their diversity, limitations, and best practices. It then proposes the conceptualization and implementation of LF 5.0, describing the selection of technologies, equipment, and the integration of physical and computational components. Section 4 discusses the main findings, including the identification of limitations in Industry 4.0-oriented learning factories and the development of an LF 5.0 model that addresses human-centricity, sustainability, open design principles and collaborative networks. Finally, Sect. 5 presents the conclusions by summarizing the main results, addressing current limitations, and proposing avenues for future research and practical application.

2 Literature Review

This section offers an integrated review of the foundational concepts for the LF 5.0 project, focusing on Industry 5.0, Open Design, and Learning Factories. It highlights Industry 5.0's shift toward human-centricity, sustainability, and collaborative human-machine interaction, as well as the European Commission's emphasis on balancing technological progress with social and environmental priorities. Open Design is presented as a catalyst for collaborative, transparent, and accessible innovation, aligning with the immersive, practice-oriented educational environments provided by Learning Factories. The convergence of these three pillars establishes a transformative framework for technical education and industrial innovation, fostering agile, flexible, and sustainable training platforms that address both current and future challenges.

2.1 Industry 5.0

Industry 5.0 marks an evolutionary step beyond Industry 4.0, with a strong focus on human-centricity, organizational resilience, and the integration of advanced technologies such as cyber-physical systems and smart manufacturing [4].

The rising interest in Industry 5.0 reflects its development as a progression from the established Industry 4.0 model and characterizing it "as an evolutionary and incremental, but crucially necessary, advance that builds upon the concept and practices of Industry 4.0" [5], although different analytical perspectives are possible.

The European Commission (EC) introduced the concept of Industry 5.0 to align with European priorities on social and environmental matters, thereby facilitating the attainment of the European Union's 2030 goals. [6]. The EC's vision positions that Industry 5.0 "complements the Industry 4.0 paradigm by promoting a research- and innovation-driven transition towards a sustainable, human-centric, and resilient industry, respecting planetary boundaries." The focus transitions from exclusive shareholder value to a broader consideration of all stakeholders engaged, essentially focusing on a sustainable industry [1]. Despite this innovative concept from the EC, some works suggest that Michael Rada first proposed the concept of Industry 5.0 on social media, later explored by various researchers and ultimately validated by the European Commission in 2021 [7].

While some authors highlight the role of sustainability, others, such as Madsen and Berg, focus on adopting a human-centric approach [7]. Additionally, a new concept of symbiosis between humans and machines has emerged, supported by several authors who advocate for human-machine collaboration and interrelation [8]. This latter concept, supported by most authors, is also based on the idea of customization, the primary attribute of Industry 5.0, which can be described as "the design and production through various sensor data that will be directly linked, providing customized products to consumers in real time" [9].

Despite the various views and perspectives regarding this new industrial revolution, there is alignment and consensus on some general aspects of this new methodology. Industry 5.0 transcends the narrow focus on efficiency and productivity characteristic of Industry 4.0, restoring and amplifying the industry's significance and impact on society, supported by the pillars of sustainability and social responsibility.

To make production more sustainable and adapt to the new industrial revolution, processes are being developed to recycle and reuse available resources. One of the goals is to reduce environmental impacts in manufacturing. For this, the implementation of technologies such as additive manufacturing is necessary, as it enables greater customization and resource optimization, reducing waste [10].

Industry 5.0 is developing global manufacturing systems by automating repetitive tasks that human workers once performed. Robots and intelligent systems are now being integrated into supply chains and production lines at an unprecedented scale. This innovative paradigm, referred to as smart manufacturing, enables designers to securely store product design files in the cloud, ensuring controlled access and facilitating the efficient allocation of manufacturing resources across multiple locations. Machine control in the factory and production lifecycle management are now carried out through cloud manufacturing systems [11]. This service-oriented model aims to integrate production capabilities with services, providing customized solutions to customers.

2.2 Open Design

The concept of Open Design (OD) has been the subject of ongoing research and exploration within the field of contemporary design. In his analysis, Abel describes OD as a broad and dynamic area whose boundaries still lack a clear definition, presenting a challenge for designers attempting to fully comprehend it [12].

The term "design" itself is notably broad and often ambiguous. John Heskett illustrates this complexity by describing four distinct possible uses of the term. He points out that, in addition to being interpreted as a noun referring to the general field of design or as a verb implying the action or thought involved in designing, the term "design" can also be understood as a noun referring to the final product or a plan or intention. In this context, the latter interpretation, "a plan or intention," will be applied [13].

Open Design is a collaborative and accessible approach to design that promotes the creation, sharing, and improvement of projects, products, or processes transparently and openly. This concept transcends the conventional boundaries of design, enabling the participation of a diverse community, including professionals, enthusiasts, and experts from various fields. Its aim is the democratization of knowledge, promoting the free exchange of ideas and resources to drive innovation and collective creativity [14].

To precisely define what OD is, it is crucial to analyze the level of openness present in a specific design project. This assessment becomes essential for comparing and contextualizing this approach to already established concepts in the design universe, such as open innovation and open source. For instance, many educational, research, and technology organizations adopt the OD concept to lower the investment in laboratories [15] and even to be an educational instrument for sustainability [16].

2.3 Learning Factory

The fundamental concept of the Learning Factory (LF) approach is to provide practical and integrated experience of design and manufacturing that is meaningful for students and trainees, enabling them to apply theoretical knowledge in a real production context. This is achieved through a variety of activities, ranging from lectures to realistic simulations of production systems. Students and trainees could analyze and improve processes, which strengthens their practical and technical understanding [17].

The task-based learning approach allows students to effectively develop technical production skills while engaging in realistic work processes. Additionally, the integration of physical and digital resources provides a holistic learning experience, in which students can visualize and understand both the practical and conceptual aspects of the manufacturing process. In this way, curricular content can be concerned with practical training.

The benefits of real-world manufacturing environments extend to both the academic education of university students and the professional development of industrial workers. Recognizing the substantial value of this approach, an increasing number of companies are adopting learning factories to enhance the qualifications of their workforce at all organizational levels, from shop floor personnel to management. The primary objective of LF's is to provide a holistic understanding of business processes while equipping participants with essential methods, concepts, and techniques. This approach enables the identification of potential areas for improvement and supports the implementation of more efficient operational processes [18]. Several LF's were oriented to Industry 4.0 [19].

The convergence of the Learning Factory, Open Design and Industry 5.0 marks a profound shift in how technology is conceived, developed, and utilized. Industry 5.0 prioritizes synergistic collaboration between humans and machines, advancing a human-centric and sustainable paradigm for industrial innovation. This shift enables the creation of more agile and adaptable production processes, which are essential for the effective design and operation of modern learning factories. Within this evolving landscape, Open Design plays a pivotal role as a catalyst for transformation. It encourages broad-based collaboration, unrestricted access to knowledge, and the democratization of design and innovation processes. By fostering transparency and the open exchange of ideas, Open Design enhances collective creativity, supporting greater customization and sustainability in the development of products and services. Promoting a feasible approach to a decentralized production system towards product customization [20]. Consequently, the convergence of these three pillars presents a promising outlook for the advancement of industry and innovation.

3 Method and Application

The methodological framework and practical analysis informing the development of LF 5.0 are grounded in a multidimensional model designed to standardize, compare, and guide Learning Factories (LFs) across key aspects such as operational structure, goals, processes, and didactics. This approach is illustrated through the examination of three diverse cases—Festo Didactic, Heilbronn, and TU Wien—which demonstrate how different LFs adapt technologies, educational strategies, and organizational models to meet evolving industrial and educational demands. Comparative analysis underscores the versatility and adaptability essential for successful LF implementation in the context of Industry 5.0, showing how best practices, open design principles, and emerging technologies can be integrated to prepare professionals for the challenges of the new industrial era.

3.1 Method

The literature reveals significant divergences regarding the morphology and objectives of a Learning Factory (LF). Notably, there are numerous disparities in the dimensions of a LF and the characteristics associated with these dimensions, as evidenced in several studies [21, 22]. To establish a foundational model and accommodate emerging changes in the field of LFs, the Collaborative Working Group (CWG), in collaboration with the Network of Innovative Learning Factories (NIL) project, established a multidimensional descriptive model. This model was created with three main objectives [23, 24]: (1) to provide a tool for delineating existing learning factories, facilitating their characterization and comparison; (2) to guide and establish guidelines for defining and setting up new learning factories, offering a clear starting point for design and creation; and (3) to promote the standardization of the LF concept, ensuring a consensual and uniform understanding.

This joint effort between the CWG and NIL aims to ensure that LFs can evolve in a consistent and standardized manner, reflecting best practices and innovations in the field. The model encompasses seven dimensions: Operational Model, Goals and Purposes, Process, Environment Configuration, Product, Didactics, and LF Metrics, which include 60 characteristics and their related attributes. The broad acceptance and universality of this model are attributed to the large number of institutions that participated in its development.

In this context and based on the work carried out by the consortium, Abele, Matternich, and Tish [2] developed a synthesis table that characterizes each LF according to its dimensions and prominent characteristics. Table 1 serves as a valuable tool for the comparative analysis of LFs, enabling a deeper understanding of their capabilities and limitations. It also facilitates the identification of best practices among different learning factories, promoting continuous improvement and innovation in various fields of activity: education, training, and research.

This framework helps map the evolution of LFs over time, highlighting how they adapt to technological changes and new industrial needs. By providing a structured and detailed overview of learning factories, this approach has become an essential reference

Table 1. Morphology of a LF according to the multidimensional descriptive model of the CIRP CWG [2].

<table>
<tr><td>2.1</td><td>Main purpose</td><td colspan="5">Education</td><td colspan="3">Vocational training</td><td colspan="6">Research</td></tr>
<tr><td>2.2</td><td>Secondary purpose</td><td colspan="5">Test environment/pilot environment</td><td>Industrial production</td><td colspan="6">Innovation Transfer</td><td colspan="2">Advertisement for production</td></tr>
<tr><td>3.1</td><td>Product Life Cycle</td><td colspan="4">Product Development</td><td>Product Planning</td><td>Prototyping</td><td rowspan="4">Manufacturing</td><td colspan="2" rowspan="4">Assembly</td><td rowspan="4">Logistics</td><td colspan="3">Recycling</td><td>Service</td></tr>
<tr><td>3.2</td><td>Factory Life Cycle</td><td>Factory concept</td><td colspan="3">Investment planning</td><td>Process planning</td><td>Ramp-Up</td><td colspan="3">Recycling</td><td>Maintenance</td></tr>
<tr><td>3.3</td><td>Order Life Cycle</td><td>Configuration & order</td><td colspan="3">Order sequencing</td><td colspan="2">Production planning and scheduling</td><td colspan="3">Picking, Packaging</td><td>Shipping</td></tr>
<tr><td>3.4</td><td>Technology Life Cycle</td><td>Planning</td><td colspan="3">Development</td><td colspan="2">Virtual testing</td><td colspan="3">Modernization</td><td>Maintenance</td></tr>
<tr><td rowspan="2">3.5</td><td rowspan="2">Indirect Functions</td><td colspan="6">Primary activities</td><td colspan="8">Secondary activities</td></tr>
<tr><td colspan="2">Supply Chain Management</td><td colspan="2">Sales</td><td>Purchasing</td><td>Services</td><td colspan="4">Facilities</td><td>HR</td><td colspan="2">Technological Innovation</td><td>Procurement</td></tr>
<tr><td>4.1</td><td>Learning Environment</td><td colspan="3">Purely physical</td><td colspan="2">Physical LF supported by digital factory</td><td colspan="3">Physical value stream of LF extended virtually</td><td colspan="6">Purely virtual</td></tr>
<tr><td>4.2</td><td>Environmental scale</td><td colspan="8">Scale down</td><td colspan="6">Life-size</td></tr>
</table>

for researchers, students, and industry professionals interested in the impact of these facilities within their respective domains.

3.2 Application

Numerous Learning Factories (LFs) have been implemented worldwide, with their most significant growth occurring in the 21st century, namely in the second decade [25], and the majority are in Europe, particularly in Germany [2, 25]. Given the impossibility of analyzing all existing LFs in detail, this study focuses on three examples – LF1: Festo Didactic Learning Factories (MPS, iCIM, CP Factory), LF2: Learning Factory for Innovation, Manufacturing and Cooperation, and LF3: TU Wien Pilot Factory Industrie 4.0 – each with distinct purposes. The analysis covers the objectives, products, and operational processes of each learning factory, using Table 4 as a reference for their characterization.

LF1: Festo Didactic Learning Factories – MPS, iCIM, CP Factory

Festo Didactic, a subsidiary of Festo Automation, has been developing learning factories since 1989. Unlike most, these learning factories are not operated by Festo itself but by its clients, which include vocational training institutions and universities. Initially, the mission of Festo Didactic was to provide training for Festo products; however, over time, the company expanded its portfolio to cover other areas.

Its first learning factory emerged from training modules for pneumatics and hydraulics, leading to the development of the Modular Production System (MPS). Created through a partnership with vocational schools, the MPS aimed to train skills not addressed in traditional pneumatics classes, particularly those related to industrial automation. Launched in 1990, the MPS is mainly used to simulate industrial environments and is characterized by a simplified process compared to real production lines, reduced size and reusable products, a modular approach, focus on assembly processes and automation technologies, and the use of industrial components. This system enables the acquisition of skills such as PLC programming, industrial machine maintenance, production process optimization, and production line configuration.

Following the MPS, Festo Didactic introduced the iCIM, which became a success and led to further solutions such as CNC machines with robotic loading, automated warehouses, flexible material transport systems, and cellular line controllers. With the rise of Industry 4.0, new needs led to the development of a new class of learning factories called CP Factory (Cyber-Physical Factory). Key features include more versatile material transport, modular layout reconfiguration without reprogramming, intelligent material flow control via RFID, cyber-physical components, an integrated MES, and cloud connectivity.

Festo Didactic learning factories produce a diverse range of products that serve as effective tools for teaching and training in industrial automation and technical skills. They are primarily used by vocational institutions and universities, operated through exercises prepared by Festo Didactic and supervised by instructors. Some universities also use these factories for research projects and practical problem-solving. The didactic environment includes extensive support materials – simulation software, multimedia learning programs, and ready-to-use exercises – providing a comprehensive and effective teaching experience [2].

Finally, to characterize Festo Didactic's learning factories, the reference framework presented in Table 2 was used.

Table 2. Morphologies of Festo Didatic LF's according to the CWG multidimensional descriptive model [2].

2.1	Main purpose	Education	Vocational training	Research					
2.2	Secondary purpose	Test environment/pilot environment	Industrial production	Innovation Transfer	Advertisement for production				
3.1	Product Life Cycle	Product Development	Product Planning	Prototyping	Manufacturing	Assembly	Logistics	Recycling	Service
3.2	Factory Life Cycle	Factory concept	Investment planning	Process planning	*Ramp-Up*			Recycling	Maintenance
3.3	Order Life Cycle	Configuration & order	Order sequencing	Production planning and scheduling				Picking, Packaging	Shipping
3.4	Technology Life Cycle	Planning	Development	Virtual testing				Modernization	Maintenance
3.5	Indirect Functions	Primary activities				Secondary activities			
		Supply Chain Management	Sales	Purchasing	Services	Facilities	HR	Technological Innovation	Procurement
4.1	Learning Environment	Purely physical	Physical LF supported by digital factory	Physical value stream of LF extended virtually	Purely virtual				
4.2	Environmental scale	Scale down	Life-size						

LF2: Learning Factory for Innovation, Manufacturing and Cooperation

In 2011, the Learning Factory for Innovation, Manufacturing and Cooperation was established in Heilbronn, Germany, as a new LF based on projects that place a real and meaningful task at the center of student activities [26], due to gaps in graduates' German students in essential areas such as knowledge acquisition, work autonomy, communication, teamwork, application of engineering knowledge, and problem-solving.

In this learning factory, all sixth-semester students participate in a fictitious company, "HHN Parts and Products," to cooperate to design and manufacture a new product based on specifications provided by instructors, including technical requirements, budget, and deadlines – realistically simulating an industrial project. Products vary each semester, all similar in size (no larger than a shoebox). While technical details are important, the ongoing process of problem-solving and organizational challenges is valued as much as the technical solution itself.

The learning factory allows students to fully simulate a real-world start-up in an authentic industrial environment. As a mandatory course, a group of students enroll in the LF project two times per year, supervised by a team of faculty and staff members. The project schedule and deadlines are standardized, even though the product changes each semester. In addition to applying and deepening factual knowledge and work methods, the LF aims to strengthen students' communication, cooperation, and interdepartmental project management skills, preparing them for future industrial employment.

Since its introduction, over 160 students have participated in the LF at Heilbronn University. A formalized evaluation process using surveys and feedback workshops has been established to improve the concept and assess student skill development. To characterize Festo Didactic's learning factories, the reference framework presented in Table 3 was used.

Table 3. Morphologies of Learning Factory for Innovation, Manufacturing and Cooperation in Heilbronn according to the CIRP CWG multidimensional descriptive model [2].

<table>
<tr><td>2.1</td><td>Main purpose</td><td colspan="5">Education</td><td colspan="3">Vocational training</td><td colspan="6">Research</td></tr>
<tr><td>2.2</td><td>Secondary purpose</td><td colspan="5">Test environment/pilot environment</td><td>Industrial production</td><td colspan="6">Innovation Transfer</td><td colspan="2">Advertisement for production</td></tr>
<tr><td>3.1</td><td>Product Life Cycle</td><td colspan="4">Product Development</td><td>Product Planning</td><td>Prototyping</td><td rowspan="4">Manufacturing</td><td rowspan="4" colspan="2">Assembly</td><td rowspan="4">Logistics</td><td colspan="3">Recycling</td><td>Service</td></tr>
<tr><td>3.2</td><td>Factory Life Cycle</td><td>Factory concept</td><td colspan="3">Investment planning</td><td>Process planning</td><td>Ramp-Up</td><td colspan="3">Recycling</td><td>Maintenance</td></tr>
<tr><td>3.3</td><td>Order Life Cycle</td><td>Configuration & order</td><td colspan="3">Order sequencing</td><td colspan="2">Production planning and scheduling</td><td colspan="3">Picking, Packaging</td><td>Shipping</td></tr>
<tr><td>3.4</td><td>Technology Life Cycle</td><td>Planning</td><td colspan="3">Development</td><td colspan="2">Virtual testing</td><td colspan="3">Modernization</td><td>Maintenance</td></tr>
<tr><td rowspan="2">3.5</td><td rowspan="2">Indirect Functions</td><td colspan="6">Primary activities</td><td colspan="8">Secondary activities</td></tr>
<tr><td colspan="2">Supply Chain Management</td><td colspan="2">Sales</td><td>Purchasing</td><td>Services</td><td colspan="4">Facilities</td><td>HR</td><td colspan="2">Technological Innovation</td><td>Procurement</td></tr>
<tr><td>4.1</td><td>Learning Environment</td><td colspan="3">Purely physical</td><td colspan="2">Physical LF supported by digital factory</td><td colspan="3">Physical value stream of LF extended virtually</td><td colspan="6">Purely virtual</td></tr>
<tr><td>4.2</td><td>Environmental scale</td><td colspan="8">Scale down</td><td colspan="6">Life-size</td></tr>
</table>

LF3: TU Wien Pilot Factory Industrie 4.0

Following the success of its first LF project, "Learning & Innovation Factory" (LIF), TU Wien (Vienna University of Technology) received another funding to install another facility, the TU Wien Pilot Factory Industry 4.0 (TU PL), involving the Institute of Management Science (IMW), the Institute of Production Engineering (IFT), and the Institute of Engineering Design and Logistics Engineering (IKL). Whereas the first initiative emphasized educational objectives, the Pilot Factory Industrie 4.0, launched in 2015, is primarily an environment for research, testing/evaluation, and demonstration. The Pilot Factory opens its doors weekly for public demonstrations, reflecting its role as an open space for innovation and technology transfer [2].

Focused on discrete manufacturing, the TU Wien Pilot Factory investigates innovative strategies for multivariate series production. In a space of less than 1.000 m^2, the process of developing an FDM 3D printer is presented comprehensively, encompassing all phases from initial design and mechanical component fabrication to assembly and final delivery to the end user. Achieving a successful transition to Industry 4.0 necessitates profound changes in production processes, which can be particularly challenging for small and medium-sized enterprises (SMEs) that may lack adequate resources, equipment, or specialized expertise. These organizations benefit from secure, industry-simulated environments where they can rigorously test and validate new technologies before integrating them into their own production systems. Within such collaborative learning settings, both students and industry trainees have the opportunity to cultivate essential methodological, social, and personal competencies required to address future challenges in manufacturing [2, 27].

Unlike the term "learning factory," the words "pilot factory" and "demonstration factory" are less defined in the literature. A pilot factory enables research, development, and prototype evaluation in an authentic environment, where it does not disrupt existing production processes, focusing on testing novel concepts and creating knowledge. A demonstration factory communicates proven concepts and cutting-edge knowledge to stakeholders and the public. The TU PF offers an innovative model that combines all three factory concepts, enabling advanced prototype development, demonstration of Industry 4.0 technologies, and practical and theoretical integration for students and professionals [27].

Thus, with the application of the reference framework, TU Wien Pilot Factory Industry 4.0 is characterized by what is presented in Table 4.

Table 4. Morphologies of the TU Wien Pilot Factory Industry 4.0 according to the model multidimensional descriptive of the CIRP CWG [2].

<table>
<tr><td>2.1</td><td>Main purpose</td><td colspan="5">Education</td><td colspan="3">Vocational training</td><td colspan="6">Research</td></tr>
<tr><td>2.2</td><td>Secondary purpose</td><td colspan="5">Test environment/pilot environment</td><td>Industrial production</td><td colspan="6">Innovation Transfer</td><td colspan="2">Advertisement for production</td></tr>
<tr><td>3.1</td><td>Product Life Cycle</td><td colspan="4">Product Development</td><td>Product Planning</td><td>Prototyping</td><td rowspan="4">Manufacturing</td><td colspan="2" rowspan="4">Assembly</td><td rowspan="4">Logistics</td><td colspan="3">Recycling</td><td>Service</td></tr>
<tr><td>3.2</td><td>Factory Life Cycle</td><td colspan="2">Factory concept</td><td colspan="2">Investment planning</td><td>Process planning</td><td>Ramp-Up</td><td colspan="3">Recycling</td><td>Maintenance</td></tr>
<tr><td>3.3</td><td>Order Life Cycle</td><td colspan="2">Configuration & order</td><td colspan="2">Order sequencing</td><td colspan="2">Production planning and scheduling</td><td colspan="3">Picking, Packaging</td><td>Shipping</td></tr>
<tr><td>3.4</td><td>Technology Life Cycle</td><td colspan="2">Planning</td><td colspan="2">Development</td><td colspan="2">Virtual testing</td><td colspan="3">Modernization</td><td>Maintenance</td></tr>
<tr><td rowspan="2">3.5</td><td rowspan="2">Indirect Functions</td><td colspan="6">Primary activities</td><td colspan="8">Secondary activities</td></tr>
<tr><td colspan="2">Supply Chain Management</td><td colspan="2">Sales</td><td>Purchasing</td><td>Services</td><td colspan="4">Facilities</td><td>HR</td><td colspan="2">Technological Innovation</td><td>Procurement</td></tr>
<tr><td>4.1</td><td>Learning Environment</td><td colspan="3">Purely physical</td><td colspan="2">Physical LF supported by digital factory</td><td colspan="3">Physical value stream of LF extended virtually</td><td colspan="6">Purely virtual</td></tr>
<tr><td>4.2</td><td>Environmental scale</td><td colspan="8">Scale down</td><td colspan="6">Life-size</td></tr>
</table>

All the analyzed learning factories follow the concept and designation developed by the consortium. However, they differ morphologically and, above all, in their specific purposes. Festo's learning factories are comprehensive structures integrating the three primary purposes: education, training, and research. The Learning Factory for

Innovation, Manufacturing and Cooperation in Heilbronn focuses mainly on university education and teaching, with research as a secondary objective. The TU Wien Pilot Factory, in turn, focuses on new concepts for multivariate series production in discrete manufacturing, prioritizing research and training, with demonstration also playing an important role.

These three factories are just a few examples of the many learning factories worldwide. Like the TU PF, which is oriented towards Industry 4.0, most LF's tend to continuously change and restructure themselves to keep pace with ongoing industrial revolutions.

4 Proposal for a LF 5.0 Model

A critical assessment of Learning Factories (LFs) designed for Industry 4.0 reveals several limitations, including insufficient human-machine integration, limited customization, low emphasis on sustainability, inadequate system connectivity, and a lack of focus on soft skills and adaptability. To address these gaps and align with the priorities of Industry 5.0 – such as human-centricity, sustainability, and continuous learning – the LF 5.0 model is proposed as an evolution of the concept. This model integrates collaborative robotics, immersive technologies, flexible manufacturing systems, and sustainability-focused practices, all underpinned by open design principles that foster transparency and innovation. The resulting framework aims to deliver a practical, adaptable, and future-ready training platform that meets both current industrial demands and the evolving expectations of society.

4.1 LF 4.0 Limitations

The introduction of Learning Factories (LFs) was a fundamental step in developing competencies for Industry 4.0 (I4.0), providing environments where students could apply theoretical knowledge to practical applications and simulate industrial situations. However, as the industrial landscape evolves toward Industry 5.0 (I5.0), it is necessary to identify and subsequently overcome the limitations of current LFs to ensure their continued relevance and effectiveness in this new industrial revolution.

Industry 4.0 is depicted by the integration of cyber-physical systems (CPS), advanced automation, and a focus on optimizing production processes. In this context, LFs have played a crucial role by offering practical means for workers to become familiar with new technologies and methodologies. Nevertheless, several shortcomings have been identified in LFs designed for Industry 4.0, which must be addressed to enable an efficient transition to Industry 5.0. The main limitations are presented in Table 5.

In summary, although Industry 4.0 LFs have contributed to participants' technical training, they exhibit several limitations that must be addressed to align LFs with the new assumptions of Industry 5.0. The most critical issues include human-machine interaction, customization, sustainability, energy efficiency, training, and system flexibility. The transition to Industry 5.0 thus demands the adoption of advanced technologies and the implementation of resilient and sustainable practices to ensure effective adaptation to new market requirements.

Table 5. Summary table of limitations of I4.0 LFs and respective approaches for I5.0.

Limitations of I4.0 LF's	Approaches towards I5.0
Weak Human-Machine Integration	• Natural interfaces (augmented reality and virtual reality) • Ergonomics at workstations (safety)
Limited customization	• Additive manufacturing technologies (3D printing) • Flexible production systems
Sustainability and Energy Efficiency	• Renewable energy • Circular economy
Lack of holistic connection	• Advanced communication platforms
Limited training and capacity building	• Continuing education • Immersive learning environments (virtual reality)
Limited resilience and flexibility	• Resilience strategies • Adaptive technologies
Weak integration with collaborative networks	• Community-based approach • Meta-Organizations • Technological platforms

4.2 LF 5.0 Model

To address the needs and characteristics that a new learning factory oriented toward Industry 5.0 and based on Open Design should encompass, a summary table was developed (Table 7). The purpose of this table is to demonstrate the main differences between the approaches of previously implemented learning factories, as presented earlier. The introduction of LFs was a fundamental step in developing competencies for Industry 4.0 by providing environments where students could apply theoretical knowledge in practical applications, simulating industrial situations. However, as we move toward a new industrial era – Industry 5.0 – it is necessary to identify and overcome the limitations of current LFs to ensure their continued relevance and effectiveness in the contemporary industrial context.

Industry 4.0 is distinguished by the integration of cyber-physical systems (CPS), advanced automation, and a focus on optimizing production processes, with LFs playing a key role in this scenario by offering practical means for workers to become familiar with new technologies and methodologies. Nevertheless, certain shortcomings have been identified in LFs designed for Industry 4.0, which must be addressed to enable an efficient transition to Industry 5.0.

Table 7 is divided into three sections: the first covers Industry 4.0 and its fundamental characteristics, the second focuses on Industry 5.0 and its new approaches, and the third includes the concept of Open Design, which should be an intrinsic feature of the new LF to be developed. Table 6 provides an assessment of the characteristics of Industry 4.0 LFs, which enabled significant advances in operational efficiency and mass production and should continue to be part of a LF 5.0. However, Industry 5.0 introduces a new paradigm, requiring deeper collaboration between humans and machines, more sophisticated customization, and a central role for sustainability.

In summary, the development of Table 6 serves as a strategic guide for implementing a new LF that not only meets the current needs of Industry 5.0 but is also prepared for future challenges. This approach seeks to establish a LF that stands as a model of innovation, efficiency, and sustainability, contributing significantly to the advancement of intelligent and collaborative production.

Table 6. Technologies and characteristics of the analyzed LFs.

	I4.0							I5.0							
	Advanced Automation	CPS	IoT	Simulation	Cloud Technology	Cybersecurity	Big Data	H - H Interaction	H – M Interaction	Sustainability	Customization	Advanced Communication	Resilience	Adaptability	OD
LF1	✓	✓	✓	✓	✓		✓		✓						
LF2		✓	✓	✓										✓	
LF3	✓	✓	✓	✓	✓		✓		✓						✓
LF 5.0	✓	✓	✓	✓	✓	✓	✓	✓	✓	✓	✓	✓	✓	✓	✓

Thus, the proposed LF 5.0 emerges as an evolution of the learning factory concept, aligning with Industry 5.0 trends and aiming to offer a practical and flexible platform that integrates advanced technologies and Open Design practices, focused on hands-on training and the adoption of sustainable approaches, using low-cost technologies and environmentally responsible practices.

To describe and characterize this LF 5.0 proposal, the reference framework was once again used, summarizing the essential characteristics and dimensions of this model. Table 7 specifies a comprehensive overview of the main aspects of this LF 5.0, including its purposes, physical configuration, and proposed functionalities. Through this analysis, it is possible to better understand the structure and objectives of the new system to be implemented, as well as to assess how it aligns with the needs and expectations of the academic and industrial environments.

Table 7. LF 5.0 morphologies according to the CWG multidimensional descriptive model.

<table>
<tr><td>2.1</td><td>Main purpose</td><td colspan="5">Education</td><td colspan="3">Vocational training</td><td colspan="6">Research</td></tr>
<tr><td>2.2</td><td>Secondary purpose</td><td colspan="5">Test environment/pilot environment</td><td>Industrial production</td><td colspan="6">Innovation Transfer</td><td colspan="2">Advertisement for production</td></tr>
<tr><td>3.1</td><td>Product Life Cycle</td><td colspan="4">Product Development</td><td>Product Planning</td><td>Prototyping</td><td rowspan="4">Manufacturing</td><td colspan="2" rowspan="4">Assembly</td><td rowspan="4">Logistics</td><td colspan="3">Recycling</td><td>Service</td></tr>
<tr><td>3.2</td><td>Factory Life Cycle</td><td>Factory concept</td><td colspan="3">Investment planning</td><td>Process planning</td><td>Ramp-Up</td><td colspan="3">Recycling</td><td>Maintenance</td></tr>
<tr><td>3.3</td><td>Order Life Cycle</td><td>Configuration & order</td><td colspan="3">Order sequencing</td><td colspan="2">Production planning and scheduling</td><td colspan="3">Picking, Packaging</td><td>Shipping</td></tr>
<tr><td>3.4</td><td>Technology Life Cycle</td><td>Planning</td><td colspan="3">Development</td><td colspan="2">Virtual testing</td><td colspan="3">Modernization</td><td>Maintenance</td></tr>
<tr><td rowspan="2">3.5</td><td rowspan="2">Indirect Functions</td><td colspan="6">Primary activities</td><td colspan="8">Secondary activities</td></tr>
<tr><td colspan="2">Supply Chain Management</td><td colspan="2">Sales</td><td>Purchasing</td><td>Services</td><td colspan="4">Facilities</td><td>HR</td><td colspan="2">Technological Innovation</td><td>Procurement</td></tr>
<tr><td>4.1</td><td>Learning Environment</td><td colspan="3">Purely physical</td><td colspan="2">Physical LF supported by digital factory</td><td colspan="3">Physical value stream of LF extended virtually</td><td colspan="6">Purely virtual</td></tr>
<tr><td>4.2</td><td>Environmental scale</td><td colspan="8">Scale down</td><td colspan="6">Life-size</td></tr>
</table>

4.3 Collaborative Networks in LF 5.0 Model

To enable a dynamic exchange of learning, knowledge, resources, and expertise among diverse stakeholders, collaborative networks represent a functional element in the LF 5.0 model. By fostering partnerships between universities, industry, and research institutions, these networks facilitate the co-creation and dissemination of best practices, technological innovations, and pedagogical strategies. Such collaboration supports the development of distributed learning environments, where participants can jointly design and implement training modules, case studies, and applied research projects. This collective approach ensures that LF 5.0 remains adaptable and responsive to the evolving needs of both industry and education, while also promoting the pooling of intellectual and material assets to accelerate innovation and customize learning experiences.

Moreover, the integration of collaborative networks within LF 5.0 aligns with the broader objectives of Industry 5.0, emphasizing human-centricity, sustainability, and resilience. These networks leverage open-source tools and digital platforms to enhance accessibility and scalability, reducing barriers to entry and promoting inclusivity across various educational and industrial contexts. By encouraging active engagement and knowledge sharing, collaborative networks help cultivate a culture of lifelong learning and collective problem-solving. This not only strengthens the technical competencies of future professionals but also fosters essential soft skills such as teamwork, communication, and adaptability, which are critical for success in complex and interconnected industrial ecosystems.

4.4 Limitations and Perspectives

While LF 5.0 presents a robust conceptual framework, its current stage is primarily theoretical. Empirical validation in real-world educational and industrial settings is needed to assess scalability and adaptability. Challenges include user training, system interoperability, and maintaining open standards. Future research should focus on pilot implementations, longitudinal studies, and the development of integrated teaching methodologies aligned with Industry 5.0 principles.

5 Conclusions

LF 5.0 represents a significant advancement in technical education, aligning with Industry 5.0's emphasis on human-centricity, sustainability, and collaborative innovation. By integrating open design, open-source solutions, and collaborative networks, the model offers a practical, accessible, and future-ready platform for technical education and training of future and current professionals. Limitations include its conceptual nature and the need for further empirical validation.

Future work should focus on the practical implementation and longitudinal assessment of LF 5.0 in real educational and industrial contexts. Furthermore, to ensure LF 5.0 relevance and impact in evolving industrial landscapes, continuous refinement of the model is mandatory.

Acknowledgements. This work has been supported by FCT - Foundation for Science and Technology within the R&D Units Project Scope: UIDB/00319/2020.

References

1. European Commission. Directorate General for Research and Innovation., Industry 5.0: towards a sustainable, human centric and resilient European industry. LU, Publications Office (2021). https://doi.org/10.2777/308407
2. Abele, E., Metternich, J., Tisch, M.: Learning factories. Springer International Publishing (2019). https://doi.org/10.1007/978-3-319-92261-4
3. Boisseau, É., Omhover, J.F., Bouchard, C.: Open-design: a state of the art review. Des. Sci. (2018). https://doi.org/10.1017/dsj.2017.25
4. Coelho, P., Bessa, C., Landeck, J., Silva, C.: Industry 5.0: the arising of a concept. In: Procedia Computer Science, Elsevier B.V., pp. 1137–1144 (2022). https://doi.org/10.1016/j.procs.2022.12.312
5. Özdemir, V., Hekim, N.: Birth of industry 5.0: making sense of big data with artificial intelligence, 'the internet of things' and next-generation technology policy. OMICS **22**(1), 65–76 (2018). https://doi.org/10.1089/omi.2017.0194
6. Alves, J., Lima, T.M., Gaspar, P.D.: Is industry 5.0 a human-centred approach? A systematic review. MDPI (2023). https://doi.org/10.3390/pr11010193
7. Madsen, D.Ø., Berg, T.: An exploratory bibliometric analysis of the birth and emergence of industry 5.0," Appl. Syst. Innovation (2021). https://doi.org/10.3390/asi4040087
8. Paschek, D., Draghici, A.: Industry 5.0 – The expected impact of next industrial revolution. Thriving on Future Education, Industry, Business and Society; Proceedings of the MakeLearn and TIIM International Conference 2019, ToKnowPress (2019)
9. Di Nardo, M., Yu, H.: Special issue 'industry 5.0: the prelude to the sixth industrial revolution. MDPI AG (2021). https://doi.org/10.3390/asi4030045
10. Adel, A.: Future of industry 5.0 in society: human-centric solutions, challenges and prospective research areas. Springer Science and Business Media Deutschland GmbH 01 Dec 2022. https://doi.org/10.1186/s13677-022-00314-5
11. Mahmood, N.H., et al.: White paper on critical and massive machine type communication towards 6G. (2020). http://arxiv.org/abs/2004.14146.
12. van Abel, B.: Open design now: why design cannot remain exclusive. BIS Publishers (2011). https://opendesignnow.org/.

13. Heskett, J.: Design. Oxford University Press, 22 Sep 2005. https://doi.org/10.1093/actrade/9780192854469.001.0001
14. Tooze, J., Baurley, S., Phillips, R., Smith, P., Foote, E., Silve, S.: Open design: contributions, solutions, processes and projects. Des. J. **17**(4), 538–559 (2014). https://doi.org/10.2752/175630614X14056185480069
15. Castro, H., et al.: Cyber-Physical systems using open design: an approach towards an open science lab for manufacturing. Procedia Comput. Sci. **196**, 381–388 (2022). https://doi.org/10.1016/j.procs.2021.12.027
16. Castro, H., et al.: Open science laboratory for manufacturing: an education tool to contribute to sustainability. Ninth International Conference on Technological Ecosystems for Enhancing Multiculturality (TEEM'21). ACM, 26 Oct 2021. https://doi.org/10.1145/3486011.3486564
17. Plorin, D., Jentsch, D., Hopf, H., Müller, E.: Advanced learning factory (aLF) -method, implementation and evaluation. In: Procedia CIRP, Elsevier B.V., pp. 13–18 (2015). https://doi.org/10.1016/j.procir.2015.02.115
18. Kreimeier, D., Morlock, F., Prinz, C., Krückhans, B., Bakir, D.C.: Holistic learning factories - a concept to train lean management, resource efficiency as well as management and organization improvement skills. In: Procedia CIRP, Elsevier B.V., pp. 184–188 (2014). https://doi.org/10.1016/j.procir.2014.01.040
19. Mion, M.B., Castro, H., Ávila, P., Bastos, J., Moreira, J.: Quo vadis learning factories? Procedia CIRP **130**, 1726–1731 (2024). https://doi.org/10.1016/j.procir.2024.10.307
20. Castro, H., Câmara, F., Ávila, P., Ferreira, L., Cruz-Cunha, M.: Product customization based on digital twin and cloud manufacturing within a decentralized production system. Procedia Comput. Sci. **239**, 2377–2384 (2024). https://doi.org/10.1016/j.procs.2024.06.431
21. Wagner, U., AlGeddawy, T., ElMaraghy, H., Müller, E.: The state-of-the-art and prospects of learning factories. In: Procedia CIRP, Elsevier B.V., pp. 109–114 (2012). https://doi.org/10.1016/j.procir.2012.07.020
22. Tisch, M., Hertle, C., Cachay, J., Abele, E., Metternich, J., Tenberg, R.: A systematic approach on developing action-oriented, competency-based Learning Factories. In: Procedia CIRP, Elsevier B.V., pp. 580–585 (2013). https://doi.org/10.1016/j.procir.2013.06.036
23. Tısch, M., Ranz, F., Abele, E., Metternıch, J., Vera, H.: Learning factory morphology – study of form and structure of an innovative learning approach in the manufacturing domain. Turk. Online J. Educ. Technol. 356–363 (2015)
24. Abele, E., et al.: Learning factories for future oriented research and education in manufacturing. CIRP Ann. Manuf. Technol. **66**(2), 803–826 (2017). https://doi.org/10.1016/j.cirp.2017.05.005
25. Callupe, M., Negri, E., Fumagalli, L.: An inclusive overview of Learning Factories around the globe. Proceedings on the 11th Conference on Learning Factories 2021, SSRN Eletron. J. (2021). https://ssrn.com/abstract=3863491
26. Balve, P., Albert, M.: Project-based learning in production engineering at the heilbronn learning factory. In: Procedia CIRP, Elsevier B.V., pp. 104–108 (2015). https://doi.org/10.1016/j.procir.2015.02.215
27. Hennig, M., Reisinger, G., Trautner, T., Hold, P., Gerhard, D., Mazak, A.: TU wien pilot factory industry 4.0. In: Procedia Manufacturing, Elsevier B.V., pp. 200–205 (2019). https://doi.org/10.1016/j.promfg.2019.03.032

AI as a Driver for Collaboration

A Brief Survey on Human-AI Collaboration for Architecture Design of Industrial Systems

Antonio Monte Pegado(✉), Luis M. Camarinha-Matos, and Andre Dionisio Rocha

NOVA School of Science and Technology, UNINOVA-CTS, and Associated Lab of Intelligent Systems (LASI), NOVA University Lisbon, 2829-516 Lisbon, Portugal
al.pegado@campus.fct.unl.pt, {cam,andre.rocha}@uninova.pt

Abstract. Industrial systems are undergoing accelerated transformation due to the convergence of artificial intelligence, cyber-physical systems, and modular software design, particularly within the vision of Industry 5.0. This shift increases uncertainty, making rigid solutions unsustainable, especially for small and medium-sized enterprises, requiring faster, more flexible design and integration. Simultaneously, the maturity of multi-agent systems and large language model-based agents is redefining possibilities for intelligent, AI-augmented design processes and context-aware software architectures. As such, this paper explores collaborative architecture design between humans and AI agents as a foundation for evolutive manufacturing concepts, where modular components interact in a logic of system of systems through autonomous, agent-based coordination. The authors emphasize architecture description methods and artifacts, human-AI collaboration, agentic traceability, and the potential of industrial data spaces. The objective is to present a brief survey on these topics, supporting scalable and resilient industrial systems that harness the complementary strengths of human and artificial agents.

Keywords: Architecture Design · Human-AI Collaboration · Evolutive Manufacturing · Multi-Agent Systems · Industry 5.0

1 Introduction

The industrial sector is undergoing rapid transformations, driven by the convergence of advanced technologies such as Artificial Intelligence (AI), Cyber-Physical Systems (CPS), and agentic software architectures. These developments are reinforced by the emerging vision of Industry 5.0 (I5.0), which emphasizes human-centric systems, resilience, and sustainability. This technological shift is reshaping how industrial systems are designed, integrated, and evolved over time.

In parallel, the complexity and uncertainty of modern industrial environments [1, 2] - particularly for Small and Medium-sized Enterprises (SMEs) that struggle to keep up with the exponential technological growth [3] - has exposed limitations in traditional software engineering methods regarding both the development and integration of new

Published by Springer Nature Switzerland AG 2026
L. M. Camarinha-Matos et al. (Eds.): PRO-VE 2025, IFIP AICT 770, pp. 55–74, 2026.
https://doi.org/10.1007/978-3-032-05673-3_4

solutions. These systems often lack the flexibility, traceability, and adaptability required to respond to dynamic environments, cross-domain interoperability, and increasing collaboration between human and collaborative technologies [4]. As a response, new forms of human-AI collaboration are emerging, facilitated by breakthroughs in Multi-Agent Systems (MAS), Large Language Models (LLMs), and collaborative networks (CNs) [5], which now offer practical implementations of autonomy, reasoning, and adaptive coordination.

At the same time, the increasing demand for modular and sustainable system design can drive renewed interest in evolutive manufacturing – intelligent and collaborative systems that respond effectively to constant changes in production requirements, exploring modular architectures and intelligent agents. One example is the concept of software symbiosis [6], where reusable software components co-evolve dynamically in a collaborative, sustainable, and context-aware manner.

The objective of this paper is to consolidate foundational concepts and methodological directions. The work adopts the Design Science Methodology (DSM) applied to systems' engineering and scalability, aiming to bridge theoretical approaches in software architecture and MAS with the practical requirements of collaborative industrial ecosystems. The work aims to identify architecture design principles and tools that promote more sustainable and scalable systems, and systemic frameworks that facilitate the co-creation, traceability, and integration of modular components across heterogeneous industrial settings.

2 Base Concepts and Research Method

This section revisits key foundational concepts offering the conceptual basis for addressing solution design and architecture challenges of manufacturing systems. It frames the rationale for exploring human-AI collaborative design, identifying critical gaps, and outlining emerging directions.

Software architecture design in manufacturing systems has long been a critical area of concern, particularly as industrial systems grow in complexity, heterogeneity, and scale [7]. Challenges persist around maintaining **traceability between high-level design artifacts and low-level implementation components**, often leading to architecture drift over time [8]. These issues worsen by the need to integrate technologies at different stages of their lifecycles, which affects system coherence and long-term maintenance. This creates barriers to sustainable evolution and validation, especially when integrating modular components.

This research takes a closer look on how manufacturing systems are built following the **Design Science Methodology**. DSM offers a structured, iterative process for building and integrating artifacts, emphasizing relevance, rigor, and utility: (i) identification of domain-specific requirements; (ii) architecture design using formal and semi-formal methods; and (iii) system implementation resorting to fitting technologies [9]. However, in current practice, these phases often remain siloed, leading to gaps in communication between multidisciplinary teams, inexistent artifact's traceability across system's lifecycle, and lack of adaptability to changing manufacturing paradigms [10, 11].

Recent advances in **Multi-Agent Systems**, particularly those leveraging **Asset Administration Shells (AAS)** [12] and **LLM-based agents** [13], present a promising direction for overcoming these limitations. Agents are no longer simple rule-based executors; they increasingly exhibit capabilities such as context-awareness, adaptive planning, and collaborative reasoning. In manufacturing, MAS can serve as cognitive middleware, enabling intelligent negotiation, resource coordination, and dynamic adaptation. When embedded within architecture design and solution layers, agents can provide runtime validation, enable Architecture-as-Code (AaC) traceability, and support cross-domain abstraction handling, in part exemplified by as exemplified by Augusto, et al., with their work on Context-Aware Systems Architecture (CaSA) [14].

Within the context of modular and evolving systems, this paper presents the example of **Software Symbiosis**, loosely inspired by **industrial symbiosis** in manufacturing ecosystems, where the outputs of one entity can serve as resources for another. The term refers to **the reuse of modular software components that interoperate to achieve shared goals or processes with increased complexity (system-of-systems)**. This symbiotic behaviour is supported by agent-mediated coordination, where modules are aware of each other's interfaces, constraints, and dependencies. In industrial environments, this enables resilient operation, and scalable evolution [15, 16], especially when components are sourced from industrial data spaces or marketplaces.

The research method adopted in this work combines **conceptual modelling**, **literature synthesis**, and insights from **applied research projects** in manufacturing contexts. Ultimately, this work aims to contribute to the emerging body of knowledge on **human-AI collaboration for architecture design** and paves the way for the adoption of **agentic** industrial systems.

3 Design Science Methodology for Systems Engineering and Scalability

To realize the vision of scalable, modular, and evolvable industrial systems, it is essential to take a look at the foundational methodologies guiding system design. A key candidate for this is the DSM, a structured approach widely adopted in engineering disciplines to drive purposeful artifact creation [9]. While DSM has demonstrated value in structuring research and development, the increasing complexity of industrial systems, driven by cyber-physical integration, AI-enabled services, and modular architectures, invites for revisiting this methodology [11].

Figure 1 illustrates an adaptation of the traditional DSM model for manufacturing systems, highlighting the interplay between Requirements, Design, and Solution. Additional ideas were introduced into the DSM representation which highlight this research focal point: the enhancement of design and knowledge base domains through collaborative human-AI tooling, linked artifacts, and evolutive mechanisms, potentially integrated with industrial data spaces and digital marketplaces.

Traditionally, DSM organizes the innovation process into three interconnected but often disjointed domains: **Requirements**, **Design**, and **Solution**. The rigor cycle ensures the scientific grounding of design choices, while the relevance cycle ensures alignment with real-world needs. However, in practice, the iterative and bi-directional nature of these cycles often fail. Artifacts such as design models, and implementation components remain poorly connected, with limited context across phases.

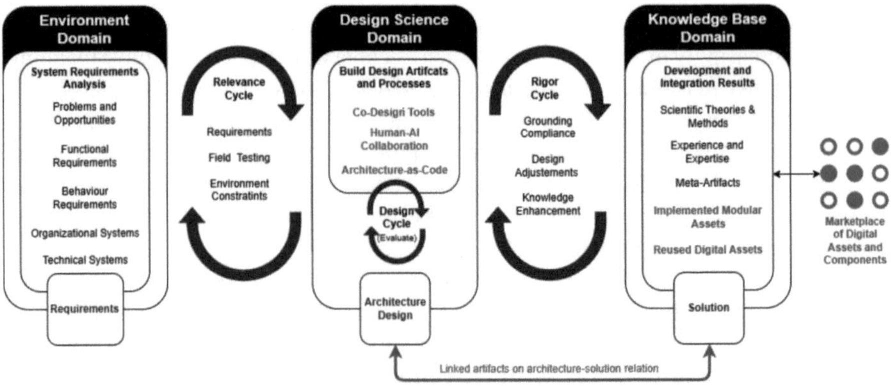

Fig. 1. Extended version of the DSM, adapted from the Design Science Methodology. This model illustrates the solution development process.

Studying system evolution and scalability scenarios allows us to identify the lack of **traceability**, with the history of decisions, rationales, and architecture intent fragmented or altogether lost, as identified by Hyun, et al. [8]. Changes made in one domain (e.g., design) propagate semantically across others (e.g., implementation), resulting in misalignments and errors. Furthermore, when systems are extended, reused, or integrated into new environments, prior knowledge embedded in past projects becomes inaccessible, requiring costly reengineering. To address this, **accountability** must become a core principle, every design decision, code change, or model evolution should be explicitly linked to the **responsible actor**, whether human or AI.

From another perspective, the human context adds further complexity. The teams responsible for these projects are inherently **multidisciplinary**, encompassing experts from software engineering, industrial automation, systems design, and operations [17]. Despite aiming for a shared outcome, they operate with distinct domain vocabularies, priorities, and epistemologies. Requirements may be expressed informally by domain experts, while architects rely on formal models, and implementers use low-level APIs.

To address this, the integration of cross-domain Large Language Models (LLMs) offers potential when appropriately trained for domain-specific tasks. These models can serve as **cognitive interfaces**, capable of **translating**, abstracting, or synthesizing artifacts across the **different knowledge domains** [18, 19], if fine-tuned with relevant architectural, engineering, or manufacturing data. Whether by generating documentation, reverse-engineering behavioural insights from existing components, LLMs can become enablers of shared understanding in complex design ecosystems.

To better understand persistent issues in systems engineering, we developed a structured taxonomy of traceability breakdowns, illustrated in Fig. 2. This representation highlights the key identified sources of disconnection across the software lifecycle. These stem from inconsistent abstractions, misaligned domains, weak artifact linkage, and lack of lifecycle context. Such challenges are further amplified in multidisciplinary teams with divergent languages and models.

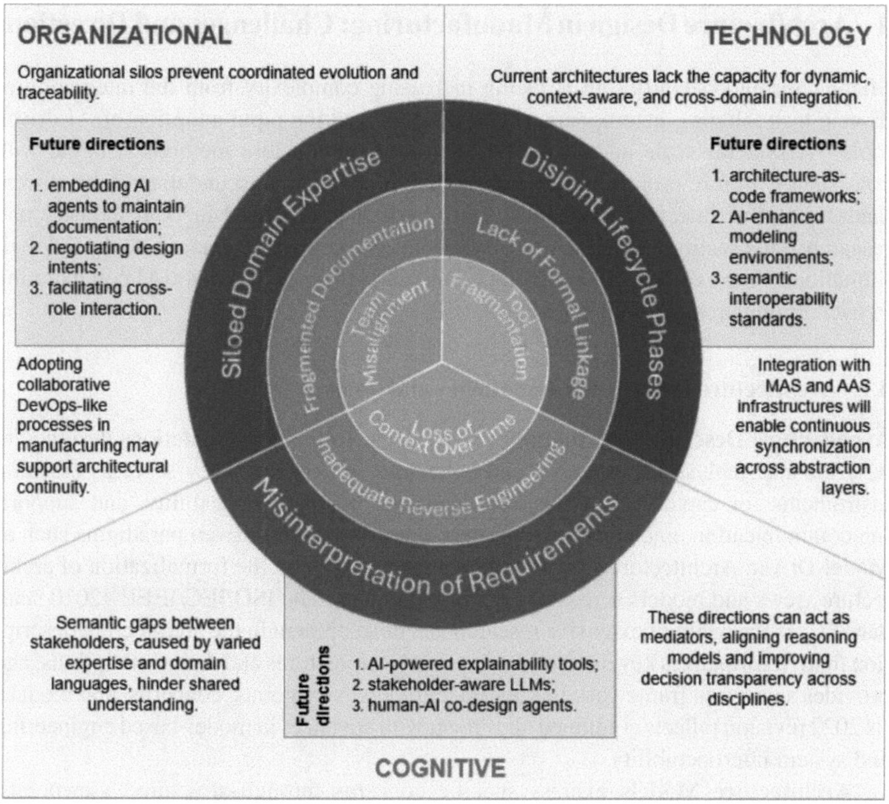

Fig. 2. Layered taxonomy of traceability breakdowns and multidisciplinary constraints in system engineering processes, visualized as a multi-depth pie chart.

Moreover, the Solution phase can be significantly enhanced through integration with **industrial data spaces and modular asset marketplaces**. Pursuing modularity or exploring evolutive paradigms, such as software symbiosis, can be significantly enhanced by access to distributed, reusable technological assets, as exemplified by Iñigo, et al. [20]. Reinventing the wheel is not an option, as such these infrastructures enable accelerated development by supporting the discovery, adaptation, and integration of a wide range of artifacts, such as software applications, ontologies, AI models, and semantic services. This approach not only reduces time-to-market and fosters interoperability but also reinforces the principles of software symbiosis and other evolutive concepts, wherein software modules are collaborative, interoperable, and interdependent within dynamic, collaborative ecosystems.

In conclusion, the DSM extended with traceability, semantic alignment, and intelligent tooling provides a foundation for architecture innovation. To fully unlock this potential, however, it is necessary to take some steps back into the **specific challenges of architecture design in manufacturing environments**, where complexity, legacy constraints, and heterogeneity further hinders system development.

4 Architecture Design in Manufacturing: Challenges and Directions

Manufacturing system design is facing increasing complexity from the integration of diverse technologies, heterogeneous components, and the rapid adoption of AI-driven tools. As systems scale and diversify, traditional architecture methods struggle with consistency. Before proposing new paradigms, it is essential to understand the current landscape of architecture languages, tools, and standards used in both industry and research. This section begins with an examination of existing semantic tools and their limitations, then explores emerging approaches and the role of human-AI collaboration in overcoming architecture challenges.

4.1 Architecture Description Languages and Tools

Architecture Description Languages (ADLs) are formal representations designed to describe and analyse the structure and behaviour of systems. They serve as essential instruments for capturing architecture decisions, enabling traceability, and supporting communication among experts. Closely related to model-driven paradigms such as Model-Driven Architectures (MDA), ADLs have supported the formalization of architecture views and models across engineering domains. The ISO/IEC/IEEE 42010 standard [21] is the result of extensive research and development in the architecture description field. It formalizes key distinctions between architectures and their descriptions, and provides a unifying framework linking stakeholders, viewpoints, concerns, and models. Its 2022 revision reflects continued alignment with advances in model-based engineering and system interoperability.

Architecture Models express specific concerns through structured viewpoints, allowing architects to articulate trade-offs and design rationales. These models are crucial for reviews, documentation, and stakeholder alignment. SysML and the C4 model provide concrete modelling layers suited for systems engineering and software architecture, respectively. **SysML** (extending UML) provides domain-specific diagrams to bridge requirements and design in domains like aerospace, automotive, and robotics [21, 23]. The **C4 model** offers a developer-centric hierarchy (Context, Container, Component, Code), simplifying communication and promoting consistent granularity across stakeholder views [24, 25].

Notable research-oriented projects shaping the ADL landscape include: (1) **OpenCAESAR** [26], from the Eclipse Foundation, offers an ontology-based framework aligned with ISO/IEC/IEEE 42010. It supports semantic modelling for formal traceability and modular viewpoints and integrates with Eclipse Capella. Its alignment with Asset Administration Shells (AAS) enhances interoperability in I5.0 contexts, making it suited for collaborative and modular engineering; (2) **Alloy**, developed at MIT by Jackson, et al. [27], is a lightweight formal language for specifying and verifying architecture constraints. Its analyser helps detect inconsistencies early, supporting modular integrity and traceability.

ADLs have evolved significantly since the 1990s, shifting from formalisms aimed at rigorously describing software architectures to more flexible, semantically rich tools suited for dynamic, multi-domain systems. While early ADLs emphasized modularity and verification, modern approaches focus on interoperability, real-time behaviour, and developer-friendly syntax. Table 1 summarizes this progression, highlighting representative ADLs and their relevance to contemporary design challenges.

The identified ADLs span from integrated MBSE environments to lightweight, domain-specific frameworks. While comprehensive platforms support end-to-end modelling and analysis, more agile tools like Structurizr and Alloy offer focused capabilities for architecture visualization and formal verification. Together, these tools form a layered support infrastructure that reflects the increasing complexity, cross-domain integration, and adaptability demands of modern systems. Table 2 provides an overview of representative tools and their alignment with current ADL practices.

Table 2. Overview of tools supporting ADLs and related work. The table details Key characteristics, ADL compatibility, State - Active (A), Research (R), Deprecated (D) -, and Maturity level - Low (L), Medium (M), High (H).

ADL Tool	Year	Description	ADLs Supported	State	Maturity	Refs.
IBM Rhapsody	1997	MBSE tool for systems engineering and code generation.	SysML, UAF, UML	A	H	[41, 42]
Acme Studio	1997	Tool for architecture interchange and style-based design.	Acme ADL	D	L	[31, 43]
Alloy Analyzer	2001	Formal verification tool for architecture constraints.	Agnostic (OMT, UML)	A	M	[44, 45]
Eclipse EMF	2002	Framework for building ADLs and modelling tools.	Agnostic (DSLs using UML)	A	H	[46, 47]
Cheddar	2003	Open-source real-time scheduling and timing analysis tool.	AADL, MARTE, Cheddar	A	M	[48, 49]
Arch Studio 5	2005	Tool suite for dynamic architectures and reconfiguration.	xADL 3.0 (XML)	D	L	[50, 51]
OSATE	2006	IDE for AADL modelling, analysis, and code generation.	AADL	A	H	[52, 53]

(continued)

Table 2. (*continued*)

ADL Tool	Year	Description	ADLs Supported	State	Maturity	Refs.
Papyrus	2008	Open-source UML/SysML with ADL-like profiles.	SysML, MARTE, ISO 42010	A	M	[54, 55]
TASTE Toolchain	2010	Toolkit for embedded systems validation and code generation.	AADL	A	M	[56]
MASIW Framework	2012	Open-source framework for safety code generation.	AADL (Ocarina), ASN.1 XML	A	M	[57, 58]
AADL Inspector	2012	Commercial tool for AADL graphical modelling and analysis.	AADL	A	M	[59, 60]
Eclipse Capella	2014	Open-source MBSE tool for industrial systems.	Arcadia DSL (UML / SysML)	A	H	[61, 62]
Structurizr	2017	Documentation tool for C4 architecture diagrams.	Structurizr DSL (C4 model)	A	M	[39, 63]
Eclipse BaSyx	2018	Implements Asset Administration Shells for I4.0/5.0 ecosystems.	AAS (RAMI 4.0)	A	M	[64, 65]

4.2 ADLs Limitations for Architecture Modelling in Manufacturing Systems

Modern manufacturing systems, especially under Industry 4.0 and CPS, face growing architecture complexity. These systems integrate heterogeneous elements, including control software, industrial equipment (e.g., robots, sensors, actuators), and human operators, across multiple abstraction layers and life cycle stages. Despite progress in ADLs and tooling, several core challenges remain unresolved.

Architecture models must support the **heterogeneous integration** of diverse physical and digital components, including co-design of embedded technology, IoT-enabled assets, human-in-the-loop interactions, and distributed CPS environments [66]. While ADLs like AADL partially address this, they lack abstractions for key elements, and toolchains such as OSATE or Papyrus demand extensive customization.

Table 1. Overview of ADLs and related work. The table details ADL Description, State - Active (A), Research (R), Deprecated (D) -, and Maturity level - Low (L), Medium (M), High (H).

ADL	Year	Description	Key Use Case	State	Maturity	Refs.
C2	1995	Hierarchical and message-based architecture style for extensible systems.	Distributed systems	D	M	[28]
Darwin	1995	Hierarchical component modelling with dynamic binding and type systems.	Distributed systems	D	L	[29]
Wright	1997	Explicit connector types and automated property checking.	Verification component interactions	D	L	[30]
Acme	1997	Extensible meta-model for style-based design and ADL interoperability.	Architecture interchange	D	M	[31, 32]
xADL 3.0	2001	XML-based language for runtime reconfiguration and versioning.	Dynamic architectures	D	L	[33]
AADL	2004	Domain-specific language for hardware/software co-design and formal analysis.	Critical embedded systems	A	H	[34, 35]
MontiArc	2010	Extensibility and ease of use to meet domain-specific requirements	Distributed systems	R	L	[36]
SBC-ADL	2017	Combines behaviour trees and contracts for validation and fault injection.	Autonomous systems testing	R	L	[37, 38]

(*continued*)

Table 1. (*continued*)

ADL	Year	Description	Key Use Case	State	Maturity	Refs.
Structurizr DSL	2017	Text-based C4 modelling for diagrams and documentation.	Software architecture visualization	A	H	[39]
DTDL	2020	JSON-LD description for smart devices, assets, spaces, and environments.	Digital Twins description	A	M	[40]

Dynamic reconfiguration, essential for adapting production lines in real time, is weakly supported, often handled outside the architecture layer, causing inconsistencies in system evolution [67].

ADLs lack support for **multi-view modelling** across domains like control, process, and communication, which is crucial for aligning engineering perspectives across the whole team. Tool silos and weak interoperability make integration difficult. **Traceability from architecture to implementation** remains limited; few tools support automated linking of models to code or configurations [8]. Formal methods like Alloy or AADL annexes are rarely applied due to complexity or limited expressiveness.

These persistent gaps demand more adaptive, collaborative modelling approaches to enhance decision-making and coherence across domains. AI-powered multi-agent systems (MAS) offer a promising solution, providing the system-level cognition needed for traceability, context-awareness across artifacts, and explainable interactions between AI and human operators (Table 3).

Table 3. Summary of key ADLs limitations for manufacturing systems.

Limitation	Description	ADLs
Heterogeneity support	Low integration of IoT, robotics, human roles, and cyber-physical systems.	C2, Wright, xADL 3.0, AADL, MontiArc, SBC-ADL, Structurizr DSL
Dynamic reconfiguration	Limited runtime adaptability and weak support for system evolution.	C2, Darwin, xADL 3.0, AADL, MontiArc
Multi-view modelling	Lack of cross-domain integration and tool interoperability.	C2, AADL, MontiArc, SBC-ADL, DTDL
Toolchain fragmentation	Tools are siloed by vendor or domain; limited interoperability.	xADL 3.0, AADL, MontiArc, DTDL
Traceability	Weak linkage between architecture and implementation.	Wright, xADL 3.0, AADL, Structurizr DSL

(*continued*)

Table 3. (*continued*)

Limitation	Description	ADLs
Industrial applicability	Formal methods underused due to complexity and limited expressiveness.	Wright, Acme, AADL, SBC-ADL
Cognitive barrier	High learning curve, specific semantic, and poor usability for non-experts.	Wright, Acme, xADL 3.0, AADL, SBC-ADL
AI integration gap	ADLs not designed for AI-in-the-loop decision-making.	All ADLs on Table 1

5 Human-AI Collaborative Design

As manufacturing systems evolve into complex, interconnected ecosystems, often referred to as systems of systems, the architecture design process faces unprecedented challenges. Traditional ADLs and associated tools, while foundational, often fall short in addressing the dynamic, heterogeneous, and collaborative nature of modern manufacturing environments. To address this, integrating Human-AI collaboration in the design process offers a promising path forward (Fig. 3), enhancing the way architectures are conceived, validated, and evolved collaboratively [68].

Fig. 3. Abstract representation of Human-AI collaboration in the Design Science Methodology applied to manufacturing systems engineering (generated in collaboration with AI).

Manufacturing environments evolve continuously, requiring **adaptable architecture strategies**. AI could be extended to support both **redesign and validation** by analyzing operational data and suggesting adjustments to optimize performance or respond to emerging requirements [69]. This continuous feedback loop between system operation and design ensures that the architecture remains resilient and aligned with organizational goals [70].

AI technologies could play a transformative role in future collaborative architectural design environments [71]. While still an emerging area of research, generative tools show potential for exploring large design spaces under user-defined constraints, aiming to meet performance, cost, and integration requirements. Similarly, **AI-powered simulation and verification** engines may eventually help reduce feedback cycles and guide designers toward more robust architectural decisions. This could be particularly valuable in manufacturing, where architectures involve complex interactions between numerous physical and cyber subsystems.

A key development is the adoption of the **AaC** paradigm. Adapted from DevOps principles, AaC treats architecture models as structured, version-controlled artifacts expressed in domain-specific languages or textual DSLs [72]. This approach enhances reproducibility, enabling collaborative workflows, validation, and automated design of system architectures. It aligns with AI tools that can analyse, generate, or refactor architecture code, enabling new forms of system intelligence and scaling.

Beyond design generation, LLMs could be developed to assist in explaining existing architecture design artifacts [73]. By incorporating domain-specific knowledge, they may support explanations for different stakeholders, potentially improving communication and understanding within multidisciplinary teams. The growing accessibility of LLM tools has increased readiness to adopt AI in daily processes. However, integration remains challenged by brittle, context-limited agents and the difficulty of aligning human and AI reasoning. More critically, organizational inertia to changing established workflows continues to hinder adoption. Addressing these constraints is key to realizing AI-integrated system design. Table 4 summarizes key activities throughout the system development process, highlighting how human expertise and AI capabilities collaborate to enhance efficiency, adaptability, and traceability in contemporary engineering workflows.

Table 4. Summary of complementary roles of humans and AI across systems engineering.

Activity	Human Role	AI Role
Requirements Engineering	Engage experts, define objectives, prioritize and negotiate conflicting needs.	Extract intent from documents/meetings, suggest structured specifications, identify inconsistencies and missing links.
Architecture Design & Decomposition	Make high-level decisions, choose patterns/styles, define constraints and quality attributes.	Recommend architectures based on prior cases, generate component structures, explore trade-offs using simulations.
Modelling & Architecture-as-Code	Define and manage architecture models, ensure domain alignment and design rationale.	Generate or refactor models from intent, maintain structural correctness, support versioning and configuration.

(continued)

Table 4. *(continued)*

Activity	Human Role	AI Role
Validation, Simulation & Analysis	Interpret results, make trade-off decisions, ensure design meets requirements.	Run formal checks or simulations, detect constraint violations, visualize behaviour and reconfiguration paths.
Traceability & Change Management	Ensure traceability across lifecycle, manage system evolution and maintain accountability.	Automate linkages between artifacts, monitor change impact, log authorship and rationale for each decision.
Communication & Documentation	Justify decisions, explain models to diverse experts, coordinate multidisciplinary teams.	Generate readable summaries, adapt content for different audiences, maintain synchronized documentation.

In summary, human-AI collaboration and advanced AI tools are beginning to redefine architecture modelling in manufacturing. By integrating AI-driven design, AaC, and cross-domain explainability, this approach addresses key ADL limitations, enabling more adaptive, collaborative, and intelligible system architectures aligned with the speed and complexity of modern engineering systems.

6 Architecture Design Toward Complex and Evolving Systems

6.1 Main Findings

This work highlights the persistent architecture challenges in modern manufacturing systems, particularly those arising from complexity, heterogeneity, and dynamic adaptation. Existing **ADLs and tools remain limited in their ability to represent, integrate, and evolve** systems effectively. Issues of fragmentation, lack of traceability, and poor interoperability hinder their application across engineering domains.

In response to these limitations, human-AI collaborative design emerges as a promising alternative. AI-enhanced tools show strong potential in augmenting design processes, automating analysis and generation, and improving communication among experts. Approaches such as AaC, generative design, and explainable AI collectively redefine how architectures are modelled, validated, and evolved. For example, AaC converts architectural models into structured, machine-readable formats, enabling automated validation, traceability, and lifecycle management. Explainable AI enhances cross-disciplinary collaboration by making system logic transparent and aligning diverse domain perspectives. These findings suggest a **shift toward traceable artifacts and collaborative architecture practices**, better suited to the demands of evolving manufacturing systems. Figure 4 represents an overview of identified opportunities and limitations across our work.

While human-AI collaboration addresses several challenges, achieving traceability and interoperability in manufacturing systems necessitates **deeper integration of AI**. This could call for the adoption of MAS and AAS as foundational components.

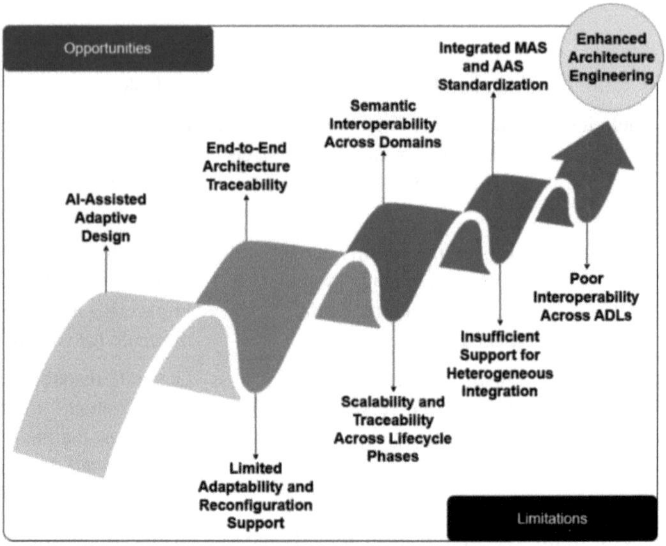

Fig. 4. Illustration of identified opportunities and limitations of architecture design processes.

6.2 Future Directions

This vision goes beyond AI supporting the design process and instead considers how systems themselves may become composed of intelligent entities. As such, it raises new questions about how to design for emergent behaviour and inter-agent collaboration.

MAS frameworks consist of autonomous agents that collaborate to achieve complex goals. Each agent can make decisions, execute tasks, negotiate execution, report system states, and share technical, behavioural, or connectivity-related information.

Realizing the potential of human-AI collaboration may require more than isolated design assistance. **AI could be embedded within systems themselves** to maintain architecture compliance, interpret context, and support informed decision-making, as suggested by initiatives like the **MAS4AI** project, which explores how modular production environments may benefit from AI-assisted support [74]. In such scenarios, AI-powered agents could evolve toward the **cognitive capabilities needed for system-wide awareness** and reasoning across design, implementation, and operation [75]. This invites for a shift from static module design to ecosystems of intelligent agents, enabling architectures to be aware, self-explanatory, and bridge human–machine understanding.

On the other hand, the **AAS** provides a standardized digital representation of industrial assets, **encapsulating** relevant information in a readable and technology-independent format. In future-oriented architectures, each component could be associated with an AAS instance that includes requirements, design models, implementation details, and agents. This structure may offer a path toward **integration across digital and physical domains** [20], supporting interoperability, traceability, and personalized user-system interaction through avatar agents.

Therefore, future work should focus on integrating AI into the industrial engineering design process to support the creation of new solutions and enable explainability across domains. This involves developing an extended AAS structure that captures both design-time and runtime artifacts, allowing for end-to-end traceability across modular components. These advances can enhance MAS by fostering greater agent collaboration and embedding system-level context awareness. Finally, critical challenges around transparency, responsibility allocation of human-AI decisions must be addressed by linking system artifacts to the collaborative design and operational history.

7 Conclusions

Architecture design in manufacturing systems remains challenged by heterogeneous components, poor traceability, and limited support for multidisciplinary collaboration. Despite the mature role of ADLs and existing tools, their limitations in handling the dynamism of evolutive system-of-systems are evident. Our findings reinforce the need for AI-assisted architectures, artifact traceability and collaborative design.

Emerging solutions lie in the integration of human-AI collaboration, where AI assists not just in generating designs but in making them aware of evolving contexts. Moving forward, system-wide cognition could be supported by intelligent MAS, capable of negotiating, contextualizing, and maintaining traceability across lifecycle stages, while the AAS presents itself as a unifying framework for this ecosystem, encapsulating digital representations, agent logic, and architecture artifacts.

This study highlights encouraging progress toward collaborative and intelligent system design. Yet, the integration of cognitive and collaborative intelligence across architecture layers remains limited. **There is a clear need to further explore synergies between manufacturing architecture, AI-driven cognition, and collaborative networks**, and to develop effective frameworks to support them.

Acknowledgments. This work was funded in part by the Portuguese Foundation for Science and Technology (FCT) under the Center of Technology and Systems (CTS) program CTS/00066.

References

1. Peres, R.S., Jia, X., Lee, J., Sun, K., Colombo, A.W., Barata, J.: Industrial artificial intelligence in industry 4.0 - systematic review, challenges and outlook. IEEE Access **8**, 220121–220139 (2020). https://doi.org/10.1109/ACCESS.2020.3042874
2. Oztemel, E., Gursev, S.: Literature review of Industry 4.0 and related technologies. J. Intell. Manuf. **31**(1), 127–182 (2020). https://doi.org/10.1007/s10845-018-1433-8
3. Abdulnour, S., Baril, C., Abdulnour, G., Gamache, S.: Implementation of Industry 4.0 Principles and Tools: Simulation and Case Study in a Manufacturing SME. Sustainability **14**(10), Art. no. 10 (2022). https://doi.org/10.3390/su14106336
4. Santos, L.M.A.L.D., et al.: Industry 4.0 collaborative networks for industrial performance. J. Manuf. Technol. Manag. **32**(2), 245–265 (2020). https://doi.org/10.1108/JMTM-04-2020-0156
5. Camarinha-Matos, L.M., Rocha, A.D., Graça, P.: Collaborative approaches in sustainable and resilient manufacturing. J. Intell. Manuf. **35**(2), 499–519 (2024). https://doi.org/10.1007/s10845-022-02060-6

6. Monte Pegado, A., Dionisio Rocha, A., Barata, J.: Enhancing software distribution and collaboration in manufacturing: developing the IMOS platform. IEEE Access **13**, 480–494 (2025). https://doi.org/10.1109/ACCESS.2024.3521867
7. Qin, Z., Lu, Y.: Self-organizing manufacturing network: a paradigm towards smart manufacturing in mass personalization. J. Manuf. Syst. **60**, 35–47 (2021). https://doi.org/10.1016/j.jmsy.2021.04.016
8. Hyun, S., Hurtado, J.A.: Traceability of architectural design decisions and software artifacts: a systematic mapping study. Found. Comput. Decis. Sci. **48**(4), 401–423 (2023). https://doi.org/10.2478/fcds-2023-0018
9. Kırmızı, M., Kocaoglu, B.: Digital transformation maturity model development framework based on design science: case studies in manufacturing industry. J. Manuf. Technol. Manag. **33**(7), 1319–1346 (2022). https://doi.org/10.1108/JMTM-11-2021-0476
10. Andersen, R., Napoleone, A., Andersen, A.-L., Brunoe, T.D., Nielsen, K.: A systematic methodology for changeable and reconfigurable manufacturing systems development. J. Manuf. Syst. **74**, 449–462 (2024). https://doi.org/10.1016/j.jmsy.2024.04.008
11. Agote-Garrido, A., Martín-Gómez, A.M., Lama-Ruiz, J.R.: Manufacturing system design in industry 5.0: incorporating sociotechnical systems and social metabolism for human-centered, sustainable, and resilient production. Systems **11**(11), Art. no. 11 (2023). https://doi.org/10.3390/systems11110537
12. Sakurada, L., Leitao, P., la Prieta, F.D.: Agent-based asset administration shell approach for digitizing industrial assets. IFAC-Pap. **55**(2), 193–198 (2022). https://doi.org/10.1016/j.ifacol.2022.04.192
13. Li, X., Wang, S., Zeng, S., Wu, Y., Yang, Y.: A survey on LLM-based multi-agent systems: workflow, infrastructure, and challenges. Vicinagearth **1**(1), 9 (2024). https://doi.org/10.1007/s44336-024-00009-2
14. Augusto, J.C., Quinde, M.J., Oguego, C.L., Giménez Manuel, J.: Context-Aware Systems Architecture (CaSA). Cybern. Syst. **53**(4), 319–345 (2022). https://doi.org/10.1080/01969722.2021.1985226
15. Torayev, A., Martínez-Arellano, G., Chaplin, J.C., Sanderson, D., Ratchev, S.: Towards modular and plug-and-produce manufacturing apps. Procedia CIRP **107**, 1257–1262 (2022). https://doi.org/10.1016/j.procir.2022.05.141
16. Vogel-Heuser, B., Neumann, E.-M., Fischer, J.: MICOSE4aPS: industrially applicable maturity metric to improve systematic reuse of control software. ACM Trans. Softw. Eng. Methodol. **31**(1), 5:1–5:24 (2021). https://doi.org/10.1145/3467896
17. Wu, Y., Zhou, L., Zheng, P., Sun, Y., Zhang, K.: A digital twin-based multidisciplinary collaborative design approach for complex engineering product development. Adv. Eng. Inform. **52**, 101635 (2022). https://doi.org/10.1016/j.aei.2022.101635
18. Zhou, X., Hu, Y., Jia, Q., Xie, R.: Cross-domain integration for general sensor data synthesis: leveraging LLMs and domain-specific generative models in collaborative environments. IEEE Sens. J. **24**(24), 42311–42326 (2024). https://doi.org/10.1109/JSEN.2024.3480932
19. Lee, J., Su, H.: A Unified Industrial Large Knowledge Model Framework in Industry 4.0 and Smart Manufacturing **1**, 41–47 (2023). https://doi.org/10.36922/ijamd.3681
20. Iñigo, M.A., et al.: Towards standardized manufacturing as a service through asset administration shell and international data spaces connectors. In: IECON 2022 – 48th Annual Conference of the IEEE Industrial Electronics Society, pp. 1–6 (2022). https://doi.org/10.1109/IECON49645.2022.9968592
21. ISO/IEC/IEEE 42010:2022(en), Software, systems and enterprise — Architecture description. Accessed: 16 Mar. 2025. https://www.iso.org/obp/ui/en/#iso:std:iso-iec-ieee:42010:ed-2:v1:en

22. Arantes, M., Bonnard, R., Mattei, A.P., de Saqui-Sannes, P.: General architecture for data analysis in industry 4.0 using SysML and model based system engineering. In: 2018 Annual IEEE International Systems Conference (SysCon), pp. 1–6 (2018). https://doi.org/10.1109/SYSCON.2018.8369574
23. Dahmann, J., et al.: SysML executable systems of system architecture definition: a working example. In: 2017 Annual IEEE International Systems Conference (SysCon), pp. 1–6 (2017). https://doi.org/10.1109/SYSCON.2017.7934816
24. Vázquez-Ingelmo, A., García-Holgado, A., García-Peñalvo, F.J.; C4 model in a Software Engineering subject to ease the comprehension of UML and the software. In: 2020 IEEE Global Engineering Education Conference (EDUCON)pp. 919–924 (2020). https://doi.org/10.1109/EDUCON45650.2020.9125335
25. Jokste, L., Kampars, J.: Comprehensible software architecture visualization with C4 model for WRM ecosystem members. In: 2024 IEEE 65th International Scientific Conference on Information Technology and Management Science of Riga Technical University (ITMS), pp. 1–5 (2024). https://doi.org/10.1109/ITMS64072.2024.10741937
26. Lab, R.; openCAESAR Enables Ontological Modeling and Analysis. openCAESAR. Accessed: 29 Mar. 2025. https://www.opencaesar.io/
27. Jackson, D.: Alloy open source language and analyzer for software modelling. Alloy. Accessed: 03 Apr. 2025. https://alloytools.org/
28. Bau, N., Endres, S., Gerz, M., Gökgöz, F.; A cloud-based architecture for an interoperable, resilient, and scalable C2 information system. In: 2018 International Conference on Military Communications and Information Systems (ICMCIS), pp. 1–7 (2018). https://doi.org/10.1109/ICMCIS.2018.8398692
29. Mohsin, A., Janjua, N.K.: A review and future directions of SOA-based software architecture modeling approaches for System of Systems. Serv. Oriented Comput. Appl. **12**(3), 183–200 (2018). https://doi.org/10.1007/s11761-018-0245-1
30. Araújo, C., Batista, T., Cavalcante, E., Oquendo, F.; Generating formal software architecture descriptions from semi-formal SysML-based models: a model-driven approach. In: Gervasi, O., Murgante, B., Misra, S., Garau, C., Blečić, I., Taniar, D., Apduhan, B.O., Rocha, A.M.A.C., Tarantino, E., Torre, C.M. (eds.) Computational Science and Its Applications – ICCSA 2021, pp. 394–410. Springer International Publishing, Cham (2021). https://doi.org/10.1007/978-3-030-86970-0_28
31. Maroui, R., Ayeb, B.: Integrating the SysML and ACME in a model driven engineering approach to verify the web service composition. In: 2015 IEEE 24th International Conference on Enabling Technologies: Infrastructure for Collaborative Enterprises, pp. 183–189 (2015). https://doi.org/10.1109/WETICE.2015.41
32. Taoufik, S.R., Tahar, B.M., Mourad, K., Faouzi, M.: UML2.0 formalization and acme verification of the qualitative properties of software architectures. In: 2016 IEEE 25th International Conference on Enabling Technologies: Infrastructure for Collaborative Enterprises (WETICE), pp. 192–197 (2016). https://doi.org/10.1109/WETICE.2016.50
33. Medvidović, N., Taylor, R.N., Dashofy, E.M.: Software architecture description revisited. IEEE Trans. Softw. Eng. **51**(3), 789–794 (2025). https://doi.org/10.1109/TSE.2025.3533387
34. Stewart, D., et al.: AADL-Based safety analysis using formal methods applied to aircraft digital systems. Reliab. Eng. Syst. Saf. **213**, 107649 (2021). https://doi.org/10.1016/j.ress.2021.107649
35. Wang, F., et al.: An approach to generate the traceability between restricted natural language requirements and AADL models. IEEE Trans. Reliab. **69**(1), 154–173 (2020). https://doi.org/10.1109/TR.2019.2936072

36. Butting, A., et al.: Systematic language extension mechanisms for the montiarc architecture description language. In: Anjorin, A., Espinoza, H. (eds.) Modelling Foundations and Applications, pp. 53–70. Springer International Publishing, Cham (2017). https://doi.org/10.1007/978-3-319-61482-3_4
37. Chen, R., Sun, S.-P., Chao, W.S.: Architecture-oriented design method for smart tourism innovative service systems. In: 2016 International Conference on Advanced Materials for Science and Engineering (ICAMSE), pp. 219–222 (2016). https://doi.org/10.1109/ICAMSE.2016.7840284
38. Ma, W.-M., Wang, H.-T., Chao, W.S.: Model-based systems engineering using structure-behavior coalescence modeling language. In: 2022 14th International Conference on Information Technology and Electrical Engineering (ICITEE), pp. 109–113 (2022). https://doi.org/10.1109/ICITEE56407.2022.9954100
39. Nicacio, J., Petrillo, F.: An approach to build consistent software architecture diagrams using devops system descriptors. In: Proceedings of the 25th International Conference on Model Driven Engineering Languages and Systems: Companion Proceedings, in MODELS '22, pp. 312–321. Association for Computing Machinery, New York, NY, USA (2022). https://doi.org/10.1145/3550356.3561567
40. Schmidt, C., Volz, F., Stojanovic, L., Sutschet, G.: Increasing interoperability between digital twin standards and specifications: transformation of DTDL to AAS. Sensors **23**(18), Art. no. 18 (2023). https://doi.org/10.3390/s23187742
41. Rott, J., et al.: Integrating hierarchical task analysis into model-based system design using airbus XHTA and IBM rational rhapsody. In: 2018 IEEE International Conference on Industrial Engineering and Engineering Management (IEEM), pp. 1856–1860 (2018). https://doi.org/10.1109/IEEM.2018.8607656
42. Batteh, J., et al.: Material production process modeling with automated modelica models from IBM rational rhapsody. Model. Conf., 158–167 (2022). https://doi.org/10.3384/ECP21186158
43. Medeiros, A.L., Cavalcante, E., Batista, T., Silva, E.: ArchSPL-MDD: An ADL-based model-driven strategy for automatic variability management. In: 2015 IX Brazilian Symposium on Components, Architectures and Reuse Software, pp. 120–129 (2015). https://doi.org/10.1109/SBCARS.2015.23
44. Wang, X., Rutle, A., Lamo, Y., Box, P.O.; Towards User-Friendly and Efficient Analysis with Alloy
45. Kafa, V., Siegburg, M., Voigtländer, J.: Exercise Task Generation for UML Class/Object Diagrams, via Alloy Model Instance Finding. In: Tait, B., Kroeze, J., Gruner, S. (eds.) ICT Education, pp. 112–128. Springer International Publishing, Cham (2020). https://doi.org/10.1007/978-3-030-35629-3_8
46. Kahani, N., Bagherzadeh, M., Dingel, J., Cordy, J.R.: The problems with eclipse modeling tools: a topic analysis of eclipse forums. In: Proceedings of the ACM/IEEE 19th International Conference on Model Driven Engineering Languages and Systems, pp. 227–237. ACM, Saint-malo France (2016). https://doi.org/10.1145/2976767.2976773
47. Sánchez Cuadrado, J., Gogolla, M.: Model Finding in the EMF Ecosystem. J. Object Technol. **19**, 10:1 (2020). https://doi.org/10.5381/jot.2020.19.2.a10
48. Fotsing, C., et al.: Cheddar Architecture Description Language
49. Dong, Y., Gou, Q., Tang, P.: Architecture-Level Schedulability Analysis with IO Constraint using AADL. In: 2021 8th International Conference on Dependable Systems and Their Applications (DSA), pp. 220–229 (2021). https://doi.org/10.1109/DSA52907.2021.00034
50. Marmsoler, D., Gidey, H.K.: FACTum studio: a tool for the axiomatic specification and verification of architectural design patterns. In: Bae, K., Ölveczky, P.C. (eds.) Formal Aspects of Component Software, pp. 279–287. Springer International Publishing, Cham (2018). https://doi.org/10.1007/978-3-030-02146-7_14

51. Li, Y., Li, Q., Wang, L., Cheng, W., Wu, T.: ADAPT: an agent-based development toolkit and operation platform for self-adaptive systems. In: 2017 IEEE Conference on Open Systems (ICOS), pp. 53–58 (2017). https://doi.org/10.1109/ICOS.2017.8280274
52. Mittal, R., Blouin, D.: OSATE-DIM solves the instance model-view update problem in AADL. In: Proceedings of the 25th International Conference on Model Driven Engineering Languages and Systems: Companion Proceedings, in MODELS '22, pp. 1–6. Association for Computing Machinery, New York, NY, USA (2022). https://doi.org/10.1145/3550356.3559083
53. Mittal, R., Blouin, D.: Facilitating AADL Model Processing and Analysis with OSATE-DIM. Ada Lett **44**(1), 53–57 (2024). https://doi.org/10.1145/3706601.3706609
54. Dupont, G., Mustafiz, S., Khendek, F., Toeroe, M.: Building domain-specific modelling environments with papyrus: an experience report. In: Proceedings of the 10th International Workshop on Modelling in Software Engineering, in MiSE '18, pp. 49–56. Association for Computing Machinery, New York, NY, USA (2018). https://doi.org/10.1145/3193954.3193962
55. Gorecki, S., Ribault, J., Zacharewicz, G., Ducq, Y., Perry, N.: Risk management and distributed simulation in Papyrus tool for decision making in industrial context. Comput. Ind. Eng. **137**, 106039 (2019). https://doi.org/10.1016/j.cie.2019.106039
56. Bardaro, G., Semprebon, A., Chiatti, A., Matteucci, M.: From models to software through automatic transformations: an AADL to ROS end-to-end toolchain. In: 2019 Third IEEE International Conference on Robotic Computing (IRC), pp. 580–585 (2019). https://doi.org/10.1109/IRC.2019.00118
57. Buzdalov, D.: Simulation of AADL models with software-in-the-loop execution. Ada Lett **36**(2), 49–53 (2017). https://doi.org/10.1145/3092893.3092902
58. Olenev, V., Lavrovskaya, I., Korobkov, I., Sheynin, Y.: Design and Simulation of Onboard SpaceWire Networks. In: 2019 24th Conference of Open Innovations Association (FRUCT), pp. 291–299 (2019). https://doi.org/10.23919/FRUCT.2019.8711908
59. Zelenov, S., Buzdalov, S.: Visualization of behavioral aspects of AADL-models. In: 2017 Computer Science and Information Technologies (CSIT), pp. 87–91 (2017). https://doi.org/10.1109/CSITechnol.2017.8312147
60. Amundson, I.: Checking compliance of AADL models with modeling guidelines using resolint. SAE Int. J. Adv. Curr. Pract. Mobil. **5**(5), 1860–1868 (2023). https://doi.org/10.4271/2023-01-0995
61. Badache, N., Roques, P.: Capella to SysML bridge: a tooled-up methodology for MBSE interoperability. In: 9th European Congress on Embedded Real Time Software and Systems (ERTS 2018), TOULOUSE, France (2018). Accessed: 23 Mar. 2025. https://hal.science/hal-01710529
62. Bouba, K., Ait Wakrime, A., Ouhammou, Y., Benaini, R.: A transformation methodology for capella to event-B models with DSL verification. J. Comput. Lang. **77**, 101241 (2023). https://doi.org/10.1016/j.cola.2023.101241
63. Thomas, R., Webb, B.: Architectural views - lecture notes in software engineering. Presented for the Software Architecture course at the University of Queensland (2025)
64. Kannoth, S., et al.: Enabling SMEs to Industry 4.0 Using the BaSyx Middleware: a case study. In: Biffl, S., Navarro, E., Löwe, W., Sirjani, M., Mirandola, R., Weyns, D. (eds.) Software Architecture, pp. 277–294. Springer International Publishing, Cham (2021). https://doi.org/10.1007/978-3-030-86044-8_19
65. Yallıç, F., Albayrak, Ö., Ünal, P.: Asset administration shell generation and usage for digital twins: a case study for non-destructive testing. In: Proceedings of the 3rd International Conference on Innovative Intelligent Industrial Production and Logistics, pp. 299–306, SCITEPRESS - Science and Technology Publications, Valletta, Malta (2022). https://doi.org/10.5220/0011561400003329

66. Sadeghi, M., Carenini, A., Corcho, O., Rossi, M., Santoro, R., Vogelsang, A.: Interoperability of heterogeneous systems of systems: from requirements to a reference architecture. J. Supercomput. **80**(7), 8954–8987 (2024). https://doi.org/10.1007/s11227-023-05774-3
67. Lee, S., Ryu, K.: Development of the architecture and reconfiguration methods for the smart, self-reconfigurable manufacturing system. Appl. Sci. **12**(10), Art. no. 10 (2022). https://doi.org/10.3390/app12105172
68. Tóth, A., Nagy, L., Kennedy, R., Bohuš, B., Abonyi, J., Ruppert, T.: The human-centric Industry 5.0 collaboration architecture. MethodsX **11**, 102260 (2023). https://doi.org/10.1016/j.mex.2023.102260
69. Mozaffar, M., et al.: Mechanistic artificial intelligence (mechanistic-AI) for modeling, design, and control of advanced manufacturing processes: Current state and perspectives. J. Mater. Process. Technol. **302**, 117485 (2022). https://doi.org/10.1016/j.jmatprotec.2021.117485
70. Castañé, G., et al.: The ASSISTANT project: AI for high level decisions in manufacturing. Int. J. Prod. Res. **61**(7), 2288–2306 (2023). https://doi.org/10.1080/00207543.2022.2069525
71. Dhar, R., Vaidhyanathan, K., Varma, V.: Can LLMs Generate Architectural Design Decisions? - An Exploratory Empirical Study. In: 2024 IEEE 21st International Conference on Software Architecture (ICSA), pp. 79–89 (2024). https://doi.org/10.1109/ICSA59870.2024.00016
72. Bucaioni, A., Di Salle, A., Iovino, L., Pelliccione, P., Raimondi, F.: Architecture as Code. In: 2025 IEEE 22nd International Conference on Software Architecture (ICSA), pp. 187–198 (2025). https://doi.org/10.1109/ICSA65012.2025.00027
73. Wu, S., Oltramari, A., Francis, J., Giles, C.L., Ritter, F.E.: Cognitive LLMs: Towards Integrating Cognitive Architectures and Large Language Models for Manufacturing Decision-making (2024). arXiv: arXiv:2408.09176. https://doi.org/10.48550/arXiv.2408.09176
74. 'Multi-Agent Systems for Pervasive Artificial Intelligence for assisting Humans in Modular Production Environments | MAS4AI | Projekt | Fact Sheet | H2020', CORDIS | European Commission. Accessed: 09 May 2025. https://cordis.europa.eu/project/id/957204
75. Xu, J., Sun, Q., Han, Q.-L., Tang, Y.: When Embodied AI Meets Industry 5.0: Human-Centered Smart Manufacturing. IEEECAA J. Autom. Sin. **12**(3), 485–501 (2025). https://doi.org/10.1109/JAS.2025.125327

The Collaborative Role of Generative Artificial Intelligence in Enterprise Architecture Modelling - Experience from Students

Sobah Abbas Petersen(✉)

Department of Computer Science, Norwegian University of Science and Technology, Trondheim, Norway
sap@ntnu.no

Abstract. Access to Generative Artificial Intelligence (GAI) applications have introduced many risks to higher education, such as assessment practices and maintaining academic integrity. Managing these risks while leveraging on the benefits of such technologies calls for new approaches to education and learning activities. This paper describes a workshop with students taking a course in Enterprise Architecture Modelling and Innovation to identify the benefits and risks of using GAI applications to create their models. While the GAI applications lacked the maturity to create correct graphical models, the students identified that these applications could play the role of a domain expert for their models. They could also act as a collaborative sparring partner and support brainstorming about the contents of the models.

Keywords: Enterprise Architecture Modelling · Generative Artificial Intelligence · Collaborative role · Domain Expert · Learning

1 Introduction

The extension of cognition and cognitive tasks to external agents have existed through history and an example of this is making notes for retrieval later. Cognitive offloading has been referred to as "the use of physical action to alter the information processing requirements of a task so as to reduce cognitive demand" [1]. In the context of learning and education, making notes and creating concept maps are examples of memory offloading tasks [2]. Until most recently external agents in most cases functioned as an external memory and the knowledge to use that information for the task at hand has been with the human. Earlier research has shown that relying too much on the Internet (or any other external agent) to store information can hinder the development of the knowledge needed to perform a task [2]. With the arrival of Artificial Intelligence (AI) and Generative Artificial Intelligence (GAI) tools such as ChatGPT from OpenAI, the external agents available today are able to do a lot more than function as an external memory or process well-defined tasks (such as calculations and simulations). These AI tools have the capability to process large amounts of information and data and create new

Published by Springer Nature Switzerland AG 2026
L. M. Camarinha-Matos et al. (Eds.): PRO-VE 2025, IFIP AICT 770, pp. 75–87, 2026.
https://doi.org/10.1007/978-3-032-05673-3_5

knowledge about almost any topic and they can interact with humans in multi-faceted ways [3, 4]. GAI tools, such as ChatGPT, have been described as extending cognition, by enhancing and extending a human's cognitive functions in ways beyond what either a human or machine could do alone [3]. The term collaborative intelligence has been used to describe the augmentation of human intelligence with AI, where the full potential of the solutions are achieved through collaboration [5].

The roles that GAI could play in learning and education has been discussed by many researchers and some of the roles that have been identified are of a collaborative nature, such as a study buddy, or a co-design agent [6, 7]. Furthermore, the possibility of GAI to support social learning in a collaborative activity is of interest to researchers and educators [7]. While the value that GAI tools bring to the educational context are significant, the concern about unethical and irresponsible use of such technologies is of concern to educators. The role that GAI tools could play in minimising the cognitive load by cognitive offloading, and how they could compromise the students' understanding of a subject is another challenge. Thus, the need to enhance awareness and knowledge among students to create value from such technologies for the benefit of their learning has magnified within the last two years.

The research goal of the study described in this paper was to explore the role of GAI in learning Enterprise Architecture Modelling and innovation in enterprises. The paper describes how students in an Enterprise Architecture and Innovation course perceive the benefits of GAI tools and how they have used them for the tasks in the course. It describes the results of a workshop conducted with the students to explore the collaborative role of GAI tools in Enterprise Architecture Modelling, where we use Enterprise Modelling methods. Enterprise Modelling is defined as the "systematic analysis and modelling of processes, organisation structures, products structures, IT-systems or any other perspective relevant for the modelling purpose" [8]. It is about understanding the real world and real-world phenomena and abstracting and conceptualising that.

The contributions of this paper include a SWOT (Strengths, Weaknesses, Opportunities, Threats) analysis of using GAI tools in Enterprise Modelling and an overview of students' perceptions of how GAI tools could add value to the course. Based on these results, a discussion about the collaborative role of GAI in Enterprise Modelling in education and beyond is included.

The rest of this paper is structured as follows: Sect. 2 provides a brief overview of human-AI collaboration in education and Enterprise Modelling; Sect. 3 describes the Enterprise Architecture Modelling and Innovation course; Sect. 4 describes the Research method; Sect. 5 describes the results; Sect. 6 discusses the results in the context of human-AI collaboration in this context and Sect. 7 concludes the paper.

2 Background

This section provides a brief overview of human-AI collaboration in education and Enterprise Modelling and the challenges related to these.

2.1 Human AI Collaboration in Education

Use of AI for idea generation, virtual peers, virtual students or other that are of the same cognitive level and who could generate novel ideas has been identified as a means of leveraging AI in education [9]. Learning is a social activity and the role of conversations as a part of the learning process has been of interest to educators. As such, ways in which students and educators could collaborate with GAI tools and how these tools could augment education have been identified [6, 7]. The GAI tools could collaborate with learners in many ways, such as by acting as possibility engines generating alternative ways to express ideas, as a collaboration coach by helping to find a solution together and as a co-designer by assisting through a design process. An approach to using GAI tools in education has also been to learn prompt engineering and to create custom GPTs, or chatbots, to support students in specific subject domains [10]. Another area where AI tools have been used in education has been to provide timely feedback through adaptive learning analytics. This is an area of growing interest and the need for upskilling educators and the acute need for policies and guidelines have been recognised [11].

2.2 Human AI Collaboration in Enterprise Modelling

Enterprise Modelling involves the systematic analysis and modelling of the different perspectives of an organisation [8] and includes the process of eliciting domain knowledge and requirements to understand the context of modelling. Domain experts play an important role in Enterprise Modelling, where they provide the knowledge for the contents of the models and evaluate the models [12, 13]. Thus, the process of creating enterprise models is a collaborative and iterative process, where the role of the domain expert contributes to the richness and correctness of the models. This process of knowledge elicitation is also similar to that of requirements elicitation in requirements engineering. Current literature suggests that as a natural process for leveraging on the capabilities of Large Language Models and GAI is the benefit from the collective knowledge of many. For example, studies have been conducted where the contributions of human domain experts have been compared with that of ChatGPT, and the domain experts confirmed that ChatGPT could provide accurate and relevant output to prepare for modelling projects [14]. Another study explored the use of ChatGPT to create a process model, or descriptions of a process model, and they concluded that ChatGPT is able to create descriptions of models, even though they are not able to produce the graphical models and that they do have value in modelling as it can assist by collaborating with domain experts to complement their explanations [13]. Another study explored if ChatGPT could be used to generate requirements for a digital twin [15].

One of the challenges faced by information models, such as Business Process Models (BPM) is keeping them updated and ensuring the inclusion of the voices of all the actors involved in the process. The possible integration of GAI through a social media platform dedicated to accompanying BPM has been explored in [16], where the role that could be played by GAI and LLMs have been considered as conversational agents, that could support the collaboration among the different actors.

The studies that have been conducted so far confirm that LLMs and GAI could play a role in Enterprise Modelling and thus, the implications of this on Enterprise Modelling methods and the competences required for conducting Enterprise Modelling are also issues for researchers. In the 4EM (4 Enterprise Modelling) method [17], which is also central to this course, LLMs could contribute to enhancing the different perspectives of the enterprise that is modelled, and therefore additional roles and activities need to be considered to enhance the modelling method [18]. Similarly, the enterprise architecture of any organisation is likely to be affected with the introduction of a new technological solutions, such as an AI application [19, 20].

Studies exploring the use of GAI in Enterprise Modelling highlight that the research area is relevant and there is a need for further studies. Some of the limitations identified in the studies are the lack of understanding of context by, e.g., ChatGPT, and that there are limitations in verifying the correctness of the information provided by them [13].

2.3 Challenges in Human AI collaboration

Challenges in integrating AI into collaborative processes have been a concern addressed by many researchers. One issue is supporting the language or communication for appropriate interactions between the humans and the AI, particularly among heterogeneous AI applications [21]. More recently, with LLMs and GAI application, the reliability and accuracy of information provided by these systems, e.g., as conversational agents, can be a challenge [16]. Issues such as bias and privacy concerns have dominated the debate among researchers and the general public. Most importantly, the need to consider not just the implementation of the AI technology, but to take into account the organisational and social contexts has been emphasised. As such, a socio-technical profiling tool for planning the integration of AI in organisations have been proposed in [22]. The trust in the system is important [11, 23] and collaborative approaches to model and appraise emotions between human and artificial agents to improve trust have been studied [24]. More specifically in the education context, GAI can provide content and solutions that are incorrect or containing errors, and this could be harmful for students [11].

3 Enterprise Architecture Modelling and Innovation Course Description

The learning goal for the course was to obtain theoretical insights and practical skills in Enterprise Architecture Modelling, service innovation and the methods for analysing organisational situations and creating Enterprise Architecture models. The students were required to identify a relevant organisational situation that they could analyse by applying theory and methods from Enterprise Modelling and to create an Enterprise Architecture model using both 4EM [17] and ArchiMate [25]. Hence, we will refer to Enterprise Modelling to imply Enterprise Architecture Modelling.

The main activities in the course included identifying a case to model, creating their enterprise models and innovating the enterprise. The minimum requirement for the enterprise model was to include three or more enterprise perspectives, e.g., processes, goals and organisational aspects. To develop students' understanding of agility in enterprises and the need for innovation in enterprises, the students were then required to apply Service Design methods to innovate one or more services, with focus on the customer or the end user. As a part of the enterprise innovation, the students were also required to develop a sustainable business model for the new service, drawing their attention to not only the economic sustainability of the organisation, but also the broader perspectives of environmental and societal sustainability [26]. Following the innovation task, they were required to enhance or adapt their enterprise models (referred to by some as "to-be" models after the innovation). The sequence of activities in the course is shown in Fig. 1.

The course described in this paper was conducted in autumn 2024 as a part of the studies in the Computer Science department. The course lasted one semester, with lectures and tutorials every week for eleven weeks.

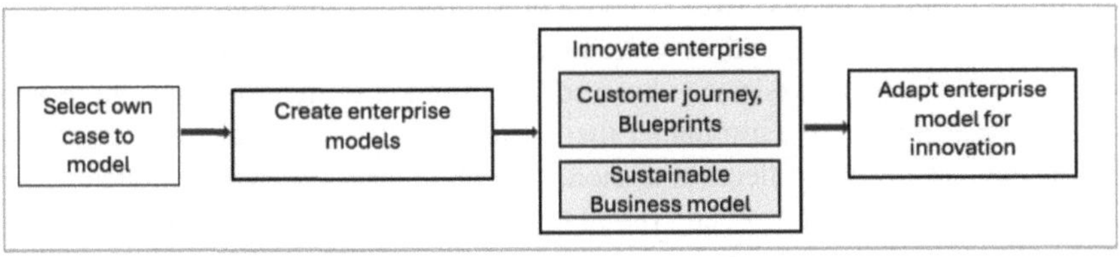

Fig. 1. Course design and activities

Every week, the students were offered three hours of lectures and two hours of tutorials. Attendance was voluntary. The students were assessed on their ability to create models and describe, discuss and reflect upon them in a final report submitted at the end of the semester. A number of learning activities were conducted during the course, including the AI workshop, presentations, peer feedback and group reflections, some of which amounted to twenty percent of the final grade. Over eighty students were registered for the course at the beginning of the semester and thirty-eight completed the course.

4 Research Method

The data for the results presented in this paper was gathered by several methods. At the beginning of the course, a survey was conducted, using an online questionnaire tool, to establish a baseline of their skills and experiences about the course contents in general. Similarly, at the end of the course, an online survey was conducted to gather data about their experience with the course. One of the areas included in the survey was their familiarity and experience with using AI tools. In addition, to explore how they could use AI tools, and to identify the strengths and weaknesses of using them for the tasks in the course, one of the tutorial sessions was used to conduct a workshop, to explore the use of these tools and to raise awareness and enhance their knowledge about the use of these tools for the tasks in the course. A mini survey using Mentimeter was conducted at the end of the workshop.

With the aims to raise awareness and knowledge about the use of AI tools, pre-emp wrong or irresponsible use of AI and to encourage open dialogue, the workshop was conducted during the third week of the course. Attending the lectures and tutorials in the course was not mandatory and hence the participation in the workshop was voluntary.

Twenty-one students participated in the workshop, which lasted two hours. The students worked in groups of 2–4 to try their preferred AI tools to perform one or more tasks in the given assignment, and we focussed on the most important task of creating an Enterprise Model using the given modelling languages. The students were given a short introduction to the aim of the workshop and what they would do in the workshop. The students were asked to work in pairs or groups, and to select an AI tool that they would use. Then they were asked to try to create an enterprise model using the modelling languages Archimate and 4EM, using the AI tool. They were asked to create their own prompts and to use around 10 minutes for this exercise. After that, they were asked to reflect on the results within their group. De Bono's Thinking Hats [27] were introduced to them to make them aware of the different perspectives to consider, so that the reflections were critical. The trial of the AI tool and reflections continued for about an hour. During this time, the teacher and the learning assistant observed and listened to the dialogues, both within and across the groups and stimulated them with questions to encourage discussions. After the exploration and reflection session, a Mentimeter survey was conducted to do a SWOT analysis and to identify any pitfalls or unsuspected dangers. This was followed by a discussion on how these tools could be used to support learning in the course.

5 Results

At the beginning of the course, over eighty students were registered for the course and forty-two students responded to the background survey. The university allows students to register and try out the courses before committing to take the course. Hence the number of students registered at the beginning of the course is less than the ones that complete the course; in this case thirty-eight completed the course. One of the questions asked in the background survey focussed on the students' experience in using GAI and the responses are shown in Fig. 2. The responses show that most of the students have used GAI tools and most of them have learned to use them by themselves. This aligns with the data from the workshop where out of the twenty-one participants in the workshop, twelve participants indicated that they had used AI applications in their courses a lot, while nine indicated that they had not used so much.

During the workshop, all but one student was engaged in exploring the use of AI tools and in discussions with their group and across the groups. One student, who had tried it earlier, appeared to be convinced that the GAI tools were not useful for the tasks in the course and for creating enterprise models. From the dialogue that was taking place among the students, we observed that this student confirmed some of the unsuccessful attempts by other students in creating their models.

The main GAI tool that the students used during the workshop was the free version of ChatGPT, Gemini and Copilot. The results of the final survey confirmed that the majority of the students used ChatGPT.

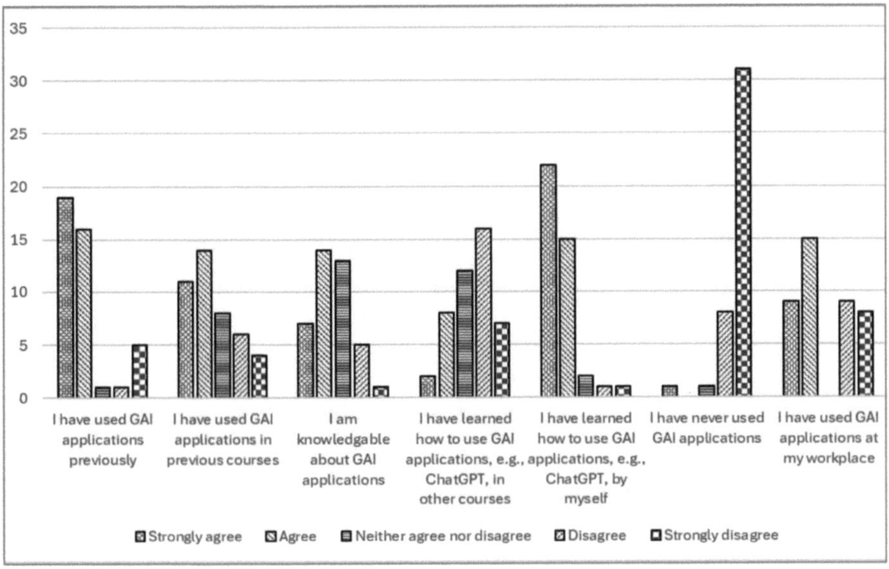

Fig. 2. Students' familiarity with GAI tools (data from survey at the beginning of the course)

5.1 Activities AI Applications Used for

Using Mentimeter, we asked the students "What kinds of activities have you used AI applications for?" The students were allowed to submit more than one response. Twenty responses were received and an overview of these are presented in Fig. 3. Several responses indicated more than one activity, e.g., coding and rewriting text. The individual responses have been grouped into the broader categories such as coding and idea generation. The numbers in paratheses indicate the no. of times they were included in the responses. The most popular activities, other than coding, are shown within a rectangle.

A similar question was asked in the final survey at the end of the course but addressing more specifically about how they actually used AI for the tasks in the course. Twenty-two out of thirty-eight students responded to the final survey (58% of the students who completed the course). An overview of the responses is shown in Fig. 4. It is clear that some of the more popular activities GAI applications were used for during the course align with what they indicated at the beginning of the course, shown in Fig. 3. The highest use of GAI tools was for text generation, including paraphrasing, summarising and translations. Idea generation was also a popular activity, e.g., for brainstorming. The responses to the final survey shown in Fig. 4 aligns with this as it appears that some of the more popular activities that GAI tools were used for during the course were also for writing the report (63.6% responded positive), for generating ideas for the case (36.4%) and for innovation of the case (27.3%). 40.9% of the students responded positively to the statement "Finding my own case to model", which also align with idea generation and brainstorming activities. These are shown within rectangles in Fig. 4. No students responded positively to the statements "I used AI tools to create my Archimate/4EM models". However, the 68.2% responded positively to the statement "Creating models

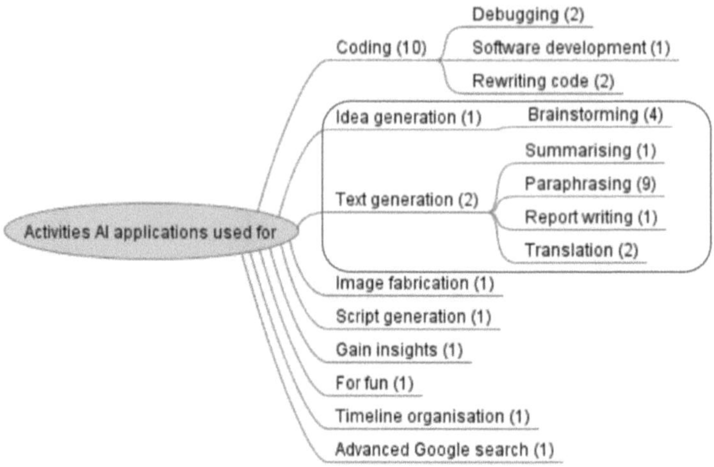

Fig. 3. Activities AI applications were used for prior to the course (data from Mentimeter survey during workshop)

in different modelling languages", which is contrary to the responses to the statements on creating Archimate and 4EM models. The tasks for the course included creating sustainable business models, customer journeys and blueprints for the innovations in the cases and therefore, this result may reflect the use of GAI tools for creating some of these models. In fact, 4.5% responded positively to the statement "I use AI tools to create my business models". Furthermore, the responses indicate that the AI tools also supported course activities other than model development, such as presentations, discussions and peer feedback.

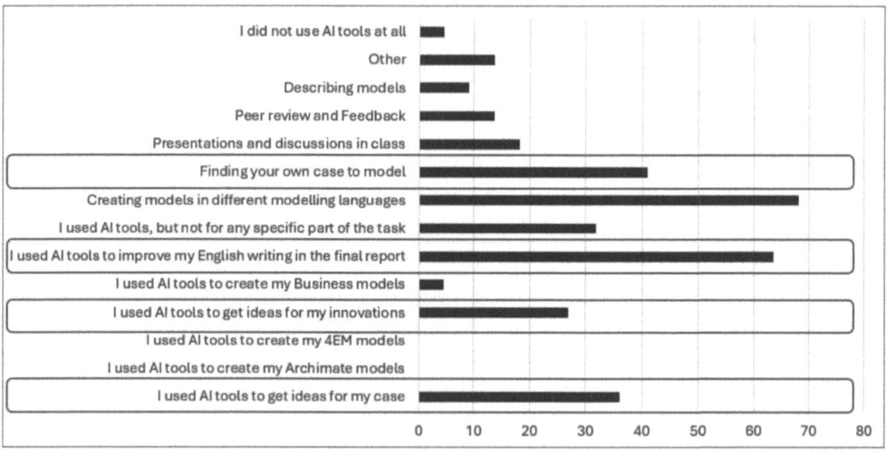

Fig. 4. Activities GAI applications were used for during the course (data from final survey at the end of the course)

5.2 SWOT Analysis

During the workshop, using Mentimeter, a SWOT analysis was conducted to identify the strengths, weaknesses, opportunities and threats related to the use of GAI tools in the course. The responses from the students are shown in Fig. 5, where the bold text indicates the points that are most relevant for the course. The strengths that were identified are well aligned with the activities that the students reported using AI tools for, as shown in Figs. 3 and 4. An additional strength that was indicated was that the AI tool could help you think of things that you hadn't thought of. The weaknesses that were identified include false information and the expertise needed to prompt the current AI applications, which also takes time. The most relevant opportunity is related to the innovation part of the tasks where new ides could be generated faster by using the GAI applications. The threats are related to the fact that the current GI tools are not able to create models, particularly using the languages that were included in the course syllabus. Hence, it could present incorrect models, even in cases where a correct description of a model may be generated. Hence, it does not help students learn the correct contents of the course. In addition, there is of course the threat of becoming overly dependent on these applications, without being able to judge correct or incorrect content that is relevant for the course.

Strenghts	Weaknesses
• **Rewrite text, paraphrasing, recap of text,** • **Translations** • Coding • **Brainstorming, Idea generation** • **Formatting and structuring report** • **Inspiration** • **It helps you think of things that you hadn't thought of before** • Checking what you know, check if answers are correct	• **False information** • Source of the information is not provided • Long answers, "a lot of yapping" • Takes a lot of time • User needs the expertise to prompt it • You have to teach it
Opportunities	**Threats**
• **How to innovate your case** • **Increased speed of idea generation** • Opportunity to complete assignment faster • As an assistant, a powerful assistant • Solution ideation • Optimise basic tasks • New perspectives, new ways of thinking • More concise texts	• **Draw the model in a wrong way. It provides a correct textual description of the model, but creates an incorrect model** • **People don't learn the contents of the course** • **Guide us to the wrong understanding** • **Wrong terminology** • Wrong information, disinformation • It will take over our jobs • People blindly trusting the systems • People won't research on their own any more • Problem of intellectual property • Generated text could be "very formal or roboty" • We may become over dependent on these systems

Fig. 5. SWOT analysis (data from Mentimeter survey during workshop, bold text indicates what is most relevant for the course)

Responses to two specific questions that followed the SWOT analysis in the workshop provided complementary content to those included in Fig. 5: "What are the main pitfalls that you have identified?" and "How do you think AI applications could contribute to the course?". The main pitfalls that were identified could be grouped into trust in the GAI applications and what it does to us. *"There is a fear that we may trust these systems blindly before we learn the theory about the subject we are learning and that we give too much credit to the answers from these systems. As such, we may never learn to do the work ourselves, which would be detrimental to our future jobs"*. An example that reflects this pitfall was experienced by a student who took the course in 2023, where the models and the report that were submitted were generated by a GAI application, and the student was unaware that the models were incorrect, that they did not use the required modelling languages and did not meet the goals of the assignment. Furthermore, the students reported that using these systems are making us dumber, less creative and we may lose the ability to do the actual work on our own.

When asked how the AI applications could contribute to the course, one response said "*nothing*". However, several other responses complemented the opportunities that were identified, including "*a friend to talk to*", "*new ways of thinking*", "*inspiration*" and that it could give a hint on how to get started on the tasks of the course. It was also noted that it could do the thinking (about the case) while the student did the modelling. Most importantly, it could help to save time doing the tasks and could explain theoretical aspects relevant to the course. It could also help to broaden the understanding of the problem domain, known as domain understanding in the context of Enterprise Modelling.

6 Discussions

The research goal of the study described in this paper was to explore the role of GAI in learning Enterprise Architecture Modelling and innovation in enterprises. The results highlight the collaborative role that GAI could play or how students could collaborate with such technologies as domain experts in a subject, or by providing new perspectives and ideas and by acting as a sparring partner to the students.

Based on the students' responses, it can be assumed that they used it in the initial phases of modelling to obtain adequate domain knowledge and the context for the models (describing their cases) as well as during the innovation phase of their enterprise. This is similar to the phases identified in [14] as creating the as-is and to-be models, which is where the role of the domain expert plays an important part. The activity of Enterprise Modelling, by definition is a collaborative activity and includes several roles, e.g., the modelling facilitator and the domain expert, and activities and interactions among the roles [12]. In this course, the students were expected to play the role of the modelling facilitator and the domain expert. It appears that the GAI tools could play the role of the domain expert in some cases or at least provide some of the knowledge of a domain expert. The GAI tools that the students used were helpful in understanding the case that they were planning to model but was of little or no help in creating the models using the Archimate or the 4EM languages. They were helpful, not only because they could suggest new ideas and contents for the case, but sometimes due to bad suggestion that sparked creativity in the student, e.g., a bad goal for the enterprise case may trigger the student to identify a better goal. Thus, they provided inspiration to the students and engaged them as a "sparring partner" as mentioned by one of the students. However, the quality of the results obtained by the students depended on the quality of the prompts used by the students, indicating new competences that were required for successful human and AI collaboration.

During the workshop, some students commented about the modelling that "*they can't actually create the models as they are. I believe they can be trained to do so with a bit of effort, but it's probably not worth it*", and "*generally, AI is not good at making models. You cannot describe a case and receive an Archimate file in return or a model with 4EM*." The dialogues among the students during the workshop indicated that some students were excited because the GAI tools provided better results after several prompts and by feeding related material. On the other hand, there were some students that questioned the excited ones if it was worth spending the time on designing good prompts or just learning to model themselves. These discussions indicate openness to a dialogue both among the students and with the teaching staff and highlighted the social aspects of the learning process. In particular, working in groups during the workshop facilitated thinking aloud, peer feedback and encouragement among the students.

Students found that ChatGPT was able to provide useful information to clarify a case that they could model, and it also provided ideas for innovating the enterprise. However, the output from the GAI tools appeared irrelevant or incorrect at times. It can be argued that GAI is not informed by observations of the real world and it may not be aligned with the real world and the desired [28]. Thus, the ability to reflect on the outputs from the GAI tools is a skill that is necessary for the students to develop, without blindly trusting them. Nevertheless, most students agreed that ChatGPT could bring in a perspective that improves the quality of the model. They also noted that since Enterprise Modelling is a multi-disciplinary activity due to the diverse domains that could be modelled, the gap in the domain knowledge could be fulfilled by ChatGPT.

An important pitfall that was identified was that *"AI usage is problematic when it comes to academic integrity, since the boundary between reference and plagiarism with AI is relatively vague"*. This statement could be interpreted as confusion from students about the appropriate and responsible use of AI tools and implies the relevance and importance of an open dialogue with students to raise their awareness about AI tools in their learning process. Thus, the workshop was aimed to address precisely such concerns from students too.

7 Concluding Remarks

This paper describes how students in an Enterprise Architecture Modelling and Innovation course perceive the benefits of GAI tools and how they have used them for the tasks in the course. It describes the results of a workshop conducted with the students to explore the collaborative role of GAI tools in Enterprise Architecture Modelling. A SWOT analysis was conducted to identify the benefits and risks of using GAI applications to create enterprise models. While the GAI applications lacked the maturity to create correct graphical models, the students identified that these applications could play the role of a domain expert for their models as well as improve the quality of their models by providing new perspectives about the case. They could also act as a collaborative sparring partner and support brainstorming about the contents of the models.

This study confirmed ways in which human and AI collaboration could benefit enterprise architecture modelling, while supporting the collaborative activities in Enterprise Modelling. The study highlighted that the human and AI collaboration could stimulate creativity and creative activities such as brainstorming and idea generation. An interesting observation is that incorrect content suggested by the GAI application could trigger critical reflection and stimulate creative thinking by the students, where the AI component could be considered as playing the role of a Socratic opponent.

The findings from this study suggest that GAI applications could support the collaborative nature of Enterprise Modelling by enhancing that in a classroom context, where the collaboration with a domain expert is unavailable. This also indicates that beyond the classroom, domain experts and enterprise modellers could benefit from using GAI applications in brainstorming, to enrich the domain knowledge and to obtain examples and use cases.

A limitation of this study is the exploratory nature of the workshop and the limited no. of participants in both the workshop and the surveys. Future workshops are planned with students taking other courses including multi-disciplinary project-based courses, to obtain a better understanding of the collaborative role of AI tools and how students collaborate with these tools to enhance their learning process.

Acknowledgements. This work is supported by the Pedagogic Academy at the university, with funding for Excellent Teaching Practitioners.

References

1. Risko, E.F., Gilbert, S.J.: Cognitive Offloading. Trends Cogn. Sci. **20**(9), 676–688 (2016)
2. Nestojko, J.F., Finley, J.R., Roediger Iii, H.L.: Extending Cognition to External Agents. Psychol, Inquiry **24**(4), 321–325 (2013)
3. Lodge, J.M., et al.: It's not like a calculator, so what is the relationship between learners and generative artificial intelligence? Learning: Research and Practice **9**(2), 117–124 (2023)
4. Koh, E., Doroudi, S.: Learning, teaching, and assessment with generative artificial intelligence: towards a plateau of productivity. Learning: Research and Practice **9**(2), 109–116 (2023)
5. Wilson, J., Daugherty, P.R.: Collaborative Intelligence: Humans and AI Are Joining Forces. Harvard Business Review 114–123 (2018)
6. Sabzalieva, E., Valentini, A.: ChatGPT and Artificial Intelligence in Higher Education. Quick Start Guide. UNESCO (2023)
7. Sharples, M.: Towards social generative AI for education: theory, practices and ethics. Learning: Research and Practice **9**(2), 159–167 (2023)
8. Vernadat, F.B.: Enterprise Modelling and Integration. In: Kosanke, K., et al. (eds.) Enterprise Inter- and Intra-Organizational Integration: Building International Consensus, pp. 25–33. Springer US, Boston, MA (2003)
9. Luckin, R., et al.: Intelligence Unleashed. An argument for AI in Education. Pearson, London (2016)
10. Huang, Q., Willems, T., Wang, P.K.: The application of GPT-4 in grading design university students' assignment and providing feedback: An exploratory study. arXiv (2025). arXiv:2409.17698.
11. Giannakos, M., et al.: The promise and challenges of generative AI in education. Behaviour & Information Technology, 1–27 (2024)
12. Persson, A., Stirna, J.: Towards Defining a Competence Profile for the Enterprise Modelling Practitioner. In: van Bommel, P. (ed.) PoEM 2010, pp. 232–245. Springer (2010)
13. Görgen, L., et al.: Large Language Models in Enterprise Modeling: Case Study and Experiences. In: 12th International Conference on Model-Based Software and Systems Engineering (MODELSWARD 2024), pp. 74–85. SCITEPRESS – Science and Technology Public., Lda (2024)

14. Sandkuhl, K., Barn, B., Barat, S.: Neural Text Generators in Enterprise Modeling: Can Chatgpt be Used as Proxy Domain Expert? in Information Systems Development, Organizational Aspects and Societal Trends (ISD2023). Lisbon, Portugal (2023).
15. Blasek, N., et al.: Large language models in requirements engineering for digital twins. In: Companion Proceedings of the 16th IFIP WG 8.1 Working Conference on the Practice of Enterprise Modeling and the 13th Enterprise Design and Engineering Working Conference. Vienna, Austria (2023)
16. Sarr, L.A., et al.: Towards the Integration of Conversational Agents Through a Social Media Platform to Enhance the Agility of BPM. In: Camarinha-Matos, L., et al. (eds.) PRO-VE 2024, pp. 36–48. Springer Nature Switzerland, Albi, France (2024)
17. Sandkuhl, K., et al.: Enterprise Modeling - Tackling Business Challenges with the 4EM Method. Springer (2023)
18. Barn, B.S., Barat, S., Sandkuhl, K.: Adaptation of Enterprise Modeling Methods for Large Language Models. Springer Nature Switzerland, Cham (2024)
19. Sayles, J.: AI and Enterprise Architecture. In: Principles of AI Governance and Model Risk Management: Master the Techniques for Ethical and Transparent AI Systems, pp. 373–382. Apress, Berkeley, CA (2024)
20. Rittelmeyer, J.D., Sandkuhl, K.: Effects of Artificial Intelligence on Enterprise Architectures - A Structured Literature Review. In: 2021 IEEE 25th International Enterprise Distributed Object Computing Workshop (EDOCW) (2021)
21. Petersen, S.A., Rao, J., Tveit, A.: Virtual Enterprises: Challenges in Selecting and Integrating Computational and Human Resources. In: AAMAS 2002, Challenges in Open Agent Environments. Bologne, Italy (2002)
22. Soares, A.L., et al.: Integrating AI in supply chain management: using a socio-technical chart to navigate unknown transformations. In: Camarinha-Matos, L., et al. (eds.) PRO-VE 2024. Springer Nature Switzerland, Albi, France (2024)
23. Gillespie, N., et al.: Trust, attitudes and use of artificial intelligence: A global study 2025. The University of Melbourne and KPMG (2025)
24. Ferrada, F., Camarinha-Matos, L.: Emotions in Human-AI Collaboration. In: Camarinha-Matos, L., et al. (ed.) PRO-VE 2024. Springer Nature Switzerland, Albi, France (2024)
25. The Open Group: ArchiMate® 3.0.1 Specification. 2012 [cited 2019 5 March]. Available from: http://pubs.opengroup.org/architecture/archimate3-doc/.
26. Joyce, A., Paquin, R.L.: The triple layered business model canvas: a tool to design more sustainable business models. J. Clean. Prod. **135**, 1474–1486 (2016)
27. De Bono, E.: Six Thinking Hats. Penguin Books, London (1985)
28. Miao, F., Holmes, W.: Guidance for generative AI in education and research. UNESCO United Nations Educational, Scientific and Cultural Organization (2023)

RELIA: Empathetic Reading Guide with Generative Artificial Intelligence

Rômulo Sherman and Sílvia Araújo(✉)

School of Arts and Humanities, University of Minho, Braga, Portugal
saraujo@elach.uminho.pt

Abstract. Critical literary reading faces significant challenges in the digital era, including declining engagement, fragmented attention, and reduced interpretive depth. This paper introduces RELIA (Reflective and Empathetic Literary Reading with Artificial Intelligence), a hybrid collaborative system between humans and AI designed to support and enrich the literary reading experience. Drawing on Bloom's Revised Taxonomy, Vygotsky's concept of scaffolding, and Digital Humanities frameworks, RELIA operates within a distributed cognition paradigm that enhances—rather than replaces—human interpretive capacities. Its architecture integrates a user-centered interface, advanced natural language processing, human–AI interoperability protocols, and scalable data infrastructures. RELIA's core innovation lies in an empathetic collaboration model that fosters both intellectual and emotional engagement through personalized dialogue with literary texts. Initial evaluations with university students show increased motivation, deeper comprehension, and higher-order critical thinking, suggesting that RELIA can serve as a resilient and ethical model for empathetic digital education. This contribution addresses key challenges in hybrid collaborative networks, including transparency, scalability, and trust, offering a transferable approach to AI-enhanced, human-centered learning across domains.

Keywords: Hybrid Collaborative Networks · Empathetic Artificial Intelligence · Digital Humanities · Critical Reading

1 Introduction

In an age of digital saturation and pervasive information flow, the practice of deep, critical, and affectively engaged reading is facing unprecedented pressure. The shift toward rapid, fragmented, and consumption-oriented media habits increasingly undermines the sustained attention and interpretive depth traditionally required by literary texts. While access to information has never been more immediate, the ability to process complex narratives, reflect on nuanced meanings, and engage emotionally with written content is steadily eroding [1]. Staying focused and motivated has become difficult for many readers today—particularly when reading challenging literary texts—due to the overwhelming presence of personalized digital distractions [2]. This transformation in media habits reflects a broader transformation in reading itself. The modern digital

Published by Springer Nature Switzerland AG 2026
L. M. Camarinha-Matos et al. (Eds.): PRO-VE 2025, IFIP AICT 770, pp. 88–103, 2026.
https://doi.org/10.1007/978-3-032-05673-3_6

environment is characterized by a shift from linear, immersive reading to non-linear, fragmented engagement— a mode increasingly driven by scanning, hyperlink browsing, and multitasking across information streams. As reading becomes more discontinuous and interface-mediated, readers are required to adopt adaptive strategies that accommodate divergent attention and fast-paced information exchange [3]. However, such strategies often privilege surface-level comprehension at the expense of critical interpretation, narrative coherence, and affective resonance, raising concerns about the long-term cognitive and educational implications of these new reading paradigms.

These evolving conditions are not merely circumstantial; they point to a deeper pedagogical misalignment. Despite increasing diversity in learners' cognitive and emotional profiles, educational systems largely persist in applying static, one-size-fits-all instructional models. These models rarely provide differentiated, responsive pathways into literary engagement— particularly for students facing challenges in comprehension, metacognition, or intrinsic motivation. While a growing body of research has explored digital interventions for supporting active reading—such as annotation tools, guided reflection, and multimodal scaffolds—most remain limited in their capacity to adapt dynamically to both the textual demands and the learner's evolving needs.

Concurrently, recent advances in natural language processing (NLP) and generative artificial intelligence offer promising avenues for designing reading environments that are not only adaptive but also interactive and emotionally responsive. These technologies can now generate real-time feedback, facilitate dialogic inquiry, and provide strategic support tailored to both the structure of the text and the cognitive-emotional profile of the reader [4]. However, this potential remains largely untapped in the realm of literary reading, where the cultivation of empathy, interpretive agency, and ethical awareness is paramount.

In response to this gap, this paper introduces RELIA (Reflective and Empathetic Literary Reading with Artificial Intelligence), a hybrid human–AI educational platform that reimagines reading as a co-constructed, emotionally rich, and critically grounded experience. Anchored in a human-centered pedagogical framework, RELIA integrates the adaptive affordances of AI with structured metacognitive scaffolding and affective guidance to support personalized, reflective, and ethically conscious engagement with complex literary texts.

The article is structured as follows: Sect. 2 reviews recent research on human–AI collaboration in education, personalized learning, and critical reading. Section 3 presents the conceptual foundations and guiding principles of the RELIA platform. Section 4 details its technical implementation and pedagogical affordances. Finally, Sect. 5 outlines future directions and broader implications for AI-mediated literacy practices.

2 Theoretical Foundation and Related Work

This section outlines the theoretical and empirical foundations of the RELIA project. It begins by addressing the decline in reading engagement and explores how human–AI partnerships can enhance reading through personalization, scaffolding, and affective support. It then examines the risks of over-personalization, the need for AI literacy, and the role of empathy in fostering critical, emotionally engaged reading. These strands converge to justify RELIA's hybrid, ethically grounded design.

2.1 Human–AI Partnerships for Personalized and Critical Reading

The 2022 PISA results revealed a sharp decline in reading performance across Europe, linked to reduced engagement and enjoyment [5]. Similar trends are seen in the U.S., where daily reading for fun among 13-year-olds dropped from 27% in 2012 to 14% in 2023 [6], and adult reading rates hit record lows. In response, educators and designers are exploring how technology—especially AI—can re-engage readers and support digital literacy [7]. AI tools like library recommendation systems offer personalization [8] but often emphasize convenience over deeper cognitive and emotional engagement. A more holistic, human-centered approach is needed to foster empathy, critical thinking, and meaningful human–AI reading interactions.

Recent scholarship highlights the potential of human–AI collaboration to transform reading practices across educational contexts. These partnerships aim to leverage the strengths of both agents: AI provides real-time adaptation, pattern recognition, and data-driven scaffolding; humans bring contextual judgment, critical inquiry, and interpretive agency [9]. This synergy supports deeper engagement and enhanced learning, provided it is guided by pedagogical frameworks that center the learner.

Bloom's Revised Taxonomy [10] provides a key framework for structuring AI-supported reading tasks, moving from basic comprehension to creative interpretation. Combined with Vygotsky's scaffolding theory [11], it highlights the value of adaptive support tailored to learners' needs. In AI-mediated settings, scaffolding can be dynamic and responsive, enabling students to progressively internalize complex strategies while preserving ownership of meaning-making. This aligns with distributed cognition theory [12], which views understanding as co-constructed through interactions between learners, tools, and environments.

2.2 Personalization in AI-Supported Reading Environments

AI's capacity for personalization allows reading materials to be tailored to learners' preferences, cognitive profiles, and developmental needs [13], making it especially valuable in inclusive contexts and for neurodiverse learners [14]. Studies show that such adaptive systems boost both comprehension and engagement, particularly for ESL students and those with attention challenges [15]. Multimodal formats like AI-narrated audiobooks also enhance motivation and academic performance [16]. However, personalization must go beyond adaptation—it should promote critical reflection and interpretive agency, not passive consumption.

2.3 Critical Engagement and AI Literacy

While conversational AI can scaffold learning, over-reliance risks reducing critical thinking and reflection [17]. Hybrid systems that foster co-construction, like Student Question Generation and AI-supported dialogue reading, enhance higher-order thinking and metacognitive skills [18]. To use these systems meaningfully, students must develop AI literacy: the ability to critically evaluate AI outputs, detect biases, and maintain an agency in interpretation. Automatic Question Generation tools further support this shift by producing tailored questions that encourage active, reflective reading while easing teachers' workload [19, 20].

2.4 Affective Dimensions of AI-Assisted Reading

Reading involves not only cognition but also emotion, ethics, and aesthetics [21]. Affective computing shows that emotionally responsive technologies can enhance motivation and depth of interpretation [22], as highlighted by Vistorte et al. [23], though ethical and cultural concerns persist. Computational empathy research explores how AI can detect and respond to emotions [24], and large language models (LLMs) can simulate emotional tone via prompts and sentiment analysis [25], though nuanced empathy remains a challenge. Frameworks like RLVER [26] and findings from CASA-based studies [27] show that people often respond empathetically to emotionally expressive chatbots, reinforcing the idea that empathy can be co-constructed in human-machine interactions. Overall, AI designed with affective intelligence can deepen engagement with literature and promote empathy, supporting its role as a space for ethical and emotional development.

2.5 Toward Ethical and Trustworthy AI Reading Companions

Reading is not solely a cognitive task—it is deeply emotional, involving empathy, ethical reflection, and aesthetic experience. As Denham [21] argues, literature invites readers into complex affective encounters marked by doubt, curiosity, and moral reflection.

Recent developments in affective computing suggest that emotionally responsive technologies can enhance motivation, retention, and interpretive depth [22]. A systematic review by Vistorte et al. [23] further highlights how AI tools—such as facial recognition and machine learning—are being used to assess and support students' emotional engagement, pointing toward more adaptive, emotion-aware learning environments. Yet, ethical concerns and cultural variability remain significant challenges.

Computational empathy research explores how artificial agents can both simulate and elicit empathy. Paiva et al. [24] define empathic agents as those able to detect a user's emotional state and respond appropriately, sometimes even prompting users to feel for the agent—suggesting new forms of affective interaction in education. Large language models (LLMs) also show potential in supporting emotionally rich dialogue. Knob et al. [25] demonstrate that models like ChatGPT and Gemini can approximate emotional tone using sentiment analysis and fine-tuned prompts. However, they caution that true empathy requires contextual sensitivity and interpretive depth.

From a learning perspective, Wang et al. [26] introduce the RLVER framework, enabling LLMs to refine empathetic responses using emotion-based feedback. Their H2HTalk benchmark shows that while LLMs handle fluent conversation, they struggle with emotional nuance over time—an issue particularly relevant to literature, where meaning often unfolds gradually and implicitly. Interestingly, human users can also develop empathy toward AI. Li et al. [27], drawing on the CASA framework, show that people often respond empathetically to emotionally expressive chatbots, reinforcing the idea that empathy can be co-constructed in human-machine interactions.

In sum, these developments support the idea t0hat AI-assisted reading, when designed with affective intelligence in mind, can foster deeper reader engagement, promote empathy, and position literature as a space for ethical inquiry and emotional growth. Rather than reducing reading to information processing, empathetic AI can expand its humanistic dimensions.

2.6 Toward RELIA – A Hybrid Framework Integrating Literary Reading and Artificial Intelligence

Despite these promising affordances, the integration of AI in reading practices also raises significant ethical challenges. Studies in human–AI interaction reveal that many systems still violate conversational maxims, lack transparency, or provide overconfident responses that undermine trust [28]. Moreover, unresolved issues concerning data privacy, algorithmic bias, and interpretability continue to limit the educational reliability of such tools [29, 30].

To address these concerns, AI reading companions must be designed with ethical intentionality. This includes ensuring that learners can view, understand, and—if needed—contest AI-generated content. It also means providing systems that are pedagogically aligned with human flourishing, supporting trust, autonomy, and critical awareness [31, 32]. Only then can AI systems act not as substitutes for human guidance, but as thoughtful collaborators in learning.

3 Research Methodology

This section outlines the methodological foundation of the RELIA project. It combines a research and development approach with user-centered design to ensure both pedagogical relevance and usability. The following components describe the design rationale, data collection strategy, experimental procedures, and the theoretical framework underpinning the system's development and evaluation.

3.1 Iterative Research and Development Process

RELIA was developed through an iterative, user-centered process grounded in action research and pedagogical theory. Nineteen master's students in Translation and Multilingual Communication at the University of Minho participated in the structured evaluation. The development followed four interconnected phases:

- Conceptualization: The theoretical and pedagogical underpinnings of RELIA were defined based on Bloom's Revised Taxonomy, Vygotsky's scaffolding, and principles of AI literacy, affective computing, and distributed cognition, to ensure that both cognitive progression and emotional engagement were adequately scaffolded.
- Design and Prototyping: Technical and pedagogical components were iteratively designed and tested, focusing on adaptive features tailored to diverse learner profiles.
- Implementation and Refinement: The full system was deployed and continuously adjusted based on user interaction data, ensuring responsiveness to cognitive and emotional signals like confusion or disengagement.
- Evaluation and Validation: Usability, perceived value, and learning impact were assessed through questionnaires, interviews, and interaction logs. Special attention was given to learner agency, critical reflection, and emotional engagement.

This cyclical and participatory approach ensured that RELIA evolved in alignment with user needs and theoretical insights.

3.2 User-Centered Design Strategy

RELIA was developed through a user-centered design approach, prioritizing the learner's cognitive, emotional, and motivational needs in literary engagement. Four principles guided this process:

- Empathetic design: Attending to the emotional and cognitive demands of reading complex literary texts
- Accessibility: Making the system usable by individuals with diverse abilities and technological familiarity
- Personalization: Adapting the reading experience to individual preferences, profiles, and learning trajectories
- Engagement: Sustaining motivation through dynamic, interactive, and meaningful encounters with the text

User research with master's students—via surveys and observation—shaped the creation of user profiles and interaction pathways. This feedback-informed process allowed RELIA to meet learner expectations while fostering AI literacy, critical thinking, and affective resonance. These principles also underpin the evaluation strategy presented in the next section.

3.3 Mixed-Methods Data Collection

RELIA's impact was evaluated using a mixed-methods approach, combining quantitative and qualitative data to capture cognitive, emotional, and usability dimensions. Nineteen master's students participated in three evaluation phases:

- Pre-RELIA: Initial questionnaire on reading habits and digital literacy.
- During-RELIA: In-app surveys and engagement data tracked usability and emotional responses.
- Post-RELIA: Final questionnaire assessed changes in comprehension, motivation, and critical engagement.

Instruments included both closed and open-ended questions, administered in a controlled setting for consistency. With informed consent, RELIA also logged interaction data (navigation, time on task, user input), supporting fine-grained analysis. Data were analyzed via descriptive statistics and thematic coding. The study followed GDPR and ethical standards, ensuring anonymization and transparency regarding AI components and data usage. This triangulated methodology linked technical performance with learning outcomes—such as deeper understanding, agency, and emotional involvement.

3.4 Integrating Learning Framework

RELIA's methodological framework combines Bloom's Revised Taxonomy, cognitive scaffolding and distributed cognition theories, and the platform's interactive structure. This integration ensures coherence between theory, pedagogy, and system design. It supports hierarchical cognitive development, real-time scaffolding, and learner agency, positioning RELIA as a hybrid, pedagogy- and AI-literate system.

This theoretical foundation is operationalized through RELIA's three-stage user experience—Contextualize, Explore, and Expand—which maps directly onto Bloom's cognitive levels (see Fig. 1). Contextualize supports remembering and understanding, drawing on Vygotskian scaffolding to provide accessible entry points. Explore fosters applying and analyzing through interactive, inquiry-based dialogue grounded in distributed cognition. Expand develops evaluating and creating, encouraging reflective autonomy and original interpretation, with AI feedback attuned to both emotional and cognitive signals.

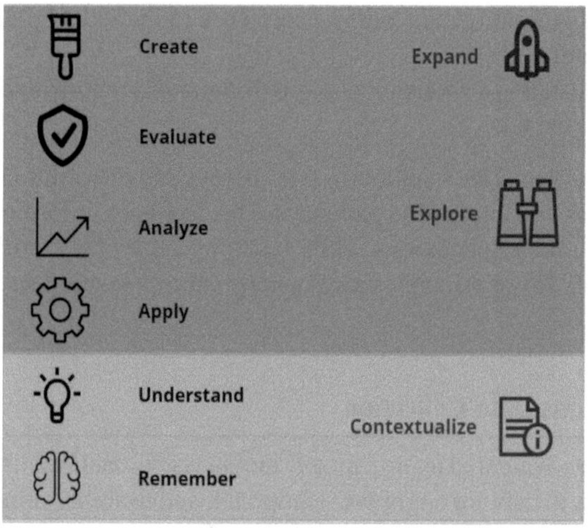

Fig. 1. Visual representation of RELIA's methodological framework, showing the alignment between Bloom's Revised Taxonomy (left) and the platform's core functionalities (Contextualize, Explore, Expand) (right). Each function supports a distinct level of cognitive engagement, scaffolding the reader's progression from basic comprehension to advanced critical and creative thinking.

RELIA's framework scaffolds learning from basic understanding to deep, creative engagement with texts. It embodies core principles of empathy, AI literacy, and human–AI collaboration, guiding both design and evaluation.

4 RELIA as a Hybrid Collaborative Reading Environment

This section presents the conceptual and technical foundations of RELIA, focusing on its architecture as a hybrid collaborative system. It details the interplay between human and AI agents, the modular infrastructure supporting adaptive interaction, and the workflow that structures the learner's journey through dialogic engagement, reflection, and feedback.

4.1 System Architecture and Conceptual Foundations

RELIA was conceived as a hybrid collaborative network, integrating human agents (readers, educators) and technological components (AI system, database, interfaces) into a cohesive ecosystem for critical literary reading. Figure 2 illustrates this architecture, highlighting how human and AI agents interact synergistically to support a dialogic and emotionally intelligent reading experience.

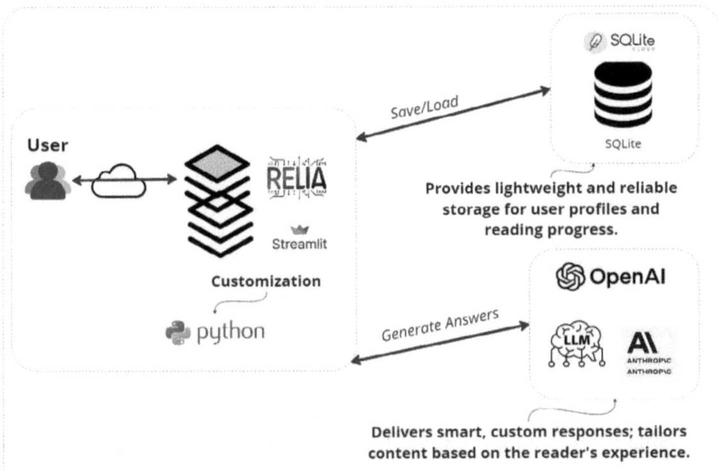

Fig. 2. General Architecture of RELIA as a hybrid collaborative network, showing the interaction between the user, the Streamlit front-end, cloud-based storage (SQLite), and AI response engines (OpenAI, Anthropic).

At its core, RELIA combines a Streamlit-based interface, a scalable cloud infrastructure, and state-of-the-art AI modules to support real-time, personalized literary interaction. The system architecture follows three major pillars:

- Real-time human-AI interaction: Through a Python-built front-end, users submit reflections, questions, and interpretations. These are processed in real time by large language models (LLMs), simulating a Socratic dialogue that supports reader insight and cognitive engagement;
- Adaptive memory and feedback loop: Interaction data—such as reading history and emotional patterns—is stored in a lightweight cloud database (SQLiteCloud). This persistent memory allows RELIA to track progress, personalize future sessions, and adapt to each reader's evolving needs. Such adaptive tracking supports individualized learning trajectories in line with the principles of personalization and reflective learning;
- Semantic and emotional processing: The system uses natural language processing (NLP) and affective analysis to tailor its responses. By assessing both semantic depth and emotional tone, RELIA generates prompts and feedback that balance intellectual challenge and affective support.

Together, these components form a distributed, adaptive learning ecosystem in which meaning is co-constructed through continuous dialogic loops between reader insight, literary text, and AI scaffolding.

4.2 Modular Design and Technical Components

Building on the architecture outlined above, this section details the modular components and technological stack that enable RELIA's reflective and emotionally attuned reading environment. The human interface is designed using user-centered principles to prioritize clarity, accessibility, and cognitive ease.

Developed with Streamlit (v1.41.0) and Python, the interface supports responsive layout design, rapid prototyping, and intuitive navigation. The AI layer, implemented in Python 3.11, includes the following modules:

- spaCy (v3.7.6) and NLTK (v3.9.1) for linguistic and stylistic analysis;
- Transformers (v4.45.2) and TensorFlow (v2.17.0) for deep learning and text generation;
- Sentiment Analysis Engine for evaluating affective tone;
- Recommendation Engine for context-aware prompts and guidance;
- Cognitive Assessment Module, aligned with Bloom's Revised Taxonomy, to dynamically adjust task complexity and scaffold critical engagement.

RELIA integrates pedagogically aligned and emotionally responsive modules, including a semantic translation engine that bridges open-ended input with structured AI queries. Its GDPR-compliant cloud infrastructure ensures secure data handling, personalized scaffolding, and session continuity.

4.3 Workflow Dynamics and Interaction Model

RELIA supports adaptive literary reading through a cycle of interaction, reflection, and feedback. After selecting a text and defining goals, users receive a personalized script and engage in empathetic dialogue with the AI. Checkpoints offer real-time feedback, while three strategies—Socratic questioning, recognition of contributions, and metacommunication—sustain a dynamic loop of engagement and adaptation (Fig. 3).

Figure 3 illustrates RELIA's workflow begins with selecting a literary work and setting reading goals, generating a personalized script. Through empathetic AI dialogue and adaptive feedback, the system supports continuous, emotionally attuned learning.

5 Empathy and Ethical Collaboration in Human–AI Literary Dialogue

This section examines how empathy is conceptualized, implemented, and ethically managed within RELIA. It explores the multi-dimensional framework of empathetic interaction, the safeguards supporting user agency and data protection, and the pedagogical strategies that ensure a balanced collaboration between human readers and AI companions.

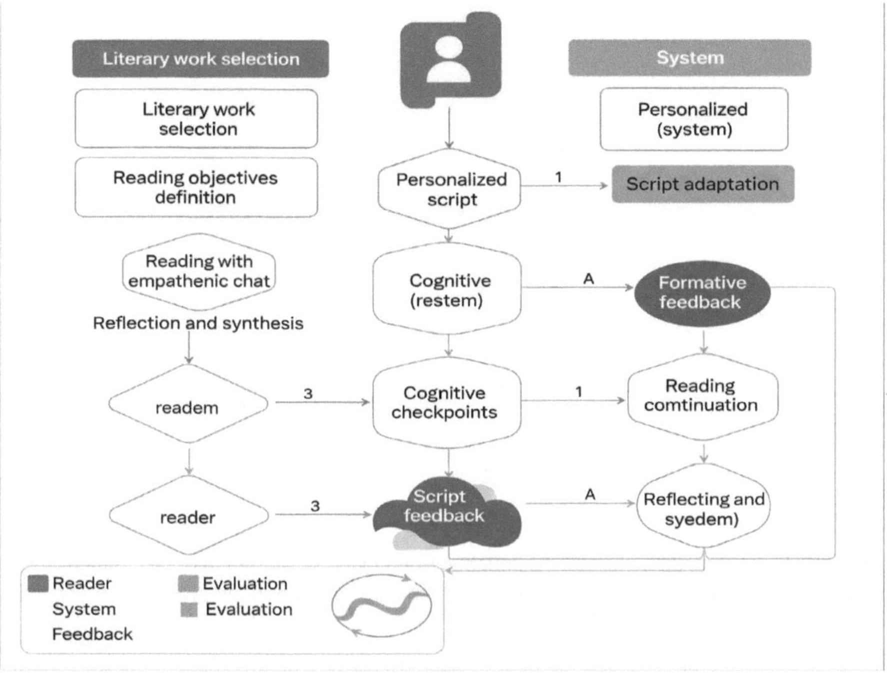

Fig. 3. RELIA's workflow and interaction process, showing the iterative cycle from initial reading goals to adaptive AI-supported dialogue and reflection.

5.1 Understanding Empathy in AI-Mediated Reading

Within RELIA, empathy operates through three interdependent dimensions (see Fig. 4): cognitive empathy, which adapts feedback to the learner's understanding; affective empathy, which responds to emotional states such as confusion or engagement; and contextual empathy, which accounts for cultural and situational factors in the reading experience.

This triadic model enables the system to engage in empathetic dialogue that supports both interpretive depth and affective engagement, fostering a learning environment where readers feel guided, understood, and respected.

5.2 Ensuring Ethical and Transparent Use of Empathetic AI

The integration of empathy into AI interactions raises critical ethical questions, which have been addressed throughout RELIA's development:

- Transparency and consent: All participants were explicitly informed about how their interaction data would be used to personalize feedback and adapt the system's responses;
- Data privacy and protection: RELIA complies with GDPR regulations, employing strong anonymization protocols to ensure that no personally identifiable data is stored or reused beyond the scope of the study;

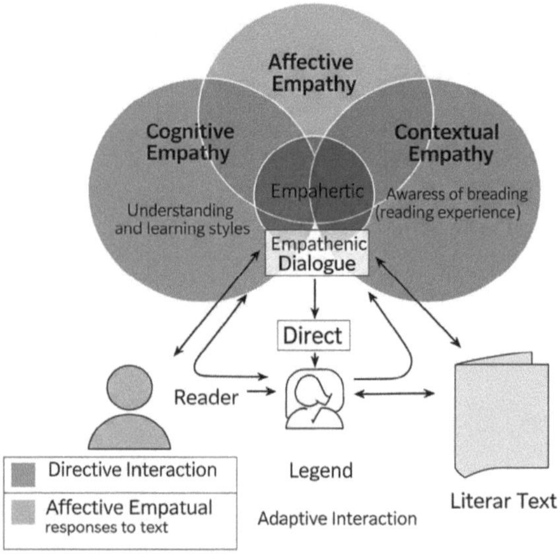

Fig. 4. RELIA's empathetic human-AI collaboration model, illustrating the three dimensions of empathy—cognitive, affective, and contextual—and their integration into the interactive reading experience between the user and the system.

- Avoiding overdependence: The system was carefully designed to support, not replace, human judgment. Readers can control the level of AI guidance and opt out of interaction at any moment;
- Bias mitigation: Particular attention was paid to the potential for algorithmic bias, especially in affective inference. RELIA was tested iteratively across diverse profiles, and real-time feedback loops were implemented to detect unintended effects or user discomfort.

These safeguards contribute to making RELIA a trustworthy and responsible educational tool, aligned with the principles of ethical AI and learner-centered design.

5.3 Balancing Learner Autonomy and AI Scaffolding

A central challenge in designing hybrid collaborative networks is to strike a meaningful balance between the learner's interpretive autonomy and the system's adaptive support. RELIA addresses this challenge through a multi-layered personalization strategy that adjusts its interventions based on real-time user data and pedagogical principles.

- Dynamic scaffolding, inspired by Vygotsky's Zone of Proximal Development [33], provides tailored prompts that fade as learner competence increases, fostering autonomy through human–AI interaction;
- Need-based intervention monitors affective and cognitive signals—like pauses or confusion—and offers minimal, timely support to maintain emotional engagement without disruption;
- With agency control, users select their preferred level of assistance, enhancing autonomy and AI literacy;

- Meanwhile, micro-personalization fine-tunes feedback styles (analytical, emotional, exploratory) in real time based on evolving learner profiles, aligning with Bloom's taxonomy and promoting deeper cognitive and emotional engagement.

Together, these adaptive mechanisms ensure that the system's support is responsive, respectful, and pedagogically sound. RELIA avoids both cognitive overload and over-reliance on AI, promoting reflective learning, emotional resonance, and the progressive development of literary competence within a transparent, learner-driven environment.

5.4 Educational Implications of Empathetic AI Collaboration

The design of RELIA integrates key themes from current debates on reading engagement, hybrid intelligence, and AI literacy. Unlike efficiency-driven personalization models, RELIA offers a dialogic, emotionally responsive, and ethically grounded reading experience. It redefines personalization as a dynamic, learner-centered process that adjusts to both cognitive and emotional cues, aligning with Vygotskian educational principles.

RELIA also operationalizes empathy by recognizing learner emotions and adapting its communication style, fostering deeper interpretive and emotional engagement. To prevent AI overreliance, it includes autonomy controls and promotes AI literacy by encouraging users to reflect critically on the tool's role. Its ethical framework ensures responsible data use, transparency, and cultural adaptability, enhancing user trust.Overall, RELIA exemplifies how generative AI can support—not replace—human interpretation. It presents a model of hybrid intelligence that combines empathy, adaptability, and critical pedagogy, with implications extending beyond literature to more ethical and human-centered forms of AI-enhanced education.

6 Evaluating Pedagogical Impact and Learner Experience

This section examines how users experienced and evaluated RELIA during the pilot implementation phase. The evaluation is structured across three complementary angles: the general patterns that emerged from survey data and platform interaction, and an in-depth learner narrative highlighting how the system fosters emotional engagement and supports learning.

6.1 Measuring Learning Outcomes and User Experience

This subsection synthesizes insights gathered through a structured questionnaire administered during the pilot phase. The data provide a multifaceted view of how students experienced RELIA—highlighting its pedagogical value, emotional resonance, and usability.

RELIA showed strong learning impact, with 50% of participants reporting improved understanding of the literary text and 72.22% feeling motivated while using the tool. System-generated questions were seen as relevant by 38.89%, with 55.56% rating them moderately or highly. Cognitive gains were notable: 44.44% reached the "comprehension" level of Bloom's Taxonomy, and 16.67% advanced to "analysis" or "creation," confirming RELIA's support for higher-order thinking through adaptive scaffolding.

Emotionally, most participants felt challenged in a positive way (83.33%) and confident using the system (66.66%), aligning with RELIA's emphasis on empathetic, affective engagement. The "Reflection Point" activity further encouraged interpretive agency, with one-third of students connecting the text to broader contexts. In terms of perceived value, users appreciated the interactive dialogue (44.44%), system questions (16.67%), and feedback (11.11%), reinforcing RELIA's learner-centered design. Challenges included formulating responses (38.89%) and maintaining engagement (27.78%), suggesting a need to refine scaffolding and AI literacy support. Overall, usability was rated positively, with 50% finding the interface intuitive and 82% approving the time structure. These findings affirm RELIA's core strengths in adaptive, dialogic, and emotionally responsive learning design.

6.2 Learner Perspective and the Transformation of Reading Engagement

Moving from statistical trends to lived experience, this subsection presents an individual learner case study to illustrate how RELIA transforms reading from a solitary task into an emotionally supported and cognitively enriching process.

Ana (a pseudonym used to protect participant confidentiality), a university student who had previously struggled with complex literary texts, engaged with RELIA over a four-week period. Initially hesitant, she soon discovered that the AI's empathetic and adaptive dialogue encouraged her to question, reflect, and forge deeper connections with the narrative. By the end of the pilot, Ana not only reported increased confidence and enjoyment in reading but also demonstrated measurable improvement in inferential comprehension scores. In her own words: *"RELIA made me feel supported and challenged at the same time. The AI was like a patient tutor that adapted to my needs, never making me feel judged or lost."*

A comparative analysis with traditional guided reading methods reinforces this experience, highlighting three key advantages of RELIA:

- In terms of personalization, traditional approaches typically rely on broad skill categories, while RELIA offers granular, dynamic support tailored to each learner's profile;
- For feedback, traditional methods deliver delayed, summative assessments, whereas RELIA integrates immediate, formative feedback into the reading process;
- Regarding scalability, conventional methods are constrained by educator availability, while RELIA enables individualized support at scale

Ana's case demonstrates how AI-enhanced environments can meaningfully integrate emotional and cognitive scaffolding, making reading more accessible, reflective, and empowering. It underscores the importance of empathetic mediation and learner agency in designing future AI-assisted educational systems.

7 Conclusion and Future Work

This concluding section summarizes RELIA's empirical, developmental, and conceptual contributions by exploring three key areas: insights from the pilot phase, future system development, and RELIA's broader implications for AI-assisted interpretive learning.

The pilot confirmed RELIA's value as a hybrid tool that supports both cognitive and emotional engagement with literature. Students reported gains in comprehension, confidence, and emotional connection, validating its foundations in scaffolding, distributed cognition, and AI literacy. However, limitations such as a small, homogenous sample and a single case study limit generalizability. Questions also remain about the system's ability to address cultural nuance and support neurodiverse learners.

Looking forward, RELIA's development will focus on expanding across linguistic, cultural, and educational contexts while preserving its core pedagogical goals. Planned improvements include a broader literary corpus, integration of Open Educational Resources, and scaffolding aligned with Universal Design for Learning. Special focus will be placed on secondary education and learners with reading or attention-related challenges. These efforts reflect RELIA's commitment to interpretive depth, emotional safety, and learner agency—offering design insights relevant to other complex learning domains like history or philosophy.

More broadly, RELIA reimagines reading as an active, co-constructed process supported by AI. Rather than automating learning, it positions AI as a partner that facilitates dialogue between cognition and emotion. When guided by ethical design and pedagogical intent, empathetic AI can deepen critical engagement without replacing human connection. RELIA thus represents not just a prototype, but a vision for education where human values and technology work in thoughtful partnership to support reflective, meaningful learning.

Acknowledgments. This work was carried out within the scope of the R&D project RELIA: Digital Transformation of Public Libraries with Artificial Intelligence, ref. 2024.07537.IACDC, supported by the measure "RE-C05-i08.m04 – Support for the launch of an R&D project program focused on the development and implementation of advanced systems in cybersecurity, artificial intelligence, and data science in public administration, as well as a scientific capacity-building program", under the Recovery and Resilience Plan (PRR), framed within the funding agreement signed between the Recovery Portugal Task Force (EMRP) and the Foundation for Science and Technology (FCT, I.P.), acting as an intermediary beneficiary.

References

1. Soni, M., Lourdusamy, A., S, D.: Investigating the role of digital tools on the proficiency of reading skills on today's generation. J. Intell. Data Anal. Comput. Stat. (2025). https://doi.org/10.46610/joidacs.2025.v02i01.002
2. Sowmya, P., Hoblida, N.S.: Reading in digital era: a study on enhancing reading skills. Int. J. Engl. Lit. Soc. Sci. (2022). https://doi.org/10.22161/ijels.75.34
3. Vorobyeva, T.: The transformation of the reading model in a digital culture. Tekst. Kniga. Knigoizdanie (2021). https://doi.org/10.17223/23062061/27/7
4. Deroy, A., Maity, S.: Generative AI and its impact on personalized intelligent tutoring systems. arXiv preprint arXiv:2410.10650 (2024). https://doi.org/10.48550/arXiv.2410.10650
5. OECD: PISA 2022 results: the state of learning and equity in education. OECD Publishing (2023)
6. Iyengar, S.: Federal data on reading for pleasure: all signs show a slump. National Endowment for the Arts (2024). https://www.arts.gov/stories/blog/2024/federal-data-reading-pleasure-all-signs-show-slump

7. Gea, N., Gulo, U., Bawamenewi, A., Gulo, W. Motivating the younger generation in reading: integrating technology in understanding digital literacy. Int. J. Educ. Elem. Psychol. (2024). https://doi.org/10.70177/ijeep.v1i3.998
8. Lin, X., Sun, Y., Zhang, Y., R, K.: Application of AI in library digital reading promotion service. In: Proc. IEEE Int. Conf. Integrated Circuits Commun. Syst. (ICICACS), pp. 1–6 (2023). https://doi.org/10.1109/ICICACS57338.2023.10100096
9. Nyholm, S.: Artificial intelligence and human enhancement: can AI technologies make us more (artificially) intelligent? Camb. Q. Healthc. Ethics, 1–13 (2023). https://doi.org/10.1017/S0963180123000464
10. Amer, A.: Reflections on Bloom's revised taxonomy. Electron. J. Res. Educ. Psychol. **4**, 213–230 (2017). https://doi.org/10.25115/EJREP.V4I8.1217
11. Shvarts, A., Bakker, A.: The early history of the scaffolding metaphor: Bernstein, Luria, Vygotsky, and before. Mind Cult. Act. **26**, 23–24 (2019). https://doi.org/10.1080/10749039.2019.1574306
12. Hollan, J., Hutchins, E., Kirsh, D.: Distributed cognition: toward a new foundation for human-computer interaction research. ACM Trans. Comput.-Hum. Interact. **7**(2), 174–196 (2000). https://doi.org/10.1145/353485.353487
13. Conati, C.: AI-driven personalization to support human-AI collaboration. In: Proc. 16th ACM SIGCHI Symp. Eng. Interact. Comput. Syst. (2024). https://doi.org/10.1145/3660515.3661324
14. Castro, G., Chiappe, A., Rodríguez, D., Sepulveda, F.: Harnessing AI for Education 4.0: drivers of personalized learning. Electron. J. e-Learn. (2024). https://doi.org/10.34190/ejel.22.5.3467
15. De Kumang, V., Sudin, A., Dr, P., Swanto, S.: Enhancing ESL learners' reading comprehension and motivation via AI-generated personalised reading texts. Int. J. e-Learn. Pract. (2024). https://doi.org/10.51200/ijelp.v7i1.5440
16. Jafarian, N.R., Kramer, A.W.: AI-assisted audio-learning improves academic achievement through motivation and reading engagement. Comput. Educ. Artif. Intell. **8**, 100357 (2025). https://doi.org/10.1016/j.caeai.2024.100357
17. Zhai, C., Wibowo, S., Li, L.D.: The effects of over-reliance on AI dialogue systems on students' cognitive abilities: a systematic review. Smart Learn. Environ. **11**, 28 (2024). https://doi.org/10.1186/s40561-024-00316-7
18. Liu, M., Zhang, J., Nyagoga, L.M., Liu, L.: Student-AI question cocreation for enhancing reading comprehension. IEEE Trans. Learn. Technol. **17**, 815–826 (2024). https://doi.org/10.1109/TLT.2023.3333439
19. Mulla, N., Gharpure, P.: Automatic question generation: a review of methodologies, datasets, evaluation metrics, and applications. Prog. Artif. Intell. **12**, 1–32 (2023). https://doi.org/10.1007/s13748-023-00295-9
20. Das, B., Majumder, M., Phadikar, S., Dey, N., Ashour, A.S.: Automatic question generation and answer assessment: a survey. Res. Pract. Technol. Enhanc. Learn. **16**(5) (2021). https://doi.org/10.1186/s41039-021-00151-1
21. Denham, A.E.: Empathy and literature. Emotion Rev. **16**(2), 84–95 (2024). https://doi.org/10.1177/17540739241233601
22. Yuvaraj, R., Mittal, R., Prince, A.A., Huang, J.S.: Affective computing for learning in education: a systematic review and bibliometric analysis. Educ. Sci. **15**(1), 65 (2025). https://doi.org/10.3390/educsci15010065
23. Vistorte, A., et al.: Integrating artificial intelligence to assess emotions in learning environments: a systematic literature review. Front. Psychol. **15** (2024). https://doi.org/10.3389/fpsyg.2024.1387089

24. Paiva, A., Leite, I., Boukricha, H., Wachsmuth, I.: Empathy in virtual agents and robots: a survey. ACM Trans. Interact. Intell. Syst. **7**(3), 1–40 (2017). Article 11, https://doi.org/10.1145/2912150
25. Knob, P.R., Scholler, L., Rigatti, J., Musse, S.R.: Are you listening to me? Fine-tuning chatbots for empathetic dialogue. arXiv preprint arXiv:2507.02537 (2025). https://doi.org/10.48550/arXiv.2507.02537
26. Wang, P., et al.: RLVER: reinforcement learning with verifiable emotion rewards for empathetic agents. arXiv preprint arXiv:2507.03112 (2025). https://doi.org/10.48550/arXiv.2507.03112
27. Li, J., Zhu, Z., Zhang, R., Lee, Y.-C.: Exploring the effects of chatbot anthropomorphism and human empathy on human prosocial behavior toward chatbots. arXiv preprint arXiv:2506.20748 (2025). https://doi.org/10.48550/arXiv.2506.20748
28. Miehling, E., et al.: Language models in dialogue: conversational maxims for human-AI interactions. arXiv preprint arXiv:2403.15115 (2024). https://doi.org/10.48550/arXiv.2403.15115
29. Jiayi, W.: Research on challenges and legal measures for personal data protection in generative AI. Sci. Law J. (2025). https://doi.org/10.23977/law.2025.040114
30. Hu, Y., A, A., Yellamati, D., Goktas, Y.: Leveraging generative AI tools for proactive risk mitigation in design. In: Proc. Annu. Reliab. Maintain. Symp. (RAMS), pp. 1–6 (2025). https://doi.org/10.1109/RAMS48127.2025.10935137
31. Savchenko, N., et al.: Personalized learning through AI: pedagogical approaches and critical insights. Contemp. Educ. Technol. (2025). https://doi.org/10.30935/cedtech/16108
32. Vössing, M., Kühl, N., Lind, M., Satzger, G.: Designing transparency for effective human-AI collaboration. Inf. Syst. Front. **24**, 877–895 (2022). https://doi.org/10.1007/s10796-022-10284-3
33. Vygotsky, L.S.: Mind in society: the development of higher psychological processes. Harvard University Press, Cambridge (1978)

Bridging the Gap: Identifying AI-Suitable Problems and Matching with Solution Providers

Thomas Schuster[1](✉) and Marian Lambert[2]

[1] Pforzheim University, Tiefenbronner Straße 65, 75175 Pforzheim, Germany
thomas.schuster@hs-pforzheim.de
[2] XPACE GmbH, Blücherstraße 32, 75177 Pforzheim, Germany
marian.lambert@xpace.de

Abstract. While many organizations are increasingly aware of the potential of artificial intelligence (AI), they often face difficulties in initiating concrete projects. A frequent challenge lies in identifying and reaching out to suitable AI implementation partners. This paper presents a structured, metadata-driven approach to facilitate that process. We develop a searchable repository of AI solution providers operating in Germany, designed to support organizations in finding relevant partners based on problem characteristics. Our core contribution lies in enabling more targeted, transparent, and effective collaboration between problem owners and solution providers. The proposed approach is evaluated through an exploratory case study. Our findings suggest that structured matchmaking mechanisms can substantially accelerate AI adoption and improve the quality of inter-organizational collaboration in digital innovation contexts.

Keywords: AI collaboration · provider matchmaking · semantic partner search · digital innovation ecosystems · interorganizational alignment · metadata enrichment

1 Introduction

Artificial Intelligence (AI) is a key driver of digital transformation in both private and public sectors. However, many organizations, regardless of size or domain, struggle to move from strategic interest in AI to actual implementation. Two challenges are particularly relevant: identifying suitable use cases for AI and finding appropriate implementation partners to realize them.

Although both aspects are important, this paper focuses on the second: enabling organizations to find suitable AI solution providers. While problem identification is highly relevant, we position it as a necessary input. Also, we plan to address it through a lightweight assessment step. The central objective of this work is to improve the matchmaking process between organizations and AI providers, thereby fostering effective collaboration.

We propose a metadata-enriched, searchable repository of AI companies operating in Germany. By linking organizational needs with provider characteristics, such as industry

Published by Springer Nature Switzerland AG 2026
L. M. Camarinha-Matos et al. (Eds.): PRO-VE 2025, IFIP AICT 770, pp. 104–118, 2026.
https://doi.org/10.1007/978-3-032-05673-3_7

focus, technological specialization, and experience, we aim to support more informed and targeted partner selection. Ultimately, our approach is intended not only to reduce search costs, but also to facilitate high-quality collaboration between problem owners and AI implementation experts.

Our guiding research question is: *How can organizations be effectively matched with AI solution providers to enable successful collaboration?*

To address this question, we follow a design science research approach: (1) we analyze existing digital innovation platforms to identify gaps in current matchmaking approaches, (2) we design and implement a metadata-enriched matchmaking system with semantic search capabilities, and (3) we evaluate the system through exploratory case studies comparing automated relevance assessments with human expert judgments.

The remainder of this paper is structured as follows: Sect. 2 provides background on AI readiness and partner matchmaking in digital ecosystems. To motivate our contribution, Sect. 3 critically examines current digital innovation platforms and identifies gaps in metadata quality, explainability, and user interaction. In Sect. 4 our tool for partner search and provider repository is described. The evaluation and discussion are presented in Sect. 5, followed by conclusions in Sect. 6.

2 AI Readiness and Adoption in Companies

This section provides background on AI readiness and partner matchmaking in digital ecosystems to contextualize our contribution.

Typical Barriers. Recent empirical studies show that AI adoption is frequently impeded by three inter-related barrier clusters: *data-related limitations*, *talent and skill gaps*, and *organizational or strategic obstacles* [3, 12]. Companies often lack sufficient, high-quality data or the data-management capabilities required for AI, while simultaneously facing shortages of employees with AI expertise [12]. On the organizational side, unclear project goals, an absent AI strategy, and legacy system constraints slow down or derail initiatives [3, 9].

Maturity and Readiness Models. To diagnose and address such barriers, numerous AI readiness or maturity models have been proposed. Most frameworks decompose readiness into multiple dimensions, typically *strategy*, *data*, *technology*, *people* and *governance*, and assess progression along four to five maturity levels [8, 9]. For instance, the Vitrine IA framework employs five levels from *exploration* to *transformation* across the above dimensions [13]. Although early models emphasised technology, recent work stresses a balanced socio-technical perspective that integrates organisational culture and change management [7, 10].

Trust, Transparency and Governance. Beyond technical readiness, trust and transparency are critical for user acceptance, especially where AI systems inform consequential decisions. A qualitative study on automated decision-making highlights concerns about bias, fairness and the "black-box" nature of many models [2]. Regulated domains (e.g., healthcare, finance, public administration) face additional governance requirements, making explainability and ethical compliance indispensable.

Implications for Our Approach. Our lightweight problem-assessment step builds on these insights. Instead of conducting a full maturity audit, we capture a minimal set of attributes (data quality, task criticality, domain context) that align with the dominant readiness dimensions and directly inform provider matching. This keeps the entry barrier low while ensuring that essential readiness factors are considered.

3 Decision Support and Matching in Digital Innovation

This section critically examines existing digital innovation platforms to identify gaps that motivate our contribution.

Digital-innovation literature offers a variety of canvases (e.g., AI Canvas) and recommender approaches. However, existing matchmaking platforms often lack transparency about provider capabilities or require significant manual effort from seekers. Moreover, fine-grained metadata that links problem descriptors to provider expertise is rarely available.

Various platforms have been developed to support AI-driven innovation by facilitating the matchmaking between problem owners and solution providers. However, many of these platforms reveal critical limitations in metadata granularity, semantic search, transparency, and user interaction.

The *KI-Marktplatz* (AI marketplace) project, for instance, connects companies and AI providers through a structured challenge–competence matching approach [5]. Companies describe their needs in free form or structured text, and providers create capability profiles, which the platform uses for automated matching. While effective within its domain focus, the metadata used for describing challenges and capabilities is relatively coarse and often unstructured, limiting the precision of matchmaking. Moreover, the underlying recommendation logic is not exposed to users, resulting in limited transparency. Interaction is largely one-directional, with little opportunity for refining or explaining the match suggestions.

Similarly, the *IIP-Ecosphere* initiative aims to build an interoperable ecosystem for AI in Industry 4.0 [6]. The project emphasizes technical integration of AI services via modular architectures and standardized interfaces. However, the platform's metadata schema primarily targets software interoperability and lacks contextual dimensions aligned with organizational use cases. No dedicated support is provided for problem formulation, semantic interpretation, or end-user decision support. As a result, users must already know what to search for, and partner discovery relies heavily on expert knowledge and manual curation.

At the European level, the *AI-on-Demand Platform* and its extensions (*StairwAI*, *DeployAI*) aim to centralize AI tools, assets, and services [1, 4, 11]. While the platform aggregates a wide range of AI resources, early versions suffered from keyword-based search and inconsistent asset descriptions. StairwAI improves usability for low-tech users by introducing natural language interaction and AI-driven matchmaking. However, its performance still depends heavily on curated metadata and knowledge bases, which may lack the granularity or standardization needed for nuanced recommendations. DeployAI seeks to improve transparency, trust, and interoperability by integrating ethical indicators and interactive navigation tools. Yet even in this advanced version, users often face a steep learning curve, and the rationale behind matches is not always inspectable.

By contrast, our approach introduces three key improvements over existing platforms: (1) a lightweight problem assessment step that captures essential contextual attributes, such as task criticality and domain, without overburdening the user, (2) an LLM-based transformation that interprets natural language inputs and enriches them with relevant semantic metadata, and (3) a retrieval and ranking mechanism optimized for use-case alignment rather than mere keyword overlap. This design allows for fine-grained, explainable, and interactive decision support, enabling transparent and low-threshold access to suitable AI partners. In doing so, it addresses core shortcomings of prior platforms and offers a practical contribution toward bridging the AI implementation gap in digital innovation ecosystems.

4 AI Provider Database and Matching

4.1 Methodology

To address our research question: *How can organizations be effectively matched with AI solution providers to enable successful collaboration?* we developed and evaluated a metadata-enriched matchmaking system. Our methodological approach comprises three main phases: (1) data collection and preprocessing to build a comprehensive provider repository, (2) design and implementation of a semantic matching algorithm with LLM-enhanced query transformation, and (3) empirical evaluation through exploratory case studies comparing human expert ratings with automated relevance assessments.

Figure 1 summarises the end-to-end logic of our approach. An *initial business problem* is first translated into a structured description by means of a lightweight *problem-assessment* step.

On this basis, it is evaluated whether the problem is *AI-suitable*. If not, organisations follow alternative solution paths. If an AI-suitable problem is identified, the process enters the section indicated in orange, and inside the dashed rectangle that marks the core contribution of this paper: **(i)** the problem is transformed into a metadata-driven *query* of our AI-provider database, **(ii)** our retrieval algorithm *ranks* the retrieved providers according to problem fit, and **(iii)** the resulting shortlist supports *partner selection and collaboration.*

The overall process steps transform an abstract, but AI-eligible business problem into a concrete, actionable recommendation of implementation partners, thereby bridging the persistent gap between organizational AI intent and real-world execution. While the three steps indicated in orange operationalize our research question of partner matching and selection.

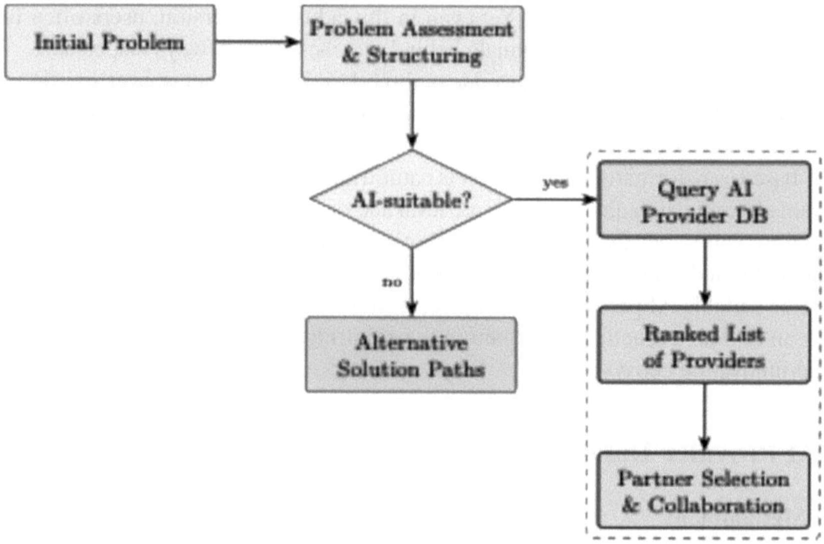

Fig. 1. From an initial business question to the selection of an AI implementation partner

4.2 Data Collection and Metadata Structure

To support our analysis, we collected structured data on AI-related projects, services, products, research activities, and organizations operating in Germany. We aggregate provider information from open registries and industry associations. The data was sourced from three public platforms: AI map Germany[1], AI map North Rhine-Westphalia[2], and start-ups listed by Applied AI institute[3]. In total, we extracted 3,983, and after consolidation we identified 3,111 unique entries.

Each entry was assigned to one of the following categories based on the type of offering:

- **project** – AI-related project
- **service** – AI-enabled service
- **product** – commercial product
- **company** – company profile
- **research** – research activity or result
- **initiative** – government or public initiative
- **platform** – technology or service platform

Of the 3,111 entries, 2,361 were assigned to project and 725 to company. The remaining 25 entries belong to platform (18), product and initiative.

For project entries, we distinguished between *active* (ongoing) and *inactive* (completed) initiatives. In addition, we reviewed websites of the associated projects and

[1] https://www.plattform-lernende-systeme.de/ki-landkarte.html.
[2] https://www.ki.nrw/ki-landkarte.
[3] https://www.appliedai-institute.de/ai-startups-deutschland.

organizations to verify classification and extract further attributes where available. We further classified the type of institution behind each offering as follows:

- **company** – private enterprise
- **university** – academic institution
- **scientific institution** – non-university research organization
- **governmental institute** – public authority or ministry
- **non-profit** – non-commercial organization
- **consortium** – multi-stakeholder partnership
- **research center** – specialized research unit

In terms of institutional affiliation, the majority of entries were associated with private enterprises (company, $n = 1781$ $n = 1781$ $n = 1781$), followed by academic institutions (university, $n = 655$ $n = 655$ $n = 655$) and non-university research organizations (scientific institution, $n = 232$ $n = 232$ $n = 232$). Additional categories included specialized research units (research center, $n = 163$ $n = 163$ $n = 163$), non-commercial organizations (non-profit, $n = 116$ $n = 116$ $n = 116$), multi-stakeholder partnerships (consortium, $n = 100$ $n = 100$ $n = 100$), and public authorities or ministries (governmental institute, $n = 64$ $n = 64$ $n = 64$). This distribution highlights the dominance of commercially oriented actors in the German AI landscape, while also underscoring the significant role of academic and public-sector institutions in shaping applied AI efforts.

Thematic analysis of the scraped provider website content indicates a clear focus on core AI technologies and their practical applications. The most frequent tags included *Artificial Intelligence* ($n = 641$ $n = 641$ $n = 641$), *Image Recognition and Understanding* ($n = 573$ $n = 573$ $n = 573$), *Data Analysis and Forecasting* ($n = 565$ $n = 565$ $n = 565$), and *Language and Text Understanding* ($n = 489$ $n = 489$ $n = 489$). Other prominent topics comprised *Human-Machine Interaction and Assistance Systems* ($n = 332$ $n = 332$ $n = 332$), *Automation* ($n = 294$ $n = 294$ $n = 294$), and *Robotics and Autonomous Systems* ($n = 245$ $n = 245$ $n = 245$). This distribution suggests that many providers position themselves at the intersection of foundational capabilities, such as data analytics, computer vision, and natural language processing, and applied domains including intelligent automation, assistive technologies, and predictive analytics.

This step represents the first phase of the preprocessing pipeline (see Fig. 2). In subsequent steps, the structured entries were transformed into a standardized JSON representation. For each record, we extracted relevant textual content and enriched it with associated metadata. Based on this representation, semantic vector embeddings were generated using the `text-embedding-3-small` model provided by OpenAI.

The resulting vectors, together with their textual source and metadata, were inserted into a Postgres instance with the `pgvector` extension enabled for efficient storage and retrieval. The ingestion process was implemented asynchronously in Python and performs batch-wise insertions.

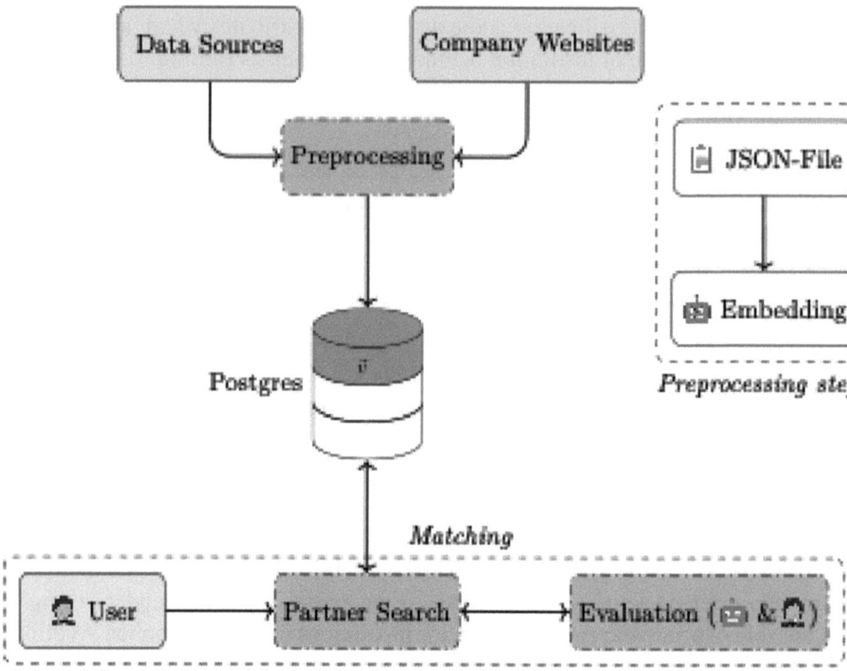

Fig. 2. AI-Matchmaking-System

4.3 Matching Algorithm and Prototype Interface

During the search process, users provide a free-text description of their use case. This input is processed by a large language model (LLM), which transforms the natural language query into a structured representation. As part of this transformation, relevant search filters are inferred – such as project category, sector, or institution type – based on predefined dimensions used during preprocessing (cf. Section 2). The structured query is then executed against our vector-based document store (Postgres), which contains embedded representations of all provider profiles (Fig. 3).

The semantic similarity search leverages dense vector matching, and the top-ranked results are further contextualized through a second LLM invocation that generates a natural language explanation of the match. This pipeline supports both structured querying and use-case–driven recommendations, enabling flexible interaction styles for different user needs.

To support user interaction, we developed a web-based application that allows users to submit free-text queries, receive structured results and concise AI-generated summaries, and explore provider matches interactively. The application is implemented using the *Next.js* framework (React 19, Tailwind CSS) and integrates with our backend via *LangChain.* It includes components for form-based input, dynamic filtering, and LLM-driven summarization. The retrieval and reasoning workflows are orchestrated using LangChain modules (`@langchain/openai`, `@langchain/community`)

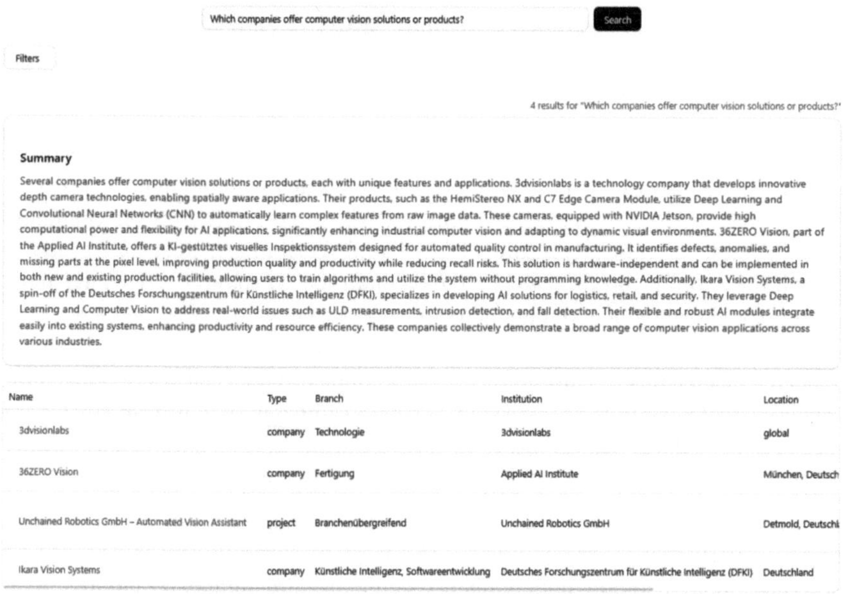

Fig. 3. User Interface of the Application Prototype

and executed client-side. The frontend architecture thus provides a reactive and extensible interface for AI-assisted problem-provider matching.

5 Evaluation

We conducted exploratory case studies with common queries to find a collaboration partner. Thus, we employed a set of practitioner-oriented requests that reflect realistic AI use cases (illustrated in Section 5.1). Each request was processed by the retrieval-and-classification (RAC) engine at the core of our prototype (see Fig. 2, and the ten highest-ranked provider entries were returned. This shortlist was then evaluated independently by two domain experts and, in parallel, assessed via an LLM-based pipeline using the `DeepEval` framework to triangulate relevance. Details of the rating scheme and reliability metrics follow below.

5.1 Use Cases

To evaluate the effectiveness and precision of our information retrieval system, we defined three representative use cases that reflect typical user intents across different application domains of artificial intelligence. Each use case is centered around a distinct query type and corresponds to a specific domain and expectation regarding the retrieved content. The following three questions serve as the starting point for our evaluation:

- *Case 1*: **Which companies offer computer vision solutions or products?** This question represents a use case from the industrial and technological application domain of

AI. The user is likely interested in startups, SMEs, or corporations that develop and provide products or services based on computer vision technologies. Relevant results must therefore not only match the technological sub-domain (*computer vision*) but also the entity type (*company*).

- *Case 2*: **Which companies are utilizing language models (LLMs)?** This use case targets the rapidly evolving field of generative AI and natural language processing. Users seek to identify commercial entities whose core offerings or technological infrastructure prominently feature LLM-based capabilities. Relevant results must match the sub-domain (*language models*) and type (*company*) and clearly indicate the practical deployment or commercialization aspect.
- *Case 3*: **What projects are exploring the use of AI in medicine?** This use case stems from the healthcare domain and focuses on applied research and development efforts. The user seeks AI projects – possibly academic, clinical, or industrial – that explore or implement artificial intelligence in a medical context. Relevant results must refer to concrete *projects* (type) and fall within the sub-domain of *AI in medicine.*

These questions allow us to assess the retrieval quality from multiple perspectives, particularly the system's ability to identify relevant results according to the user's underlying intent, including both domain-specific and structural expectations.

Table 1 presents the formal rating definitions of our evaluation scheme for user queries and retrieved results. Each result is rated according to its alignment with the user's primary intent, specifically evaluating match on sub-domain, entity type, and any additional constraints. The scheme differentiates between four levels of relevance.

Table 1. Relevance Scoring Scheme for Use Case Matching

Rating	Score	Definition	Type	Domain	Constraints
irrelevant	0.00	Does *not* match the user's *primary intent*—wrong sub-domain *and* wrong entity type, even if additional attributes match.	✗	✗	?
low	0.33	Matches one intent axis (sub-domain *or* entity type) but misses the other completely.	✗	✓	?
medium	0.66	Matches both sub-domain *and* type, but misses an additional constraint (e.g., location, status, size).	✓	✓	✗
high	1.00	Fully aligns with *all* explicit constraints—type, sub-domain, and every additional filter.	✓	✓	✓

To illustrate the practical application of our rating scheme (cf. Table 1), we briefly outline representative examples for each category. An *irrelevant* result (0.00) might return "RoboGroup ABC", a robotics research group, for the query *"computer vision startup in South Germany"*, thus failing to match both domain and entity type. A *low* score (0.33) may apply when only one intent axis is matched – for instance, "Visio Institute", a research institute in the right domain but of the wrong type. A *medium* rating (0.66) could result from "OptiSight North GmbH", a computer vision startup located in the wrong region. A *high* score (1.00) is assigned if all explicit constraints are met, such as with "VisionPro South GmbH", a fictitious computer vision startup based in South Germany.

5.2 Results

Table 2 summarizes the relevance scores assigned by our two human experts (Human Score 1 and Human Score 2) alongside the automated DeepEval ratings, averaged across all three use cases and broken down by result set size (top 3, top 5, and top 10). Overall, human raters gave mean scores of 0.78 and 0.80, respectively, whereas DeepEval yielded a somewhat lower average of 0.70.

Looking at the top 3 results per case, we see that our "self-query" strategy (in which the system first reformulates the user's free-text query via the LLM and additionally sets metadata filters) achieved perfect alignment with both human raters for Case 1 (computer vision) (1.00 / 1.00), while the direct-query method scored 0.78 / 0.89. DeepEval likewise favored the self-query variant (0.80 vs. 0.63).

In contrast, for Case 2 (language-model providers), direct querying outperformed self-query both by humans (0.78 / 0.89 vs. 0.77 / 0.89) and by DeepEval (0.44 vs. 0.21). Case 3 (AI in healthcare) showed strong DeepEval performance on direct querying (0.83) but lower human agreement on the self-query method (0.33 / 0.55).

Case 1: Which companies offer computer vision solutions or products?

Case 2: Which companies are utilizing language models (LLMs)?

Case 3: What projects are exploring the use of AI in medicine?

Expanding to the top 5 and top 10 results reveals similar patterns: the self-query approach maintains parity or outperforms direct querying in Case 1, while Case 2 consistently favors direct querying. Case 3 continues to show the largest gap between automated and expert judgments, particularly for self-query at larger result depths (e.g. DeepEval = 0.82 for top 5, compared to human means of 0.46 and 0.53).

Figure 4 reports Kendall's τ as a measure of inter-rater reliability and the agreement between human ratings and the DeepEval system. Across all cases, the two human raters achieved moderate agreement ($\tau = 0.59$), while correlations between human and system scores were lower ($\tau = 0.34$ for Human Score 1 vs. DeepEval, $\tau = 0.06$ for Human Score 2 vs. DeepEval; Fig. 4a).

When broken down by use case, the highest human–system alignment occurred in the **computer vision** scenario, with a Kendall's τ of 0.66 0.66 0.66 between Human Score 1 and DeepEval (Fig. 4c). In contrast, the **AI in healthcare** case showed weak or even negative correspondence between human and machine judgments ($\tau = 0.30$ and $\tau = -0.05$, respectively; Fig. 4b). The **language model** use case exhibited moderately

Table 2. Human and System Ratings for Use Case Methods

Use Case	Method	Human Score 1	Human Score 2	Deepeval Score
All Cases (avg.)	–	0.78	0.80	0.70
Top 3 Results				
Case 1	direct	0.78	0.89	0.63
Case 1	selfquery	1.00	1.00	0.80
Case 2	direct	0.78	0.89	0.44
Case 2	selfquery	0.77	0.89	0.21
Case 3	direct	0.78	0.66	0.83
Case 3	selfquery	0.33	0.55	0.70
Top 5 Results				
Case 1	direct	0.87	0.86	0.76
Case 1	selfquery	0.87	1.00	0.76
Case 2	direct	0.80	0.93	0.53
Case 2	selfquery	0.73	0.80	0.25
Case 3	direct	0.87	0.73	0.86
Case 3	selfquery	0.46	0.53	0.82
Top 10 Results				
Case 1	direct	0.87	0.86	0.72
Case 1	selfquery	0.83	1.00	0.70
Case 2	direct	0.86	0.97	0.72
Case 2	selfquery	0.76	0.76	0.37
Case 3	direct	0.80	0.66	0.88
Case 3	selfquery	0.53	0.56	0.81

consistent results, with Kendall's τ ranging from 0.54 0.54 0.54 to 0.57 0.57 0.57 across all pairwise comparisons (Fig. 4d).

Taken together, these results demonstrate that our metadata-driven, LLM-mediated matching pipeline achieves high precision for technology-focused queries (computer vision and language models), particularly when leveraging the self-query reformulation step. In more complex, domain-specific contexts such as healthcare, expert judgments diverge more sharply from the LLM proxy, highlighting opportunities to refine either the automated evaluation framework or the underlying metadata filters for regulated sectors.

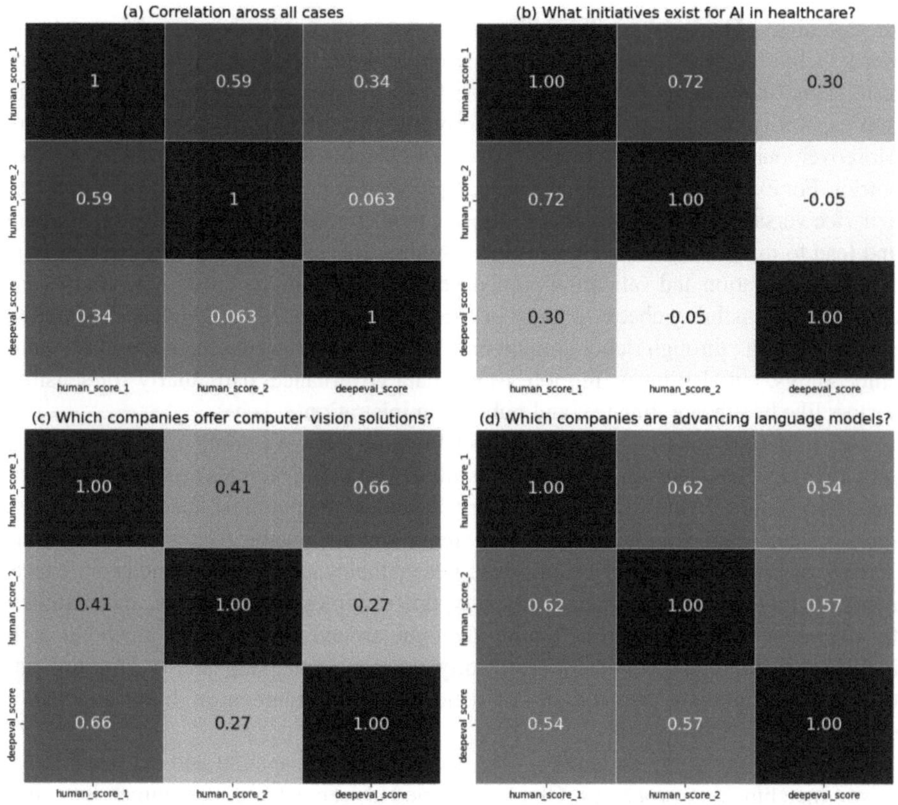

Fig. 4. Kendall rank correlations between Human Score 1, Human Score 2 and DeepEval across (a) all cases, and broken down by use case: (b) AI in healthcare, (c) computer vision, (d) language models.

5.3 Discussion

The results of our exploratory study offer a nuanced perspective on how metadata-guided query strategies and semantic retrieval affect perceived relevance in searching collaboration partner for AI solution implementation. First, the presented metadata-driven matching approach supports semantically structured queries that go beyond traditional keyword search by explicitly incorporating contextual and typological constraints. This design aligns with theoretical frameworks emphasizing user-centered, context-aware decision support. In practice, our evaluation demonstrates that semantically guided query strategies – combined with embedding-based retrieval – achieve higher human-rated relevance across all use cases, particularly in technology-driven domains such as computer vision and natural language processing (cf. Table 2). These findings suggest that embedding domain-specific metadata and leveraging semantic similarity mechanisms can help close the gap between organizational needs and available AI solutions, ultimately enhancing the precision and relevance of the matchmaking process.

Nonetheless, several limitations emerged from our evaluation. The divergence between human experts and automated (`DeepEval`) assessments underscores current shortcomings. The results indicate that while our system reliably captures straightforward, technologically explicit queries, it struggles with nuanced, context-sensitive criteria. This likely stems from limitations in both the metadata structures and the current capability of retrieval systems to interpret highly specific or ambiguous contexts. Moreover, our manual review revealed occasional inconsistencies in the underlying data entries. For example, entities labeled as companies that in fact refer to research projects, and vice versa. Such type misclassifications can distort semantic similarity calculations and lead to misleading match suggestions. Addressing this issue will require more rigorous data curation and validation procedures, including stricter entity type control and automated plausibility checks. Future iterations should thus not only enhance metadata granularity, e.g., through richer domain ontologies or supervised refinement of semantic embeddings, but also invest in more robust data governance, particularly for sensitive sectors like healthcare, finance, and public administration.

An important lesson for practical collaboration between companies and solution providers emerges from our study: successful matchmaking requires more than technical capability alone. Organizations must clearly articulate their context-specific constraints, such as operational complexity, regulatory requirements, or ethical considerations. Conversely, AI providers must transparently represent their capabilities beyond generic technological labels, clarifying their domain expertise, deployment contexts, and readiness for regulated environments. Facilitating dialogue around these detailed attributes early in the matchmaking process can significantly enhance partnership quality, aligning with theoretical insights on the necessity of socio-technical alignment in digital innovation ecosystems.

Moreover, our study underscores the necessity for transparent and explainable AI-driven matchmaking processes. Given the varied agreement between human and automated evaluations, it becomes evident that relying solely on black-box metrics is insufficient. Implementing clear explanations of why particular matches are recommended and enabling interactive user-driven refinement of search queries and filters will increase trust and adoption. This aligns well with broader theoretical discussions on transparency and explainability as critical factors for user acceptance of AI systems.

In sum, our study presents practical and theoretical implications on effectively connecting organizational AI ambitions with suitable providers. While our initial evaluation confirms the practical utility and conceptual soundness of the metadata-driven matching approach, it also reveals methodological and technical areas for improvement. Continued engagement with real-world use cases and iterative development based on organizational feedback remain vital next steps for evolving this matchmaking system into a robust facilitator of AI-driven innovation partnerships.

6 Conclusion and Outlook

This paper introduced a structured matchmaking framework designed to help organizations effectively connect with suitable AI solution providers. Our main contributions include the development of a lightweight problem assessment method, the design of a metadata-driven query transformation process, and the implementation of an interactive provider-matching prototype that facilitates targeted and efficient collaboration.

Returning to our guiding research question, our findings demonstrate that metadata-enriched semantic retrieval combined with LLM-enhanced query transformation can significantly improve match relevance compared to traditional keyword-based approaches. In particular, our evaluation focused on the second phase of the assessment framework – the AI-specific matching process – where we analyzed how structured queries and metadata-guided semantic retrieval support the generation of ranked provider recommendations. Human relevance assessments across multiple use cases indicate that semantically enriched queries outperform baseline strategies in aligning with user expectations, confirming that even lightweight structuring of business queries and constraints significantly improves the interpretability and effectiveness of automated AI matchmaking systems.

Building on these findings, future research directions can further enhance our structured matchmaking approach between organizations and AI solution providers. Specifically, extending the current lightweight problem assessment step and improving the transformation process of business requirements into structured queries remain crucial areas for refinement.

In the immediate future, we intend to deepen the role of large language models (LLMs) in interpreting user-defined problem statements. This involves enhancing the initial steps in the pipeline, the transition from informal input to a structured representation of the problem context and its AI relevance. By leveraging advanced natural language understanding techniques, we aim to refine the extraction of nuanced user intents, leading to more precise and contextually relevant provider recommendations.

Additionally, we plan to expand the depth and breadth of provider data by integrating further authoritative sources and exploring potential API integrations. By continuously enriching the database with up-to-date, granular metadata about solution providers, we seek to maintain and even increase the precision and reliability of the matching system.

Lastly, the practical deployment of our matchmaking prototype, supported by real-world usage data, is planned. Conducting longitudinal studies based on user interactions and feedback will allow us to iteratively optimize the system, ensuring its relevance and utility in diverse organizational contexts.

These planned extensions aim not only to further bridge the gap between strategic AI ambitions and practical implementations but also to foster an ecosystem characterized by transparency, efficiency, and successful collaboration in the rapidly evolving AI landscape.

References

1. AI4EU Consortium: A european AI on demand platform and ecosystem, https://cordis.europa.eu/project/id/825619 (2019). https://doi.org/10.3030/825619
2. Booyse, D., Scheepers, C.B.: Barriers to adopting automated organisational decision-making through the use of artificial intelligence. Manag. Res. Rev. **47**(1), 64–85 (2023). https://doi.org/10.1108/MRR-09-2021-0701
3. Cubric, M.: Drivers, barriers and social considerations for AI adoption in business and management: a tertiary study. Technol. Soc. **62**, 101257 (2020). https://doi.org/10.1016/j.techsoc.2020.101257

4. DeployAI Consortium: Development and deployment of the european AI-on-demand platform, https://cordis.europa.eu/project/id/101146490 (2024)
5. Dumitrescu, R., et al.: KI-marktplatz: Das Ökosystem für künstliche Intelligenz in der Produktentstehung. Zeitschrift Für Wirtschaftlichen Fabrikbetrieb **115**, 1–2, 86–90 (2020). https://doi.org/10.3139/104.112240
6. Eichelberger, H., et al.: Developing an AI-enabled IIoT platform - lessons learned from early use case validation. In: Batista, T., et al. (eds.) Software architecture. ECSA 2022 tracks and workshops, pp. 265–283. Springer International Publishing, Cham (2022)
7. Horvat, D., Heimberger, H.: AI readiness: an integrated socio-technical framework. In: Proceedings of the 11th international conference on production research – americas (ICPR americas), pp. 548–557 (2023). https://doi.org/10.1007/978-3-031-36121-0_69
8. Sadiq, R.B., et al.: Artificial intelligence maturity model: a systematic literature review. PeerJ. Comp. Sci. **7**, e661 (2021). https://doi.org/10.7717/peerj-cs.661
9. Schuster, T., et al.: Maturity models for the assessment of artificial intelligence in small and medium-sized enterprises. In: Wrycza, S., Maślankowski, J. (eds.) Digital Transformation, pp. 22–36. Springer International Publishing, Cham (2021). https://doi.org/10.1007/978-3-030-85893-3_2
10. Schuster, T., Waidelich, L.: Maturity of artificial intelligence in SMEs: privacy and ethics dimensions. In: Camarinha-Matos, L.M., et al. (eds.) Collaborative Networks in Digitalization and Society 5.0, pp. 274–286. Springer International Publishing, Cham (2022). https://doi.org/10.1007/978-3-031-14844-6_22
11. StairwAI Consortium: Stairway to AI: Ease the engagement of low-tech users to the AI-on-demand platform through AI, https://cordis.europa.eu/project/id/101017142 (2021). https://doi.org/10.3030/101017142
12. Uren, V., Edwards, J.S.: Technology readiness and the organizational journey towards AI adoption: an empirical study. Int. J. Inf. Manage. **68**, 102588 (2023). https://doi.org/10.1016/j.ijinfomgt.2022.102588
13. Artificial intelligence maturity framework and assessment tool. Vitrine IA Québec (2021)

Collaborative Risk and Crisis Management

Study on the Identification of Risk Elements of Collaborative Networks Based on Power Grid Feasibility Study Reports

Yanan Xiao[1], Wenxin Mu[1], Minghong Liu[2], Xianing Jin[3], and Juanqiong Gou[1](✉)

[1] Beijing Jiaotong University, Beijing, China
{24120585,wxmu,jqgou}@bjtu.edu.cn

[2] State Grid Xinjiang Economic and Technological Research Institute, Urumqi, China

[3] State Grid Economic and Technological Research Institute Co., Ltd., Beijing, China

Abstract. Most of the current collaborative network risk studies focus on modelling risks in the project implementation phase, rarely using data analysis methods, and the identification of risks inevitably lags behind. This study addresses the problem of risk element identification in complex network scenarios, based on the grid feasibility study, and constructs a multi-layer network of risk elements based on unstructured data analysis. The network contains risk element layer, risk structure layer and collaborative network layer, which realises potential risk identification and prevention in the project reserve stage. The main research contents are as follows: 1) constructing the risk element layer using TF-IDF algorithm and co-occurrence analysis; 2) building the risk structure layer and completing the cross-layer association through text similarity and keyword matching; 3) establishing the collaborative network layer and completing the cross-layer association by leveraging semantic matching methods. Finally, a case study of a provincial grid company's production technical reform project confirms the model's validity and practical utility, which provides a scientific basis for risk management and responsibility allocation of power grid projects.

Keywords: collaborative networks · risk identification · risk networks · NLP

1 Introduction

The collaborative network of power grid enterprises may closely connect multiple parties to enhance the reliability of the power grid, and its risk-resistant ability is crucial to the development of the power grid industry, which is currently facing major challenges in collaborative network risk management [1]. The majority of extant collaborative network risk studies concentrate on the risks in the project implementation phase, and the identification of risks inevitably lags behind. The feasibility study report, as a key document

This work was supported by the Science and Technology Project of State Grid Corporation of China (Grant No. 1400-202456284A-1-1-ZN, Research on the collaborative allocation and feedback control technology of project reservation for business optimization).

Published by Springer Nature Switzerland AG 2026
L. M. Camarinha-Matos et al. (Eds.): PRO-VE 2025, IFIP AICT 770, pp. 121–136, 2026.
https://doi.org/10.1007/978-3-032-05673-3_8

prior to project implementation, contains a substantial amount of risk information; however, the conventional risk assessment method is challenging to elucidate the potential relationship between this information, particularly in the context of multi-departmental collaboration, where risk elements are dispersed and the definition of risk responsibility is ambiguous. In order to address the aforementioned issues, this study proposes the construction of a multi-layer network of risk elements, based on multi-source data including grid feasibility study reports. The objective of this construction is to establish a systematic and intelligent collaborative network risk identification system, with the aim of identifying and preventing potential risks in the project reserve phase.

In the field of grid research, risk identification is typically achieved through the utilisation of multi-source data fusion techniques, natural language processing (NLP) techniques, and deep learning techniques. Multi-source data fusion techniques have the capacity to integrate different sources and types of data, thereby providing a more comprehensive risk assessment [2, 3]. NLP techniques are particularly suitable for processing large amounts of textual data in the grid domain, such as feasibility study reports, equipment operation logs, accident reports, and so forth, which usually contain rich risk information [4, 5]. Conversely, deep learning techniques employ feature learning and pattern recognition on grid operation data to identify potential risks by constructing a multi-layer neural network structure [6, 7]. However, these techniques require substantial amounts of labelled data.

As demonstrated by extant research, progress has been made in the field of grid risk identification. However, the unstructured data format in the grid domain is complex and rich in jargon, which hinders the capture of potential risks. Furthermore, research into risk identification for the grid cooperative network is inadequate, and the allocation of risk responsibility faces numerous challenges. Therefore, this study proposes a cross-layer and multi-dimensional Risk Factors Multilayer Network Model (RFMNM), constructed using multi-source text data and NLP technology. It is noteworthy that the system not only accurately identifies the risk elements in the feasibility study report, but also clarifies the responsible parties for the risks through the traceability mechanism of the collaborative network. This provides a new perspective and methodology for the risk management of grid enterprises.

This paper is organized as follows: Sect. 1 describes the need for constructing a multi-layer network model of risk identification and the limitations of existing research. Section 2 reviews the research on risk network construction and describes the application of NLP techniques in risk management. Section 3 discusses the methodology for constructing the risk network model. Section 4 validates our approach using the example of a provincial grid company. Section 5 summarises the research results and shortcomings of this paper.

2 Literature Review

Risk networks, which are formed by the interactions and associations between risk factors within complex systems, have received extensive attention across various fields [8]. Many studies have focused on constructing and analysing risk networks within these systems.

In project management, [9] proposed a risk propagation model for project portfolio networks considering risk perception, while [10] explored network topology modification to minimize risks in computer networks. In aviation safety, [11] proposed a text mining-based safety risk identification model, and [12] developed a flight training risk network model through text mining and ensemble algorithms. Risk networks are also applied to financial contagion studies. For instance, [13] examined oil market risk impacts on financial systems using complex networks, and [14] developed a risk contagion model for dynamic multilayer financial networks. Furthermore, the method of constructing risk networks to identify risk elements and propagation paths has been widely utilised across diverse fields, including fisheries [15], metro construction [16], and urban systems [15]. However, the extant literature predominantly addresses siloed systems and overlooks cross-stakeholder risk dependencies in collaborative settings, such as power grid development. This oversight has the effect of limiting effective holistic risk governance in multi-stakeholder projects.

Text mining and NLP techniques have proven effective in extracting insights from unstructured text data, particularly for risk factor identification and network construction [17].

On the one hand, text mining enables the extraction of valuable patterns from textual data, facilitating hidden risk identification in project documentation. For instance, [18] combined text mining with event evolutionary graphs for comprehensive risk analysis, while [19] employed an improved LDA topic model and Bayesian networks for chemical safety risk identification. The technique has been widely implemented across domains. For example, [20] built knowledge graphs using text mining techniques from accident reports for railway risk assessment, [21] proposed a novel text mining approach for power distribution risk identification, and [22] created a text mining and network analytics framework to automatically extract and analyse risk factors from aviation accident reports. Moreover, NLP can enhance risk management by enabling computer interpretation of technical documents. For instance, [23] developed an NLP-based approach to automatically identify quality risk factors in steel structures through construction reports, and [24] pioneered an NLP-based approach for improved comorbidity risk prediction from EHR data. Similarly, [25] applied NLP and machine learning to credit risk assessment in validation reports. For complex scenarios, researchers increasingly combine NLP with deep learning models to boost prediction accuracy [22, 26, 27].

While existing studies highlight text mining and NLP's value in risk network construction, they typically focus on isolated sectors or specific risk types. Notably, research on risk element identification in collaborative networks - particularly using power grid feasibility reports - remains scarce. This study addresses this gap by developing a novel NLP-based method for risk element extraction in collaborative networks.

Focusing on the power industry, we construct a specialized risk network model that precisely captures risk characteristics and traceability paths in grid projects. Our approach provides both innovative technical tools and enhanced decision-support capabilities for power industry risk management.

3 Methodology

The objective of this study is to construct a cross-layer, multi-dimensional risk element multilayer network model, which is designed to identify and analyse risks under complex cooperative networks. The methodology of the study encompasses the design of risk element multilayer network, the construction of risk element corpus, the extraction of risk key structures, the alignment of cooperative networks and the application of the model. The construction process is illustrated in Fig. 1, and the specific steps are as follows:

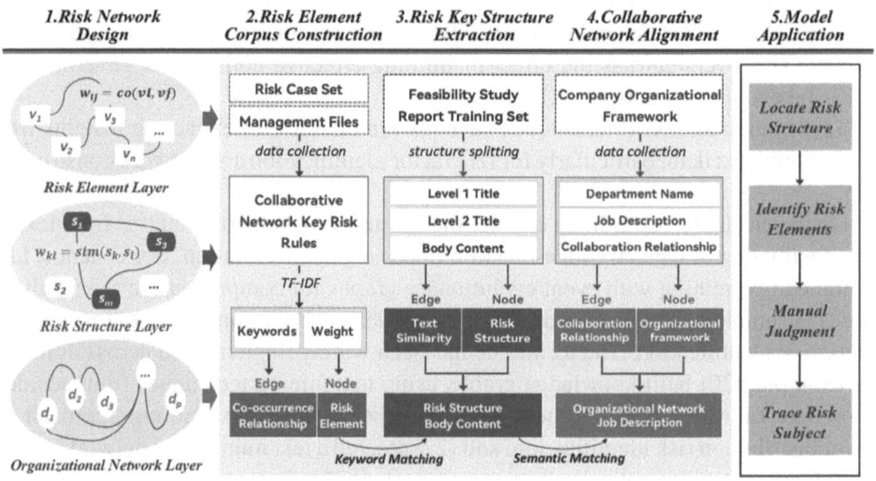

Fig. 1. Model architecture

- **Risk Network Design:** Develop a comprehensive multi-layer network model consisting of a risk element layer, a risk structure layer, and a collaborative network layer. Define the inter-layer mapping relationships to facilitate interactions among these layers.
- **Risk Element Corpus Construction:** Create a corpus of risk elements and establish a structured collection of these elements through keyword extraction and co-occurrence analysis, ensuring a comprehensive representation of potential risks.
- **Risk Key Structure Extraction:** Utilize text similarity computation and keyword matching techniques to identify and extract the key structures associated with risks.
- **Collaborative Network Alignment:** Manually integrate the organizational framework and business processes to create a collaborative network. This alignment will facilitate the tracing of risk responsibility across departments and ensure coherent risk management.
- **Model Application:** Apply the developed model to a grid feasibility study reports in order to identify potential risk elements and assess risk levels, thereby achieving traceability to relevant risk subject departments.

3.1 Risk Network Design

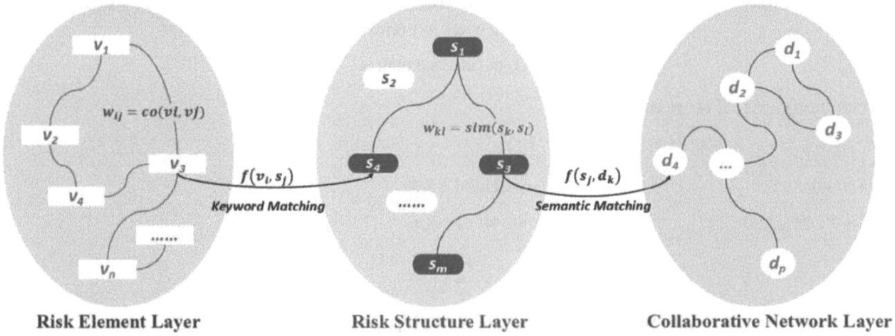

Fig. 2. Schematic diagram of risk network model

The risk element multilayer network encompasses the risk element layer, the risk structure layer and the collaborative network layer. The model structure is shown in Fig. 2.

- The risk element layer is utilised for the identification and quantification of fundamental risk points, thereby furnishing the entire model with essential risk information.
- The risk structure layer occupies a central transitional position, interconnected with the risk element layer via keyword matching and intimately linked with the collaborative network layer through semantic matching. This layer plays a pivotal role in the integration of risk elements, facilitating their transmission to the collaborative network layer.
- The collaborative network layer is utilised for the purpose of displaying the company's organisational structure and departmental collaboration. It facilitates the reception of risk structure layer information through semantic matching, the tracing of the risk subject department, and the provision of a clear basis for risk management and responsibility allocation.

1) Definition of risk element layer

The risk element layer can be defined as a weighted undirected graph $G_1 = (V, E_{co})$, where the set of nodes V contains all the risk element keywords and their weights, and the edges in the set of edges E_{co} are built by calculating the number of co-occurrences of different risk elements in the same risk rule. The weights of the edges are determined by the co-occurrence matrix $co(v_i, v_j)$. An edge exists between two nodes only when the number of co-occurrences exceeds a threshold ϕ, thus reflecting the actual correlation between the risk elements. The magnitude of the co-occurrence relationship can be quantified by w_{ij}. It can be demonstrated that an increase in the number of co-occurrences corresponds to a strengthening of the correlation between the two risk elements (Table 1).

2) Definition of risk structure layer

Table 1. Definition of risk element layer

Definition	Description
$V = \{v_1, v2, \ldots, vn\}, vi = (ki, wi)$	the set of risk element nodes, where k_i denotes the risk keyword and w_i denotes its corresponding weight
$co(v_i, v_j) = \begin{cases} \text{CoOccurrence}(v_i, v_j), & \text{if co -occurring} \\ 0 & otherwise \end{cases}$	co-occurrence matrix
$w_{ij} = co(vi, vj)$	weight of a side
$Eco \subseteq V \times V, ifw_{ij} \geq \phi$	the set of edges

Table 2. Definition of risk structure layer

Definition	Description
$S = \{s1, s2, \ldots, sm\}, s_i = (t_i, c_i)$	the set of risk structure nodes, where t_i is the secondary title and c_i is the corresponding body content
$\text{sim}(s_k, s_l) = \begin{cases} \text{TextSimilarity}(c_k, c_l), \text{if } s_k \neq s_l \\ 0, \text{if } s_k = s_l \end{cases}$	similarity matrix
$w_{kl} = sim(s_k, s_l)$	weight of a side
$\text{Esim} \subseteq S \times S, ifw_{kl} \geq \theta$	the set of edges

The risk structure layer can be defined as a weighted undirected graph $G_2 = (S, E_{sim})$, specifically, the set of nodes S contains all the secondary titles as risk structures and their corresponding body contents. The edges in the set of edges E_{sim} are constructed through calculation of the textual similarity between the corresponding body contents of different risk structures. The weight of the edges, w_{kl}, is determined by the similarity matrix $\text{sim}(s_k, s_l)$, and an edge exists between two nodes only when the similarity exceeds the threshold value, θ. This reflects the textual correlation between the risk key structures (Table 2).

3) Definition of collaborative network layer

Table 3. Definition of collaborative network layer

Definition	Description
$D = \{d1, d2, \ldots, dp\}, d_i = (n_i, r_i)$	the set of collaborative network nodes, where n_i is the name of the department and r_i is the job description
$collab(d_i, d_j) = \begin{cases} 1, & ifd_i andd_j \text{collaborate} \\ 0 & otherwise \end{cases}$	similarity matrix
$\text{Ecollab} \subseteq D \times D, ifcallab(di, dj) = 1$	the set of edges

The collaborative network layer can be defined as an undirected graph $G_3 = (D, E_{collab})$, where the set of nodes D contains all the departments and their job descriptions, and the set of edges E_{collab} represents the collaborative relationships between departments. These collaborative relationships are obtained by manually sorting out the actual business processes without edge weights, and an edge e_{ij} is established between departments d_i and d_j if they collaborate in a business process (Table 3).

4) Definition of the mapping relationship between the risk element layer and the risk structure layer

Table 4. Definition of the mapping relationship between the risk element layer and the risk structure layer

Definition	Description
$V = \{v_1, v2, \ldots, vn\}, vi = (ki, wi)$	the set of risk element nodes
$S = \{s1, s2, \ldots, sm\}, s_i = (t_i, c_i)$	the set of risk structure nodes
$f(v_i, s_j) = \sum_{k_i \in c_j} w_i$	mapping function
$e_{ij} \in E_{\text{map}}$, *iff* $(v_i, s_j) > \tau$	the set of mapping edges

The mapping relationship between the risk element layer and the risk structure layer is achieved by means of keyword matching. It is important to note that the set V denotes the pre-constructed risk element nodes, and the set S denotes the pre-constructed risk structure nodes. The mapping function $f(v_i, s_j)$ calculates the matching weight between the risk element keyword v_i and the risk structure s_j by summing up the weights of all the risk element keywords matched in the body content. This reflects the strength of the body content in carrying the semantics of the risk element. In the event that $f(v_i, s_j)$ exceeds the pre-established threshold τ, it is deduced that a mapping relationship exists between v_i and s_j. Consequently, an edge e_{ij} is established within the set of mapping edges E_{map}, with the weight of the edge being $f(v_i, s_j)$. In the absence of such a relationship, a mapping relationship cannot be established. This mapping relationship reflects the semantic relatedness between risk elements and risk critical structures, thus enabling semantic connectivity between the risk element and risk structure layers (Table 4).

5) Definition of the mapping relationship between the risk structure layer and the collaborative network layer

Table 5. Definition of the mapping relationship between the risk structure layer and the collaborative network layer

Definition	Description
$S = \{s1, s2, \ldots, sm\}, s_i = (t_i, c_i)$	the set of risk structure nodes
$D = \{d1, d2, \ldots, dp\}, d_i = (n_i, r_i)$	the set of collaborative network nodes
$f(s_j, d_k) = \cos(\text{BertEmbedding}(c_j), \text{BertEmbedding}(r_k))$	mapping function
$e_{jk} \in E_{\text{map}}, \text{if} f(s_j, d_k) > \theta$	the set of mapping edges

The mapping relationship between the risk structure layer and the collaborative network layer is achieved through the use of semantic mapping. Specifically, word embedding is performed by the BERT word embedding technique on the body content c_j corresponding to the risk structure and the departmental job descriptions r_k in the collaborative network layer. The cosine similarity between the two is then computed to obtain the mapping weight $f\left(s_j, d_k\right)$. In the event that $f\left(s_j, d_k\right)$ exceeds the preset threshold θ, it is to be considered that a mapping relationship exists between the risk-critical structure s_j and the department d_k, and a mapping edge e_{jk} is being created with the weight of $f\left(s_j, d_k\right)$. In the absence of such a relationship, a mapping relationship cannot be established. This mapping relationship reflects the correlation between the risk structure and the organisational departments, thus enabling a semantic connection between the risk structure layer and the collaborative network layer (Table 5).

3.2 Risk Element Corpus Construction

The first task in constructing a multi-layer network model of risk elements is to extract and organise the risk elements to form a structured corpus of risk elements. The process of constructing the risk element layer is as follows:

- **Keyword extraction:** Based on the management documents and case sets, the risk rules are extracted manually. The extracted risk rules are analysed using the TF-IDF algorithm, which can identify the keywords that are representative of the document content and their importance weights by calculating the frequency of words in the document and the inverse document frequency, forming a collection of risk element keywords and their weights.
- **Association relationship construction:** by calculating the co-occurrence of risk elements in the risk rules, the correlation relationship between risk elements is constructed. Specifically, if two risk elements co-occur in the same risk rule, it is considered that there is a co-occurrence relationship between them, and the strength of the co-occurrence relationship is measured by the frequency of co-occurrence, i.e., the more times two risk elements co-occur, the stronger the correlation.

3.3 Risk Key Structure Extraction

The extraction of risk key structures provides fundamental data support for the model, while also establishing the correlation between risk structures and the mapping relationship between risk elements and risk structures. The specific steps are outlined below:

- **Risk structure extraction:** Each report in the FEASIBILITY STUDY REPORTS training set is structured using the pdfplumber [28], splitting it into first-level headings, secondary headings and corresponding body contents, and merging its corresponding body content by second-level headings. The extracted second-level headings are defined as risk structures, which together with the collated body contents constitute a collection of nodes in the risk structure layer.
- **Association relationship construction:** Based on the processed structured data, the text similarity between the body contents of each node is calculated to quantify the

semantic relevance of different risk structures, and this is used as the edge weight, so as to construct an association network of risk structures based on text similarity.

- **Mapping relationship building:** Firstly, the body content is subjected to word splitting, with the pre-constructed corpus of risk elements then being used to match the splitting results word by word. The weights of the successfully matched keywords are then summed up, with the resultant value being indicative of the semantic carrying strength of the risk structure to the risk elements. When the value reaches or exceeds a certain threshold, it can be concluded that there is a valid correlation between the two, and the matching weight is taken as the mapping weight. This enables a quantitative connection between the risk elements and the risk structure to be established. It is important to note that not all risk structures are mapped to risk elements. Therefore, the risk structures identified by keyword matching are defined as "critical risk structures", which indicate a high potential risk likelihood. This process integrates domain knowledge with keyword weights to reflect the importance differences of different risk structures and achieves data-driven semantic quantitative matching.

3.4 Collaborative Network Alignment

In order to correlate the risk structure layer with the collaborative network layer and to ensure that the model reflects the actual business processes and organisational structure, the collaborative network alignment process is as follows:

- **Collaborative network building:** The company's business processes and organisational framework are to be organised manually. This will allow the composition of the departments, their responsibilities and the business collaboration relationships between them to be sorted out in detail. The objective of this process is to construct a collaborative network layer that accurately reflects the company's internal operations, with departments represented as nodes and inter-departmental collaboration relationships depicted as edges. The establishment of a collaborative network provides the necessary infrastructure to support the subsequent mapping of risk structures and ensures that the model aligns with the actual business scenarios.
- **Mapping relationship building:** In order to establish the association between the risk structure layer and the collaborative network layer, the following process is undertaken. Firstly, the description of the responsibilities of each department in the collaborative network and the body content of the risk structure in the risk structure layer is processed. Then, the text information is semantically encoded using the BERT word embedding technique. Finally, the cosine similarity between them is calculated. In the event that the similarity exceeds a predefined threshold, a mapping relationship is deemed to exist between the risk key structure and the corresponding department. Consequently, the similarity value is designated as the weight of the edge. This approach not only establishes a semantic association between the risk structure and the organisational department, but also quantifies the closeness between the two through the weight values.

3.5 Model Application

This section details the process of applying the multi-layer network model of risk elements, validating the validity and usefulness of the model.

- **Data preprocessing:** Firstly, it is important to note that a feasibility study report test document is structurally split into three distinct sections: primary headings, secondary headings and body content. Furthermore, the body content is subjected to word splitting in order to transform the raw text into a format suitable for model processing.
- **Model application:** Firstly, the critical risk structures are located through the use of keyword matching technology, and in-depth text mining is then employed to identify content semantically similar to the known risk elements, thus identifying potential risk points. The risk level of these potential risk points is then determined through manual intervention to ensure the accuracy of the risk assessment. Finally, the risk subject is clarified by reliance on the traceability mechanism of the model. That is to say, the main responsible departments are identified, providing clear guidelines for risk management and responsibility allocation.
- **Evaluation of application effectiveness:** The effectiveness of the application of the model is assessed in two main ways: firstly, the degree of match between the risk points identified through the model and the actual risk points, and secondly, through the subjective evaluation of business personnel. This comprehensive evaluation not only validates the technical performance of the model, but also ensures its practical effectiveness and operability in real business settings.

4 Case Study

4.1 Background Introduction

The power industry is characterised by its intricate nature and specialised character, necessitating the collaborative efforts of numerous departments. This intricate system is susceptible to significant risks, which can have a substantial impact on the efficiency of project execution and the safety of enterprise operations. Consequently, this study has selected the production technical reform project of a provincial grid company as a case study, as it is highly representative of the grid industry and has more complete data records for in-depth analysis. A comprehensive collection of relevant management documents, risk case sets and organisational business process documents was assembled, and 10 randomly selected risk-free feasibility study reports were utilised as a training set to analyse collaborative network risks in power grid enterprises.

4.2 Model Construction

Data preparation: Through manual analysis of management documents and risk case sets, this study distilled approximately 30 risk rule entries pertinent to the "production technology renovation" initiative. Pdfplumber [28] was utilized to extract primary and secondary headings, as well as body content, from the feasibility study report training set, and these elements were integrated to form risk structure data. Collaborative network data was derived through manual organization of the company's business processes and organizational structure. The data description is presented in the Table 1.

In order to achieve systematic risk analysis from micro risk elements to macro organisational structure, this study proposes the construction of a three-layer network model. This comprises a risk element layer, a risk structure layer and a collaborative network layer. The risk element layer functions as the base layer, constructing a risk element association network through the utilisation of co-occurrence analysis. The risk structure layer, situated in the middle, establishes a semantic network by employing text similarity computation. The collaborative network layer, representing the business layer, generates a departmental collaborative network based on real business processes. In order to achieve cross-layer association, the model embeds knowledge from the risk element layer to the risk structure layer through keyword matching, and aligns the risk structure layer to the collaboration network layer through semantic similarity matching (Table 6).

Table 6. Description of collected data

Applicable Level	Source	Fields Included	Example
Risk Element Layer	management documents and risk case sets	Applicable Objects	Production Technical Reform Project
		Risk Rules	Check whether the project content contains keywords, such as "overhaul"
Risk Structure Layer	feasibility study report training set	Primary Title	1.Project Overview, etc.
		Secondary Title	1.1 Compilation Basis
		Merged body Content	(1) The contacts of the terminal block are in rolling contact, and it was found that the contact surface between the rotating core…
Risk Structure Layer	company organizational framework	Department Name	Development Planning Department
		Job Description	Responsible for distribution network planning…
		Collaboration Objects	Materials Department, Equipment Management Department

The results of the model construction are demonstrated in Fig. 3.

As illustrated in the figure, purple nodes represent risk elements, green nodes denote risk structures, and blue nodes are indicative of business units within the collaborative

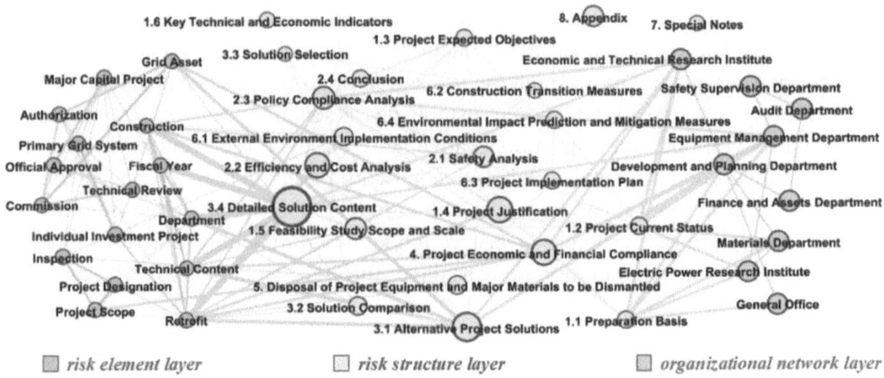

Fig. 3. Risk network model construction result

network. The size of the circle is a measure of node importance, while the thickness of the connecting line signifies the correlation between the nodes.

The model comprises 47 nodes, including 16 risk element nodes, 22 risk structure nodes, and 9 business unit nodes. It also covers 196 relationships. As indicated by the strong correlation between "3.4 Detailed Solution Content" and risk elements such as "Retrofit" and "Technical Content", it is evident that the technical programme is dependent on the contents of the production technical reform project. The "Development and Planning Department" and the "Economic and Technical Research Institute" have an average correlation strength of 0.93 with the risk structure layer, thereby highlighting their central position in the company's risk governance.

4.3 Model Application

The test set for this study is a randomly selected feasibility study report on the production technical reform project. The report was firstly structurally split to extract the primary title, secondary title and body content. The body content was then processed with word splitting. As a case in point, Fig. 4 illustrates the outcome of the text processing for Sect. 3 of the test set.

The risk structure entitled "3.1 Alternative Project Solutions" can be accurately located through the implementation of structured processing. It is evident that, in consideration of the outcomes derived from textual content segmentation, the model has the capacity to facilitate the identification of potential risk elements through the implementation of semantic matching and mapping functions. This includes, by way of illustration, the terms "Primary Grid System" and "Retrofit". Subsequently, a manual judgement is made to determine the risk level of potential risk points. In the event of identified risk, the model's mechanism for traceability will determine the department responsible for the risk, thereby providing a clear foundation for subsequent risk management and responsibility allocation.

The risk points identified by the model have been shown to have a high rate of accuracy, while feedback from frontline business personnel on the model output results also indicates that the model has strong applicability in actual business scenarios.

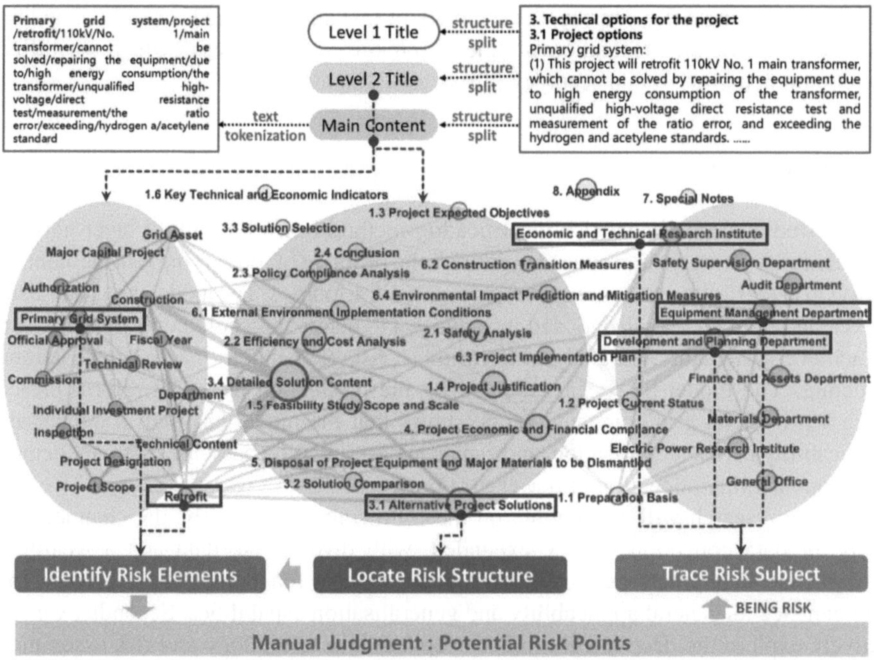

Fig. 4. Risk network model application results

5 Discussion

This study has made significant progress in the area of collaborative network risk assessment for power grid companies, but it also has certain limitations. On the positive side, this study selected the production technical reform project from a certain power company as a case study, fully demonstrating the applicability of the research results in actual business scenarios and deeply revealing the core challenges of risk management in the power grid industry, thereby providing a clear direction for model application. Additionally, compared to traditional risk assessment methods that rely on historical data and expert experience, this study utilises text mining and NLP technologies to extract risk factors from unstructured data in feasibility reports, overcoming the limitations of traditional methods in handling complex text data and achieving more timely and accurate risk identification. Finally, the risk network model innovatively combines risk factors, risk structure and collaborative networks. This multi-layer architecture not only reflects the complexity of risks but also traces the risk subject departments through collaborative networks, providing power grid companies with a more comprehensive and in-depth risk assessment method.

However, this study also has limitations. Firstly, it focuses on identifying risk factors from text without conducting an in-depth assessment of the severity of these risks. Consequently, the study can only provide a basis for risk identification and cannot directly support risk quantification or resource allocation. Secondly, the model relies heavily on historical data and expert experience, which may limit its ability to respond quickly and adapt to emerging risks. Thirdly, the accuracy of text similarity and semantic matching techniques in complex textual environments remains to be improved, which may affect the comprehensiveness and accuracy of risk assessments.

6 Conclusion

In this study, an intelligent risk identification method based on a multi-layer network model of risk elements is proposed to address the problem of identifying risk elements of power grid feasibility study under complex network scenarios. The model integrates data-driven and domain knowledge, and introduces a dynamic threshold control mechanism to achieve systematic risk analysis from micro risk elements to macro organisational structure. The model has been validated by the production technical reform project from a provincial grid company, which shows that the model has high accuracy and applicability in risk identification, and can provide a scientific basis for risk management and responsibility allocation of power grid projects.

Future research will concentrate on the following areas. Firstly, the channels and scope of data collection will be expanded, with diverse risk data and a wealth of project cases being incorporated to strengthen the data foundation of the model. This will enhance its general applicability and generalisation capabilities. Secondly, we will actively explore the deep integration of deep learning technology and risk assessment models to build a risk assessment system with dynamic adaptability, thereby improving the model's risk prediction capabilities and adaptability to dynamic changes. Finally, the development of risk assessment tools and platforms that are more intuitive and user-friendly is essential for grid company professionals to effectively apply research findings to practical risk management work. This, in turn, will improve the efficiency and effectiveness of risk management in grid companies and support the grid industry's sustainable long-term development in the face of complex and evolving risk challenges.

References

1. Camarinha-Matos, L.M., Rocha, A.D., Graça, P.: Collaborative approaches in sustainable and resilient manufacturing. J. Intell. Manuf. **35**(2), 499–519 (2024). https://doi.org/10.1007/s10845-022-02060-6
2. Zhang, H., Fang, C., Li, S., Zhang, R., Zhao, H.: A meteorological risk identification and early warning model for power system based on multi-source data fusion. Proceedings of the 2024 4th International Signal Processing, Communications and Engineering Management Conference (ISPCEM 2024), pp. 598–602 (2024). https://doi.org/10.1109/ISPCEM64498.2024.00108
3. Han, J., et al.: Risk identification method for power payment based on joint analysis of multi-source data. Proceedings of the 2024 10th International Conference on Systems and Informatics (ICSAI 2024) (2024). https://doi.org/10.1109/ICSAI65059.2024.10893736
4. Lei, S., He, J., Zhao, Z., Wu, L.: Text mining and fault risk identification in power transformers based on deep semantic learning. 2024 3rd International Conference on Energy, Power and Electrical Technology (ICEPET 2024), 1800–1803 (2024). https://doi.org/10.1109/ICEPET61938.2024.10627201

5. Li, S.-X., Chen, H.-L., Liu, L., Lu, J.: Research on risk identification technology for power system supply chain based on knowledge graph. Proceedings of the 2024 International Conference on Machine Learning and Cybernetics (ICMLC 2024), pp. 152–156 (2024). https://doi.org/10.1109/ICMLC63072.2024.10935164
6. Ma, F., Liu, Y., Wang, B., Jia, R., Ma, H.: Research on intelligent identification method of distribution grid operation safety risk based on semantic feature parsing. Int. J. Electr. Power Energy Syst. **160**, 110139 (2024). https://doi.org/10.1016/j.ijepes.2024.110139
7. Shen, W., Wang, Y., Yao, C., Zhou, Z., Jin, G.: Research on a data risk identification technology based on machine learning. 2024 5th International Conference on Artificial Intelligence and Electromechanical Automation (AIEA 2024), pp. 404–409 (2024). https://doi.org/10.1109/AIEA62095.2024.10692359
8. Yang, X., Wei, X., Cai, J.: Constructing a composite ecological security pattern through blind zone reduction and ecological risk networks: A case study of the Middle Yangtze River Urban Agglomeration. China. Sustainability **17**(11), 5099 (2025). https://doi.org/10.3390/SU17115099
9. Bai, L., Wang, C., Sun, Y., Xie, X., Tang, T., Xie, Q.: Project portfolio network risk propagation modeling: A risk perception perspective. IEEE Trans. Eng. Manage. **71**, 14608–14620 (2024). https://doi.org/10.1109/TEM.2024.3455310
10. Shiroky, A.: Risk management in the design of computer network topology. Lect. Notes Comput. Sci. **14123**, 375–386 (2024). https://doi.org/10.1007/978-3-031-50482-2_29
11. Zhang, H., Wang, Q.: Risk identification model of aviation system based on text mining and risk propagation. Eksploatacja i Niezawodnosc **27**(1), 192767 (2025). https://doi.org/10.17531/ein/192767
12. Zhuang, Z., Hou, Y., Yang, L., Gong, J., Wang, L.: Toward safer flight training: The data-driven modeling of accident risk network using text mining based on deep learning. Int. J. Computat. Intel. Sys. **17**(1), 291 (2024). https://doi.org/10.1007/s44196-024-00705-3
13. Wang, K., Wen, F., Gong, X.: Oil prices and systemic financial risk: a complex network analysis. Energy **293**, 130672 (2024). https://doi.org/10.1016/j.energy.2024.130672
14. Jin, Q., Sun, L., Chen, Y., Hu, Z.-L.: Financial risk contagion based on dynamic multi-layer network between banks and firms. Physica A **638**, 129624 (2024). https://doi.org/10.1016/j.physa.2024.129624
15. Zhang, G., Feng, W.: Generation and evolution process of urban systemic risk based on the complex network theory and its application in rainfall scenario. SSRN (2024). https://doi.org/10.2139/ssrn.4719212
16. Xu, N., Hu, Y., Zhang, B., Chang, H., Guo, C., Zhou, X.: Safety-risk transmission assessment based on a factor-event network for metro construction projects. Nat. Hazard. Rev. **25**(1), 04023056 (2024). https://doi.org/10.1061/NHREFO.NHENG-1884
17. Li, A., Wang, Y., Chen, H.: AI driven cardiovascular risk prediction using NLP and large language models for personalized medicine in athletes. SLAS Technology **32**, 100286 (2025). https://doi.org/10.1016/j.slast.2025.100286
18. Zhou, Z., Guo, J., Huang, J.: Chemical safety risk identification and analysis based on improved LDA topic model and Bayesian networks. Appl. Sci. **15**(11), 6197 (2025). https://doi.org/10.3390/app15116197
19. Liu, C., Yang, S.: Using text mining to establish knowledge graph from accident/incident reports in risk assessment. Expert Syst. Appl. **207**, 117991 (2022). https://doi.org/10.1016/j.eswa.2022.117991
20. Zhou, Y., Ge, J., Chen, J., Bai, Z.: Risk prediction for operational environments of power distribution equipment based on inspection text mining. Gaodianya Jishu/High Voltage Engineering **48**(4), 1213–1225 (2022). https://doi.org/10.13336/j.1003-6520.hve.20211924

21. Xing, Y., et al.: Discovering latent themes in aviation safety reports using text mining and network analytics. Int. J. Transport. Sci. Technol. **16**, 292–316 (2024). https://doi.org/10.1016/j.ijtst.2024.02.009
22. Bu, Z., Ye, S.: Network security risk evaluation and inducement analysis based on bayesian method. In: 2024 5th Information Communication Technologies Conference (ICTC), pp. 70–75. IEEE (2024). https://doi.org/10.1109/ICTC61510.2024.10601785
23. Zhao, Y., Zhang, J., Mu, E.: NLP-based approach for identifying quality risk factors in steel structure construction. Buildings **14**(11), 3493 (2024). https://doi.org/10.3390/buildings14113493
24. Hameed, T., et al.: An NLP-enhanced approach to test comorbidities risk scoring based on unstructured health data for hospital readmissions prediction. Proceedings of the 16th International Joint Conference on Biomedical Engineering Systems and Technologies (BIOSTEC 2023), pp. 649–659 (2023). https://doi.org/10.5220/0011944500003414
25. Liu, L., Shi, L.: An intelligent risk mining method by whole process-oriented risk analysis model. Proceedings of the 2024 16th International Conference on Machine Learning and Computing (ICMLC 2024), pp. 616–620 (2024). https://doi.org/10.1145/3651671.3651779
26. Lis, S., Kubkowski, M., Borkowska, O., Serwa, D., Kurpanik, J.: Analyzing Credit Risk Model Problems through NLP-Based Clustering and Machine Learning: Insights from Validation Reports. arXiv (2023)
27. Parikh, P., Penfield, J., Barker, R., McGowan, B., Mallon, J.R.: NLP-based ergonomics MSD risk root cause analysis and risk controls recommendation. Ergonomics **68**(7), 1124–1136 (2025). https://doi.org/10.1080/00140139.2024.2394510
28. pdfplumber: pdfplumber: A Python library for extracting and analyzing PDF content [Computer software] (2024). https://github.com/jsvine/pdfplumber

Research on Risk Management System of Grid Reserve Project Based on Human-Computer Collaboration

Xina Zhu[1], Wenxin Mu[1], Wanyu Li[1], Xianing Jin[2], and Juanqiong Gou[1(✉)]

[1] Beijing Jiaotong University, Beijing, China
{24120593,wxmu,24125578,jqgou}@bjtu.edu.cn
[2] State Grid Economic and Technological Research Institute Co., Ltd., Beijing, China

Abstract. In the research field of grid risk management, a combination of information systems and manual work is usually used. As the power grid continues to evolve, the use of artificial intelligence (AI) is gradually increasing, the patterns of efficient Human-AI collaboration become a crucial research problem. Management interface risks in the power grid industry are the type of risks that are likely to occur during the project feasibility study review stage. Once these risks occur, they will have a certain degree of impact on each business process node in the subsequent stages of the project. This study aims to explore how these risks can be managed through effective collaboration between human and AI. First, this paper examines human-computer division of labor criteria for management interface risks, with a particular focus on rule-driven tasks. Second, we propose a "composite algorithm", which integrates cosine similarity, BERT similarity, hybrid similarity and APRIORI algorithm. This algorithm enables risk rule extraction, risk keyword extraction, risk structure matching and risk correlation identification, ultimately constructing a risk rule base. Finally, the effectiveness of this human-AI collaborative risk management method is verified using an enterprise in the power sector as a case study. This paper is innovative at the field level, the application level and the organizational management level.

Keywords: Human-AI collaboration network · risk management system · composite algorithm · risk rule base

1 Introduction

Human-Machine Collaboration (HMC) has emerged in multiple fields [1, 2]. In the field of renewable energy, Human-Computer Collaboration combines AI analytics with human decision-making expertise to enhance energy system resilience and sustainability [1]. In the manufacturing sector, collaborative networks (CNs) play a key role in the

This work is supported by Science and Technology Project of the SGCC (Grant No. 52060025002A-188-ZN, Research on Multi-dimensional Goal Decision-making and Dynamic Control Technology for Corporate Planning Oriented to Strategic Missions).

Published by Springer Nature Switzerland AG 2026
L. M. Camarinha-Matos et al. (Eds.): PRO-VE 2025, IFIP AICT 770, pp. 137–153, 2026.
https://doi.org/10.1007/978-3-032-05673-3_9

Industry 5.0 trend [3]. For example, in industrial environments, the integration of continuous learning and object detection algorithms sets a new standard for intelligent HMC systems [2]. The pervasive use of AI agents in the workplace has transformed employee interactions with technology, providing new perspectives on AI implementation in collaborative environments [4].

As the scale of power grid project construction expands annually [5], project management interface risks are frequent. Management interface risks, including management interface confusion, management interface cross, management hierarchy cross, duplication of construction, and frequent establishment, have a decisive impact on the project investment decision. However, they are often neglected due to their hidden nature and complexity. And the monitoring and identification of these risks often begin after they have already occurred or become apparent [6], leading to a lag in risk oversight. The rationality and accuracy of the feasibility study report (FSR) is the basis for the construction of the project [7]. Effectively mining the risk correlation relationship of the management interface from the FSR at the feasibility study review stage is a front-end type of risk management strategy, which can effectively reduce the possibility of risk occurrence in the business process line during the implementation of the project, such as the distortion of the technical and economic budgets, and the high incidence of repetitive inputs.

Presently, the prevalent risk identification mainly applies two modes of manual analysis or machine processing, while the management interface risk identification in the power grid industry relies solely on manual analysis. The manual mode relies on expert experience for document review and risk assessment, which is inefficient and subjective; while machine mode is difficult to parse semantically, so a human-computer collaboration system is essential.

This study achieved a triple breakthrough at the innovative level, as follows:

- Innovation in the field: A correlation analysis framework for the management interface risk of power grid projects is proposed, which fills the shortage of research on the identification of risk correlation relationship in the field of power grid.
- Innovation in application: The granularity of risk correlation analysis is refined from the traditional project management dimension to the semantic unit of documents, realizing the application of risk correlation relationship analysis at the level of FSR.
- Innovation in organizational management: Proposing a human-computer collaborative risk identification paradigm, breaking through the traditional single human or machine dominated cognitive boundaries.

The rest of the article is structured as follows. In the second part, the related research is briefly introduced. In the third part, a human-computer collaboration-based risk management methodology system is constructed to clarify the human-computer division of labor criteria and the implementation steps of this methodology. In the fourth part, for the case of a grid industry enterprise, the risk keywords are extracted and matched with the structure of the FSR, the rule base is constructed, and the relationship between the rules and risks is stored in the graph database, so as to generate the association map of "project-frequent itemset-rule-risk-structure of the FSR" in order to validate the validity of the methodology system. Finally, the fifth part summarizes the paper.

2 Related Works

Human-Computer Collaborative Networks. Artificial Intelligence (AI) offers great potential in organizations, and focusing on the interaction and complementary interoperability between humans and AI will be a key way to realize this potential [8]. [9] emphasizes AI's strengths in information processing and human capabilities in abstract decision making. It also discusses how these complementary strengths can be utilized to achieve human-machine cooperation.

Human-computer CNs are divided into macro and micro. At a macro level, CNs are networks of organizations, people, and other entities that are largely autonomous, geographically distributed, and heterogeneous in terms of their operating environments, cultures, social capital, and goals. Participants in a collaborative network share information, resources and responsibilities in order to achieve common or compatible goals, and the interaction of the parties is realized through computer networks [10]. At the micro level, the value of human-computer collaboration lies in effectively uniting the strengths of humans and machines to ensure effective and rational task allocation between humans and machines [11].

The development of human-computer CNs at the micro level has undergone a paradigm shift from instrumental assistance to cognitive collaboration. Early research focused on human-computer division of labor for mechanical tasks [12], and the main literature in human-computer task assignment research utilizes mathematical models and optimization algorithms [13]. With the evolution of AI technology, the collaboration form is gradually evolving towards dynamic adaptive collaborative systems. [14] found that HMC in organizations undergoes a three-stage evolution of "tool substitution-complementary capabilities-cognitive enhancement".

Various manifestations of CNs have been studied in different branches of science such as computer science, computer engineering, and management [15]. [16] focused on the application of AI in the field of human resource management. [1] has realized the application of human-machine CNs in the energy ecosystem. [17] detailed the application of human-computer collaboration in a variety of areas such as text generation, story creation, and artistic drawing. [18] studied the application of human-computer collaboration in general-purpose tasks using image classification as a specific case study.

Risk Management. Risk management can be defined as a process involving several stages, including risk identification, risk analysis, and risk evaluation, to achieve preventive control before an accident occurs, assessment of hazards and impacts during an accident, and emergency response and feedback after an accident.

With the development of the power market and the increase in the complexity of power grids, risk management research has evolved continuously, aiming at guaranteeing the safe and stable operation of power grids and the sustainable development of enterprises.

In terms of the construction of the risk assessment indicator system, [19] built an effective asset risk assessment system, which comprehensively covers all kinds of risk factors faced by power grid enterprises. [20] built a system of indicators for assessing the risks and benefits of grid investment, to provide a basis for investment decision-making. [21] established a three-dimensional multi-layered risk assessment system for the power purchase business of the grid agent to cope with the uncertainties in market transactions.

In terms of risk assessment and prediction methods, [22] applies intelligent algorithms such as PSO and FAHP to construct a risk prediction model and set up a three-level early warning mechanism to promote risk management towards intelligence and real-time development.

In terms of grid failure risk response strategies, [23] proposed to integrate grid operation-guided and structure-driven modeling strategies to effectively reduce cascading fault sizes and enhance grid robustness and resilience.

In summary, research on the criteria for the human-machine division of labor in human-machine CNs has become more comprehensive, and such networks are increasingly utilized across various fields. However, there are fewer studies in the related literature in the field of risk management. The risk assessment index system, assessment and prediction methods, and risk response strategies of the power grid industry have been studied in the field. Therefore, this paper will supplement the shortcomings of human-computer collaborative network research in the field of risk management by constructing the human-computer division of labor standard for the study of the risk of the management interface of the grid reserve project through the literature-driven method, and completing the study of the correlation relationship between the risk factors and the risk of the management interface through the APIRORI algorithm, and ultimately building a human-computer collaborative risk management system.

3 Methodology

In this paper, we construct a risk management methodology system based on human-computer collaboration. Through the complementary advantages of human experience and machine algorithms, to jointly complete risk management of grid reserve projects, see Fig. 1.

3.1 Human-Computer Division of Labor Criteria Setting

Theoretical Basis Extraction. A human-computer collaborative system consists of human and machine algorithms which work together to accomplish a complex task. The first step to realize effective collaboration is to ensure effective task allocation. Optimize the performance of that risk management framework by establishing human-computer collaboration division of labor criteria.

A large body of literature has addressed the human-machine division of labor and the advantages of humans versus machines. [11] stated that humans are uniquely equipped with cognitive and reasoning abilities to handle highly flexible tasks; while machines can complement humans in tasks that require great strength, long hours of work, high speed and high precision. [24] identified task complexity as a key factor in human-machine task allocation, arguing that machines excel at performing routine tasks guided by explicit rules, while non-routine tasks involving problem solving and complex communication pose a continuous challenge to automation. [25] similarly pointed out that machines can replace humans in the performance of everyday tasks, which can be summarized as a series of specific activities performed according to well-defined instructions and procedures. [17] noted that deep learning techniques play an important role in alleviating heavy and tedious human tasks.

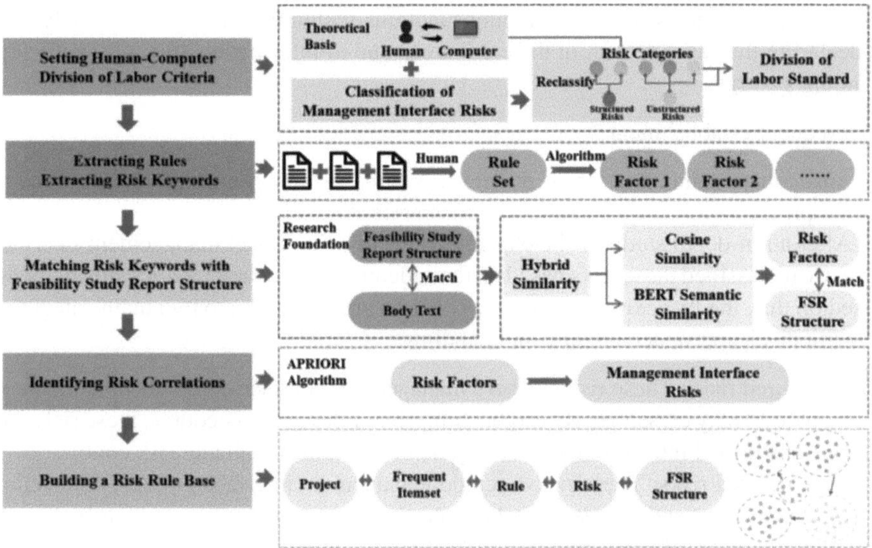

Fig. 1. Technical Architecture Diagram

Grid Reserve Program Management Interface Risks Classification. At the feasibility study stage of the project, the reserve project management process is characterized by unclear boundaries and overlapping of special projects, ill-defined levels of project reporting, multiple establishments of the same project, and frequent establishment and modification of the project. Depending on the actual situation, in the reserve program business scenario, management interface risks can include five types of risk events: management interface confusion, management interface cross, management hierarchy cross, duplication of construction, and frequent establishment.

The definition of the five categories of management interface risks is given below as:

(1) Management interface confusion

Misidentification of project attributes during the project declaration stage can lead to incorrect categorization into non-matching special management categories.

(2) Management interface cross

The same construction content was duplicated in different projects or unreasonably split into separate projects as a result of unclear definition of project content.

(3) Management hierarchy crosses

The vertical management system's approval levels for feasibility studies at the headquarters and its units are inappropriate.

(4) Duplication of construction

Implementing projects with overlapping functions within the same power supply area or declaring the same project in different areas due to information silos or insufficient planning synergy.

(5) Frequent establishment

The inadequate demonstration of project feasibility results in multiple declarations of similar projects.

After an in-depth study of the characteristics of grid project management interface risks, we reclassified these risks based on their identification characteristics and methods. Based on this, the five existing categories of risks are grouped into two main categories to facilitate clearer understanding and handling:

(1) Structured risks: These risks involve management interface confusion and management hierarchy crossings. By establishing clear rules and procedures, these risks can be transformed into actionable management tasks, thus realizing risk control.
(2) Unstructured risks: These risks include management interface crosses, duplication of construction and frequent establishment. They are not easily defined by simple rules and often rely on semantic similarity analysis and human experience for identification and treatment. Owing to the complexity and uncertainty of such risks, their management requires more specialized knowledge and flexible response strategies.

Division of Labor Standard Setting. Based on the document "A Company's Circular" to classify the risk. The power grid project can be divided into 16 projects according to professional management, such as power grid infrastructure, power grid small infrastructure, production technology reform. Since the production technology reform project is more numerous and more widely applied in the actual situation, this paper takes this project as an example for research.

Analyse the relevant laws, regulations, national industry standards and the in-depth regulations of the feasibility study of the reserve project and other documents, and combine the experience of experts for the extraction of management interface risks rules, which refer to statements in documents related to risk identification. It is found that the rules extracted from various management documents are concentrated in the two categories of management interface confusion and management hierarchy cross. That is, through the machine identification method by logical judgment and keyword matching, the above two types of rule-driven tasks can be accomplished to complete the risk identification. As for the three types of management interface cross, duplication of construction and frequent establishment risks, there is no exact rule basis for risk identification, and it requires manual empirical judgment.

Based on the above analysis, we categorize the risk association relationship identification tasks into two types: rule-driven tasks and experience-driven tasks. This paper focuses on rule-driven tasks and studies the reasonable division of labor between humans and machine algorithms in such tasks under the guidance of the theoretical basis of human-computer division of labor criteria, and constructs a risk rule database. In such tasks, the human-computer decision boundaries are shown in Fig. 2.

(1) The source of the rules is twofold, first, by manually extracting relevant items from various documents, second, by relying on the experience of experts based on actual situations in which management interface risks have occurred in the past; (2) Risk

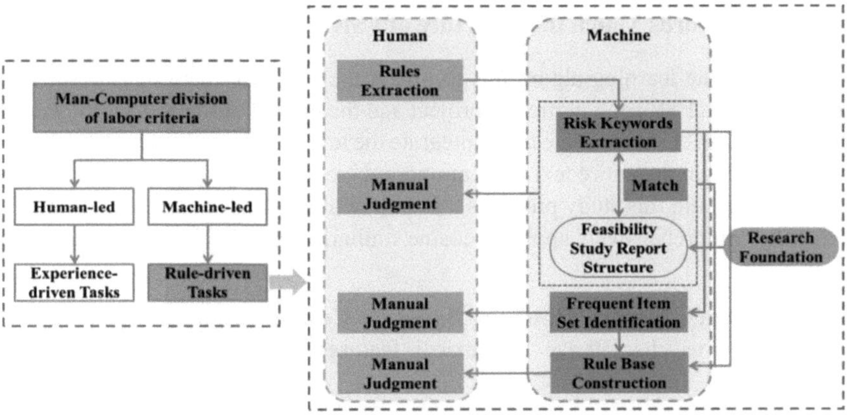

Fig. 2. Decision-making boundaries for humans and machines

keywords are extracted by machine algorithms; (3) The matching of risk keywords with the structure of such project's FSRs is realized by machine algorithms; (4) Frequent item sets are identified by APRIORI algorithm to find out the most probable risk; (5) In practice, the risk keywords, the matching results with FSRs, and the set of risk frequent items need to be judged manually.

3.2 Rule Extraction and Risk Keyword Extraction

The rules in this paper are derived from expert experience and documents such as relevant laws, regulations, national industry standards and the in-depth regulations of feasibility study of reserve projects, from which the rules on management interface risks are manually extracted to constitute a rule set. Risk keywords, that is, words extracted from each rule that directly localize management interface risks. Since the accuracy of keywords has a large impact on the subsequent keyword matching, in this paper, based on the pre-defined customized dictionary and deactivated thesaurus of the grid industry management interface risks domain, the rules are subdivided into multiple risk factors, namely, risk keywords.

Specifically, the automated process of extracting risk factor keywords from grid project rule names is realized through code. As one of the technical tools used in data analysis, jieba has been widely applied in the field of Chinese natural language processing and can be used in scenarios such as text mining, sentiment analysis, and information retrieval [26]. Firstly, the rule name is accurately separated by jieba Chinese lexical tool combined with power grid terminology dictionary, and then the words that contain non-Chinese and English characters, such as numbers, symbols, spaces, etc. are filtered out by regular expressions. The processed keywords are intercepted in the order of occurrence of the first 10 as risk factors, and finally the original rule name and the extracted keywords are spliced horizontally to generate a structured result table. The output is directly used for subsequent risk correlation relationship analysis and graph construction.

The extracted risk keywords are handed over to experts to check for accuracy.

3.3 Risk Keywords Match the Structure of FSR

Through machine learning algorithms to match the similarity between the secondary titles of multiple FSRs of a particular project and the outline of feasibility study compilation of the project. At the same time, integrate the text of different FSRs under the same structure to obtain the entire text content under the outline of a specific FSR. Based on this research result, this study proposes a hybrid similarity index for text similarity calculation by comprehensively applying cosine similarity and BERT pre-trained language model.

Word Frequency Feature Matching Based on Cosine Similarity. Using term frequency model to characterize the lexical features of the text, the specific steps are:

(1) Text preprocessing: Filter Chinese and English characters by regular expressions, accurately separate words based on the jieba lexical tool combined with the domain customized dictionaries, and eliminate stop words and numeric characters.
(2) Vector space modeling: Integrate the regular risk factor keywords and body content keywords into a corpus, and use the CountVectorizer method to convert the text data into a word frequency matrix.
(3) Similarity calculation: For each rule, the cosine similarity between its risk factor keyword vector and each body content keyword vector is calculated in turn.

BERT-Based Semantic Feature Extraction. As a pre-trained model based on multi-layer bidirectional Transformers, BERT can generate context-aware word embeddings. By calculating the distance between embedded vectors, it can effectively measure semantic similarity and demonstrate its ability to capture deep semantic associations in multilingual tasks [27]. Sentence-BERT, based on BERT, generates sentence embeddings through a twin network structure and pooling operations, retaining BERT's contextual understanding advantages. It can accurately capture deep semantic associations at the sentence level in tasks such as semantic text similarity [28]. In order to capture deep semantic associations, a pre-trained BERT model is used to generate semantic embeddings with context-awareness, the specific steps are:

(1) Text preprocessing: The method is the same as the text preprocessing process of cosine similarity.
(2) Embedding Generation: Utilize the BERT model to convert each text into semantic vectors.
(3) Semantic Similarity Calculation: For each rule, after obtaining its corresponding BERT semantic vector, the cosine similarity between this vector and the BERT semantic vectors of the text under the secondary headings of all FSRs will be calculated in turn, see Eq. (1).

$$Sim_{BERT} = \frac{R_{BERT} \cdot C_{BERT}}{R_{\mathrm{BERT}} \cdot C_{BERT}} \tag{1}$$

Let the semantic vector of rule keywords be $\mathrm{R_{BERT}}$ and the semantic vector of body text be $\mathrm{C_{BERT}}$.

Hybrid Similarity Fusion Strategy. Since the cosine similarity algorithm can well measure the degree of lexical overlap, and the BERT semantic similarity algorithm is good at capturing the deep semantic associations, this study proposes a hybrid similarity computation method based on the fusion of word-frequency features and semantic features in order to balance the lexical accuracy and semantic generalization ability. The designed hybrid similarity calculation is Eq. (2):

$$Sim_{Hybrid} = \alpha \cdot Sim_{cosin} + (1 - \alpha) \cdot Sim_{BERT} \quad (2)$$

where $\alpha = 0.5$ is determined based on the expert's empirical judgment of the matching results.

3.4 APRIORI Algorithm to Identify Risk Correlation Relationship

First, the rule data is loaded and the risk factors and corresponding management interface risks for each rule are extracted to construct the transactional dataset. Transaction data is converted to Boolean matrix by TransactionEncoder to realize the structured encoding of data. Second, the APRIORI algorithm is applied to mine the frequent item sets, set the minimum support threshold to 0.05 to filter the low-frequency combinations, and generate association rules with a confidence level of no less than 50%. In order to focus on the core management risks, the code filters out the rules that contain only "management interface confusion" or "management hierarchy cross" as the consequents through ensemble operations to eliminate irrelevant noise.

As above, the results of the identification of risk correlation relationship are also judged by expert experience for reasonableness, and inappropriate frequent item sets are added, deleted, or modified.

3.5 Risk Rule Base Construction

In this study, we design a rule knowledge base based on Neo4j graph database, structurally store the associations among special projects, frequent itemsets, rules, risks and FSR structure entities according to the algorithms of the above rule extraction, risk keyword extraction, matching of risk keywords and feasibility study structure, and generate the association mapping of "projects-frequent itemsets-rules-risks-FSR structure" association mapping. The data model of the rule base is designed as follows:

(1) Node Design
   1) Project: Indicates different specialties.
   2) RiskStructure: The second-level title of the FSR.
   3) RiskRule: Indicates the specific rules extracted from laws and regulations, depth requirements of the study and other documents.
   4) FrequentItemset: Indicates the frequent itemset of the risk factor combinations extracted from the rules pointing to the management interface risks.
   5) ManagementRisk: Indicates management interface risks.

(2) Relationship Design

1) CONTAINS: Connects project and frequent itemsets, indicating that a project contains multiple frequent itemsets.
2) ASSOCIATED_WITH: Connecting frequent itemsets and risk rules, indicating that a risk rule can be derived from multiple frequent itemsets.
3) LEADS_TO: Connects risk rules and management interface risks, the consequents of a risk rule is management interface risks.
4) INCLUDES_IN: Connects management interface risks and FSR risk structure, indicating that management interface risks are included in the specific structure of FSR.

4 Case Verification

4.1 Case Selection

This paper chooses a grid industry enterprise as the study case. There are three reasons: first, the selected company is a core enterprise in China's power industry, which has a very high industry representation; second, the enterprise has a great deal of information such as FSRs and rule documents, which cover a large amount of detailed information on risk factors and management interface risks; moreover, the electric power industry requires a high degree of security, and risk management is of vital importance.

4.2 Risk Keyword Extraction and FSR Structure Matching

The rules are categorized and organized separately according to the project. Since the accuracy of the keywords has a great impact on the subsequent keyword matching work, in this paper, on the basis of predefined custom dictionaries and deactivated thesaurus of the risk areas of the management interface risks of the power grid industry, the rules are divided into words, and multiple risk factors, namely the risk keywords, are extracted from each rule. See Table 1.

The text content under the integrated secondary heading structure is matched with the similarity of each risk factor in the rules extracted in this paper, and identify the three secondary heading structures corresponding to a certain rule with the highest similarity, so as to realize the matching mapping between the rules and the FSR structure, and thus locate the management interface risks more precisely.

Similarly, using the example of the production technology reform project, some of the results of using cosine similarity to match the structure of the feasibility study are shown in Table 2.

Some of the results of researchable structure matching using BERT semantic similarity are shown in Table 3.

It can be seen that there is a large difference between the matching results of the two methods, and the possibility of the cosine similarity value is the same, so this paper adopts the hybrid similarity formula, see Table 4.

The similarity comparison of the three methods is shown in Fig. 3.

For each rule, set a corresponding feasible structural standard answer. Use three metrics—Precision, Recall, and F1 score—to quantitatively evaluate machine learning performance. Precision represents the proportion of true positives among all candidate

Table 1. Partial data display of production technology reform project

Rule name	Management interface risks	Risk factor 1	Risk factor 2	Risk factor 3	Risk factor 4 …
Whether grid primary and power supply technical reform projects with a single investment of 20 million yuan and above are restricted projects	management hierarchy cross	single investment	grid primary	Power Supply Technology Reform Project	restricted projects
New grid infrastructure: The name of the project contains "main transformer reconstruction", "main transformer replacement"; the content contains "main transformer replacement"; the main transformer's new capacity is 50% or more of the original.	management interface confusion	New Grid Infrastructure	the name of the project	main transformer	Reconstruction …

entries; Recall represents the proportion of standard answers retrieved among all rules; F1 score is the harmonic mean of accuracy and recall. Specifically, the mixed similarity method achieves an accuracy of 26%, a recall of 79%, and an F1 score of 40%; the BERT similarity method achieves metrics of 18%, 53%, and 26%; and the cosine similarity method produces metrics of 6%, 18%, and 9%. It is evident that the mixed similarity method outperforms the two individual methods. Subsequently, the matching results of the algorithm need to be judged and corrected manually.

4.3 Identification of Risk Correlation Relationship

Next, we combine the "Risk factor" and "Management interface risks" corresponding to each "Rule name" in Table 1 of Sect. 4.2 into transaction data. The effectiveness

Table 2. Cosine similarity matching results (partial)

Rule name	Match Ranking	secondary heading	Sim_{cosin}
Whether grid primary and power supply technical reform projects with a single investment of 20 million yuan and above are restricted projects	1	8.Appendix	0
	2	7.Note on Special Matters	0
	3	1.2Description of The Current Situation	0
New grid infrastructure: The name of the project contains "main transformer reconstruction", "main transformer replacement"; the content contains "main transformer replacement"; the main transformer's new capacity is 50% or more of the original.	1	3.4Program Details	0.48
	2	1.2Description of The Current Situation	0.38
	3	1.4Rationale for The Project	0.38

Table 3. BERT similarity matching results (partial)

Rule name	Match Ranking	secondary heading	Sim_{BERT}
Whether grid primary and power supply technical reform projects with a single investment of 20 million yuan and above are restricted projects	1	7.Note on Special Matters	0.93
	2	3.3.Program Options	0.91
	3	8.Appendix	0.87
New grid infrastructure: The name of the project contains "main transformer reconstruction", "main transformer replacement"; the content contains "main transformer replacement"; the main transformer's new capacity is 50% or more of the original.	1	3.3.Program Options	0.94
	2	7.Note on Special Matters	0.94
	3	8.Appendix	0.89

of the association rule mining results depends on the setting of the support and confidence threshold size, if the setting is too low then a large amount of result data will be obtained and no effective information can be extracted, whereas if the setting is too high then a small amount of data will be obtained, which will result in the omission of key information. Considering the small size of this dataset, the support level is appropriately increased in order to avoid generating more useless rules as well as avoiding too much fragmentation of the results. Meanwhile, based on the amount of data as well as the test results, repeated iterations and analysis are carried out so as to determine the

Table 4. Hybrid similarity matching results (partial)

Rule name	Match Ranking	secondary heading	Sim cosin	Sim BERT	Sim Hybrid
Whether grid primary and power supply technical reform projects with a single investment of 20 million yuan and above are restricted projects	1	7. Note on Special Matters	0	0.93	0.46
	2	3.3. Program Options	0	0.91	0.45
	3	8. Appendix	0	0.87	0.44
New grid infrastructure: The name of the project contains "main transformer reconstruction", "main transformer replacement"; the content contains "main transformer replacement"; the main transformer's new capacity is 50% or more of the original	1	3.4 Program Details	0.48	0.67	0.57
	2	6.2 Construction transition measures	0.38	0.74	0.56
	3	1.2 Description of The Current Situation	0	0.69	0.53

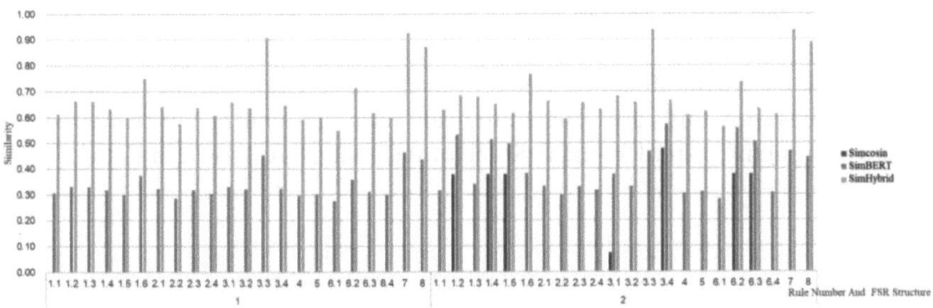

Fig. 3. Data Comparison Chart (partial)

appropriate threshold value. In this paper, the support threshold is finally set at 0.05 to filter out the frequently occurring itemsets. Based on the frequent item set, association rules are generated and the minimum confidence threshold is set to 0.5 to filter out rules with strong associations. In addition, restricting consequences to rules that are reserved only for management interface risks to ensure that risk keywords are causally related to management interface risks.

Again, taking the production technology reform project as an example, some of the association rule data are shown in Table 5.

Table 5. Association Rules

Serial number	Rules	Support	Confidence	Lift
1	{total investment, the name of the project} = > {management interface confusion}	0.06	1	3.09
2	{restricted projects, single investment} = > {management hierarchy cross}	0.06	1	1.48
3	{new grid infrastructure project, the name of the project, details} = > {management interface confusion}	0.06	1	3.09

It shows that management interface confusion risks are usually related to the total investment and the project name, and risk avoidance requires scrutinizing the relevant study structure in relation to them; management hierarchy cross risks are closely related to whether the project is restricted projects or not, and to the project's individual investment.

4.4 Risk Rule Base Construction

Apply the rule base data model designed in Sect. 3.5 to complete the construction of the risk rule base for this case. The stored rule base can realize the risk conduction traceability through Cypher language. Some of the results are shown in Fig. 4.

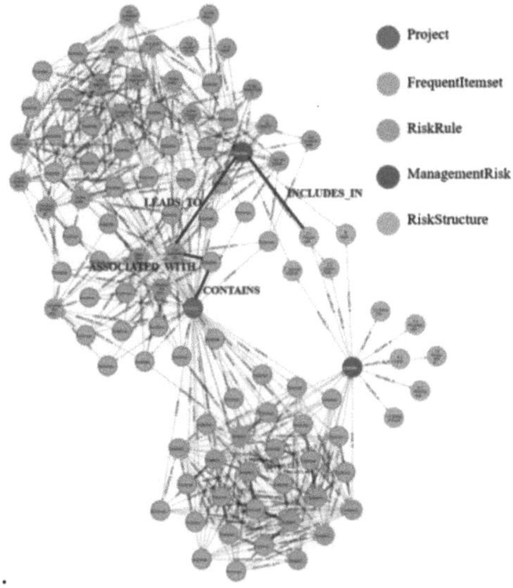

Fig. 4. Management interface risks rule base (partial)

5 Conclusion

Focusing on management interface risks in the power grid industry, this study proposes a risk management system based on human-computer collaboration, aiming to effectively deal with such risks in the feasibility study review stage. The study first clarifies the human-computer division of labor criteria, focuses on rule-driven tasks, accomplishes risk management through human and multiple algorithms, and constructs a risk rule base. Then the effectiveness of the method is verified through case studies.

However, this study is limited by the small size of the dataset and relies on empirical judgments of key parameters, which may affect the generality and robustness of its findings. Future research directions can consider increasing the sample size and incorporating project data from different regions and different types of grid enterprises into the research scope, so as to significantly enhance the general applicability and reliability of the research conclusions. In addition, on the basis of the current study, researchers can further explore the human-computer collaboration mode in experience-driven tasks and optimize the human-computer collaboration mechanism, so as to more comprehensively deal with the various types of risks that may be encountered in the grid project management interface.

At the same time, in view of the continuous progress and rapid development of AI and big data technology, future research can also try to introduce more advanced and accurate algorithms and models. Through these technical means, the accuracy of risk identification, correlation analysis and prediction can be further improved, thus providing more powerful technical support for the risk management of power grid projects.

References

1. Adu-Kankam, K.O., Camarinha-Matos, L.M., Obeng, E.: Hybrid collaborative networks in energy ecosystems. In: Navigating Unpredictability: Collaborative Networks in Non-linear Worlds. PRO-VE 2024, Pt I. IFIP AICT, vol. 726, pp. 3–21. Springer International Publishing Ag (2024). https://doi.org/10.1007/978-3-031-71739-0_1
2. Fan, Y., Antonelli, D., Simeone, A.: Continual Learning for human-machine collaboration in VUCA environments. In: Navigating Unpredictability: Collaborative Networks in Non-linear Worlds. PRO-VE 2024, Pt I. IFIP AICT, vol. 726, pp. 68–81. Springer International Publishing Ag (2024). https://doi.org/10.1007/978-3-031-71739-0_5
3. Graca, P., Camarinha-Matos, L.M.: Influence of collaboration in sustainable manufacturing networks. In: Collaborative Networks in Digitalization and Society 5.0, PRO-VE 2022. IFIP AICT, vol. 662, pp. 3–17. Springer International Publishing Ag (2022). https://doi.org/10.1007/978-3-031-14844-6_1
4. Schulte, A., Klat, W., Suesse, T.: How does the implementation of AI agents affect human agents' job profiles? Insights from two industrial cases. In: PRO-VE 2022. IFIP AICT, vol. 662, pp. 313–320. Springer International Publishing Ag (2022) https://doi.org/10.1007/978-3-031-14844-6_25
5. Lin, L., Ge, Q., Han, Y.: Infrared image segmentation technology for electrical equipment based on genetic algorithm and fuzzy C-Class mean. In: Wu, H., Li, H. (eds.) ICCAID 2023, p. 92. SPIE, Qingdao, China (2024). https://doi.org/10.1117/12.3026495
6. He, F., Ji, L., Li, C.: Grid disaster risk identification based on social network analysis. Reliab. Eng. Syst. Saf. **256**, 110756 (2025). https://doi.org/10.1016/j.ress.2024.110756
7. Li, Y., Liu, H., Guo, J.: The stakeholder analysis of progress management in prophase of the hydropower project. In: Ma, M. (ed.) SSR 2013, Pt 1. Advances in Social and Behavioral Sciences, vol. 1, pp. 222–228. Singapore Management & Sports Science Inst Pte Ltd, Singapore (2013)
8. Fabri, L., Haeckel, B., Oberlaender, A.M., Rieg, M., Stohr, A.: Disentangling human-AI hybrids conceptualizing the interworking of humans and AI-enabled systems. Bus. Inf. Syst. Eng. **65**(6), 623–641 (2023). https://doi.org/10.1007/s12599-023-00810-1
9. van den Bosch, K., Schoonderwoerd, T., Blankendaal, R., Neerincx M.: Six challenges for human-AI co-learning. In: Sottilare, R.A., Schwarz, J. (eds.) AIS 2019. Lecture Notes in Computer Science, vol. 11597, pp. 572–589. Springer International Publishing Ag (2019). https://doi.org/10.1007/978-3-030-22341-0_45
10. Camarinha-Matos, L.M., Afsarmanesh, H., Galeano, N., Molina, A.: Collaborative networked organizations – Concepts and practice in manufacturing enterprises. Comput. Industr. Eng. **57**(1), 46–60 (2009). https://doi.org/10.1016/j.cie.2008.11.024
11. Hu, B., Chen, J.: Optimal task allocation for human-machine collaborative manufacturing systems. IEEE Robot. Autom. Lett. **2**(4), 1933–1940 (2017). https://doi.org/10.1109/LRA.2017.2714981
12. Cheng, Y., Sun, F., Zhang, Y., Tao, F.: Task allocation in manufacturing: a review. J. Ind. Inf. Integr. **15**, 207–218 (2019). https://doi.org/10.1016/j.jii.2018.08.001
13. Cai, M., Liang, R., Luo, X., Liu, C.: Task allocation strategies considering task matching and ergonomics in the human-robot collaborative hybrid assembly cell. Int. J. Prod. Res. **61**(21), 7213–7232 (2023). https://doi.org/10.1080/00207543.2022.2147234
14. Raisch, S., Krakowski, S.: Artificial intelligence and management: the automation–augmentation paradox. AMR **46**(1), 192–210 (2021). https://doi.org/10.5465/amr.2018.0072
15. Camarinha-Matos, L., Afsarmanesh, H.: Collaborative networks: a new scientific discipline. J. Intell. Manuf. **16**(4–5), 439–452 (2005). https://doi.org/10.1007/s10845-005-1656-3

16. Chowdhury, S., et al.: Unlocking the value of artificial intelligence in human resource management through AI capability framework. Human Resour. Manage. Rev. **33**(1), 100899 (2023). https://doi.org/10.1016/j.hrmr.2022.100899
17. Mahmud, B., Hong, G., Fong, B.: A Study of human-AI symbiosis for creative work: recent developments and future directions in deep learning. ACM Trans. Multimed. Comput. Commun. Appl. **20**(2), 47 (2024). https://doi.org/10.1145/3542698
18. Fuegener, A., Grahl, J., Gupta, A., Ketter, W.: Cognitive challenges in human-artificial intelligence collaboration: investigating the path toward productive delegation. Inf. Syst. Res. **33**(2), 678–696 (2022). https://doi.org/10.1287/isre.2021.1079
19. Ye, Y., Lin, H., Ruan, D., Zhu, Y., Zhang, C.: Research on effective asset risk assessment of power grid enterprises based on LBWA-vague set. In: I&CPS Asia, pp. 50–54. IEEE, Chongqing, China (2023). https://doi.org/10.1109/ICPSAsia58343.2023.10294484
20. Gao, C., Wang, X., Li, D., Han, C., You, W., Zhao, Y.: A novel hybrid power-grid investment optimization model with collaborative consideration of risk and benefit. Energies **16**(20), 7215 (2023). https://doi.org/10.3390/en16207215
21. Huang, Q., Jiang, M., Bi, M., Xue, B., Liu, T., Zhou, Y.: Research on power purchase risk measurement and grading evaluation of grid enterprises based on improved BWM-Cloud model under agency mode. Int. J. Low-Carbon Technol. **20**, 568–579 (2025). https://doi.org/10.1093/ijlct/ctaf010
22. Zhang, Y., Du, Y., Zhou, Y., Liu, H., Zhou, P., Jiao, J.: Digital grid investment risk prediction and identification under PSO-FAHP based intelligent algorithm. In: PEAI 2024, pp. 641–651. Assoc Computing Machinery, New York (2024). https://doi.org/10.1145/3674225.3674342
23. Salama, M., El-Dakhakhni, W., Tait, M.: Systemic risk mitigation strategy for power grid cascade failures using constrained spectral clustering. Int. J. Crit. Infrastruct. Prot. **42**, 100622 (2023). https://doi.org/10.1016/j.ijcip.2023.100622
24. Zhang, Y., Jiang, H., Gong, Q.: Dynamics of human-machine task allocation in intelligent production processes: a case study. Comput. Ind. Eng. **194**, 110354 (2024). https://doi.org/10.1016/j.cie.2024.110354
25. Gong, Q.: Machine endowment cost model: task assignment between humans and machines. Hum. Soc. Sci. Commun. **10**(1), 129 (2023)
26. Zhang, N.: Design of movie data visualization system based on web crawler. J. Phys.: Conf. Ser. **1971**, 012029 (2021). https://doi.org/10.1088/1742-6596/1971/1/012029
27. Bao, W., Che, H., Zhang, J.: Will Go at SemEval-2020 Task 3: an accurate model for predicting the (Graded) effect of context in word similarity based on BERT. In: Herbelot, A., Zhu, X., Palmer, A., Schneider, N., May, J., Shutova, E. (eds.) SemEval-2020, pp. 301–306. ACL, Stroudsburg (2020)
28. Reimers, N., Gurevych, I.: Sentence-BERT: sentence embeddings using siamese BERT-networks, In: EMNLP-IJCNLP 2019, pp. 3982–3992. ACL, Stroudsburg (2019)

Enhancing Organizational Antifragility Through Financial and Market Strength Capabilities

Ariane Avila[1], Gustavo Dalmarco[1(✉)], Ricardo Zimmermann[1], and Rosanna Fornasiero[2]

[1] INESC TEC, Porto, Portugal
{ariane.avila,Gustavo.dalmarco,ricardo.a.zimmermann}@inescte.pt
[2] National Research Council, Roma, Italy
rossana.fornasiero@cnr.it

Abstract. This study investigates the antifragility of organizations, especially in strategic sectors highly exposed to disruptive events. Based on a qualitative approach with case studies in the wine and textile sectors in Portugal, the findings indicate that financial and market strength, as resilience capabilities, operate interdependently and are reinforced by digital maturity and supply chain integration. Companies with financial robustness and strong market intelligence tend to be more agile in strategically investing and reallocating resources during crises. The research adopts an expanded definition of antifragility, which incorporates resilience, innovation, and strategic reconfiguration in the face of disruptions. It concludes that organizational antifragility results from the articulation of financial resources, market intelligence, and digital collaboration, offering a sustainable competitive advantage in the face of uncertainty. The study contributes to theoretical debates and provides practical recommendations for managers and policymakers.

Keyword: Resilience Capabilities · Antifragility · Financial Strength · Market Strength

1 Introduction

In an increasingly volatile, complex, and interconnected world, organizations face growing pressure to develop capabilities that go beyond the mere ability to withstand external shocks. Climate emergencies, pandemics, political and trade crises, and technological uncertainties demand organizational forms capable of operating with stability, adapting quickly, and ideally evolving positively in the face of disruptions. In this context, academic and managerial interest in the concepts of resilience and antifragility has grown, particularly as applied to organisations that integrate human intelligence and collaborative digital systems in their structures and decision-making processes.

Published by Springer Nature Switzerland AG 2026
L. M. Camarinha-Matos et al. (Eds.): PRO-VE 2025, IFIP AICT 770, pp. 154–165, 2026.
https://doi.org/10.1007/978-3-032-05673-3_10

In this context, this article investigates how financial strength and market strength capabilities interact to reinforce the antifragility of organizations, especially in strategic sectors highly exposed to disruptive events. The analysis is grounded in the theoretical foundations of dynamic capabilities [2, 23], organizational resilience [3, 21], and disruption management in supply chains [4, 16], aligning with an integrative perspective that views these capabilities as complementary elements to generate adaptive advantages in high-uncertainty environments.

Although the literature often differentiates between the concepts of resilience and antifragility, this study considers them in an integrated manner. According to [15] and [21], resilience refers to an organization's ability to withstand disturbances and return to its prior state of functioning. Antifragility, as proposed by [21], goes further, it represents the ability to benefit from disorder, learning, and strengthening from it. For the purposes of this research, we adopt an expanded and operational definition of antifragility that incorporates resilience, considering it the ability of organizations to persist, adapt, or transform in the face of change and disruptive events [14, 20, 25]. This integrated approach enables us to observe not only resistance or recovery, but also the innovation, learning, and strategic reconfiguration processes triggered by external events.

Theoretically, this study contributes to emerging debates on resilience and antifragility by proposing an integrated analytical model that links financial and market capabilities in organizational environments. By considering antifragility as a continuum of strategic response, from persistence to transformation, the study broadens the understanding of organizational adaptation mechanisms in complex and unstable environments [6, 25]. Moreover, although the literature on supply chain resilience is extensive, studies often address the concept broadly or focus on operational capabilities (e.g., flexibility, visibility). This research contributes by focusing on two specific capabilities, financial strength and market strength, which are less explored as determinants of resilience in industrial sectors.

Based on that, the research is guided by the following question: How do financial strength and market strength capabilities contribute to the antifragility of organizations in the face of disruptive events? To investigate this question, we conducted a qualitative multiple-case study in two strategic sectors of the Portuguese economy: the wine and textile industries. These sectors were chosen due to their historical, social, and economic relevance in Portugal, as well as their high exposure to challenges such as climate change, global supply chain disruptions, and sustainability-related regulatory transitions. Both also display interorganizational collaborative dynamics and increasing levels of digitalization, making them representative of organizations in real contexts.

Data collection involved three complementary qualitative techniques: (i) analysis of secondary data, including sector association reports, strategic documents, scientific publications, and governmental sources; (ii) direct observation of organizational practices during technical visits and sectoral events; and (iii) focus groups with representatives from companies, support institutions, public entities, and experts from both sectors (one focus group per sector). The combination of these approaches enabled us to capture different dimensions of the phenomenon under study, focusing on narratives, practices, and perceptions regarding responsiveness and transformation in the face of crises.

Organizations, focus of this study, are characterized by the combination of human intelligence and algorithms, decision-support systems, and collaborative digital platforms. The use of technologies such as artificial intelligence, IoT, analytics, and blockchain does not replace human action but complements it, enhancing monitoring, forecasting, and strategic response capabilities [1, 13]. In such organizations, intangible resources such as data and shared knowledge become central to building resilience and, as we argue, antifragility.

The results reveal that financial and market strength capabilities do not operate in isolation but mutually reinforce one another in building antifragile organizational responses. For example, companies with financial robustness were able to invest in innovation, digitalization, and supplier diversification during the crisis, while those with well-developed market intelligence quickly redirected these resources to strategic areas. Moreover, companies with trusted relationships with clients and partners were able to renegotiate deadlines, adjust offerings, and maintain revenue during critical moments, which in turn bolstered their financial stability.

2 Literature Review

2.1 From Dynamic Capabilities to Resilience Capabilities

The theory of dynamic capabilities [23] emphasizes strategic adaptability as a key factor for achieving sustainable competitive advantage in volatile and uncertain markets. According to [2], builds on this by systematizing the concept and proposing that dynamic capabilities are composed of multiple dimensions that work together to enable continuous adaptation.

In contexts of extreme uncertainty, such as health crises or geopolitical shifts, dynamic capabilities become essential not only for maintaining competitiveness but also for enabling innovation and strategic transformation. [6, 25] argue that such capabilities can be replicable in high-velocity environments, but competitive advantage lies in an organization's ability to apply them with agility and at the right moment. This perspective is directly linked to resilience, as the rapid and effective reconfiguration in the face of disruptions is a clear indicator of dynamic capabilities in action.

Considering this, resilience is the ability of an organization to withstand, absorb, and recover from disruptive events while maintaining acceptable levels of functioning and performance. According to [21], supply chain resilience involves capabilities of adaptation, response, and recovery, which enable firms not only to endure shocks but also to learn and evolve from them. This perspective is expanded by [3], who introduce dimensions such as robustness, redundancy, rapidity, and resources, forming a multidimensional framework to assess resilience in complex systems.

The literature suggests that resilience should be understood as a combination of structural and relational competencies. [25] highlight factors such as agility, visibility, and flexibility as essential for a resilient supply chain. Furthermore, emphasize that resilience is a dynamic process, involving continuous adaptation to changing environmental conditions and requiring organizational routines oriented toward learning.

Building on this theoretical foundation, this study specifically examines the dynamic capabilities of market strength and financial strength, understood as critical enablers of organizational resilience and antifragility. In highly volatile and uncertain environments, such as those shaped by systemic crises or supply chain disruptions, these capabilities allow organizations not only to absorb shocks but also to strategically reposition themselves.

Financial strength was defined as the organization's ability to absorb financial shocks and reallocate resources, both in the short and long term, to sustain or improve performance. Elements such as liquidity, credit access, budget flexibility, and contractual renegotiation capacity emerged as key components of this dimension [9, 11]. Market strength, in turn, refers to the ability to anticipate and respond to changes in external demands and conditions, maintain stable relationships with strategic customers and suppliers, and explore new market opportunities even in adverse contexts [7, 17].

2.2 The Relationship Between Resilience and Antifragility: An Integrated Approach

Over recent decades, organizational resilience has become a critical capability in environments marked by uncertainty, disruption, and volatility. Traditionally, resilience is understood as the ability to withstand, absorb impacts, and recover, returning to a functional state after adverse events [3, 21]. However, the contemporary context, characterized by systemic crises, accelerated technological change, and complex disruptions, demands a broader and more evolutionary perspective.

In this study, we adopt an expanded and operational definition of antifragility, aligned with [25], which incorporates resilience as a foundational component. Antifragility, in this sense, is not only about overcoming adversity but about the ability to persist, adapt, and transform in the face of change and external shocks. This integrated approach allows us to observe not only resistance or recovery, but also the processes of innovation, organizational learning, and strategic reconfiguration triggered by disruption.

Resilience thus functions as an operational prerequisite for antifragility. Resilient organizations are able to maintain operations and safeguard critical assets during crises; however, only antifragile organizations can leverage such moments to evolve, creating new organizational forms, practices, and structures. While resilience focuses on robustness and a return to the status quo, antifragility emphasizes continuous improvement through adversity [22].

Recent literature has emphasized that resilience and antifragility are not dichotomous, but progressive [8]. [25] proposes that the transition from a resilient to an antifragile system depends on an organization's ability to combine intelligent redundancy, strategic experimentation, decentralized decision-making, and collaborative learning. In supply chains, this translates into practices such as multi-sourcing, digital traceability, collaborative networks, and predictive simulations [4, 16].

Moreover, by integrating the antifragility perspective, we broaden the analytical scope of resilience: from a capability for operational continuity to a lever for sustainable competitive advantage. Antifragile organizations develop, over time, an adaptive memory, based on the intelligent collection, dissemination, and use of information, that allows them to turn threats into strategic opportunities.

Therefore, rather than treating resilience and antifragility as separate capabilities, this research supports a continuous and integrated approach, in which resilience provides the foundation, and antifragility represents a higher evolutionary stage. In contexts marked by unpredictable events, such as pandemics, wars, logistical crises, and protectionist policies, antifragile organizations are able to turn vulnerabilities into strategic opportunities. This perspective enables a better understanding of how organizations not only survive but grow stronger and innovate through disruption.

3 Methodology

This research is part of the RISE-SME project, funded by the European Union through the Horizon Europe research and innovation program under Grant Agreement number 101138645. The project is based on a comprehensive analysis of various resilience capabilities within industrial supply chains (adaptability & flexibility, efficiency, visibility, redundancy, market strength, financial strength, response, transform). During the interpretation of results, it was observed that market strength and financial strength capabilities consistently stood out across the cases analyzed. Considering this finding, the present study focuses specifically on an in-depth examination of these two capabilities, aiming to understand how they contribute to building organizational resilience in the face of disruptive events.

Thus, to achieve the objective of investigating how financial strength and market strength capabilities interact to reinforce the antifragility of organizations, especially in strategic sectors highly exposed to disruptive events, we chose two economic activity sectors: the wine sector and the textile sector. According to [27], sectors can be categorized based on the essentiality index, which serves as an indicator of economic protection against the impacts of measures implemented during disruptive periods, such as the COVID-19 lockdown.

Guided by this indicator, our methodological approach focused on these two sectors at opposite ends of the spectrum: the textile sector, identified as having low essentiality, and the agri-food sector, recognized as highly essential. Within the agri-food sector, we specifically chose to analyse the wine industry for convenience.

Considering that, data collection involved three complementary qualitative techniques designed to ensure a comprehensive and contextualized understanding of resilience capabilities. This multi-method approach follows the principles of triangulation to enhance the credibility and depth of qualitative research [10, 19]. The combination of these approaches enabled us to capture different dimensions of the phenomenon under study, focusing on narratives, practices, and perceptions regarding responsiveness and transformation in the face of crises.

First, the analysis of secondary data included a wide array of documentary sources such as reports from industry associations, strategic documents, academic articles, and governmental publications. This type of documentary analysis is as it helps to contextualize findings and corroborate data from other sources [26].

Second, direct observation was carried out during technical visits to firms and at sectoral events such as workshops and conferences. This method allowed researchers to observe routines, behaviors, and interactions in situ, capturing tacit elements of organizational practice. As highlighted by [12], observation contributes to understanding the real-world context of organizational processes, especially those not easily articulated by participants.

Third, focus groups were conducted with stakeholders from companies, support institutions, public entities, and academic or technical experts. Thus, in the context of this research, representativeness was conceived in a qualitative sense, not tied to statistical generalization criteria, but rather to the diversity and relevance of participants for the study's objectives. Therefore, the aim was to ensure a plurality of perspectives through the composition of focus groups with representatives from the four helices proposed by the quadruple helix theory [5] which highlights the importance of interactions among these actors to foster innovation, sustainable development, and social well-being. The balanced presence of participants from these four helices ensured that the discussions reflected different interests and social roles, enriching the analyses and enabling the capture of more complex dynamics regarding financial and market resilience capabilities in the industrial sectors studied.

These group discussions enabled the collection of diverse and interactive insights on resilience strategies and sectoral responses to disruptions. According to [18], focus groups are particularly effective in exploratory research as they stimulate collective reflection, highlight consensus and divergence, and generate rich qualitative data through interaction (Table 1).

Table 1. Focus Group sessions information

Sector	Date	Local	Duration (hours)	Number of participants
Textile	November, 2024	Portugal	3,5	12
Wine	December, 2024	Portugal	2,5	11

Most studies on resilience adopt quantitative methods and large surveys. By employing focus groups, this study deepens the understanding of perceptions, sectoral dynamics, and causal mechanisms, generating insights that would hardly emerge from traditional quantitative analyses. This enriches the understanding of *how* and *why* these specific capabilities influence resilience.

4 Results and Discussion

Based on the focus groups conducted, we gathered practical insights into the importance of financial strength and market strength as key elements of resilience in the sectors analysed (Table 2). Participants assessed, on a scale from 1 to 5, the level of development of various indicators associated with resilience capabilities. The results reveal that, in the textile sector, there is a high level of maturity in both domains, with notable scores for access to medium- and long-term financial resources (4.8) and stable relationships with clients (4.7), reflecting a scenario of structural solidity and stability in commercial relationships.

In the wine sector, participants also acknowledged the importance of financial and market strength, although with slightly lower average scores compared to the textile sector. Access to short-term financial resources (4.3) and client relationships (4.5) were positively evaluated, indicating a resilient foundation, though with greater variation across indicators. The lowest score was given to the capacity to establish new partnerships and access new markets (3.7), highlighting an opportunity for strategic development. These qualitative assessments, resulting from direct engagement with sector stakeholders, provide valuable evidence about the internal and relational capabilities that support or constrain companies' responses to disruptive events.

Table 2. Description of capabilities

	Capability	Indicator	Grade	Mean
Textile Sector	Financial Strength	have access to resources (short-term) to mitigate the impacts of supply chain interruptions	4,5	4,6
		have access to resources (medium/long-term) to invest in changes prompted by the event	4,8	
	Market Strength	have a stable relationship with suppliers	4,5	4,6
		have a stable relationship with customers	4,7	
		establish new partnerships or access new markets	4,5	
Wine Sector	Financial Strength	have access to resources (short-term) to mitigate the impacts of supply chain interruptions	4,3	4,1
		have access to resources (medium/long-term) to invest in changes prompted by the event	3,9	
	Market Strength	have a stable relationship with suppliers	4,2	4,1
		have a stable relationship with customers	4,5	
		establish new partnerships or access new markets	3,7	

5 Textile Sector: Conservative Resilience

From the perspective of dynamic capabilities [23], the textile sector demonstrates maturity in identifying, integrating, and reconfiguring resources to cope with disruptions. The high scores attributed to financial strength and market strength show that companies in this sector place great importance on maintaining liquidity and access to both short- and long-term resources, as well as stable relationships with clients and suppliers, while also actively seeking new partnerships and markets. These capabilities indicate a consolidated competitive position and reflect competencies to reconfigure strategies in the face of crises, reinforcing the sector's adaptability.

From the standpoint of resilience capabilities, the textile sector emphasizes preparation and rapid response to disruptive events. Financial strength allows firms to absorb shocks, while market strength helps maintain trust across the supply chain. However, transformation capability was considered less relevant, suggesting a tendency toward stability rather than radical innovation. Thus, in terms of antifragility [22], the sector appears to remain within the sphere of classical resilience—enduring and recovering—rather than advancing toward positive evolution in the face of crisis. This may be related to the traditional character of the sector, with less agile structures for deep transformations. In this context, we propose:

Proposition 1: In traditional sectors, where the combination of financial and market strength supports solid resilience but limits organizational transformation, the result is an adaptive and conservative response to disruptions.

6 Wine Sector: Moving Toward Antifragility

Through the lens of dynamic capabilities, the wine sector demonstrates competencies oriented toward adapting and integrating resources in volatile contexts. Market strength capabilities, such as consolidated relationships with clients and suppliers, reveal a strategic focus on maintaining distribution channels and diversifying markets. While financial strength is also relevant, it scores slightly lower than in the textile sector, indicating some limitations in pursuing long-term strategic investments. Nonetheless, these capabilities provide a solid foundation for responding to the environmental and economic threats that characterize the sector.

In terms of resilience capabilities, the wine sector faces more systemic risks, such as environmental and political crises, which require not only recovery but continuous transformation. As such, there is potential for antifragility, as companies that adopt digital practices and new technologies may not only withstand disruptions but emerge stronger. The emphasis on sustainable practices, commercial digitalization, and adaptation to direct-to-consumer channels suggests a move toward strategic reconfiguration. In this context, we propose:

Proposition 2: In sectors highly exposed to systemic risks and external pressure for innovation, the presence of market strength combined with moderate financial strength promotes adaptation and stimulates transformation, enabling organizations to evolve toward antifragile behaviour in the face of disruptions.

7 Sectoral Comparison: Stability vs. Transformation

When comparing the two sectors, both value preparation and response capabilities, with financial and market strength standing out as common pillars of resilience. However, the textile sector adopts a more conservative stance, focused on stabilization and continuity, reflecting a more robust and less transformational profile. The wine sector, on the other hand, shows greater openness to adaptive transformation, integrating sustainability and digitalization dimensions that can catalyse antifragile capabilities.

While the textile sector relies heavily on internal resources and established relationships to resist shocks, the wine sector is more sensitive to external environments and more likely to reconfigure practices in response to change. From the perspective of antifragility, this positions the wine sector one step ahead, as it transforms vulnerabilities into strategic advantages. The ability to learn from adverse events and incorporate innovations suggests a more dynamic evolution potential, in contrast to the greater adaptive rigidity observed in the textile sector. In this context, we propose:

Proposition 3: Organizational resilience based on financial and market strength manifests differently depending on the sector's openness to transformation—being conservative and stabilizing in traditional sectors (such as textiles), and evolutionary and antifragile in sectors facing environmental and technological pressures (such as wine).

Furthermore, these differences can be better understood when analysed through the lens of the essentiality index proposed by the [27], which classifies sectors based on the degree of economic protection they receive during disruptive events, such as the COVID-19 pandemic. The textile sector, identified as having low essentiality, was among the first to experience operational shutdowns and among the last to resume activity [24]. This limited institutional prioritization translated into reduced access to emergency support measures, supply chain continuity, and policy-driven incentives, pushing firms to rely predominantly on internal resources, particularly financial reserves and pre-existing market relationships, to maintain operations. As a result, organizations in this sector adopted conservative resilience strategies, focused on survival and damage containment, with minimal room for experimentation or structural transformation. The high scores in financial and market strength observed in the textile sector reflect this emphasis on stability and preservation, rather than on adaptability or innovation.

In contrast, the wine sector, positioned within the broader agri-food ecosystem, was classified as highly essential, allowing it to maintain operations even during the strictest phases of lockdown. This designation resulted in greater operational continuity, preferential logistical access, and targeted institutional support, including subsidies and trade facilitation. Such conditions provided not only a safety net for firms but also a window of opportunity to invest in strategic adjustments, such as the digitalization of sales channels, reconfiguration of distribution networks, and engagement with more sustainable and resilient supply practices. Despite scoring lower in financial capacity, wine sector firms leveraged their market strength and the relative stability of institutional backing to explore transformative pathways, enabling them not just to recover, but to evolve, an essential characteristic of antifragility.

Thus, when observed through the essentiality lens, it becomes evident that institutional positioning and external support mechanisms critically shape the strategic room for manoeuvre available to firms during crises. While both sectors exhibit strong foundational capabilities, their trajectories diverge according to how their economic role is perceived and supported at the policy level. Antifragility, in this sense, is not merely a function of internal resources, but also of the enabling environment that allows organizations to take calculated risks, innovate, and grow stronger from disruption. In this context, we propose:

Proposition 4: Highly essential sectors tend to develop greater antifragility due to stronger institutional support and operational continuity during crises, while low-essentiality sectors adopt more conservative strategies, limiting their potential for transformation.

8 Conclusion

This study aimed to investigate how financial strength and market strength capabilities interact to reinforce organizational antifragility, especially in strategic sectors highly exposed to disruptive events. Based on the comparative analysis between the textile and wine sectors, it was observed that these two capabilities operate in complementary ways, though influenced by the sectoral context. In the textile sector, financial robustness and stable commercial ties support consolidated resilience, yet one that is oriented toward maintenance and recovery, with limited openness to transformation. In contrast, in the wine sector, market strength plays a central role in adaptation and innovation, while financial strength, although more limited, contributes to a more agile and evolutionary response to disruptions.

These differences can be better understood when analysed through the lens of the essentiality index proposed by the [27], which classifies sectors according to their level of economic protection during crises. The textile sector, categorized as low essentiality, faced greater restrictions and less institutional support during the pandemic, leading to more conservative resilience strategies. In contrast, the wine sector, as part of the highly essential agri-food ecosystem, benefited from greater operational continuity and external support, creating conditions for developing more transformation-oriented capabilities, a pathway that favors antifragility.

By methodologically focusing on two sectors at opposite ends of the essentiality spectrum, it was possible to demonstrate that the interaction between financial and market strength not only sustains resilience but can also act as a catalyst for antifragility, provided that the institutional environment and sectoral culture support strategic reconfiguration. In the wine sector, this interaction is evident in the ability to diversify markets, adopt technologies, and adapt to new forms of consumption. In the textile sector, however, the same combination, although solid, still operates under a predominantly defensive logic. Thus, organizational antifragility depends not only on the existence of these capabilities but also on the willingness to use them to transform vulnerabilities into strategic advantages.

From a practical standpoint, the results offer guidance for managers and policy-makers. Rather than focusing exclusively on contingency plans, it is advisable to adopt capacity development approaches, with targeted investments in digital systems, flexible financial structures, and market intelligence applied to decision-making. The experience of the analysed sectors shows that building antifragility also involves co-creation with stakeholders, collaborative governance, and continuous learning from crises.

However, one limitation of this research concerns the small number of sectors analyzed, which may restrict the generalizability of the results to other industrial contexts. Additionally, the data was collected through focus groups, relying on participants' subjective perceptions, which may introduce interpretative biases. Future studies using quantitative approaches and larger samples could complement and deepen the findings presented here.

Given these limitations, future studies are recommended to expand the analysis to a larger number of sectors with varying levels of essentiality, allowing for greater generalizability of the results. Moreover, it is suggested that the propositions be tested as hypotheses with quantitative methods. The use of quantitative approaches, such as surveys or statistical models, could complement the perceptions gathered from the focus groups, providing greater robustness to the conclusions and enabling the identification of broader patterns in the interaction between organizational capabilities and antifragility across different contexts. Furthermore, comparative studies between countries or regions with different institutional structures could also enrich the understanding of the factors that influence the strengthening of organizational antifragility in diverse contexts.

In conclusion, this research reinforces the idea that organizational antifragility results from the strategic articulation of financial and market strength, mediated by digital technologies and collaborative networks. Organizations that can harmonize these elements are better positioned not only to withstand disruptions but to emerge stronger, more innovative, and better adapted to new realities. By recognizing the value of error, instability, and transformation, these organizations stop fearing change and start using it as a source of sustainable competitive advantage.

References

1. Alyasein, O.I.Y., Ojha, D., Sadeghi, K.: Supply chain digitalization, innovation capability, and organizational agility: the moderating role of institutionalization and supply chain integration. Ind. Mark. Manage. **125**, 215–225 (2025)
2. Barreto, I.: Dynamic capabilities: a review of past research and an agenda for the future. J. Manag. **36**(1), 256–280 (2010)
3. Bruneau, M., et al.: A framework to quantitatively assess and enhance the seismic resilience of communities. Earthq. Spectra **19**(4), 733–752 (2003)
4. Bode, C., Wagner, S.M.: Structural drivers of upstream supply chain complexity and the frequency of supply chain disruptions. J. Oper. Manag. **36**(1), 215–228 (2015). https://doi.org/10.1016/j.jom.2014.12.004
5. Carayannis, E.G., Campbell, D.F.J.: 'Mode 3' and 'Quadruple Helix': toward a 21st century fractal innovation ecosystem. Int. J. Technol. Manage. **46**(3–4), 201–234 (2009)
6. Castillo, C.: Is there a theory of supply chain resilience? A bibliometric analysis of the literature. Int. J. Oper. Prod. Manag. **43**(1), 22–47 (2023)
7. Cavusgil, S.T., Deligonul, S.Z.: Dynamic capabilities framework and its transformative contributions. J. Int. Bus. Stud. 1–10 (2024)
8. Conz, E., Magnani, G.: A dynamic perspective on the resilience–organizational performance relationship: a meta-analysis of the empirical literature. Int. J. Manag. Rev. **22**(2), 184–208 (2020)
9. Craighead, C.W., Blackhurst, J., Rungtusanatham, M.J., Handfield, R.B.: The severity of supply chain disruptions: design characteristics and mitigation capabilities. Decis. Sci. **38**(1), 131–156 (2007)

10. Denzin, N.K.: The Research Act: A Theoretical Introduction to Sociological Methods. McGraw-Hill (1978).
11. Dickens, J.M., Uvet, H., Anderson, J.R., Ponomarov, S.Y., Nowicki, D.R.: An empirical examination on firm innovativeness and supply chain resilience: the role of information sharing from a dynamic capabilities view. Knowl. Process. Manag. **31**(4), 295–308 (2024)
12. Flick, U.: An Introduction to Qualitative Research, 5th edn. Sage (2014)
13. Hald, K.S., Coslugeanu, P.: The preliminary supply chain lessons of the COVID-19 disruption—What is the role of digital technologies? Oper. Manag. Res. **15**(1), 282–297 (2022)
14. Hamel, G., Välikangas, L.: The quest for resilience. Harv. Bus. Rev. **81**(9), 52–63 (2003)
15. Holling, C.S.: Resilience and stability of ecological systems (1973)
16. Ivanov, D., Dolgui, A., Sokolov, B., Ivanova, M., Rozhkov, M.: Supply chain disruptions and resilience: a major review and future research agenda. Ann. Operat. Res. **293**(1), 313–344 (2020). https://doi.org/10.1007/s10479-020-03912-1
17. Matthews, R., Rutherford, B.N., Edmondson, D., Matthews, L.: Uncertainty in industrial markets: the COVID-19 pandemic. Ind. Mark. Manage. **102**, 364–376 (2022)
18. Morgan, D.L.: Focus Groups as Qualitative Research, 2nd edn. Sage (1997)
19. Patton, M.Q.: Qualitative Research & Evaluation Methods, 3rd edn. Sage (2002)
20. Pettit, T.J., Fiksel, J., Croxton, K.L.: Ensuring supply chain resilience: development and implementation of an assessment tool. J. Bus. Logist. **31**(1), 1–21 (2010)
21. Ponomarov, S.Y., Holcomb, M.C.: Understanding the concept of supply chain resilience. Int. J. Logist. Manage. **20**(1), 124–143 (2009)
22. Taleb, N.N.: Antifragile: Things That Gain from Disorder. Random House, New York (2012)
23. Teece, D.J., Pisano, G., Schuen, A.: Dynamic capabilities and strategic management. Strateg. Manag. J. **18**(7), 509–533 (1997)
24. UNCTAD: Textile and garment supply chains in times of COVID-19: Challenges for developing countries. United Nations Conference on Trade and Development (2020)
25. Wieland, A., Durach, C.F.: Two perspectives on supply chain resilience. J. Bus. Logist. **42**(3), 315–322 (2021)
26. Yin, R.K.: Case Study Research and Applications: Design and Methods, 6th edn. Sage (2018)
27. OECD: OECD Services Trade Restrictiveness Index: Policy Trends up to 2025. OECD Publishing, Paris (2025). https://doi.org/10.1787/9953845b-en

AI for Logistics and Supply Chain Management

Socio-Technical AI Maturity in Supply Chains: Insights from the Pulp and Paper Sector

Fernanda Freitas[1], Ricardo Zimmermann[2], Gaudencio Freires[1], Fabio Couto[2,3], Cristiano Fontes[1], António Lucas Soares[2,3], Gustavo Dalmarco[2], Donna Rhodes[4], and Jorão Gomes Jr.[5(✉)]

[1] Federal University of Bahia, Salvador, Bahia, Brazil
{fernanda.cassia,francisco.gaudencio,cfontes}@ufba.br
[2] INESC TEC – Institute for Systems and Computer Engineering, Technology and Science, Porto, Portugal
{ricardo.a.zimmermann,fabio.couto,antonio.l.soares, gustavo.dalmarco}@inesctec.pt
[3] Faculty of Engineering, University of Porto, Porto, Portugal
[4] Sociotechnical Systems Research Center, Massachusetts Institute of Technology, Cambridge, MA, USA
rhodes@mit.edu
[5] Vienna University of Economics and Business, Vienna, Austria
jorao.gomes.junior@wu.ac.at

Abstract. The integration of AI in supply chains offers opportunities to enhance efficiency, sustainability, and decision-making. However, effective implementation requires attention to both technical and socio-technical aspects. This study examines AI maturity in the pulp and paper sector using the SC-STAI profiling tool, assessing AI integration across technical, social, human, and organizational domains. Based on nine case studies from Brazil and Portugal, the research identifies key areas for improvement and highlights uneven AI adoption. Findings show that performance and resilience are most impacted, while job role adoption remains the lowest. The study emphasizes the importance of Socio-Technical AI Maturity Models in guiding responsible AI adoption and improving socio-technical alignment in supply chains, contributing to a better understanding of AI readiness in traditional industries and demonstrating the SC-STAI tool's applicability for strategic AI planning.

Keywords: AI-based System Design · Maturity Models · Socio-Technical Systems · Supply Chain Management · Digital Transformation

1 Introduction

Recent developments in Artificial Intelligence (AI) integration within Supply Chains (SCs) have advanced human-computer interaction and fostered new B2B collaborative strategies [5]. However, effective adoption extends beyond technical deployment and

Published by Springer Nature Switzerland AG 2026
L. M. Camarinha-Matos et al. (Eds.): PRO-VE 2025, IFIP AICT 770, pp. 169–184, 2026.
https://doi.org/10.1007/978-3-032-05673-3_11

must consider the social, organizational, and human dimensions [5]. Understanding AI maturity in SCs is therefore critical to ensure its sustainable integration and maintain human oversight. Although prior research has explored inter-organizational learning [6], trust [7], and collaborative sustainability [8], comprehensive frameworks that account for both technical and social aspects of AI integration remain limited [5].

This study investigates AI integration maturity through a socio-technical lens using nine case studies from the pulp and paper sector in Brazil and Portugal. The demand for pulp and paper materials continues to grow due to their widespread use in everyday products, despite increasing concerns about their environmental impact. Global paper production has risen from just over 60 million metric tons in 1961 to nearly 200 million metric tons in 2022 [1]. While the share of recycled paper has grown, most production still relies on cellulose extracted from wood, a market valued at over USD 160 billion [1]. The pulp and paper industry faces complex challenges related to sustainability, efficiency, and competitiveness. Rising demand, combined with environmental and economic pressures, drives the need for innovative solutions [2]. AI offers promising avenues for addressing these issues [2, 3]. In these SCs, AI can support real-time monitoring of emissions, water and energy usage, and other environmental indicators. It also enhances operational efficiency through predictive maintenance, resource optimization, and quality control. Moreover, AI can improve SC coordination and visibility across stakeholders [4].

This work applies the Supply Chain Socio-Technical AI (SC-STAI) profiling tool to evaluate current integration levels and identify improvement opportunities in the pulp and paper sector. The aim of this paper is twofold: (i) to assess the AI integration landscape in the pulp and paper industry in Brazil and Portugal; and (ii) to evaluate the applicability and refinement needs of the SC-STAI profiling tool as a Socio-Technical AI Maturity Model (STAI-MM). The results indicate that companies have different levels of AI adoption regarding its impact on the socio-technical dimensions. The findings demonstrate that the performance and resilience dimensions present the clearest evidence of AI's current impact on SCs, while the job role dimension has the lowest adoption levels among the companies under investigation. Finally, the results allowed an evaluation of the tool used, the identification of improvements in the diagnostic process and the definition of the next steps in the implementation of the SC-STAI profiling tool.

The remainder of the paper is structured as follows: Sect. 2 reviews related literature; Sect. 3 outlines the methodology; Sect. 4 presents findings and discussion; and Sect. 5 concludes the study.

2 Literature Review

The integration of AI in SCs has been growing in recent years, offering new opportunities to improve coordination, efficiency, sustainability, and decision-making, but successful AI adoption cannot be viewed solely from a technocentric perspective. The literature consistently highlights enabling factors like technological readiness, data quality, governance, and legal and ethical compliance as prerequisites for successful integration [19, 26, 27]. Moreover, and despite human and organizational factors being also acknowledged e.g., in terms of training, upskilling, and reskilling, broader organizational practices such as change management, organizational workflow alignment, and stakeholder involvement are still inconsistently addressed [14, 19, 29–32].

AI Maturity Models (AI-MMs) have surged to guide AI adoption by defining structured stages of integration, typically from early experimentation to advanced levels of optimization and transformation [9–11]. These models commonly assess maturity dimensions including strategy and governance, technology, data, skills, processes, and increasingly, ethics and regulation [9–12]. Additionally, some of the recent AI-MMs explicitly address concerns with transparency, explainability, and bias mitigation [19], and recommend documenting ethical decisions and AI development practices [28]. However, these models remain largely technocentric, as AI-MMs overlook the process of embedding AI into complex socio-organizational environments, aligning AI adoption with evolving human roles, or supporting collaborative human-AI interactions within organizations and across SC networks.

In the SCM domain specifically, multiple contributions propose frameworks that link AI to SC resilience, optimization, and strategic value [13–18]. For example, [13] outlines multiple AI roles in SCM, [14] identifies critical success factors for AI integration in food SCs, and [16] present models for Human-AI Collaboration (HAIC) that account for varying levels of autonomy and responsible integration. Other works map AI's contributions to operational resilience, scenario simulation, compliance, supplier management, and customer engagement [15, 17]. Although these frameworks advance the knowledge base on AI use in SCs, they mostly highlight the technical or functional aspects of AI integration, whereas socio-organizational variables like human-AI trust, transformation of job roles, or governance of collaborative AI systems remain peripheral or fragmented in current models.

Socio-Technical Systems (STS) theory and Responsible AI (RAI) principles offer a broader lens to address these challenges: STS design proposes the co-optimization of technical, social, organizational, and ecosystem subsystems to achieve sustainable and context-sensitive innovation [5]; RAI complements this by defining governance structures and ethical standards (e.g., fairness, transparency, accountability, and robustness) that should guide AI development and deployment [16, 19, 20]. Furthermore, Human-AI collaboration literature adds supplementary nuance by characterizing interaction patterns, shared decision-making processes, and the concept of augmented intelligence where AI improves human agency [21–25]. Despite this wealth of conceptual insight, the operationalization of these principles into actionable AI-MMs for SCM remains limited.

As demonstrated, there are multiple gaps in existing academic literature. First, while AI-MMs provide structured pathways for AI adoption, they tend to stress technical indicators and overlook important socio-technical dynamics. Second, the integration of RAI principles into AI-MMs remains inconsistent and lacks operational specificity. Third, socio-technical design frameworks and human-centered perspectives are not well translated into tools that supply chain organizations can use to diagnose or plan their AI strategies. Finally, there are few empirical studies that apply and test socio-technical maturity models in traditional industrial sectors as is the pulp and paper sector, leaving open questions about socio-technical AI-MM's practical relevance and applicability.

As a result, the paper addresses these gaps by applying and evaluating the SC-STAI profiling tool, which is a Socio-technical AI-MM, within the pulp and paper SC sector in Brazil and Portugal. The SC-STAI integrates human, social, and organizational dimensions with technical maturity, and incorporates principles from both STS and RAI frameworks. The tool provides a structured diagnostic approach to assess AI integration, as organizations can visualize their current state (as-is state) and define strategic paths (to-be state) toward human-centered and responsible AI adoption. Through nine case studies, this paper evaluates the current AI maturity landscape and the practical utility of the SC-STAI tool as a boundary object for multi-stakeholder alignment and strategic planning in AI-enabled SCs.

3 Methodological Approach

Considering the limitations identified in the literature on AI-MMs, RAI, and the STS dynamics of AI adoption, this study applies the SC-STAI profiling tool [5]. Drawing from existing AI-MMs, SC-STAI adopts a stage-gated stance to AI integration, but it extends these AI-MMs by incorporating ethical, human-centered, and contextual organizational considerations, all of which are underscored in RAI and STS perspectives. Additionally, SC-STAI responds to practical challenges in AI adoption highlighted in the literature on enablers and barriers, offering a strategic diagnostic framework for the alignment of technological, social, and organizational readiness.

Figure 1 depicts the visual conceptualization of the SC-STAI. SC-STAI is structured within three socio-technical dimensions: human, social, and organizational. Each dimension is divided into three sub-dimensions: job role, capability, decision-making (human); sustainability, resilience, performance (organisational); trust, visibility, collaboration (social). Within each sub-dimension, the tool proposes three cumulative AI integration levels, reflecting increasing degrees of integration and HAIC: fixed roles, adapting roles, roles crafting (job role); AI technical competence, AI adaptive competence, Human-AI knowledge sharing (capability); human oversight, integrated human-AI, networked human-AI (decision-making); AI resource consumption optimisation, AI supporting design of sustainable products-services, AI managed circular economy (sustainability); risk prediction, human-AI driven mitigation planning, AI driven mitigation actions (resilience); AI support operational efficiency, AI impacting strategic activities, AI drives innovation and business opportunities (performance); human-human, human-AI, AI-AI (trust); data-enabled, predictive, extended and synthesised (visibility); AI-managed collaboration, AI as teammate, AI-based discovery of collaboration forms (collaboration). As a mapping and boundary object, the SC-STAI helps SC stakeholders visualize the current ("as-is") and target ("to-be") states of the AI integration journey.

Regarding its use, the tool can be applied by a company to outline its strategic AI roadmap, or by a focal company in an SC, together with key partners, to outline the SC-AI strategy. Based on the STS design framework for future organizations [33], this tool is intended to be used at the strategic (purpose, governance, ecosystem, organization) and operational (technology, social system) design levels. Furthermore, according to this framework, the tool addresses all four proposed subsystems to be designed: technical, organizational, social, and ecosystem. The SC-STAI tool can be used as an instrument within any systems design methodology, from general design thinking methods to systems approaches to change management [30, 34], such as the Soft Systems Methodology and its recent variations [35]. The tool can be used first to map the desirable properties of the SC system to be developed, then to characterize the current situation, and then to help define the roadmap. This tool can be seen as an "artifact" that enables knowledge sharing and collective action by SC stakeholders, assuming multidisciplinary and interdisciplinary perspectives [36].

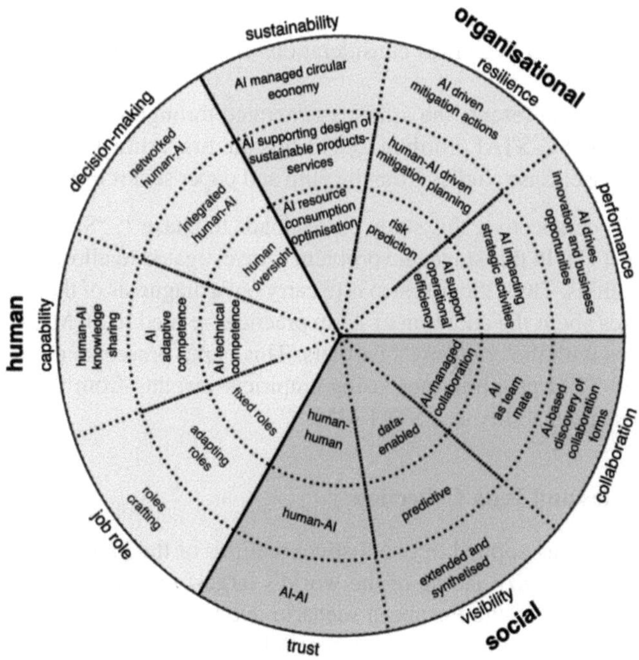

Fig. 1. SC-STAI model [5].

3.1 SC-STAI as an Artifact of Design Science Research

This study employs a Design Science Research (DSR) methodology where the SC-STAI profiling tool is the main artifact. As described by [37], the DSR methodology comprises six activities: problem identification and motivation, definition of solution objectives, design and development, demonstration, evaluation, and communication.

In the context of AI integration in SCM, DSR facilitates the systematic design and evaluation of artifacts that address identified socio-technical challenges and points of improvement. The research process follows the DSR Grid proposed by [38], emphasizing six core dimensions: Problem Description, Input Knowledge, Research Process, Key Concepts, Solution Description, and Output Knowledge.

Artifact evaluation adopts the approach outlined by [39], involving simultaneous assessment concurrent evaluation throughout the DSR process: assessing/evaluating problem identification (Eval 1), assessing evaluating solution design (Eval 2), assessing/evaluating solution instantiation (Eval 3), and assessing/evaluating solution in use (Eval 4). This allows for continuous artifact refinement based on stakeholder feedback and changing requirements.

In this paper, we synthesize the DSR model by [40] and the SC-STAI profiling tool by [5], providing a structured approach to evaluate the SC-STAI as an STAI-MM. To do so, we outline our four main components:

1. Problem Space: Outlines the socio-technical challenges of AI integration in SCM, including business needs, organizational context, and stakeholder requirements.
2. Design Space: Socio-Technical considerations across human, social, and organizational dimensions.
3. Solution Space: Represents the artifacts generated through the DSR process. In our case, we use the SC-STAI profiling tool as it is the first artifact to be evaluated.
4. Knowledge Base: Case studies from the pulp and paper sector in Brazil and Portugal.

From a DSR perspective, this study corresponds to phase 1, "Solution Incubation", as suggested by [41]. In this stage, the problem is investigated to allow the identification of possible solutions. Thus, the first step is to carry out a diagnosis of the current situation of the companies about the adoption of AI in practices related to SCM and in managing the relationships with the company's partners. This paper presents an initial evaluation cycle of the SC-STAI profiling tool, using empirical insights from the case studies to refine the tool's applicability as a STAI-MM.

3.2 Case Studies and Data Collection

The SC-STAI tool was applied in two distinct realities of the paper and pulp sector, in Brazil and Portugal. Brazil is one of the world's largest producers of cellulose, while Portugal has stood out in the European scenario due to innovation in the sector. In the Brazilian context, the case of the paper and cellulose industry ecosystem in three states (Bahia, São Paulo and Espírito Santo) was analyzed, which has shown significant growth in recent years. Seven cases from the region participate in this phase of the study. In Portugal, the case of the forestry sector was analyzed, where information was collected from two of the largest companies in the paper and pulp sector in the country.

Responses were collected from the nine case studies during May 2025. We labeled the cases from A to I. Cases A–G were collected from large companies in Brazil on 15/05/2025. Cases H and I were collected from large companies in Portugal on 19/05/2025. The objective was to position the companies in the SC-STAI profiling tool. Companies answered questions related to the three dimensions of technology use and nine sub-dimensions of the model. Companies that reported not using AI in a given sub-dimension were classified as 0. For each dimension, respondents reported the current level of technology use/impact, as shown in Table 1.

Table 1. Data collection instrument structure.

Dimension	Sub-dimension	Questions*	Level
Human	Decision-making	Does not apply to our company	0
		Our employees rely on AI for suggestions but make the final decisions themselves.	1

(*continued*)

Table 1. (*continued*)

Dimension	Sub-dimension	Questions*	Level
		Decisions are made jointly by humans and AI, with both contributing equally to the outcome.	2
		AI systems and humans from different departments (internally) or companies (externally) work together to make decisions across the supply chain.	3
	Capability	Does not apply to our company	0
		Our staff have the skills to understand and use AI tools in their daily work.	1
		Our teams actively update their AI knowledge and adjust to new AI features or tools.	2
		People and AI learn from each other, for example, by using human feedback to improve AI and AI insights to guide training.	3
	Job role	Does not apply to our company	0
		We have clearly defined roles for people interacting with AI tools in the supply chain.	1
		Our employees change or adapt their responsibilities as AI capabilities evolve.	2
		Our employees regularly rethink and reshape their roles to work better with AI, both individually and across teams.	3
Social	Trust	Does not apply to our company	0
		The use of AI has affected (positively or negatively) trust among colleagues (internally) or partners (externally).	1
		Our employees and partners trust AI enough to follow their recommendations or decisions.	2
		AI systems interact directly, in our company and with partners, and we trust those interactions to be reliable.	3
	Visibility	Does not apply to our company	0
		AI has helped us to improve the quality or quantity of information we share with partners.	1
		Our AI systems anticipate supply chain issues or opportunities before they happen.	2
		We use AI to generate future scenarios to guide supply chain decisions.	3
	Collaboration	Does not apply to our company	0

(*continued*)

Table 1. (*continued*)

Dimension	Sub-dimension	Questions*	Level
		Some interactions or processes between supply chain partners are managed by AI systems (e.g. scheduling, ordering).	1
		Our employees (and supply chain partners) work together with AI systems to solve problems or complete tasks collaboratively.	2
		AI has helped us to find new or better ways to collaborate internally and externally.	3
Organisational	Performance	Does not apply to our company	0
		AI has mainly helped us with repetitive tasks or reducing errors and costs.	1
		AI has been used to support strategic decisions and to plan business activities.	2
		AI is a source of innovation and competitive advantage for our company in our supply chain.	3
	Resilience	Does not apply to our company	0
		AI has helped us identify risks or potential disruptions in the supply chain.	1
		AI tools have helped us decide how to respond to supply chain risks or issues.	2
		AI has played a central role in managing and adapting our risk response strategies.	3
	Sustainability	Does not apply to our company	0
		AI has been used to improve efficiency and reduce waste in supply chain operations.	1
		AI contributes to the development/design of more sustainable products or processes.	2
		We use AI to help manage product life cycles and support circular or regenerative business models.	3

* The questions were translated into Portuguese.

4 Results and Discussion

The objectives of this study are twofold: to analyze the current state of AI adoption in the pulp and paper sector in Brazil and Portugal (RQ1) and evaluate the applicability and refinement needs of the SC-STAI profiling tool as an STAI-MM (RQ2). Therefore, this section is divided into two parts. First, an analysis and discussion of the responses obtained from the case studies is carried out to contribute to RQ1. The second part focuses on the analysis of the tool itself to contribute to its development to answer RQ2.

As mentioned in the methodology section, this article represents the first stage of the application of a DSR approach thus these two analyses are fundamental to inform the next stages: the adoption of AI in the cases studied and to further develop the SC-STAI profiling tool.

4.1 Case Studies Analysis

The analysis of responses obtained for each case study was conducted with the purpose of mapping the current level of AI integration in each of the nine sub-dimensions of the SC-STAI profiling tool. Table 2 presents the level adoption/impact of each sub dimension of the model for the nine cases. It presents the results obtained from the survey conducted with professionals (specialists, coordinators, and managers from each analyzed case), divided into three aspects: dimension, sub-dimension, and the values assigned to each of the nine cases (A to I). The last row presents the overall average values for each case, making it possible to carry out analyses.

There was substantial variation in the maturity of AI integration among the companies. Overall average scores ranged from 0.9 (Companies H and I) to 2.6 (Company F). The analysis of the cases showed the existence of three clusters: low adoption, intermediate adoption and advanced adoption. Figure 2 presents the results.

Six companies (A, C, D, E, H, I) compose the low adoption cluster, presenting average levels below 1.5, representing 66.7% of the sample. Companies H and I showed the lowest levels, at an early stage, with minimal operational integration.

Companies B and G exhibited moderate levels and are part of the intermediate adoption cluster, representing 22.2% of the sample. Company B demonstrated balanced maturity, with strong performance and resilience. Company G stood out in capability, collaboration, and performance, but had limited integration in job roles and visibility.

Table 2. Levels of adoption/impact of each dimension by case.

Dimension	Sub-dimension	A	B	C	D	E	F	G	H	I
Human	Decision-making	1	2	1	1	1	1	1	1	1
	Capability	3	1	0	1	2	3	3	1	1
	Job role	0	2	0	1	2	3	0	0	0
Social	Trust	0	2	1	2	1	3	2	1	1
	Visibility	1	2	1	1	1	3	1	1	1
	Collaboration	1	1	3	1	1	3	3	1	1
Organisational	Performance	3	3	2	3	1	3	3	1	1
	Resilience	3	3	3	1	1	3	1	1	1
	Sustainability	1	2	1	1	1	1	2	1	1
Average		1,4	2,0	1,3	1,3	1,2	2,6	1,8	0,9	0,9

Company F was an outlier with a significantly higher average score (2.6), representing 11.1% of the sample. It is considered the most mature in AI integration and forms the advanced adoption cluster alone.

The analysis highlighted a prioritization of certain subdimensions over others, revealing disparities in maturity levels both within the same dimension and between different dimensions.

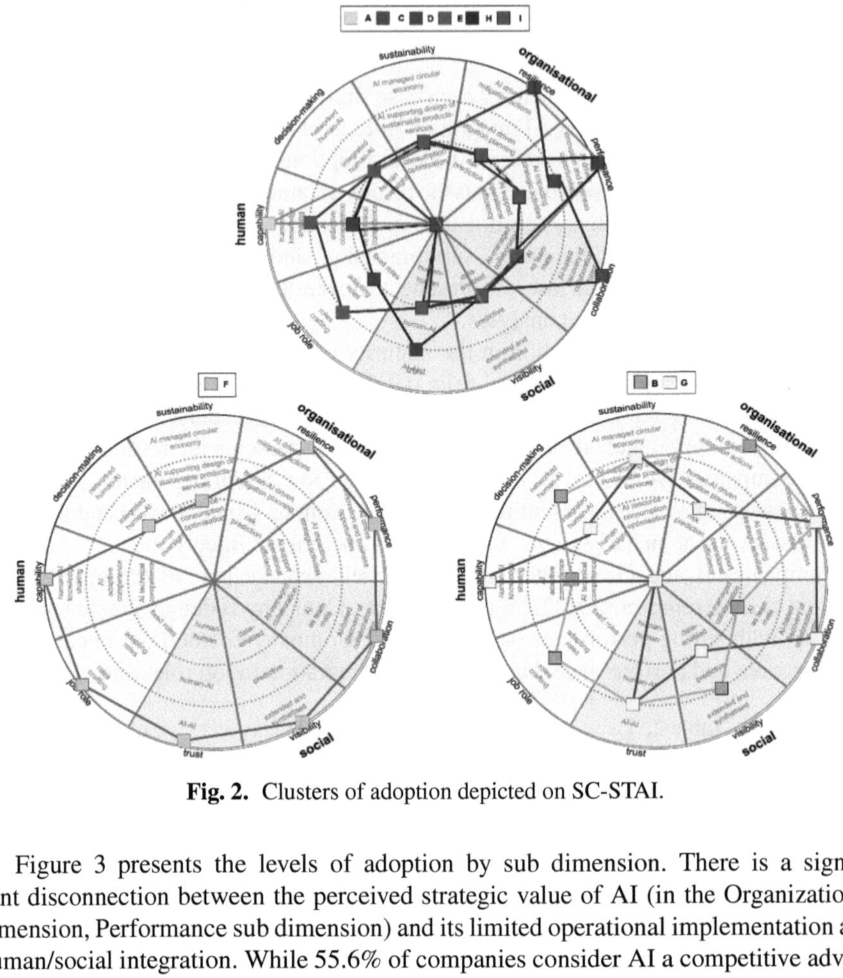

Fig. 2. Clusters of adoption depicted on SC-STAI.

Figure 3 presents the levels of adoption by sub dimension. There is a significant disconnection between the perceived strategic value of AI (in the Organizational dimension, Performance sub dimension) and its limited operational implementation and human/social integration. While 55.6% of companies consider AI a competitive advantage in its current stage of implementation (Level 3 in Performance), only 11.1% have achieved collaborative human-AI decision-making (Level 2 in Decision-making, Human dimension), and the majority (55.6%) have yet to redefine job roles (Level 0 in Job role, Human dimension). This suggests that recognition of AI's strategic benefits precedes its operational integration and transformation of human and social aspects. Barriers related to resources, skills, or organizational culture may hinder full implementation.

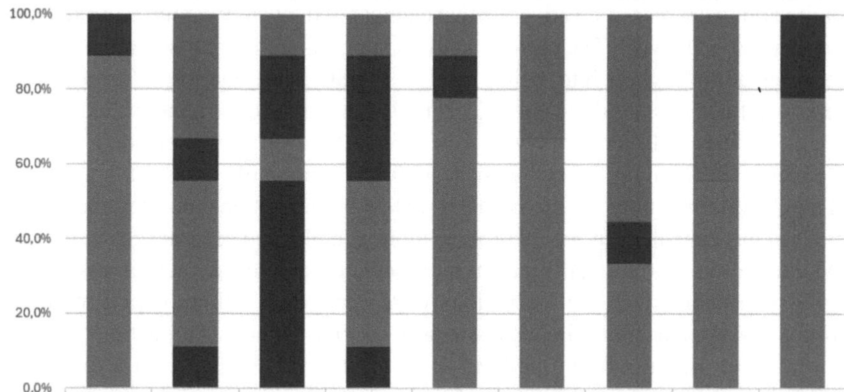

	Decision-making	Capability	Job role	Trust	Visibility	Collaboration	Performance	Resilience	Sustainability
■ Level 3	0,0%	33,3%	11,1%	11,1%	11,1%	33,3%	55,6%	44,4%	0,0%
■ Level 2	11,1%	11,1%	22,2%	33,3%	11,1%	0,0%	11,1%	0,0%	22,2%
■ Level 1	88,9%	44,4%	11,1%	44,4%	77,8%	66,7%	33,3%	55,6%	77,8%
■ Level 0	0,0%	11,1%	55,6%	11,1%	0,0%	0,0%	0,0%	0,0%	0,0%

Fig. 3. Levels of adoption by sub dimension.

The predominance of Level 1 in Decision-making (Human dimension) for 88.9% of companies, even among those with high Performance (Organizational dimension), indicates a cautious approach to AI integration in decision-making. Organizations value AI insights but maintain human control over critical decisions. This reflects an early-stage collaborative model in which AI supports decision-making but does not replace or equally share responsibility with humans.

The lowest maturity levels were observed in the Job role (Human dimension) and, in many cases, across the Social dimension (Trust, Visibility, Collaboration). This suggests that transforming job roles and integrating AI into trust and relationships within the SC remain significant challenges that must be overcome to reach higher levels of overall maturity.

The wide variation in adoption levels within the same sector indicates that internal organizational factors, such as AI development capabilities (Capability, Human dimension), organizational culture, and strategic commitment, are more decisive in AI adoption success than industry-specific characteristics. Company F, with a high internal capability (Capability Level 3), demonstrates the highest overall maturity, reaching advanced levels across almost all dimensions. In contrast, Companies H and I, which exhibit low capability levels (Level 1), show the lowest overall adoption levels and consistently low profiles.

4.2 SC-STAI Tool Critical Analysis

Two points for improvement were found for the next DSR cycle after applying the tool to nine case studies.

Refine the sub-scales of the SC-STAI. Positioning companies accurately within the predefined levels (0 to 3) for each sub-dimension proved challenging. Companies often exhibit varying degrees of AI adoption that cannot be adequately captured through binary or strictly defined levels. The current analysis suggests it is unrealistic to position most companies at the highest integration level of the SC-STAI due to the complexity and diversity in their AI adoption stages. This indicates the need to refine the existing radar levels. Introducing a Likert scale (with 5 or 7 points) for each sub dimension would enable more precise positioning, allowing nuanced differentiation of cases within the profiling tool and facilitating more detailed analyses. Defining transitional or intermediate stages for partial implementations would provide more granular and accurate characterizations of AI integration. Currently, the lack of intermediate stages makes self-assessment challenging, especially since the evaluations were conducted without expert moderation. Additionally, the current tool does not clearly specify the necessary actions companies should take to progress from one level to the next (e.g., moving from level 1 to level 2). This was not in the initial scope of the tool, as it requires road mapping capabilities. However, some sort of guidelines to produce recommendations to cross the gap AS-IS/TO-BE would improve the effectiveness of the tool.

Introduce Quantitative Vectors for Positioning and Decision-Making. Developing clear quantitative guidelines for companies to evaluate their positions on the radar would address issues such as overlapping responses and data noise. Currently, companies occasionally "skip" levels during AI adoption. For instance, in the "Performance" sub-dimension, reaching level 3 implies that companies already leverage AI as a strategic advantage and support strategic decisions, requirements typically aligned with level 2. A structured overview of the decision-making processes needed for progression between stages is essential. To address this, each SC-STAI level should incorporate specific pre-requisites, such as minimum revenue thresholds, a defined percentage of AI ecosystem integration, or employee counts. Only after meeting all defined criteria should companies advance to the next level. Utilizing clear analytical vectors, key performance indicators, and metrics to define both qualitative and quantitative characteristics of each SC-STAI level would significantly improve assessment clarity, consistency, and facilitate a unified understanding of AI integration benchmarks. For example, in [29], the authors' AI Trust Maturity Model provides the necessary documentation relevant for assessing each maturity dimension, alongside metrics of evaluation, e.g., Explainability documentation and metrics of evaluation. Additionally, [42] developed an Industry 4.0 Maturity Model that includes vectors of analysis for every dimension, i.e., specific capability areas within the dimensions that support targeted maturity improvements and clarify the areas of analysis. Similar levels must be defined to STAI-MMs.

5 Conclusion

The application of the SC-STAI profiling tool in nine case studies in the pulp and paper sector, covering companies in Brazil and Portugal, revealed challenges and opportunities in adopting AI in SCM. The analysis of clusters related to the level of adoption (low, intermediate, and advanced) highlights socio-technical barriers and strategic pathways to enhance AI maturity in the sector.

In the low adoption group (companies A, C, D, E, H, and I), AI is primarily used for basic and routine operational tasks. Low scores in Trust, Visibility, and Collaboration indicate challenges beyond technical limitations, including the lack of training, resistance to change, and an unclear strategic value associated with AI. It is essential that AI be perceived as a collaboration tool rather than a threat to human labor, helping overcome cultural barriers and fostering a culture of collaboration and continuous learning. Despite these challenges, some organizations have begun to recognize the potential of AI and invest in enhancing human skills, beginning the process of digital transformation. Advancing this process requires ongoing workforce training, revising roles and responsibilities, and strengthening organizational culture to foster trust and transparency for a more strategic AI adoption.

In the intermediate adoption cluster, comprising companies B and G, there is a balance between operational performance and initial collaboration with AI. There are visible advances in Performance, Resilience, Capability, and Collaboration; however, challenges related to AI autonomy and its integration into strategic functions persist. Although AI's benefits are acknowledged, the absence of structured processes and clear metrics hinders progress. In this context, expanding human-AI collaboration in strategic decisions and accelerating its integration across various business areas are crucial steps forward.

In the advanced adoption cluster, company F demonstrates strong AI integration, showcasing technological maturity and alignment. However, there is still room to deepen sustainability and circularity practices by leveraging AI as a catalyst for sustainable innovation. Strengthening its role in sustainable practices and the circular economy represents a promising path to maximizing the value of AI-enabled technologies.

Driving innovation, resilience and sustainability requires overcoming cultural barriers, promoting continuous training and redefining roles. The SC-STAI is a valuable diagnostic tool, but its effectiveness depends on ongoing adaptation to digital transformations. Establishing clear metrics, building trust, and aligning AI with business objectives will ensure that its full potential is used to improve operations and drive sustainable innovation in the SCs. A balanced approach between technical and human factors is crucial for AI to deliver long-term strategic impact.

As next steps, it is necessary to refine the SC-STAI subscales and introduce quantitative vectors for positioning and decision-making. These levels should be defined to improve the SC-STAI towards a STAI-MM.

Acknowledgements. The authors acknowledge the National Council for Scientific and Technological Development (Conselho Nacional de Desenvolvimento Científico e Tecnológico, CNPq-BRAZIL – Knowledge Brazil Program – Support for Network Projects – 444535/2024-1) for their financial support.

References

1. STATISTA: Global pulp industry – statistics & facts. Statista. https://www.statista.com/topics/7345/pulp-industry/. Accessed 11 Sep 2024
2. Del Rio, D.F., et al.: Decarbonizing the pulp and paper industry: a critical and systematic review of sociotechnical developments and policy options. Renew. Sustain. Energy Rev. **167**, 112706 (2022). https://doi.org/10.1016/j.rser.2022.112706

3. Kar, A.K., Choudhary, S.K., Singh, V.K.: How can artificial intelligence impact sustainability: a systematic literature review. J. Clean. Prod. **376**, 134120 (2022). https://doi.org/10.1016/j.jclepro.2022.134120
4. Weisz, E., Herold, D.M., Ostern, N.K., Payne, R., Kummer, S.: Artificial intelligence (AI) for supply chain collaboration: implications on information sharing and trust. Online Inf. Rev. **49**(1), 164–181 (2025). https://doi.org/10.1108/OIR-02-2024-0083
5. Soares, A.L., Gomes, J., Zimmermann, R., Rhodes, D., Dorner, V.: Integrating AI in supply chain management: using a socio-technical chart to navigate unknown transformations. In: Camarinha-Matos, L.M., Ortiz, A., Boucher, X., Barthe-Delanoë, A.M. (eds.) Navigating Unpredictability: Collaborative Networks in Non-linear Worlds, vol. 726, pp. 12–23. Springer, Cham (2024). https://doi.org/10.1007/978-3-031-71739-0_2
6. Knoppen, D., Christiaanse, E., Huysman, M.H.: Supply chain relationships: exploring the linkage between inter-organisational adaptation and learning. J. Purch. Supply Manag. **16**, 195–205 (2010). https://doi.org/10.1016/j.pursup.2010.03.001
7. Tejpal, G., Garg, R.K., Sachdeva, A.: Trust among supply chain partners: a review. Meas. Bus. Excell. **17**(1), 51–71 (2013). https://doi.org/10.1108/13683041311311365
8. Chen, L., Zhao, X., Tang, O., Price, L., Zhang, S., Zhu, W.: Supply chain collaboration for sustainability: a literature review and future research agenda. Int. J. Prod. Econ. **194**, 73–87 (2017). https://doi.org/10.1016/j.ijpe.2017.04.005
9. Hartikainen, M., Väänänen, K., Olsson, T.: Towards a human-centred artificial intelligence maturity model. In: Extended Abstracts of the 2023 CHI Conference on Human Factors in Computing Systems, Hamburg, Germany, pp. 1–7 (2023). https://doi.org/10.1145/3544549.3585752
10. Sadiq, R.B., Safie, N., Abd Rahman, A.H., Goudarzi, S.: Artificial intelligence maturity model: a systematic literature review. PeerJ Comput. Sci. **7**, e661 (2021). https://doi.org/10.7717/peerj-cs.661
11. Nick, G., Zeleny, K., Kovács, T., Járvás, T., Pocsarovszky, K., Kő, A.: Artificial intelligence enriched industry 4.0 readiness in manufacturing: the extended CCMS2.0e maturity model. Product. Manuf. Res. **12**, 2357683 (2024). https://doi.org/10.1080/21693277.2024.2357683
12. Das, S.D., Bala, P.K., Mishra, A.N.: Towards defining a trustworthy artificial intelligence system development maturity model. J. Comput. Inform. Syst. **64**, 775–796 (2024). https://doi.org/10.1080/08874417.2023.2251443
13. Hendriksen, C.: Artificial intelligence for supply chain management: disruptive innovation or innovative disruption? J. Supply Chain Manag. **59**, 65–76 (2023). https://doi.org/10.1111/jscm.12304
14. Dora, M., Kumar, A., Mangla, S.K., Pant, A., Kamal, M.M.: Critical success factors influencing artificial intelligence adoption in food supply chains. Int. J. Prod. Res. **60**, 4621–4640 (2022). https://doi.org/10.1080/00207543.2021.1959665
15. Riad, M., Naimi, M., Okar, C.: Enhancing supply chain resilience through artificial intelligence: developing a comprehensive conceptual framework for AI implementation and supply chain optimization. Logistics **8**, 111 (2024). https://doi.org/10.3390/logistics8040111
16. Yaroson, E.V., Abadie, A., Roux, M.: Human-artificial intelligence collaboration in supply chain outcomes: the mediating role of responsible artificial intelligence. Ann. Oper. Res. (2025). https://doi.org/10.1007/s10479-025-06534-7
17. Sharma, R., Shishodia, A., Gunasekaran, A., Min, H., Munim, Z.H.: The role of artificial intelligence in supply chain management: mapping the territory. Int. J. Prod. Res. **60**, 7527–7550 (2022). https://doi.org/10.1080/00207543.2022.2029611
18. Modgil, S., Gupta, S., Stekelorum, R., Laguir, I.: AI technologies and their impact on supply chain resilience during COVID-19. Int. J. Phys. Distrib. Logist. Manag. **52**, 130–149 (2022). https://doi.org/10.1108/IJPDLM-12-2020-0434

19. Akbarighatar, P., Pappas, I., Vassilakopoulou, P.: A sociotechnical perspective for responsible AI maturity models: findings from a mixed-method literature review. Int. J. Inf. Manag. Data Insights **3**, 100193 (2023). https://doi.org/10.1016/j.jjimei.2023.100193
20. Reuel, A., et al.: Responsible AI in the Global Context: Maturity Model and Survey. arXiv preprint (2024). https://doi.org/10.48550/ARXIV.2410.09985
21. Gomez, C., Cho, S.M., Ke, S., Huang, C.-M., Unberath, M.: Human-AI collaboration is not very collaborative yet: a taxonomy of interaction patterns in AI-assisted decision making from a systematic review. Front. Comput. Sci. **6**, 1521066 (2025). https://doi.org/10.3389/fcomp.2024.1521066
22. Loske, D., Klumpp, M.: Intelligent and efficient? An empirical analysis of human–AI collaboration for truck drivers in retail logistics. Int. J. Logist. Manag. **32**, 1356–1383 (2021). https://doi.org/10.1108/IJLM-03-2020-0149
23. Richter, A., Schwabe, G.: There is No 'AI' in 'TEAM'! Or is there? – Towards meaningful human-AI collaboration. Australas. J. Inf. Syst. (2025). https://doi.org/10.3127/ajis.v29.5753
24. Sun, X., Song, Y.: Unlocking the synergy: increasing productivity through Human-AI collaboration in the industry 5.0 Era. Comput. Ind. Eng. **200**, 110657 (2025). https://doi.org/10.1016/j.cie.2024.110657
25. Schmager, S., Pappas, I.O., Vassilakopoulou, P.: Understanding Human-Centred AI: a review of its defining elements and a research agenda. Behav. Inf. Technol. (2025). https://doi.org/10.1080/0144929X.2024.2448719
26. Ramdhani, Y.L., Surendro, K.: Development of AI governance model in enterprises based on CMMI model structure. In: Proceedings of the 2022 International Conference Information Technology System Innovation (ICITSI), pp. 145–150. Bandung, Indonesia (2022). https://doi.org/10.1109/ICITSI56531.2022.9970981
27. Colangelo, E., Fries, C., Hinrichsen, T.-F., Szaller, Á., Nick, G.: Maturity model for AI in smart production planning and control system. Procedia CIRP **107**, 493–498 (2022). https://doi.org/10.1016/j.procir.2022.05.014
28. Hansen, H.F., Lillesund, E., Mikalef, P., Altwaijry, N: Understanding artificial intelligence diffusion through an AI capability maturity model. Inf. Syst. Front. **26**, 2147–2163 (2024). https://doi.org/10.1007/s10796-024-10528-4
29. Mylrea, M., Robinson, N.: Artificial Intelligence (AI) trust framework and maturity model: applying an entropy lens to improve security, privacy, and ethical AI. Entropy **25**, 1429 (2023). https://doi.org/10.3390/e25101429
30. Schuster, T., Waidelich, L.: Maturity of artificial intelligence in SMEs: privacy and ethics dimensions. In: Camarinha-Matos, L.M., Ortiz, A., Boucher, X., Osório, A.L. (eds.) Collaborative Networks in Digitalization and Society 5.0, pp. 274–286. Springer, Cham (2022). https://doi.org/10.1007/978-3-031-14844-6_22
31. Van Hoek, R.: Insight from industry-early lessons learned about AI adoption in core procurement processes, directions for managers and researchers. Supply Chain Manage.: An Int. J. **29**, 794–803 (2024). https://doi.org/10.1108/SCM-02-2024-0143
32. Herrmann, T., Pfeiffer, S.: Keeping the organization in the loop as a general concept for human-centered AI: the example of medical imaging. In: Proceedings of the Hawaii International Conference System Science (2023). https://doi.org/10.24251/HICSS.2023.644
33. Pasmore, W., Winby, S., Mohrman, S.A., Vanasse, R.: Reflections: sociotechnical systems design and organization change. J. Change Manag. **19**(2), 67–85 (2018). https://doi.org/10.1080/14697017.2018.1553761
34. Reynolds, M., Holwell, S.: Systems Approaches to Managing Change: A Practical Guide. Springer, London (2010). https://doi.org/10.1007/978-1-84882-809-4
35. Paucar-Caceres, A., Jerardino-Wiesenborn, B.: A bridge for two views: Checkland's soft systems methodology and Maturana's ontology of the observer. J. Oper. Res. Soc. **71**(4), 660–672 (2020)

36. Rebentisch, E.S., Soares, A.L., Rhodes, D.H., Zimmerman, R.A., Cardoso, J.L.F.P.: On the use of sociotechnical systems design in industry: digital transformation processes and artifacts. In: Proceedings of the 8th Socio-Technical Perspective in IS Development, p. 14 (2022)
37. Peffers, K., Tuunanen, T., Rothenberger, A.M., Chatterjee, S.: A design science research methodology for information systems research. J. Manage. Inf. Syst. **24**, 45–78 (2007). https://doi.org/10.2753/MIS0742-1222240302
38. vom Brocke, J., Hevner, A., Maedche, A.: Introduction to design science research. In: vom Brocke, J., Hevner, A., Maedche, A. (eds.) Design Science Research. Cases, pp. 1–13. Springer, Cham (2020). https://doi.org/10.1007/978-3-030-46781-4_1
39. Sonnenberg, C., vom Brocke, J.: Evaluations in the science of the artificial – reconsidering the build-evaluate pattern in design science research. In: Peffers, K., Rothenberger, M., Kuechler, B. (eds.) Design Science Research in Information Systems. Advances in Theory and Practice (DESRIST 2012), LNCS, vol. 7286. Springer, Berlin, Heidelberg (2012). https://doi.org/10.1007/978-3-642-29863-9_28
40. Hevner, A.R., March, S.T., Park, J., Ram, S.: Design science in information systems research. Manage. Inform. Syst. Quart. **28**, 75–105 (2004). https://doi.org/10.2307/25148625
41. Holmström, J.B., Ketokivi, M., Hameri, A.-P.: Bridging practice and theory: a design science approach. Decis. Sci. **40**(1) (2009). https://ssrn.com/abstract=1346889
42. Senna, P., Barros, A.C., Roca, J., Azevedo, A.: Development of a digital maturity model for Industry 4.0 based on the technology-organization-environment framework. Comput. Ind. Eng. **185**, 109645 (2023). https://doi.org/10.1016/j.cie.2023.109645

Collaborating with Algorithms: AI for Collaborative Supply Chain Management

Fabio Couto[1,2(✉)], Mariana Curado Malta[1,2], and António Lucas Soares[1,2]

[1] Institute for Systems and Computer Engineering, Technology and Science (INESC TEC), R. Dr. Roberto Frias, Porto, Portugal
{fabio.couto,mariana.c.malta,antonio.l.soares}@inesctec.pt

[2] Faculty of Engineering, University of Porto (FEUP), R. Dr. Roberto Frias, Porto, Portugal

Abstract. Artificial Intelligence (AI) integration in supply chain systems is growing, and with it grows its potential impact on inter-organisational collaborative networks. We review existing literature on how different AI archetypes (*Reflexive, Anticipatory, Supervisory, Prescriptive*) could support Collaborative Supply Chain Management (CSCM) activities, and how they impact information sharing, collaborative decision-making, and trust among supply chain partners at different integration levels. Adopting a sociotechnical perspective, we synthesise existing literature and map the archetypes along four levels of AI integration, varying in scope and decision autonomy. The results are conceptual frameworks demonstrating how AI impacts collaboration dynamics as it evolves from a decision-support tool to an autonomous coordination agent. Findings show differentiated effects along archetypes and integration levels, with implications for CSCM governance, transparency, and resilience. We contribute to the discussion on human-AI collaboration in CSCM and offer a baseline for research on the human-centric values of Industry 5.0.

Keywords: Artificial Intelligence Integration · Collaborative Supply Chain Management · Human-AI Collaboration · Sociotechnical Systems

1 Introduction

What happens when intelligent machines start negotiating delivery schedules, reassigning inventory, and flagging supplier risks not as mere tools, but as actors within a network of supply chain organisations? This is no longer a speculative question. In the age of Artificial Intelligence (AI), supply chains are progressing from linear pipelines into adaptive, collaborative ecosystems, where decision- making is progressively shared between human actors and artificial agents [1].

The integration of AI-based technologies in Supply Chain Management (SCM) is changing how organisations collaborate throughout networks [2, 3], with benefits in visibility, predictive insights, and coordination [4], while there is increasing Volatility, Uncertainty, Complexity and Ambiguity (VUCA environments), paired with swift AI

Published by Springer Nature Switzerland AG 2026
L. M. Camarinha-Matos et al. (Eds.): PRO-VE 2025, IFIP AICT 770, pp. 185–200, 2026.
https://doi.org/10.1007/978-3-032-05673-3_12

advancements [5]. In this paper, AI is understood as "the ability of a machine to learn from experience, adjust to new inputs, and perform human-like tasks" [6, p. 63].

We concentrate on Collaborative Supply Chain Management (CSCM), a model of inter-organisational cooperation based on collective goals, information sharing, and mutual performance improvement [7]. These practices take place within collaborative networks, where coordination is no longer restricted to bilateral relationships (*ad-hoc* collaboration), but arises from dynamic, multi-actor interactions ranging from defined and linked to integrated and extended collaboration [8].

Concurrently, the introduction of Industry 5.0 and offsprings such as the concept of Organisation 5.0, brings a cultural and technological move from the technocentric automation and efficiency keywords of Industry 4.0 to the broader inclusion of resilience, sustainability, and human-centric design [9, 10]. In this context, CSCM becomes a context and test bed for reimagining how humans and AI systems can co-create value beyond automated transactions [4, 11]. AI technologies offer new avenues for improving coordination, transparency, and trust among supply chain partners, and a growing body of literature has been investigating the intersection of AI and CSCM practices [3]. However, despite growing interest in AI adoption within CSCM [3, 4, 12] and to the best of our knowledge, there are no academic contributions analysing the impact that different types of AI systems have on collaborative dynamics, nor the CSCM activities they could support.

To address this gap, we adopt a sociotechnical perspective [13, 14] and propose a detailed analysis based on four AI archetypes that reflect how AI systems differ in functional roles, decision autonomy and interactions with humans and organisational actors: Reflexive, Anticipatory, Supervisory and Prescriptive AI [15, 16]. Instead of considering AI as a static object, we examine how different types of AI are situated within CSCM practices, going from decision support to autonomous coordination. Mapped across four levels of AI integration [13], the paper explores how each archetype impacts information sharing, collaborative decision-making, and trust. This paper contributes new perspectives to the organisational and relational transformations taking place as AI walks towards being an increasingly autonomous collaborative agent in CSCM.

The remainder of this paper is organised as follows. We begin with an overview of relevant topics and similar works (Sect. 2). Then comes the definition of the research problem, research question and methodology (Sect. 3). Sections 4 and 5 present and discuss the results. Finally, in Sect. 6, we conclude by highlighting the research implications and suggesting future research avenues.

2 Background

2.1 AI-Enabled Collaboration in Supply Chain Networks

This paper combines three interlinked conceptual lenses, consisting of AI system archetypes, AI integration levels, and supply chain relationship levels, to analyse how AI systems reshape the conditions for inter-organizational collaboration in socio-technical terms.

AI systems are not immovable, meaning that their role in CSCM depends on how they are configured regarding autonomy, analytical capability, and interaction with human actors [4]. The concept of AI archetypes describes this reality, and we define them as generalised, reusable models or patterns of AI system behaviour, architecture, or interaction, which serve as a reference for designing, analysing, or categorising AI-based systems. Departing from the work of [15], Reflexive and Anticipatory AI systems primarily support decision-making by augmenting human insight, while Supervisory and Prescriptive AI systems embody more autonomous and adaptive forms of agency. These archetypes differ in function and in the kind of collaboration they facilitate, which goes from reactive assistance to proactive and autonomous coordination.

However, AI's collaborative potential is not exclusively determined by its technical profile, because it is also dependant on how deeply AI systems are embedded into organizational processes and decision structures [13]. Drawing on the sociotechnical framework of [13], we interpret four AI integration levels as different configurations of scope and agency: Human Sherlock, Robot Watson, Robot Cartographer, Chess Grandmaster, and Artificial Ecosystem (Table 1). These levels act as deployment contexts that influence how AI archetypes are operationalised, besides how much impact they have on collaborative outcomes.

Table 1. AI Integration framework for supply chains (Source: [13], p. 70).

	Partial Integration	Full Integration
Assistive Role	1 – Human Sherlock, Robot Watson: AI provides insights for specific supply chain activities like inventory management, supporting human-led decision-making.	2 – Robot Cartographer: AI provides end-to-end supply chain visibility and generates insights for decision-making, but strategic decisions are still made by humans.
Autonomous Role	3 – Chess Grandmaster: AI takes charge of specific activities like supplier selection or inventory replenishment, but humans retain the final approval authority.	4 – Artificial Ecosystem: AI takes charge of end-to-end supply chain management, from demand forecasting to delivery, with minimal human intervention.

Finally, partnerships in supply chains take place at different levels of information and decision systems integration, as well as business process integration [17], from simple data exchange to strategic co-planning; these relationships go through an initial stage of communication (e.g. order placement), evolving then to the coordination between partners (e.g. shared inventory levels, demand), subsequently reaching a cooperation stage (highly integrated business processes), and lastly achieving a state of inter-organisational collaboration (routine involvement in strategic, tactical and operational decisions), each stage with its norms, expectations, and information flows. The success of AI systems depends on the social infrastructure of the collaboration, namely the shared goals, trust, collaborative governance, and also adaptive capacity.

The convergence of these three conceptual layers configures our lenses for studying how AI mediates CSCM: the archetypes describe what AI is, the integration levels describe where AI sits in the organisation, and the inter-organisational partnership stages describe the collaborative readiness of the supply chain network. It is at the junction of these layers that one starts to understand the application of AI, and its role in transforming the collaborative logic of supply chains.

2.2 Similar Works

[3] conduct a systematic literature review on AI applications in CSCM over the past decade, using the SCOR model (Plan, Source, Make, Deliver, Return, Enable) as the analysis framework. Based on this structure, they propose six future research priorities: hybrid intelligence, ethical aspects, system hybridisation, the physical internet, AI for the "Make" process, and resource sharing. The study also categorizes AI technologies by methodological families: machine learning (ML), expert systems, fuzzy logic, multi-agent systems (MAS), and decision support systems (DSS); and distinguishes between symbolic and sub-symbolic approaches. Each type of AI is linked to specific collaborative functions, such as MAS for decentralized sourcing negotiations and ML for demand forecasting. The authors highlight the fragmented and interdisciplinary nature of the field and call for greater integration of insights across operations research, information systems, and organizational theory.

[4] offer a conceptual and managerial lens on AI's role in supporting supply chain collaboration, with a focus on information sharing and trust. They argue that successful CSCM requires alignment between three factors: AI capabilities, information quality, and trust. A key challenge lies in transitioning trust from interpersonal and interorganizational relationships toward trust in AI systems. To address this, they propose a five-stage framework of AI collaboration, from Complementary to Autonomous and Replacing applications, making a parallelism with the levels of automation in other fields i.e. vehicles. The framework outlines the technical and managerial capabilities needed at different stages and highlights transparency and explainability as essential for building trust in AI systems.

[12] present an applied framework for Intelligent Collaborative Supply Chain Management (iCSCM), developed in the context of a university holding company. While narrower in scope, the study gives emphasis to the structural and behavioural requirements for AI-supported collaboration in knowledge-intensive, cross-sectoral ecosystems. Their iCSCM model integrates structural dimensions (e.g., ICT infrastructure, workflow, control systems) with behavioural enablers (e.g., leadership, culture, trust). The authors argue that predictive analytics, real-time communication tools, and adaptive systems can improve collaboration along multiple supply chain functions, and that human factors like trust and organizational readiness remain pivotal to successful AI adoption in CSCM contexts.

3 Research Design

The literature so far provides a foundation for understanding the evolution of AI in CSCM: [3] offer a systematic mapping of the research field; [4] develop an AI CSCM framework grounded in trust and information exchange; [12] highlight the integration of AI into collaborative supply chain organisational workflows and governance. However, a common limitation in these contributions is the absence of an explicit sociotechnical perspective that accounts for the mutual shaping of technological capabilities and social systems [14]. Limited attention has been paid to how different AI archetypes and AI integration levels interact to produce collaborative outcomes.

It is then necessary to analyse how each AI archetype can be integrated in CSCM and then explore the influence each archetype and AI integration level have on CSCM dimensions. Regarding the influence on CSCM dimensions, our attention is steered to information sharing, collaborative decision-making, and trust; these CSCM dimensions are identified in the literature as baselines to successful inter-organisational collaboration. Prior research indicates that the quality and degree of information sharing and the level of trust among supply chain partners are indicators of collaborative performance and resilience [4]: trust affects the willingness to share sensitive data and to act collaboratively, whereas information sharing supports visibility, alignment, and coordination across the supply chain network [4].

Simultaneously, collaborative decision-making is gaining importance due to increasingly complex and powerful AI-based systems contributing to data analysis, predictive modelling and prescriptive coordination [3, 12]. As an example, Machine Learning (ML) applications for supply chain decision-making have seen a surge of interest since 2022, driven in part by the growing attention to Large Language Models (LLMs) [3]. These systems expand AI's role from supporting operational tasks to influencing strategic choices, which directly impacts how partners negotiate, allocate resources, and respond to disruptions [2, 13]; decision-making is evolving from exclusively human-led to a co-mediation by algorithmic agents [13].

For the above reasons, those CSCM dimensions are three interdependent components that reflect sociotechnical and operational aspects of collaboration assisted by AI systems, with that being the rationale for our choice. The Research Question that drives this research is"Which CSCM activities could the AI archetypes support, and how would it impact information sharing, collaborative decision-making and trust at different levels of integration?".

This study adopts a narrative literature review approach [18, 19], allowing a theory-driven, integrative exploration of relevant scholarly work across disciplines like SCM, information systems, organisational studies, operations research and HAIC [3, 19]. The search was conducted in Google Scholar and SCOPUS using the queries:'artificial intelligence' AND'collaborative supply chain', considering exclusively English-written peer-reviewed journal papers and conference proceedings. The papers were filtered according to their relevance for this study. Furthermore, and to complement traditional literature review methods, we used an LLM in an augmentative co-ideation process [20] to brainstorm possible applications of AI for CSCM: human-generated ideas were based on scholarly sources identified during the literature review, and used as a reference point in this process; AI's suggestions were critically assessed for relevance and conceptual fit, and then validated against existing academic literature. The co-ideation process involved an iterative human-AI exchange, with LLM's ideas of AI applications for CSCM being filtered, refined and expanded, recurring to academic evidence and considering theoretical alignment. Figure 1 depicts the methodology used in this paper. The results are presented in the following sections.

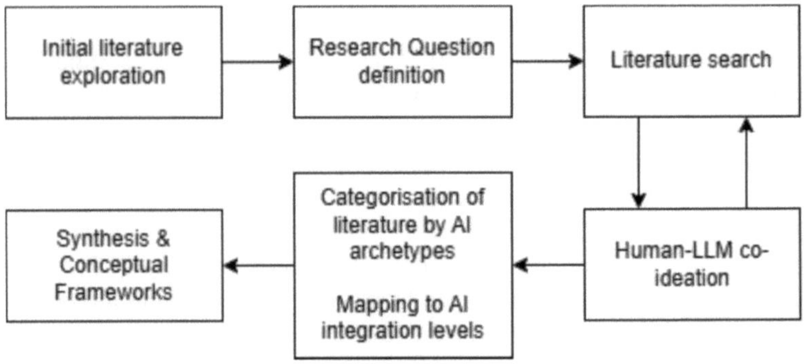

Fig. 1. Schema of the methodology (Source: own elaboration)

4 AI Archetypes in Collaborative Supply Chain Management

Reflexive AI. Within CSCM, *Reflexive AI* systems could support tasks of **Collaborative Scenario Analysis** [21] in which partners simulate multiple outcomes based on shared inputs, improving collective preparedness without altering control hierarchies. This archetype can simulate scenarios using historical and static inputs, assisting collaborative planning by generating comparable options, but always leaving final evaluation and selection to humans, as these systems do not act, but inform. It links with *Reflexive AI*'s analytical support role. It can also support **Cost-Benefit Sharing** [22] in which it offers structured models to assess contribution-benefit between echelons and partners, promoting transparency in value distribution. This archetype helps calculate and present the proportional gains or investments among supply chain actors using rule-based computations derived from historical data. However, humans interpret and negotiate the final distribution of costs and benefits. The AI system here acts as an impartial calculator, not a negotiator or actor. It could also support **Collaborative Production Scheduling** [23, 24] based on shared forecasts, thus reducing bottlenecks and inefficiencies through coordination. This archetype can help optimise production plans based on available data and constraints across supply chain partners. Even though it supports synchronisation efforts, it does not execute or enforce the plan. Therefore, it impacts alignment amongst partners, but it depends on human coordination.

Anticipatory AI. Within CSCM, *Anticipatory AI* can take the form of **Early Warning Systems** [25] that alert partners to deviations (e.g., demand surges, weather alerts) based on upstream data and thus support preventive coordination, e.g. planning of production schedules. While the AI system may alert supply chain actors after detecting anomalies, it does not prescribe or execute responses. Anticipation is applied here to inform and support coordinated human action. It can also support **Collaborative Contingency Planning** [24, 25], e.g. consisting of predictive models informing collaborative"what-if" planning to craft shared resilience strategies. The AI system forecasts future risk scenarios, providing shared situational awareness amongst partners, with humans assuming the decision-making. It anticipates problems to support human-led planning. It could also support **Risk Sharing** [26, 27] to anticipate demand variability or supplier reliability and thus inform decisions about contractual risk allocation or shared safety stocks. The system estimates future exposure or variability, helping partners distribute risk more equitably. It informs contracts or agreements but doesn't enforce them. In this case, this archetype helps craft inter-organisational policies.

Supervisory AI. Within CSCM, *Supervisory AI* systems can support tasks such as **Inter Organisational Negotiation** [28] through MAS architectures that imitate human negotiation logic. In MAS setups, AI agents can represent organisations and negotiate parameters (e.g., pricing, lead times, transportation, stock optimisation) within defined constraints. This goes beyond recommending options, as the system acts on behalf of stakeholders under circumscribed rules; supervisory AI takes the initiative but still within controlled boundaries. It can also support **Policy Adaptation** [29] through learning from past interactions [30] (deviations or failures in collaborative performance. e.g., stockouts or delays) in a process of inter-organisational learning [31] and proposes new coordination rules, meaning it contributes to long-term alignment and not just short-term optimisation (e.g. predictive maintenance of shared resources).

Prescriptive AI. Within CSCM, *Prescriptive AI* systems could be applied in support of **Self-Organising Logistics Networks** [12, 32] that represent distributed intelligence, where multiple AI agents collaborate across organisational boundaries to allocate resources, reroute goods, or balance inventories. This is the most advanced case, in which decentralised AI agents coordinate between organisations through mutual collaboration of intelligent agents and not exclusively with humans.

Table 2 summarises the points discussed in this section.

Table 2. Description of AI archetypes and their applications in CSCM (Source: own elaboration)

AI Archetype	Main Function	Level of Autonomy	Example Application(s) in CSCM
Reflexive	Recommendation of optimal actions	Low	Collaborative scenario analysis, Cost-benefit sharing, Collaborative production scheduling
Anticipatory	Forecasting of future states and trends	Low	Early warning systems, Collaborative contingency planning, Risk sharing
Supervisory	Control system	Medium	Inter-organisational negotiation, Policy adaptation
Prescriptive	Autonomous management	High	Self-organising logistics networks

5 AI Archetypes and Human-AI Collaboration in Supply Chains Towards Hybrid Actor Networks

The different levels of AI integration represent more than technological deployments, to include organisational logics and human sensemaking that guide how AI systems are positioned about human actors, thus being considered a sociotechnical phenomenon [13, 14]. AI's impact on CSCM dimensions like information sharing, collaborative decision-making, and trust, differs along different levels of AI integration [13], and those differences will be addressed in the following subsections.

Information Sharing. The integration of AI technologies changed the scale, frequency, and quality of information sharing in CSCM [4]. As AI systems evolve along different levels of integration [13], there are differences in what, how, when and why information is exchanged, and data circulates inter-organisations.

In assistive and partial AI integration scenarios (Quadrant 1 of [13] – *Human Sherlock, Robot Watson*), *Reflexive AI* provides insights for specific activities, supporting human-led decision-making. At this stage, partners in CSCM may use such AI to generate data-driven recommendations for e.g. shipment scheduling or inventory control [4], but information sharing at this stage is still essentially governed by human actors, who may rely on semi-structured methods (e.g., periodic updates via phone, shared spreadsheets, or email coordination) [33]. Reflexive AI systems can offer real-time visibility within individual organisations, but at this stage that visibility is not systematically extended across supply chain partners. Instead, it configures a scenario of near real-time analysis among partners, augmenting collective awareness, and the actual dissemination and integration of information across organisations is still episodic, bilateral, and reactive.

In assistive and full AI integration scenarios (Quadrant 2 of [13] – *Robot Cartographer*), *Anticipatory AI* generates insights for decision-making. However, humans still make strategic decisions, as AI is used to analyse historical data and make forecasts to identify potential disruptions or optimise inventory levels. At this stage, partners in CSCM start exchanging more complex and forward-looking information like demand predictions or production schedules, as the AI system automates data entry and analysis, cleaning and consolidation [4]. From this stage on, information sharing is done via cloud platforms, shared dashboards or databases, as partners are increasingly more open to share operational data by seeing the potential for efficiency and responsiveness gains through the reduction of manual interventions [4].

In autonomous and partial AI integration scenarios (Quadrant 3 of [13] – *Chess Grandmaster*), *Supervisory AI* takes charge of specific activities. Still, humans are in the loop and thus can overrule system actions, as the system focuses on automatic information sharing and real-time insights. At this stage, CSCM partners use AI-generated data and real-time visibility to collaboratively deliberate on inventory optimisation, scenario planning (e.g. transportation planning) or predictive maintenance [4]. Information sharing is seen as a strategic asset amongst supply chain partners for informed decision-making and to leverage collective intelligence [4]. Information flows in this quadrant are continuous, bidirectional, and responsive, as organisations develop collective alignment around shared KPIs and adaptive workflows.

In autonomous and full AI integration scenarios (Quadrant 4 of [13] – *Artificial Ecosystem*), *Prescriptive AI* takes charge of end-to-end CSCM activities, with minimal human intervention, as the goal is to optimise information flows across supply chain partners. At this stage, there is a fully integrated collaboration system, with centralised information sharing platforms that streamline information sharing while enabling cost reductions [4]. AI is used to autonomously organise logistics networks, routing shipments, managing inventory and making purchases [4]. Information sharing is imperative, as data from the supply chain partners is what enables autonomous AI systems to identify improvement areas, test new strategies and monitor collaboration performance [4]. AI systems in this quadrant autonomously exchange, interpret, and act on information along the supply chain network, with automated and self-regulated information sharing, being optimisable through feedback loops [34].

Collaborative Decision-Making. Collaborative decision-making is one of the main dimensions of CSCM, and it requires coordination, negotiation, and alignment among supply chain partners that have different individual goals and constraints, in most cases collaborating with the motivation of achieving higher profits and benefiting individually [33]. Within HAIC, AI systems changed how decisions are made, by whom, under what circumstances, and with what degree of transparency and shared control [6, 35], all of which differ according to each AI integration stage.

In the first quadrant [13], *Reflexive AI* systems act mainly as a decision support tool, processing data to identify patterns, provide recommendations, and support collaborative deliberation processes between the different human.partners in a supply chain [36]. At this stage, decision-making remains a human task, with AI exclusively as a supportive tool within traditional collaborative processes, where AI insights are used to inform human negotiations. Therefore, AI is considered a neutral advisor, devoid of any strategic agency, and humans reach agreements using consensus [37, 38]. In this initial phase, the incorporation of AI reflects a collaborative augmentation model [39] in which *Reflexive AI* facilitates coordination but does not modify the structures of decision authority.

In the second quadrant [13], *Anticipatory AI* systems use predictive analytics and real-time data to support collective situational awareness. AI has a more active role in collaborative decision-making. The supply chain partners start relying on AI outputs to inform and precondition their decision space, because although humans make decisions, AI plays a pre-structuring role through guiding deliberation, e.g. via simulation and what-if analysis [35]. Within this AI integration stage, *Anticipatory AI* supports more proactive forms of collaboration, but confidence in the predictive models and the quality of shared data is needed [14, 40].

In the third quadrant [13], *Supervisory AI* gains delimited autonomy in restricted decision domains, meaning AI may propose or execute decisions in routine or lower risk situations, with human actors overseeing and intervening if exceptions arise. This phase introduces a hybrid governance model, where human and AI agents manage decision-making responsibilities [41], indicating that delegation protocols must be enforced, override rights, and escalation paths shared with all supply chain partners. In this context, the risk of misalignment between algorithmic logic and human intention becomes higher if transparency is not safeguarded regarding the explainability of AI decisions [4].

In the fourth quadrant [13], *Prescriptive AI* systems take autonomous control of decision-making across the entire supply chain network, as AI agents embedded in different partner organisations negotiate, coordinate, and execute decisions without human intervention. Consequently, collaborative decision-making becomes based on machine-to-machine interactions, with human actors adopting a strategic oversight role [2, 13, 42]. This is the most potentially disruptive stage, carrying its challenges, such as possible disagreements between inter-organisational AI agents, or responsibility for potential failures. Because of that, the decision logics must be codified, auditable, and aligned with shared governance principles [33, 43]. Without that, these AI agents can wear away transparency and amplify power asymmetries [44, 45], indicating that collaboration is no longer built through inter-human relations, but through pre-programmed rules and algorithmic contracts [46, 47].

Trust. Traditional supply chain collaboration relies on interpersonal and inter-organisational trust, built through relational history, contractual obligations, and mutual dependence [33]. As AI systems are embedded into collaborative workflows, a new layer emerges: trust in AI systems themselves [4]. The evolution from human-mediated to AI-mediated information sharing changes collaboration dynamics, as they evolve from an initial relational trust among human actors to system-level trust in technology; this change brings new requirements for AI technologies, which must be transparent, interoperable and have defined governance mechanisms [4, 48].

In the first quadrant [13], and from an organisational perspective, AI is seen as a relief mechanism, meaning that it takes charge of routine activities and frees humans to focus on more strategic tasks, bringing benefits in terms of operational efficiency. However, and regarding a more collaborative perspective, *Reflexive AI* instils only partial trust amongst supply chain partners and thus is used as a complement to existing systems [4]; in this stage of integration, one of the downsides of AI is the emergence of a possible skills gap, which could consequently lead to an eventual resistance to change and hesitation by employees by fear of the unknown [13]. At this integration level, trust in AI is conditional and dependent on human oversight and social validation (see the framework for AI socialisation by [48]).

In the second quadrant [13], and from an organisational perspective, *Anticipatory AI* is seen as a tool, being an instrument that increases human capabilities and a robust extension of human decision-making; it leads to a reduction of manual errors and contributes to operational efficiency by automating routine tasks. The supply chain partners increasingly trust these AI systems and see them as augmentative applications, namely in the domain of data analysis [4]; from the perspective of employees, fear arises that the integration of such AI applications could lead to job displacement as a consequence of automation of specific procedures, e.g. those that involve data analysis or planning [13]. Trust here is situational and performance-based because it grows as AI consistently delivers reliable insights but remains fragile in the face of system errors or a lack of explainability.

In the third quadrant [13], and from an organisational perspective, *Supervisory AI* is seen as a partner, being a collaborator that works synergistically alongside humans and having shared responsibilities; consequently, the decision quality is improved when compared to non-AI-assisted decisions. There is now a high level of trust in AI amongst supply chain partners, who use these systems in a logic of Human-AI collaboration [4]. At the individual level, there could be both the risk of AI overreliance by human decision-makers and the risk of distrust and resistance by employees, who might feel overly monitored or unfairly treated [13]. At this point, trust becomes a dynamic construct, conditioned by human–machine calibration [49], AI system transparency, and perceived fairness in decision-making processes.

In the fourth quadrant [13], and from an organisational perspective, *Prescriptive AI* is seen as an actor, with autonomy for decision-making and with active participation in CSCM; due to its agency, this archetype might provoke changes in inter and intra-organisational roles and responsibilities. The supply chain partners have the highest trust in these AI systems as they work together to execute collaborative activities [4]. However, the agency of the *Prescriptive AI* systems leads to challenges regarding accountability and control, especially when hurtful decisions are made that can have severe financial and human impacts; AI governance mechanisms must be put in place to prevent such outcomes [13, 15]. In this context, trust must be institutionalised through AI governance frameworks, third-party validation, and shared ethical standards embedded into system design.

5.1 The Supply Chain as a Hybrid Human-Artificial Actors Network

The four AI archetypes, as mapped along the AI integration levels and collaboration dimensions, demonstrate how AI restructures CSCM functionally and relationally, by changing how decisions are made, who holds agency, and what forms of trust arise. To understand these changes holistically, one could frame them within the broader concept of a Hybrid Human-Artificial Actor (HHAA) network. Such networks are composed of human and artificial agents, each contributing different capabilities to decision-making, coordination, and adaptation: human actors bring contextual knowledge, negotiation skills, or ethical reasoning; artificial actors (e.g., AI systems) offer speed, scalability, and pattern recognition.

The levels of AI integration outlined before can be interpreted as stages in the evolution of HHAA networks: as supply chains move from *Reflexive* to *Prescriptive AI* archetypes, collaboration moves along a spectrum composed of partial AI integration and human-dominated coordination (Human Actors Network), full integration of AI (Hybrid Human Actors Network), and ever-more machine-mediated cooperation (Hybrid Human-Artificial Actors Network), and that entails redefinitions of governance, accountability, and shared purpose. In this context, CSCM moves past isolated transactions and reaches a phase of distributed cognition and collaborative sensemaking between human and artificial actors. Reflexive and Anticipatory AI archetypes are meant to assist human decision-makers (Human Actors), whereas Supervisory AI is inserted in a scenario of higher integration in which humans ultimately stay in the loop and can override system decisions (Hybrid Actors), and Prescriptive AI introduces more generalized decision-making autonomy in a full integration scenario (Artificial Actors). Nevertheless, the question of whether or not to have humans in the loop depends on the decision context, as humans might be out of some loops e.g. in lower risk and high reward scenario loops, but there are other loops in which human involvement is still necessary up to this day (as a decision-maker or as an overseer) [50]. These changes take place as AI technologies evolve and acquire new capabilities and challenge the assumption that human-out-of-the-loop scenarios must be avoided; in certain cases, keeping humans in the loop unnecessarily can introduce lag and thus decrease agility and responsiveness [50]. As [50] put it, when learning to ride a bicycle, it is prudent to use training wheels (humans-in-the-loop), but it is as important to envision the day in which the training wheels can be safely removed (humans-out-of-the-loop).

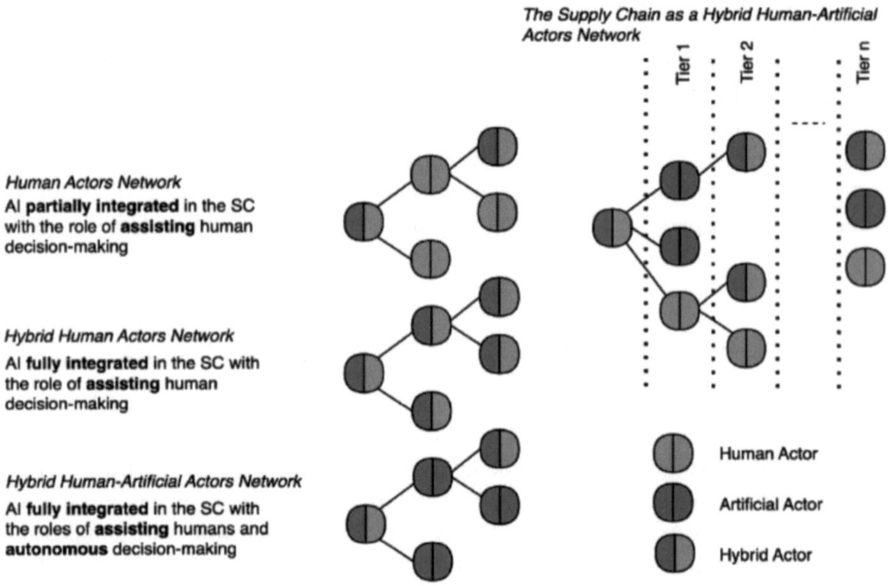

Fig. 2. Levels of AI integration in different types of Actor networks (Source: own elaboration)

As illustrated in Fig. 2, fully integrated HHAA networks converge the complementary strengths of humans and AI. In some cases, artificial actors might communicate or work alongside hybrid or human actors, creating a context of humans-in-the-loop (artificial actor – human/hybrid actor), and in other cases communicate and work with other artificial actors in a context of humans-out-of-a-specific-loop (artificial actor – artificial actor). When designed with attention to trust, transparency, and collaboration, such networks hold the potential to positively impact resilience, adaptability, and collective performance in complex collaborative supply chain environments (e.g. via supply chain Data Spaces initiatives [51]).

Table 3 summarises the points discussed in this section.

Table 3. Impact of different AI archetypes and integration levels in CSCM dimensions (Source: own elaboration)

AI Archetype	Level of AI Integration	Information Sharing	Collaborative Decision-Making	Trust	Type of Actor
Reflexive	Human Sherlock, Robot Watson	Episodic, Bilateral, Reactive	Collaborative augmentation	Depends on human oversight and social validation	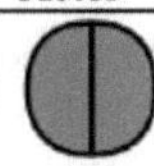
Anticipatory	Robot Cartographer	Systematic, Frequent	Proactive collaboration	Situational, Performance-based	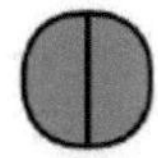
Supervisory	Chess Grandmaster	Continuous, Bidirectional, Responsive	Hybrid governance	Dynamic, depending on Human-Machine Calibration, Transparency and Fairness	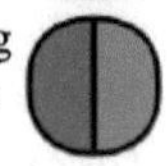
Prescriptive	Artificial Ecosystem	Real-time, Machine-to-Machine, Ecosystem-wide	Machine-to-Machine	System-level	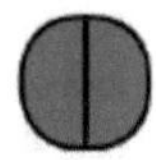

6 Conclusions and Future Work

This paper presents an investigation of how different types of AI (*Reflexive*, *Anticipatory*, *Supervisory*, and *Prescriptive*) could be integrated in CSCM practices and how they impact collaboration dimensions, including information sharing, collaborative decision-making, and trust. Through a sociotechnical lens, the paper suggests a mapping of the archetypes along four levels of AI integration and interprets how AI systems progress from decision-support tools to autonomous agents in collaborative supply chain networks, introducing the idea of HHAA networks.

The main contributions of this paper are the reusable conceptual frameworks that synthesise existing academic literature, categorise AI's collaborative role in CSCM and introduce the concept of HHAA networks in supply chains, which supports researchers and practitioners assessing the alignment between AI capabilities and CSCM needs; the frameworks demonstrate how different types of AI systems could support CSCM activities and their impact on inter-organisational coordination mechanisms and relational dynamics. Moreover, the frameworks contribute to developing more human-centred, resilient and sustainable collaborative supply chains towards Industry 5.0, in which AI-based actors will be increasingly integrated with gradually higher levels of agency.

Future research could explore more applications of AI for CSCM (Table 2), namely regarding the less represented archetypes (*Supervisory* and *Prescriptive*), and expand the framework on the impact of AI archetypes (Table 2) to include other CSCM dimensions not analysed. Finally, HHAA networks highlight the interconnectedness and interdependence of human and artificial elements within complex socio-technical systems.

Understanding and analysing these networks can provide insights into how AI and human agency interact to shape behaviours, outcomes, and socio-technical transformations. Therefore, a further exploration of HHAA networks (e.g. nodes properties, inter-actor relationships, properties of meta-level HHAA networks) would encourage cooperation across organisational borders and contribute to building trust among the highly fragmented stakeholders within the supply chain (Fig. 2).

Acknowledgements. This work is co-financed by Component 5 – Capitalization and Business Innovation of core funding for Technology and Innovation Centres (CTI), integrated in the Resilience Dimension of the Recovery and Resilience Plan within the scope of the Recovery and Resilience Mechanism (MRR) of the European Union (EU), framed in the Next Generation EU, for the period 2021 – 2026, with reference 21.

References

1. Schmidt, L., Pehlke, M., Jansen, M.: Ai-enhanced qoc-analysis: a framework for transparent and insightful decision-making. In: Working Conference on Virtual Enterprises, Springer (2024)
2. Soares, L., Gomes Jr, J., Zimmermann, R., Rhodes, D., Dorner, V.: Integrating AI in supply chain management: using a socio-technical chart to navigate unknown transformations. In: Working Conference on Virtual Enterprises. Springer (2024)
3. Nitsche, A.-M., Franczyk, B., Schumann, C.-A., Reuther, K.: A decade of artificial intelligence for supply chain collaboration: Past, present, and future research agenda. Logist. Res. **17**(1) (2024)
4. Weisz, E., Herold, D.M., Ostern, N.K., Payne, R., Kummer, S.: Artificial intelligence (ai) for supply chain collaboration: implications on information sharing and trust. Online Inform. Rev. **49**(1) (2024)
5. Zamani, E.D., Smyth, C., Gupta, S., Dennehy, D.: Artificial intelligence and big data analytics for supply chain resilience: a systematic literature review. Ann. Operat. Res. **327**(2) (2023)
6. Duan, Y., Edwards, J.S., Dwivedi, Y.K.: Artificial intelligence for decision making in the era of big data–evolution, challenges and research agenda. Int. J. Inform. Manage. **48** (2019)
7. Attaran, M., Attaran, S.: Collaborative supply chain management: the most promising practice for building efficient and sustainable supply chains. Bus. Process Manag. J. **13**(3) (2007)
8. Bititci, U.S., Martinez, V., Albores, P., Parung, J.: Creating and managing value in collaborative networks. Int. J. Phys. Distribut. Logist. Manage. **34**(3/4) (2004)
9. Latino, M.E.: A maturity model for assessing the implementation of industry 5.0 in manufacturing SMES: learning from theory and practice. Technol. Forecast. Soc. Change **214** (2025)
10. Korte, P., Kobert, M., Süße, T.: Digital leadership from the perspective of organization 5.0: an analysis of key action fields towards green, resilient, and human-centered digitalization. In: Working Conference on Virtual Enterprises. Springer (2024)
11. Carminati, L., Pirola, F., Lagorio, A., Cimini, C., Jurczuk, A., Boucher, X.: Skills, technical and organizational support needed for collaborative networks 5.0. In: Working Conference on Virtual Enterprises. Springer (2024)
12. Phuengrod, S., Wannapiroon, P., Nilsook, P.: Intelligent collaborative supply chain management (ICSCM). In: IEEE International Conference on Cybernetics and Innovations (ICCI). IEEE (2024)

13. Hendriksen, C.: Artificial intelligence for supply chain management: disruptive innovation or innovative disruption? J. Supply Chain Manag. **59**(3) (2023)
14. Herrmann, T., Pfeiffer, S.: Keeping the organization in the loop: a socio-technical extension of human-centered artificial intelligence. Ai Soc. **38**(4) (2023)
15. Baird, A., Maruping, L.M.: The next generation of research on is use: A theoretical framework of delegation to and from agentic is artifacts. MIS Quart. **45**(1) (2021)
16. Strunk, J.A., Banh, L., Nissen, A., Strobel, G., Smolnik, S.: To delegate or not to delegate? factors influencing human-agentic is interaction. In: ICIS 2024 Proceedings, Association for Information Systems (2024)
17. Muckstadt, J.A., Murray, D.H., Rappold, J.A., Collins, D.E.: Guidelines for collaborative supply chain system design and operation. Inform. Syst. Front. **3** (2001)
18. Cronin, P., Ryan, F., Coughlan, M.: Undertaking a literature review: a step-by-step approach. British J. Nurs. **17**(1) (2008)
19. Boell, S.K., Cecez-Kecmanovic, D.: On being 'systematic' in literature reviews in is. J. Inform. Technol. **30**(2) (2015)
20. Baltà-Salvador, R., El-Madafri, I., Brasó-Vives, E., Peña, M.: Empowering engineering students through artificial intelligence (AI): blended human–AI creative ideation processes with chatgpt. Comput. Applicat. Eng. Educ. **33**(1) (2025)
21. Pérez-Perales, D., Boza, A., Alarcón, F., Gómez-Gasquet, P.: Mathematical programming-based methodology for the evaluation of supply chain collaborative planning scenarios. Ann. Operat. Res. **337**(1) (2024)
22. Niemsakul, J., Islam, S., Singkarin, D., Somboonwiwat, T.: Cost-benefit sharing in healthcare supply chain collaboration. Int. J. Logist. Syst. Manage. **30** (2018)
23. Mielcarek, P., Piekarczyk, A.: Synchronized scheduling and order processing as the leverage of digital supply chain transformation process. Manage. Product. Eng. Rev. **15**(4) (2024)
24. Esteso, A., Alemany, M., ´Ortiz, A., Lezoche, M.: Collaborative optimization tool for sustainable planning of an agricultural supply chain preserving farmers' independence. In: Working Conference on Virtual Enterprises. Springer (2022)
25. Khan, R.S., Sirazy, M.R.M., Das, R., Rahman, S.: An AI and ml-enabled framework for proactive risk mitigation and resilience optimization in global supply chains during national emergencies. Sage Sci. Rev. Appl. Mach. Learn. **5**(2) (2022)
26. Wang, D., Yu, A.: Supply chain resources and economic security based on artificial intelligence and blockchain multi-channel technology. Int. J. Inform. Technol. Syst. Approach **16**(3) (2023)
27. Ahmed, W., Khan, M.A., Najmi, A., Khan, S.A.: Strategizing risk information sharing framework among supply chain partners for financial performance. Supply Chain Forum: An Int. J. **24** (2023)
28. Moghadam, F.S., Zarandi, M.F.: Mitigating bullwhip effect in an agent-based supply chain through a fuzzy reverse ultimatum game negotiation module. Appl. Soft Comput. **116** (2022)
29. Richey Jr, R.G., Chowdhury, S., Davis-Sramek, B., Giannakis, M., Dwivedi, Y.K.: Artificial intelligence in logistics and supply chain management: a primer and roadmap for research (2023)
30. Modgil, S., Singh, R.K., Hannibal, C.: Artificial intelligence for supply chain resilience: learning from covid-19. Int. J. Logist. Manage. **33**(4) (2022)
31. Lehoux, N., D'Amours, S., Langevin, A.: Inter-firm collaborations and supply chain coordination: review of key elements and case study. Product. Plann. Control **25**(10) (2014)
32. Gerrits, B., van Heeswijk, W., Mes, M.: Towards self-organizing logistics in transportation: a literature review and typology. Int. Transact. Operat. Res. **31**(3) (2024)
33. Simatupang, T.M., Sridharan, R.: The collaborative supply chain. Int. J. Logist. Manage. **13**(1) (2002)

34. Pedreschi, D., et al.: Human-AI coevolution. Artificial Intelligence (2024)
35. Gomez, C., Cho, S.M., Ke, S., Huang, C.-M., Unberath, M.: Human-AI collaboration is not very collaborative yet: a taxonomy of interaction patterns in AI-assisted decision making from a systematic review. Front. Comput. Sci. **6** (2025)
36. Tessler, M.H., et al.: Ai can help humans find common ground in democratic deliberation. Science **386**(6719) (2024)
37. Karacapilidis, N., Papadias, D.: Computer supported argumentation and collaborative decision making: the hermes system. Inform. Syst. **26**(4) (2001)
38. Chiang, C.-W., Lu, Z., Li, Z., Yin, M.: Are two heads better than one in ai- assisted decision making? comparing the behavior and performance of groups and individuals in human-AI collaborative recidivism risk assessment. In: Proceedings of the 2023 CHI Conference on Human Factors in Computing Systems (2023)
39. Grønsund, T., Aanestad, M.: Augmenting the algorithm: Emerging human-in-the-loop work configurations. J. Strateg. Inform. Syst. **29**(2) (2020)
40. Chong, L., Zhang, G., Goucher-Lambert, K., Kotovsky, K., Cagan, J.: Human confidence in artificial intelligence and in themselves: the evolution and impact of confidence on adoption of AI advice. Comput. Hum. Behav. **127** (2022)
41. Lima, G., Grgić-Hlača, N., Cha, M.: Human perceptions on moral responsibility of AI: A case study in AI-assisted bail decision-making. In: Proceedings of the 2021 CHI Conference on Human Factors in Computing Systems (2021)
42. Kuziemski, M., Misuraca, G.: AI governance in the public sector: three tales from the frontiers of automated decision-making in democratic settings. Telecommun. Policy **44**(6) (2020)
43. Tamò-Larrieux, A.: Decision-making by machines: Is the 'law of everything' enough? Comput. Law Secur. Rev. **41** (2021)
44. Ren, M., Chen, N., Qiu, H.: Human-machine collaborative decision-making: an evolutionary roadmap based on cognitive intelligence. Int. J. Soc. Robot. **15**(7) (2023)
45. Maas, J.: Machine learning and power relations. AI & Soc. **38**(4) (2023)
46. Rahwan, I.: Society-in-the-loop: programming the algorithmic social contract. Ethics Inform. Technol. **20**(1), 5–14 (2017)
47. Scholz, L.H.: Algorithmic contracts. Stan. Tech. L. Rev. **20** (2017)
48. Makarius, E.E., Mukherjee, D., Fox, J.D., Fox, A.K.: Rising with the machines: a sociotechnical framework for bringing artificial intelligence into the organization. J. Bus. Res. **120** (2020)
49. Wang, Y., Guo, J., Zeng, S., Mao, Q., Lu, Z., Wang, Z.: Human-machine trust and calibration based on human-in-the-loop experiment. In: 4th International Conference on System Reliability and Safety Engineering (SRSE). IEEE (2022)
50. Muyskens, K., Ma, Y., Menikoff, J., Hallinan, J., Savulescu, J.: When can we kick (some) humans "out of the loop"? an examination of the use of AI in medical imaging for lumbar spinal stenosis. Asian Bioethics Rev. **17**(1) (2025)
51. Padberg, J.: Catena-x's contribution to sustainability in the automotive supply chain. In: International Conference on Drives and Energy Systems of Tomorrow, pp. 141–154. Springer (2025)

A Conceptual Framework to Design Patterns of Horizontal Collaboration in Co-opetitive Logistics Partnerships

Leandro Carvalho[1,2](✉), Jorge Freire de Sousa[1,2], and Jorge Pinho de Sousa[1,2]

[1] Faculdade de Engenharia da Universidade do Porto, Porto, Portugal
leandromec@yahoo.com.br, jfsousa@fe.up.pt,
jorge.p.sousa@inesctec.pt

[2] INESC TEC, Porto, Portugal

Abstract. Despite the recognised potential of horizontal collaboration in logistics to reduce inefficiencies, and the increasing academic interest in this topic, in practice many initiatives fail. One of the main reasons for this failure is the poor strategy planning and governance organisation. This paper addresses this gap proposing a comprehensive conceptual framework to support the design and implementation of a common strategy for the stakeholders of such partnerships. The research employs qualitative methods, drawing on interviews and the case analysis of existent initiatives. The proposed framework involves the main phases of the strategic formulation, deciding the stakeholder engagement, strategic formulation, operational implementation, and business model elaboration. It serves as a road map for stakeholders to avoid common mistakes and accelerate the deployment of cooperative partnerships.

Keywords: Horizontal collaboration · co-opetition · business models · logistics · governance · conceptual frameworks

1 Introduction

Logistics is an essential activity not only for ensuring product availability and affordability, but also for fostering economic growth, job creation, regional development, and social inclusion. However, logistic activities also generate significant negative impacts on society and the environment, including greenhouse gas emissions, visual pollution, accidents, traffic congestion, and high energy consumption. These negative impacts or externalities are often exacerbated by inefficient planning, often leading to freight vehicles operating empty or only partially loaded.

Horizontal collaboration arises in logistics as an alternative to reduce these inefficiencies through strategic alliances between companies that share common activities within the same leg of the transport, by sharing resources, infrastructure, or even purchase orders [1], differing from vertical collaboration where partners operate in complementary stages of a service provision. Literature on this subject suggests that collaborative models have

Published by Springer Nature Switzerland AG 2026
L. M. Camarinha-Matos et al. (Eds.): PRO-VE 2025, IFIP AICT 770, pp. 201–217, 2026.
https://doi.org/10.1007/978-3-032-05673-3_13

the potential for companies to reduce costs, expand markets, increase load factors, and enhance customer services [2]. Additionally, reducing inefficiencies in the transport of goods, these partnerships can reduce externalities benefiting cities, the society in general and the environment [3].

But, although there is considerable and increasing research on this field reinforcing the benefits of horizontal collaboration in logistics [4], several of these initiatives fail in the early stages, especially those fostered by external sponsors [5]. Planning and governance problems, including inadequate process management, unclear role definition, and poor monitoring mechanisms [2, 6, 7], lead to wasted energy and resources when a partnership collapses, often in its early stages, and discourage companies from engaging in new ventures. When participating companies are competitors (a scenario referred to as co-opetition), the management and governance of the partnerships are even more demanding, especially when it comes to building trust among participants and managing the exchange of sensitive information.

To tackle these issues, this work first seeks to identify the critical measurable and non-measurable factors that influence the success of these types of partnerships. Moreover, it aims to provide a guide to support the design of horizontal collaboration initiatives, preventing companies from repeating past mistakes. For this purpose, the paper proposes a conceptual framework organized in 4 phases, to define and organize patterns of horizontal collaboration in logistics. The main outcome of the framework will be a business model, to guide companies in transforming strategy into logistic activities.

The research methodology consists of a literature review, semi-structured interviews with urban logistics experts (both academics and practitioners), and case studies examining partnerships in real-world contexts. These methods helped us to deepen conceptual understanding, revisit assumptions, and yield new insights on the subject. Ultimately, the proposed framework will be partially validated through the analysis of the real-world case studies, demonstrating its applicability and relevance in practical settings.

The paper is organized as follows: Sect. 2 contextualizes co-opetition in horizontal collaboration in logistics; Sect. 3 describes the main inputs of the interviews for the framework; Sect. 4 presents the proposed conceptual framework; Sect. 5 applies the framework in the case studies; and Sect. 6 presents the contributions and conclusions of this work.

2 Co-opetition in Logistics Horizontal Collaborations

Managing horizontal collaborations is considerably more complex than managing vertical relationships, particularly when the participating firms are competitors [8]. Traditionally, companies have focused on developing competitive advantages over rivals. In co-opetitive partnerships, firms collaborate to create value, while simultaneously competing on how to share the resulting gains, a mindset that contrasts with conventional strategies aimed at market dominance. Shifting from the traditional thinking to this hybrid approach presents significant challenges for managers. However, once these barriers are overcome, numerous benefits emerge.

Through co-opetition companies can share assets and fleet utilization, avoiding empty backhauls or at least increasing load factors. In an economic perspective this may result in economies of scale, lowering variable costs (fuel, freight) and operating expenses. Co-opetition can boost overall chain profitability, creating win-win relationships.

Operationally, co-opetition can enhance vehicle and warehouse utilization by reducing empty miles and lowering the cost per unit shipped. It also mitigates the operational risks associated with transport.

Considering the strategic perspective, co-opetition stimulates joint innovation and development cooperation since it reduces innovation risks. Likewise, it fosters knowledge and best practices exchange. It also creates opportunities for market expansion and customer service improvement.

Moreover, as sustainability becomes a strategic priority, companies are increasingly addressing the social and environmental impacts of their operations. Objectives and key performance indicators (KPIs) related to transport externalities are being integrated into strategic planning, with companies publishing sustainability reports that include actions aimed at improving their social and environmental performance. Co-opetition offers a feasible approach to reducing CO_2 emissions, lowering energy consumption, and promoting joint green practices.

Nevertheless, co-opetition based initiatives can fail for a variety of reasons. Changes in the external environment may diminish the benefits for one or more partners. Moreover, agreements are often terminated when any participant perceives the allocation of costs or benefits as inequitable.

In some cases, companies coordinate their actions for their mutual benefit to the detriment of consumers, with partnerships that can be characterized as collusions [9], approaching the threshold of cartel formation or monopoly (sanctioned under applicable regional and international legislation).

However, the co-opetition literature suggests that one of the primary reasons such initiatives are discontinued, or never implemented, is the lack of trust among the parties involved [10–12].

Organizational trust tends to be substantially lower in horizontal alliances than in vertical ones [11]. The paradox of simultaneously competing and cooperating with other firms generates tensions among participants. Such tensions arise from various factors, including uncertainty regarding a competitor's intentions and the fear of opportunistic behaviour [13].

Therefore, companies that intend to engage in a horizontal collaboration initiative must plan how to prepare their employees for the resulting tensions and foster an environment of trust with their partners. [14] suggests that, prior to launching any collaboration, it is essential to ensure strategic alignment among all participating firms. [15] further argues that appropriate governance mechanisms must be implemented to prevent conflicts and deter opportunistic behaviour, thereby building trust. The development of formal procedures and regulations within co-opetition initiatives helps reduce tensions and strengthen trust.

To operationalize governance in co-opetitive partnerships, many consortia appoint a 'trusted intermediary', for example, a liability-limited company (LLC), to mediate responsibilities and objectives [3]. Employing a trusted external intermediary can further enhance confidence among collaborating partners [16]. Third-party not-for-profit organizations help bridge gaps between competitors, ease tensions, and shift firms' agendas beyond immediate economic gains, to include social and environmental objectives [17].

[18] highlight the importance of firms realigning their strategies and reconfiguring their internal processes to engage in co-opetition. It is necessary to embed collaboration into the "architecture" of the firm through co-opetitive business models that both create and capture value [19]. [8] argue that firms should evaluate the strategic opportunities afforded by co-opetition by comparing the alternative outcomes of participating in such partnerships versus remaining independent.

This study proposes a methodology for companies to adapt their strategies and internal processes to participate in co-opetitive horizontal collaborations through the analysis of their business models.

3 Research Methodology

This qualitative study is exploratory in nature, due to the limited availability of robust literature on governance and business models in co-opetitive horizontal collaborations within logistics. To address this gap, interviews were conducted with experts from both academia and industry. These interviews enriched the conceptual foundation of the research and revealed key practical challenges faced in real-world applications.

As part of a qualitative inquiry, interviews were employed not merely as a data-collection method but as a knowledge-construction process [20]. Whereas structured interviews aim to capture precise, codifiable data and unstructured interviews seek to explore phenomena without any pre-existing categorization [21], this study opted for a semi-structured format [22], employing predefined themes while giving respondents the flexibility to elaborate on the topics under discussion.

We conducted 11 semi-structured interviews (30/60 minutes) with academics and practitioners across Europe, South America, and Asia, exploring drivers, barriers, and enablers of horizontal collaboration.

3.1 Insights from Interviews

The insights from interviews can be organized through four main themes, presented in Table 1 below: (1) enabling mechanisms; (2) value drivers; (3) barriers, and (4) strategic orientation. A deepen discussion about these themes was used as basis for the framework crafting. The last column of the table shows how these inputs are correlated to the framework (the phases of the framework presented here will be duly explained later in the paper).

Theme 1 – Enabling Mechanisms. Most interviewees argue that governments and public entities can have an important role in enhancing collaboration, through incentives or regulations. However, one researcher warns that the public sector should contribute as a regulator in the process and not be the main actor. Suggestions also included low-emission zones or time windows that favour consolidated deliveries (e.g., dedicated lanes, priority parking for joint carriers). In parallel, authorities could penalize companies refusing to collaborate (higher fees or bans). Crucially, many argued that if society gains (less congestion or pollution) while companies incur costs (double handling, new hubs), then financial support or subsidies are justified.

Most respondents also referred the need of a third party to manage the collaboration. They highlight the importance of a neutral element to foster trust between participants, manage operations in a fair way and equally distribute the gains and costs of the partnership. Companies often waste trust by launching full-scale networks that fail. Instead, pilots run by universities or industry consortia can demonstrate benefits in a low-risk setting. Interviewees recommended starting small experiences (by, for example, sharing one vehicle or distribution route) and expanding these experiences if they are successful.

Theme 2 – Value Drivers. There is a consensus between interviewers that horizontal collaboration can benefit the environment and the society, reducing the externalities of logistic activities. They noted dramatic cuts in vehicles, emissions and congestion when firms share deliveries. Reduction of emissions is the positive aspect most mentioned, revealing that improvement in the environmental footprint is an expected outcome. Moreover, interviewees highlighted fewer trucks on city streets and better use of parking and warehouse space under collaboration.

Nonetheless, economic sustainability leads to some concerns. Interviewees stressed that while the *system* (society) gains via higher efficiency and less pollution, the direct benefits of individual firms may decrease. One group argued that efficiency gains typically outweigh start-up costs, yielding net profit. Another pointed out that without subsidies or incentives, extra handling costs can make projects unprofitable for companies. These contrasting views underscore a trade-off: horizontal schemes boost overall sustainability, but companies are worried about their share of the costs. As one respondent remarks, while society is clearly benefited, companies are faced with the main challenges.

Table 1. Interviews summary

THEMES	MAIN INSIGHTS	CONTRIBUTION FOR FRAMEWORK
1 – ENABLING MECHANISMS	- Enablers & Incentives - Role of Third Parties	- Phase 1 (Stakeholders Engagement) - Phase 3 (Operational Planning)
2 – VALUE DRIVERS	- Sustainability Impacts - Economic Benefits & Trade-offs	- Phase 2 (Strategy Formulation)
3 - BARRIERS	- Operational & Structural Barriers - Cultural Barriers (Trust & Data Sharing)	- Phase 1 (Stakeholder Engagement) - Phase 3 (Operational Planning)
4 – STRATEGIC ORIENTATION	- Strategic Implications - Co-opetition mindset - Leadership	- Phase 2 (Strategy Formulation) - Phase 4 (Design of the Business Model)

Even though, interviewees enumerate a set of benefits companies may have in these partnerships such as fuller vehicles cutting transport costs, higher service quality, geographic reach, economies of scale, and access to new clients. For example, experts noted that collaboration is especially natural when expensive assets (such as airplanes or containers in ships) can be pooled, since cost savings justify the effort. They also observed "circular" effects: shared use prolongs asset life and reduces waste. Some pointed to reduced manpower costs (fewer trips imply less driver labour) and faster innovation through joint business cases.

Theme 3 – Barriers. The general perception is that horizontal collaboration has a huge potential for global benefits, however, for several reasons projects did not last after the trial phases, and some of them have not even started. Experts mentioned numerous practical obstacles. A frequent theme was the existence of mismatched operations: collaborating firms typically have different schedules, parcel sizes and IT systems. Likewise, highly customised fleets (built around specific products or customers) leave little spare capacity to share. Some billing methods also prevent pooling: most carriers charge per kilometre, so sharing routes would cut their billed distance, leading them to "lose money if they are not running with their [own] cars". Additionally, companies often cannot easily quantify the payoff. In particular, small and medium firms lack sophisticated models to simulate a shared network, so they hesitate to invest without guaranteed return. Some companies also express concern that close collaboration may violate competition laws, particularly regarding the risk of forming cartels or monopolistic structures.

However, mistrust emerges as the most frequently mentioned and decisive barrier to successful horizontal collaboration. Interviews argue that a legacy of "information is power," where companies accumulate data and view rivals with suspicion. This leads to confusion over confidentiality: one interviewee said firms "don't know how to differentiate open from classified information," so by default they share nothing. One expert contrasted this with theory: under transactional-cost logic, firms avoid partnerships (opportunism dominates), but in a network paradigm we need to change people's mindset towards shared value.

Theme 4 – Strategic orientation. Experts agree that implementing co-opetitive collaboration requires a fundamental strategic shift. Most emphasized reframing competition as expanding the pie rather than fighting over the slices. One interviewee explained that companies must see that collectively growing the market (the "big pie") and then sharing it, is easier than slugging it out for a piece of a limited market. They suggest it could be useful to generate scenarios or make simulations to show companies the long-term benefits of cooperation (increased profits and market share) versus the "business-as-usual" fight. A closely related issue was the call for strong leadership and governance: firms must decide who governs the collaboration (a manager, board or trustee), what the rules are, and how decisions are made. This reflects the earlier referred point on third parties, but here focused on competitive strategy. Several interviewees also referred to the internal company culture: CEOs and boards must visibly endorse collaboration and align incentives across departments.

4 The Framework

A framework provides the foundational structure for developing an idea, concept, or system and serves as a powerful tool for understanding complex phenomena. In this study, we apply established theories to real-world initiatives, using a 4 phases framework to encompass the core attributes of horizontal collaboration, see Figure 1.

The first three phases of the framework cover the key decisions stakeholders make when organizing the partnership. The fourth phase examines how the partnership established in the preceding phases influences the companies' strategies and how their activities should be reconfigured through the development of a tailored business model. As a central element of the framework, this business model must be adapted to the specific features of the logistics processes. The framework also implies some iterative feedback where the partners agree on formal checkpoints, each combining a concrete milestone and an associated KPI, to validate progress before moving on.

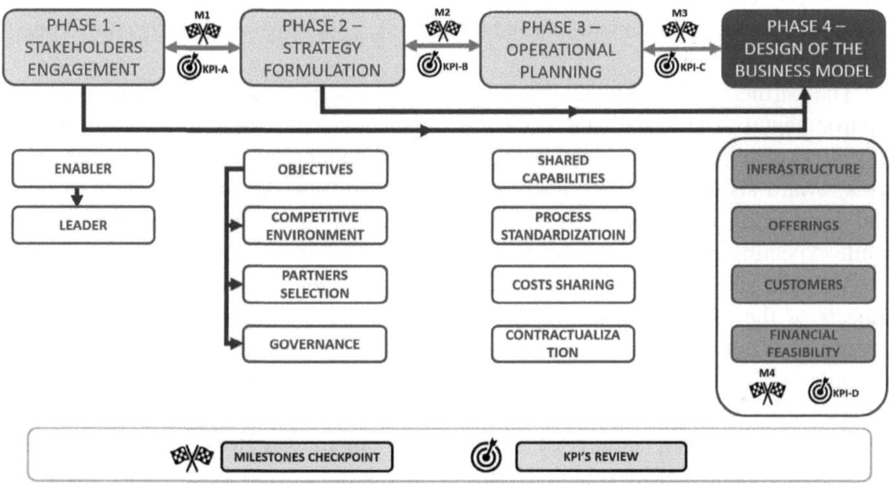

Fig. 1. Framework for horizontal collaboration in logistics

Phase 1 – Stakeholder Engagement. In the logistics context, stakeholders comprise both the actors directly engaged in operations and those indirectly impacted by supply chain activities. In this research we will consider five groups of stakeholders in logistic activities: (1) Shippers; (2) Receivers; (3) Logistic Service Providers, (4) Governments and Regulatory Authorities, and (5) Citizens/Tourists. The different ways in which each stakeholder responds to the impacts of urban logistics give rise to distinct sets of preferences and expectations. This multiplicity of interests often leads to tensions in stakeholder relationships and the most effective way to minimize these tensions is through stakeholder participation in the development of the initiatives. The stakeholder roles, expectations, and needs must be defined from the beginning, with regular co-design meetings to ensure alignment. As many interviewers noted, collaboration often fails because roles and incentives are unclear and, as a result, companies mistrust each other.

The choice of a partnership enabler significantly shapes the collaboration from start to finish. [5] argue that public-sector–sponsored systematic horizontal logistics collaborations (SHLCs) are more prone to failure than privately initiated horizontal logistics collaborations (HLCs), due to factors such as poor cost-benefit communication, inadequate shipper pooling, enabler-induced decoupling, selection errors, and conflicting sponsor/facilitator/shipper goals.

At this stage, the governance model for the collaboration is drafted, including the appointment of a leader responsible for overseeing the partnership. In simpler arrangements, such as backhauling, the shippers or receivers themselves may manage the collaboration, others may be led by the logistic operator. However, in more complex setups involving extensive sharing of assets and information, both interviews and case studies highlight the critical importance of management by a third party.

Phase 2 – Strategy Formulation. To maximize the likelihood of success, strategic alignment among partners must be secured at the project's inception. In this initial phase, it is advisable to define a shared vision and mission to establish a common language around the partnership's intentions and aspirations, with the overall partnership strategy being then co-created.

The partnership's strategic objectives can be categorized as economic, social, or environmental. The initiative's enabler strongly influences the prioritization of these objectives. Government or state-owned sponsored collaborations typically steer objectives toward social and environmental outcomes, shifting the focus away from financial results. Conversely, privately initiated partnerships prioritize economic performance while expecting externalities reduction as an important complementary benefit.

The next step is the evaluation of the competitive environment. One of the defining aspects of the partnership's development is deciding if the partnership will be "co-opetitive" or not. The literature review and experts emphasize that establishing a shared vision and a co-opetitive mindset presents significant hurdles. Moreover, companies must evaluate scenarios across the local economy (fuel costs, freight rates, city centre mobility fees), society, technology, and the environment. It is also crucial to understand the specific features of logistic deliveries in the region, as well as the rivals' behaviour and market power. Experts further highlighted the importance of examining relevant regulations, especially those governing competition and antitrust laws.

Stakeholders then must establish clear rules for partner selection. Determining the number of participants is critical in shaping operational complexity. Some types of horizontal-collaboration initiatives require a limited number of partners. Furthermore, partners should be chosen based on the benefits and opportunities they bring, balanced against the costs and risks of their inclusion. It is also necessary to establish in the contract the rules for entering and exiting the partnership.

There are many aspects that must be considered in terms of governance. The first is whether or not to appoint a trustee, or third party. This entity will manage sensitive information and organize the operationalization of the partnership, as well as assess potential power asymmetries and create balancing mechanisms. The trustee may be an external company, or a hybrid body drawn from the management structures of the participating companies, such as a joint board of directors. Furthermore, the governance model can be centralised, with the trustee making all decisions, or decentralised, with companies participating in decision-making processes either by consensus or by majority voting. It should be the decision-maker's responsibility to define ownership of the facilities and equipment, designate who monitors performance, determine who manages day-to-day operations, and establish how the partner interface with customers will work. Finally, this body plays the fundamental role of proposing how benefits and costs will be shared.

Phase 3 – Operational Planning. This phase operationalizes the collaboration. Although it follows strategic planning, practical insights gained during execution may prompt a strategic review.

The "shared capabilities" component of this phase captures the tangible and intangible assets that partners agree to pool: vehicles, warehouses, handling equipment, IT platforms, and skilled personnel. Interviews repeatedly flagged "operational incompatibility" as a barrier, as firms often bring differently configured fleets or siloed IT systems, and therefore mapping and harmonizing these capabilities up front is vital. Partners will decide which digital enablers will be used such as data sharing platforms, route optimization software, internet of things for real time tracking, blockchain for transparency and dashboards monitoring. Nonetheless, it is necessary to document each partner's asset specifications (truck types, load capacities, warehouse availability), creating a transparent inventory that underpins all downstream planning.

Process standardization involves defining and harmonizing the workflows, tasks, and hand-offs that each partner will perform in the collaboration. It involves organising operations, predicting difficulties and building trust between participants. The stakeholders will define the scope of standardisation (packages sizes, electronic data interchange, route planning, order intake), the sequence in which each task occurs (for example: order – packaging – consolidation – transport – deliver), the responsible for each task, the quality metrics and control mechanisms, and the responsible for customer communication and corrective actions. Co-opetitive horizontal collaboration involves multiple departments within companies. Clearly predefined processes prevent unnecessary friction by ensuring that all stakeholders know exactly, for example, when consolidation will occur, the volume to be loaded, and the package dimensions.

Negotiating how costs and benefits are split was flagged by interviewees as one of the fiercest sticking points. One common mistake is focusing on social and environmental outcomes and not defining the financial impact for companies in the beginning of the partnership development. It is necessary to model scenarios using pilot data to test different allocation methods and then agree on a mechanism that all partners consider fair. The literature has extensively studied this aspect and offering several alternatives to fairly share savings and expenses through techniques such as proportional allocation, linear allocation and game theory approaches. This fairness is an essential step to booster trust between partners.

Finally, all the above agreements are bundled into contracts that specify entry/exit conditions, liability clauses, governance roles, data-sharing covenants, and antitrust safeguards. For some simple forms of collaboration, no formal contracts are required, and companies usually only need non-disclose agreements (NDA) to safeguard confidential information. However, interviewees stress that mere verbal agreements leave too much room for opportunistic behaviour. Ideally an external part, not necessarily the LLC, should suggest the conditions in the contract, which must be signed in consensus between partners. This will create legal scaffolding that enforces commitments, mitigates risk, and reassures all stakeholders.

Phase 4 – Design of the business model. The business model plays a central and integrative role by translating the strategic intent and operational plans into a coherent structure that governs how value is created, delivered, and captured within a horizontal collaboration initiative. In alignment with both the literature on horizontal collaboration and the insights gathered from interviews, this phase reflects a maturation point where decisions made in earlier phases are consolidated into a shared operational logic.

Strategic formulation must establish a common language that fosters intra- and inter-departmental dialogue, encourages employee commitment, and generates synergies in pursuit of a shared objective [23]. Although the business model is an outcome of the strategy, it does not, by itself, constitute the strategy [24]; while strategy articulates 'why' and 'what,' the business model details 'how' firms organize their activities to deliver on that strategy.

Thus, the business model is a strategic concept that helps to clarify and structure the organization's main activities for value creation. In other words, analysing a corporation's business model involves examining the underlying logic of the business and understanding how the strategy is deployed to achieve the desired outcomes.

[25] organize the business model into nine building blocks that span its four core domains: customers, value proposition, infrastructure, and financial viability. Since this seminal framework's inception, business-model architectures have evolved from designs founded on competitive advantage to those embracing horizontal collaboration and the co-opetitive creation and capture of value.

In this work, we adapt the Business Model Canvas proposed by the Straightsol project [26] for logistics initiatives, that adds to the traditional Osterwalder canvas a tenth building block, Externalities (see Fig. 2). This block more transparently captures the societal and environmental impacts of urban logistics within the value-creation framework. By situating "externalities" alongside "value propositions", the model forces firms to evaluate benefits and costs for all stakeholders, not just customers.

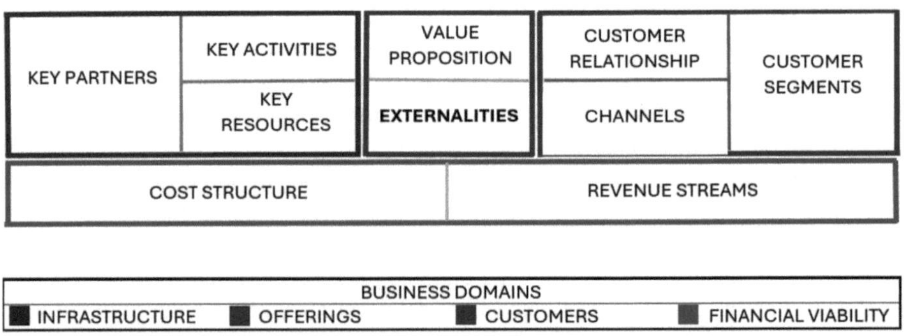

Fig. 2. Business model for logistics horizontal collaboration

Using this business model within our framework will enable us to understand how the core activities of the participating firms are organized and to assess whether their planning is coherent and robust. Moreover, by defining the key characteristics of a business model, one can compare the operations of different firms with distinct objectives and strategies. As [27] define, the business model can help measure, observe, and compare a firm's underlying business logic.

Variations in any of the aspects described in the previous 3 phases will directly or indirectly influence the final business model design. Stakeholder Engagement (Phase 1) is directly related to Key Partners. Strategy Formulation (Phase 2) feed into Value Propositions, Customer Segments, Customer relationship, Channels, and Externalities. Operational Planning (Phase 3) directly influences Key Activities, Key Resources, Cost Structure and Revenue Streams. In combination, decisions made in the phases 1 to 3 may create several different architectures of business models.

For example, an initiative created by a municipality (phase 1 – enablers) and led by a research group (phase 1) sustained by a centralized governance (Phase 2) usually focus on offerings related to externalities, considers citizens as main customers and use public structure as key resources, putting the financial viability for companies in second plan.

Or let us suppose the case of three automotive companies (phase 1 – enablers/leaders) creating a steering committee with rotating leadership (phase 2 – governance) in a pooling network (Phase 3 – shared capabilities) to cut freight costs by 15% through a 30% reduction in empty-truck miles (phase 2 – objectives). This partnership must focus on key resources (pooled fleet), key activities (coordinated routing, just-in-sequence scheduling, quarterly steering-committee leadership handover), channels (direct dispatch through shared real time transportation management system), externalities (reduced CO2 emissions), and cost structure (reduced fuel and labour costs).

Feedback loops. Feedback mechanisms transform this framework from a linear checklist into a truly adaptive, learning system, operating throughout the entire framework. At the end of each phase, a concrete milestone is defined and paired with one or more KPIs. Progression to the next phase can take place only when those KPIs meet their targets. The bidirectional arrows in the diagram indicate that insights from downstream phases can flow back upstream. Over multiple cycles, whether within a single large partnership or across successive projects, organizations accumulate robust data on what works and what does not. These lessons inform updated targets, smarter process designs, and more realistic business models for future collaborations.

For example, in Phase 3, a potential milestone is the resource readiness certification, measured by a resource utilization readiness KPI that quantifies the percentage of agreed-upon assets that are ready for joint service. In Phase 4, the investment return milestone can be tracked via the target ROI (return on investment) KPI.

5 Case Studies

This section analyses two case studies in the logistics business sector, using the central concepts of horizontal collaboration, as defined by our framework. Thus, this analysis is part of the framework validation. The information used in these case studies was gathered through interviewees with the company element leading the partnerships and through document analysis. Both projects are connected, describing how one company evolves in the operationalisation of collaboration. This company developed a project with a low level of intensity and, after this experience, invested in a more complex type of horizontal collaboration with co-opetition.

5.1 Case Studie 1 - Backhauling

This horizontal collaboration initiative was developed by the supply chain department of a big multinational company. For confidentiality reasons, the names of the companies are not disclosed in this article.

Company C is a big multinational in the food sector. They have several factories in Brazil producing a diverse range of products, distributed by a complex network throughout the country, serving from small retailers to big supermarkets. The company started participating in a quite simple type of horizontal collaboration, the backhauling. In these initiatives, the same vehicle carries products from one factory of Company C located in City 1 to its distribution centre in City 2, where the parcels are unloaded. The same truck returns to City 1 loaded with products from Company D (see Fig. 3 below). This cycle aims at reducting / eliminating empty returning trips.

In this type of horizontal collaboration, a minimum amount of information is shared. Companies only discuss the type of vehicle, the loading date and the route. In this partnership, companies C and D define the date, origin and destination, and the logistic service provider designs the route. As a result, only the supply chain departments from both shippers will lead the project and exchange information. In this context, the logistic service provider (LSP) has obviously an essential role in the partnership. Each leg of the operation is organized individually, between each shipper and the logistic service provider. As a result, shippers do not share any information system. Each shipper manages his part of the operation, this meaning they do not discuss package sizing, load factor, freight prices or type of products transported.

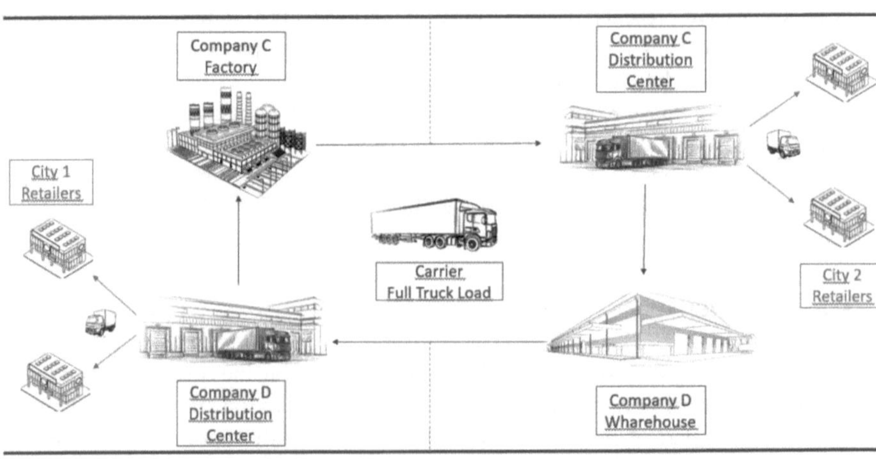

Fig. 3. Case Study 1: Backhauling

The project objective is to positively impact the financial sustainability of the firm through a reduction in freight costs. Externalities such as reduction in CO2 emissions are direct outcomes of the initiative. However, the increase in the global efficiency of the operation results in significant indirect benefits, such as less energy consumption and fewer trucks traveling on roads and circulating in cities. Company C is pleased with the results of this venture and expanded it to 5 new bilateral partnerships. Both shippers lead the project and exchange information. Figure 4 shows the application and assessment of this case study through the proposed framework.

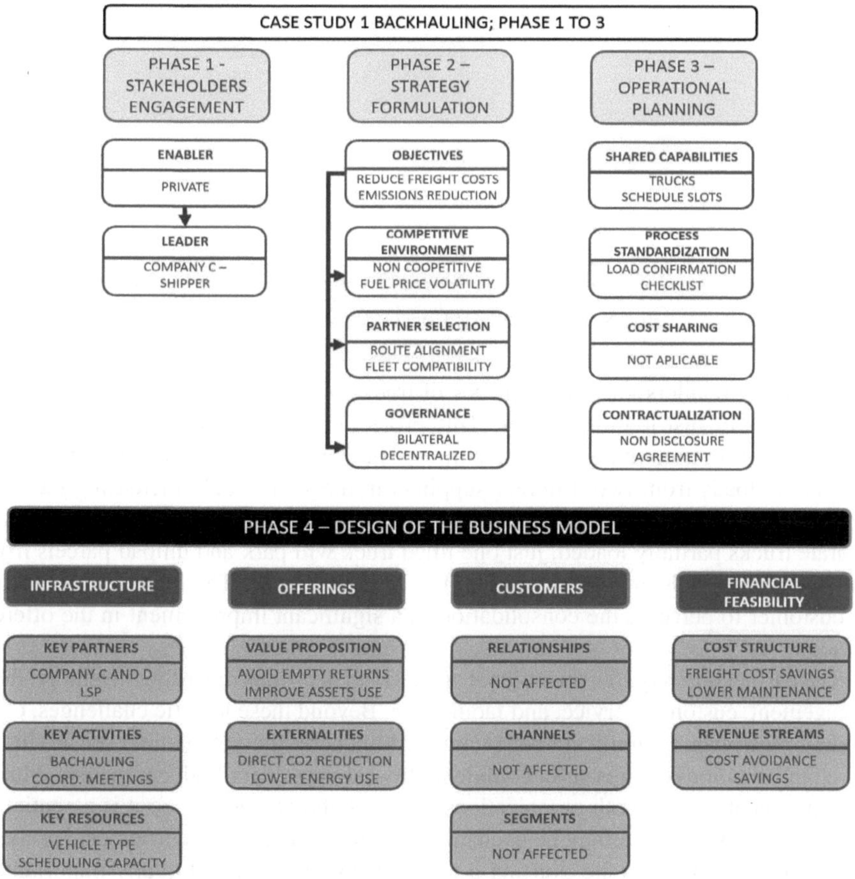

Fig. 4. Application of the framework to Case Study 1.

5.2 Case Studie 2 – Consolidation by Shippers

After the success of the backhauling project, Company C developed the necessary knowledge, skills and confidence to create a new project to consolidate load with another shipper for deliveries to big retailers. Compared to backhauling, consolidation requires more planning, information sharing, participation of internal departments, a new cost and benefit-sharing system and a trustworthy environment.

In this initiative, Company C consolidates the freight, and shares the same vehicle with Company E, a competitor in the main segments of products, for deliveries to supermarkets or big distribution centres, as described in Fig. 5 below.

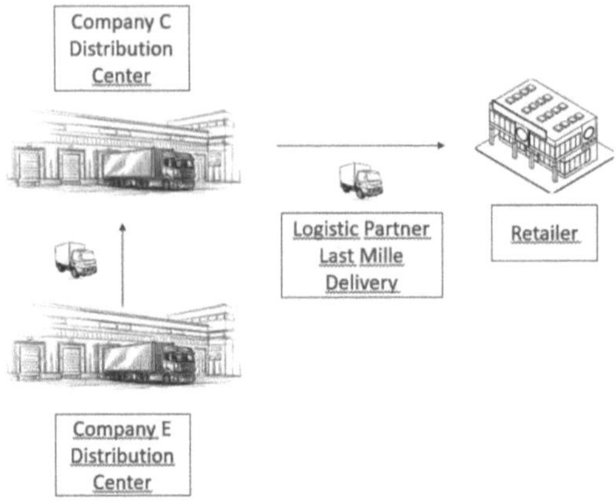

Fig. 5. Case Study 1: Consolidation by shippers

Often, big retailers keep long queues of trucks waiting for unloading packages in supermarkets or distribution centres. This project emerged to minimize losses from this long waiting time in receivers' facilities. The idea of this consolidation project is to combine loads from two different suppliers in the same truck, increasing the load factor. The receiver is also benefited from faster deliveries. Rather than unloading two separate trucks partially loaded, just one filled truck will park and unload parcels from both companies, reducing the number of trucks in the queue. The interviewee expects the customer to perceive the consolidation as a significant improvement in the offered service.

The partnership requires operational and tactical decisions regarding inventory, fleet management, customer service, and facility use. Beyond these logistic challenges, consolidation involves a significant behavioural component: the volume and sensitivity of shared information requires strict confidentiality safeguards for both companies. Multiple departments across both organizations must collaborate closely, so it is essential to clearly define which data may be exchanged. To foster a secure environment for these interactions, the partners are drafting a comprehensive contract. Equally important, a culture of trust must be actively cultivated.

The first trials indicate a clear increase in efficiency, reducing costs and CO2 emissions. The company is considering expanding the consolidation project, now studying new partnerships in the region and analysing by simulations different scenarios (in particular, concerning the distances between shippers) to assure profitability for the consolidation, see Fig. 6.

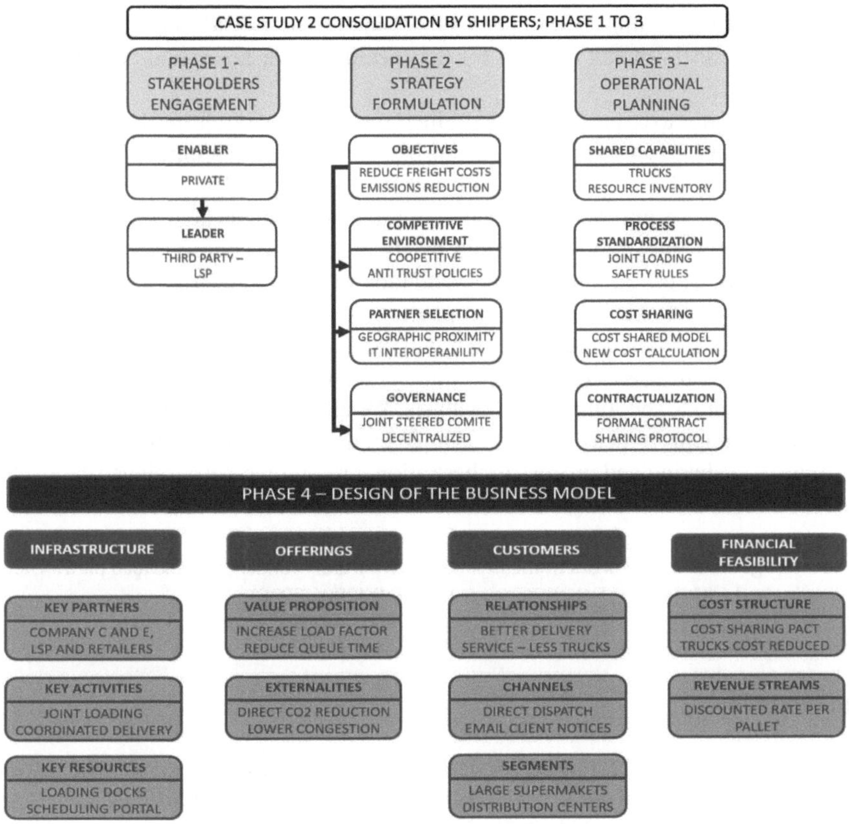

Fig. 6. Application of the framework to Case Study 2

6 Conclusion

This paper provides a theoretical contribution to the field, by a framework providing companies with knowledge and guidelines for launching horizontal collaboration partnerships in logistics. It aims to be a starting point to discuss business planning in the area and advise and guide companies seeking to participate in such type of initiatives.

First, we presented and discussed the concept of co-opetition in horizontal collaboration in logistics, its potential benefits and main barriers for implementation.

Then, a representative set of semi-structured interviews provided qualified input for crafting the framework. The discussion arose themes related to enabling mechanisms, value drivers, barriers, and strategic orientation.

Then, the paper presented a proposal of framework based on four main steps: Stakeholders Engagement → Strategy Formulation → Operational Planning → Design of the Business Model. This framework maps the critical decisions leaders must make – from selecting partners to executing operations – guided throughout by a unified strategic vision. By embedding clear milestones and KPIs at every transition, the framework provides practitioners and regulators with a precise roadmap to sidestep common pitfalls and steer co-opetitive ventures toward lasting, sustainable success. Moreover, we propose a customised business model adapted for the specificities of horizontal collaboration in logistics.

This work aims to be an advance in the literature on co-opetition and business models, due to the numerous cases of failure of horizontal collaboration initiatives in logistics, mainly caused by the incipient application of these concepts. The proposed framework also seeks to be a helpful planning method for managers in this field.

The scope of the study was limited by its geographic concentration and number of case studies. Thus, a more detailed validation of the framework is needed, and we therefore intend to test it in a set of companies in the logistics sector, seeking to start a horizontal collaboration. Future research will expand the application of the framework to other geographical areas, companies, and types of collaboration, potentially using qualitative methods and longitudinal analysis. We also intend to explore the digital and information systems dimensions, for example by designing collaborative platforms for real-time data sharing and process orchestration, prototyping permissioned-blockchain smart contracts to automate governance rules and assess their impacts.

Acknowledgements. This work of the first author is partially funded by Fundação para a Ciência e Tecnologia (FCT), Portugal, through grant PD/BD/142906/2018.

References

1. Cleophas, C., Cottrill, C., Ehmke, J.F., Tierney, K.: Collaborative urban transportation: Recent advances in theory and practice. Eur. J. Oper. Res. **273**(3), 801–816 (2019)
2. Cruijssen, F., Cools, M., Dullaert, W.: Horizontal cooperation in logistics: opportunities and impediments. Transp. Res. Part E Logist. Transp. Rev. **43**(2), 129–142 (2007)
3. Pan, S., Trentesaux, D., Ballot, E., Huang, G.Q.: Horizontal collaborative transport: Survey of solutions and practical implementation issues. Int. J. Prod. Res. **57**(15–16), 5340–5361 (2019)
4. Abideen, A.Z., Sorooshian, S., Sundram, V.P.K., Mohammed, A.: Collaborative insights on horizontal logistics to integrate supply chain planning and transportation logistics planning – A systematic review and thematic mapping. J. Open Innov. Technol. Mark. Complex. **9**(2), 100066 (2023)
5. Sternberg, H., Linan, I., Prockl, G., Norrman, A.: Tragedy of the facilitated commons: a multiple-case study of failure in systematic horizontal logistics collaboration. J. Supply Chain Manag. **58**(4), 30–57 (2022)
6. Verstrepen, S., Cools, M., Cruijssen, F., Dullaert, W.: A dynamic framework for managing horizontal cooperation in logistics. Int. J. Logist. Syst. Manag. **5**(3–4), 228–248 (2009)
7. Leitner, R., Meizer, F., Prochazka, M., Sihn, W.: Structural concepts for horizontal cooperation to increase efficiency in logistics. CIRP J. Manuf. Sci. Technol. **4**(3), 332–337 (2011)
8. Brandenburger, A., Nalebuff, B.: The rules of co-opetition. Harv. Bus. Rev. **99**(1), 48–57 (2021)
9. Walley, K.: Coopetition: an introduction to the subject and an agenda for research. Int. Stud. Manag. Organ. **37**(2), 11–31 (2007)
10. Rindfleisch, A.: Organizational trust and interfirm cooperation: an examination of horizontal versus vertical alliances. Mark. Lett. **11**(1), 81–95 (2000)

11. Lascaux, A.: Coopetition and trust: what we know, where to go next. Ind. Mark. Manag. **84**, 2–18 (2020)
12. McAllister, D.J.: Affect- and cognition-based trust as foundations for interpersonal cooperation in organizations. Acad. Manag. J. **38**(1), 24–59 (1995)
13. Pomponi, F., Fratocchi, L., Tafuri, S.R.: Trust development and horizontal collaboration in logistics: a theory based evolutionary framework. Supply Chain Manag. **20**(1), 83–97 (2015)
14. Pomponi, F., Fratocchi, L., Tafuri, S.R., Palumbo, M.: Horizontal collaboration in logistics: a comprehensive framework. Res. Logist. Prod. **3**(4), 243–254 (2013)
15. Cruijssen, F.: Cross-chain collaboration in logistics: looking back and ahead. In: Price, C.C. (ed.): Springer, Tilburg, the Netherlands (2020)
16. Lindholm, M., Browne, M.: Local authority cooperation with urban freight stakeholders: a comparison of partnership approaches. Eur. J. Transp. Infrastruct. Res. **13**(1), 20–38 (2013)
17. Mirzabeiki, V., Qile, H., Sarpong, D.: Sustainability-driven co-opetition in supply chains as strategic capabilities: drivers, facilitators, and barriers. Int. J. Prod. Res. **61**(14), 4826–4852 (2023)
18. Limoubpratum, C., Shee, H., Ahsan, K.: Sustainable distribution through coopetition strategy. Int. J. Logist. Res. Appl. **18**(5), 424–441 (2015)
19. Ritala, P., Golnam, A., Wegmann, A.: Coopetition-based business models: the case of Amazon.com. Ind. Mark. Manag. **43**(2), 236–249 (2014)
20. Kvale, S.: Doing Interviews. Sage, London (2008)
21. Denzin, N.K., Lincoln, Y.S.: Collecting and Interpreting Qualitative Materials. Sage Publications, Thousand Oaks, CA (1998)
22. Rabionet, S.E.: How I learned to design and conduct semi-structured interviews: an ongoing and continuous journey. Qual. Rep. **16**(2), 563–566 (2011)
23. Carvalho, L., Sousa, J.F.d.: Strategic alignment in a public transport operator: a case study at STCP. In: XIII EURO Working Group on Transportation Meeting, p. 10. University of Padova, Padova (2009)
24. Casadesus-Masanell, R., Ricart, J.E.: From strategy to business models and onto tactics. Long Range Plann. **43**(2), 195–215 (2010)
25. Osterwalder, A., Pigneur, Y.: Business Model Generation, 6th edn. John Wiley & Sons, Hoboken (2010)
26. Straightsol: Straightsol Report Summary. Norway (2015)
27. Osterwalder, A., Pigneur, Y., Tucci, C.L.: Clarifying business models: origins, present, and future of the concept. Commun. Assoc. Inf. Syst. **16**, 1–40 (2005)

Technologies for Adaptable Collaborative Networks

A Digital Twin System to Enable Better Healthcare Management

Simone Gitto(✉), Ginevra Giuliani, and Alberto Lasciarrea

Department of Information Engineering and Mathematics, University of Siena, Via Roma 56, 53100 Siena, Italy
{simone.gitto,ginevra.giuliani2,alberto.lasciarrea}@unisi.it

Abstract. The healthcare sector faces complex challenges exacerbated by tight timelines and fragmented data. Uncertainty, underutilized resources, overcrowding and inadequate information are common problems for decision-makers. In resolving such matters, a Digital Twin, a detailed digital replica of the healthcare system, offers a promising solution. This technology models patient inflows and determines congestion levels and resource and service use to simulate, forecast, and optimize healthcare behaviors. We show the reliability of our system by modelling a complex organization such as one of the Local Health Authority (ASL) of Tuscany. Our Digital Twin system could enable proactive and deliberative-driven decisions by supporting the evaluation of system impacts and optimizing resource utilization. Moreover, the Digital Twin enhances system resilience while improving the decision-making process with the additional data provided through feedback. Such a tool may enable better strategic and optimal resource use.

Keywords: Digital Twin · healthcare management · decision support system

1 Background

Hospital systems worldwide have encountered increasingly complex problems in the modern era. The aging population, high prevalence of chronic diseases, increased financial constraints, and a general shortage of healthcare providers are structural problems that undermine the long-term sustainability and efficiency of health services [1]. Widening disparities in access to care accentuate these problems; the insufficiency of facilities in some places and the desire for greater specialized and integrated care shape this need [2].

Meanwhile, technological advancement has dramatically changed how these problems play out. Digital transformation—including telemedicine, AI, big data, and Digital Twins—provides additional options to deal healthcare challenges in a more nimble, predictive, and connected manner [3, 4]. These technologies can be successfully adopted only after more fundamental organizational transformations. Spending on workforce development is fundamental so that professionals in the healthcare sector can use and interpret modern digital frameworks. Equally important is developing high-quality, interoperable data systems to support the seamless exchange of clinical information [5].

Published by Springer Nature Switzerland AG 2026
L. M. Camarinha-Matos et al. (Eds.): PRO-VE 2025, IFIP AICT 770, pp. 221–237, 2026.
https://doi.org/10.1007/978-3-032-05673-3_14

Additionally, innovation cannot be technological alone. New decision-support tools like the Digital Twin are needed in today's healthcare systems because of the serious risks and inefficiencies they face despite their promising potential. Healthcare data is still inconsistent and fragmented; it is frequently recorded with different standards and levels of completeness and dispersed across heterogeneous systems. This fragmentation leads to a substantial loss of valuable information, forcing managers to rely more on intuition than on objective, data-driven analyses. Decision-making processes are often heuristic and reactive, lacking systematic methods to anticipate outcomes [1, 6]. At the same time, organizational learning is sluggish and delicate since the effects of every decision can only be assessed after considerable delays [4, 6]. Additionally, the system's efficiency is strained and operational bottlenecks, such as the ongoing overcrowding in emergency rooms and specialized services, compromise service quality [1, 3]. A significant barrier is the lack of integration among different data flows, which prevents a unified, coordinated vision of healthcare activities [2, 7]. Moreover, many healthcare organizations still operate with outdated IT infrastructures and face cultural resistance to innovation, limiting their ability to adopt advanced analytical solutions [2, 5, 8].

In this context, we raise the following research question: *What technologies can be implemented to support healthcare decision makers in optimizing resources, improving operational efficiency, and promoting a data-driven approach to governance?*

Understanding these levers is fundamental for enhancing operational efficiency and health service outcomes. To address this, we propose the use of a Digital Twin—a virtual replica of healthcare systems capable of simulating processes, forecasting outcomes, and supporting data-driven decision-making. This model offers a revolutionary opportunity to overcome structural constraints and redesign healthcare governance according to proactive, evidence-based, and predictive principles. It reduces uncertainty, accelerates response times, and provides a dynamic simulation environment where strategic decisions can be tested in advance, offering strong analytical support for planning and resource allocation [3, 9, 10]. Additionally, they allow managers to access real-time performance indicators, predictive insights, and quantitative evaluations of operational scenarios to optimize resources, reduce inefficiencies, and design sustainable interventions [4, 7, 9]. In this sense, Digital Twins go beyond technical simulation, offering actionable intelligence across various levels of healthcare management [11–13].

We design this real-time system based on the experience of a complex organization such as one of the Local Health Authority of Tuscany (Italy). Local Health Authorities (Aziende Sanitarie Locali, or ASLs) are public organizations that manage and coordinate the delivery of hospital-based and territorial healthcare services within defined geographic areas in the Italian National Health Service.

Digital Twin could help enable proactive and deliberative-driven decisions by supporting the evaluation of system impacts and optimizing resource utilization. By simulating care pathways and policy choices in advance, it enables a shift from reactive problem-solving to anticipatory decision-making, contributing to a more intelligent, inclusive, and efficient healthcare system [3, 8, 10].

2 Digital Twin

The concept of the Digital Twin originated in the 1960s when NASA used it to simulate the operational conditions of spacecraft during the Apollo program [9]. However, the term "Digital Twin" was formally introduced in 2003 [9]. The key feature distinguishing a Digital Twin from a simple model or simulation is the bidirectional data connection between the physical entity and its virtual counterpart; this connection is real-time and dynamic [4, 7, 9, 10]. Data flows from the physical object to its virtual twin, returning information or processes to the physical entity [9]. The virtual model constantly adapts to changes in online data and can predict the future of its physical counterpart [4, 7].

The main characteristics of a Digital Twin include the ability to simulate behaviors [7, 9], monitor current status [7, 9], analyze performance [9], identify issues [7], forecast potential future states [4, 7, 9], optimize processes or resources [3, 7, 9], allowing to support decision-makers [3, 7, 9, 12]. The implementation of a Digital Twin relies on the integration of several enabling technologies [7, 9, 10], including:

- Internet of Things (IoT) collects large volumes of real-time data through sensors embedded in the physical entity [4, 7, 10];
- Artificial Intelligence (AI) and Machine Learning (ML) to analyze data, build predictive models, detect anomalies, and generate valuable insights [3, 7, 9];
- Big Data technologies for managing and analyzing large sets of collected data [3, 4, 7, 9, 10];
- Simulation technologies replicate the behavior of the physical entity in the virtual world [7, 9, 10];
- Cloud Computing stores and processes data and models [4, 7, 9].

2.1 Digital Twins for Healthcare Management

The Digital Twin (DT) concept first emerged as a transformative technology within the evolution of Industry 4.0, initially finding applications in sectors like manufacturing and automotive. In recent years, however, this paradigm has rapidly expanded into the healthcare domain, giving rise to what is now known as Digital Twin for Health (DT4H) [8]. Practical applications of Digital Twins in healthcare include multiple domains [13]:

- Hospital Management & Care Coordination: optimizing patient flow, resource allocation, and staff coordination through real-time simulation;
- Medical Device Design: testing devices virtually (e.g., "Living Heart Project") before prototyping;
- Biomarker and Drug Discovery: simulating patient-drug interactions to accelerate research and reduce reliance on lab trials;
- Biomanufacturing: ensuring consistency and quality in biologics, vaccines, and tissue production;
- Surgical Planning: visualizing procedures with patient-specific DTs to improve precision;
- Clinical Trials: using virtual patients for synthetic control arms and treatment simulations;
- Personalized Medicine: enabling real-time treatment customization based on dynamic personal profiles;

- Wellness & Preventive Care: integrating data from wearables for continuous monitoring, especially in elderly or high-risk populations.

Healthcare Digital Twins can be classified into two main categories [3]:

- Human-body Digital Twins: virtual replicas of individual persons based on biological, physiological, genomic, and clinical data, valid for personalized diagnosis, treatment simulation, and predictive medicine.
- Medical Digital Twins: virtual models of medical devices, healthcare facilities, or hospital processes used to optimize operational efficiency, equipment management, and hospital design [14].

Beyond this classification, DTs provide a more precise and agile approach to administering care in medicine. Their integration with Cyber-Physical Healthcare Systems (CPHS)—which merge digital technologies to physical medical devices, infrastructures, and workflows—marks a significant leap forward [8].

This technological fusion improves diagnosis, treatment, and patient management, facilitates resource and operational efficiency, and builds healthy systems. DTs, more than just technological upgrades, mark a transformation to healthcare paradigms: they shift the focus from post-hoc "reactive" measures to proactive ones and from a one-size-fits-all "standardized" approach to tailored "personalized" care [8].

2.2 Literature Review

Digital Twin (DT) technology is rapidly emerging as a transformative innovation in the healthcare sector, enabling real-time simulation, predictive analytics, and personalized treatment through virtual models that mirror physical entities. This literature review synthesizes key findings from recent studies to offer an overview of the current state and future potential of DT applications in healthcare.

A foundational review [4] focused on using DT technologies to construct patient-specific models to support diagnosis and personalized care. The findings reveal an exponential increase in DT-related research in healthcare, particularly from 2010 onwards, with the United States, the United Kingdom, and China leading in publication volume. Key application domains include cardiovascular diseases, orthopedics, surgery, and pharmaceutical research. The review concluded that DT technology has already achieved significant early applications and is expected to play an increasingly central role in real-time monitoring, dynamic analysis, and precision medicine.

Building on this, the broader landscape of current and prospective DT applications in healthcare has been examined in [12]. The study emphasized the potential of DTs to proactively anticipate and prevent medical errors, thereby improving patient outcomes and reducing clinical risk.

Similarly, a review [10] highlighted how DTs can enhance healthcare systems. It emphasized the role of DT in delivering personalized treatment plans by integrating real-time data, advanced analytics, and virtual simulation. By facilitating early intervention, DTs can help prevent adverse health events, thereby significantly improving the quality and efficiency of care delivery.

Finally, a comprehensive Digital Twin framework for intelligent and context-aware healthcare systems was proposed in [11]. Their framework aims to integrate DTs with real-time analytics to enhance healthcare delivery. A use case involving ECG-based heart rhythm classification was presented for real-time health monitoring and early detection of cardiac anomalies. The study compared five different algorithms and found that neural network-based models—such as Long Short-Term Memory (LSTM), Convolutional Neural Networks (CNN), and Multi-Layer Perceptron (MLP)—outperformed traditional machine learning techniques in processing ECG data, demonstrating the effectiveness of advanced AI within DT frameworks.

While these studies collectively underscore the potential of DTs to support and enhance specific aspects of clinical care, such as diagnosis, treatment, and patient monitoring, they remain focused mainly on isolated components or functions within the healthcare system. In contrast, the Digital Twin system we propose is conceived as an organizational-level innovation, designed to represent the full complexity of a Local Health Authority. Rather than targeting a single clinical domain or technological application, our framework aims to digitally replicate a healthcare organization's entire structure and set of processes. This includes patient flow, resource allocation, departmental coordination, and system-wide performance monitoring.

By broadening the scope from specialized clinical functions to systemic organizational processes, our approach leverages the full potential of DT technology as a tool not only for improving care delivery but also for enabling strategic governance, operational efficiency, and dynamic decision-making. This marks a pivotal shift in the evolution of Digital Twins from supporting tools at the micro level to strategic assets for health system transformation.

3 Method

3.1 Description, Concept and Objectives

In contrast with the literature highlighted in the previous section, which primarily focuses on Digital Twins for specific clinical tasks, often with fragmented applications, we propose a novel system designed to model healthcare organizations as complex, adaptive systems with a holistic approach. Figure 1 introduces the envisioned system and the interaction between its components.

The envisioned Digital Twin is a dynamic and modular simulation system that reconstructs the healthcare delivery ecosystem across both its structural and behavioral dimensions. It integrates heterogeneous data streams, from population demographics and epidemiological trends to service capacity, facility geography, and clinical pathways, to create a real-time, data-driven mirror of the healthcare environment.

Inputs to the system include clinical, geographic, and administrative data—along with the constraints that must drive the solution, like e.g. budget, protocols and policies. On the demand side, the model incorporates patient demographics, comorbidities, healthcare service usage, and inferred health needs, derived from historical records and predictive modeling such as prescriptions and outpatient visits. On the supply side, it maps the distribution of healthcare providers, including general practitioners and specialists, their facility capacities, time-based availability (such as working hours and appointment slots), and systemic constraints like policy restrictions and governance frameworks. Additional layers of spatial and behavioral data—such as high-resolution population density maps and routing networks—enable realistic modeling of patient mobility, service accessibility, and location-based inequalities.

These data streams feed into a stochastic simulation engine that reproduces healthcare behaviors across time and space. Synthetic patients, generated from regional demographic and epidemiological profiles, are assigned probabilistic health events and geographical locations. Upon simulated need (such as symptom onset), patients interact with virtual general practitioners who serve as gatekeepers and initiate referrals within the simulated care network. The Digital Twin models the full patient journey—including scheduling, waiting, travel, abandonment, and care delivery—while accounting for feedback effects and emergent behaviors.

By leveraging this structure, the system enables dynamic waiting list simulation, allowing for the projection of wait times under varying demand and supply conditions. It supports the identification of spatial and temporal mismatches between supply and demand, along with the measurement of service access using real routing networks and time-based constraints.

A distinctive feature of the Digital Twin is its iterative learning capability. Machine learning algorithms continuously compare predicted and actual outcomes, adjusting internal parameters to improve forecasting accuracy over time. Through this feedback loop, each real-world decision and its consequences refine the model's future projections, progressively aligning the Twin with systemic realities.

The impact of possible resource allocation strategies, such as adding capacity in underserved areas, adjusting GP referral rules, or centralizing services, can be evaluated within the simulation. The system also supports cost modeling, quantifying dimensions such as travel time, missed appointments, and opportunity costs. Behavioral responses such as opting for private care, appointment abandonment, or system re-entry are included.

Structural policy levers, including prioritization strategies, distance-based incentives, and no-show penalties, can also be encoded to simulate governance and operational rules. Governance scenarios such as prioritization protocols or provider-specific scheduling can be tested without impacting live operations. These capabilities allow for the simulation of many scenarios, from seasonal surges and pandemic responses to structural changes such as opening a community health center or redistributing general practitioners. Downstream impacts on congestion, patient flow, and cost-effectiveness can be evaluated in a controlled environment. By merging simulation, real-time data ingestion, and predictive modeling, the Digital Twin represents a shift from reactive service management to proactive, evidence-based system design. It enables institutions to plan, test, and optimize healthcare strategies with a level of foresight and precision that traditional tools cannot offer.

Designed to be modular and scalable, the architecture can initially target specific domains, such as outpatient care, emergency services, or chronic disease management, before expanding to broader territorial or functional scopes. This makes it adaptable for local health authorities, regional agencies, or national-level digital health strategies.

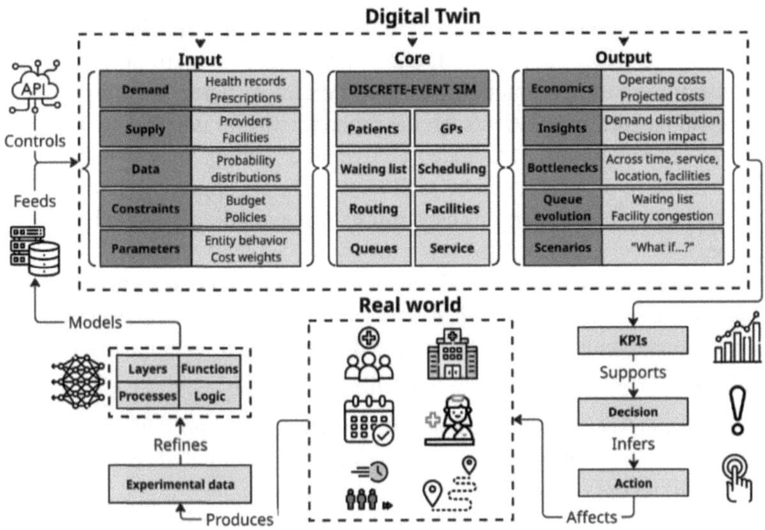

Fig. 1. Functional block diagram

Ultimately, the Digital Twin serves as a living, evolving platform—a computational laboratory for health system managers to explore decisions, improve resilience, and pursue sustainable and equitable health outcomes at scale.

At the core of the system lies a Discrete-Event Simulation (DES) model, built around agents: patients, general practitioners (GPs), healthcare providers, and coordination entities. The model is designed to dynamically simulate the interaction between demand and supply for outpatient services, with particular emphasis on waiting lists, spatial distribution of providers, and patient decision-making.

The simulation starts with the generation of synthetic patients, crafted to realistically reflect the real population in terms of demographic, clinical, and geographical characteristics, and each patient's journey is thoroughly traced.

The Digital Twin integrates behavioral, spatial, and organizational components to realistically represent how the healthcare system evolves over time. It also includes feedback and learning mechanisms that allow the model to adapt to observed data, narrowing the gap between simulation and real-world dynamics.

The following sections detail this architecture across its main modules: the simulation pathway (Sect. 3.2), data sources (Sect. 3.3), learning mechanisms (Sect. 3.4), system output (Sect. 3.5) and extensibility and integration (Sect. 3.6). The DT is currently implemented in the MATLAB/Simulink suite, although migration to a dedicated framework and software stack (e.g., Python or Rust) for scalability is undergoing consideration.

3.2 Simulation Pathway

At the core of the simulation lies a multi-agent system in which each agent represents a key actor in the healthcare process. The simulation proceeds in discrete time steps. In each cycle, health events are triggered for a subset of patients, who then consult their

GP. The GP issues referral requests, each associated with a specialty and an urgency level. Available providers are queried, and appointment slots are proposed to patients using a multicriteria utility function that incorporates distance, waiting time, urgency, and contingent constraints. Patients decide probabilistically whether to accept or reject the proposal. Accepted slots are added to dynamic waiting lists, while cancellations return slots to the pool, which can be reallocated. On the appointment date, the patient travels to the facility and undergoes care simulation, including modeled congestion and service time.

Patients are generated synthetically using a calibrated Poisson process, where the arrival rate is extracted from historical data from general practitioners. Each synthetic entity is instantiated with a vector of attributes drawn from either empirical or analytically derived probability distributions. These attributes include:

- Demographics: Age, gender, nationality, household city and municipality.
- Health Profile: Probabilistically sampled illness and estimated severity, informed by historical GP records, along with comorbidity data.
- Spatial Embedding: The patient's location is sampled from high-resolution population density maps. These maps are produced using a hybrid geospatial model: census-derived statistics are combined with machine-learning-inferred building footprints from satellite imagery. Density points are segmented by demographic strata to allow stratified sampling across administrative units.
- Behavioral Willingness: Each patient is assigned a dynamic cost-aversion profile, representing their tolerance to waiting times and travel distance, which also depends on the type of illness and its relative severity. This behavioral layer, critical to capturing patient attrition, employs a nonlinear decision function. Calibrated on empirical rejection and dropout rates, the function outputs a probability that governs the patient's willingness to remain in the public queue vs. abandoning, for example, diverting to private care.

General practitioners perform a triage evaluation and have defined practice locations, behavioral profiles, and referral tendencies. This process assigns a priority class to the patient and, where clinically appropriate, proposes an appointment. Same-day scheduling logic triggers an immediate assignment (if accepted); otherwise, the patient is enrolled into a deferred scheduling mechanism.

The queuing module (waiting list) is structured as a set of priority-aware FIFO buffers—one per class and destination—driven by a resource-aware event handler. Patients enrolled in deferred queues periodically undergo a logical reassessment of their willingness to wait. This reassessment is governed by a decaying probability function that considers elapsed waiting time and travel distance, similarly to the aforementioned one. Each iteration executes a Bernoulli trial that defines if the patient exits the queue, hence releasing the slot. Released slots are retroactively redistributed to remaining patients in strict priority order.

This dynamic enables a feedback loop where high waiting times and excessive travel burdens systematically degrade patient compliance. As a result, queue structure and facility load dynamically co-evolve with the system's state.

System coordinators play a supervisory role, dynamically reallocating slots based on waiting list evolution and patient abandonment patterns.

Moreover, unannounced drop-out dynamics (and hence unexpected empty slots on delivery day) are also considered—and calibrated through historical data—to further enhance the model's coherence with a real-world scenario.

Each facility is modeled as a spatially embedded service node with distinct operational features. For example, each facility may contain multiple treatment lines, each represented as a server-queue system whose behavior is governed by a set of attributes. Attributes include:

- Daily activity schedule and slot capacity
- Queuing structure (e.g., walk-in buffers or scheduled FIFO)
- Service time, modeled via empirical distribution functions fitted to observed durations. This also considers whether the server/patient duo can rely on electronic health records, or when a complete anamnesis is required.

Upon admission, patients are routed to the appropriate line. At route path completion, a terminal node logs the patient's total experience, including waiting time, travel cost, and any behavioral penalties accrued due to abandonment or rescheduling.

Spatial realism is ensured by tight integration with OpenStreetMap (OSM) and OSRM (Open Source Routing Machine), which are deployed locally for low-latency, high-accuracy routing. This infrastructure enables precise estimation of travel time and distance for each patient-provider pair, identification of underserved zones, and simulation of behavior sensitive to accessibility, such as increased no-show or lateness rates for longer or more complex routes. The geospatial model includes:

- Up-to-date OSM data with administrative overlays;
- Public transportation;
- Road class segmentation (e.g., urban vs. rural);
- Topographic constraints (e.g., mountainous areas, limited-access zones).

This layer also informs the cost function in the patient behavior module, ensuring that spatial burden is not a generic scalar but a function of real accessibility, where metrics on geographic access are robust and decision-relevant.

3.3 Data Sources

The system ingests a combination of census data, administrative health records and geospatial service registries. These data allow for the generation of synthetic patients sampled from distributions that reproduce observed frequencies by age group and pathology type, while maintaining geographic representativeness. Calibration is based on historical event rates and care patterns.

The simulation is grounded in a comprehensive data backbone that enables empirical calibration:

- Population Registry: Age, sex, nationality, and municipal-level residence for the full population.
- GP Prescription Dataset: Clinical demand; includes suspected diagnosis, priority, target service, requested regime, date and time, and historical comorbidity data.

- Delivered Services Dataset: Empirical supply; timestamped logs of executed appointments, including facility, priority, public or private regime, and type of care. A cross-reference to the Prescription Dataset is also available, giving a measurement for waiting times of accepted appointments.
- Geospatial Density Database: Meta-derived and stratified by demographic segment. The segmentation includes overall, women, men, children (0–5), youth (15–24), elderly (60 +), and women of reproductive age (15–49).
- Administrative Boundaries: Aligned with the national health system structure, ensuring traceability from regional authorities to individual municipalities.

3.4 Learning Mechanisms

A key component of the Digital Twin is its ability to evolve in response to empirical discrepancies between expected and observed outcomes—a process akin to semi-live feedback. Rather than running on rigid deterministic rules, the simulator compares its forecasts against real-world indicators such as waiting times, no-show rates, and abandonment frequencies. Discrepancies act as signals for model refinement.

This forms the basis for a closed-loop learning mechanism. If, for example, a simulation predicts that reallocating capacity will reduce waiting times but actual data shows the opposite, the system adjusts internal components such as patient heuristics, referral logic, or bottleneck definitions. Over time, this coevolution reduces model drift and enhances reliability.

In more advanced configurations, this loop can be coupled with online learning algorithms. These allow for the dynamic tuning of behavioral policies or scheduling rules based on performance metrics, using KPIs such as equity indices and access times as reward signals. While not fully autonomous, this significantly increases the responsiveness and adaptability of the simulation.

3.5 System Outputs

The value of the Digital Twin is ultimately measured by the utility of its outputs. The system delivers actionable intelligence across strategic, tactical, and operational levels.

Outputs include performance dashboards tracking metrics such as accessibility, equity, congestion, and system load across time, geography, and specialty. Comparative analytics allow stakeholders to weigh the trade-offs of different interventions, such as adding diagnostic slots in underserved zones versus adjusting GP referral patterns. Predictive maps identify emerging stress zones, unmet demand clusters, or likely abandonment hotspots. Behavioral forecasts estimate no-show likelihoods or dropout risks based on patient histories or journey complexity. Resilience metrics evaluate system performance under stressors such as flu outbreaks or infrastructure failures.

The system also generates narrative visualizations—including animated patient journeys or synthetic case studies—to facilitate communication with stakeholders and policymakers. These outputs are interactive: users can ask scenario-based questions, such as "What if we close a rural clinic?" or "What if we centralize diagnostics?", and receive quantifiable, interpretable results.

3.6 Extensibility and Integration

The system is built for extensibility and integration. It supports REST APIs for external control and data exchange, modular plug-ins for integration with dashboards, machine learning models, or planning tools, and dual simulation models for both long-term planning and real-time rescheduling.

Each component—from demand generation to routing, scheduling, or policy modeling—is implemented as a separate module or microservice with well-defined interfaces. This allows for modular development, selective replacement, and parallel execution, making it possible to experiment with different models (such as alternative behavioral assumptions or scheduling strategies) without altering the system's core.

Standard data formats ensure interoperability, with, for example, Fast Healthcare Interoperability Resources (FHIR) used for clinical entities and GeoJSON for spatial data. Adapters support communication with legacy systems and regional data warehouses. The twin can run in standalone mode or be orchestrated as part of a broader decision-support workflow.

Scalability is addressed through containerized deployments and simulation sharding. The architecture supports variable levels of granularity, from macro-level flows across regions down to detailed modeling of individual facilities and patient trajectories.

This architectural approach is foundational to the system's practical utility, as it allows the Digital Twin to evolve in parallel with the healthcare environment it represents. In complex and evolving healthcare ecosystems, rigid architectures quickly become obsolete or misaligned with policy and organizational needs. Extensibility ensures that new paradigms (such as analytical methods, data streams, or operational priorities) can be incorporated without destabilizing the system or undergoing massive restructuring.

Integration, on the other hand, enables the Digital Twin to function as part of a wider digital health infrastructure. Rather than operating in isolation—as a standalone on-call computational unit—it can ingest live data, trigger external workflows, or return outputs to institutional dashboards and operational platforms. This makes the model usable not only for retrospective or hypothetical analysis, but also as a live decision-support tool embedded in real-time governance processes.

This design makes the Digital Twin a foundation for collaborative development. It becomes not just a tool, but a platform for health authorities, managers, researchers, and technology providers to jointly build and iterate upon.

4 Results

To provide the reliability of our system, we have developed it based on real data. We calibrate the models according to the logics and rules of previous sections, based on 1 year of historic data. After calibrating the models, we generate 5 different simulated scenarios according to resource allocation configurations. The baseline service capacity was incrementally augmented by 10% and 20%, and two prioritization strategies—ξ_1 and ξ_2, that were discussed with health managers. These strategies govern the allocation logic for additional resources (i.e., medical personnel and service slots): ξ_1 prioritizes centralization, favoring larger and more accessible facilities, while ξ_2 supports a more distributed, network-oriented healthcare model.

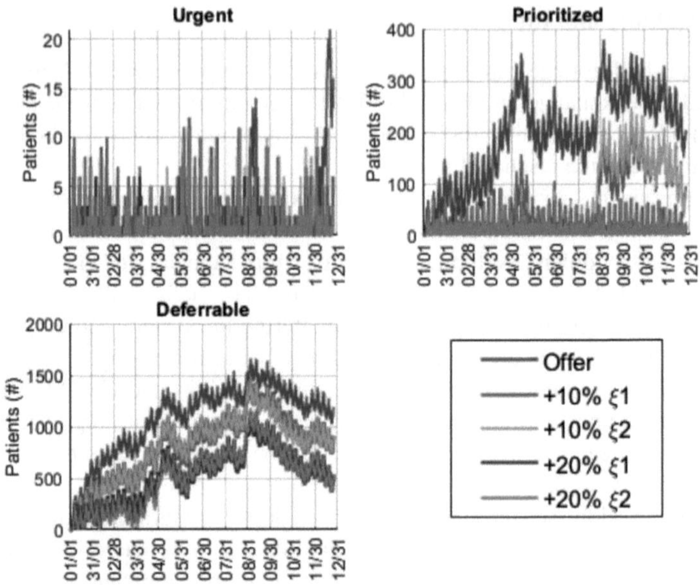

Fig. 2. Evolution of the number of patients in waiting list over one year, considering prioritization strategies ξ_1 and ξ_2.

Figures 2 and 3 present the evolution of waiting lists over a full year. Fig. 2 displays the total number of patients awaiting service, while Fig. 3 reports the average waiting time for patients on each corresponding day. Both figures disaggregate results by patient priority class, as defined by medical protocols: Urgent, Prioritized, and Deferrable. Upon receiving a referral from their general practitioner, each patient is classified into one of these categories, which dictates the maximum allowable waiting time for public service delivery. If this threshold is exceeded, patients may seek private care and request reimbursement—an outcome that carries significant cost implications for the healthcare system. To safeguard Urgent care delivery, resource allocation policies must reserve capacity for this class, often at the expense of Prioritized and Deferrable patients, who tend to experience longer delays.

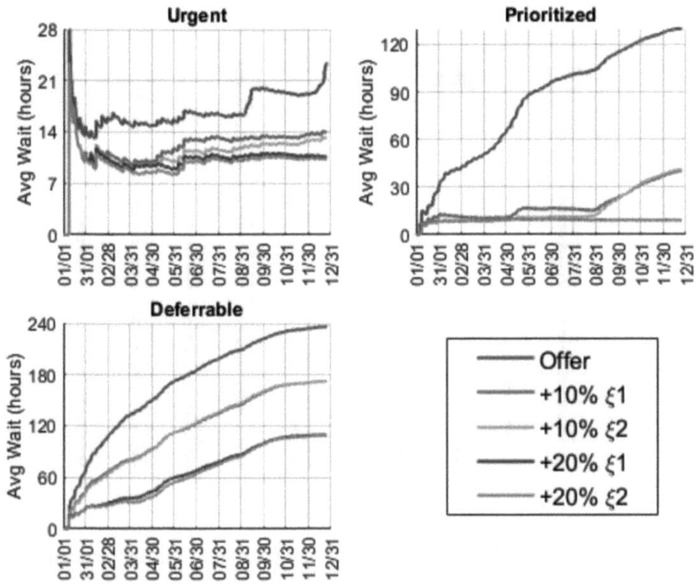

Fig. 3. Evolution of average stay in the waiting list, over one year, considering prioritization strategies ξ_1 and ξ_2.

Figure 4 displays the cumulative number of waiting days from the patients' perspective, aggregated by facility. The analysis again spans one year and compares the four augmented scenarios against the baseline configuration. The bar chart highlights the 20 facilities that demonstrated the largest absolute reduction in waiting time under any of the augmented setups. The model also considers the travel distance that the patient endures to reach the facility, and various penalties due to e.g. dismissal or waiting list dropout. With the appropriate coefficients, these measures can be combined into a single fictitious cost that represents the patient's satisfaction.

Lastly, Fig. 5 illustrates the evolution of average queue length across clinics, expressed in waiting time, as a daily average. This metric captures the in-facility congestion on treatment days, reflecting both patient demand and operational scheduling choices (e.g., overbooking as a buffer for no-shows or tight deadlines). The figure reports results for a single scenario—the 10% augmentation under ξ_1—to explore intra-facility dynamics in more detail. Queue lengths are also influenced by scheduled follow-up appointments, which are planned and are hence not subjected to the same maximum delay thresholds as initial referrals. Each line in the graph corresponds to a single facility, where service times follow an exponential distribution, with mean and variance estimated from historical performance data.

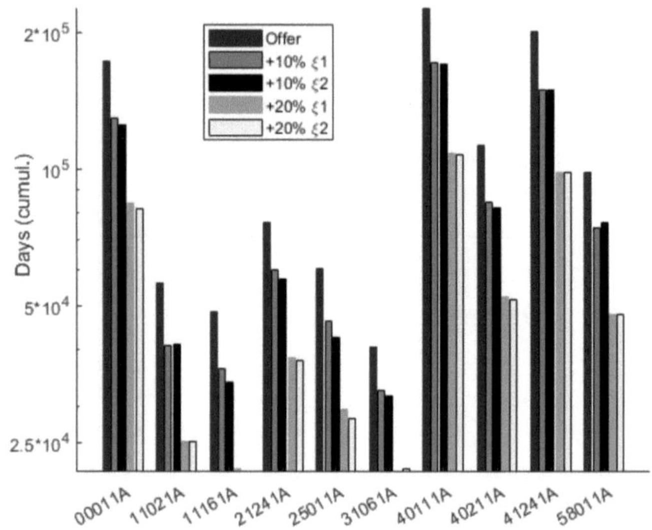

Fig. 4. Cumulative wait for service by facility over one year, considering prioritization strategies ξ_1 and ξ_2.

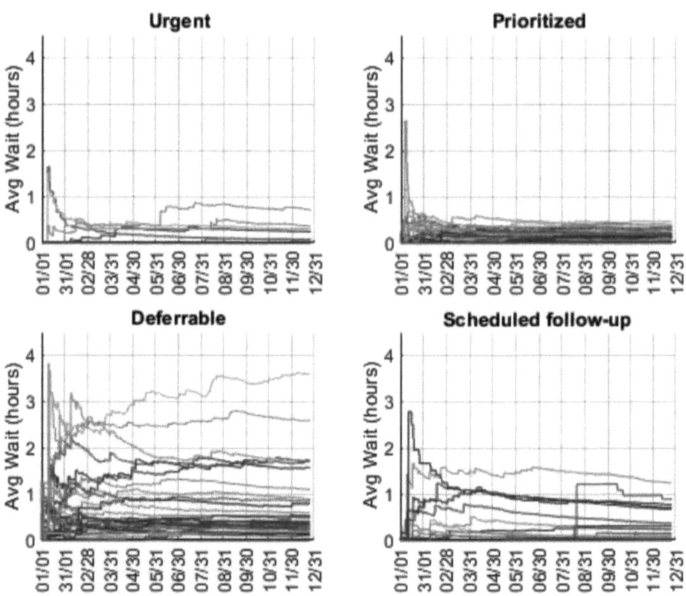

Fig. 5. Evolution of in-clinic queues as average daily wait, one year, + 10% ξ_1.

5 Conclusion and Further Developments

This proposal outlines a Digital Twin designed as both a mirror and a planning engine for healthcare systems. By simulating patients, providers, geography, and governance, it enables a level of decision support far beyond traditional dashboards or reports.

Further steps involve validating synthetic demand models against real data, testing core scheduling mechanisms for representative specialties, and collaborating with clinicians and administrators to define realistic behavioral rules and decision thresholds.

The long-term aim is to develop a fully operational platform that can run high-fidelity simulations and support regional health authorities in both routine management and structural transformation. Adopting demand-oriented and problem-oriented approaches, coupled with strengthened top-level design and systematic planning, the proposed digital twin allows for increasingly supporting the high-quality development of healthcare management. We believe that through the joint efforts of society, this digital twin will contribute to building a more equitable, higher-quality, and more sustainable health ecosystem.

5.1 Multiparadigm Approach

The implementation of the Digital Twin system presented in this study is mostly based on DES, which provides a powerful and flexible framework to model healthcare workflows at a practical level (e.g., patient referral chains, waiting lists, scheduling systems, and resource allocation at facility level). However, as the complexity of the healthcare domain often spans across operational, behavioral, and systemic dimensions [15], a multi-paradigm simulation approach becomes particularly valuable to extend the capabilities of the system in a modular and scalable way.

In a multi-paradigm simulation framework, distinct modeling paradigms—primarily DES, agent-based modeling (ABM), and system dynamics (SD)—are combined, each addressing different scales, data granularities, and abstraction levels. For instance, system dynamics can be leveraged at the macro level to represent long-term trends such as population aging, chronic disease progression, or policy-level capacity planning. These models are typically formulated using differential equations and allow for the analysis of feedback loops and nonlinear dynamics, which are harder to capture through DES alone.

At the micro level, agent-based models can be introduced to simulate individual actors—patients, general practitioners, care managers—each endowed with specific rules, preferences, and adaptive behavior. ABM is particularly suited for capturing heterogeneity, autonomy, and emergent phenomena, such as behavioral changes in response to waiting times, routing policies, or localized incentives.

The integration of these paradigms introduces several technical and conceptual challenges, particularly related to synchronization, data consistency, and modular communication. From a temporal perspective, synchronization between models operating at different time resolutions (e.g., continuous-time SD vs. event-driven DES) requires a coupling mechanism. This can involve establishing a central simulation clock with adjustable resolution, where discrete events can trigger updates in SD stocks or ABM agent states, and vice versa. For example, a sudden surge in patient arrivals (captured by a SD inflow) may generate new patient agents in the ABM module, who are then processed in the DES system according to available resources and scheduling logic.

Information flow between modules must also be carefully managed. Interface variables (such as global congestion indices, capacity thresholds, or cumulative performance indicators) act as bridges between paradigms. These variables may be computed in one module and used as inputs or control signals in another. For instance, a SD model may track long-term demand saturation and trigger resource scaling policies that reconfigure the DES logic (e.g., opening new facilities or reprioritizing queues). Alternatively, emergent agent-level behaviors in the ABM module can be aggregated and fed back into SD loops to adjust policy assumptions.

Calibration and validation across paradigms require consistent use of shared data sources and simulation artifacts. Agent-level parameters, such as compliance rates or risk profiles, may be derived from population-level statistics modeled in SD, while time-to-event distributions in DES can be refined using synthetic traces generated by ABM agents. Iterative experimentation plays a crucial role: scenarios explored in one module may define boundary conditions for another, and model refinement often proceeds through staged coupling rather than monolithic integration.

5.2 Future Challenges

As the envisioned DT is grounded in a variegated and structured data backbone, it is important to acknowledge several challenges that arise in real-world implementation—particularly when scaling or replicating the approach across different regions.

Data acquisition, though feasible in this pilot setting through integration with SSN (Servizio Sanitario Nazionale) databases and public repositories, remains a significant hurdle in broader applications. While administrative registries and service logs are often available within institutional silos, data fragmentation, latency in access, and legal ambiguity in secondary use can obstruct unified modeling efforts. Not all healthcare systems provide the same degree of granularity or continuity, and might hence require an array of bespoke adaptations.

Interoperability further complicates integration: different providers, regions, and information systems adopt heterogeneous data formats, classification schemes—as an example, nationwide migration to HL7 is still ongoing—and database architectures. Harmonizing these inputs demands considerable ETL (Extract, Transform, Load) engineering and often relies on ad hoc mappings that may introduce noise, bias, errors, or procedural bugs—which might require significant effort to identify and mitigate.

Data governance is equally critical. The sensitive nature of health information imposes strict requirements around privacy, security, and ethical use: although synthetic patient generation minimizes reidentification risks, upstream access to identifiable data (e.g., for calibration or validation) still requires robust safeguards. This includes anonymization pipelines, controlled environments, and most importantly formal legal agreements for PNRR compliance (e.g., DPIAs and DPO oversight). Moreover, ensuring data quality and semantic accuracy remains a nontrivial technical and organizational task, especially across institutions.

Another challenge is real-time responsiveness. While the model currently operates on batch-fed historical data with periodic updates, extending its capabilities toward real-time feedback loops demands infrastructural upgrades and integration with live streaming systems, which are not yet universally available. To mitigate the runtime complexity, the proposed DT allocates as much of the computational burden as possible to before simulation (e.g., pre-calculated distance matrix for all patient-facility permutations), but the challenge of optimization remains a crucial factor which must be considered—both from a hardware and software perspective.

Finally, the long-term sustainability and governance of such a Digital Twin system pose structural challenges. Questions arise about who might maintain and fund the system, how updates are managed, and how its outputs are interpreted and acted upon within health governance frameworks. Embedding the Twin as a decision-support instrument requires not only technical reliability but also institutional trust, interpretability, and transparency in how its recommendations are generated: an agreed-upon procedural handbook is the bare minimum to be expected.

References

1. Jones, C.H., Dolsten, M.: Healthcare on the brink: navigating the challenges of an aging society in the United States. npj Aging **10**(1), 22 (2024)
2. Malviya, R., Sundram, S., Dhanaraj, R.K., Kadry, S. (eds.): Digital transformation in healthcare 5.0: Volume 1: IoT, AI and Digital Twin. Walter de Gruyter GmbH & Co KG (2024)
3. Li, T., Shen, Y., Li, Y., Zhang, Y., Wu, S.: The status quo and future prospects of digital twins for healthcare. EngMed **1**(3), 100042 (2024)
4. Sun, T., He, X., Li, Z.: Digital twin in healthcare: recent updates and challenges. Digit. Health **9**, 20552076221149652 (2023)
5. Momani, A.: Implications of Artificial Intelligence on health data privacy and confidentiality (2025). arXiv, arXiv-2501
6. Meijer, C., Uh, H.W., El Bouhaddani, S.: Digital twins in healthcare: methodological challenges and opportunities. J. Pers. Med. **13**(10), 1522 (2023)
7. Haleem, A., Javaid, M., Singh, R.P., Suman, R.: Exploring the revolution in healthcare systems through the applications of digital twin technology. Biomed. Technol. **4**, 28–38 (2023)
8. Roopa, M.S., Venugopal, K.R.: Digital twins for cyber-physical healthcare systems: architecture, requirements, systematic analysis and future prospects. IEEE Access (2025)
9. Hassani, H., Huang, X., MacFeely, S.: Impactful digital twin in the healthcare revolution. Big Data Cogn. Comput. **6**(3), 83 (2022)
10. Vallée, A.: Digital twin for healthcare systems. Front. Digit. Health **5**, 1253050 (2023)
11. Elayan, H., Aloqaily, M., Guizani, M.: Digital twin for intelligent context-aware IoT healthcare systems. IEEE Internet Things J. **8**(23), 16749–16757 (2021)
12. Erol, T., Mendi, A.F., Doğan, D.: The digital twin revolution in healthcare. In 2020 4th int. Symp. Multidiscip. Stud. Innov. Technol. (ISMSIT) (pp. 1–7). IEEE (2020)
13. Katsoulakis, E., et al.: Digital twins for health: a scoping review. NPJ Digit. Med. **7**(1), 77 (2024)
14. Elkefi, S., Asan, O.: Digital twins for managing health care systems: rapid literature review. J. Med. Internet Res. **24**(8), e37641 (2022)
15. Rodríguez-Aguilar R., Marmolejo-Saucedo J.A.: Conceptual framework of digital health public emergency system: digital twins and multiparadigm simulation. EAI Endorsed Trans. Pervasive Health Technol. (2020)

IT Applications, Systems, and Services Towards an Agnostic Digital Ecosystem

A. Luís Osório[1(✉)], Carlos Gonçalves[1], Paula Urze[2], and Mário Pinheiro[1]

[1] ISEL - IPL, Polytechnic University of Lisbon, UnIRE and POLITEC&ID, Lisbon, Portugal
{aosorio,cgoncalves}@deetc.isel.ipl.pt, mario.pinheiro@isel.pt
[2] FCT, NOVA University of Lisbon, CIUHCT, Lisbon, Portugal
pcu@fct.unl.pt

Abstract. The trend towards a thorough immersion in a digital society raises unresolved research questions about reliability, trustworthiness, integration, security, and scalability under an agnostic underlying technology supporting base. With daily activities quasi-exclusively supported by digital assets from various suppliers/vendors, establish a critical technology base that needs to be integrated, operated, and updated in response to business management decisions. The lack of an open, holistic digital framework based on open standards creates dependencies on critical digital technology, which can be an obstacle to business development. This paper extends the ISoS framework by revisiting its definition, positioning a conceptual definition of application that is separated from implementation by an ISoS service element. The paper further clarifies the ISoS computing technology artifacts structure developed in the SINCRO national driver enforcement network project. The ISoS framework is argued as a technology strategy to logically structure the overall digital technology base, from sensors, shopfloor machines, roadside equipment, on-premises data center infrastructure, and public cloud deployments, under unified digital-related vendor-agnostic technology artifacts management.

Keywords: Collaborative Networks · Informatics System and Informatics System of Informatics Systems · Distributed Informatics Systems · Interoperability · Integration · Agnostic IT

1 Introduction

The last two decades have seen significant contributions from the industry, with computing-based products and services offered for free to achieve the network effect [1]. The offering of unprecedented and valuable AI tools, the "*twenty-first-century calculator*", is an example. Following previous advancements, such as social networks, citizens are increasingly relying on AI tools without a regulated framework, raising the question of whether they can trust the services offered. Moreover, given the market concentration of digital critical infrastructures in a few companies with the power of countries, the question arises whether arbitrary private decisions threaten public governance and democracy,

Published by Springer Nature Switzerland AG 2026
L. M. Camarinha-Matos et al. (Eds.): PRO-VE 2025, IFIP AICT 770, pp. 238–253, 2026.
https://doi.org/10.1007/978-3-032-05673-3_15

with similarities to the thesis that "... *overreliance on consultancies harms public interest....*" [2]. While not a central concern in our research, we recognize the importance of strengthening the agnostic dimension for IT, driven by public research investment independent of specific business interests. The open-source community, while an interesting strategy for achieving the network effect, has been essential and can improve with public investment to respond to open models and technology consensus required by the integrated digital.

Nevertheless, open-source dynamics are not immune to risks, as many companies have experienced disruptions in the open-source or open specifications ecosystem when the leading company or consortium decides to close it. The cases of Flash, maintained by Adobe, or Java applets deprecation [3], developed by Sun Microsystems (now Oracle), are paradigmatic examples of the risks associated with deprecated technologies when a significant dependency already exists. Another case is the introduction of a business license when an immense community trusts an open-source initiative. The recent cases of Docker[1] and Terraform[2] are also surprising to the open-source community, with an unexpected shift from community-driven to business-driven strategy. In the case of Terraform, the model change preceded the acquisition of HashiCorp by IBM, leading to the OpenTofu open-source community based on a branch of the Terraform code base just before the license changed. The concern is not related to the fairness of the move, but rather the risks of impact on the contributing community and user members, particularly regarding their expectations.

Society has always responded to unbalanced moves by joining community efforts to develop countermeasures. However, such community efforts require moderation, from State awareness and strategic investments [4], with the foundation set by the example of US DARPA, which catalyzed the Internet. In a more recent study by the same author [5], the author cites John M. Keynes to emphasize the moderating or power value of guiding public policies in the economy. Her contribution, from an economic perspective, centered on smart innovation and inclusive growth, corroborates the importance of reasserting authority over digital infrastructures in enhancing market competitiveness by investing in open standards.

There are examples of public-led strategies addressing the holistic digital landscape, as seen in the case of the Australian Data and Digital Government Strategy [6]. However, implementing an agnostic ICT, or information technology (IT), raises foundational questions concerning the lack of formal business technology alignment standards models. Despite research from a decade ago, which favored a model for managing the transition to public cloud [7], researchers have more recently examined the unpredictability of public cloud costs in light of the lack of a formal and standardized governance framework for deployment and management models [8]. Moreover, a recent report from the Brussels-based think tank Centre on Regulation in Europe (CERRE) on competition and regulation of cloud computing services gives special consideration to vendor lock-in and switching costs [9]. The report also acknowledges the increasing predominance of hyperscalers.

[1] https://www.docker.com/pricing/.

[2] https://www.hashicorp.com/ja/pricing?tab=terraform.

In this paper, we examine the potential weaknesses of countries or blocs in managing their digital sovereignty, questioning digital technology concepts and strategies grounded in previous ISoS research [10]. Moreover, as a contribution to a multidisciplinary reading, we emphasize the semantics of commonly used terms in contributing to the safe and rigorous grounding of political, social, legal, business, and technological strategic discussions. We clarify groups of computing artifacts based on any technology or size. We abstract groups of technology artifacts as Service elements. The service element is grounded in SOA [11] and service systems [12], defined as a specific structure with its entities being the computing artifacts that interact to generate value. In this research, we clarify the service concept, which encompasses the various semantics it adopts, depending on the discourse context.

Questioning SOA, the technology artifacts are embedded in ISoS services, converging products to unified interfaces, programmatic (API), and application implementation (App). Fig. 1 depicts, on the left, a monolith ISoS service while, on the right, a microservice in the ISoS model, where size is not a service model issue.

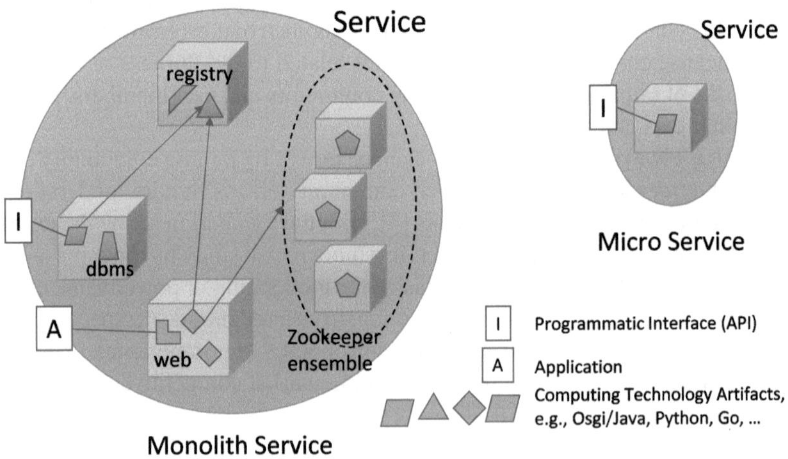

Fig. 1. On questioning the size of a service, from monolith to microservice

From the ISoS framework viewpoint, the strategy is not based on the atomic abstraction size, but on the formalized and implemented programmatic interfaces (API) and applications. The proposed clarification suggests confining software engineering contributions within the ISoS service borders. However, the crucial question is how to relate an informatics system (ISystem) to an information system, the core concept central to IT or ICT research. In the previous paper [13], we argued that an information system is a sociotechnical system that addresses both business and technology strategic concepts in positioning the idea for a business system.

In this paper, we revisit the application definition by "splitting" it from the implementation. The proposal follows model-driven design and specification of user applications, using *low-code* or *no-code* model-driven practices. OutSystems, Camunda, Bonita, or

Mendix are paradigmatic examples of this trend. Some have recently adopted generative AI to help generate user interfaces and automate the generation of implementation aspects [14].

The research was developed within the context of the SINCRO (national road traffic enforcement network) project, a publicly funded research initiative aimed at establishing a Portuguese national road traffic enforcement system based on an agnostic technology infrastructure, incorporating roadside cyber-physical equipment and IT distributed computing elements. The central research question is how to establish the anostic IT, and the hypothesis explored in this paper is the separation of the application concept from its technology implementation. What we refer to as an agnostic digital ecosystem means that competing products can join the IT ecosystem without dependency restrictions; a vendor lock-in-less IT.

The remaining paper is organized in Sect. 2, where we present and discuss related research. Section 3 positions the ISoS framework by redefining application as the abstraction and formalization of user access to implemented functionalities. Section 4 discusses the proposed contributions in the context of the SINCRO and HORUS projects, and Sect. 5 presents conclusions and further research.

2 Related Research

Community developments gained growing importance over the last two or three decades, in some cases with key contributions that have shaped the IT ecosystem. By the IT ecosystem, we refer to the de facto collaborative network of products, services, suppliers, and in-house teams from both business and technology, serving as key actors in digital transformation. The web and cloud have triggered innovation by introducing the scale, reliability, and (cyber)security dimensions as primary challenges. Furthermore, AI research has been reshaping the global web platform with intelligence over the past few decades. The Internet, powered by a unified TCP/IP networking infrastructure made possible by public DARPA investments, has become the canonical "wiring" for connecting everything in the digital world, an example of public investment [15]. An oversimplification emerged in business and scientific discourse, creating a sense of simplicity in the evolution of organizations' IT and society, leading to fast and free access to services, which became the underlying elements of the digital society. Social networks are a paradigmatic example of novel services that scale due to the free offering model. Moreover, achieve the network effect by inviting others to register. Even public administration adhered to the trend as a cost-effective mechanism to convey the political message. More recently, society has become aware of the risks associated with concentration, with the paradigmatic unauthorized sharing of personal data in the Analythica case [16] marking a significant milestone in shifting attitudes. The USA and the EU blocs started questioning concentration and developing new policies to impose order in the public's best interest. The complementary sociological perspective on sustainable technology entrepreneurship and innovation advocates for modern business development to achieve long-term competitiveness [17]. However, the research identifies a weak performance of R&D in creating value in ICT/IT domains for Serbia. The study and the broader EU research reported by Draghi [15], which identifies an 80% dependency on digital technology, raise questions about the way technology entrepreneurship and innovation have been conducted. The research [18] introduces sustainable technology entrepreneurship, refining the conceptual framework for a sustainable society, economy, organization, and people within the context of technology and management. Furthermore, as advocated in [19], systems engineering is necessary to address the complexity of software engineering, exemplified by the World Wide Web, which is the most significant information system. By establishing a formal border for computing technology artifacts, the ISoS framework adopted in the SINCRO project develops an agnostic IT of heterogeneity encapsulated in an ISoS service as atomic elements of an informatics system (ISystem).

The last three decades have seen a paradigm shift in science and engineering, driven by companies that scale to hyper-dimensions and R&D investments comparable to large governments or unions. The case of Alphabet, the parent company of Google, invested approximately $49 billion in R&D expenditures in 2024, with an upward trend since 2013 [20]. The $49 billion allocated to a single business company, compared to the EU's R&D expenditure of €381 billion in 2023 [21], should prompt questioning of the potential reasons behind the few businesses that tend to hold the power to reshape the future of digital society. For a rigorous comparison, it is worth noting that the EU R&D budget encompasses a broader range of research domains.

Our research, based on empirical results from projects with industry, contributed to the development of a technology-agnostic strategy, as seen in projects such as Brisa/ITSIBus [22], SINCRO/ISoS [23], and FORDESI SITL-IoT [24, 25]. A key contribution was defining and agreeing with potential suppliers' open data models and programmatic interfaces to reshape the underlying technology landscape, making it vendor lock-in-free.

Unfortunately, public administration appears to be operating '*after the loss*' to reinstate the competition authority, with the hope of changing course through the adoption of open standards. This would create a democratic market where any startup with a valuable product has the same opportunity as a large company. The question is how to value the paramount role of a large company, such as Alphabet/Google, in leading Kubernetes, which is making a reality the 90s idea of a distributed operating system (DOS) [26]. The idea and investment in Kubernetes infrastructure were motivated by Google's internal need to cope with scale [27]. It is impressive to see the fast-growing dynamics from research and industry around concepts introduced by Kubernetes, a Cloud Native Computing Foundation (CNCF) community project, which, as of May 2025, has attracted the impressive 3,794 contributors. Kubernetes has overshadowed other significant scientific contributions to the challenging goal of making distributed computing more accessible under the Open Container Initiative (OCI) Container concept [28]. The cloud computing paradigm, discussed in the context of real-time industrial systems [29], also applies to the back-office IT landscape.

Nevertheless, computing science and engineering, or the adopted informatics engineering terminology, require clarification of terms and concepts to facilitate a seamless interdisciplinary understanding and collaboration. For a fine-tuned clarification, we suggest separating computer science and engineering from computing science and engineering with the fundamental premise that the complexity of the computing domain makes an independent body of knowledge. A cyberphysical system, e.g., a computer, requires electrotechnical competencies that a computing engineer tends to be less familiar with.

Returning to the operating systems and distributed operating systems of the 90s, we summarize the responsibility of the informatics (computing) engineering as establishing a reliable distributed computing ecosystem. The distributed computing ecosystem relies on well-founded operating system abstractions that manage computer resources. Through a standard application programming interface (API) named System Calls, these abstractions provide the foundation for operationalizing software constructs called informatics systems, which implement business or user applications. Google's Kubernetes vision, driven by internal needs to address the scale of offered cloud services [27], is considered the de facto standard due to the considerable investment of the large development community. Kubernetes has contributed to the concretization of the 90s distributed operating system, pushing the Internet/web platform to a novel dimension by revisiting the on-premises (CAPEX) approach with an intelligent cloud provider lock-in-less adoption (OPEX) if it develops the necessary open standards [1].

Figure 2 depicts the two key infrastructure concepts: i) the operating system abstracting processing (CPU, GPU, NNP), memory, and input/output resources of a single node on the left, and ii) a cluster abstracting the same kind of resources on one or more nodes wired by a TCP/IP (internet) communication infrastructure. The Kubernetes ecosystem has served as the seed for numerous open-source initiatives and products that are associated with the DevOps (development and operations) vision for the lifecycle management of applications, is contributing to question the trend to move for public cloud instead of an intelligent balance with on-premises, adopting what is known as hybrid-cloud [30]. The decision to move to the public cloud is questionable, given the risks associated with the 'First-mover disadvantage,' which suggests the possibility of high costs and uncertainties for adopters of under-consolidated public services offerings. One recurring disadvantage is the lack of a regulated and secure infrastructure, which allows companies to move freely across public cloud providers without restrictions, as discussed in [31] as barriers to switching cloud providers.

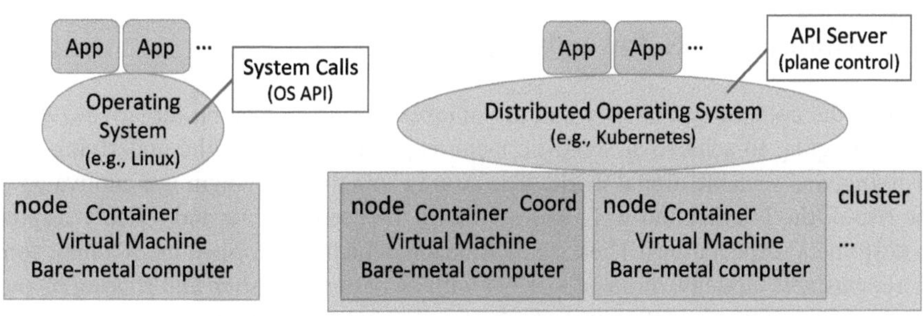

Fig. 2. Revisiting cloud computing with the 90s distributed operating system

The operating system is centered on the process object, which provides abstraction functionalities made available by the system call, similar to an application programming interface (API). The distributed operating system (DOS), based on Kubernetes, manages the central object, the pod, through the API server, which is identical to the OS system calls. The main difference is that processes in an OS are restricted to a single computer, whereas pods can be deployed on distributed nodes. In other words, the OS enables the execution of applications' computing logic on the same computer. The application running on the DOS has its computational logic in containers within pods deployed across cluster nodes. The cluster nodes can be on-premises or, if justified by a technical and business assessment, hosted on a public cloud provider.

Kubernetes focuses on abstracting a scalable (distributed operating system) execution environment for containerized applications. A common understanding of an application refers to a program or a set of programs, also called software, that implements a set of functionalities accessible to (business) users. In other words, what Kubernetes refers to as containerized applications is depicted in Fig. 1 as computing technology artifacts inside containers and logically modelled by the ISoS service entity. Our approach follows the idea of delimiting software engineering to a service abstraction, considering a service as an atomic entity that can be of any complexity, as discussed in [32]. Considering the service entity as a closed box follows the SOA principle, defined three decades ago by Jim Waldo [33], which envisions any commodity embedding computing capabilities as a findable entity. At the same time, all register in a registry service, making this an adaptive complex system of systems. While challenging, the encapsulation of a diverse range of payloads, including computing technology artifacts, is gaining momentum with Kubernetes in addressing distribution and scalability. Moreover, the fast-evolving embedding of AI into citizens' lives and organizations needing distributed computing resouces, dealing with data volume and diversity, model training and fine-tuning, scalability and elasticity, storage and throughput, and networking, can take advantage of the emerging Cloud Native (CN) and Artificial Intelligence (AI) [34]. Cloud-native is nothing more than an updated arrangement of the best-tailored computer resources available on-premises, on public providers, or even leveraging the growing computing potential of personal laptops, e.g., by deploying some computational logic to a web assembly runtime initially targeted to web browsers and more recently to agile high-performance computing (HPC) based on OCI containers [35].

3 Positioning ISoS Towards the Agnostic IT

Despite the computing maturity and the number of standardization initiatives, we are still struggling to achieve an agnostic technology ecosystem for the underlying, fast-evolving, and scalable digital world. The cloud computing paradigm was motivated by the rise of the Internet and web, and driven by the need to scale and reliably respond to customers' expectations. The case of Amazon, which transformed its excellent commerce business strategy, initiated in 1994 with an online bookshop and sharing its own need being pioneer the offering in 2006 of web services known as Amazon Web Services (AWS) with Elastic Compute Cloud (EC2) and Simple Storage Service (S3), as percursos of what is now known as cloud computing [36]. For some reason, only a few, including Google, understood the high margins that could be achieved by investing in on-premises infrastructure and simultaneously investing in an ecosystem that invites others to transition from CAPEX to OPEX, without questioning the maturity of computing and communication technologies or the risks of depending on others to scale their business.

The incorporation of generative AI features for automatically generating business process models in the ISO/IEC standard Business Process Model and Notation

(BPMN) language or user interface forms can be found in the Camunda BPM platform [37]. Grounded on large language models (LLM) for generative artificial intelligence approaches, [38] proposes the Large Process Model (LPM), combining LLMs with knowledge-based systems and automated reasoning for business process management (BPM) and automation. However, adopting AI features deepens the complexity of the supporting technology artifacts and how competing vendors can offer partial contributions. All integrate to establish a consistent, secure, and reliable IT. The question, therefore, is how to structure heterogeneous computing artifacts that potentially require computer-specific resources, such as CPU, GPU, or a neural network processor (NNP), without compromising the agnostic dimension for the organization's IT.

Following the ISoS strict structuration of computing technology artifacts into service abstractions and the redefinition of application, an organization's digital is suggested to evolve for a unified standard user interface as the initial entry authentication step to access the ISoS desktop, depicted in Fig. 3.

Any user authenticates through a single sign-on (SSO) mechanism into the organization's portal and, based- on their respective profile, views and accesses the relevant applications or application hierarchies. The administration application is visible at the desktop only for ISoS IT users with the administration role.

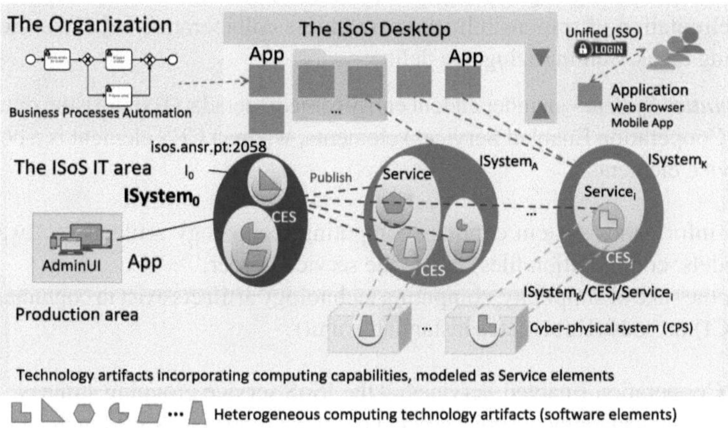

Fig. 3. The proposed unified ISoS applications desktop

As depicted in Fig. 3, applications can be generated from business process models or generative AI mechanisms, resulting in the application entity with the required metadata and configuration mechanisms. The application entity holds the mechanisms to invoke application implementations (through ISoS service technology artifacts) and present user interaction flows, e.g., in a web browser, on a mobile device, or a simple command-line interface. Another aspect of the ISoS strategy is to consider that some cyber components of a cyberphysical system, or all the CPS cyber components, can be modeled as an ISoS service entity. This move establishes a unified strategy for any organization, public or private, and across all sectors to develop a comprehensive cross-organizational

IT system, spanning from back-office applications to production area applications and cyber-physical systems.

To accurately position ISoS, specific terms and concepts require clarification for a more comprehensive, cross-disciplinary understanding. The study of information systems in the context of organizations has a long tradition. Submitting "*information system concept*" to Google search, the AI Overview reports as of the writing of the paper with "*… is a network of components that collect, process, store, and distribute information to support decision-making and other administrative duties within an organization*". On the other hand, the NIST[3] glossary defines information system as a "*Discrete set of information resources organized for the collection, processing, maintenance, use, sharing, dissemination, or disposition of information.*" Both definitions position information system centered on data management strategy, rather than a formal approach to technology management. However, if crossing with information technology product in the same glossary, "*A discrete, identifiable information technology asset (e.g., hardware, software, firmware) …*", it is possible to infer the opposite. Furthermore, in the same glossary, application is defined as "*A hardware/software system …*", meaning it encompasses both the computer and the computing logic (software) that implements and responds to user or business requirements.

Therefore, given the informatics engineering youthfulness, in the Anglo-Saxon terminology of computing engineering, it is essential to position core concepts towards a formal delimitation of responsibilities for seamless collaboration between science and engineering areas. Summarizing, we define:

- ***Informatics System*** - an independent entity (object metadata) comprising one or more CES (Cooperation Enabled Services) elements, where a CES element is a composite of service elements.
  - An informatics system confines computing technology artifacts (software, data models, configuration files) inside the service border;
  - For the sake of simplicity, computing technology artifacts exist in container images (OCI) or pods (Kubernetes instantiable unit)
- ***CES*** (Cooperation Enabled Services) – the ISoS service grouping strategy.
- ***Service*** – the leaf element (object metadata) of an informatics system tree that implements zero or more programmatic interfaces (I), the API concept (implementation of computing accessed functionalities), and zero or more applications (implementation of user functionalities, UI).
- ***Interface (I)*** – implemented interface (object metadata) defined in some interface definition language.
  - An interface object includes the metadata that a programmatic client requires to construct the accessing proxy.
- ***Application (A, App)*** – Is the entity (object metadata) formalizing user functionalities, and how the implementation is accessed, e.g., the URL for the entry web page.

[3] https://csrc.nist.gov/glossary (US National Institute of Standards and Technology).

  - Our definition of application suggests a change in the commonly adopted semantics. Most used semantics consider the application tightly bound to the implementation. We propose to separate the contexts.

- ***Informatics System of Systems*** (***ISoS***) is our proposal for formalizing an organization's information technology (IT) area.

  - Formalizes an IT based on the meta-informatics system, ***ISystem$_0$***, as a metadata registry, accessed under security credentials on port 2058, e.g., *isos.ansr.pt:2058*, for the SINCRO case, as depicted in Fig. 3.

As discussed in the introduction, the differentiation of the microservice concept is not considered relevant for the ISoS framework. The informatics system engineer determines whether the service element is a small piece of software, such as a simple REST API, or a complex suite of computing technology artifacts, for example, migrating a legacy monolithic system in the ISoS context. The ISoS framework suggests a formal structuration for the growing complexity and risks of the digital underlying infrastructure, with a potential grading of responsibilities for informatics engineers and other participating competencies. The grading is facilitated by encapsulating computing technology artifacts into the service abstraction, which can play the lowest systemic responsibility level. Our proposal to formalize the application object as a distinct entity, decoupled from technology implementation, opens up a space for standardization and convergence of a universal user interaction language. As a first approach, the application entity object holds the data required for application invocation, e.g., its entry URL. The strategy enables engineers to create mechanisms for multivendor setups, with products plugging into a standard, agnostic digital infrastructure.

The proposed extension of ISoS, which involves formalizing the user application concept beyond the programmatic interface, aims to facilitate the establishment of a unified digital ecosystem for layperson users. At the same time, technology heterogeneity is hidden by adopting containerization for computing technology artifacts, which are essentially software parts composed of computing programs, making it possible to establish higher-level constructs without requiring complex changes to legacy assets. Figure 4 depicts the simplest informatics system, based on a single CES and a service element, which we hypothesize abstracts a legacy system.

The private-led Kubernetes cloud infrastructure, as a community initiative, incorporates interesting concepts that can contribute to a public-led technology (through public administration investment), sociotechnical developments, and business strategy. This approach, where public open standards moderate business dynamics, fosters a compliant European agnostic digital ecosystem. The idea opposes a business management thinking ground on the principle that technology is not a problem. However, despite investing in interoperability, the state of the digital technology landscape already follows a software-centric approach, leading to unique products whose interoperability needs to be addressed, rather than a systemic approach where products integrate into a cooperative digital landscape. By cooperative digital landscape, we mean interoperability by design, meaning that (informatics) systems engineers structure software under standard patterns, not depending on developer technical skills or beliefs, but developing for passing conformance processes. Interestingly, the 2018 OECD report [39] suggests a digital government policy framework (DGPF) based on six premises for digital government: i) Digital by design, ii) data-driven public sector, iii) government as a platform, iv) open by default, v) user-driven, and vi) proactiveness, in what we argue the ISoS framework is a contribution.

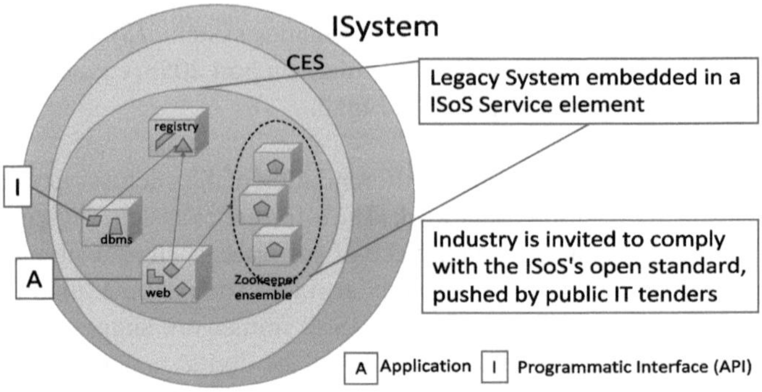

Fig. 4. Computing technology artifacts exist in ISoS's service elements

In the following chapter, we report on the application and results from the ANSR/SINCRO and BP/HORUS research projects, which are committed to questioning the agnostic digital technology validated in both public (ANSR/SINCRO) and private (BP/HORUS) contexts.

4 The SINCRO and HORUS Cases

Despite the numerous conceptual, development, and runtime frameworks, integrating computing technology artifacts from different vendors and across various technology frameworks or platforms is a costly and risky endeavor. The long-discussed and researched interoperability continues to be a recurring concern in achieving the integration of disparate, heterogeneous computing-based products and remains a challenge to researchers. More recently, AI has raised concerns about ethics, accountability, security, and interoperability for cooperation among AI systems by introducing dynamic interoperability in the context of systems of CPS (SoCPS) [40]. In the SINCRO project, citizen trustworthiness is a challenging problem related to AI-based vehicle identification confidence and the possibility of generating a false-positive notification that could result in a fine for a driver. The projects SINCRO, within the context of the Portuguese national road traffic enforcement network, and HORUS, for detecting outstanding vehicle fuel payments, utilize AI-based vehicle identification. Moreover, despite AI having gained growing importance, our research is committed to challenging an agnostic extended IT, considering both back-office and cyber-physical systems (CPS), in both cases, for roadside CPS equipment to detect and generate evidence of traffic rule violations and for fuel station payment enforcement. One question was developing a national infrastructure that incorporates road cyber-physical systems and back-office informatics systems in a unified IT system. On the assumption that for each public tender to renew or extend the network, no constraint shall exist concerning specific technology, product, or service supplied by one particular business company. Moreover, the maintenance and changes to back-office systems (informatics systems) should be supervised by the national road safety authority (ANSR) in a seamless collaborative network [36]. The Makewise company, which offers the vehicle identification product 'Plate.Vision[4], version 2 as a service, is an example of a company that joined SINCRO project efforts to contribute to defining the standard API (YAML file lpr-apiI-v1.0.3.yaml). Following the first phase of the SINCRO project in 2010, we evolved from 2022 to 2024 to unify execution granularity based on the ISoS service concept. We suggest encapsulating computing technology artifacts into container images following the Open Container Initiative (OCI) image and runtime standards to facilitate industry adherence. Furthermore, while a container composite is restricted to the same node, the pod prepares a group of containers for the distributed Kubernetes context. Therefore, adopting the Pod concept answers the distribution case, allowing ISoS service elements to be deployed on a Kubernetes cluster and, in this way, being ready to incorporate distributed informatics systems.

Figure 5 depicts the two products: i) Carmen from Adaptive Recognition and ii) Plate. Vision from Makewise.

Both products incorporate updated AI implementations that can evolve through product upgrades without compromising existing dependencies from other service elements of the same or another informatics system. The ISystem_0 and the associated metadata for service elements can dynamically resolve dependencies between informatics systems, enabling the retrieval of a reference to an API implementation, interface (I), and adapting client service access. The interoperability of ISoS services faces a similar impedance mismatch in client proxies as discussed in the research on microservice-oriented database systems [41]. Nevertheless, in our approach, the metadata associated with an ISoS service, namely the data needed to create an interoperability proxy, contributes to improving adaptability between heterogeneous implementations.

For the case of encapsulating Carmen's C and Java language code base, we adopted encapsulating the computing technology artifacts in an OCI container image. On the other hand, the Makewise company containerized the Plate.Vision's computing logic and resources were available in a pod. Both implementations are based on heterogeneous technology options, depending on the informatics systems development companies' culture, hidden by the ISoS service concept, ranging from a simple microservice or an uber package of computing technology artifacts, including complementary resources like configuration files, as discussed. The adopted strategy proves a viable path to invite companies developing informatics systems to unify the delivery of market offerings.

[4] https://makewise.pt/plate-vision-2/.

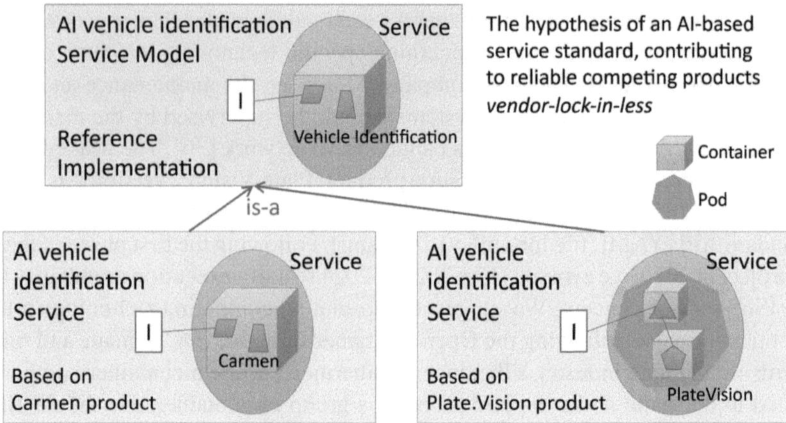

Fig. 5. The validated open-standard vehicle identification service

5 Conclusions and Further Research

The paper presents and discusses the formalization of an application to the ISoS framework towards a multivendor strategy for accessing a compound of functionalities implemented by an ISoS service. The research introduces recent contributions from computer virtualization, such as adopting containers and clusters with nodes running pods with containers. We argue that Kubernetes clusters establish the 90s distributed operating system, making cloud computing a streamlined infrastructure supporting the challenged agnostic IT.

The paper further proposes boosting public investment in making practical open standards through reference implementation that "imposes" on the market a framework towards competing tenders where start-ups and SME have opportunities to grow through public tenders adjusted to their bidding business size risks. In the SINCRO project, a vehicle identification ISoS service was validated by collaborating companies, who adapted their products to comply with open-API standard interfaces. The ISoS service encapsulation using OCI containers or Kubernetes pods establishes market-supplying elements that can be assembled into CES and thus form Informatics systems as isolated formal computing responsibility borders registered on the $ISystem_0$.

The hypothetical adoption of the ISoS framework as the standard structuration of an IT area, making any computing technology artifact, needs further research. This would be accompanied by the industry's adherence to migrating their products as ISoS service elements. Our open research question is whether the ISoS ISystem concept, with its CES made of service elements, should be incorporated as an operating or distributed operating system native managed entity. From previous research and adherence so far from industry, public, and private IT professionals, we identify the bases to succeed. The apparent success of the Kubernetes operator concept, as evidenced by the numerous open-source initiatives, supports the hypothesis that an ISoS ISystem operator can effectively manage informatics system objects, making this research valuable. Furthermore, the agnostic IT success relies on the public IT professional willing to precede tenders from investments to invite the industry to converge on replaceable/substitutable (open-standard) products (ISystems) or parts of products (services or CES elements) as a way to make effective the long-discussed intelligent public procurement [42].

Acknowledgments. This work is partly supported by research grants from ANSR/SINCRO, 2010–2012, 2022–2024, and BP/HORUS from 2013, led by IPL/ISEL/UnIRE and GIATSI research groups. National funds partially support this paper through the FCT - Fundação para a Ciência e a Tecnologia, I.P., Research Center in Communication Studies and CIUHCT - Interuniversity Center for the History of Science and Technology, NOVA University (UIDB/00286/2020).

References

1. Biglaiser, G., Crémer, J., Mantovani, A.: The economics of the cloud, tech. rep. Toulouse School Econ. (2024)
2. Radanovic, I.: The big con: how the consulting industry weakens our businesses, infantilizes our governments, and warps our economies - review (2024)
3. Skrodzki, M.: How the deprecation of java applets affected online visualization frameworks - a case study. In: VisGap - The Gap between Visualization Research and Visualization Software (Gillmann, C., Krone, M., Reina, G., Wischgoll, T. (eds.). The Eurographics Association (2020)
4. Mazzucato, M.: The entrepreneurial state debunking public vs. private sector myths (2013)
5. Mazzucato, M.: Building the entrepreneurial state: a new framework for envisioning and evaluating a mission-oriented public sector (2015)
6. Government, A.: Data and digital gobernment strategy – the data and digital vision for a world-class APS to 2030," 2023
7. Alkhalil, A., Sahandi, R., John, D.: A review of the current level of support to aid decisions for migrating to cloud computing. In: Proceedings of the International Conference on Internet of Things and Cloud Computing, ICC '16, (New York, NY, USA), Association for Computing Machinery (2016). https://doi.org/10.1145/2896387.2896443
8. Manganelli, A., Schnurr, D.: Competition and regulation of cloud computing services: economic analysis and review of EU policies," tech. rep., Centre on Regulation in Europe (CERRE) (2024). Accessed: 02 June 2025
9. Manganelli, A., Schnurr, D.: Competition and regulation of cloud computing services: economic analysis and review of EU policies (2024)
10. Osório, A.L., Belloum, A., Afsarmanesh, H., Camarinha-Matos, L.M.: Agnostic informatics system of systems: the open isos services framework. In: Collaboration in a Data-Rich World, (Cham), pp. 407–420, Springer Int. Pub. (2017). https://doi.org/10.1007/978-3-319-65151-4_37
11. Wollrath, A., Riggs, R., Waldo, J.: A distributed object model for the JavaTM system. In: Proceedings of the 2nd Conference on USENIX Conference on Object-Oriented Technologies (COOTS) - Volume 2, COOTS '96, (USA), p. 17, USENIX Association (1996)
12. Stoshikj, M., Kryvinska, N., Strauss, C.: Service systems and service innovation: two pillars of service science. Procedia Computer Science, vol. 83, pp. 212–220, 2016. The 7th International Conference on Ambient Systems, Networks and Technologies (ANT 2016) / The 6th International Conference on Sustainable Energy Information Technology (SEIT-2016) / Affiliated Workshops

13. Osório, A.L., Rabelo, R.J., Gonçalves, C.: A business technology alignment strategy for digital collaborative networks. In: Collaborative Networks in Digitalization and Society 5.0 (L. M. Camarinha-Matos, X. Boucher, and A. Ortiz, eds.), (Cham), pp. 380–397, Springer Nature Switzerland (2023)
14. Liu, Y., et al.: An empirical study on low code programming using traditional vs large language model support (2024)
15. Draghi, M.: The future of european competitiveness - a competitiveness strategy for Europe," tech. rep., European Commission, Part A of the Draghi Report (2024)
16. Brown, A.J.: Should I stay or should I leave?": exploring (Dis)continued facebook use after the cambridge analytica scandal. Social Media + Society, vol. 6, no. 1, p. 2056305120913884 (2020). https://doi.org/10.1177/2056305120913884
17. Jakšic, M.L., Marinkovic, S., Rakicévic, J.: Sustainable technology entrepreneurship and development - the case of Serbia. Manage. J. Theory Pract. Manage. **70**, 65–73 (2014). https://doi.org/10.7595/management.fon.2014.0004
18. F.T.S. Group: 2025 tech trends report, tech. rep. Future Today Strategy Group, (2025). 18th edition, comprehensive foresight report
19. Sommerville, I.: Software Engineering. Pearson, 9 ed. (2010)
20. Alphabet, S.: Research and development expenditure from 2007 to 2023. (2024). Accessed on 30 May 2025
21. Eurostat. EU spent â,¬381.4 billion on R&D in 2023 (2024). https://ec.europa.eu/eurostat/web/products-eurostat-news/w/ddn-20241211-2. Accessed: 2025–06–02
22. Osório, A.L., et al.: Open multi-technology service oriented architectur for "its" business models: the ITSIBus etoll services. In: Collaborative Networks and Their Breeding Environments (Camarinha-Matos, L.M., Afsarmanesh, H., Ortiz, A. eds.). (Boston, MA), pp. 439–446, Springer US (2005)
23. Gonçalves, C., Dias, T., Osório, A.L., Camarinha-Matos, L.M.: A multi-supplier collaborative monitoring framework for informatics system of systems. In: Collaborative Networks in Digitalization and Society 5.0, (Cham), pp. 44–53, Springer International Publishing (2022). https://doi.org/10.1007/978-3-031-14844-6_4
24. Gonçalves, C., Osório, A.L., Camarinha-Matos, L.M., Dias, T., Tavares, J.: A collaborative cyber-physical microservices platform – the SITL-IoT Case. In: Smart and Sustainable Collaborative Networks 4.0, (Cham), pp. 411–420, Springer International Publishing (2021). https://doi.org/10.1007/978-3-030-85969-5_38
25. Osório, A.L., Camarinha-Matos, L.M., Dias, T., Gonçalves, C., Tavares, J.: Open and collaborative micro services in digital transformation. In: Smart and Sustainable Collaborative Networks 4.0, (Cham), pp. 393–402, Springer International Publishing (2021). https://doi.org/10.1007/978-3-030-85969-5_36
26. Tanenbaum, A.S., Van Renesse, R.: Distributed operating systems. ACM Comput. Surv. **17**(4), 419–470 (1985). https://doi.org/10.1145/6041.6074
27. Burns, B., Grant, B., Oppenheimer, D., Brewer, E., Wilkes, J.: Borg, omega, and kubernetes. Commun. ACM **59**(5), 50–57 (2016). https://doi.org/10.1145/2890784
28. Initiative, O.C.: Open container initiative. https://opencontainers.org/ (2025). Accessed: 02 June 2025
29. Queiroz, R., Cruz, T., Mendes, J., Sousa, P., Simoes, P.: Container-based virtualization for real-time industrial systems - a systematic review. ÃCM Comput. Surv. (2023). https://doi.org/10.1145/3617591
30. Alonso, J., et al.: Understanding the challenges and novel architectural models of multi-cloud native applications â€" a systematic literature review. J. Cloud Comput. **12**(1), 6 (2023). https://doi.org/10.1186/s13677-022-00367-6
31. Ofcom: Cloud services market study - final report, tech. rep., Office of Communications (Ofcom). (2023). Accessed: 02 June 2025

32. Zimmermann, O.: An Architectural Decision Modeling Framework for Service Oriented Architecture Design. Phd thesis, Universität Stuttgart (2009). https://doi.org/10.18419/opus-2665
33. Waldo, J.: Alive and well: jini technology today. Computer **33**(6), 107–109 (2000). https://doi.org/10.1109/2.846324
34. Zaalouk, A., et al.: Cloud native Artificial Intelligence," tech. rep., Cloud Native Comput. Found. (CNCF) (2024)
35. Chadha, M., Krueger, N., John, J., Jindal, A., Gerndt, M., Benedict, S.: Exploring the use of webassembly in HPC. In: Proceedings of the 28th ACM SIGPLAN Annual Symposium on Principles and Practice of Parallel Programming, PPoPP '23, (New York, NY, USA), pp. 92–106, Association for Computing Machinery (2023) https://doi.org/10.1145/3572848.3577436
36. Carreno, A.M.: Analyzing Amazon's evolution from an online bookstore to a global tech giant (2024). https://doi.org/10.5281/zenodo.14649218
37. Senathipathi, S.: Revolutionizing insurance policy administration: AI-driven low-code automation in guidewire policycenter with Camunda & Python. **36**, 11–26 (2023)
38. Kampik, T., et al.: Large process models: a vision for business process management in the age of generative AI. KI - Künstliche Intelligenz (2024). https://doi.org/10.1007/s13218-024-00863-8
39. OECD: The OECD digital government policy framework: six dimensions of a digital government. Tech. Rep. 2, OECD Publishing (2020). https://doi.org/10.1787/f64fed2a-en
40. Nilsson, J., Javed, S., Albertsson, K., Delsing, J., Liwicki, M., Sandin, F.: AI concepts for system of systems dynamic interoperability. Sensors (2024). https://doi.org/10.3390/s24092921
41. Laigner, R., Zhou, Y., Salles, M.A.V., Liu, Y., Kalinowski, M.: Data management in microservices: state of the practice, challenges, and research directions. Proc. VLDB Endow. **14**(13), 3348–3361 (2021). https://doi.org/10.14778/3484224.3484232
42. OECD: Integrating responsible business conduct in public procurement, tech. rep. OECD Publishing (2020). https://doi.org/10.1787/02682b01-en

A Blockchain-Integrated Deep Learning Approach for Robust Anomaly Detection in IoT Systems

Chaima Khalfaoui(✉)

AODB Group, Paris, France
khalfaoui.chayma@gmail.com

Abstract. The proliferation of IoT systems has introduced significant challenges related to security, scalability, and real-time decision-making. While AI-based techniques, particularly those relying on Deep Learning, have shown strong capabilities for anomaly detection, they remain vulnerable to adversarial attacks and require substantial computational resources for retraining. To address these limitations, we propose a secure and scalable anomaly detection framework that combines AI with Blockchain technology. The proposed approach integrates two complementary modules governed by a unified global detection policy: one for proactive device monitoring and another for real-time anomaly detection. A hybrid Off-chain/On-chain strategy is employed to optimize performance-training and modelling are performed off-chain, while detection decisions are executed on-chain through smart contracts. This design ensures transparent, decentralized, and verifiable outcomes. Experimental validation conducted using the IBRL dataset demonstrates that our framework achieves high detection accuracy, reduces latency and energy consumption, and outperforms existing methods in terms of reliability and computational efficiency.

Keywords: IoT · Blockchain networks · Smart contracts · Anomaly detection · Stochastic processing · Deep Learning

1 Introduction

General Context. IoT systems have revolutionized various domains, significantly improving the daily lives of users in areas such as healthcare, smart cities, and vehicular networks [1, 2]. These advanced systems create intelligent environments, enabling seamless remote monitoring and control through smart devices. However, as the number of smart devices is projected to exceed 14 billion by 2024, with ongoing exponential growth to meet market demands [3], the security of IoT systems has emerged as a critical concern. It is now widely recognized as one of the greatest challenges of this decade [4]. IoT devices, often characterized by limited memory and computing power, are highly

Published by Springer Nature Switzerland AG 2026
L. M. Camarinha-Matos et al. (Eds.): PRO-VE 2025, IFIP AICT 770, pp. 254–277, 2026.
https://doi.org/10.1007/978-3-032-05673-3_16

susceptible to random faults and cyber-attacks, given the hostile deployment environments [5], resulting in inevitable anomalies in the processed data. These anomalies can manifest as incorrect readings, corrupted data or unexpected components behaviours, undermining the reliability and accuracy of the collected data and subsequent analysis. The establishment of effective early detection mechanisms for these anomalies is paramount to ensure reliable functioning of services and uphold the overall security of the devices and the network. This measure plays a pivotal role in creating a trusted IoT environment. Deep Learning-based approaches have lately emerged as effective solutions for large-scale anomaly detection. DL models excel in learning various data features and using them to make accurate decisions about unseen future data [6]. However, the growing popularity of DL models also exposes them to significant security issues. Machine Learning models are vulnerable to a wide range of adversarial attack that aim to compromise their integrity. Adversarial attacks can occur at different stages, including during model training, testing, and post-deployment processing. These attacks seek to manipulate legitimate input data to mislead the model, resulting in inaccurate results and anomalies. Common types of attacks include membership inference attacks, model inversion attacks, model evasion attacks, and model extraction attacks [7]. It is of paramount importance to establish secure and reliable services. By doing so, several potential risks can be effectively mitigated, contributing to ensure trustworthy IoT systems. Meanwhile, Blockchain has emerged as a highly promising technology that enables autonomous software services and ensures reliable information exchange while maintaining a high level of availability and transparency. This technology has the capability to capture the entire lifecycle of Deep Learning models, as it documents every stage from creation to updating and usage [8]. However, existing works have not fully exploited the potential of combining both techniques to enhance anomaly detection in IoT due to the challenges associated with their integration. Indeed, both Blockchain and DL impose demanding requirements in terms of energy consumption and processing time while IoT systems need to deliver information intact, at the right time, and with minimal cost and delay. Therefore, developing such a system requires careful consideration of the associated challenges. In this paper, we introduce a new hybrid detection approach designed for IoT systems.

Main Contributions. In our previous work [9], we proposed a trust-based decentralized access control approach for IoT data management systems. The approach allowed to predict insider malicious entities in IoT systems based on their observed behaviour and using probabilistic Bayesian modelling and stochastic Markov modelling. Evaluation results showed efficient prediction of dishonest entities compared to other trust-based management approaches. However, we recognized that while the results from our initial article showcased good detection performances, it fell short of meeting in considering two criteria: the real-time demands of IoT scenarios and the evolving nature of attacks in IoT environments. Indeed, the performances quickly decreased when the network scalability is increasing. Therefore, while we consider proactive anomaly prediction solutions are valuable in securing IoT systems, they are not sufficient to address the challenging needs of IoT environments. To overcome the identified limitations, we propose a secure anomaly detection approach that ensures reliable data communication within IoT systems. Our solution combines Blockchain and Deep Learning through two interrelated modules operating under a unified detection policy. The first module enables proactive device monitoring, while the second ensures real-time anomaly detection. By integrating both proactive and reactive mechanisms, the system fosters a secure and efficient IoT environment. Beyond accurate decision-making, our approach aims to reduce both time and cost by optimizing module deployment and minimizing data flow. The detection modelling phase is executed off-chain, while decision-making is handled on-chain via smart contracts, ensuring trustworthy and verifiable results. This architectural choice improves scalability and facilitates integration into diverse IoT contexts. To summarize, our work offers several distinct contributions: A comprehensive analysis of Blockchain-based anomaly detection methods in IoT, detailing their specifications, strengths, and limitations. A decentralized Blockchain-IoT architecture that secures both applications and services, with Blockchain as an active structural component fostering trust and resilience. A formal modelling of the anomaly detection task as a multi-objective minimization problem with simultaneous constraints. An Off-chain/On-chain detection strategy leveraging stochastic device monitoring to reduce Blockchain computation and enhance scalability. Extensive empirical validation on the Intel Berkeley Research Lab dataset, demonstrating the effectiveness and real-world applicability of the proposed approach.

2 Background

This section provides a concise yet comprehensive overview of Blockchain technology, a core component of our proposed approach. Blockchain is built upon a decentralized peer-to-peer architecture, where nodes collaborate to verify and store transactions in blocks. Each block contains a sequence of transactions and is cryptographically linked to the previous one, forming a tamper-evident "block-chain." When a node adds a new block, it broadcasts it across the network to ensure data consistency among all participants [10]. Two central functionalities characterize Blockchain systems: the mining process and the consensus mechanism [11, 12]. These are supported by key security mechanisms, including Merkle trees, time-stamping, and cryptographic hashing. Common consensus protocols include Proof of Work and Proof of Stake. Bitcoin, introduced by Nakamoto [13], was the first Blockchain-based digital currency and utilizes PoW. Its success catalysed a wave of Blockchain applications across sectors such as identity management, electronic records, and remote-control systems, demonstrating Blockchain's potential to improve security and efficiency. Nick Szabo later extended this potential by proposing smart contracts, leading to the development of Ethereum, the first platform designed to execute such contracts [14]. Today, Ethereum remains the most widely used platform for decentralized applications. It relies on the Ethereum Virtual Machine (EVM) and uses Gas to measure and charge for computational tasks. Smart contracts, once deployed, function autonomously, enforcing predefined rules and agreements without external intervention. Other platforms such as [15, 16] have also emerged. They contribute to the development of autonomous and trust less processes. However, the execution of smart contracts is often resource-intensive, making it a costly process. To optimize resource usage, it is important to prioritize practical activities that have value, such as solving mathematical problems and conducting machine learning exercises [17]. This ensures that energy is not waste on futile tasks. In this section, we present a comprehensive review of DL-based anomaly detection solutions in the IoT. These solutions can be broadly categorized into three main types based on the source of anomalies: fault detection, event detection, and intrusion detection [18]. Additionally, a more detailed classification based on the recognition technique further divides them into five major categories: statistical methods [19], density-based methods [20], distance-based methods [21], clustering methods [22], and Machine Learning methods [23]. In our study, we specifically focus on ML-based anomaly detection approaches. To facilitate this analysis, we introduce three new sub-categories based on the architectural structure used for model deployment: smart contracts [24–28], Blockchain ledger [29–31], and traditional architectures [32–36]. Table 1. Provides a comparative analysis of these solutions, taking into account key parameters such as type of anomaly, detection strategy, utilized dataset, Blockchain platform, intended use of the Blockchain technology, targeted security features, and computational performance.

2.1 Anomaly Detection Based on Smart Contracts

Smart contracts have played a significant role in advancing anomaly detection approaches for IoT systems. Demertzis *et al.* [24] proposed an anomaly detection approach for Industrial IoT data by implementing an auto-encoder neural network embedded in a smart contract. The authors conducted evaluations using multiple datasets to ensure the reliability of their conclusions. Although the results demonstrated higher precision values compared to other models like SVM and iForest, the obtained accuracy rates were deemed insufficient for large-scale deployment. Additionally, the proposed approach incurred high computational expenses due to the complexity of the neural network architecture. Similarly, Alkadi *et al.* [26] developed a decision support framework that enables distributed intrusion detection in IoT networks using Blockchain and smart contracts. They employed LSTM algorithms and utilized the BoT-IoT datasets as input. The framework showed a lower false alarm rate in comparison to other ML algorithms such as SVM and Naive Bayes. Gupta *et al.* [27] introduced a DL-based scheme for detecting malicious smart contracts in IoT environments. Their classifier used an open Google BigQuery dataset and achieved a precision rate of up to 0.91% in identifying vulnerabilities. Saveetha *et al.* [28] aimed to explore the security potential of integrating Blockchain technology with intrusion detection systems. They initially employed an Ethereum Classic dataset, utilizing transaction attributes as input parameters. Subsequently, they employed RNN algorithms to identify specific types of Blockchain attacks. The study concluded that configuration variables alone were insufficient for accurate detection, and suggested to incorporate data from external sources to enhance the efficiency of the approach.

2.2 Anomaly Detection Based on Blockchain

During our examination of the research conducted by Podgorelec *et al.* [29], Kim *et al.* [30], and Odiathevar *et al.* [31], we observed a common trend in the incorporation of Blockchain technology in anomaly detection mechanisms. Most of the reviewed studies utilized Blockchain either as a database to supply input data for DL algorithms or as a secure storage tool to preserve decision-making results. However, a notable gap in research was identified, as none of these studies explored the potential of Blockchain technology in establishing a secure execution environment for anomaly detection services. Several factors contribute to this gap. The first reason can be associated to the costly nature of the Blockchain technology. Its implementation and maintenance expenses are significant, especially considering the complex verification and validation process required to support Blockchain security features. Secondly, the modelling and processing of DL algorithms within the Blockchain involve substantial delays and computational complexity. These challenges hinder large scale integration of Blockchain in IoT environment, particularly in the context of anomaly detection.

2.3 Anomaly Detection Based on Traditional Architectures

Recent literature has introduced various anomaly detection systems for IoT, primarily relying on centralized architectures [32–36]. However, such architectures raise significant concerns due to their vulnerability to attacks, particularly those exploiting single points of failure. Zhou et al. [33] proposed a predictive model combining Monte Carlo Markov Chains with a CNN to identify contaminated sources based on sparse concentration measurements. Evaluations on synthetic data showed high accuracy and a speedup of nearly twentyfold compared to traditional deep learning models. Similarly, Khodaei et al. [34] developed a detection model that integrates MCMC with an SVM for classifying breast cancer DNA genes. Their approach included a dimension reduction phase to preserve features while minimizing input size, yielding high classification accuracy with low computational overhead. Despite their promising performance, these models face limitations. Designed for domain-specific applications, they require substantial adaptation before being applied to broader IoT use cases.

2.4 Paper Positioning

To address the previously identified challenges, we propose a novel Blockchain-based approach for anomaly detection in IoT systems. Our method combines classification techniques, specifically Markov chains and DL, with an On-chain/Off-chain deployment strategy to ensure timely identification of malicious devices and anomalous data. The approach is designed to optimize key constraints, such as energy efficiency, response time, and computational performance.

3 Architecture Overview and Threat Model

3.1 System Architecture

The IoT system we aim to secure through our detection approach is implemented within a Blockchain-based architecture inspired from our work in [9]. In order to facilitate understanding, we provide a comprehensive description of the architecture's layers, as well as the components that constitute both the IoT system and the anomaly detection approach. This detailed overview enables a structured visualization of how our anomaly detection approach seamlessly integrates with the IoT system, thereby reinforcing its overall security and reliability. The selection of this architecture is primarily motivated by its modularity which facilitate the deployment of customized services through smart contracts and the seamless integration of various components as plugins. As illustrated in Fig. 1, the architecture consists of a hierarchically 3-layered structure consisting of the Perception layer, the Network layer, and the Storage layer, each serving a specific purpose. The role of each layer is described as follows.

- In the Perception layer, interconnected IoT devices such as sensors and actuators play a crucial role. These devices are responsible for collecting massive amounts of environmental data that represent observations of physical events and communicate them to the upper layer. We designate, by $D = \{d_1, d_2, d_3, ..., d_D\}$ the set of deployed IoT devices, and by $A = \{a_1, a_2, a_t, ..., a_A\}$ the set of all observations collected during a temporal period T. To ensure the integrity of data transmission, trusted Oracles enable the communication between the two layers. As in other studies, it is presumed that interdomain data transfer across wireless gateways is secure and WiFi is utilized as the transmitting and routing technology.

- The Network layer comprehends the Blockchain network, which includes miner nodes, a shared ledger, and smart contracts. This layer establishes a secure and trustworthy environment for the deployed services to exchange, process, and store transactions. Participant nodes within the Blockchain network analyze and process the traffic data received from the Perception layer, applying predefined anomaly detection policies specified in the smart contracts. For simplicity, we assume that each device transmits one observation per time slot, and each observation is encapsulated in a single transaction.

We designate, by $V = \{v_1, v_2, v_3, ..., v_V\}$ the set of participating nodes, by $K = \{k_1, k_2, k_t, ..., k_K\}$ the set of transactions processed during the period T. The processed data and decision results are then hashed and transmitted through Oracles to the upper layer, while the communication details are stored as transactions in the shared ledger for transparency and auditability.

- Lastly, the Storage layer consists of servers and data centers that provide long-term storage services. Data from the Network layer is routed to the Storage layer, where secure servers maintain the traceability of processed data and support the implementation of IoT end-user applications or data analytics. This layer plays a crucial role in providing efficient data management within the overall architecture.

3.2 Network Related Constraints

The Blockchain network operates under certain constraints that govern its performance. These constraints include:

- Transaction storage capacity: Each transaction in the blockchain has a predefined maximum storage capacity, which determines the maximum amount of data it can fit per observation. Transactions that surpass this storage capacity are not accepted.
- Transaction processing latency: Each transaction is subject to a maximum processing time limit, known as the maximum latency threshold. The value of this threshold is

Table 1. Relative comparison of the state of the art: Machine Learning based anomaly detection in IoT-driven applications using smart contracts, Blockchain, and other architectures.

Author	Year	Shortcomings	Data				Detection approach					Blockchain			Security & Performances features					
			Domain	Dataset	Attack	Fault	ML model	Preprocessing method	Training mode	Integration with BLC	Compared with	Blockchain Platform	Ledger	Smart Contract	Scalability	Integrity	Availability	Accuracy	Complexity	Delay
[24]	2020	-Considered only static data -Used imprecise decision thresholds	IoT for Industry 4.0	Water dataset	✓	✗	AE NN	One class	Inside	Inside	IFM SVM MCD	Ethereum	✓	✓	Low	High	High	Low	High	High
[25]	2021	-Based on staticical decision rules - Limited to detecting one type of errors	IoT for logistics	IBRL	✗	✓	Local	Basic	Inside	Inside	None	Hyperledgrer	✓	✓	Low	High	High	High	Low	Low
[26]	2021	-Only data is protected through BLC - The detection service is centralised, vulnerable to all point of failure attacks	IoT	UNSW NB15 BoTIoT	✓	✓	BiLSTM	Filtering	Outside	Outside	IFM SVM	Ethereum	✓	✓	High	High	Low	Low	High	High
[27]	2022	-The detection process is not secured	IoT	Google BigQuery	✓	✗	LSTM	Basic	Outside	Outside	ANN GRU	Ethereum	✓	✓	High	Low	Low	High	High	High
[28]	2022	-Considered only configuration data -Absence of comparing techniques	IoT	ETC logs	✓	✗	MLP LSM	Basic	Inside	Inside	None	Ethereum	✓	✓	Low	Low	Low	Low	NM	NM
[29]	2020	-Detection results are not reliable -Detection model for only one context -Unsupervised learning with BLC engendered high delays	IoT for Personal use	10 Tx Address logs	✗	✓	RF	None	Inside	inside	None	Ethereum	✓	✗	Low	Low	Low	Low	High	High
[30]	2021	-Input data is protected, while its treatment is left vulnerable -Semi-supervised training cost is high	IoT for Finances	Bitcoin Mainnet	✓	✗	AE	None	Outside	Outside	OC-SVM DNN, LR	Bitcoin	✓	✗	Low	Low	Low	High	High	High
[31]	2022	-Distributed system did not consider decentralized decision making to protect the detection service -Evaluation based on synthesized data	IoT	UNSW-NB15 NSL-KDD	✓	✗	SLFN Bayesian Random AE	Normalize	Inside	Inside	GMM KNN Bayesian GMM	Local	✓	✗	High	Low	High	High	Low	Low
[32]	2020	-Unsupervised learning engendered high delays -Centralized detection process	IoT for Smart cities	IBRL, Yahoo	✗	✓	Hybrid VAE	Basic	NA	NA	LSTM GGU SVM	NA	✗	✗	High	High	Low	High	High	High
[33]	2021	-Tested with only simulated datasets -Based on a centralized architecture	IoT for Environment	Synthetic data	✗	✓	CNN	MCMC	NA	NA	FNN	NA	✗	✗	Low	Low	Low	High	High	High
[37]	2021	-Centralized architecture vulnerable to all single point of failure	IoT	IBRL LUCE PDG	✗	✓	OCSVM	dimension reduction	NA	NA	SVM KCPA	NA	✗	✗	High	Low	Low	High	Low	Low
[35]	2021	-Lacks of integrity-preserving service for storing and exchanging data	IoT for Mechanics	MTruk	✓	✗	ANN	None	NA	NA	[38]	NA	✗	✗	High	Low	High	Low	NM	NM
[36]	2022	-Limited number of learning inputs -Centralized architecture vulnerable to all single point of failure attacks	IoT for Smart cities	IBRL	✗	✓	Multi-obj Gaussian	MLE	NA	NA	[39]	NA	✗	✗	Low	Low	Low	High	Low	Low
		Our Proposal	**IoT**	**IBRL**	✗	✓	**MLP**	**MCMC**	**Outside**	**Inside**	**KNN GNB**	**Ethereum**	✓	✓	**High**	**High**	**High**	**High**	**Low**	**Low**

** NM = Not Mentioned, NA = Not Applicable.

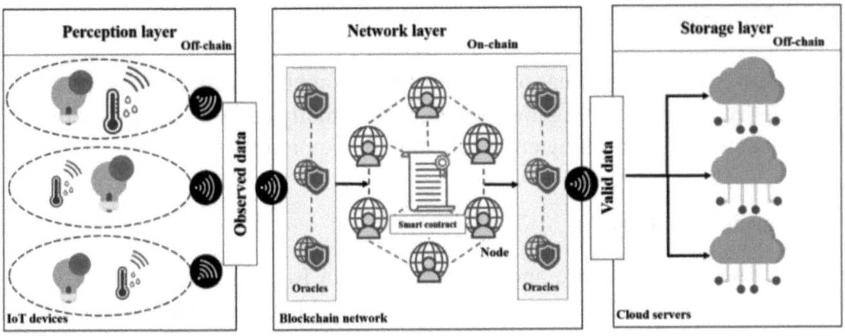

Fig. 1. System Architecture

determined during the configuration phase and can be adjusted based on the network's needs. Transactions exceeding the fixed threshold are rejected by the network.
- Validating nodes threshold: A minimum number of nodes within the network must participate in the validation process. This requirement is defined during the network's configuration phase. Failing to attain the minimum number of node validation threshold, result in a consensus failure, leading to their rejection by the network.

3.3 Threat Model

The objective of this paper is to enhance the security of IoT systems by implementing efficient and reliable anomaly detection approach based on Blockchain and Deep Learning. The vulnerabilities and attacks primarily focus on data integrity, where attackers compromise DL models and manipulate the processed data within the model. We investigate two distinct adversarial attacks. The first attack surface is focused on the IoT devices layer, while the second attack surface targets the Network layer. The main attacks that we consider within our approach are as follows:

- *False Data Injection Attack:* occurs in the perception layer, where an external adversarial entity would attempt to gain control over one or more IoT devices and deliberately submits inaccurate data, replacing the correct data that was originally collected. This malicious action not only compromises the data collection process but also has implications for all subsequent data processes and security procedures.
- *Evasion Model Attack:* occurs in the network layer, where an internal malicious entity that is already known to the system as a participating node in the Blockchain network and possessing access to the DL model would attempt to illegitimacy manipulate the anomaly detection decisions. By influencing other network nodes and gradually replacing their smart contract copies of the authentic DL model with a corrupted version that is trained to classify normal data as anomalous and anomalous data as normal. As a result, the malicious entity gains majority control within the network, compromising the accuracy and effectiveness of the entire detection process.

4 Problem Statement

In this section, we present a clear overview of the anomaly detection problem in IoT. By formulating hypotheses, setting constraints, and formally defining the problem, we lay a solid foundation for designing and evaluating our approach.

4.1 Research Hypothesis

Achieving efficient and secure anomaly detection in IoT requires minimizing energy consumption and response times while maintaining high computational performance in decision-making. Balancing these factors ensures optimal resource use and system effectiveness. In this context, we argue that combining Blockchain and Deep Learning in a detection framework, though complex, can yield reliable and cost-effective decisions provided that the computational burden is effectively distributed across system components. This vision is guided by the following principles: At the IoT device level: Compromised devices can produce large volumes of corrupted data, degrading system performance. As frequent targets of attacks exploiting hardware and software vulnerabilities, these devices should be filtered early. Early elimination reduces the data volume to be processed on-chain, alleviating both computational and security loads at the Blockchain level without compromising detection performance. At the Blockchain level: Transaction validation across distributed nodes is energy-intensive, especially when handling large data volumes and complex computations. To mitigate this, only critical operations should be executed on-chain. Moreover, since the computational cost of DL models scales with the number of input parameters and network connections, we hypothesize that reducing model complexity (e.g., fewer neurons and layers) can accelerate convergence, lower energy consumption, and reduce latency. This assumption is supported by [40], which links DL model structure to required training data volume and quality.

4.2 Problem Modelling

The definition of the optimization problem involves the use of a multi-objective optimization function, denoted as f. This function comprises three individual objective functions, namely f1, f2, and f3. In the subsequent, we provide a formal description of each of these four functions.

- The multi-objective optimization function, denoted f, comprises three distinct objective functions: f1, f2, and f3. Formally, this function can be defined by Eq. (1).

$$\text{Minimize}\, f(M) = min(f_1, f_2, f_3) \text{ subject to } \forall M \in \Omega, C_1, C_2, C_3 \quad (1)$$

M denotes a vector of solution models within the solution space, each representing an instance of the decision variables, while Ω defines the finite-dimensional feasible solution space. The objective function f_1 measures the loss, quantifying the detection error to be minimized in order to enhance accuracy. Function f_2 computes the average operational effort during the detection process, aimed at minimizing energy consumption.

Function f_3 calculates the average latency of the detection process, which is minimized to improve system responsiveness. The constraints C_1, C_2, and C_3 correspond to the Blockchain's resource limitations: C_1 relates to the maximum transaction processing time, C_2 to the minimum number of validating nodes required per transaction, and C_3 to the transaction storage capacity.

- The loss function uses the mean squared error in order to evaluate the effectiveness of the detection model. This metric is commonly employed to assess the performance of detection models [41], particularly in classification problems involving numerical variables. Thus, Eq. (2) defines the first objective function to minimize, aiming to optimize the accuracy of the detection.

$$f_1 = \frac{1}{2}(E_{mse} + CON_{on})$$
$$\text{subject to } E_{mse} = \frac{1}{K}\sum_{i=1}^{K}\left(Y_i - Y_i'\right)^2,\ CON_{on} = \sum_{j=1}^{CN} cnx_j \times \frac{100}{CNX} \quad (2)$$
$$CNX$$

where: *Emse* denotes the mean squared error, computed as the average of the squared differences between predicted and expected values. *CNX* refers to the total number of possible connections in the Deep Learning model, while *CNXon* represents the proportion of active connections. Y and $\sim Y$ are the vectors of predicted and model-classified observations, respectively. Cnx_i is a binary indicator for each connection, equal to 1 if the connection is active and 0 otherwise.

- The Operational effort function quantifies the cost associated with anomaly detection operations executed in the blockchain, which is a critical factor that needs to be considered in the model construction phase. This cost is directly influenced by the processed data size and is evaluated using a specific metric based on the platform used. In our case, we adopt the Ethereum platform, where the Gas metric represents the cost. Hence, the second objective function f2 aims to minimize the average cost required to execute all transactions within a given period. It can be mathematically expressed using Eq. (3) where G returns the gas cost of a transaction. By minimizing this function, we aim to reduce the total cost of transactions and thus preserve energy and resources.

$$f_2 = \sum_{i=1}^{K} G(k_i) \quad (3)$$

- The latency function calculates the average time the Blockchain network takes to verify, execute, and validate a set of transactions. In our context, executing a transaction involves data analysis and decision-making via Deep Learning. Two methods are typically used to measure periodic latency: (1) aggregating the time taken by all nodes (cooperative model), and (2) treating node collaboration as a black box, measuring latency as the delay between task reception and completion. We adopt the second method and integrate it into the **third objective function** (f_3) of our multi-objective optimization model, as defined in Eq. (4). This function captures the total processing time for all transactions over a period t, with Q representing the delay for a single transaction, including verification, execution, and detection. Minimizing f_3 aims to reduce overall processing time and improve system performance.

5 Proposed Approach for an Optimized Anomaly Detection

This section introduces the proposed anomaly detection approach to address the formulated minimization problem. Section 5.1 describes the detection policy, while Section 5.2 outlines the methodology used to develop the solution.

5.1 Anomaly Detection Policy

The anomaly detection policy AD is comprised of two sub-policies: the device detection sub-policy and the observation detection sub-policy. Each of these includes a detection phase including classification rules and a reaction phase defining the actions to apply for each case. The policy AD can be expressed as:

$$policy_{AD} = (detection_{dev}, reaction_{dev}, detection_{obs}, reaction_{obs}) \tag{4}$$

where: $policy_{AD}$ represents the global anomaly detection policy defined by the quadruplet $detection_{dev}$, $reaction_{dev}$, $detection_{obs}$, $reaction_{obs}$, $detection_{dev}$ is a judgement function that assigns to each device a trust class according to its past behavioral, $detection_{obs}$ is a judgment function responsible for classifying the emitted observations based on a predefined set of rules, $reaction_{dev}$ is an agreement function that specifies the required actions to be taken when a malicious device is identified and $reaction_{obs}$ is an agreement function that specifies the necessary actions to be taken when an anomalous data is discovered.

5.1.1 Detection Policy for Devices

The device detection policy aims to classify the devices, identify the malicious ones and discard them from the system at an early stage.

Classification of a device: A device is classified either as malicious or as honest based on its behaviour and the defined judgment constraints as expressed as in Eqs. (5), (6) and (7).

$$\text{detection}_{\text{dev}} = \begin{cases} \text{malicious, if Constraint } (j_1) \\ \text{honest, if Constraint } (j_2) \end{cases} \tag{5}$$

With:

$$Constraint(j_1) = (\forall a \in A, \text{decision}_{\text{obs}}(a) = \text{anomalous} \rightarrow \text{true}) \vee (\text{Problems} \rightarrow \text{true}) \tag{6}$$

$$Constraint(j_2) = (\exists a \in A, \text{decision}_{\text{obs}}(a) = \text{normal} \rightarrow \text{true}) \wedge (\text{Problems} \rightarrow \text{false}) \tag{7}$$

Constraints j1 and j2 are the judgment rules for classifying a device, Problems indicates common problems that may occur, such as receiving outdated and empty data fields.

Reaction plan: Devices identified as malicious are prohibited from participating in the data collecting, as shown in Eq. (8). All the interactions with a malicious device are dropped before reaching the DL detection phase.

$$\text{reaction}_{\text{dev}} = \{ \text{Drop, if malicious ; Transfer, if normal} \tag{8}$$

5.1.2 Detection Policy for Observations

The observations' detection policy intends to rapidly identify anomalies produced in the data and conduct appropriate countermeasures.

Classification of an observation: An observation is categorized as normal if it meets the normality acceptance criteria or as anomalous if it exceeds the acceptability limits and as suspicious otherwise. In real-world, observations are commonly correlated, therefore a sudden decrease or increase in values must be regarded as suspicious.

Reaction plan: The hash of each normal data is published into the Blockchain network, and the data itself is sent for storage. However, if it is considered anomalous, the deployment is refused and a message alerting the blockchain of the identified anomaly is transmitted. In case the data is suspicious, its associated hash is stored, and an alert is shared over the Blockchain, such as:

$$\text{reaction}_{obs} = \begin{cases} (1) \wedge (2), \text{ if normal} \\ (1) \wedge (2) \wedge (3), \text{ if suspicious} \\ (3) \wedge (4), \text{ if anomalous} \end{cases} \tag{9}$$

With the following actions ①: proceed to sharing the hash of the data in the Blockchain. ②: proceed to transferring the data for storage. ③: proceed to sharing an alert over the Blockchain network. ④: proceed to reject the data.

5.2 Methodology

In this section, we elaborate the anomaly detection methodology. An overview of the communication process between the system components is illustrated in Fig. 2.

5.2.1 Global Process Overview

We aim to present a clear chronological overview of the operational steps to performing the detection of anomalies. We list Off-chain and On-chain tasks separately as follows:

Off-chain process

Step ①: historical data of each device is used as input of the Markov chain process to generate a decision vector. The obtained vector contains a classification of the devices.
Step ②: The second step presents the DL modelling. It includes the data cleaning, the model training, evaluating and parameters adjusting.

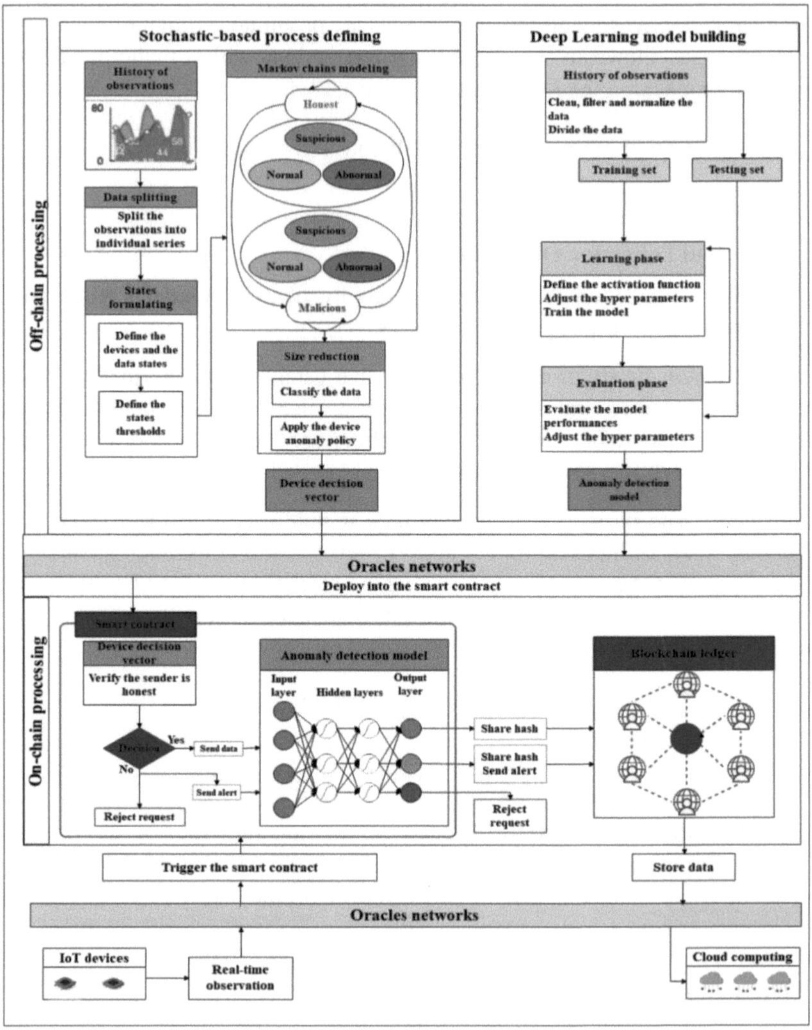

Fig. 2. Overview of the communication flow in the proposed anomaly detection approach

Step ③: The third step consists of deploying the device decision vector and the DL turnkey model in a smart contract.
Step ④: The fourth step is data gathering. The IoT devices start collection data from the environment and uploading it to the Blockchain via a network of trusted oracles.

On-chain process

Step ⑤: The fifth step consists of triggering the smart contract. When a new data reaches the Blockchain, the anomaly detection smart contract is activated to evaluate the resource that data sending resource.

Step ⑥/a: If the device is judged malicious, the data is rejected, and the detection process is concluded.
Step ⑥/b: If it is honest, the data is forwarded for classification.
Step ⑦: This step involves classifying the data into one of the three following states: normal, suspicious or anomalous.
Step ⑧/a: If the observation is considered normal, the data is stored in the cloud, and its hash is conserved in the Blockchain.
Step ⑧/b: If it is considered suspicious, the data is saved in the cloud, its hash is conserved in the blockchain, however an alert is shared in the network.
Step ⑧/c: If the observation is considered malicious, the data is rejected, and an alert is shared in the Blockchain.

5.2.2 Stochastic Process

The proposed method evaluates data anomaly detection through early device classification and lightweight dimensionality reduction. It involves transforming IoT device observations into Markov chains, which are then used to construct device decision vectors for identifying malicious behaviour. The process begins with defining interval states, where we use a border generator method, originally introduced in [42], and adapt it to handle multi-state stochastic processes—extending beyond the original birth-death process limitation. Currently, interval cardinalities are manually set based on the data's nature and scale. We recommend a compromise that ensures states are mutually exclusive and collectively exhaustive. Typically, 2 to 4 intervals are used in Markov-based detection approaches [43].

Markov Chains Modelling: We now consider the stochastic process X = {Xt, t ∈ T} governed by a stationary discrete Monte Carlo Markov chain. X can be expressed using the following 4 elements: The inite-state space: S = {s1, s2,.., sN} with N states, that can be obtained using the border generator method. The initial probabilities are directly derived from the history of collected observations. The probability transition matrix P, also known as the transition probability distribution and denoted (P = pij). The matrix presents the probability of transitioning from a current state si to the next state sj and can be expressed as follows:

$$p_{ij} = P\{x_{t+1} = s_j | x_t = s_i\} \tag{10}$$

With x_t, the current state, and satisfying the constraints of Eq. (11). And Eq. (12).

$$p_{ij} \geq 0, i, j \leq N \tag{11}$$

$$\sum_{j=1}^{N} p_{ij} = 1, 1 \leq i \leq N \tag{12}$$

And the steady-states can be deduced from the Markov chains. They indicate the long term predicted behaviour of each device, which we use as the devices decisions vector.

$$\lim_{n \to \infty} P^n = \pi \tag{13}$$

5.2.3 Deep Learning Modelling

The DL model is developed over the three following phases:

Preprocessing phase: This step enhances data quality and reduces estimation bias through normalization. We apply the min-max scaling technique for normalization.

$$\frac{X + X_{min}}{X_{max} + X_{min}} \tag{14}$$

Learning phase: The model is trained to differentiate normal from malicious behavior by optimizing weights and biases to minimize the loss function.

Evaluation phase: We test the built model with new observations and evaluate it using performance metrics such as the Mean Square Error detailed in the previous sections.

6 Experiments

6.1 Evaluation Metrics, Dataset and System Settings

This section outlines the experimental setup. Table 2 summarizes the dataset, Table 3 lists the Blockchain parameters, and Table 4 presents the Deep Learning configuration.

Evaluation. To evaluate anomaly detection performance, we use three standard metrics: Accuracy, measuring the proportion of correctly classified samples (reliable only with balanced data), Precision, indicating the proportion of correctly identified anomalous or normal samples among those classified as such, and Recall, representing the model's ability to detect actual anomalies. Dataset description: We use the publicly available Intel Berkeley Research Lab (IBRL) dataset [44], widely adopted in anomaly detection studies [25, 32, 45]. It contains data from 54 sensors deployed at the University of California's research lab, recording temperature, humidity, light, and voltage over 36 days.

For comparability with related work, we focus on 3 types per sensor: temperature, humidity and voltage.

We employ a Markov chain process to construct the device decision vector. Acceptance thresholds and interval boundaries were defined based on dataset characteristics and insights from related work, with missing values completed using the generator method described in Sect. 5.2.2. As a result, normal temperature values were set between 0 °C and 40 °C, and humidity between 0% and 100%. For the device decision vector, a minimum safety interval of [20, 80] was established devices with a maliciousness distribution of 20% or higher are classified as malicious.

Deep Learning Model: To determine the most appropriate machine learning model for our anomaly detection task, we evaluated the performance of three widely used classifiers KNN, Gaussian GNB, and MLP on a dedicated subset of the IBRL dataset.

As shown in Fig. 3a, the MLP exhibits a slightly higher model building time of 1.9 s compared to 1.71 and 1.02 s for KNN and GNB, respectively. This difference is mainly attributed to the complexity of the neural architecture.

Nevertheless, as illustrated in Fig. 3b, this marginal increase in processing time is acceptable, given that model training is only performed once during deployment. More

Table 2. IBRL Dataset description

Parameters	Values
Observation period	35 days
Collection interval time	30 seconds per epoch
Number of instances	1048576 observations
Number of attributes	8 attributes
Types of anomalies	Constant, Noise and Burst

Table 3. Blockchain parameters

Parameters and tools	Values
Ethereum network	Ropsten
Consensus protocol	Proof of Work
Number of nodes	11 nodes
Average miner tip	2,425 Gwei
Smart contract	Solidity V.0.8.0
Oracle API	web3.js

Table 4. DL parameters

Parameters	Values
DL network	MLP
Training set	80% of the dataset
Test set	20% of the dataset
Weights optimizer	ADAM gradient
Activation function	ReLU
Number of hidden Layers	3 layers
Number of neurons per layer	11
Learning rate	0.01 - constant

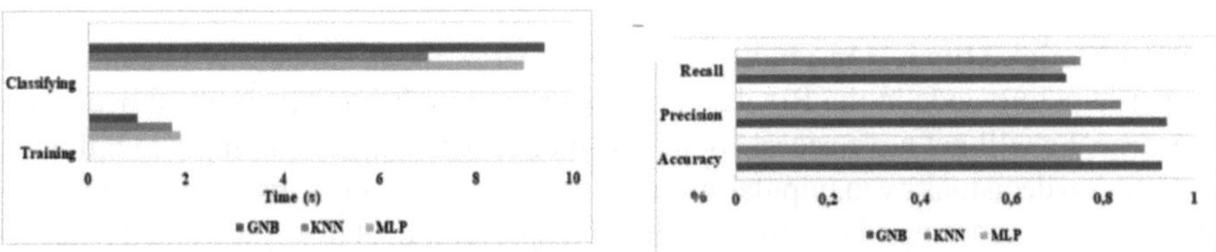

(a) Time cost comparison between GNB, KNN and MLP in training the model and classifying data

(b) Performance evaluation of GNB, KNN and MLP using Recall, Precision and Accuracy metrics

Fig. 3. Performances comparison between: KNN, GNB and MLP classifiers

critically, MLP achieved the best results across all key performance metrics, including accuracy, precision, and recall. Considering its superior predictive capabilities and the acceptable computational overhead, the MLP is selected as the classifier for our anomaly detection system, offering the best compromise.

6.2 Threat Model

To demonstrate the robustness of our approach against data integrity threats, we evaluate two types of adversarial attacks targeting both the data and the model. These attacks are carried out on two distinct surfaces: the first occurs at the IoT device layer, and the second targets the network layer.

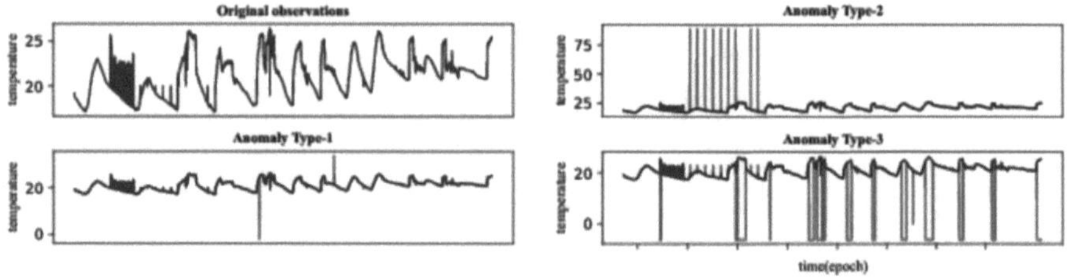

Fig. 4. Example of injected anomalies in a segment of observations: sensor 8 - temperature)

False Data Injection Attack (Off-chain): The adversarial entity is assumed to be unknown to the system. The attacker seeks to compromise one or more IoT devices by submitting false data instead of the correct sensor readings. To simulate this behaviour, we adopt a widely used anomaly injection method, as implemented in prior works using the IBRL dataset [5, 46]. Three main types of anomalies are injected: Type-1 (Burst), representing rare values significantly higher or lower than normal; Type-2 (Noise), consisting of isolated, irregular spikes; and Type-3 (Constant), where consecutive observations form an abnormally high or low series. These anomalies are illustrated in Fig. 4, which shows a normal sequence of temperature readings from sensor eight, modified separately with each anomaly type each resulting in a distinct pattern. To reflect real-world attacks, we also introduce a 4th type, referred to as Mixed anomalies, that combines the previous 3.

Evasion Model Attack (On-chain): In this scenario, the hostile entity is assumed to be a participating node in the Blockchain network whose behaviour evolved over time. Otherwise, he will not have access to the DL-model. The attacker attempts to influence the detection decisions by manipulating some network nodes and substituting their smart contract copies of the true DL-model with a corrupt DL-model that was trained to detect normal data as anomalous and anomalous data as normal. To carry out this attack, we gradually replace deployed copies of smart contracts with corrupt versions.

6.3 Evaluation Results

The evaluation is divided into three parts: (1) the efficiency performance of the approach, including computing and time costs; (2) its effectiveness against False Data Injection Attacks; and (3) its effectiveness against Evasion Model Attacks.

6.3.1 Efficiency Performance of the Approach

Figure 5 presents both the anomaly detection accuracy in normal (attack-free) contexts and the corresponding average runtime.

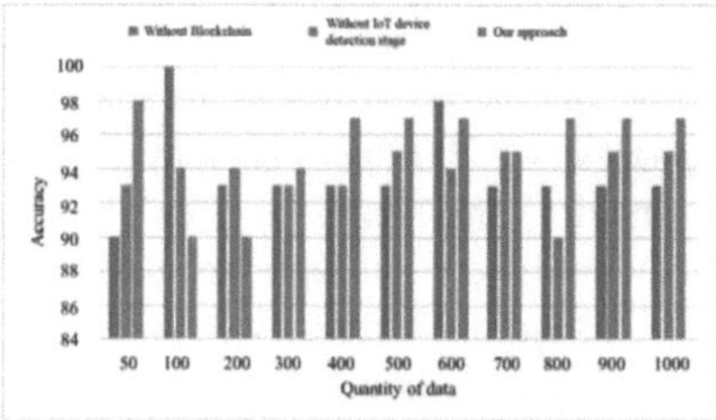

(a) Temperature

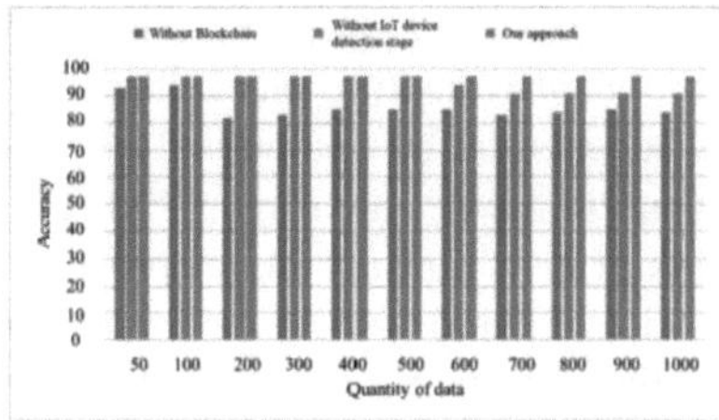

(b) Humidity

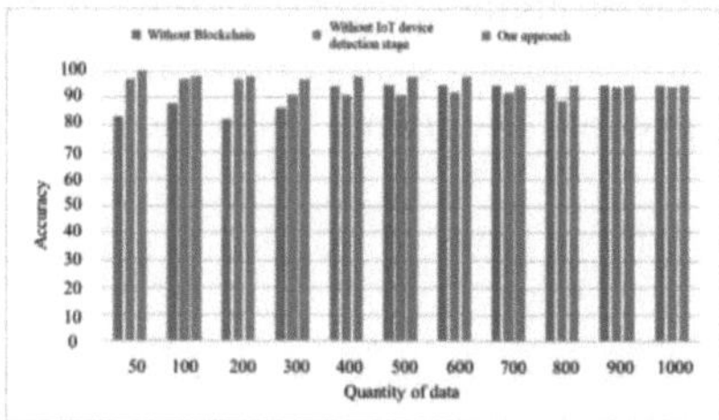

(c) Voltage

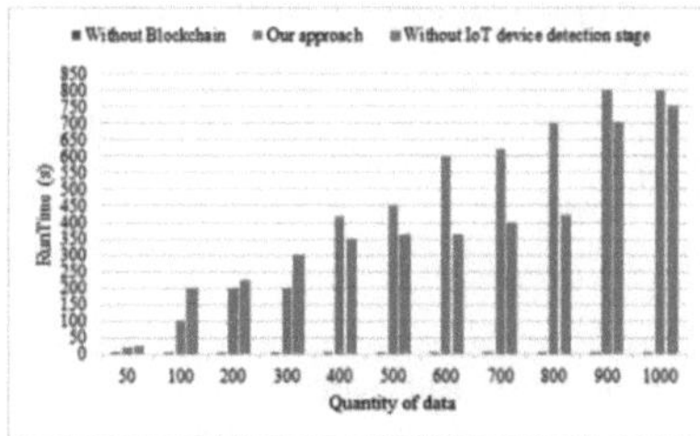

(d) Average Runtime

Fig. 5. Accuracy and Average Runtime comparison using (a) Temperature, (b) Humidity, (c) Voltage observations and (d) Average Runtime

Three configurations were evaluated: our proposed approach, its centralized version ("Without Blockchain"), and a DL-based solution without early IoT device detection ("Without IoT device detection stage"). As shown in Fig. 5a, b and c, all three approaches yield comparable classification performance across temperature, humidity, and voltage data. However, Fig. 5d highlights significant differences in convergence time. The Blockchain-based solutions require more time than the centralized one, due to the additional steps of data verification, validation, and propagation inherent to Blockchain. This effect is further amplified by the use of a public testnet in our experiments. Therefore, transactions are validated by community miners, who are often overloaded with prior validations. We estimate that the execution time shown in the figure could be reduced tenfold if the approach were deployed on a private blockchain, a reasonable trade-off considering the enhanced overall security.

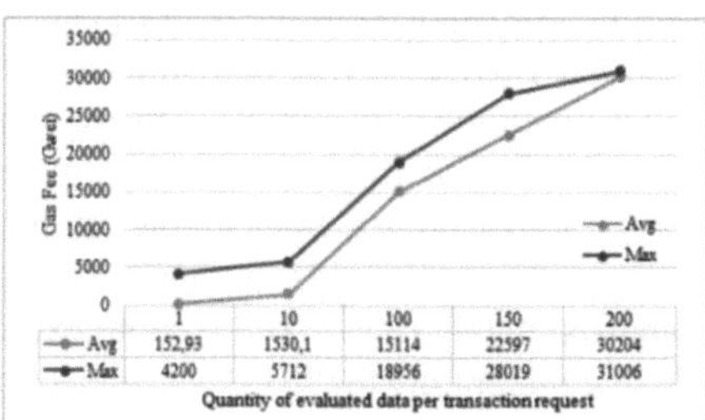

	1	10	100	150	200
Avg	152,93	1530,1	15114	22597	30204
Max	4200	5712	18956	28019	31006

(a) Gas fee evaluation

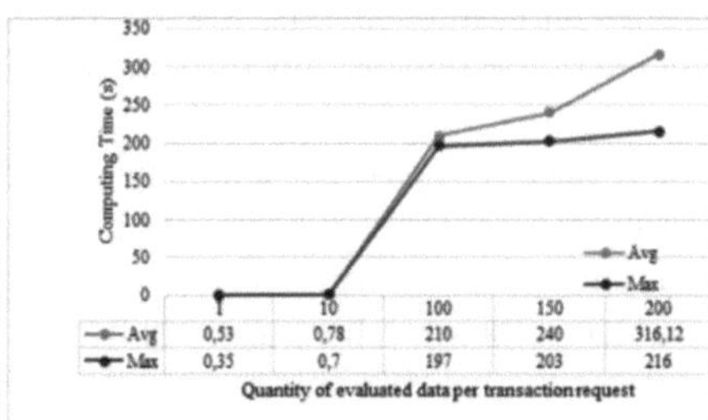

	1	10	100	150	200
Avg	0,53	0,78	210	240	316,12
Max	0,35	0,7	197	203	216

(b) Time cost evaluation

Fig. 6. Gas fee and time cost comparison using max priority and average priority transactions

Computing Cost: As previously noted, Gas fee estimation is more critical than execution time when evaluating Blockchain-based approaches. In Fig. 6a, we assess the scalability of our method by computing the Gas cost for processing 200 data observations. Two transaction types are shown: "Max" (maximum priority) and "Avg" (average priority). Max-priority transactions are processed faster but incur higher costs, approximately 4200 gwei, compared to 153 gwei for non-priority ones. This large discrepancy stems from gas fee fluctuations for storing 1 kB of data, ranging between 135 and 185 gwei. Moreover, since the miner tip is applied only once per transaction, increasing the data volume does not proportionally raise the total gas cost. Figure 6b presents the corresponding execution time. Initially low (under 10 s), the transaction time increases sharply between 10 and 100 s, before stabilizing, reflecting the typical behaviour of network congestion under load.

Time Complexity:

- On-chain, the overall computing complexity is the sum of the processing times for IoT device detection and data anomaly detection. The device detection has linear complexity, as it involves verifying a one-dimensional table. The Deep Learning model's processing time corresponds to a single evaluation round and can be approximated by the time complexity of the MSE computation.

Table 5. Time complexity evaluation

	IoT device detection	Data device detection	Overall time complexity
Processing	$O(n)$	$O(n^2)$	$O(n) + O(n^2) \approx O(n^2)$
Modeling	$O(n^2)$	$O(n^3)$	$O(n^3) + O(n^2) \approx O(n^3)$

- Off-chain, the overall modelling complexity is computed as the sum of the time required for IoT device detection and data anomaly detection. The device detection relies on Markov chains, where modelling time corresponds to the convergence of prediction estimates. Since all chains are stationary and converge to a unique distribution after n iterations, the time complexity is quadratic with respect to the number of devices ($O(D^2)$). The anomaly detection model uses an MLP network, composed of multiple connected layers. As noted in [47], the worst-case time complexity for a minimal network with one hidden layer is $O(n^2)$. Extending this to a network with N layers, the overall complexity becomes approximately $O(n^3)$. These complexities are summarized in Table 5, and we conclude that integrating the IoT device detection phase does not significantly increase the global computational delay of the DL model.

6.3.2 Approach Effectiveness Performance Against False Data Injection Attack

In this experiment, the four anomalies described in the Off-chain adversarial scenario were injected at a standard rate of 5%, commonly used in anomaly detection studies. Based on the results in Fig. 6, several observations can be made. First, Type-1 anomalies are the easiest to detect across all sensor types. As shown in Fig. 6a, temperature data achieves 95% True Positive Rate (TPR) with only 0.05% False Positive Rate (FPR). In humidity (Fig. 6b), TPR remains above 77%, while voltage readings (Fig. 6c) reach up to 98% TPR with 0.01% FPR in the final evaluation phase. For Type-2 anomalies, TPR gradually increases, eventually exceeding 95% across all three metrics—temperature, humidity, and voltage. In contrast, Type-3 anomalies yield lower detection rates, especially for humidity and voltage. However, TPRs of 80% (temperature), 90% (humidity), and 75% (voltage) are still considered acceptable. These results suggest that the proposed approach is highly effective at detecting Type-1 and Type-2 anomalies, while slightly less performant on Type-3. Given that Type-1 anomalies represent rare extreme values, their distinction from normal data can be challenging—making the slight drop in performance reasonable. Additionally, the approach performs robustly under mixed anomaly conditions, which closely reflect real-world scenarios.

Table 6. Post-evasion accuracy evaluation

Corrupt nodes	Quantity of data (%)						
	1	40	60	80	100	150	200
2	100	96.0	96.0	95.1	96.0	89.4	86.3
6	0	4.0	11.9	6.3	2.1	2.1	2.1
11	0	2.7	3.4	3.5	1.46	3.2	7.5

6.3.3 Effectiveness Performance of the Approach Against Evasion Model Attack

To assess the reliability of the Blockchain ecosystem in deploying security services, we simulate an On-chain adversarial scenario in which the anomaly detection model is progressively replaced by a compromised version across network nodes. As shown in Table 6, the Blockchain's ability to reject incorrect decisions depends on the number of compromised nodes. With six corrupted nodes, the system begins to produce erroneous outputs an expected outcome given that the PoW consensus relies on majority rule. While a faulty model contributes to disrupting the Blockchain's global consistency, some inaccuracies may also stem from other factors. For instance, with 200 data points, the accuracy rate in a network with 11 compromised nodes expected to be zero, remains above 7%. In summary, our experiment with 11 nodes shows that the attacker can undermine the system after gaining control of half the network. However, such an attack becomes significantly more difficult in larger Blockchain networks.

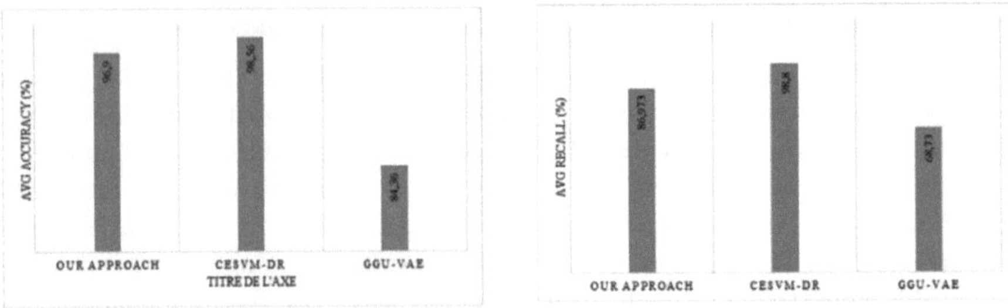

(a) Average accuracy rates (b) Average recall rates

Fig. 7. Average performance comparison with related works in terms of Accuracy and Recall

6.3.4 Comparative Evaluation

In this section, we compare our work to two related research on anomaly detection in IoT using machine learning. Both utilized IBRL datasets during the evaluation process. In the first proposal [37], we denote CESVMDR, authors presented a lightweight Anomaly Detection Scheme employing data dimension reduction and One Class Support Vector Machine algorithm. The second research work [32], we denote GGU-VAE, presented an anomaly detection method for critical IoT systems using GRU-based Gaussian Mixture VAE. As shown in Fig. 7. In terms of realized accuracy rates, comparative study demonstrates that our proposal outperforms GGU-VAE work. Regarding CESVM-DR, we both obtain the same processing time complexity O(n2), despite the fact that our technique utilizes Blockchain to improve service reliability and data integrity. However, their accuracy results surpass slightly ours, we assume that the disparity in accuracy results is mostly attributable to the extreme dimension reduction module that was applied to the data, resulting in a tiny sample size to analyse.

7 Conclusion and Future Works

Due to the lack of trust in the IoT environment, the design of a performant, yet reliable anomaly detection approach is crucial but challenging. In this research paper, we examined the problem of securing anomaly detection services in IoT. We formulated the problem as a multi-objective problem including minimizing the system effectiveness and reducing delay and computing costs. The approach consists of two complementary security modules. The first module introduces a stochastic-based device classification and filtering. This proactive device monitoring aims to lighten the data detection process without compromising its integrity. The second module provides real-time data anomaly detection using Deep Learning. We propose to perform the modelling of the approach outside of the Blockchain to save processing time. In contrast, decision making is managed collaboratively by the Blockchain nodes through smart contracts to guarantee trustworthy and verifiable results. Experimental evaluations demonstrated that the proposed Off-chain/On-chain strategy increases the system scalability while reducing excessive computing waste. Additional, obtained results demonstrated our approach resistance capacities to many ML adversarial attacks. For future works, we want to investigate alternative consensus protocols to achieve faster results with less computing complexity.

Acknowledgments. This work was partly supported by grants from the Troyes University of Technology, Eurelis company and AODB Group.

References

1. Silva, D., et al.: A management architecture for iot smart solutions: design and implementation. J. Netw. Syst. Manage. **30**(2), 1–30 (2022)
2. Farman, H., Jan, B., Khan, Z., Koubaa, A.: A smart energy-based source location privacy preservation model for internet of things-based vehicular ad hoc networks. Trans. Emerg. Telecommun. Technol. **33**(2), 3973 (2022)
3. Cisco, U.: Cisco annual internet report (2018–2023) white paper. Cisco: San Jose, CA, USA (2020)
4. Cui, L., et al.: Security and privacy-enhanced federated learning for anomaly detection in iot infrastructures. IEEE Trans. Ind. Inf. (2021)
5. Xie, M., Hu, J., Guo, S.: Segment-based anomaly detection with approximated sample covariance matrix in wireless sensor networks. IEEE Trans. Parallel Distrib. Syst. **26**(2), 574–583 (2014)
6. Shahhosseini, M., Mashayekhi, H., Rezvani, M.: A deep learning approach for botnet detection using raw network traffic data. J. Netw. Syst. Manage. **30**(3), 1–23 (2022)
7. Zhang, G., Liu, B., Zhu, T., Zhou, A., Zhou, W.: Visual privacy attacks and defenses in deep learning: a survey. Artif. Intell. Rev. (2021). https://doi.org/10.1007/s10462-021-10123-y
8. Shafay, M., Ahmad, R.W., Salah, K., Yaqoob, I., Jayaraman, R., Omar, M.: Blockchain for deep learning: review and open challenges. Clust. Comput. 1–25 (2022)
9. Khalfaoui, C., Ayed, S., Esseghir, M.: A stochastic approach for an enhanced trust management in a decentralized healthcare environment. In: 2020 16th International Conference on Wireless and Mobile Computing, Networking and Communications (WiMob), pp. 26–31 (2020). IEEE
10. Dixit, A., Deval, V., Dwivedi, V., Norta, A., Draheim, D.: Towards user-centred and legally relevant smartcontract development: A systematic literature review. J. Ind. Inf. Integrat. 100314 (2022)
11. Berdik, D., Otoum, S., Schmidt, N., Porter, D., Jararweh, Y.: A survey on blockchain for information systems management and security. Inf. Process. Manage. **58**(1), 102397 (2021)
12. Fu, X., Wang, H., Shi, P.: A survey of blockchain consensus algorithms: mechanism, design and applications. Sci. China Inf. Sci. **64**(2), 1–15 (2021)
13. Nakamoto, S.: Bitcoin: a peer-to-peer electronic cash system. Decentralized Bus. Rev. (2008)
14. Buterin, V., et al.: Ethereum white paper. GitHub Repository **1**, 22–23 (2013)
15. Dhillon, V., Metcalf, D., Hooper, M.: The hyperledger project. In: Blockchain Enabled Applications, pp. 139–149. Springer, (2017)
16. Brown, R.G., Carlyle, J., Grigg, I., Hearn, M.: Corda: an introduction. R3 CEV **1**(15), 14 (2016)
17. Sharma, P., Jindal, R., Borah, M.D.: A review of smart contract-based platforms, applications, and challenges. Cluster Comput. (2021). https://doi.org/10.1007/s10586-021-03491-1
18. Samara, M.A., Bennis, I., Abouaissa, A., Lorenz, P.: A survey of outlier detection techniques in iot: review and classification. J. Sens. Actuator Netw. **11**(1), 4 (2022)
19. Bouyeddou, B., Harrou, F., Kadri, B., Sun, Y.: Detecting network cyber-attacks using an integrated statistical approach. Clust. Comput. **24**(2), 1435–1453 (2021)
20. Zhang, H., Zhou, W.: A two-stage virtual machine abnormal behavior-based anomaly detection mechanism. Clust. Comput. **25**(1), 203–214 (2022)

21. Cook, A.A., Mısırlı, G., Fan, Z.: Anomaly detection for iot time-series data: a survey. IEEE Internet Things J. **7**(7), 6481–6494 (2019)
22. Li, J., Izakian, H., Pedrycz, W., Jamal, I.: Clusteringbased anomaly detection in multivariate time series data. Appl. Soft Comput. **100**, 106919 (2021)
23. Kwon, D., Kim, H., Kim, J., Suh, S.C., Kim, I., Kim, K.J.: A survey of deep learning-based network anomaly detection. Clust. Comput. **22**(1), 949–961 (2019)
24. Demertzis, K., Iliadis, L., Tziritas, N., Kikiras, P.: Anomaly detection via blockchained deep learning smart contracts in industry 4.0. Neural Comput. Appl. **32**(23), 17361–17378 (2020). https://doi.org/10.1007/s00521-020-05189-8
25. Ahmed, M., Taconet, C., Ould, M., Chabridon, S., Bouzeghoub, A.: Iot data qualification for a logistic chain traceability smart contract. Sensors **21**(6), 2239 (2021)
26. Alkadi, O., Moustafa, N., Turnbull, B., Choo, K.- K.R.: A deep blockchain framework-enabled collaborative intrusion detection for protecting IoT and cloud networks. IEEE Internet Things J. **8**(12), 9463–9472 (2020)
27. Gupta, R., Patel, M.M., Shukla, A., Tanwar, S.: Deep learning-based malicious smart contract detection scheme for internet of things environment. Comput. Electr. Eng. 107583 (2021)
28. Saveetha, D., Maragatham, G.: Design of blockchain enabled intrusion detection model for detecting security attacks using deep learning. Pattern Recogn. Lett. **153**, 24–28 (2022)
29. Podgorelec, B., Turkanovi´c, M., Karakatiˇc, S.: A machine learning-based method for automated blockchain transaction signing including personalized anomaly detection. Sensors **20**(1), 147 (2020)
30. Kim, J., et al.: Anomaly detection based on traffic monitoring for secure blockchain networking. In: 2021 IEEE International Conference on Blockchain and Cryptocurrency (ICBC), pp. 1–9 (2021). IEEE
31. Odiathevar, M., Seah, W.K., Frean, M.: A bayesian approach to distributed anomaly detection in edge ai networks. IEEE Transactions on Parallel and Distributed Systems (2022)
32. Guo, Y., Ji, T., Wang, Q., Yu, L., Min, G., Li, P.: Unsupervised anomaly detection in iot systems for smart cities. IEEE Transactions on Network Science and Engineering 7(4), 2231–2242 (2020)
33. Zhou, Z., Tartakovsky, D.M.: Markov chain monte carlo with neural network surrogates: application to contaminant source identification. Stoch. Env. Res. Risk Assess. **35**(3), 639–651 (2021)
34. Khodaei, A., Feizi-Derakhshi, M.-R., MozaffariTazehkand, B.: A markov chain-based feature extraction method for classification and identification of cancerous dna sequences. BioImpacts BI **11**(2), 87 (2021)
35. Ba-hutair, M.N., Bouguettaya, A., Neiat, A.G.: Multiperspective trust management framework for crowdsourced iot services. IEEE Transactions on Services Computing (2021)
36. Xu, Z., Guo, Y., Saleh, J.H.: Multi-objective optimization for sensor placement: an integrated combinatorial approach with reduced order model and gaussian process. Measurement 187, 110370 (2022)
37. Zamry, N.M., Zainal, A., Rassam, M.A., Alkhammash, E.H., Ghaleb, F.A., Saeed, F.: Lightweight anomaly detection scheme using incremental principal component analysis and support vector machine. Sensors **21**(23), 8017 (2021)
38. Bao, F., Chen, I.-R.: Dynamic trust management for internet of things applications. In: Proceedings of the 2012 International Workshop on Self-aware Internet of Things, pp. 1–6 (2012)
39. Chaloner, K., Verdinelli, I.: Bayesian experimental design: A review. Statistical Science, 273–304 (1995)
40. Zanchettin, C., Ludermir, T.B., Almeida, L.M.: Hybrid training method for mlp: optimization of architecture and training. IEEE Transactions on Systems, Man, and Cybernetics, Part B (Cybernetics) **41**(4), 1097–1109 (2011)

41. Huber, R., Schwaiger, R., Mayer, H.A.: On the role of regularization parameters in fitness functions for evolutionary designed artificial neural networks. In: World Congress on Neural Networks, pp. 1063–1066 (1996). Lawrence Erlbaum Associates Inc.
42. Saligrama, V., Konrad, J., Jodoin, P.-M.: Video anomaly identification. IEEE Signal Process. Mag. **27**(5), 18–33 (2010)
43. Han, J.G., Park, T.H., Moon, Y.H., Eom, I.K.: Efficient markov feature extraction method for image splicing detection using maximization and threshold expansion. J. Electron. Imaging **25**(2), 023031 (2016)
44. Intel Berkeley Research Lab. http://db.csail.mit.edu/labdata/labdata.html. Accessed: 2022–03–09
45. Abid, A., Masmoudi, A., Kachouri, A., Mahfoudhi, A.: Outlier detection in wireless sensor networks based on optics method for events and errors identification. Wireless Pers. Commun. **97**(1), 1503–1515 (2017)
46. Rassam, M.A., Zainal, A., Maarof, M.A.: One-class principal component classifier for anomaly detection in wireless sensor network. In: 2012 Fourth International Conference on Computational Aspects of Social Networks (CASoN), pp. 271–276 (2012). IEEE
47. Al-Rousan, N., Al-Najjar, H.: Optimizing the performance of mlp and svr predictors based on logical oring and experimental ranking equation. J. Chin. Inst. Eng. **44**(2), 149–157 (2021)

Unified Model for Complex IT Infrastructures Governance: SCAFE Case Study

Rabia Azzi[1(✉)], Punita Raj[2], Ioana Filipas[3], François Marmier[2], Chaima Khalfaoui[1], Mathieu Gros[1], and Bertrand Rose[2]

[1] Groupe AODB - Alliance of Digital Builders, SCAFE Company, Paris, France
rabia.azzi@scafe.io, {chaima.khalfaoui,mathieu.gros}@aodb.com
[2] University of Strasbourg, Icube CNRS 7357, 67412 Illkirch, France
{marmier,bertrand.rose}@unistra.fr
[3] University of Strasbourg, BETA CNRS, 7522, 67085 Strasbourg Cedex, France
filipas@unistra.fr

Abstract. Modern IT infrastructure's complexity significantly hinders comprehensive visibility and operational management across heterogeneous environments. Current monitoring systems suffer from fragmentation and limited interoperability, creating governance gaps across DevOps, Cloud, and Cybersecurity domains. This paper proposes a unified governance model and methodology for complex IT infrastructures, structuring knowledge from these three domains. Our approach centers on the Cockpit decision-support framework, which models IT ecosystems through knowledge-based representation and prioritizes actions via standardized indicators. The industrial case study at SCAFE validates this approach through four pilot implementations, demonstrating successful data aggregation from diverse sources, including Jira, cost management, and performance monitoring tools. Results show effective consolidation of availability, performance, cost, and security metrics across multiple vendors, bridging isolated environments and promoting consistent monitoring practices. The paper concludes with a discussion of the results, implications, and future research directions.

Keywords: Cloud · Cybersecurity · DevOps · Governance automation · Interoperability · IT infrastructure · Strategic decision planning

1 Introduction

Enterprise IT structures undergo quick transformation due to cloud computing, DevOps automation, containerization, and AI integration, leading to heterogeneous, highly scalable infrastructure environments [1]. Organizations in present times use a combination of public, private, hybrid, and multi-cloud systems, which require separate evaluation of performance and compliance at the same time while maintaining different cost standards [2]. Therefore, operational fragmentation occurs as a result of the flexibility, which allows both innovation and speed [3]. Organizations distribute their monitoring systems across different specialized tools that each focus on individual layers or providers, which

Published by Springer Nature Switzerland AG 2026
L. M. Camarinha-Matos et al. (Eds.): PRO-VE 2025, IFIP AICT 770, pp. 278–292, 2026.
https://doi.org/10.1007/978-3-032-05673-3_17

leads to fragmented data storage and limited operational visibility [4]. Decision-makers, together with IT teams, face challenges when trying to merge essential performance indicators, which include system availability, resource performance, security posture, and financial overhead [5]. Organizations also face difficulties in quick incident response and budget management and policy enforcement due to the lack of an integrated, consolidated view of all platforms.

The fragmented approach leads to poor cooperation among organizations. The organizations work with various performance indicators along with unique tracking tools, which results in strategic misalignment and operational disintegration [6]. The main challenge occurs from the failure to merge dissimilar data sources into a coordinated structure that produces actionable insights [7]. Modern monitoring solutions do not offer system independence from particular manufacturers or platforms. They cannot establish real-time relationships between multiple monitoring indicators. The result of this failure fosters operational risk together with impaired agility and suboptimal resource management across organizations. Thus, the paper introduces Cockpit as a centralized oversight platform which integrates technology along with analytical insights for comprehensive visibility. The tool operates as one integrated display to unite and connect information across Jira (project tracking), performance probes (latency, uptime), and financial analytics systems (cost tracking). The strategic planning capabilities of Cockpit become pertinent by visualizing multiple dimensions of metrics through its unified dashboards, which permit cross-metric comparisons such as operations performance, cost expenditure, system risk levels, and uptime statuses. These capabilities bridge operational silos through the system, strengthens transparency, and accelerate effective decision-making processes among technical staff and business personnel. Moreover, the paper explains the design rationale along with the architecture and functional features of Cockpit systems. The paper also demonstrates experimental validity through the deployment of Cockpit in multiple real-world pilot projects across different organizational fields. The evaluation proves that the platform can reduce fragmentation by standardizing monitoring while enabling continuous improvement in enterprise IT governance. The introduction of Cockpit sets a major advancement toward organizational operational intelligence capabilities, which use artificial intelligence through complex digital scenarios.

2 Literature Review

This section examines the current state of IT monitoring and governance solutions, structured around four key themes to provide a comprehensive understanding of existing approaches and their limitations. The analysis reveals critical gaps that motivate our unified governance approach for complex IT infrastructures.

2.1 Evolution of IT Monitoring in Heterogeneous Environments

Modern IT monitoring advances directly with the evolution of IT structures, which shifted from dedicated on-site systems to dispersed cloud-based systems [8]. IT monitoring started as a basic centralized method with easy upkeep that studied CPU behaviour and memory performance and uptime status inside single data facilities [9]. When organizations started adopting virtualization and implementing cloud computing solutions together with DevOps practices, the monitoring environment became much harder to manage. The inclusion of public and private clouds and on-premises systems together with containerized applications and serverless functions has made monitoring operations highly difficult. The monitoring environment faces difficulties with irregular data structures together with multiple integrated development systems and fragmented performance measurements spread across various providers and delivery networks [10]. Modern information systems face limited relevant understanding from traditional monitoring frameworks since these tools cannot normalize data among different domains. The need for real-time visibility, together with compliance adherence and security monitoring, has increased the importance of integrated system oversight. Moreover, the operational governance utilizes real-time monitoring as its strategic component after moving past its role as a reactive system for failure detection [11]. Thus, continuous delivery together with agile development requires system-wide monitoring at all times in ways that reflect present-day deployment complexity and dynamic structure. Contemporary IT monitoring requires solutions that provide efficient technical capabilities alongside flexibility and independence between vendors and multi-platform visibility [12]. The evolutionary pattern shows that it is necessary to develop a framework to unify fragmented visibility and establish monitoring as a fundamental decision-making foundation for enterprises across the board.

Despite significant advances in technologies, the literature highlights persistent structural and semantic limitations that hinder unified governance across complex infrastructures. One of the main shortcomings is the lack of interoperability between tools and domains, particularly in heterogeneous, multi-cloud environments where DevOps, Cloud, and Cybersecurity operate with distinct logics, data formats, and objectives. Current solutions often remain tied to specific suppliers or limited to a single layer of the stack, preventing the correlation of performance, security, and cost metrics within a coherent governance framework. In addition, dashboards and monitoring platforms tend to focus on reactive alerts or technical indicators, without supporting higher-level decision-making or strategic alignment. The absence of an integration model further limits data aggregation, automation, and intelligent reasoning across domains. In addition, the literature points to a disconnect between operational oversight and strategic governance, particularly in organizations where fragmented tools and inconsistent reporting create decision-making silos. These gaps highlight the need for a meta-platform capable of unifying information flows, standardizing indicators, and integrating contextual knowledge to support both operational monitoring and real-time strategic foresight.

2.2 Tools and Platforms for Integrated IT Oversight

With the advancement of IT in many sectors, there are multiple tools and platforms to support integrated IT oversight due to digital infrastructure complexities and numerous operational environments [13]. Infrastructure observability emerged from traditional monitoring solutions, including Nagios, Zabbix, and Icinga, to deliver basic availability and performance metrics. These tools struggle to directly monitor cloud environments, container orchestration, and service mesh operations; thus, enterprises adopted API-focused platforms as a replacement [14]. The Kubernetes-based environment extensively adopts Prometheus together with Grafana, which operate as cloud-native solutions for delivering robust metric collection and visualization functions. ASI offers dashboard customization and alert automation capabilities to organizations, but organizations must invest substantial work to connect their different clouds into one system. The commercial solutions Datadog, New Relic, and Dynatrace provide full-stack observability between infrastructure along with applications and user experience and feature built-in AI for anomaly detection and performance analysis capabilities [15]. The separate nature of performance data and security information, and cost data across various software domains and tools remains an ongoing substantial challenge. Enterprise entities with cloud operations spanning multiple providers experience a heightened version of this issue when using standalone DevOps systems. The log and data aggregation of Splunk and Elastic Stack attempts to overcome this challenge but does not provide domain-independent governance and genuine operational unity for insights [16]. Decentralized monitoring architectures have emerged through the development of orchestration layers along with service mesh observability tools, particularly Istio and Linkerd [17]. Extended visibility into microservices follows through specialized tools, although their narrow field of operation makes overall system insight challenging. The growing market demand for a meta-platform that unifies different gear together while standardizing multiple data streams and presents single operational views. Such platforms will help achieve essential business value through extensibility along with automation and semantic correlation features to support organizations that want improved oversight capabilities, tool consolidation, and better decisions.

2.3 Gaps in Current Monitoring and Governance Solutions

With the continuous advancement of new tools and solutions, multiple essential gaps persist in IT monitoring systems and platforms, which create barriers to the thorough governance of various infrastructure types [13]. The major challenge arises from the limited communication abilities of tools, which remain strongly tied to various technology types and cloud vendor solutions. Operation visibility becomes limited due to performance analytics, security measurements, and cost reports [18]. Fragmentation within security tools makes it difficult to trace incidents and damages situational awareness while slowing down the response time for detecting abnormal events or security breaches. The observation of multiple domains falls short due to insufficient coordinated capabilities [19]. Most application monitoring and infrastructure tracking solutions have limited capability to connect the entire stack across cloud provisioning through end-user experiences. There are a few tools to implement governance capabilities, which include both compliance monitoring and risk-scoring features and policy enforcement functions. These tools are Azure Policy, AWS Config, HashiCorp Sentinel, Open Policy Agent (OPA), Prisma Cloud by Palo Alto Networks, etc. The division between technical and governance control elements produces hindered decision-making processes alongside higher operational risks [20]. Several current platforms experience challenges when trying to normalize their data inputs. The combination of diverse systems creates numerous different logging methods alongside different monitoring specifications and outcome monitoring signals. Transmission and semantic comparison tools work beyond manual data connections or specialized adapter maintenance to stop organizations from facing scalability issues while adding complexity [21]. However, operation systems today show limited flexibility when operating in changing environments. Current monitoring systems also face challenges when monitoring short-lived workloads because of microservices, serverless computing adoption, transient states, and dependent relationships. Organizations become more vulnerable and experience degraded operational quality due to these undetected system points.

The present-day solutions usually fail to put user needs at their core. Technical dashboards and alerts commonly exist as systems with restricted relevance for strategic stakeholders of the business. The separation between operational monitoring and enterprise-level decision-making creates an operational gap, which is worsened since organizations lack data governance frameworks for consistent business unit representation [22]. Anomaly detection capabilities are implemented through machine learning by some platforms, yet they offer minimal automated capabilities and continuous system improvement functions. Thus, the systems need to adopt an immediate requirement for detecting operational disruptions together with automated action plans which adapt according to changing operational behaviours. Therefore, the current industry needs powerful unified tools to unite different data foundations through semantic operations to deliver real-time cross-department governance.

2.4 Role of Data Aggregation and Dashboards in Decision Support

Decision support across the modern IT ecosystem is driven through data aggregation solutions that integrate with dashboard systems. Modern distributed and complex IT infrastructure environments with multiple cloud providers, on-premise components, and hybrid deployments demand critical data aggregation and presentation in usable formats [23]. Various organizations obtain complete picture awareness by uniting data from multiple systems, including performance monitors, security logs, incident trackers, and financial databases, through integrated data aggregation [4]. Information unification delivers improved operational visibility and allows decision-making authorities to notice hidden patterns and relationships which would have otherwise stayed hidden [24]. Thus, strategic intervention becomes necessary when analyzing the correlation between infrastructure cost increases after deployment changes and security alerts that appear. It becomes impossible for decision-makers to understand data connections when data aggregation does not occur [25]. The aggregated data become meaningful indicators, which dashboards present to diverse stakeholders through their functional visual interface.

Therefore, the organizations need high-level information with KPIs showing cost data, compliance metrics, and performance metrics, whereas engineers need more detailed data streams for debugging and optimization functions. This way, the users can personalize dashboards and perform filtering operations to create content that suits each professional team. It leads to operational agility and receives substantial support from real-time dashboards since they enable fast responses when abnormal conditions or deviations occur [26]. The system helps organizations conduct proactive governance through alerts that show trends along with simulated scenarios. The latest advanced dashboards integrate embedded analytics that combine with machine learning capabilities to enable users to see future outcomes along with their capacity to adjust their actions based upon changing situations [27]. Decision support effectiveness depends heavily on the quality standards which underline the data dashboard. Data mistrust, along with misinterpretation, occurs when data formats are not aligned semantically or present inconsistent formats [28]. Therefore, establishing strong mapping systems through ontologies became more critical for dashboard developers to deliver consistent, dependable findings to users. User-centred dashboard integration into IT governance platforms enhances teamwork while ensuring better performance tracking and speeds up decision-making that uses datasets. Such design principles make dashboards operate as a single control system which connects raw system data with strategic operational knowledge across complex technological domains.

2.5 Towards Smart Monitoring: AI and Analytics Integration

The implementation of AI systems with advanced analytics enables IT governance to adopt smarter adaptive oversight that is called "smart monitoring". Modern IT governance now benefits from a substantial transformation which transitions beyond traditional rule-based monitoring into data-driven proactive decision-making capacities [29]. The real-time analysis of large data volumes by AI systems identifies abnormal patterns together with predictive system behaviour modelling from learned patterns, which benefits both response time and decreases MTTR [30]. The transformation in IT monitoring stems from the combination of intricate and vast modern IT infrastructure deployments that occur in hybrid as well as multi-cloud setups. Threshold-based alert systems produce two problems by causing alert overload along with the failure to identify essential system indicators [31]. Across systems, AI models consisting of machine learning algorithms and neural networks use advanced capabilities to discover minimal discrepancies in standard conduct, which allows for early detection of system failures and security breaches. Through advanced analytics, decision-makers gain access to predictive information and the original causes of problems. The combination of time-series forecasting approaches enables organizations to predict system outages and infrastructure requirements [32]. The clustering systems also identify incidents, which subsequently determine maintenance sequences. Strategic IT management uses these abilities to move beyond static historical data and set parameters for better decision-making at a strategic level. Moreover, AI implementation makes it possible to convert basic monitoring dashboards into smart centers for control [33]. Operating dashboard activity with AI functions presents automated suggestions together with visual assessments of forthcoming operational effects and scenario modelling capabilities that help users make operational decisions. Semantic data interpretation, when applied to these insights, increases their contextual understanding, thus enabling businesses to merge technical events with their operational goals [34].

The performance of AI combined with analytics in smart monitoring depends entirely on the quality together with the structure of input data. Structured contextual data requires the essential synergy of semantic frameworks because such data supports better performance and training of AI models. Through their unified operation, these technologies develop an automatic monitoring system that constructs itself through time for persistent policy development alongside operational agility.

2.6 Research Gap and Motivation

There is extensive progress in IT monitoring tools and frameworks, but large gaps remain in existing solutions, which reduce their effectiveness while impairing their scalability and interoperability, primarily when operating within heterogeneous dynamic environments [24]. Multiple current platforms maintain a limited application scope since they concentrate on working with particular cloud providers, operational tools, or performance metrics, thus restricting their use in hybrid and multi-cloud environments [28]. Standalone systems in monitoring create multiple fragmented viewpoints while duplicate work occurs with insufficient understanding about data across multiple business units and system layers. Semantic interoperability stands as the biggest limitation that impacts this solution [30]. The proprietary data formats and restrictive schemas in monitoring systems create obstacles to joining different monitoring sources and adding new monitoring tools because substantial manual reconfiguration procedures are needed [13]. The limited connection between data systems makes organizations struggle to identify cross-domain problems, and they fail to comprehend the total operational risks and performance inefficiencies. Most current platforms show data visually through dashboards yet provide limited meaningful insights [34]. The displayed raw data or loosely interconnected metrics on dashboards do not show a direct connection to business objectives and governance policies and strategic planning. Therefore, high-level decision-making becomes impeded when these systems restrict usefulness because such restrictions create misalignment between IT operations and enterprise goals.

The evolving nature of modern IT ecosystems poses persistent issues for the establishment and maintenance of steady monitoring methods alongside compliance standards [4]. Businesses encounter monitoring dilemmas when implementing new services or expansion levels since their conventional monitoring frameworks lack the speed to provide instant domain-wide visibility and policy implementation capabilities [21]. This presents an immediate requirement for development frameworks which can adjust to infrastructure evolution by using operational insights and regulatory and organizational standards while learning from operational data.

This analysis reveals three critical gaps: (i) semantic interoperability limitations across DevOps, Cloud, and Cybersecurity domains prevent effective correlation of performance, security, and cost metrics; (ii) the disconnect between operational monitoring and strategic governance creates decision-making silos; (iii) current solutions lack dynamic adaptability required for maintaining domain-wide visibility and policy compliance in rapidly evolving IT ecosystems. These gaps create an immediate requirement for unified governance frameworks that can adapt to infrastructure evolution while maintaining operational insights and regulatory standards, directly motivating our proposed approach.

3 Methodology: Unified Governance Model

This section presents our unified governance model designed to address the integration challenges across DevOps, Cloud, and Cybersecurity domains identified in the literature review. The model provides a systematic approach to achieving cross-domain visibility and decision support in complex IT infrastructures.

3.1 Conceptual Framework

To address the integration challenge across the three domains (Cloud, DevOps, and Cybersecurity) which has been clearly identified as a gap in the literature, we propose the conceptual model shown in Fig. 1. The conceptual model of the Cockpit platform is based on the integration and correlation of data streams across three operational domains through a modular data architecture that supports unified IT governance. Rather than relying on complex ontological frameworks, the model adopts a connector-based integration paradigm that ensures interoperability at the system level through standardized data collection, transformation, and consolidation mechanisms.

The model addresses the semantic interoperability challenge identified in the literature by implementing a pragmatic approach that balances technical feasibility with governance requirements. Unlike traditional approaches that attempt full semantic unification, our model focuses on syntactic harmonization while preserving domain-specific contexts. This design decision allows for fast deployment and maintenance, as well as for the nature of modern IT ecosystems.

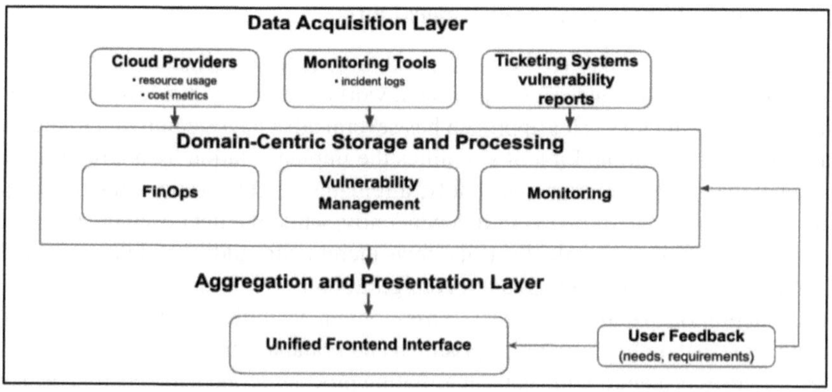

Fig. 1. Three-layer conceptual architecture of the Cockpit platform for cross-domain IT governance

3.2 Three-Layer Architecture

The Cockpit platform is structured around three core layers that collectively enable unified governance across heterogeneous IT environments:

Data Acquisition Layer. This layer contains the purpose-specific connectors that interact with heterogeneous external systems, such as cloud providers, monitoring applications, ticketing tools, and security solutions. Every connector retrieves specific datasets (resource usage metrics, cost information, incident logs, vulnerability reports, and performance indicators). The connector model offers a pluggable integration mechanism, which enables organizations to introduce new data sources without modifying the core components of the platform. Consistent ingestion of data from various technology stacks is also possible through standard API protocols and data extraction methods.

Domain-Centric Storage and Processing. The collected data is organized and flown to domain-specific Data Storage Models, e.g., the FinOps model for spend management, the Vulnerability Management model for security oversight, and the Monitoring model for operation performance. This model, maintaining the contextuality of the datasets, enables domain-based analytics and processing workflow. Every domain module incorporates specific data models and logic to support the particular needs of that governance, again ensuring that domain knowledge is not lost but can still be correlated across domains.

Aggregation and Presentation Layer. At the consolidation step, domain datasets are retrieved, cross-referenced, and served through APIs to a single frontend interface. Rather than performing semantic inference, the system supports syntactical harmonization via schema alignment and normalization pipelines for multi-domain visualization and decision support. These are used to standardize Key Performance Indicators (KPI) and metrics, which can be interpreted consistently across domains, supporting strategic and operational oversight.

3.3 Integration Paradigm and Interoperability

The proposed model addresses the interoperability issues highlighted in the literature using a connector-based integration approach, working at the syntax level, while maintaining domain semantics. This approach has several advantages compared to the traditional semantic integration. First, it simplifies the implementation by not requiring full ontological mapping of domains. Secondly, it remains flexible, as domain-specific processing logic is capable of evolving independently, while the data exchange interfaces are kept stable. Third, it is scalable, as it allows incremental addition of new domains or data sources without causing a global reconfiguration.

The integration paradigm enables cross-domain visibility with no need of deep semantic representation, presenting a practical and scalable approach to dynamic governance. It focuses on centralizing data, automating processes, and temp posting decisions in context in complex and changing IT landscapes with the help of extensible connectors and decoupled data pipelines. This architectural style allows maintainable and scalable development for different technological ecosystems.

3.4 Validation Approach

To demonstrate the proposed Unified Governance Model and the underlying Cockpit platform, we have implemented and tested a set of pilot experiments in different operational scenarios in the SCAFE industry. Each pilot intended to validate the potential of integration between the DevOps, Cloud and Cybersecurity areas, tackling in particular some issues such as tool integration, inter-organizational collaboration, service continuity, and process unification. The pilot deployments present empirical evidence of the model's usefulness in practice and its suitability for different organizational contexts and governance needs.

The validation approach factors in various dimensions such as the technical integration capability, operational efficiency, and the strategic fit to the business objectives. This holistic validation process is capable of addressing both technical infrastructure interoperability problems and governance issues, as identified from the literature, and provides a strong basis for integrated IT governance in complex infrastructures.

4 Application Case

4.1 Validation Approach

The validation of the Cockpit framework was performed at SCAFE, which is a digital services company based in France and offers expertise in complex IT infrastructure management. The assessment included four independent pilot deployments on governance requirements in the areas of Cloud, DevOps, and Cybersecurity. All pilots followed an experimental protocol using pre-established metrics, collection of baseline information, and post-implementation assessments over a 12-month period.

Fig. 2. Unified multi-cloud supervision interface: Cockpit platform

The operational interface of the Cockpit platform (see Fig. 2) presents consistent monitoring across multi-cloud environments. It consolidates indicators such as its budget, the level of vulnerability, the traceability of incidents, support tickets, and financial indicators with providers (AWS, Scaleway, Azure…). Primary analysis functions are monthly cost predictions, application-system availability monitoring, and resource-usage analysis.

4.2 Pilot Implementation Results

Pilot 1: Dashboard Consolidation and Tool Unification. The first pilot focused on the problem of unifying disparate monitoring tools through a centralized interface to obtain real-time visibility and automate customer communication. This approach leveraged data sources provided by tools like Jira for ticket management, project management systems like Tempo for tracking time, cloud billing platforms, and SLA monitoring systems via the three-layer Cockpit architecture with ad-hoc connectors for each data source. Jira tickets across multi-cloud environments contain various interdependencies, including performance degradation, CI/CD pipeline errors, cluster version mismatches, and shared infrastructure resource conflicts. Cockpit platform help resolves this complexity by matching up metadata from monitoring systems, deployment histories, application logs, and budget data, which consequently allows for smart ticket classification and prioritization based on business priorities. The findings showed that it decreased ticket volume from an average of 150 tickets per month at baseline to 98 tickets per month (35% decrease), decreased invoicing reconciliation requests from 5 per month to 1 (80% decrease), and reduced accounting reconciliation processes time from 8 days to 4 days (50% acceleration). These refinements demonstrate improved operational visibility and decreased operational cognitive load for operations teams by displaying consolidated information.

Pilot 2: Inter-Company Collaboration Protocols. The second pilot established standardized collaboration protocols with external digital service provider partners. The pilot introduced structured cooperation procedures between project scoping and deployment with a focus on technical and financial alignment, service standardization, and certification enhancement. The results covered a 25% reduction of project scoping time (4–3 weeks average), a 40% diminution of rework for initial deployment phases, and the introduction of three new service offerings related to FinOps and Green IT. This pilot targets directly collaboration issues across organizational boundaries by provisioning shared governance, minimizing frictions among internal and external parties, and showing the ability of the platform to support collaborative networks across organizational borders.

Pilot 3: Aligning Services and Structuring Governance. The third pilot confirmed and expanded on the partnership-based approach developed in the second pilot through harmonized protocols and engaging stakeholders. Standardized deliverables and shared responsibility matrix use promoted operational cadence across Cloud, DevOps, and Cybersecurity. The pilot confirmed the repeatability of the collaborative model with a second partner, decreased deployment errors by 30% when compared with the pre-implementation baseline, and increased cost transparency by including sustainability indicators. However, the full practice unification is still missing, especially on semantic interoperability and automatic enforcement of policies in real-time, and can be considered as future works.

Pilot 4: Unified Methodology for Maintaining in Operational Condition (MCO). The fourth pilot integrated operational maintenance approaches in the three domains into a single MCO model. Among these were a proactive maintenance timeline partially automating time tracking, dynamic resource reallocation, and automated cost effectiveness well above the contractual obligations under the SLA. This initial pilot also increased MCO projects by 200% from 5 to over 15 a year, had a 93% resolution rate of critical incidents, and decreased the average downtime of critical services by 25% from 4 to 3 h. However, full automation in monitoring and billing is still problematic because of growth in the number of projects and maintaining team stability, implying scalability concerns in future implementations.

4.3 Evaluation Framework and Quantitative Results

The selected Key Performance Indicators (KPIs) are a representation of three dimensions of governance performance across the collaborative network context. Key operational efficiency dashboard metrics include ticket volume reduction and processing time improvements, which map directly to the platform's agility to process the flow of information and minimize overhead spend. Quality indicators related to collaboration include reduction of scoping time, minimization of rework, and improvements in inter-team synchronization, thus evidence of the capacity of the framework in enhancing collaborative networks between internal teams and external service providers. Reliability metrics center around incident resolution and reduced downtime, showing the platform's success in providing service uptime over large, distributed environments.

The quantitative results show that the Cockpit platform is able to give a concrete answer to the issues found in the state of the art. The deficiencies of existing monitoring systems (in particular the fragmentation of tools, the absence of a common repository, and the lack of relationship between technical data and strategic objectives) are addressed by this approach. Centralizing performance, security, and cost data in a single interface ensures complex environments are not only clearer to comprehend but also that critical, cross-departmental decisions are more effectively informed. Such metrics are highly relevant to the core platform objectives related to reducing fragmentation, increasing visibility, and improving the decision-making process in heterogeneous IT environments.

4.4 Qualitative Evaluation and User Feedback

In addition to the quantitative and operational results, a second evaluation phase has been launched based on gathering feedback from users who have interacted with the platform in their day-to-day activities. The feedback is collected via structured forms sent to various stakeholders, covering technical, functional, and decision-making profiles. The aim of this approach is to assess the effective appropriation of Cockpit, the perceived relevance of the indicators, ease of use, and the perceived added value in the coordination, anticipation, and analysis processes.

This qualitative evaluation phase enables measurement of the extent to which the platform helps to overcome the obstacles identified in the literature, particularly in terms of organizational compartmentalization, the lack of semantic interoperability, and the weak link between operational monitoring and strategic governance. It also provides critical elements for adjusting future developments to the system, enhancing the ergonomics of the interfaces, and refining the implementation model according to business contexts.

5 Discussion, Conclusion, Perspective

The originality of this work lies in the construction of a governance model that is not limited to the aggregation of data but is based on a formalization of knowledge. This approach ensures real interoperability between the Cloud, DevOps, and Cybersecurity domains and initiates dynamic, adaptive, and strategy-oriented governance. The results of the pilots attest to the operability of this vision while highlighting certain limits that need to be overcome, particularly with regard to the industrialization of processes, the native integration of cybersecurity into decision flows, and the customization of dashboards according to user profiles.

Current limitations include incomplete semantic interoperability between domains and challenges in scaling automated governance policies to support larger collaborative networks. The pilots revealed that while syntactic harmonization effectively addresses immediate integration needs, semantic unification remains essential for advanced automation capabilities. Additionally, the increasing complexity of multi-organizational collaborations requires more sophisticated governance frameworks that can adapt to diverse regulatory and operational requirements across different sectors.

Future research will focus on enhancing semantic integration capabilities through ontology-driven approaches and developing more sophisticated automation frameworks to support larger-scale deployments across extended collaborative networks. This work represents a significant step towards intelligent governance of complex IT infrastructures, demonstrating that unifying technological domains via a structuring model and an appropriate operational tool can not only improve supervision but also transform strategic management methods in a multi-cloud and highly distributed context. The current results, enriched by future feedback, pave the way for a gradual generalization of the model, as well as the exploration of new automation, simulation, and learning capabilities through the integration of advanced artificial intelligence mechanisms.

Acknowledgment. The authors would like to thank SCAFE, a subsidiary of the AODB Group, for its commitment in designing and testing the approach presented in this study. Exchanges with the operational teams and feedback from the projects carried out provided invaluable input, both for anchoring the methodology in the field and for the gradual construction of the evaluation model.

References

1. Asad, F., Jackson, D.: The Role of Artificial Intelligence in Modernizing Enterprise Architecture Through Cloud and DevOps (2024)
2. Anh, N.H.: Hybrid cloud migration strategies: balancing flexibility, security, and cost in a multi-cloud environment. Trans. Machi. Learn. Artif. Intel. Adv. Intel. Sys. **14**(10), 14–26 (2024)
3. Ojha, D., Struckell, E., Acharya, C., Patel, P.C.: Managing environmental turbulence through innovation speed and operational flexibility in B2B service organizations. J. Bus. Indus. Market. **36**(9), 1627–1645 (2021)
4. Ngcobo, K., Bhengu, S., Mudau, A., Thango, B., Lerato, M.: Enterprise data management: Types, sources, and real-time applications to enhance business performance-a systematic review. Systematic Review (2024)

5. Gadekar, R., Sarkar, B., Gadekar, A.: Key performance indicator based dynamic decision-making framework for sustainable Industry 4.0 implementation risks evaluation: reference to the Indian manufacturing industries. Annals of Operations Research **318**(1), 189–249 (2022)
6. Bellisario, A., Pavlov, A., van der Steen, M.P.: The role of performance measurement in aligning operations with strategy: sustaining cognitive processes of internal alignment. Int J. Operat. Prod. Manage. **41**(12), 1879–1907 (2021)
7. Chandra, C.M.B.: From Silos to Synergy: Delivering Unified Data Insights across Disparate Business Units (2024)
8. Mathur, P.: Cloud computing infrastructure, platforms, and software for scientific research. High Performance Computing in Biomimetics: Modeling, Architecture and Applications, 89–127 (2024)
9. Shih, W.C., Yang, C.T., Ranjan, R., Chiang, C.I.: Implementation and evaluation of a container management platform on Docker: Hadoop deployment as an example. Clust. Comput. **24**(4), 3421–3430 (2021)
10. Zhang, J.: Evaluation of Application Migration from Cloud to On-Premise (2024)
11. Abikoye, B.E., Akinwunmi, T., Adelaja, A.O., Umeorah, S.C., Ogunsuji, Y.M.: Real-time financial monitoring systems: Enhancing risk management through continuous oversight. GSC Adv. Res. Rev. **20**(1), 465–476 (2024)
12. Makokha, F.: A Vendor Neutral Quality of Service Monitoring Model for Software as a Service Cloud Computing Solutions (Doctoral dissertation, University of Nairobi) (2022)
13. Das, D.K.: Exploring the symbiotic relationship between digital transformation, infrastructure, service delivery, and governance for smart sustainable cities. Smart Cities **7**(2), 806–835 (2024)
14. Verginadis, Y.: A review of monitoring probes for cloud computing continuum. In: International Conference on Advanced Information Networking and Applications, pp. 631–643. Springer International Publishing, Cham (2023)
15. Öztürk, M.: Refactoring strategies for optimizing and consolidating telemetry systems (Doctoral dissertation, FH Vorarlberg (Fachhochschule Vorarlberg) (2024)
16. Jaju, I.: Maximizing DevOps Scalability in Complex Software Systems: Maximizing DevOps Scalability in Complex Software Systems (2023)
17. Souza, A.: Observability and Monitoring. In: Tech Leadership Playbook: Building and Sustaining High-Impact Technology Teams, pp. 171–191. Apress, Berkeley, CA (2024)
18. Jangjou, M., Sohrabi, M.K.: A comprehensive survey on security challenges in different network layers in cloud computing. Archiv. Computat. Methods Eng. **29**(6), 3587–3608 (2022)
19. Ahmad, A., Maynard, S.B., Desouza, K.C., Kotsias, J., Whitty, M.T., Baskerville, R.L.: How can organizations develop situation awareness for incident response: A case study of management practice. Comput. Secur. **101**, 102122 (2021)
20. Singh, M.M.K., Chandna, M., Kongala, V.Y.Y.: Risk Management Framework for Cloud Migration and Selection of Suitable Cloud Service Provider. Adv. Enterp. Technol. Risk Assessm. 283 (2024)
21. Vernadat, F., Molina, A., Panetto, H., Weichhart, G.: Outlook and future trends. In: Interoperability Principles and Standards: Applications to Collaborative and Automated Systems, pp. 297–320. Springer Nature Switzerland, Cham (2025)
22. Akano, O.A., Hanson, E., Nwakile, C., Esiri, A.E.: Designing real-time safety monitoring dashboards for industrial operations: a data-driven approach. Global J. Res. Sci. Technol. **2**(02), 001–009 (2024)
23. Hosen, M.S., et al.: Data-driven decision making: advanced database systems for business intelligence. Nanotechnology Perceptions **20**(3), 687–704 (2024)
24. Angelo, L.: Unlocking Hidden Value: A Framework for Transforming Dark Data in Organizational Decision-Making. Available at SSRN 5032778 (2024)

25. González-Granadillo, G., González-Zarzosa, S., Diaz, R.: Security information and event management (SIEM): Analysis, trends, and usage in critical infrastructures. Sensors **21**(14), 4759 (2021)
26. Navinchandran, M., Sharp, M.E., Brundage, M.P., Sexton, T.B.: Discovering critical KPI factors from natural language in maintenance work orders. J. Intel. Manufact. 1–19 (2022)
27. Amaro, R., Pereira, R., Mira da Silva, M.: DevOps metrics and KPIs: a multivocal literature review. ACM Comput. Surv. **56**(9), 1–41 (2024)
28. Podobnikar, T.: Bridging Perceived and Actual Data Quality: Automating the Framework for Governance Reliability. Geosciences **15**(4), 117 (2025)
29. Miller, T., et al.: Integrating artificial intelligence agents with the internet of things for enhanced environmental monitoring: applications in water quality and climate data. Electronics **14**(4), 696 (2025)
30. Sheikh, N.: AI-Driven Observability: Enhancing System Reliability and Performance. J. Artif. Intel. Gener. Sci. (JAIGS) **7**(01), 229–239 (2024). ISSN: 3006-4023
31. Shrivastava, S., Agrawal, Y.: Multi-Cloud Deployments and Hybrid Cloud Architecture (2024)
32. Mirshekali, H., Santos, A.Q., Shaker, H.R.: A survey of time-series prediction for digitally enabled maintenance of electrical grids. Energies **16**(17), 6332 (2023)
33. Siddiqui, A.H., et al.: Harnessing Big Data: Strategic Insights for IT Management. Int. J. Adv. Comp. Sci. Appl. **15**(7) (2024)
34. Gavric, A.: Enhancing process understanding through multimodal data analysis and extended reality. In: PoEM Companion (2023)

People-Centred & AI-Driven Processes and Environments of Tomorrow

A Method to Design Human-Centered AI Teammates

Wenqiang Li[1], Juanqiong Gou[1(✉)], Luis M. Camarinha-Matos[2], and Fangcong Zhang[1]

[1] School of Economics and Management, Beijing Jiaotong University, Beijing, China
{wenqli,jqgou,fangczhang}@bjtu.edu.cn

[2] School of Science and Technology, Uninova-CTS and LASI, NOVA University Lisbon, Campus de Caparica, Monte Caparica, Portugal
cam@uninova.pt

Abstract. Recent developments of artificial intelligence (AI) have open up significant opportunities for organizations to adopt human–AI collaboration, enhancing the efficiency of complex collaborative decision-making. Within this hybrid human–AI team paradigm, the concept of AI teammates is gaining increasing recognition. Despite their practical potential, organizations still face various challenges when introducing AI teammates, including insufficient consideration of user needs, unclear application scenarios, limited use of human experiential knowledge, and concerns around privacy and ethics. To address these issues, this study adopts the Design Science Research (DSR) methodology and incorporates principles from Human-Centered AI (HCAI) to propose a structured method for analyzing and designing AI teammates in complex collaborative decision-making contexts. The method emphasizes active involvement of business staff and systematically supports the acquisition and structured representation of experiential knowledge, facilitating the effective design and deployment of AI teammates. The feasibility and effectiveness of the method are demonstrated through experimental validation. Theoretically, this research contributes to the methodological foundations of HCAI and advances the integration of human experiential knowledge into AI systems. Practically, it offers a business-staff-driven design approach that enhances organizational intelligence and supports the adoption of AI technologies in complex decision-making situations.

Keywords: Human-Centered AI · AI Teammate · Experiential Knowledge · Hybrid collaborative networks · Design Science Research

1 Introduction

In today's highly volatile and uncertain organizational environment, dynamic decision-making is a must in enterprise operations [1, 2]. Operations under such conditions are often characterized by high complexity, unstructuredness, temporal variability, and knowledge intensity. Johnson et al. (2022) [3] define such operations as complex unstructured problems, which require cross-departmental collaboration and the balancing of

Published by Springer Nature Switzerland AG 2026
L. M. Camarinha-Matos et al. (Eds.): PRO-VE 2025, IFIP AICT 770, pp. 295–312, 2026.
https://doi.org/10.1007/978-3-032-05673-3_18

multiple, often conflicting, objectives. This study refers to them collectively as complex collaborative decisions.

Despite some undesirable consequences of human-AI collaboration (HAC) as indicated in [4], the cognitive and knowledge-based complementarity between humans and artificial intelligence (AI) systems provides a methodological foundation for the formation of Human–AI Collaboration teams, which have demonstrated superior performance in addressing complex collaborative decisions [2, 5]. Within the HAC paradigm, AI systems contribute through efficient information processing and pattern recognition, while humans provide contextual understanding and value judgment, resulting in decision outcomes that surpass those achievable by either party alone [5].

However, integrating AI as a "teammate" in organizational collaborative decision-making still faces multiple challenges. On one hand, most AI development has focused on algorithmic performance while neglecting end-user needs [6], resulting in a weak alignment between model outputs and business scenarios and limiting collaboration effectiveness [7–10]. On the other hand, AI deployment raises concerns regarding privacy, ethical responsibility, diminished human autonomy, and skill degradation [11]. In response, the paradigm of Human-Centered AI (HCAI) has been widely advocated, emphasizing continuous user involvement to ensure that AI serves to augment rather than replace human intelligence [11].

HCAI promotes the systematic integration of human experiential knowledge into AI system design. Prior studies have shown that incorporating such knowledge not only mitigates issues of data sparsity and incompleteness [12] but also improves model interpretability and performance, thereby advancing responsible and ethical AI practices [3]. More importantly, in complex collaborative decision-making contexts, experiential knowledge is often key to generating high-quality strategies [1]. Yet, from a human-centered perspective, how to effectively couple tacit personal experience with explicit organizational knowledge and translate them into AI-consumable representations and reasoning mechanisms remains a pressing research challenge [3].

In response, this study addresses the following research question:

RQ1: *How can organizations adopt AI to enhance complex collaborative decision-making in a staff-centered perspective?*

RQ2: *How can business staff's experiential knowledge be systematically embedded into AI teammates?*

To this end, we adopt a design science research (DSR) approach and propose the HCAI–guided analysis and design method for complex collaborative decision-making (HCAI-CDM Method). Theoretically, this research extends the methodological foundations of human-centered AI by addressing the core issue of embedding experiential knowledge into AI systems. Practically, it offers a structured, business-staff-oriented method for designing AI teammates to enhance organizational intelligence and improve user acceptance in complex decision situations. Notably, the proposed method is specifically designed for analyzing and designing AI Agents based on large language models (LLMs).

The remainder of this paper is structured as follows: Section 2 reviews relevant literature and theoretical foundations; Section 3 outlines the DSR methodology employed;

Section 4 details the proposed HCAI-CDM method; Section 5 presents an experimental evaluation of the method; and Section 6 concludes with a summary of theoretical contributions, practical implications, and directions for future research.

2 Literature Review

Teamwork collaboration has long been recognized as a crucial mechanism for organizations to navigate complex, dynamic, and knowledge-intensive business environments. Through the exchange and integration of knowledge among team members, effective collective decisions can be formed to address complex collaborative problems [4, 13]. In recent years, the rapid development of artificial intelligence (AI)—especially large language model (LLM)-driven conversational agents such as ChatGPT and ERNIE Bot—has provided new opportunities for addressing these problems via Human–AI Collaboration (HAC). By extending human cognitive and analytical boundaries, HAC offers a promising paradigm for tackling complex collaborative decision-making.

Raisch et al. (2024), drawing on behavioral theory of the firm, compare three modes of organizational problem-solving: human collaboration, pure AI solutions, and human–AI collaboration. Their findings suggest that human-only teams tend to generate deeper solutions, while AI-driven solutions offer broader coverage; HAC, in turn, achieves both depth and breadth [5]. In practice, humans are increasingly viewing AI not merely as a tool but as a collaborative teammate—an evolution driven by AI's growing capacity for perception, cognition, decision-making, and action [14, 15], particularly in uncertain and dynamic contexts.

As AI technologies continue to permeate organizational and societal spheres, both industry and academia are converging on the need to move beyond technology-centric design models toward Human-Centered AI (HCAI) [6]. HCAI emphasizes the centrality of human needs, values, capabilities, and roles, and calls for continuous user engagement to ensure AI enhances rather than replaces human agency [11]. It encompasses key dimensions such as user control over decisions, human-compatible interpretability, and augmented human intelligence through human–machine collaboration [11]. Besides a new approach to design AI systems, it is also necessary to "reimagine the work" or "re-architecting the work" [16, 17].

The HCAI philosophy is being widely embraced as a guiding principle in AI development. Recent international AI governance initiatives—such as the European Union's AI Act (2024) [18]—explicitly identify HCAI as a foundational pillar for responsible and ethical AI adoption. Leading academic institutions such as Stanford University, UC Berkeley, and MIT have also established dedicated research centers on Human-Centered AI. Researchers have increasingly investigated HCAI's theoretical foundations and practical applications [19]. Increasingly, the architecture design of AI systems is no longer the exclusive domain of computer science experts; instead, meaningful contributions are emerging from fields such as management, organizational theory, psychology and other social sciences, which requires a multi-disciplinary dialogue.

Despite these advances, current literature lacks systematic, actionable, and generalizable methods to guide organizations in embedding AI teammates into business practices under complex collaborative settings. While prior studies emphasize the importance of incorporating human experiential knowledge into AI design [12, 14], there remains a critical gap in how to effectively integrate this form of tacit knowledge with HCAI-oriented development. Specifically, there is a need for structured methods that enable the transformation of human experience into AI-relevant knowledge representations and reasoning mechanisms.

This study aims to bridge these gaps by proposing a human-centered and systematic approach that supports organizations in introducing and utilizing AI teammates in complex collaborative decision-making. The proposed method enables the acquisition and formalization of experiential knowledge and its organic integration into AI design.

3 Research Method

This study adopts the Design Science Research (DSR) paradigm, which emphasizes the construction and evaluation of artifacts to solve real-world problems [20]. Specifically, following the process proposed by Kolfschote and De Vreede (2009) [21], the study integrates the theory from Participatory Design (PD) [22], emphasizing active involvement of both users and experts to ensure practical relevance [23].

To address the challenges of complex collaborative decision-making, the method incorporates tools such as the collaborative situation meta-model [24], Decision Model and Notation (DMN) [25], and the Human–AI Team (HAT) meta-model [26]. To tackle the architectural challenges of LLM-based AI teammates, it further introduces task chain and chain of thought (CoT) to structure AI behaviors, while supporting low-code AI agent platforms to facilitate implementation by business professionals.

To evaluate the method, a serious-game [27] inspired manufacturing simulation system was employed. Developed jointly by an edtech company and a university in China, the system replicates complex decision environments to foster applied learning. Participants applied the proposed HCAI-CDM method within this simulation to design and deploy AI teammates, verifying its feasibility and effectiveness.

4 Developing the HCAI-CDM Method

This study follows the core attributes and fundamental components of the analytical method proposed by Braun et al. (2005) [28], using its operational characteristics to guide the design and articulation of the HCAI-CDM method. To enhance the usability and reusability of the HCAI-CDM method, five key components are systematically structured: Activities, Roles, Tools, Instructions, and Results. As illustrated in Fig. 1, these elements collectively form the structural framework of the HCAI-CDM method. The detailed content of the Instructions will be further elaborated in subsequent subsections.

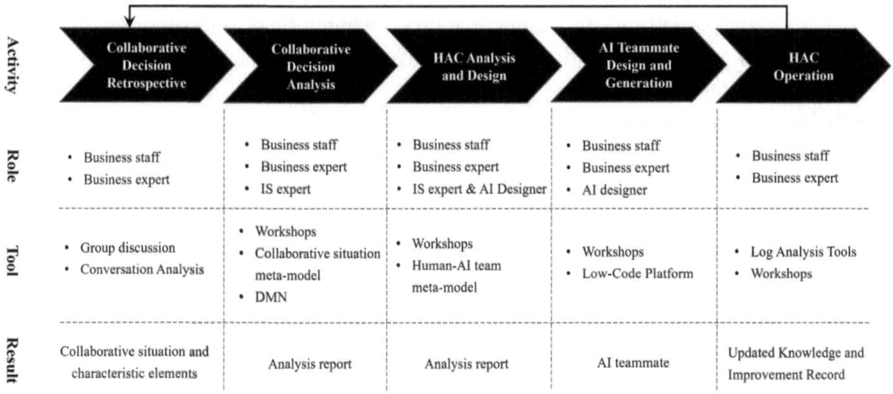

Fig. 1. HCAI-CDM Method

4.1 Activity 1: Collaborative Decision Retrospective

In complex collaborative decision-making, business staff begin with situation awareness [1] and typically collaborate with others to advance problem resolution [5]. Fügener et al. (2021) define this process as the integration of individual knowledge into collective opinions through group intelligence to generate effective solutions [4]. Given the rich experiential knowledge and multi-party collaboration involved, the first step of the HCAI-CDM method is to retrospect the collaborative decision process, identify the situations, and extract key elements. This step also initiates the transformation of experiential knowledge into context-sensitive knowledge. The analysis follows a core principle: systematic translation of practical experience into reusable knowledge. The HCAI-CDM method offers two analytical perspectives for collaborative decision retrospection:

(1) Multi-party meeting perspective

Organizations typically address complex decisions through meetings among stakeholders. The widespread use of platforms like Zoom and Tencent Meeting enables the capture of rich collaborative dynamics. To extract key patterns the following steps were considered: Step 1: Twenty experienced MBA students engaged in manufacturing business simulation were organized in five groups. Each group recorded ~5 hours of discussion. Step 2: The research team analyzed three recordings (~15 hours) using conversation analysis to identify key features and analytical methods. Step 3: The remaining two recordings (~10 hours) were used to validate those findings.

Collaborative decisions were typically characterized by cross-departmental coordination around complex decisions, frequent communication and confirmation, and potential misalignment of departmental goals. Key conversational patterns included overlapping talk, interruptions, repeated exchanges, and clarification efforts. During the analysis, business staff and experts first identify key decision events based on the characteristics of collaborative decision-making and conversational turn-taking patterns. They then determine the specific target situations and assign situation names according to business characteristics.

(2) Business activity perspective

Collaborative situations often emerge at process handoffs or intersections. Attention should be paid to nodes requiring frequent cross-functional communication via tools like WeChat or calls.

(3) Integrated framework

By combining both perspectives, business experts analyze: (a) the initiators and goals of collaboration, (b) participant roles and affiliations, (c) individual goals and contributions, (d) extracted key business knowledge, and (e) joint decisions that require multi-party agreement. The result of Activity 1 is the collaborative situation and the above five characteristic elements.

4.2 Activity 2: Collaborative Decision Analysis

Based on the retrospective analysis of collaborative decision-making, business staff and business experts are required to conduct a deeper examination of the complex collaborative decision processes. This stage is not only critical for the integration and abstraction of knowledge, but also serves as a key point for synthesizing experiential knowledge with theoretical insights. It also necessitates the involvement of information systems (IS) experts to provide modeling support. The analysis at this stage comprises two sub-activities - collaborative situation definition and collaborative decision analysis – followed by a mapping between the collaborative situation model and the DMN notation. The result of Activity 2 is the collaborative decision-making analysis report.

(1) Collaborative situation definition

This study builds upon the collaborative situation metamodel proposed by Benaben et al. (2019) [24], drawing on selected elements to develop a structured approach for business staff and business experts to define collaborative situations. As illustrated in Table 1, key elements are clearly described along with actionable guidance to support systematic situation definition.

(2) Collaborative decision analysis

Following the definition of the collaborative situation, a detailed analysis of both individual and joint decision-making is required. This phase focuses on uncovering the interdependencies among decisions, the supporting knowledge, and the underlying logic structures.

To support this process, this study employs DMN—a standardized graphical language for modeling both human and automated decisions. DMN facilitates the clear articulation of decision logic at various organizational levels and emphasizes collaborative decisions, decision governance, and the representation of business knowledge [25]. The DMN framework includes two main components:

(1) Decision Requirements Diagram (DRD): Specifies decision inputs, interdependencies, and supporting knowledge models and sources. In this context, business experts and operational staff define the knowledge models, drawing on domain expertise and business documentation [25].
(2) Decision Logic: Encodes the rules that govern decisions. DMN primarily uses Decision Tables for formalizing rule sets, but also supports algorithms, and business rule sets to extend logic expressions [25]. This analysis serves as structured input for AI teammate design and bridges human experiential knowledge with machine-executable representations.

Table 1. Explanations and instructions for the collaborative situation metamodel.

Elements	Explanations (E) and Instructions (I)
Context	E: The environment of collaboration, including physical and virtual components and their characteristics, along with embedded opportunities (e.g., technologies, policies) and threats (e.g., uncertainty, conflicts). I: Based on *analysis point a*, describe contextual features (time, location, system state, etc.) and identify key opportunities and threats.
Objective	E: The core business goal driving collaboration. I: Clearly define and, where possible, quantify the goal (*analysis point a*).
Partner	E: Stakeholders from different departments or organizations involved in the situation. I: Abstract individuals into role-based representations with shared goals (e.g., "Production Manager") per *analysis point b.*
Sub-objective	E: Distinct goals or task demands of different collaborators. I: Specify measurable sub-goals for each partner to capture coordination complexity (*analysis point c*).
Resource	E: Knowledge and data supporting decisions; includes theoretical and experiential knowledge. I: Identify and name knowledge types (e.g., "MRP theory") and relevant data per *analysis point d*; assess contextual relevance if using LLMs.
Activity 1)Participant decision 2)Collaborative decision	E: Decision-making behaviors, both individual and joint, within collaboration. I: Map decision sequences and collaborative processes aligned with sub-goals (*analysis point e*).

Note: Analysis points a through e are grounded in the integrated framework presented in Section (3) of Activity 1: Collaborative Decision Retrospective.

(3) Mapping definition between the collaborative situation model and DMN

To systematically establish the relationship between collaborative situation elements and DMN-based decision model components, we formalize the mapping as follows:

(a) ***Element definitions*****:** Let the collaborative situation be defined as $CS = (A, R_D, R_K, P, C, O_{\text{obj}}, S_{\text{obj}})$, where A denotes the set of activities; R_D, the set of data resources; R_K, the set of knowledge resources; P, the set of participants (partners); C, the set of contextual elements; O_{obj}, the set of situation-level objectives; and S_{obj}, the set of sub-objectives. Let the decision model be defined as $DMN = (I, B, D, K, O)$, where I represents the set of input data; B, the set of business knowledge models; D, the set of decisions and sub-decisions; K, the set of knowledge sources; and O, the set of output results.

(b) ***Mapping functions*****:** Define a set of mapping functions as:

$$\varphi_1 : A \to P(D), \varphi_2 : R_D \to \mathcal{P}(I), \varphi_3 : R_K \to \mathcal{P}(B), \varphi_4 : \mathcal{P} \cup R_K \to \mathcal{P}(K) \quad (1)$$

where $\mathcal{P}(\cdot)$ denotes the power set, allowing for many-to-many mappings. Based on these mappings, the corresponding DMN model can be derived as:

$$DMN = \left(\bigcup_{a \in A} \varphi_1(a), \bigcup_{r \in R_D} \varphi_2(r), \bigcup_{k \in R_K} \varphi_3(k), \bigcup_{x \in P \cup R_K} \varphi_4(x) \right) \quad (2)$$

(c) Mapping properties

Completeness : $\forall (a, r, k, p) \in (A, R_D, R_K, P), \exists \big(d, i, b, k'\big) \in (D, I, B, K)$, then,

$$\varphi_1(a) \in \mathcal{P}(D), \varphi_2(r) \in \mathcal{P}(I), \varphi_3(k) \in \mathcal{P}(B), \varphi_4(p \,\text{or}\, k) \in \mathcal{P}(K) \quad (3)$$

Traceability:

$$\forall m \in D \cup I \cup B \cup K, \exists e \in A \cup R_D \cup R_K \cup P, \text{then,} m \in \varphi_i(e)(i = 1, 2, 3, 4) \quad (4)$$

$$\mathit{Scalability} : \mathit{If}\ CS' \supseteq CS, \mathit{then}, DMN' \supseteq DMN \quad (5)$$

To illustrate the mapping process, consider a promotion decision scenario. The collaborative situation includes the activity "evaluate employee performance," the data resource "performance records," the knowledge resource "promotion criteria," and the participant "HR manager." These elements are mapped to the DMN model as follows: the activity corresponds to the decision "promote or not," performance records serve as input data, promotion criteria as the business knowledge model, and the HR manager as a knowledge source.

4.3 Activity 3: HAC Analysis and Design

In Activity 3, business staff and business experts are required to identify suitable AI teammates based on the outputs of Activities 1 and 2 and further analyze the human–AI collaboration process to clarify the roles and responsibilities of humans and AI agents in joint tasks. This phase of analysis and design serves as a foundational step toward the implementation of the AI system and the intelligent application of organizational knowledge. It demands not only the in-depth engagement and knowledge contributions of business staff and experts but also the collaborative involvement of IS specialists and AI designers—where the former provide modeling support, and the latter assess the feasibility and rationality of HAC analysis and design from a technical perspective.

This phase draws on the Human–AI Collaborative Team (HAC Team) meta-model [26] to extract key modeling elements, thereby offering structured support and methodological guidance for the two sub-activities, "HAC Analysis" and "HAC Design". Tables 2 and 3 present the critical elements of these activities and corresponding operational guidelines. The result of Activity 3 is the HAC analysis and design report.

Table 2. Explanations and instructions for HAC analysis

Elements	Explanations and instructions
Context	E: In HAC analysis, Context defines the boundary of human–AI collaborative decision-making, covering both physical and virtual task conditions. I: Context analysis should include (1) the spatiotemporal setting and platform environment where collaboration occurs, and (2) the appropriateness of AI involvement under uncertain or dynamic situations.
AI teammate identification	E: AI teammate identification is grounded in the characteristics of collaborative decision tasks, including task selection and functional definition. I: Analyze each task by: (1) Type: a) Rule-based/repetitive; b) Data-intensive; c) Complex but modelable; d) Creativity/cognition-driven. → (a)(b) suit AI execution; (c) for AI-assisted with human validation; (d) human-led with AI support. (2) Risk: High-stakes tasks favor AI support over automation. (3) Exclusions: Identify tasks unsuitable for AI, e.g., emotional or ethical decisions. Combined analysis defines the AI teammate's name, role, and function.
PCDE	E: PCDE describes AI teammate capabilities in terms of Perception, Cognition, Decision, and Execution. I: These capabilities are mapped as follows. Perception refers to information acquisition and identification, aligned with data input. Cognition involves processing and reasoning, linked to business knowledge models. Decision corresponds to one or more nodes in the DMN decision logic. Execution reflects expected actions and system outputs.

(1) HAC analysis

(2) Mapping definition of HAC analysis elements

To systematically establish the relationships between HAC analysis elements, collaborative situation components, and DMN (Decision Model and Notation) components, we define the following formal mapping:

(a) Element definition: Let the set of HAC analysis elements be defined as $\mathcal{H} = \{Cxt, AI, PCDE = \{P_{\mathrm{AI}}, C_{\mathrm{AI}}, D_{\mathrm{AI}}, E_{\mathrm{AI}}\}\}$, where Cxt denotes the contextual element, AI refers to the identification of AI teammates, and $PCDE$ includes P_{AI} (Perception), C_{AI} (Cognition), D_{AI} (Decision), and E_{AI} (Execution).

(b) Mapping functions: We define a mapping function:

$$\Psi : (CS, DMN) \rightarrow \mathcal{H} \tag{6}$$

Specifically: $\Psi_1(C) \mapsto \boldsymbol{Cxt},\ \Psi_2(D) \mapsto \boldsymbol{AI},\ \Psi_3(I,B,D,O) \mapsto \boldsymbol{PCDE}$

The PCDE sub-elements correspond as follows:

$$P_{AI} \leftarrow I, C_{AI} \leftarrow B, D_{AI} \leftarrow D, E_{AI} \leftarrow O \tag{7}$$

(c) Mapping properties

$$\textbf{Completeness}: \forall \boldsymbol{h} \in \mathcal{H}, \exists(\mathcal{E}_1, \mathcal{E}_2) \in (CS, DMN), \Psi(\mathcal{E}_1, \mathcal{E}_2) = \boldsymbol{h} \tag{8}$$

$$\textit{Traceability}: \forall \boldsymbol{h} \in \mathcal{H}, \exists!(\mathcal{E}_1, \mathcal{E}_2) \in (CS, DMN), \Psi^{-1}(\boldsymbol{h}) = (\mathcal{E}_1, \mathcal{E}_2) \tag{9}$$

$$\textbf{Scalability}: \Psi'(CS', DMN') \supseteq \Psi(CS, DMN) \text{ 当 } CS' \supseteq CS, DMN' \supseteq DMN \tag{10}$$

In the promotion decision scenario, elements from the collaborative situation and DMN model are systematically mapped to HAC analysis components. The contextual factor "Promotion opportunity" maps to *Cxt*, and the decision node "whether to promote" identifies the need for an AI teammate. Within the PCDE structure: "performance records" correspond to perception (P_{AI}), "promotion criteria" to cognition (C_{AI}), the decision "whether to promote" to decision-making (D_{AI}), and the outcome "promote / not promote" to execution (E_{AI}).

(3) HAC design

(4) Mapping definition of HAC design elements

To systematically establish the relationships between HAC design elements and components from the collaborative situation (CS), decision model (DMN), and HAC analysis (H), we define the following formal mapping framework:

(a) Element definitions: Let $Z = \left(R_{AI}, C_{AI}, R_{AI\_RES}, R_H, C_H, O_{HAT}, A_{AI}, A_H\right)$, where R_{AI}, C_{AI}, and R_{AI_RES} denote the roles, capabilities, and responsibilities of AI teammates, respectively; R_H and C_H refer to the roles and capabilities of human participants; O_{HAT} is the set of objectives for the Human–AI Team; $A_{AI} = \left(A^{task}, A^{data}, A^{know}\right)$ represents AI activities related to task execution, data processing, and knowledge utilization; and A_H denotes the human activity set.

(b) Mapping functions: Define the overall mapping function as:

$$\Theta : (CS, DMN, \mathcal{H}) \rightarrow Z \tag{11}$$

Sub-mappings are defined as:

$$\begin{aligned} &\Theta_1 : AI \rightarrow \left(R_{AI}, C_{AI}, R_{AI\_RES}\right) \\ &\Theta_2 : (D, K, AI) \rightarrow (R_H, C_H) \\ &\Theta_3 : \left(O_{obj}, S_{obj}, AI\right) \rightarrow O_{HAT} \\ &\Theta_4 : PCDE \rightarrow A_{AI} = \left(A^{task}, A^{data}, A^{know}\right) \\ &\Theta_5 : (D, I, PCDE) \rightarrow A_H \end{aligned} \tag{12}$$

Within the AI activity structure A_{AI}, elements are derived as follows:

$$P_{AI} \rightarrow A^{data}, C_{AI} \rightarrow A^{know}, \{D_{AI}, E_{AI}\} \rightarrow A^{task} \tag{13}$$

Table 3. Explanations and instructions for HAC design

Elements	Explanations & Instructions
AI Role	E: Define the AI teammate's role in collaborative tasks (e.g., executor, advisor, monitor). I: Based on HAC analysis and task features, assign the AI a clear functional role aligned with its contribution (e.g., action, suggestion, oversight).
AI Capability	E: Outline the AI's task scope and capability boundaries. I: Specify capabilities across perception, cognition, prediction, decision, execution, and generation, using concrete examples tied to real situations.
AI Responsibility	E: Describe the AI's responsibilities in the collaboration (e.g., data analysis, forecasting, execution). I: Match responsibilities to the AI's role and capabilities; e.g., a forecasting AI supports strategic planning.
Human Role	E: Define the role of human actors in the HAC team, particularly in oversight or high-stakes decisions. I: Align human roles with tasks where experience, judgment, or ethical reasoning is critical.
Human Responsibility	E: Identify the specific responsibilities of humans during collaboration. I: Clarify their tasks and intervention points, ensuring complementarity with AI functions.
HAT Objective	E: Articulate the intended goals of the human–AI team within the given context. I: Set measurable, situation-specific goals that reflect team objectives and role distributions.
AI Activity • Task • Knowledge • Data	E: Detail the AI teammate's decision tasks and supporting knowledge/data. I: Specify: (1) tasks (clearly labeled); (2) knowledge (rules/models); (3) data (inputs and sources).
Human Activity • Task • Data	E: Describe the human's decision tasks in interaction with AI. I: Define (1) tasks before/after AI actions, and (2) required data, indicating dependencies on AI outputs or systems.

(c) Mapping properties

$$\textbf{Completeness}: \forall z \in Z, \exists (CS, DMN, \mathcal{H}), z \in \Theta(CS, DMN, \mathcal{H}) \quad (14)$$

$$\textbf{Traceability}: \forall z \in Z, \exists! (\mathcal{E}_1, \mathcal{E}_2, \mathcal{E}_3) \in (CS, DMN, \mathcal{H}), z \in \Theta(\mathcal{E}_1, \mathcal{E}_2, \mathcal{E}_3) \quad (15)$$

Scalability : *if* $CS' \supseteq CS, DMN' \supseteq DMN, \mathcal{H}' \supseteq \mathcal{H}$, *then*,

$$\Theta\left(CS', DMN', \mathcal{H}'\right) \supseteq \Theta(CS, DMN, \mathcal{H}) \quad (16)$$

In the promotion decision scenario, the AI teammate is designed as a decision support agent with capabilities (C_{AI}) in perception, cognition, and decision-making. Its responsibilities ($R_{\text{AI\_RES}}$) include processing performance data, applying promotion criteria, and generating recommendations. The human participant (R_{H}), the HR manager, has capabilities (C_{H}) in contextual judgment and evaluating AI outputs. The Human–AI Team's objective (O_{HAT}) is to enhance the efficiency and fairness of the promotion process. The AI's activities (A_{AI})—data processing (A^{data}), knowledge use (A^{know}), and task execution (A^{task})—are derived from HAC analysis elements: perception (performance records), cognition (promotion criteria), and decision-making ("promote or not" judgment). Human activities (A_{H}) involve interpreting AI suggestions and making the final decision.

4.4 Activity 4: AI Teammate Design and Generation

Traditional AI agents, often based on rule sets or decision trees, struggle to handle the complexity and variability of collaborative business situations. Recent advances in large language models (LLMs) offer a new pathway for building intelligent, adaptive AI agents capable of perception, decision-making, task execution, and human interaction. These agents can dynamically learn, transfer knowledge, and flexibly invoke tools to meet diverse task demands.

Activity 4 focuses on the structured design and instantiation of AI teammates based on the LLM-agent architecture. While AI designers lead this stage, the method emphasizes deep involvement of business staff and experts in designing task and CoT to ensure alignment with business needs and support human-centered AI development. In fact, one of the main challenges here is the continuous evolution of AI technology. The LLM-agent framework includes two key components: (1) Task Chain: a structured sequence of planning, decision-making, and execution steps that define agent actions; (2) CoT: composed of perception, memory, and reasoning mechanisms that support step-by-step problem-solving. In this method, task chains are derived from AI Activities in the HAC design phase; perception CoT aligns with required data inputs; memory CoT with domain knowledge and DMN-defined knowledge sources; and reasoning CoT with logical rules and structured representations. These elements form the agent's cognitive-action foundation.

The HCAI-CDM method supports the implementation of executable AI teammate prototypes via low-code development platforms. With the advancement of the LLM systems, platforms such as Langflow and Dify now provide powerful capabilities for rapid prototyping and visual configuration of intelligent agents, facilitating co-design between technical AI developers and business stakeholders. These platforms typically support three core functions: workflow orchestration, prompt engineering, and tool invocation. In this context, the AI task chain can be directly translated into a workflow structure, the thinking chain can inform the construction of structured prompt templates, and the tool invocation module can be configured according to the capability requirements of the AI teammate, enabling integrated and extensible functionality. The result of Activity 4 is concrete AI teammates.

4.5 Activity 5: HAC Operation

Following the development and deployment of AI teammates, business staff engage in substantive collaboration with AI agents to address complex decision-making tasks. This human–AI collaboration can occur through natural language dialogues, interface interactions, or embedded task coordination, reflecting joint activities such as perception, evaluation, deliberation, and resolution. During this phase, the human–AI interaction system (e.g., instant messaging platforms) is expected to comprehensively record all interactions between business users and AI teammates, including dialogue transcripts, task execution steps, decision rationales, feedback, and instances of conflicts or revisions. These interaction logs constitute a critical data source for post-hoc analysis. Through structured analysis of these logs, several key insights can be derived: (1) newly acquired experiential knowledge by business staff; (2) suggestions for improving AI teammate design; (3) knowledge gaps in decision-making processes; and (4) weaknesses in AI reasoning, judgment, or output generation.

These findings inform the iterative refinement of AI teammates, enabling dynamic adjustments to model parameters, knowledge base structures, and inference mechanisms to enhance adaptability and decision quality across contexts. Moreover, the process facilitates the continuous externalization and intelligent evolution of experiential knowledge, potentially supporting mutual growth between AI teammates and human collaborators. The result of Activity 5 is the updated knowledge of AI teammates and the improvement strategies for AI teammates.

5 Evaluating the HCAI-CDM Method

To evaluate the value and feasibility of the proposed HCAI-CDM method, a three-week experimental study was conducted. The experiment involved a team of five master's and doctoral students in information management, each possessing basic competencies in systems analysis and AI application.

Performed activities:

- Week 1: Team members assumed different business roles (e.g., sales, production, finance) and engaged with a manufacturing simulation platform to carry out business operations, thereby gaining familiarity with the domain logic and decision-making processes. All activities were recorded using Tencent Meeting to facilitate subsequent analysis.
- Week 2: The research team introduced and trained the experimental team on the HCAI-CDM method. The experimental team then conducted systematic analysis and design of AI teammates based on the scenarios within the simulation system. During this phase, the researchers acted as AI designers to guide and support the design process.
- Week 3: The experimental team conducted human–AI collaborative experiments using the AI teammates they had developed. They simulated decision-making tasks and proposed continuous refinements based on observed collaboration issues. Due to space constraints, only key results are presented here; additional materials are available upon request.

In Activity 1: Collaborative Decision Retrospective, the experimental team identified "order selection" as a representative collaborative situation. In Activity 2: Collaborative Decision Analysis, the experimental team modeled the collaborative situation (Fig. 2) and developed a corresponding DMN-based decision model (Fig. 3), where orange nodes represent sales decisions, blue for production, green for finance, and purple for cross-functional decisions. For example, the sales team's order screening logic involved: (1) Identifying eligible product categories; (2) Defining a set of candidate orders $\{X_1, \ldots, X_n\}$ with corresponding unit prices $\{Y_1, \ldots, Y_n\}$, and sorting them in descending order of Y; (3) Outputting key order details, such as client name, payment ratio, product, price, quantity, expected delivery, and penalty terms.

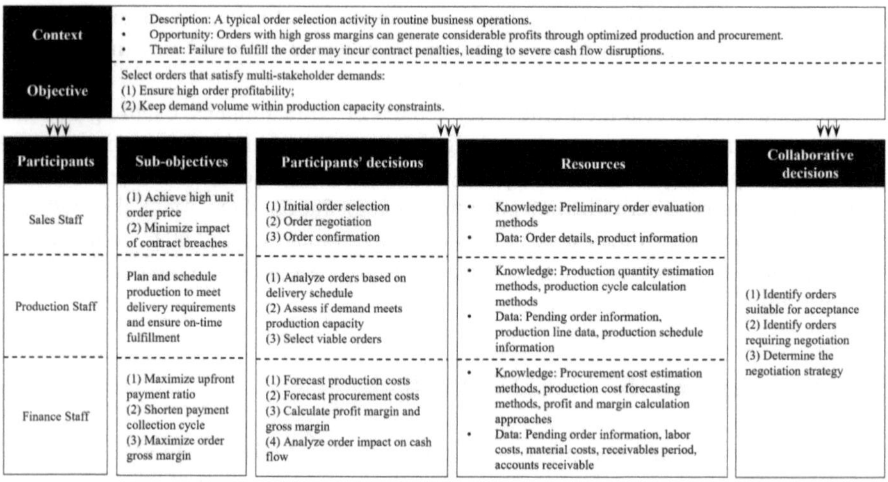

Fig. 2. Collaborative situation model of order selection

In Activity 3: HAC Analysis and Design, the experimental team analyzed possible AI teammates for the order selection task and developed various Human–AI Team (HAT) models. From the sales perspective, they identified the "Order Pre-selection AI Teammate (Sales)" and specified its role, capabilities, responsibilities, and collaboration with human team members (Fig. 4). In Activity 4: AI Teammate Design and Generation, the experimental team defined the task chain and thinking chain for the AI teammate based on the HAC design, and used the low-code platform Dify to build a functional prototype (Fig. 5).

In Activity 5: HAC Operation, the experimental team reinitiated the manufacturing simulation to evaluate the effectiveness of the constructed AI teammate. During this phase, the team identified a key limitation: warehouse inventory data had not been considered in the decision logic. As a result, they proposed expanding the team to include warehouse stakeholders and designed a new AI teammate—"Inventory Analysis AI Teammate"—to enhance the overall collaborative decision-making process. Following the introduction of the new AI teammate, the experimental team reported smoother execution of order acquisition tasks, increased company revenue, and reduced costs

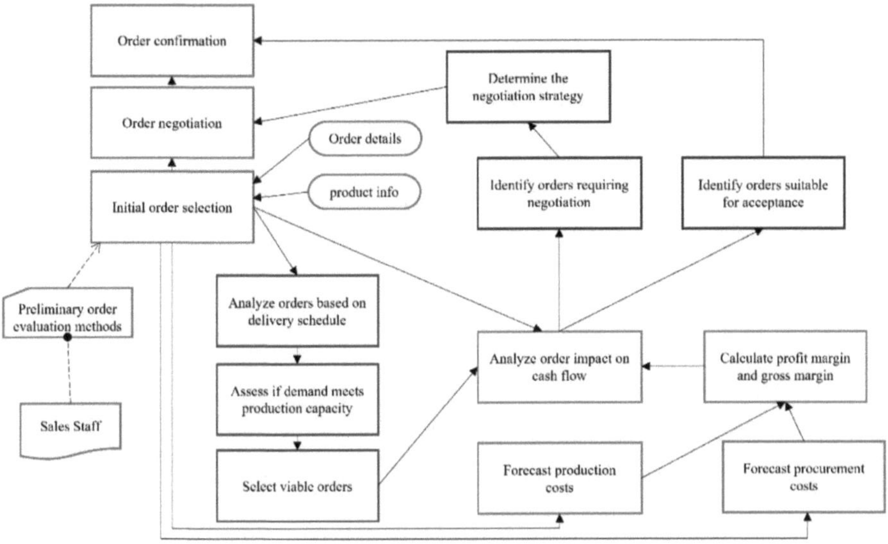

Fig. 3. DMN of order selection

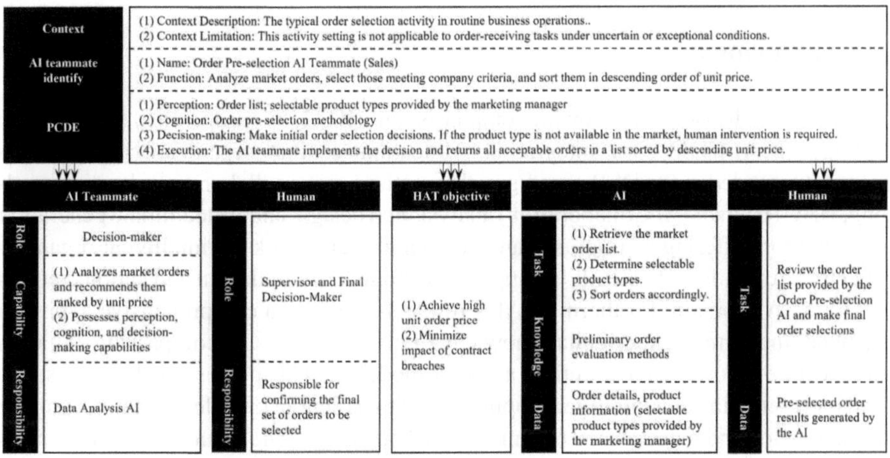

Fig. 4. HAC analysis and design from the sales perspective

through more comprehensive decision-making. However, the team also noted the continuous emergence of new requirements and AI teammate optimization strategies, highlighting the necessity of agile AI teammate operation in today's complex and dynamic decision-making environments.

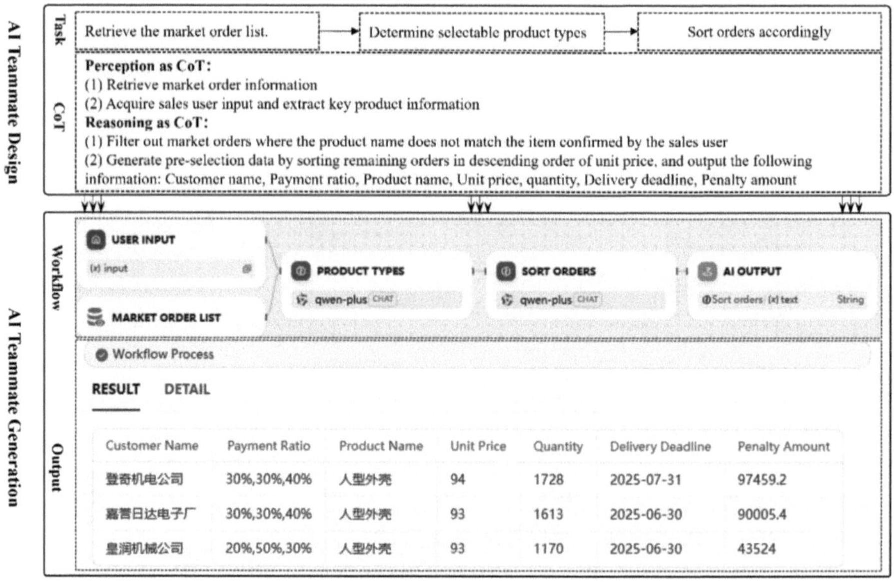

Fig. 5. AI teammate design and generation

6 Conclusions

This study addresses the growing emphasis on HCAI by proposing a systematic method—HCAI-CDM—for integrating AI teammates into organizational decision-making. Grounded in the DSR paradigm, this method spans collaborative situation modeling, HAC (Human–AI Collaboration) analysis and design, and AI teammate generation and operation, offering a structured and actionable framework for intelligent organizational transformation. It extends the application boundaries of design and action theories [29] to the AI domain. Furthermore, this research provides a comprehensive approach to embedding human experiential knowledge into AI systems, encompassing situation retrospection, knowledge extraction, and task modeling. This process enables the structured representation and intelligent application of experiential knowledge, supporting the externalization and reuse of tacit organizational knowledge. The method also emphasizes the active participation of business staff across the AI lifecycle, transforming them from passive users into co-designers and intelligent feedback providers. This shift enhances system adaptability, user understanding, and trust. Practically, HCAI-CDM offers organizations an operational pathway to develop AI teammates that exhibit knowledge adaptability, improved decision quality, and greater user involvement. This study has yet to be validated in real-world organizational settings. Future research should assess the practical effectiveness of HCAI-CDM in actual business environments. Moreover, subsequent work should explore cognitive alignment, ethical interaction, and trust mechanisms in HAC to advance the theoretical and methodological foundations of HCAI.

Acknowledgments. The presented research work has been supported by the "National Natural Science Foundation of China (61972029)", the "Fundamental Research Funds for the Central Universities (B24YJS00220) and the "Portuguese Foundation for Science and Technology" through the project CTS/00066.

References

1. Baran, B.E., Woznyj, H.M.: Managing VUCA: The human dynamics of agility. Organizational Dynamics. **50**, 100787 (2021). https://doi.org/10.1016/j.orgdyn.2020.100787
2. Jarrahi, M.H.: Artificial intelligence and the future of work: Human-AI symbiosis in organizational decision making. Business Horizons. **61**, 577–586 (2018). https://doi.org/10.1016/j.bushor.2018.03.007
3. Johnson, M., Albizri, A., Harfouche, A., Fosso-Wamba, S.: Integrating human knowledge into artificial intelligence for complex and ill-structured problems: Informed artificial intelligence. Int. J. Info. Manage. **64**, 102479 (2022). https://doi.org/10.1016/j.ijinfomgt.2022.102479
4. Fügener, A., Grahl, J., Gupta, A., Ketter, W.: Will Humans-in-the-Loop Become Borgs? Merits and Pitfalls of Working with AI. MISQ. **45**, 1527–1556 (2021). https://doi.org/10.25300/MISQ/2021/16553.
5. Raisch, S., Fomina, K.: Combining Human and Artificial Intelligence: Hybrid Problem-Solving in Organizations. Acad. Manage. Rev. amr.2021.0421 (2024). https://doi.org/10.5465/amr.2021.0421
6. Shneiderman, B.: Human-Centered Artificial Intelligence: Three Fresh Ideas. THCI. 109–124 (2020). https://doi.org/10.17705/1thci.00131
7. Alsheibani, S., Cheung, Y., Messom, C.: Factors Inhibiting the Adoption of Artificial Intelligence at organizational-level: A Preliminary Investigation. Presented at the Americas Conference on Information Systems 2019, Cancun (2019)
8. Davenport, T.H., Ronanki, R.: Artificial Intelligence for the Real World (2018)
9. Mao, H., Zhang, T., Tang, Q.: Research framework for determining how artificial intelligence enables information technology service management for business model resilience. Sustainability. **13**, 11496 (2021). https://doi.org/10.3390/su132011496
10. Siu, H.C., et al.: Evaluation of Human-AI Teams for Learned and Rule-Based Agents in Hanabi (2021). https://doi.org/10.48550/arXiv.2107.07630
11. Xu, W., Gao, Z., Ge, L.: New research paradigms and agenda of human factors science in the intelligence era. Acta Psychologica Sinica. **56**, 363 (2024). https://doi.org/10.3724/SP.J.1041.2024.00363
12. Harfouche, A., Quinio, B., Saba, M., Saba, P.B.: The Recursive Theory of Knowledge Augmentation: Integrating human intuition and knowledge in Artificial Intelligence to augment organizational knowledge. Inf Syst Front. **25**, 55–70 (2023). https://doi.org/10.1007/s10796-022-10352-8
13. Camarinha-Matos, L.M., Afsarmanesh, H.: The Evolution Path to Collaborative Networks 4.0. In: Advancing Research in Information and Communication Technology. IFIP AICT, vol 600. Springer, Cham (2021). https://doi.org/10.1007/978-3-030-81701-5_7
14. Zheng, Q., Gou, J., Camarinha-Matos, L.M., Zhang, J.Z., Zhang, X.: Digital capability requirements and improvement strategies: Organizational socialization of AI teammates. Info. Proc. Manage. **60**, 103504 (2023). https://doi.org/10.1016/j.ipm.2023.103504
15. Hemmer, P., Schemmer, M., Vössing, M., Kühl, N.: Human-AI Complementarity in Hybrid Intelligence Systems: A Structured Literature Review (2021), Twenty-fifth Pacific Asia Conference on Information Systems, Dubai, UAE, PACIS (2021)

16. Richter, S., Richter, A.: Human-AI Collaboration in the Metaverse – How to Research the Future of Work? In: Proceedings of ECIS 2024-32nd European Conference on Information Systems. Paphos, Cyprus (2024)
17. Deloitte Insights: The social enterprise in a world disrupted: Leading the shift from survive to thrive, https://www2.deloitte.com/content/dam/insights/us/articles/6935_2021-HC-Trends/di_human-capital-trends.pdf (2021)
18. European Union: Regulation (EU) 2024/1689 of the European Parliament and of the Council of 13 June 2024 laying down harmonised rules on artificial intelligence (Artificial Intelligence Act). EUR-Lex. https://eur-lex.europa.eu/eli/reg/2024/1689/oj. Accessed 22 May 2025
19. Ridley, M.: Human-centered explainable artificial intelligence: An Annual Review of Information Science and Technology (ARIST) paper. Asso for Info Science & Tech. asi.24889 (2024). https://doi.org/10.1002/asi.24889
20. Hevner, March: Park, Ram: Design Science in Information Systems Research. MIS Quarterly. **28**, 75 (2004). https://doi.org/10.2307/25148625
21. Kolfschoten, G.L., De Vreede, G.-J.: A design approach for collaboration processes: a multi-method design science study in collaboration engineering. J. Manage. Info. Sys. **26**, 225–256 (2009). https://doi.org/10.2753/MIS0742-1222260109
22. Schön, E.-M., Thomaschewski, J., Escalona, M.J.: Agile requirements engineering: a systematic literature review. Comp. Stand. Interf. **49**, 79–91 (2017). https://doi.org/10.1016/j.csi.2016.08.011
23. Roccetti, M., Prandi, C., Mirri, S., Salomoni, P.: Designing human-centric software artifacts with future users: a case study. Hum. Cent. Comput. Inf. Sci. **10**, 8 (2020). https://doi.org/10.1186/s13673-020-0213-6
24. Benaben, F., et al.: A Tentative Framework for Risk and Opportunity Detection in A Collaborative Environment Based on Data Interpretation. Presented at the Hawaii International Conference on System Sciences (2019). https://doi.org/10.24251/HICSS.2019.369
25. OMG: Decision Modeling and Notation1.4. (2023). https://www.omg.org/spec/DMN/1.4/About-DMN
26. Miller, M.E., Rusnock, C.F.: Integrating Artificial and Human Intelligence through Agent Oriented Systems Design. CRC Press, Boca Raton (2024). https://doi.org/10.1201/9781003428183
27. Graafland, M., Schraagen, J.M., Schijven, M.P.: Systematic review of serious games for medical education and surgical skills training. British Journal of Surgery. **99**, 1322–1330 (2012). https://doi.org/10.1002/bjs.8819
28. Braun, C., Wortmann, F., Hafner, M., Winter, R.: Method construction - a core approach to organizational engineering. In: Proceedings of the 2005 ACM symposium on Applied computing. pp. 1295–1299. ACM, Santa Fe New Mexico (2005). https://doi.org/10.1145/1066677.1066971
29. Gregor: The Nature of Theory in Information Systems. MIS Quarterly. **30**, 611 (2006). https://doi.org/10.2307/25148742

Co-Designing Digitally-Enhanced and Inclusive Patient Pathways in Dental Care: A Case Study Combining Modelling, Simulation and Collaborative Innovation

Raksmey Phan[1(✉)], Edlecio Moreno[2], and Xavier Boucher[1]

[1] Mines Saint-Etienne, Univ Clermont Auvergne, INP Clermont Auvergne, CNRS, UMR 6158, LIMOS, Saint-Etienne, France
{raksmey.phan,xavier.boucher}@mines-stetienne.fr
[2] Mines Saint-Etienne, Saint-Etienne, France
edlecio.moreno@mines-stetienne.fr

Abstract. This article presents a method dedicated to the design of collaborative healthcare processes in the context of dental centres by combining qualitative and quantitative approaches. Collaboration is addressed as a way to improve process efficiency and as component of the design approach. This design approach articulates the use of modelling and simulation of patient flows, together with a participative and inclusive approach applied in the case study of a dental centre, with the aim to improve the patient pathway. The patient experience deeply depends on how the centre is organised. For this reason, Design Thinking tools were used to collaboratively involve professionals and patients in identifying areas for improvement: job descriptions, organisation of spaces, ergonomics of treatment rooms, etc., with the aim of designing the dental centre 'of the future'. Several organisational models were then simulated, using FlexSim software to assess the impact of the various collaborative scenarios considered. This real case study led to the construction of a new centre at the end of 2024, partially based on these recommendations. This work shows how digitally-powered modelling tools, combined with participatory and collaborative design approaches, supports personalized, ethical, and inclusive service transformation.

Keywords: Human-Centreed Innovation · Patient Pathway Optimization · Dental Centre Design · Inclusive Healthcare Transformation

1 Introduction

The transformation of healthcare systems increasingly depends on collaborative networks that integrate human expertise with digital technologies. In this context, this article presents a case study of a collaborative enterprise network formed by a federation of dental centres. The focus is a transformation project led by AESIO Santé, aimed at redesigning its centres through a more explicit and structured model of collaboration.

Published by Springer Nature Switzerland AG 2026
L. M. Camarinha-Matos et al. (Eds.): PRO-VE 2025, IFIP AICT 770, pp. 313–331, 2026.
https://doi.org/10.1007/978-3-032-05673-3_19

In many dental clinics, coordination remains largely informal, relying on tacit knowledge, interpersonal arrangements, and legacy practices. The heterogeneity of tools, procedures, and infrastructures—often inherited from successive mergers—generates inefficiencies, discontinuities in care, and inconsistencies in service quality. This paper explores the potential benefits of deliberately structured, digitally-enabled collaboration to enhance both organisational performance and patient outcomes. The innovation process adopted is rooted in a mixed-methods approach, drawing upon concepts from ergonomics, social psychology, applied mathematics, and organisational sciences and implemented within a Living Lab framework. Digital tools such as FlexSim were used to simulate various organisational configurations, assess their performance with respect to key performance indicators (KPIs), and validate proposed changes against operational constraints. The integration of human-centred practices with simulation-based modelling fosters service innovation while empowering practitioners in their daily work.

The AESIO Santé dental care network provides a relevant context for investigating collaborative healthcare systems. As a multi-site organisation with shared goals and centralised digital tools, it offers a living laboratory to explore how coordination, knowledge sharing and service consistency can be achieved throughout distributed structures. The case study highlights key challenges of collaborative networks, such as balancing local autonomy with standardisation and aligning diverse professional roles through shared workflows and technologies. Rather than optimising a single site, this research aims to produce transferable insights into the design and governance of federated care networks. By combining field observation, participatory design and simulation, it demonstrates how collaborative principles—such as co-construction, real-time coordination, and integration of user needs—can be embedded into the operational fabric of complex healthcare ecosystems.

The project already led to two key strategic outcomes: (i) the development of an architectural and functional program for a new dental centre scheduled to open in late 2024; and (ii) the design of a centralised information system to support coordination of all sites in the network. By investigating how collaboration can be made explicit and systemic in a multi-site healthcare organisation, this study contributes to the development of human-centred and digitally enhanced care models—aligned with values of inclusion, work-life quality, and operational efficiency.

The remainder of this article is structured as follows. Section 2 presents the conceptual and theoretical foundations of our approach. Section 3 introduces the methodological framework. Section 4 details the case study conducted in the AESIO Santé network. Section 5 presents both the qualitative transformation outputs and the results of scenario-based simulations. Finally, Sect. 6 discusses the implications and concludes with perspectives for future work.

2 Related Works: Digitally-Enhanced Collaborative Networks for Healthcare Innovation

Collaborative networks are increasingly recognised as essential structures within healthcare systems, enhancing patient care through improved coordination, resource optimisation and knowledge sharing [1]. Recent studies highlighted their value in strengthening organisational resilience and responsiveness in complex and rapidly evolving healthcare environments. Notably, collaborative networks enable a shift from informal and implicit to explicit and formal collaboration through conceptual tools. Such tools support healthcare workers in developing effective collaboration in complex systems [2] to increase operational efficiency and achieve better patient outcomes. Additionally, computationally aided collaborative networks based on advanced simulation and optimisation approaches help reducing operational bottlenecks and enhancing patients' satisfaction in various healthcare settings [3]. Adopting collaborative network paradigms appears crucial to foster innovation, agility, and patient-centred care.

The integration of digital technologies into healthcare systems has given rise to new forms of collaboration between human actors and intelligent systems. This human-digital collaboration is increasingly recognised as a key enabler of agility, responsiveness, and personalisation in care delivery [4]. For instance, [5] proposes the concept of a learning healthcare system, in which collaboration between humans and intelligent systems is essential to enhance responsiveness to rapid changes. Digital tools—ranging from decision support systems to simulation environments and intelligent planning—no longer serve as passive assistants; rather, they act as active and adaptive collaborators in both clinical and operational processes [4], where AI and digital technologies become cognitive partners in healthcare, promoting more personalised and responsive medicine. In collaborative healthcare networks, such technologies improve workflow transparency, support coordination among distributed teams and enable real-time adaptation to patient needs and resource constraints. Recent studies [3] demonstrate how digital platforms and simulation frameworks can enhance collaborative decision-making in contexts of elderly care, home healthcare services, or outpatient scheduling. These examples underscore the growing role of artificial intelligence and discrete-event simulation in orchestrating interactions among clinicians, administrative staff, and digital agents, thereby reducing waiting times, improving patient satisfaction, and distributing workload more efficiently. Ultimately, human-digital collaboration not only redefines technological tools but also transforms the very nature of cooperation, turning tacit coordination into explicit, data-driven, and adaptive processes.

In complex and dynamic organisational environments such as healthcare systems, collaboration has traditionally relied on informal coordination mechanisms, tacit routines, and local adjustments [6]. But as size and heterogeneity grow - and especially so in multi-site or multidisciplinary contexts - such an implicit form of collaboration is increasingly under strain. Moving on to an explicit form necessitates formalisation of work interactions into common procedures, ordered communication protocols and standardised roles. [2] offers a typology of modes of collaboration, ranging from informal through to ordered, in healthcare organisations. Management sciences and ergonomics have long emphasised the critical role of regulatory mechanisms in supporting coherence and resilience in collective activity, especially under conditions of variability and uncertainty [7]. These contributions highlight that, beyond technical tools, the effectiveness of collaboration is determined by the organisational infrastructure-clarity of responsibilities, transparency of decision-making processes, and alignment of actor interfaces. Making collaboration explicit facilitates not only task coordination, but also mutual understanding, accountability and collective adaptability in real time. From this perspective, formal models of cooperation are not intended to eliminate the flexibility of human judgement, but rather to provide a shared reference framework that enhances collective performance and reduces ambiguity in increasingly interconnected work environments.

Innovation in healthcare systems increasingly relies on participatory and multidisciplinary approaches to ensure the effectiveness and sustainability of transformation initiatives. Methods such as Living Labs, Design Thinking, and Human-Centred Design have proven particularly well suited, as they involve end-users—patients, healthcare professionals, and administrative staff—from the earliest stages of solution design [8, 9]. Ergonomics and work psychology allow us to take into account the realities of daily activity and offer analytical and experimental approaches that allow us to finely evaluate the conditions of engagement, the regulatory mechanisms in the activity and the factors of resistance or adhesion to transformations. With the social sciences, which shed light on organizational dynamics and the conditions of acceptability, these approaches foster a shared understanding of needs and constraints while stimulating collective creativity, thereby facilitating the integration of qualitative and quantitative methodologies. In parallel, quantitative approaches such as operations research and simulation provide rigorous tools for evaluating organisational alternatives and supporting decision-making. The relevance of using simulation tools such as AnyLogic and FlexSim to assess organisational resilience in healthcare has been demonstrated in [10, 11]. The integration of these disciplines thus enables the design of more suitable, better accepted and more sustainable solutions in healthcare environments [12].

Dental centres have particular organisational features making them unique among outpatient-care structures. Organising considers high versatility of actors (dentists, assistants, administration), space modularity and strong ergonomic constraints as regards posture, technical device handling and space configuration. These particularities make patient pathway very sensitive to workload mismatches, appointment cancellations or task interruptions. Various studies tackle optimisation of pathways in dental practices using operation research approaches, including dynamic appointment scheduling, queue management and resource planning [13, 14]. Besides, flow simulation approaches, commonly complemented with organisational engineering tools, allow virtual testing of possible spatial and temporal configurations. These tools allow their respective performance and worker well-being to be evaluated and support collaborative decision-taking [15].

In summary, while the literature provides valuable insights into collaborative healthcare networks and the role of digital technologies, important limitations persist. Participatory design approaches are often disconnected from quantitative evaluation tools such as simulation, reducing their potential for operational transformation. Moreover, the formalisation of collaboration across heterogeneous, multi-site healthcare structures remains underexplored. Finally, few empirical studies combine ergonomic fieldwork with simulation-based organisational analysis. This study addresses these gaps by proposing an integrated methodology that bridges participatory co-design, ergonomic diagnostics, and discrete-event simulation to support the inclusive and efficient redesign of patient pathways in a federated dental care network.

3 A Structured Research Methodology, Articulating Qualitative and Quantitative Approaches

The innovation approach used in this project is systemic and multidisciplinary. It is based on integrating qualitative, participatory, non-participatory and quantitative methods. The aim is to build a deep understanding of existing dental centre organisation and co-develop and test plausible improvement scenarios. Utilising ergonomics, work psychology and organisational science principles, the method includes semi-structured interviewing, observation in the field and surveys to evaluate mental workload, causes of stress and levels of coping strategy adoption. Four complementary elements were established: ergonomic analysis of actual work activity, qualitative interviewing, co-design workshops and organisational simulation. These are explained in more detail below and their integration is described in Sect. 3.5.

3.1 Ergonomic Approach and Observation of Real Work Activity

The ergonomic investigation in this project is grounded in activity-centred ergonomics and seeks to understand work as practiced in context rather than as officially prescript. It highlights the dynamic and adaptive nature of professional practice and takes into account real-time adjustments to changing organisational, material, and cognitive boundaries. For this investigation, direct observation in multiple dental centres employed systematic ergonomic grids as a data collection tool. These observations measured patient flow, bodily moves, sequential tasks and interruptions to tasks, postural requirements, and staff member-to-staff member interactions. Particular emphasis was given to identify invisible causes of strain factors; including cognitive load from multitasking, workspace limitation or tool-sharing competition. Two theoretical perspectives were used to frame the analysis: Karasek's "Job Demand–Control" model [16] to identify exposure to psychosocial hazards and Sweller's cognitive load theory [17] to guide an assessment of mental overload associated with organisational fragmentation and resource-sharing. These direct observations formed a diagnostic base line, demonstrating an organisational build-up of micro-adjustments required to sustain continuity of care yet never formalised and reinforced. They also allowed priority areas for organisational redesign to be identified.

3.2 Semi-Structured Interviews with Healthcare Professionals

Semi-structured interviews were conducted to complement field observations by capturing professionals' subjective perspectives, decision-making logics, and lived experience of constraints and workarounds. Although observations revealed what was being worn and the symptoms of overwork and dysfunction, interviews provided a richer understanding of the causes and how and why teams adapted. The interviews followed the structure of a theme-centred interview and focused on patient pathways, the division of tasks, interactions within the team, use of digital tools and brain-storming for improvements. Dentists, dental assistants, receptionists, and centre managers participated. The discussions brought to light recurring challenges such as unclear role boundaries, cognitive overload, limited process visibility, and the informal coping mechanisms and local workarounds developed to handle daily disruptions. The interviews also served to validate or nuance hypotheses from the field observations. For instance, a centre that appeared to function smoothly during observation was later described by staff as submitted to intense hidden pressure from phone management and administrative backlog. This methodological triangulation enriched the overall analysis, ensuring that the proposed transformations would be aligned with both observed workflows and professionals' expressed needs.

3.3 Co-Design Workshops (Design Thinking)

The Design Thinking (DT) sessions organized within the framework of this project are part of an interdisciplinary and interprofessional co-construction approach, mobilizing user-centred design principles and collaborative innovation, combining qualitative and quantitative tools. This approach aims to actively involve healthcare system users – professionals and patients – in analyzing dysfunctions and generating concrete and adapted solutions. Specifically, three sessions were initially planned, bringing together dentists, dental assistants, reception staff, and member patients. However, due to scheduling constraints, only one session gathering all stakeholders could be organized at the end of the project, with the others being conducted with only part of the participants. Participants were invited to share their experiences, identify friction points in the patient journey and, then, collectively imagine improvements in the form of organizational or spatial scenarios (role distribution, space layout, tracking tools, etc.). DT, as an inductive, iterative and visual method, open the opportunity to build consensus, debate divergent representations and strengthen adherence to the proposed transformations. This approach also reinforced the dynamics of change by valuing the experiential knowledge of professionals and establishing a structured dialogue space between different professions.

3.4 Modelling and Simulation of Organizational Scenarios

The last methodological component of the project is based on modelling and simulating organizational scenarios using digital tools (*FlexSim* and *AnyLogic*). This approach aims to objectify the impacts of different work organization configurations on the overall performance of the centre: patient transit times, resource availability, staff workload, and flow efficiency. The modelling relies on a reasoned abstraction of a dental centre's functioning, integrating patient flows, workstations (care, reception, sterilization), service times (care, rescheduling, movement), as well as human and material constraints. The tested scenarios, derived from field observations and co-design workshops, were simulated for different centre formats (3, 5, and 6 cabinets), with probabilistic laws calibrated from observed data. This approach allows for a statistically repeatable, objective comparative evaluation of organizational options in a controlled environment. It serves as a decision-support tool, complementary to ergonomic analysis, by enabling the anticipation of systemic effects of organizational choices before their actual implementation and identifying compromises between performance, work comfort or quality of service.

3.5 Methodological Articulation

The research methodology follows an iterative and integrative logic, where qualitative and quantitative approaches are not deployed sequentially but continuously in interaction. Observations, interviews, co-design workshops and simulation were interwoven throughout the project, allowing each insight to refine or redirect the ongoing process. This articulation ensures methodological consistency and alignment with the complexity of real-world healthcare systems.

Table 1 summarises the methodological framework, highlighting the core activities and key outputs of each phase. It illustrates how the multi-method strategy supports a comprehensive understanding of the current system while guiding the co-design and assessment of alternative organisational models. This approach enables the design of solutions that are context-sensitive, operationally tested, and user-accepted. Its iterative nature supports both rigour and adaptability, making it suitable for other complex healthcare settings seeking to improve coordination and workflow.

Table 1. Methodology Summary

Phases	Activities	Results Expectation
3.1 Observations	- Systematic observations in several dental centres - Use of structured grids (patient flows, interruptions, gestures, postures)	Provides a situated understanding of professional practices as they unfold in real time, rather than as they are formally prescribed. Emphasises the adaptive nature of work within dynamic constraints, and supports the identification of latent sources of strain, thus informing areas for potential redesign.
3.2 Semi-Structured Interviews	- Interviews with dentists, dental assistants, and receptionists - Elicitation of perceived constraints, adaptations, and informal practices - Thematic cross-analysis	Captures the subjective experience of professionals, uncovering how they interpret, adapt to, and manage structural constraints. Validates or nuances observational hypotheses and adds depth to the diagnosis by revealing invisible tensions, coping strategies, and misalignments between formal structures and actual functioning.
3.3 Co-Design	- Collaborative workshops with healthcare professionals and patients - Scenario generation and prototyping of new layouts, processes, and roles	Facilitates the transformation of field insights into actionable proposals through structured, iterative, and collaborative sessions. Supports mutual understanding across professional roles and integrates user perspectives into the design of organisational and spatial alternatives, strengthening stakeholder engagement.
3.4 Digital Modeling and simulation	- Simulation of organisational scenarios - Parameter calibration based on field data - Evaluation of scenarios across multiple centre sizes - Analysis of KPIs: total patient pathway time, waiting times, workload distribution	Offers a formal and quantitative environment to assess organisational configurations under controlled conditions. Complements qualitative methods by enabling prospective evaluation of scenarios, supporting decision-making, and anticipating systemic implications of organisational choices.

4 Practical Examples of Collaborative Networks in Dental Care Centres

4.1 Study Case Presentation

A dental care centre is a multidisciplinary facility dedicated to the prevention, diagnosis and treatment of oral diseases. Unlike private practices, these centres operate as collaborative environments, bringing together dentists, assistants and administrative teams within a common organisational framework. Each treatment room - or practice - is equipped with a dental chair, instruments and a computer workstation where the surgeon performs his or her procedures, assisted by a dental assistant in charge of preparation, chairside assistance, disinfection and, sometimes, reception or sterilisation. Administrative staff - mainly receptionists - handle patient relations, appointments and billing, while some centres also appoint a site manager to coordinate day-to-day operations. These centres cure a very diverse patient population and are increasingly faced with challenges relating to service quality, team coordination and overall efficiency. In this context, it becomes essential to review their organisational models. This study is based on in-depth observations of four dental centres in the AESIO Santé network, each with distinct characteristics in terms of size, staff and day-to-day operations. Centre #1, a moderately sized facility with around four to five practices, operates with a compact team. It struggles to maintain steady coverage during staff absences, often resorting to temporarily shifting personnel without a sustainable, long-term fix. This ad hoc approach tends to create friction when unexpected absences occur, ultimately disrupting the smooth delivery of patient care. Centre #2, the largest of the two, with six or more surgeries, has a broader staff base—including several dental assistants and three receptionists. However, the assistants frequently find themselves stretched thin, balancing both clinical duties and administrative tasks, which adds strain and makes workload management a persistent challenge. This results in regular interruptions to the workflow. Centre #3, which is medium to large (5–6 practices), works with a dentist-assistant pair and follows a flexible model with redeployment between sites. However, the absence of either party in these pairs has a direct impact on the provision of care. Finally, centre #4, the smallest (2 to 3 practices), illustrates great fragility: care, reception and supervision tasks are often managed by a single person, leading to operational isolation and increased vulnerability to disruption.

Taken together, these four cases offer a representative overview of the common challenges mutualist dental centres face today—particularly around team resilience, clarity of roles and structural organization.

4.2 Mixed Methodological Implementation

The analysis of the current organization of dental centres is based on a qualitative field approach, using tools from real work ergonomics, user-centred design, and participatory research. The objective was to build a fine, contextualized, and shared understanding of activity conditions in the centres. Visits were conducted in all centres, allowing direct observations of work situations. These visits were complemented by semi-structured interviews with various stakeholders: dental assistants, dentists, reception staff, and centre managers. In parallel, a documentary analysis (job descriptions, schedules, layout plans, testimonials) and verbatim collection enriched the analysis. Several tools were used: ergonomic observation grids, mental map (see Fig. 1), flow mapping, photographs, and activity/mental load matrices. This approach was extended by a Design Thinking session, bringing together professionals, patients, engineers, and institutional representatives. It allowed validation of findings, prioritization of pain points, and construction of transformation pathways consistent with the ground reality.

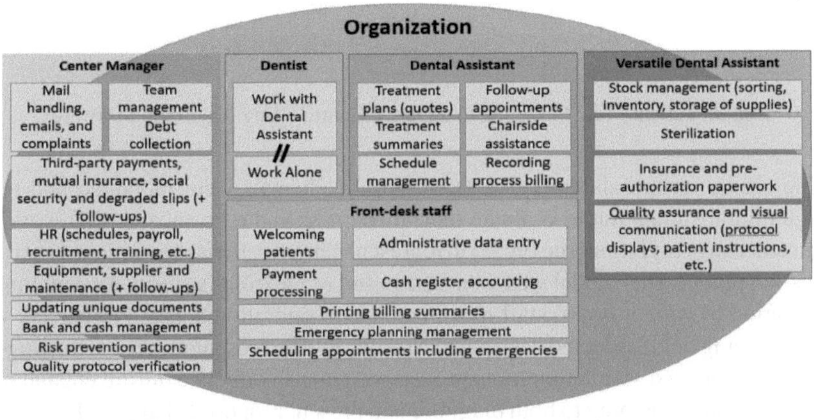

Fig. 1. Diagram of the Organization of a Large Dental Health Centre with Different Positions and Associated Tasks

The project also integrated a qualitative collection of patient experience to identify subjective perceptions related to reception, clarity of the patient journey, comfort, and care coordination. This opinion survey, conducted through open questionnaires, informal exchanges during centre visits, and participatory workshops - notably during the Design Thinking session - allowed verification of the correspondence between observed organizational dysfunctions and user perceptions. The feedback reveals a reception experience that, while generally friendly, often feels disorganized and hard for patients to navigate. Many express confusion—particularly at Centre #4—about the steps involved in their care. Long and unpredictable wait times are another recurring issue, especially when no assistant is present. On the other hand, patients tend to feel more at ease when familiar practitioners and assistants work together, seeing it as a sign of reliable, high-quality care. Overall, there's a strong push for clearer communication, easier access to information and digital tools that help patients keep track of where they are in the process. These insights echo internal observations and underscore the urgency of rethinking spatial layout and workflow. They also validate the broader goal of co-designing a dental centre model that is transparent, efficient, and focused on delivering a seamless user experience.

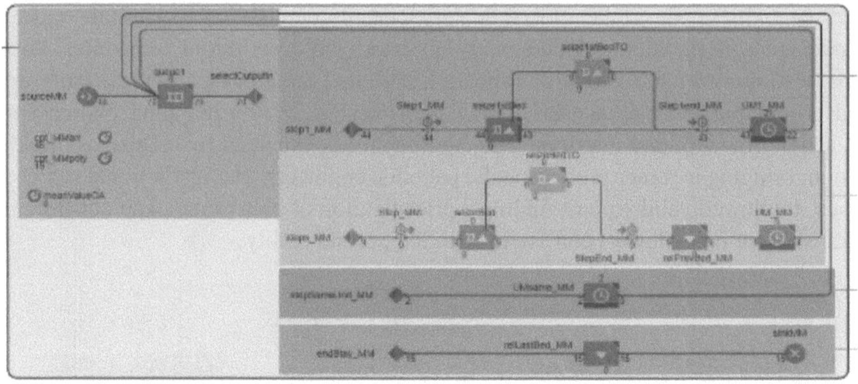

Fig. 2. Patient Flow Modeling in a Dental Centre Using AnyLogic Software

The change proposals emerging from these exchanges were modelled and tested through digital simulation to evaluate their robustness and relevance. A first work was conducted using AnyLogic (see Fig. 2) to represent patient pathways and identify primary congestion points. This model was then transposed to FlexSim (see Fig. 3), enabling 3D visualization of patient flows, staff movements, and saturation zones. Parameters were calibrated using field-collected data, and the results will be presented in the following sections. Modelling and simulation tools proved particularly effective during engagements with professionals, helping to both diagnose and present proposed changes. These methods enabled teams to visualise the organisational effects of various scenarios in real time, allowing layout changes, staffing models and patient flow adjustments to be tested safely without disrupting day-to-day operations. The simulations identified bottlenecks, predicted the impact on waiting times and workloads and measured the potential gains from the redesigns. Based on real data and scientific rigour, this approach improved the quality of the dialogue and played a key role in gaining staff support for the recommendations.

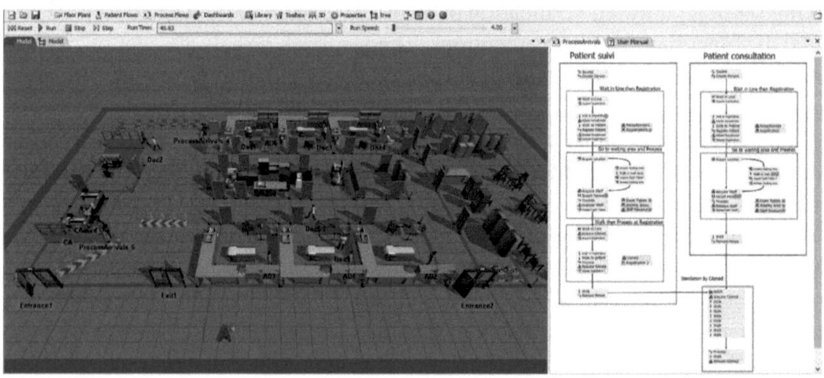

Fig. 3. Simulation of a Dental Centre with 6 Offices Using FlexSim Software

5 Simulation Results and Empirical Insights

5.1 Results of Qualitative Analysis

Following the observation visits and semi-structured interviews, the current functioning of dental care centres is summarized in Table 2. This table highlights a series of structural weaknesses common to the four centres, notably constrained polyvalence, lack of standardization, and overload in case of absence. Each site has developed its own localized approach, though how sustainable these strategies are in the long run varies. Sites #2 and #3 show greater adaptability when it comes to moving staff around, while site #4 continues to grapple with deeper structural weaknesses. Site #1 is quicker to react but still relies too much on individual initiatives. Taken together, these patterns point to a clear need for a shared model—one that's strong, scalable, and flexible enough to handle disruptions, clarify roles, and shore up day-to-day operations. Observations at the various dental centres revealed deviations from the normal patient pathway. Each centre adapts its strategies on a day-to-day basis, depending on its human resources.

Table 2. Summary Table of the Current Functioning of Centres

Aspect of the Process	Common to 4 centres
Appointment Scheduling	Dependence on duo assistant/practitioner; little delegation
Patient Reception	Frequent interventions by dental assistants in support
Chair-side Care	Frequent interruptions; practitioners sometimes alone
Follow-up Planning	Often ensured by the dedicated assistant of the practitioner
Multiple Roles/Versatility	Strong polyvalence: reception, care, administrative tasks
Absence Management	Few replacements; systematic overload
Standardization of Practices	No inter-centre standardization observed
Centre	Specificities
#1	- Assistants sometimes take follow-up appointments - Assistants occasionally reinforce reception - Care slows down in case of absence - Planning sometimes delayed due to lack of availability - Versatility present in case of absence - Internal replacement when possible - Reactive, local organization
#2	- High call volume, pressure on reception - 3 to 4 people needed to avoid overload - Assistant presence essential, but often absent - Planning deemed non-delegable - Very high workload at reception and in care - Rare replacements, but internal mobility - Specific tasks but practices not formalized

(*continued*)

Table 2. (*continued*)

#3	- Possible support from other centres for appointment scheduling - Replacements by assistants from neighboring centres - Often unbalanced partnerships - Planning adjusted according to urgency - Frequent cross-centre versatility and reinforcement - Recurring absences, poorly compensated - Local practices without standardization
#4	- A single assistant manages everything (scheduling, reception, care) - Extreme organizational fragility - Practitioners often alone, chronic overload - No planning support - Involuntary versatility, without support - No organized replacement - Empirical organization, dependent on individuals

This form of flexible operation may be useful from time to time, but it makes it difficult to clearly define everyone's roles - particularly for dental assistants (DAs). Especially when the centres have to adapt too regularly, it is detrimental to the coherence and functioning of the department. Dental assistants have to carry out multiple tasks that disrupt the workflow, cause delays and fragment the care process. Juggling clinical work, reception, administration and sterilisation all at the same time reduces the efficiency of ADs, slowing down patient flow and weakening team dynamics.

These findings from the qualitative analysis were then tested through quantitative modeling. The objective was to objectify the organizational impacts observed and to test, through simulation, different scenarios for the layout and distribution of tasks. To this end, four organizational models were tested, including scenarios with a dedicated sterilization assistant and specific reception staff.

5.2 Results of Quantitative Evaluation of Organisational Scenarios

We present the outcomes of a quantitative evaluation based on discrete-event simulations conducted with FlexSim and AnyLogic. The aim was to assess the operational performance of different organizational models in dental centres, under realistic constraints observed in four AESIO Santé sites (Monistrol-sur-Loire, Saint-Chamond, Romans-sur-Isère, and Malauzat). Four organizational models were compared: *AD Model, CAmed Model, Mixte Model* and *Stéri Model.*

AD Model (Baseline): This is now the minimum requirement in most AESIO centres. ADs are in charge of everything what concerns the patient (both on the clinical as well as the administrative part) from sterilisation and appointments, to billing, and chasing up reimbursements. This multitasking leads to frequent workflow interruptions, increased workload, and inefficiencies in both care delivery and patient processing time. *CAmed Model*: In this scenario, administrative workload (appointment scheduling, billing, handling quotes and reimbursement requests) is partially transferred to a specialized front-desk role called 'Chargé d'Accueil Médicalisée' (CAmed). These staff members, with hybrid training in administrative and medical coordination, handle all patient intake, reimbursement procedures, and document preparation. Clinical procedure and post treatment function are the central tasks of the ADs. It is an operational model to promote front-office efficiency with consideration of the physical presence of assistants. *Mixed Model*: Here, ADs and CAmeds can assist each other when staffing shortages occur, although each's role is clearly defined. *Stéri Model:* One assistant is dedicated to sterilization. This configuration allows ADs to fully focus on clinical care. By reducing distractions, this model seeks to enhance clinical efficiency.

These models were instantiated on two centre sizes (3 and 5 dental units) in Table 3 and Table 4, following layouts and organizational dynamics derived from field observations and ergonomic studies. Each model was simulated over a virtual one-year horizon. We propose to focus on three key performance indicators (KPIs): (1) Total patient pathway time from check-in to check-out (Total Time (min)); (2) Waiting time due to unavailability of rooms (Wait Time – Room (min)); and (3) Waiting time due to unavailability of personnel (Wait Time – Personnel (min)). To model patient arrivals, we use a Poisson process, while task durations were modelled with triangular distributions based on empirical data.

In the AD models, patient wait times tend to be high due to staff being stretched thin—dental assistants are tasked with both rescheduling appointments and managing equipment sterilization. Yet, treatment can't begin unless both the assistant and the dentist are present in the room. As a result, patients often have to wait for the AD to become available, which in turn delays the availability of treatment rooms for other patients in the waiting area. The CAmed and Stéri models yield the best performance, as ADs are no longer in charge of sterilization and can dedicate their full working time to patient care. However, the CAmed model proves difficult to implement in practice: front-desk staff (CA) already face a high administrative workload, and in small dental centres, there is typically only one CA. It would be unrealistic for this person to leave the reception desk to handle sterilization tasks, since no one else would be available to welcome and guide incoming patients. Moreover, CAs are required to perform numerous administrative duties in parallel with front-desk responsibilities. The Stéri model thus appears even more efficient in real-life settings, as the administrative workload of CAs was not fully considered in the simulation processes. Its only drawback lies in the need to hire an additional staff member.

Table 3. Small Centre – 3 Dental Units

Configuration	Total Time (min)	Wait Time – Room (min)	Wait Time – Personnel (min)
AD (Baseline)	91.0	51.2	8.86
CAmed	77.2	39.7	6.66
Mixte	88.1	49.0	8.20
Stéri	76.1	38.8	6.63

Table 4. Medium Centre – 5 Dental Units

Configuration	Total Time (min)	Wait Time – Room (min)	Wait Time – Personnel (min)
AD (Baseline)	89.4	49.0	8.37
CAmed	76.5	37.2	5.58
Mixte	86.3	46.5	7.56
Stéri	74.7	35.3	5.15

These results are aligned with qualitative field findings, which highlight role fragmentation, workstation interruptions, and lack of ergonomic adequacy as recurring sources of inefficiency.

5.3 Interpretations

Qualitative studies carried out in centres #1, #2, #3, and #4 unveil an important gap between theoretical structure and real-life practice. In practice, local and informal logics rather than theoretical organization underlie the functioning. At #2, for instance, management of tasks is subject to days and people on duty, whereas at #4 one person manages the entire patient pathway without precise role definitions. This is evidence of a high level of personalization within working practices with little in place as stable organizational mechanisms to cushion uncertainties or ensure continuity in services offered. This absence of structuring generates frequent breakpoints in the patient pathway, especially on absences, interruptions, or activity peaks. None of the centres have a formalised substitution system in place. At #1 and #3, periodic readjustments try to be made (inter-centre reinforcements, internal redeployment), but are unstable. At #4, an alternative solution does not exist, leaving the centre at risk of shutdown in case of absence. Even in a better-equipped centre such as #2, absences generate chronic overload. The consequences are direct: delayed treatment, broken treatments, chaotic rescheduling, and higher mental load on the existing teams.

At the same time, all centres studied have restricted staff versatility, most notably for dental assistants, who load up clinical responsibilities (chair-side support), logistical tasks (sterilization and material handling), administration (scheduling and estimates), and even reception on occasion. Such versatility, neither formal nor expected, causes indefiniteness in responsibility assignment, activity disorganization, and diffused organizational tension. At #2, it is occasionally necessary to mobilize up to four individuals at reception in order to contain the workload, whereas at #4, the operational separation is so great that one absence is detrimental to the functioning of the centre as a whole. Frequent interruptions during essential activities, e.g., management of treatment sheets or planning, heighten this disorganization and disrupt quality of patient follow-ups.

This informal functioning, highly dependent on individual experience, makes the centres vulnerable to turnover or lack of transmission. There is neither a common reference framework nor a shared visualization of processes (mapping, flowcharts, digital tracking tools). The significant heterogeneity of practices between centres – and sometimes even between practitioners – prevents any standardization, any pooling of tools, and complicates the implementation of common digital or organizational solutions. Finally, the absence of operational performance indicators (journey time, staff availability, office occupancy) prevents effective resource and flow management.

5.4 Preconisations

To enhance the quality of the patient journey within dental centres, several key areas for improvement have been identified through ergonomic assessments, staff interviews, patient feedback, and digital simulations.

Firstly, appointment scheduling must be optimised. The implementation of intelligent digital systems for managing consultation slots can help reduce patient waiting times and alleviate episodic staff overload. Introducing a structured triage process would further support the effective orientation of patients based on the urgency and nature of care required, thereby facilitating a more efficient allocation of human and material resources. *Secondly*, it is recommended to reorganize centre spaces to minimize unnecessary movements and improve interaction fluidity between different areas (reception, treatment rooms, sterilization, administrative offices). To reduce interruptions and allow medical staff to focus on their care tasks, it is recommended to clearly distinguish between clinical and administrative functions. This will make it easier to distribute roles and tasks between ADs and administrative staff. For example, it would be appropriate to create an administrative position that coordinates administrative tasks to reduce the mental burden on clinical teams, thereby improving the quality of care and creating a more peaceful working environment. This specialization could also improve professional satisfaction by clarifying responsibilities and reducing stress related to work overload. *Thirdly*, integrating enhanced collaborative practices, supported by digital tools facilitating instant and secure communication between professionals, would be beneficial. These systems would improve real-time sharing of patient-related information, thus optimizing clinical and administrative decisions. Moreover, regularly implementing experience feedback and interprofessional exchange sessions would foster a continuous improvement culture and strengthen team spirit. *Finally*, it's essential to plan for change support at every stage of the transformation. Even when organizational changes aim to improve service or workplace comfort, they can generate uncertainty, resistance, or additional emotional strain. Support must be multifaceted: training on new tools or processes, psychological support if necessary, spaces for team expression, and recognition of successful adjustments. Such an approach not only facilitates the adoption of changes, but also preserves the motivation and health at work of the professionals involved.

These recommendations offer a clear potential for improving the overall functioning of dental centres, both from an operational efficiency perspective and in terms of team comfort and overall patient satisfaction.

6 Theoretical Results and Analytical Insights

Beyond the specific case study findings, the simulation results can be interpreted through the lens of Human-Centred Design. They underscore the importance of organisational configurations that reflect users' real constraints and practices. Reduced workflow interruptions, clarified roles, and improved fluidity indicate increased system usability and acceptance—hallmarks of a design process that integrates experiential knowledge.

Secondly, Design Thinking structured an inclusive and iterative innovation process. Through co-design workshops, field-based challenges were articulated and transformed into simulation-ready solutions. The ideation and prototyping phases helped translate tacit knowledge into operational scenarios, reinforcing both the realism and applicability of the models—confirming the value of Design Thinking as a collaborative engineering method in complex environments.

Finally, insights from work psychology and ergonomics enrich the interpretation of simulation results. Karasek's demand–control model suggests that clearer role distribution and fewer interruptions may improve the regulation of work demands and support autonomy. Sweller's cognitive load theory further explains how multitasking and fragmented tasks increase mental strain, whereas streamlined workflows reduce cognitive overload. Although psychosocial effects were not measured directly, these models frame the organisational impact on work quality and sustainability.

Beyond interpretation, the approach surfaced informal tensions and fostered cross-role understanding through shared scenario testing. By grounding collaboration in real practices, co-design and simulation helped build collective ownership and improve coordination. Methodologically, the study demonstrates how combining human-centred design, simulation, and work psychology offers both conceptual clarity and empirical robustness. It also provides a practical, replicable framework to test and refine care scenarios before implementation, reducing risk and enhancing stakeholder alignment.

7 Discussion and Conclusion

This work illustrates the complementarity between qualitative and quantitative tools. It highlights the advantages of combining participatory and collaborative methodologies with digital modelling and simulation tools to help identifying and defining the work organization in four dental centres. Thus, this article presents a concrete collaboration for the transformation of often tacit cooperation into clear, transparent and streamlined processes.

Dental centres are, by nature, collaborative environments where continuous improvement of work processes is essential to increase efficiency and quality of care. This project adopts a multidisciplinary innovation approach, mobilizing organizational management, ergonomics, and mathematical modelling to strengthen team synergy. Field observations highlighted significant ergonomic and structural dysfunctions, particularly with regard to space layout and task distribution. These shortcomings have a direct impact on workload, staff well-being and quality of service. To address these issues, the proposed solution relies on better physical delineation of reception, sterilization and treatment areas, as well as more precise adjustment of tools to actual workflow needs. This next-generation dental centre embodies this vision by focusing on "hybrid digitalization," which harmoniously combines human intelligence and smart technologies. At the intersection of collaborative design and hands-on experimentation, the project also incorporates insights from work psychology to better understand daily routines. By identifying the sources of stress and cognitive overload, it offers targeted solutions that bring clarity, control, and meaning to work—all levers for ethical and sustainable change. This interdisciplinary method supports long-term engagement and encourages adoption of innovative practices. A new centre is currently under construction, incorporating many of the project's key proposals, alongside the rollout of an integrated information system—marking a concrete step toward structured, collaborative care.

The study offers a practical roadmap for decision-makers aiming to improve care delivery. It highlights the importance of co-design and anticipatory evaluation, showing that sustainable change emerges from participatory processes aligned with local realities and supported by simulation-based evidence.

In conclusion, this project demonstrates that making collaborative practices explicit—through a fusion of social science insights and advanced digital tools—is a timely and effective path toward greater organizational performance and improved care quality in dental centres.

8 Limitations and Future Work

This study offers valuable insights for developing more collaborative and inclusive dental care processes, while acknowledging certain limitations. The analysis was conducted exclusively within AESIO Santé centres, which may limit the transferability of the results to other settings with different organizations or patient profiles. The mixed methodological approach—combining interviews, observations, and simulations—enriched our understanding of the dynamics at work. However, the short data collection period and the limited number of scenarios modelled in FlexSim may have overlooked certain underlying trends or unexpected variations in daily practices. To strengthen the scope of the findings, future research would benefit from incorporating a more diverse panel of dental centres, varying their sizes, geographic locations, and demographic characteristics. Conducting longitudinal studies would also provide a better understanding of the evolution of organizational transformations over time. Finally, the improvement of simulation tools – notably through the integration of real-time data and predictive systems based on artificial intelligence – could improve the responsiveness of devices and promote more precise adaptation of the patient journey to constantly evolving clinical and operational needs.

Acknowledgements. This work was conducted within the MedTechLab® of Mines Saint-Etienne, in collaboration with AESIO Santé. The authors extend their sincere thanks to all dental and administrative professionals who generously contributed their time, insights, and engagement throughout the study. They would like to especially acknowledge Johanna Clerc and Nathalie Hospital for their support in fieldwork and coordination, as well as Olivier Lenfant for his role in the modelling and simulation work.

References

1. Camarinha-Matos, L.M., Afsarmanesh, H., (eds.): Collaborative Networks: Reference Modeling. Springer, New York (2008). https://doi.org/10.1007/978-0-387-79426-6
2. D'Amour, D., et al.: A model and typology of collaboration between professionals in healthcare organizations. BMC Health Ser. Res. **8**, Article no. 188. Springer, Cham (2008). https://doi.org/10.1186/1472-6963-8-188
3. Dessevre, G., Martinez, C., Zhang, L., Bortolaso, C., Fontanili, F.: Analysis of a Collaborative Resilient Solution Based on Real-Time Re-Optimization for Home Health Care Routes Subject to Disruptions by Discrete Event Simulation. In: Camarinha-Matos, L.M., Boucher, X., Ortiz, A. (eds.) Collaborative Networks in Digitalization and Society 5.0 (PRO-VE 2023). IFIP Advances in Information and Communication Technology, vol. 688, pp. 563–574. Springer, Cham (2023). https://doi.org/10.1007/978-3-031-42622-3_40
4. Topol, E.J.: High-performance medicine: the convergence of human and artificial intelligence. Nature Medicine **25**(1), 44–56. Springer Nature, London (2019). https://doi.org/10.1038/s41591-018-0300-7
5. Coiera, E.: The forgetting health system. Learning Health Systems **1**(4), e10023. Springer Nature, Cham (2017). https://doi.org/10.1002/lrh2.10023
6. Mintzberg, H.: The Structuring of Organizations. In: Asch, D., Bowman, C. (eds.) Readings in Strategic Management. LNTCS, vol. 688, pp. 322–352. Springer, London (1989). https://doi.org/10.1007/978-1-349-20317-8_23
7. Clot, Y., Faïta, D.: Genres et styles en analyse du travail. Concepts et méthodes. Travailler, **4**, 7–42. Springer Nature, Cham (2000)
8. Schuurman, D., De Marez, L., Ballon, P.: The impact of living lab methodology on open innovation contributions and outcomes. Technology Innovation Management Review **6**(1), 7–16. Springer, Cham (2016). https://doi.org/10.22215/timreview/956
9. Brown, T.: Change by Design: How Design Thinking Transforms Organizations and Inspires Innovation. HarperBusiness, New York (2009)
10. Friesen, M.R., McLeod, R.D.: A survey of agent-based modeling of hospital environments. IEEE Access **2**(1), 227–233. IEEE, Piscataway (2014). https://doi.org/10.1109/ACCESS.2014.2313957
11. Al-Ashwal, R.H., Ayoep, F.A.Z.B., Omar, N.B.: Experimenting patient flow using computer simulation. In: Mohamed Ali, M., Wahid, H., Mohd Subha, N., Sahlan, S., Md Yunus, M., Wahap, A. (eds.) Modeling, Design and Simulation of Systems (AsiaSim 2017). Communications in Computer and Information Science, vol. 751, pp. 506–515. Springer, Singapore (2017). https://doi.org/10.1007/978-981-10-6463-0_48
12. Lamé, G., Crowe, S., Komashie, A., Royston, G.: Joining forces: the value of design partnering with operational research to improve healthcare delivery. Design Science **9**, e4. Springer Nature, Cham (2023). https://doi.org/10.1017/dsj.2023.2
13. Ala, A., Chen, F.: Appointment scheduling problem in complexity systems of the healthcare services: a comprehensive review. J. Healthc. Eng. **2022**, Article ID 5819813. Springer Nature, Cham (2022). https://doi.org/10.1155/2022/5819813
14. Jun, J.B., Jacobson, S.H., Swisher, J.R.: Application of discrete-event simulation in health care clinics: a survey. J. Operat. Res. Soc. **50**(2), 109–123. Springer, London (1999). https://doi.org/10.1057/palgrave.jors.2600669
15. Günal, M.M., Pidd, M.: Discrete event simulation for performance modelling in health care: a review of the literature. Journal of Simulation **4**(1), 42–51. Springer, London (2010). https://doi.org/10.1057/jos.2009.25

16. Karasek, R.A.: Job Demands, Job Decision Latitude, and Mental Strain: Implications for Job Redesign. Administrative Science Quarterly **24**(2), 285–308. Springer, Chicago (1979). https://doi.org/10.2307/2392498
17. Sweller, J., van Merrienboer, J.J.G., Paas, F.G.W.C.: Cognitive Architecture and Instructional Design. Educational Psychology Review **10**(3), 251–296. Springer, London (1998). https://doi.org/10.1023/A:1022193728205

Centralised or Decentralised? Decision Factors for Healthcare Supply Chain Configurations

Elena Pessot(✉) and Jacopo Lolli

Department of Information Engineering and Mathematics, University of Siena, Siena, Italy
{elena.pessot,jacopo.lolli}@unisi.it

Abstract. The challenges in ensuring effective and timely access to medicines and healthcare products, while balancing with efficiency pressures, require a careful design and structuring of Healthcare Supply Chains (HSC)s. This study investigates the key factors influencing configuration decisions in HSC, focusing on the trade-off between centralised and decentralised models. Using the Analytic Hierarchy Process (AHP) methodology, technological and organisational criteria guiding decision-making were evaluated through expert input. Results of AHP show that technological enablers - especially integrated systems and warehouse automation - favour centralised HSC models, while organisational elements like training and collaboration support decentralised ones. Overall, the centralised configuration emerged as the preferred alternative, with a global priority of 62.77%, highlighting its efficiency and cost-saving potential. These findings provide actionable insights for managers of healthcare systems to optimise supply chain structures.

Keywords: Healthcare supply chain · Centralised configuration · Decentralised configuration · Decision-making

1 Introduction

Healthcare systems are under increasing pressure to limit operational costs while maintaining high service levels. A significant yet often underestimated area for improvement lies in the management of the logistic flows in the overall Healthcare Supply Chain (HSC), aiming at ensuring safe, effective, and timely access to medicines and healthcare products. The HSC is a complex network that encompasses a diverse range of stakeholders – including raw material suppliers, manufacturers (primary and secondary), distributors, wholesalers, logistics providers, pharmacies, hospitals, and ultimately, patients [1, 2]. Historically, hospitals and pharmacies prioritise clinical care over logistical efficiency, despite logistics constitute over 30% of hospital expenditures [3]. As healthcare costs rise due to aging populations, technological advancements, and the consequences of the COVID-19 pandemic, supply chain optimisation has become a strategic imperative [4, 5]

Moreover, the HSC operates within a highly regulated environment, managing products often characterised by specific handling requirements, such as temperature control (and the cold chain management), short shelf-lives, and high value, while facing challenges like counterfeiting and the need for rigorous traceability [6, 7].

Published by Springer Nature Switzerland AG 2026
L. M. Camarinha-Matos et al. (Eds.): PRO-VE 2025, IFIP AICT 770, pp. 332–343, 2026.
https://doi.org/10.1007/978-3-032-05673-3_20

A fundamental strategic decision within HSC management is its structural configuration, and especially the choice between centralised and decentralised models [1, 8]. A centralised supply chain typically consolidates key functions like procurement, inventory management, warehousing, and distribution decision-making into a single or limited number of hubs, providing medical goods to more hospitals. Conversely, a decentralised structure distributes these functions across multiple facilities, often regional or local, granting greater autonomy to individual HSC logistics units.

The selection between these configurations involves balancing trade-offs and context-dependent factors. The optimal configuration is indeed influenced by factors such as the market geography, the regulatory frameworks, the inventory management settings, the performance management systems, and the strategic priorities like cost efficiency versus customisation [7, 9, 10]. For example, the Italian healthcare system has undergone a structural shift from a decentralised to a more centralised model, particularly in logistics and procurement, with regional consortia operating shared warehouses and integrated services for groups of hospitals [11].

Given the critical impact of supply chain design on efficiency, resilience, and ultimately patient access and safety, a clear understanding of the main factors involved, and the applicability of implementing centralised versus decentralised models, is pivotal. While numerous studies addressed aspects of HSC design [12, 13], further research is needed in enquiring the centralisation-decentralisation dichotomy and their appropriateness in relation to different decision elements for research and practice.

This study aims to identify the most influential factors in selecting a supply chain configuration for HSC and to assess which configuration - centralised or decentralised - is generally preferred. By applying the Analytic Hierarchy Process (AHP), we provide a structured evaluation of these drivers from a group of healthcare logistics experts.

2 Theoretical Background

The HSC encompasses the complete lifecycle of medical goods, from the procurement operations to the distribution to patient delivery. It includes internal hospital logistics (micro-logistics) and external supplier interactions (macro-logistics). The design of a HSC network is a critical strategic issue influencing overall performance, encompassing decisions on facility location, material flow and performance management [7, 9, 10]. The product flows handled by healthcare companies include drugs, medical devices, and economic goods, with their logistics having a significant impact on patients' therapies and health conditions [13, 14].

Among the possible design choices, the Decentralised configuration and the Centralised configuration are the most used and debated ones.

In the Decentralised Configuration, each hospital manages its own logistics processes, from purchasing to storage and distribution. This model typically allows for enhanced responsiveness, greater flexibility and autonomy to respond to local demands, shorter lead times, and thus rapid response to emergencies [4, 15]. Moreover, a decentralised HSC configuration reduces transportation distances and costs, and potentially improves the overall supply resilience through network dispersion [16]. Results from recent studies show that disruption risks, such as geopolitical instability and pandemics, lead to significant impacts especially in global supply chain design [4]. Conversely, main challenges of decentralisation concern achieving economies of scale with duplication of efforts, higher unit costs, and potentially increased overall inventory and operational burden if not managed effectively [17, 18]. A key issue is also the complexity in standardisation and harmonisation of manufacturing protocols, quality testing, and release procedures across multiple sites to ensure product consistency and regulatory compliance [19, 20]. The low level of standardisation could be particularly critical in complex manufacturing and delivery tasks like cell and gene therapies. Nevertheless, some studies show that decentralised point-of-care (POC) or regional manufacturing models are considered advantageous for therapies requiring rapid turnaround times, high personalisation, or serving areas with poor cold chain logistics [16].

In the Centralised Configuration, logistics and procurement are managed through a regional or inter-hospital hub. Centralised models are frequently associated with cost advantages through economies of scale in procurement and manufacturing, with lower operational and facility costs, streamlined standardisation, easier quality control implementation, and potentially optimised inventory levels across the network [21, 22]. Mathematical modelling is often employed to find optimal warehouse locations, with studies demonstrating cost-effectiveness for centralised hubs in regions with high demand density [23]. There is also an emphasis on the use of advanced information and automation technologies. However, potential drawbacks of centralised models include reduced flexibility, slower response times to local market needs or disruptions, higher transportation costs to distant locations, and potential vulnerability of single hubs [24]. Moreover, centralisation requires substantial upfront investment and coordination.

The two models can be present also in the same national healthcare context, e.g. the Italian one. For example, the Area Vasta Emilia Nord consortium and the Tuscany region's ESTAR are two examples of centralisation, leveraging centralised solutions as big warehouses and integrated IT systems. The majority of regional contexts opted for the decentralised configuration to ensure a higher flexibility and responsiveness to local demand [6, 11].

In general, neither a centralised nor decentralised configuration is demonstrated being inherently superior for all HSC. Extant literature highlights several factors that can influence configuration decisions. These include both organisational issues, such as the organisational behaviours of healthcare facilities and the intensity of outsourcing, and the adoption of technologies and information systems [13].

Table 1 summarises the factors identified from extant studies as the most important to be considered in HSC configuration choices. The specific elements were retrieved from a literature review of main decisions influencing information and product flows in the HSC, or leading to a specific supply chain configuration, and investigated in multi-criteria analyses.

Specifically, this study considers only the determinants internal to the supply chain, and excludes environmental factors such as the regulatory framework and the demographical and geographical variables. This focus was motivated by the willingness to exclude the factors that are often outside managerial control, are less actionable and can introduce complexity without a clear impact on internal configurational choices. Moreover, environmental factors are often treated as constraints or boundary conditions, and not as primary decision criteria in the configuration choices.

Table 1. List of factors supporting HSC configuration choices from literature.

Dimension	Factors	Definition	References
Technology	Adoption of technologies to support data collection, sharing and analysis	Technologies that support data collection, sharing and management (e.g., Enterprise Resource Planning, Big data analytics, Artificial Intelligence)	[19, 25, 26]
	Adoption of technologies to support warehouse operations	Technologies that substitute/helps humans in repetitive task and improve operations efficiency (e.g., AGV, pick to light)	[25]
	Adoption of technologies for traceability	Technologies that improve the traceability of drugs and medical products (e.g., RFID, blockchain) between SC members	[19, 25–27]
	Adoption of integrated information systems between SC members	It refers to the real-time exchange of information through information systems among SC members to optimise SC performance	[12, 19, 26, 28]
Organisation	Outsourcing of logistics processes	It refers to the choice of outsourcing warehousing and distribution processes (or part of them) to a third-party provider	[15]
	Investments in training	Training of employees in functional skills development, cross-functional skills, technologies, and lean practices	[19, 26–28]
	Adoption of risk- and reward-sharing mechanisms between SC members	Adoption of risk and reward sharing through a contractual mechanism	[10, 28]
	Adoption of collaborative behaviours and decision-making between SC members	Trust-based collaboration between SC members, aimed to reliable forecasts, shared planning, and decision-making	[10, 28]

The factors identified in the Table 1, addressing both operational efficiency and collaborative structuring, were considered in the following investigation.

3 Research Method

3.1 Research Design

This study adopts AHP to investigate the main enablers of specific configuration decisions for HSC.

AHP [29] is a widely used multi-criteria decision-making method, using the subjective opinions of experts as inputs [30]. Decision makers assign a weight to different evaluation criteria and ranks alternatives, based on a number of criteria that can be either quantitative or qualitative [31]. This method was selected as it has a hierarchical structure adaptable to different decision-making situations and is particularly suited for complex decision problems involving expert judgment, including supply chain management.

Other studies adopt AHP for exploring different issues in the HSC, e.g. Mehralian et al. [28] applied the method to prioritise factors that characterise pharma supply chain coordination; Silva and Mattos [32] studied the classification of the key factors for the implementation of a drug traceability system; Hossain et al. [19] used AHP to rank barriers in the healthcare supply chain; and Khlie and Abdullah [24] applied the method to determine the optimal layout for the hospital supply chain.

The choice of AHP as a methodology is suitable for the HSC context as it involves numerous competing objectives and stakeholders perspective. Moreover, we considered the need to ensure a transparent and replicable prioritisation of criteria guiding the choice of HSC configuration, and the importance of providing actionable results to decision-makers with experts' judgement on "what matters most" in combining both organisational and technological factors.

The research questions guiding this study, and the following problem structuring, were formulated as follows:

RQ1. Which factors (criteria) are the most important in adopting a specific HSC configuration?

RQ2. Based on the weight of each criterion, which configuration (between decentralised and centralised HSC) is preferable, as well as the preferred configuration with respect to each criterion?

3.2 Problem Structuring

The first step in AHP requires to structure the problem hierarchically, with the three levels of goal, criteria and alternatives. In this study, the AHP hierarchy was structured as follows:

- Goal: adoption of a preferred HSC configuration;
- Criteria: the eight factors (denominated from C1 to C8), divided in four technological factors and four organisational factors, as defined in Table 1;
- Alternatives: two alternatives per each criterion, i.e. the decentralised configuration (denominated A1), with each hospital acting as an individual actor; and the centralised configuration (denominated A2), with the centralisation of procurement and logistics processes in hubs.

3.3 Data Collection

The second step included the design of a questionnaire to be submitted to healthcare logistics experts, and the following survey data collection. The questionnaire was firstly tested by two expert scholars.

According to AHP, n(n−1)/2 pairwise comparisons are necessary, with n equal to the number of criteria [29]. Thus, the questions were structured to include a total of 28 pairwise comparisons among criteria and 8 comparisons of configuration preference per criterion. For the first part of the questionnaire, inquiring the most important factors in adopting a specific HSC configuration, each question reported a scale where 1 means "equal importance", 9 means "extreme importance" of the factor on the left compared to the factor on the right (and vice versa 9). For the second part of the questionnaire, inquiring the preferred configuration between decentralised and centralised per each criterion, the respondents had a scale where 1 means "equally preferable" between the two configurations, 9 means "extremely preferable" of the decentralised supply chain compared to the centralised supply chain, and 9 on the opposite side means "extremely preferable" of the centralised supply chain compared to the decentralised supply chain. Once tested, the questionnaire was administered online and a total of 26 responses were gathered.

Respondents included scholars (46%), healthcare professionals (35%) and consultants (19%). The majority of them (51%) has more than 10 years of working or research experience (with 38% more than 20 years of experience). All respondents are Italian, aiming to ensure a common contextual (demographical, geographical and political) framework.

3.4 Analysis and Validation

The procedure known as the approximate AHP method [33], was carried out step by step as follows:

1. Determination of relative priorities (weights or importance) for the criteria;
2. Consistency estimation;
3. Determination of local priorities (preferences) for the alternatives;
4. Determination of overall priorities.

Pairwise comparison matrices were populated using the geometric mean of responses. Subsequently, to get the relative priorities (weights), the mean of the rows was recorded after the normalisation of the matrix [29, 33], obtaining the order of importance of criteria in the adoption of a HSC configuration.

Consistency ratios were calculated for the criteria matrix, with the resulting consistency ratio (C.R.), i.e. the ratio between the consistency index (C.I.) of the comparison matrix and the average consistency index (R.I.) of many randomly filled matrices [33], equal to $CR = 0.0252$, well below the acceptable 0.1 threshold [29]. This small value of inconsistency also indicates that the approximate method is able to provide a valid estimate of the overall weights [33].

Subsequently, local priorities for each configuration relative to each factor were determined. Since there are only two options to evaluate per each criterion, consistency in comparison matrices is guaranteed [33]. Finally, overall preferences were derived through weighted aggregation of the eight criteria.

Table 2 shows the final weights and overall priorities per each criterion (C1-C8) and alternative configuration (A1, A2).

Table 2. Overall priorities.

	C1	C2	C3	C4	C5	C6	C7	C8	
Weights	0.1281	0.1414	0.1193	0.1559	0.0769	0.1251	0.1161	0.1372	Overall
A1	0.3413	0.2354	0.2725	0.2737	0.2788	0.5455	0.5	0.5276	0.3723
A2	0.6587	0.7646	0.7275	0.7263	0.7212	0.4545	0.5	0.4724	0.6277

Finally, the AHP method (non-approximated) was implemented using the Super Decisions software to make the results more robust. This decision support software was selected as a result of its widespread reference by many authors [33, 34]. The same results were obtained, confirming robustness.

4 Results

4.1 Importance of Criteria in HSC Configuration

The ranking of factors resulting from the experts opinions and the AHP application is shown in Table 3.

Table 3. HSC configuration factors ranking.

Rank	Factors (criteria)	Dimension	Weight (%)
1°	Adoption of integrated information systems between SC members	Technology	15.59%
2°	Adoption of technologies to support warehouse operations	Technology	14.14%
3°	Adoption of collaborative behaviours and decision-making between SC members	Organisation	13.72%
4°	Adoption of technologies to support data collection, sharing and analysis	Technology	12.81%
5°	Investments in training	Organisation	12.51%
6°	Adoption of technologies for traceability	Technology	11.93%
7°	Adoption of risk- and reward-sharing mechanisms between SC members	Organisation	11.61%
8°	Outsourcing of logistics processes	Organisation	7.69%

Interestingly, the results from the data analysis revealed that technological factors, and especially the use of integrated information systems and warehouse technologies, are the most important factors determining the choice of a configuration.

Nevertheless, organisational factors are still considered pivotal in the choice of a specific configuration. Specifically, the adoption of collaborative behaviours and decision-making between SC members demonstrate being a key driver in the design process. In general, technological criteria slightly outweighed organisational ones (54.47% vs. 45.53%), emphasising the importance of the availability of digital infrastructure and automation to consider specific configurations.

4.2 Results on Preferable HSC Configuration

The results of AHP method also outlined the preferred configuration according to each factor, as summarised in Table 4.

Table 4. Preferred HSC configuration.

Factors (criteria)	Dimension	Preferred configuration (alternative)	Local priorities (preference)
Adoption of integrated information systems between SC members	Technology	Centralised	72.63%
Adoption of technologies to support warehouse operations	Technology	Centralised	76.46%
Adoption of collaborative behaviours and decision-making between SC members	Organisation	Decentralised	52.76%
Adoption of technologies to support data collection, sharing and analysis	Technology	Centralised	65.87%
Investments in training	Organisation	Decentralised	54.55 %
Adoption of technologies for traceability	Technology	Centralised	72.75 %
Adoption of risk- and reward-sharing mechanisms between SC members	Organisation	-	50%
Outsourcing of logistics processes	Organisation	Centralised	72.12%

The two factors that already emerged as the most important ones, i.e. the adoption of integrated information systems between SC members and the adoption of technologies to support warehouse operations, are both preferred in the centralised configuration (72.63% and 76.46%, respectively). Conversely, the first organisational factor, i.e. the adoption of collaborative and decision-making behaviour among CS members, is slightly preferred in the decentralised configuration (52.76%). Technologies and outsourcing of logistics processes are largely preferential in the centralised setting. This result could be explained by the need of optimising flows in the centralised HSC model, leading to the choice of adopting integrating technologies and the use of logistics providers. However, the adoption of risk- and reward-sharing mechanisms between SC members do not strongly favour either configuration, demonstrating their importance for both centralised and decentralised HSC.

Considering the importance of the criteria and the related preferable HSC model, the centralised configuration results the preferred one with an overall priority of 62.77%.

5 Discussion and Conclusions

This research identified and prioritised eight key factors that influence HSC configuration decisions. Answering to RQ1, the most important factors in adopting a specific HSC configuration are the Adoption of integrated information systems between SC members, the Adoption of technologies to support warehouse operations, and the Adoption of collaborative behaviours and decision-making between SC members. Answering to RQ2, it emerged that centralised models are generally preferred, particularly when organisations have the capacity to implement advanced technologies and integrated systems. However, decentralisation retains strategic value in contexts where collaboration, training, and local adaptability are critical.

The findings validate the importance of technological infrastructure in supporting centralised HSC models. Integrated information systems, data analytics and warehouse automation provide clear advantages in terms of efficiency while improving service quality [19]. Technologies for traceability enhance regulatory compliance and product safety that are pivotal in pharmaceutical logistics. Moreover, these results confirm the increasing interest (and application) in research and practice of digital health networks and Healthcare 4.0 solutions. Digital technologies are increasingly adopted to foster the integration of different HSC actors at different supply chain levels, enabling effective communication and coordination, interoperability and more efficient operational flows of information, products, and services [35]. Thus, HSC centralised configuration are confirmed as preferred configuration when technologies are adopted to achieve higher efficiency.

Organisational factors such as collaborative behaviours among SC members and training were more closely associated with decentralised systems. Most notably, fostering education for healthcare professionals is crucial for HSC to operate successfully [7]. Collaborations often rely on localised knowledge and trustworthy relationships in production, procurement, and distribution [9]. Partnership help to preserve mutual trust in more distributed settings, aimed to reliable forecasts, shared planning, and decision-making [36]. Thus, more decentralised settings are actionable when organisational factors are well-established and guide the decision-making.

Interestingly, outsourcing was rated as the least important factor. This may reflect the willingness to maintain internal control over logistics and develop the decision-making process on HSC design and optimisation as core expertise [37].

Overall, the study highlights the nuanced trade-offs between the typical efficiency of centralised settings and the typical flexibility and collaborative structuring of decentralised configurations. A hybrid approach toward socio-technical systems may be optimal, by leveraging and merging 1) centralised hubs for standardised functions and the support of integrated information systema and automation technologies, aiming at operational efficiency, and 2) decentralised "spokes", with more flexible operations and services where more customisation or faster emergency responses are required, based on collaborative structuring and operators' skills development.

5.1 Implications

Results of the study contribute to advance research and practice in the design and implementation of effective HSC configurations.

From an academic standpoint, results contribute to the literature on the HSC design and optimisation with a focus on the decision-making process, enquiring the centralisation-decentralisation dichotomy with the most important factors.

From a practitioners standpoint, these findings provide actionable insights for managers of healthcare systems to optimise supply chain structures. Centralised models can be considered when integrated information systems and advanced warehouse technologies and data analytics ensure efficiency, while a decentralised HSC configuration mainly requires collaborative behaviours and training for more flexible and rapid logistics. Policymakers can promote investments in integrated IT infrastructure to support regional logistics hubs, while supporting collaborative practices and specialised training in distributed warehouses. Moreover, HSC logistics planners can adopt AHP as a multi-criteria method to guide resource allocation and configuration decisions in the specific HSC logistics.

5.2 Limitations

Limitations of this study include the type of criteria considered in the analysis, the modest sample size and the focus on the Italian healthcare system.

First, this study focused on technological and organisational criteria. We considered that environmental factors are often treated as constraints or boundary conditions, and not as primary decision criteria in the choice of the supply chain configuration. Future research could enlarge the selection of criteria to include environmental factors such as infrastructure, regulations, complexity of the competitive environment.

Second, future investigations could replicate the methodology in different national or regional contexts, and include contextual factors such as healthcare system structure, population and geography in the set of determinants guiding the specific configuration and design choices.

Finally, follow-up investigations with empirical case studies or scenario-based modelling could complement the AHP findings. Studies could investigate whether the prevalence of technological criteria, and the centralised configuration, correspond to the most advantageous model in terms of cost savings, operational flows and higher service levels of different healthcare products.

References

1. Battini, D., Zennaro, I., Aldrighetti, R., Sgarbossa, F.: Centralised healthcare supply networks for efficient and sustainable drug management: an Italian case study. Int. J. Integr. Supply Manag. **13**, 394–417 (2020)
2. Rivard-Royer, H., Landry, S., Beaulieu, M.: Hybrid stockless: a case study: lessons for healthcare supply chain integration. Int. J. Oper. Prod. Manag. **22**, 412–424 (2002)
3. Volland, J., Fügener, A., Schoenfelder, J., Brunner, J.O.: Material logistics in hospitals: a literature review. Omega **69**, 82–101 (2017)
4. Božić, D., Šego, D., Stanković, R., Šafran, M.: Logistics in healthcare: a selected review of literature from 2010 to 2022. Transp. Res. Procedia **64**, 288–298 (2022)
5. Pinna, R., Carrus, P.P., Marras, F.: Emerging trends in healthcare supply chain management—an Italian experience. In: Ganguly, K. (ed.) Applications of Contemporary Management Approaches in Supply Chains, pp. 117–137. Business Science Reference, Hershey (2015)
6. Baglio, M., Dallari, F., Garagiola, E.: Pharma Supply Chain in Italia. Modelli distributive e strategie di outsourcing. LIUC Business School (2017). https://www.liucbs.it/wp-content/uploads/Pharmalogistics.pdf
7. Dixit, A., Routroy, S., Dubey, S.K.: A systematic literature review of healthcare supply chain and implications of future research. Int. J. Pharm. Healthc. Mark. **14**, 119–157 (2019)
8. Azzi, A., Persona, A., Sgarbossa, F., Bonin, M.: Drug inventory management and distribution: outsourcing logistics to third-party providers. Strat. Outsourcing Int. J. **6**, 48–64 (2013)
9. Narayana, S.A., Pati, R.K., Vrat, P.: Managerial research on the pharmaceutical supply chain–A critical review and some insights for future directions. J. Purch. Supply Manag. **20**, 18–40 (2014)
10. Singh, R.K., Kumar, R., Kumar, P.: Strategic issues in pharmaceutical supply chains: a review. Int. J. Pharm. Healthc. Mark. **10**, 234–257 (2016)
11. Aldrighetti, R., Zennaro, I., Finco, S., Battini, D.: Healthcare supply chain simulation with disruption considerations: a case study from Northern Italy. Global J. Flex. Syst. Manag. **20**(Suppl 1), 81–102 (2019)
12. Sathiya, V., et al.: Reshaping healthcare supply chain using chain-of-things technology and key lessons experienced from COVID-19 pandemic. Socio-Econ. Plan. Sci. **85**, 101510 (2023)
13. Pinna, R., Carrus, P.P., Marras, F.: The drug logistics process: an innovative experience. TQM J. **27**, 214–230 (2015)
14. World Health Organization: What are medical devices? (2023). https://www.who.int/teams/health-product-policy-and-standards/assistive-and-medical-technology/medical-devices/nomenclature
15. Das, D., Datta, A., Kumar, P., Kazancoglu, Y., Ram, M.: Building supply chain resilience in the era of COVID-19: An AHP-DEMATEL approach. Oper. Manag. Res. 1–19 (2021)
16. Mansur, A., Vanany, I., Arvitrida, N.I.: Horizontal collaboration in a decentralised system: Indonesian blood supply chain. Supply Chain Forum Int. J. **24**, 334–350 (2023)
17. Bhakoo, V., Chan, C.: Collaborative implementation of e-business processes within the healthcare supply chain: the Monash Pharmacy Project. Supply Chain Manag. Int. J. **16**, 184–193 (2011)
18. Kumar, A., Mani, V., Jain, V., Gupta, H., Venkatesh, V.G.: Managing healthcare supply chain through artificial intelligence (AI): A study of critical success factors. Comput. Ind. Eng. **175**, 108815 (2023)

19. Hossain, M.K., Thakur, V.: Benchmarking health-care supply chain by implementing Industry 4.0: a fuzzy-AHP-DEMATEL approach. Benchmarking Int. J. **28**, 556–581 (2021)
20. Kelle, P., Woosley, J., Schneider, H.: Pharmaceutical supply chain specifics and inventory solutions for a hospital case. Oper. Res. Health Care **1**, 54–63 (2012)
21. Jung, H., Jeon, J., Choi, H.: Important factors in the development of biopharmaceutical logistics centers. Asian J. Shipp. Logist. **37**, 301–306 (2021)
22. Mathew, J., John, J., Kumar, S.: New trends in healthcare supply chain. In: Annals of POMS Conference Proceedings, Denver, pp. 1–10 (2013)
23. Jahani, H., Chaleshtori, A.E., Khaksar, S.M.S., Aghaie, A., Sheu, J.B.: COVID-19 vaccine distribution planning using a congested queuing system—A real case from Australia. Transp. Res. Part E Logist. Transp. Rev. **163**, 102749 (2022)
24. Khlie, K., Abdullah, A.: Redesigning the hospital supply chain for enhanced performance using a lean methodology. Int. J. Ind. Eng. **12**, 917–927 (2013)
25. Bentahar, O., Benzidia, S., Bourlakis, M.: A green supply chain taxonomy in healthcare: critical factors for a proactive approach. Int. J. Logist. Manag. **34**, 60–83 (2023)
26. Gupta, A., Singh, R.K., Gupta, S.: Developing human resource for the digitization of logistics operations: readiness index framework. Int. J. Manpow. **43**, 355–379 (2022)
27. Papalexi, M., Bamford, D., Nikitas, A., Breen, L., Tipi, N.: Pharmaceutical supply chains and management innovation? Supply Chain Manag. Int. J. **27**, 485–508 (2021)
28. Mehralian, G., Moosivand, A., Emadi, S., Asgharian, R.: Developing a coordination framework for pharmaceutical supply chain: using analytical hierarchy process. Int. J. Logist. Syst. Manag. **26**, 277–293 (2017)
29. Saaty, R.W.: The analytic hierarchy process—what it is and how it is used. Math. Model. **9**, 161–176 (1987)
30. Brunelli, M.: Introduction to the analytic hierarchy process. Springer, Heidelberg (2014)
31. Ravindran, A.R. (ed.): Multiple criteria decision making in supply chain management. CRC Press, Boca Raton (2016)
32. Silva, R.B.D., Mattos, C.A.D.: Critical success factors of a drug traceability system for creating value in a pharmaceutical supply chain (PSC). Int. J. Environ. Res. Public Health **16**, 1972 (2019)
33. Kulakowski, K.: Understanding the analytic hierarchy process. CRC Press, Boca Raton (2020)
34. Stofkova, J., Krejnus, M., Stofkova, K.R., Malega, P., Binasova, V.: Use of the analytic hierarchy process and selected methods in the managerial decision-making process in the context of sustainable development. Sustainability **14**, 11546 (2022)
35. Benevento, E., Stefanini, A., Aloini, D., Dulmin, R., Mininno, V.: Beyond digital technologies: investigating the barriers to supply chain integration of healthcare organizations. IEEE Trans. Eng. Manag. **71**, 13660–13672 (2023)
36. Singh, R.K.: Modelling of critical factors for responsiveness in supply chain. J. Manuf. Technol. Manag. **26**, 868–888 (2015)
37. Pessot, E., De Togni, G.: A framework for the collaborative evaluation of service outsourcing contracts in pharmaceutical logistics. In: Boosting Collaborative Networks 4.0: 21st IFIP WG 5.5 Working Conference on Virtual Enterprises, PRO-VE 2020, Valencia, Spain, November 23–25, 2020, Proceedings 21, pp. 623–633. Springer International Publishing (2020)

Interdisciplinary Collaboration for Designing with Intelligence: A Qualitative Study on the Development of AI Tools for Home Adaptation for Older Adults

Daniele Spoladore[1](✉), Federica Romagnoli[2], Atieh Mahroo[1,3], Teresa Villani[2], Tiziana Ferrante[2], and Marco Sacco[1]

[1] Institute of Intelligent Industrial Technologies and Systems for Advanced Manufacturing (STIIMA), National Research Council of Italy (CNR), Lecco, Italy
{daniele.spoladore,atieh.mahroo,marco.sacco}@cnr.it

[2] Department of Planning, Design, Technology of Architecture (PDTA), Sapienza University of Rome, Rome, Italy
{federica.romagnoli,teresa.villani,tiziana.ferrante}@uniroma1.it

[3] Department of Informatics, Systems and Communication, University of Milano-Bicocca, Milan, Italy

Abstract. Reconfiguring homes for older adults or individuals with limited autonomy poses major challenges, requiring collaboration among architects, clinicians, caregivers, and technology experts. Integrating these disciplines into a unified workflow is complex. AI-based technologies can support this process through collaborative decision-making tools, but must reflect the actual needs of professionals. This paper presents a questionnaire developed to identify such needs. Administered to 20 professionals, the study explored their roles, challenges in home reconfiguration, use of medical data, knowledge of assistive technologies, and expectations for AI tools, especially regarding integration with current systems, enhancing collaboration, and the capabilities AI should provide. Preliminary results indicate a strong willingness to adopt AI-based systems and the role of multidisciplinary collaboration: collaboration between healthcare professionals and architects emerges as an important aspect (for understanding occupants' needs and assisting in selecting suitable assistive technologies), while applying accessibility regulations in real contexts can benefit from AI-mediated expertise.

Keyword: Domestic environment reconfiguration · AI-based Decision Support System · Requirements elicitation · Interdisciplinary collaboration · Qualitative study

1 Introduction

Population ageing is a social issue afflicting both Western and Eastern countries and implying major challenges. In a recent report [1], the World Health Organization (WHO) underlined that ageing is a generalized issue that impacts every country's economy and

Published by Springer Nature Switzerland AG 2026
L. M. Camarinha-Matos et al. (Eds.): PRO-VE 2025, IFIP AICT 770, pp. 344–359, 2026.
https://doi.org/10.1007/978-3-032-05673-3_21

health systems. The current number of people aged 60 is estimated to be 1.4 billion, which is expected to rise to 2.1 billion in 2025. People aged 80 or older are expected to reach 426 million globally by 2050. Even though this demographic shift started in high-income countries, even low- and middle-income countries are experiencing this change nowadays. Therefore, by 2025, more than 60% of the global population aged 60 or more will live in low- and middle-income countries. More older adults have a significant impact on national healthcare systems, since longer lives often imply the development of chronic health conditions and disabilities, which ultimately significantly affect the elderly's ability to live autonomously.

In high-income countries, the ageing population issue has started to be tackled with different approaches: in the EU, active ageing has emerged as a paradigm involving physical and cognitive activities to support people's abilities retention, to prevent health conditions' exacerbations [2]. Moreover, Ambient Assisted Living (AAL) [3] leverages Artificial Intelligence (AI), Internet of Things (IoT), and Context Awareness capabilities to develop "smart" domestic environments – i.e., physical infrastructures that can support older adults in living autonomously by assisting them and, possibly, foreseeing their needs [4, 5]. While active ageing indications are mainly driven by medical professionals, AAL reconfiguration of living environments requires the physical environment to be redesigned, taking into account several factors (e.g., the occupant's health condition, the selection and deployment of sets of sensors, actuators, aids, and assistive technologies, etc.). This task is far from trivial, and designers and architects, on their own, may not possess all the necessary competencies to fulfil an effective domestic environment reconfiguration, which necessarily implies a tight cooperation among other professionals and stakeholders, such as clinicians, caregivers, and occupants, as well as a solid understanding of aids and assistive devices' functionalities. In such a complex context, AI can support architects and designers in reconfiguration tasks. In particular, an intelligent system may enable architects' understanding of clinical and health data, helping them select the most suitable assistive technologies and guiding them in their deployment within the physical space. Nevertheless, the development of a new AI-enabled system requires eliciting architects' and designers' practical and operational needs, and understanding how to support them in cooperating with different stakeholders and, ultimately, in making decisions for domestic environments' personalization and reconfiguration. Therefore, the research question underlying this paper is how AI can be beneficial to architects facing the home adaptation issues for older adults.

To this purpose, this work presents a preliminary survey conducted with 20 professionals. A questionnaire was administered to investigate several aspects of their experiences in domestic reconfiguration, possible difficulties related to collaboration and data acquisition from the other stakeholders involved, and their expectations and considerations regarding the role of AI-based systems in domestic environment reconfiguration tasks.

The remainder of this paper is organized as follows: Sect. 2 provides the theoretical background for the problem at hand, focusing in particular on the role of multidisciplinary cooperation for smart environments and domestic environments' reconfiguration, and on the role of AI-based technologies in such a context. Section 3 presents the questionnaire, details the experiment, and reports the results gathered. Section 4 discusses the results in the light of recent literature and highlights some fundamental implications. Section 5 proposes an architecture of an AI-based system for reconfiguring domestic environments, based on the experiment's findings. Finally, the Conclusions summarize the main outcomes of this study.

2 Related Work

This Section surveys the recent advancements in domestic environments reconfiguration for certain categories of people, and its multidisciplinary and cooperative characteristics, underlining the role of architects and designers.

2.1 Making the Environment "Smart" for People with Special Needs

With the rise of AAL and smart homes, the possibility of providing users with special needs with tailored services – enabled by IoT and AI technologies – started to be investigated. Although many architectures were designed, the problem of the physical deployment of AAL and smart solutions was soon detected [6, 7].

Nevertheless, in the past 15 years, many smart environments have been designed for people with special needs and older adults – partially embracing the need for physical and cognitive training foreseen by the active ageing paradigm [8, 9]. Also, the impulse from IoT, monitoring technologies of Ambient Intelligence, and the increasing availability of digital applications opened the possibility of developing tailored environments and highly-monitored solutions [10, 11]. However, the focus of the personalization is rarely placed on the physical domestic environment, which continues to pose deployment challenges.

There are several technological barriers that slow the real-world deployment of smart environments. Although technologies have made significant progress in the last two decades, their maturity is not adequate for large-scale deployment (e.g., they are not yet completely reliable or real-world deployment reveals issues not detectable in laboratory environments) [12, 13]. Also, once deployed, AAL solutions may prove to be hard to maintain for non-technical users (including older adults), which increases costs and reduces feasibility [14, 15]. Alongside technological barriers, physical environment's constraints are still a persistent issue: the physical layout and infrastructure of homes or care facilities can hinder the installation and operation of sensors, devices, and communication networks. Older buildings may lack the necessary wiring or space for new technologies, and environmental factors like interference or poor connectivity can disrupt system performance [13, 16].

Finally, architects and designers, who are ultimately called to redesign the environment to meet the user's specific needs, may not have all the necessary competencies: for instance, they may not be aware of assistive technologies or aids' specific features and their impact on the end users; nor do they have knowledge of older adults' health conditions and their needs, which may limit their choices in reconfiguring a room [17, 18].

Therefore, more research needs to be conducted on the necessities raised by the real-world deployment of AAL-tailored solutions. The first step involves investigating the real challenges faced by architects and designers while tackling such a task.

2.2 AAL Solutions: A Multidisciplinary and Collaborative Activity

AAL solutions must address a wide range of users' needs, which usually imply physical and cognitive disabilities hindering everyday activities. The design and development of effective AAL solutions is thus a complex task, and it must rely on many inputs. These solutions need to rely on a multidisciplinary approach, enabled by the cooperation among the different professionals involved: clinicians and rehabilitators, caregivers, technologists and technicians, computer scientists, and architects and designers. Only transdisciplinary and interdisciplinary collaboration enables a holistic understanding and innovative problem-solving by bringing together all the parties involved in smart environment reconfiguration processes [19, 20].

In particular, architects and designers are "the first line" in reconfiguring domestic environments for people with special needs. Besides tackling physical barriers for people with limited mobility (e.g., making bathrooms and kitchens accessible to wheelchair users, placing aids such as grab bars, etc.) [21] and adjusting the environment for occupants with sensory-related disabilities (e.g., adapting the environments and the indoor spaces for people with vision-related impairments) [22], architects are now – and, increasingly, in the near future – challenged with the impairments deriving from chronic conditions. Age-related impairments cover a wide range of sensory (e.g., hearing and sight loss), mobility (e.g., decreased muscle strength, reduced balance, etc.), cognitive (memory loss, mild cognitive impairment, etc.), and functional impairments (which involve difficulties in carrying out daily activities such as cooking, cleaning, bathing, dressing, etc.). Designing a domestic environment capable of addressing specific users' conditions and needs requires flexible tools for personalization [23, 24]. Moreover, it would require architects and designers to be up to date on assistive technologies, aids, and digital technologies that can act as supports – the "gerontechnological innovations" [25]. Finally, architects may be asked to know policy and legislation on disability, which is often fragmented and insufficient.

Therefore, these professionals could benefit from a cooperative approach, capable of supporting them in acquiring and sharing knowledge with other stakeholders – which impacts the reconfiguration process at some point. Such an approach can be enabled by AI technologies, which – to some extent – are already being used for empowering older adults in living autonomously using smart technologies [17, 18, 26, 27].

3 Investigating Architects' Opinions and Expectations on the Role of AI in Domestic Environment Reconfiguration

This Section introduces the aim and the tool adopted to investigate architects and designers' needs and challenges, perceptions, opinions, and expectations on the reconfiguration activity and the role AI should play.

3.1 Participants

The questionnaire was developed following Nielsen Normal Guidelines [28] and administered to 20 architects (aged between 26 and 35) – belonging to a network of former students from the Faculty of Architecture at Sapienza University of Rome, with already significant working experience and currently practicing across various regions of Italy. The questionnaire was administered using free online tools, and the collected data were anonymized by removing any meaningful identifiers and replacing them with IDs [29]. The sample size was determined according to [30].

3.2 Results

This subsection presents the questionnaire results, starting with the composition of the participants' sample and its characteristics, then delving into the parts that compose the questionnaire.

Sample's working experience. The majority of the architects (12) reported a working experience between 6 and years, with 8 participants indicating less than 5 years working experience. It is interesting to observe that almost all architects have already faced domestic reconfiguration projects (18). However, only a minority (3) have worked in reconfiguration projects for older adults with special needs or frailty. Figure 1 represents participants' answers graphically.

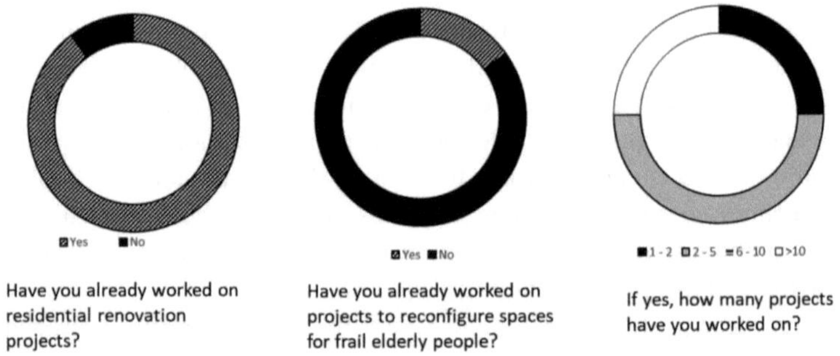

Fig. 1. Participants' answers regarding their work in domestic environments reconfiguration.

Sample's perceived competences. The questionnaire also investigates two fundamental aspects of architects' expertise: their knowledge of the current regulations for residential settings and their confidence in their knowledge and abilities for the reconfiguration of domestic environments for older adults and/or persons with special needs. While most of the participants indicated a good or higher knowledge of the regulations (13), the majority of the sample specified having only a *basic knowledge* of designing accessible and inclusive spaces for elderly people (14), with 2 participants indicating *no competencies* at all. Figure 2 summarizes the results.

Sample's digital competencies. Another relevant feature of architects and designers' work activity is the ability to use design software with a reasonable degree of confidence. A professional use of design software is far from trivial; therefore, the questionnaire investigated this aspect and asked for more specifics (i.e., which software participants use in their work). All participants rated their knowledge of design software as "good" or

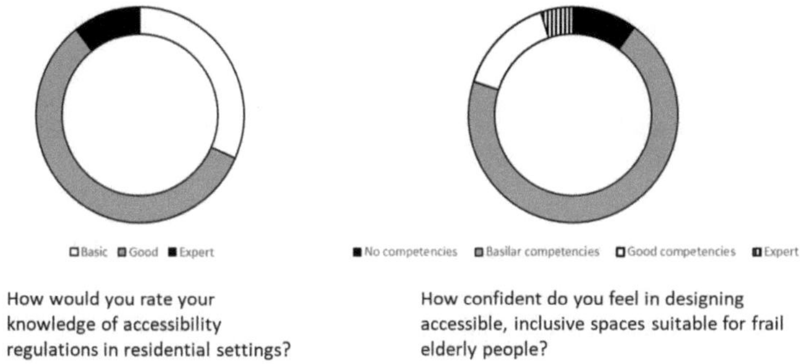

Fig. 2. Participants' answers regarding their knowledge of regulations and confidence in reconfiguring environments for the elderly.

"expert" and provided a list of currently used software. Figure 3 represents these results in a graphic form.

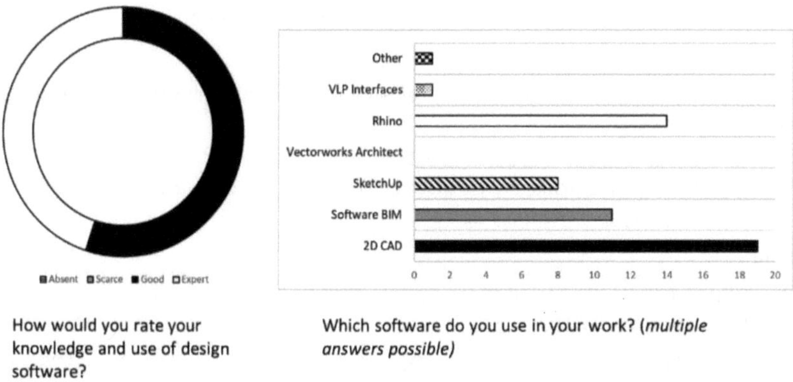

Fig. 3. Participants' digital competencies and software used during their working activity.

Regarding the types of software used by participants, 2D CAD solutions are those adopted by almost the totality (19), with Rhino (a 3D modeller) and BIM software (e.g., Revit, Archicad, Edificius, etc.) used by 14 and 11 participants, respectively. Although professionals vary in using lesser-known software solutions, they do not use Vectorworks Architect.

Living spaces reconfiguration – Difficulties. Six questionnaire items investigated the difficulties or barriers participants faced (or expect to face) when reconfiguring a domestic environment for people characterized by special needs. Participants were asked to rate the importance of each statement, selecting from a Likert scale ranging from 1 ("Not important") to 5 ("Extremely important"). Table 1 summarizes the results.

As the Table illustrates, all items scored higher than 3 ("Moderately important"), indicating that pre-existing architectural barriers (e.g., load-bearing walls, columns, thresholds, etc.) are considered the most cumbersome elements to overcome.

Table 1. Professionals' perception of barriers and difficulties when reconfiguring living environments for older adults.

Among the difficulties you have encountered (or would expect to encounter) in reconfiguring domestic spaces for frail elderly people, how would you rate their importance?

#	Item	AVG	ST.D.
1.1	Pre-existing architectural barriers	4.2	0.69
1.2	Difficulty in sourcing suitable aids or furniture	3.75	0.55
1.3	Complexity in applying accessibility and safety regulations	3.65	0.87
1.4	Client/user budget limitations	3.7	0.80
1.5	Difficulty in communicating with the client or family members	3.15	0.93

Living spaces reconfiguration – Health & aids. Eight questionnaire items addressed the role attributed to the occupants' health status, availability, and knowledge about aids and assistive technologies, and the opportunity of balancing aesthetics with functionality – while being limited by a budget. Table 2 summarizes the results.

Table 2. Professionals' perception of the role of occupants' health status information and aids in a reconfiguration process.

	For the following statements, please indicate your level of agreement on a scale from 1 (strongly disagree) to 5 (strongly agree):		
#	**Item**	**AVG**	**ST.D.**
2.1	Gathering detailed information about the elderly person's health status and specific needs is a complex process.	3.5	1.05
2.2	Identifying the most suitable aids (e.g., grab bars, patient lifts) is difficult.	2.75	0.91
2.3	Balancing functionality and aesthetics in the home is a significant challenge.	3.55	0.94
2.4	Accessibility regulations and guidelines are complex to interpret and apply.	2.85	0.93
2.5	Communication with the elderly person's family members often leads to misunderstandings.	3	1.07
2.6	Managing project costs and timelines is problematic.	3.35	0.98
2.7	The availability of devices, aids, and innovative solutions is limited.	3.1	0.85
2.8	Integrating devices or aids into the domestic space is difficult.	3.3	0.86

It is interesting to observe that, although higher than 2, two items scored less than 3; moreover, contrary to the previous questionnaire section, standard deviation values are higher, and average values never reach 4.

Using AI – professionals' willingness. Two questions asked participants whether they would use an AI tool to reconfigure a domestic environment for older adults and the elderly with special necessities. The questions allowed the selection of one of three possible answers, as depicted in Table 3.

Table 3. Professionals' willingness to adopt AI tools.

Item	Not willing	Moderately willing	Completely willing
To what extent are you willing to adopt AI-based tools in your professional practice?	0	8	12
Item	**No**	**Maybe**	**Yes**
Do you consider that an AI-powered intelligent system, integrated with CAD tools, could effectively support you in reconfiguring domestic spaces for frail elderly individuals?	0	2	18

These simple questions' results indicate professionals' marked tendency toward the adoption of AI systems, with the belief that such tools could be supportive in the reconfiguration tasks.

AI expectations – characteristics. The questionnaire then explores the characteristics an AI tool should have, according to participants. A set of seven items is provided, and professionals are asked to state the importance of each statement, selecting from a Likert scale ranging from 1 ("Not important") to 5 ("Extremely important"). Table 4 synthesizes the results. Table 4 illustrates the results.

The list of characteristics and features proposed are all considered "Moderately important" or higher (>3); the integration with existing CAD software, update information and guidelines on the regulations, and a database of aids and assistive devices scored better than the other items.

AI expectations – functions. The expected functions of an AI system supporting the reconfiguration of domestic environments are then addressed. Six items are ranked in importance (using the same Likert scale of Tables 1, 2, and 4) by professionals. Table 5 reports the results.

Two items stand out: simulating the elderly interaction within the environment and AI-assisted optimization of indoor space. Nevertheless, it is worth observing that there is no homogeneity in the answers, as the standard deviations for these two items are higher than the others.s

Multidisciplinary collaboration. The role the AI system should play among the stakeholders and actors that are usually involved in a domestic environment reconfiguration process is then investigated. Participants are asked to grade the importance of eight items. Table 6 illustrates the results.

Table 4. The characteristics an AI system should have, according to participants.

Among the following features of a system designed to assist you in reconfiguring a domestic environment for a frail elderly person, please indicate the ones you consider most important on a scale from 1 (not at all important) to 5 (extremely important).

#	**Item**	**AVG**	**ST.D.**
4.1	A system that provides personalized recommendations for devices, aids, and modifications based on the elderly person's health status.	3.8	0.69
4.2	A system that is integrated with widely used 2D and 3D CAD tools.	4.15	0.81
4.3	A system that offers an up-to-date database of devices, aids, and innovative solutions.	4.25	0.55
4.4	A system that facilitates communication and collaboration with the elderly person's family members.	3.6	0.82
4.5	A system that provides updated information on accessibility regulations and guidelines.	4.15	0.67
4.6	A system that automatically estimates the costs associated with the proposed construction work.	3.9	0.91
4.7	A system that incorporates input from the elderly person's medical professionals.	3.9	0.64

Table 5. The functions an AI system should have, according to participants.

Among the following features of a system designed to assist you in reconfiguring a domestic environment for a frail elderly person, please indicate the ones you consider most important on a scale from 1 (not at all important) to 5 (extremely important).

#	Item	AVG	ST.D.
5.1	AI should be An AI-based system should facilitate collaboration with social workers elderly person's health status to generate design proposals.	3.35	1.08
5.2	AI should be able to simulate the elderly person's interaction with the redesigned space (e.g., through virtual reality).	4	0.72

(continued)

Table 5. *(continued)*

Among the following features of a system designed to assist you in reconfiguring a domestic environment for a frail elderly person, please indicate the ones you consider most important on a scale from 1 (not at all important) to 5 (extremely important).

#	Item	AVG	ST.D.
5.3	AI should be able to optimize the layout of the space to maximize accessibility and safety.	4	0.85
5.4	AI should be able to learn from the preferences of the elderly person and their family members to personalize the design.	3.7	0.73
5.5	AI should be able to identify innovative and unconventional solutions to accessibility challenges.	3.7	0.8
5.6	AI should be able to assess the emotional and psychological impact of the design on the elderly person.	3.55	1.05

4 Discussion

4.1 Contextualizing Domestic Environment Reconfiguration: A Challenging Task

Professionals underlined their knowledge of (local) regulations and norms pertaining to the domestic setting's accessibility (13 participants rated their knowledge as "good" or "expert", and did not rate this issue as one of the most relevant in Table 2, item 2.4). However, when asked about what AI could do to ease the domestic environment reconfiguration activity (items 4.5, 5.1, and 5.5), architects underlined the supportive role an AI-based tool can play in applying the regulations within a real reconfiguration project. Field studies and many other research studies [31–34] underline the difficulties in applying regulation in real projects, since each domestic environment presents unique features. Therefore, being supported by a "smart agent" – capable of interpreting, adapting, and applying regulations to specific cases – is perceived as a significant enhancement for this type of task. Moreover, considering the multidisciplinary characteristics of domestic environment reconfiguration (which also emerged as expected supports in Tables 4 and 5), a system capable of taking into account a variety of inputs for the correct and best interpretation of accessibility regulations is considered a plus.

Another relevant challenge that emerges from the answers provided by professionals is related to aids and assistive technologies (as seen in items 1.2, 4.1, and 6.3). As mentioned in Sect. 2, the reconfiguration for older adults and/or persons with special needs often requires specific knowledge of the assistive technologies and aids, with a focus on their functions – i.e., the "positive effect" they are supposed to grant to their users. However, architects and designers do not necessarily possess this knowledge, and there is also a lack of valid methods and instruments for the selection of assistive

Table 6. The way in which AI systems can support multidisciplinary cooperation.

For the following statements regarding your expectations about the role of Artificial Intelligence (AI), please indicate their level of importance on a scale from 1 (not at all important) to 5 (extremely important).

#	Item	AVG	ST.D.
6.1	An AI-based system should facilitate collaboration with healthcare professionals (e.g., occupational therapists, geriatricians, physicians) in the design of spaces for elderly individuals.	3.95	0.75
6.2	An AI-based system should facilitate collaboration with social workers to support in understanding the elderly person's social and family context.	3.35	0.87
6.3	An AI-based system should facilitate collaboration with experts in home automation and assistive technologies to integrate innovative solutions.	3.95	0.68
6.4	An AI-based system should facilitate communication and information exchange among the various professionals involved.	3.95	0.82
6.5	An AI-based system should provide tools for the joint sharing and visualization of design projects.	3.9	1.11
6.6	An AI-based system should be able to integrate the different perspectives and recommendations of professionals to generate an optimized design.	4	0.79
6.7	AI should be able to identify potential conflicts or inconsistencies among the recommendations of different professionals.	4.1	0.71
6.8	AI should be able to generate reports and documentation that facilitate communication with the elderly person and their family members.	3.8	0.89

technologies [35, 36]. Thus, an AI system should support professionals in providing suitable assistive devices, technologies, and aid options for the reconfiguration project (and the occupant's needs) at hand. Professionals' answers underline the complexity of reconfiguring domestic environments for older adults. In particular, the need to adapt and deploy accessibility regulations in a real context and the selection of the most suitable aids call for a multidisciplinary smart system, capable of conveying experts' experiences and knowledge to support architects.

4.2 Accounting for Occupants' Health Conditions: A Collaborative and Multidisciplinary Task

As a corollary of the previous findings, architects and designers facing reconfigurations for people with impaired health conditions step into a field of knowledge that is still considered highly specialized and is not yet included in their traditional educational curricula (as the average scores for items 5.1 and 6.2 underline). Nevertheless, in light of current socio-demographic trends, design activities will increasingly require an understanding of a person's health status and specific needs related to physical or cognitive frailty, in order to identify which aids and assistive technologies could be effectively deployed in her/his domestic environment. This issue emerged clearly from Table 6 (item 6.1) and, more marginally, from Tables 4 (items 4.1, 4.3, and 4.7) and 5 (item 5.1). Once again, the solution to this issue relies on a multidisciplinary approach to reconfiguration, which must result in a collaborative (and multi-domain) system, capable of reasoning over different professionals' opinions, recommendations, and suggestions and elaborating the most suitable solution. Also, this aspect of the AI tool emerged in Table 6 (items 6.6 and 6.7), when professionals rated the integrations of different stakeholders' perspectives higher than any other item in the Table.

4.3 Multidisciplinary Collaboration and AI "Inevitability"

From the results of Tables 3 and 5, it is evident how the sample of architects was willing to adopt AI tools for domestic environment reconfiguration; furthermore, Tables 5 and 6 clearly indicate that they are well-aware of the areas in which AI can be of any help. It is also worth observing that participants rated all collaboration items of Table 6 higher than "3".

Thus, it is plausible to conclude that AI is considered "inevitable" in architects' jobs and that professionals are aware of its role as a multidisciplinary collaboration-fostering tool and a "smart assistant" for very peculiar tasks (i.e., those discussed in Sect. 4.1). These results are in line with recent studies, which underline how AI can support collaboration and enhance human creativity [37, 38]. The results are also aligned with recent studies indicating that AI integration in the architectural design process is well-accepted and positively influenced by AI's perceived usefulness [39, 40]. In light of these studies, the proposed questionnaire sheds light on what is perceived as useful when tackling the problem at hand. In fact, Table 5's scores highlighted maximizing space optimization for occupant's accessibility and safety (according to regulations) and the possibility of adopting virtual representations of the reconfigured environments to simulate occupants' interactions. While the first aspect has been addressed in the previous subsections, the opportunity to simulate the reconfigured environment was only partially hinted at by item 4.2 (which investigated AI's possibility to integrate with existing architectural software and scored more than average ("4.15")). In this regard, it is worth noticing that the issue of adopting virtual reality to simulate domestic environments in AAL contexts is an ongoing research activity [18, 41, 42]; nevertheless, virtual reality in architecture is mostly used in educational contexts [43, 44] and customer engagement [45], since it faces challenges such as high costs, motion sickness, and integration difficulties.

4.4 Limitations

This study presents some limitations. The most evident limitation consists in the sample of participants' provenance – all architects are from Italy – and demography – all architects are younger than 35. Although experienced, the majority of architects did not have significant experience with the reconfiguration of spaces for non-self-sufficient older adults. This could, in part, explain why item 5.1 scored less than other expected AI functions.

Nevertheless, it is necessary to observe that the sample is a cross-section of the "future" experts, i.e., those architects who will (soon) be dealing with reconfiguration challenges, many of which will likely arise from the mismatch between the existing housing stock and the needs of an increasingly ageing population [46]. Also, considering that Italy is the European country with the highest percentage of the elderly, the results contribute to highlighting a deficiency in prospective architects' academic preparation. A second limitation is the lack of involvement of other stakeholders in this survey: although this study is specifically focused on architects, different questionnaires should investigate other stakeholders' perspectives on the topic at hand. The last limitation is connected to the preliminary nature of this study: Tables 5 and 6 could only provide a limited number of items, which ultimately limited participants' answers to a specific set of options. Other qualitative methods (e.g., interviews, open questions, etc.) may elicit different results.

5 Conclusions and Future Works

This preliminary study explored the perspectives and expectations of a sample of young Italian architects regarding the integration of AI tools in domestic environment reconfiguration for older adults with special needs. The findings highlight a strong willingness among professionals to adopt AI-based systems, particularly those capable of supporting multidisciplinary collaboration, regulatory interpretation, and selection of assistive technologies. The results underscore the need for intelligent tools that can bridge knowledge gaps between architectural practice and clinical or technological domains, thereby enhancing the effectiveness and personalization of reconfiguration projects.

Future work will focus on expanding the participant sample to include a broader age and geographic diversity, as well as professionals from other fields involved in the reconfiguration process (e.g., clinicians, occupational therapists, caregivers, etc.). Moreover, the development of a prototype AI-based support system, aligned with the requirements identified in this study, will be a central goal. This prototype will be iteratively tested and refined through co-design methodologies involving end users. Additional qualitative research methods, such as in-depth interviews or participatory workshops, will also be employed to further investigate professionals' needs and validate the functionalities proposed.

Acknowledgements. This paper was developed within the project funded by Next Generation EU - "Age-It - Ageing well in an ageing society" project (PE0000015), National Recovery and Resilience Plan (NRRP) - PE8 - Mission 4, C2, Intervention 1.3". The views and opinions expressed are only those of the authors and do not necessarily reflect those of the European Union or the European Commission. Neither the European Union nor the European Commission can be held responsible for them.

References

1. World Health Organization: UN Decade of Healthy Ageing: Plan of Action. (2020)

2. Foster, L., Walker, A.: Active ageing across the life course: towards a comprehensive approach to prevention. Biomed Res Int. (2021). https://doi.org/10.1155/2021/6650414
3. Costa, R., et al.: Ambient assisted living. In: 3rd Symposium of Ubiquitous Computing and Ambient Intelligence 2008. pp. 86–94. Springer Berlin Heidelberg, Berlin, Heidelberg (2009). https://doi.org/10.1007/978-3-540-85867-6_10
4. Cook, D.J., Das, S.K.: How smart are our environments? An updated look at the state of the art. Pervasive Mob. Comput. **3**, 53–73 (2007). https://doi.org/10.1016/j.pmcj.2006.12.001
5. Spoladore, D., Arlati, S., Colombo, V., Modoni, G., Sacco, M.: A Semantic-enabled smart home for AAL and continuity of care. In: Studies in Computational Intelligence (2021). https://doi.org/10.1007/978-981-15-9897-5_17
6. Bellmunt, J., Tiberghien, T., Mokhtari, M., Aloulou, H., Endelin, R.: Technical challenges towards an AAL large scale deployment. Presented at the (2015). https://doi.org/10.1007/978-3-319-19312-0_1
7. Barsocchi, P.: Evaluating indoor localization systems for AAL environments. Presented at the (2013). https://doi.org/10.1007/978-3-642-37419-7_1
8. Konstantinidis Evdokimos I., Antonis, B., Walter, H., Paul, P., Bamidis Panagiotis, D.: Integration of cognitive and physical training in a smart home environment for the elderly people. Presented at the (2010). https://doi.org/10.3233/978-1-60750-588-4-58
9. Santos, O.C.: Beyond cognitive and affective issues: designing smart learning environments for psychomotor personalized learning. In: Learning, Design, and Technology. pp. 3309–3332. Springer International Publishing, Cham (2023). https://doi.org/10.1007/978-3-319-17461-7_8
10. Hajjaji, Y., Boulila, W., Farah, I.R., Romdhani, I., Hussain, A.: Big data and IoT-based applications in smart environments: a systematic review. Comput. Sci. Rev. **39**, 100318 (2021). https://doi.org/10.1016/j.cosrev.2020.100318
11. Souri, A., Hussien, A., Hoseyninezhad, M., Norouzi, M.: A systematic review of IoT communication strategies for an efficient smart environment. Trans. Emerg. Telecommun. Technol. (2022). https://doi.org/10.1002/ett.3736
12. Dasios, A., Gavalas, D., Pantziou, G., Konstantopoulos, C.: Hands-on experiences in deploying cost-effective ambient-assisted living systems. Sensors. **15**, 14487–14512 (2015). https://doi.org/10.3390/s150614487
13. Márquez, G., Taramasco, C.: Barriers and facilitators of ambient assisted living systems: a systematic literature review. Int. J. Environ. Res. Public Health **20**, 5020 (2023). https://doi.org/10.3390/ijerph20065020
14. Wagner, S., et al.: CareStore platform for seamless deployment of ambient assisted living applications and devices. In: Proceedings of the ICTs for improving Patients Rehabilitation Research Techniques. IEEE (2013). https://doi.org/10.4108/icst.pervasivehealth.2013.252110
15. Aloulou, H., et al.: Deployment of assistive living technology in a nursing home environment: methods and lessons learned. BMC Med. Inform. Decis. Mak. **13**, 42 (2013). https://doi.org/10.1186/1472-6947-13-42
16. Musri, N.I.F., Osman, R., Hamid, N.H.A., Razak, F.H.A.: Adoption barriers of assistive ambient technology: a systematic literature review. Presented at the (2024). https://doi.org/10.1007/978-981-99-7339-2_18
17. Spoladore, D., et al.: Customizing seniors' living spaces: a design support system for reconfiguring bedrooms integrating ambient assisted living solutions. Presented at the (2024). https://doi.org/10.1007/978-3-031-62849-8_46
18. Spoladore, D., Mahroo, A., Sacco, M., Ferrante, T., Romagnoli, F., Villani, T.: Reconfiguring domestic environments: a decision support system for ambient assisted living. In: 2024 IEEE

International Conference on Metrology for eXtended Reality, Artificial Intelligence and Neural Engineering (MetroXRAINE). pp. 89–94. IEEE (2024). https://doi.org/10.1109/MetroXRAINE62247.2024.10795971

19. Zhu, N., et al.: Bridging e-health and the internet of things: the SPHERE project. IEEE Intell. Syst. **30**, 39–46 (2015). https://doi.org/10.1109/MIS.2015.57
20. Boger, J., et al.: Principles for fostering the transdisciplinary development of assistive technologies. Disabil. Rehabil. Assist. Technol. **12**, 480–490 (2017). https://doi.org/10.3109/17483107.2016.1151953
21. Tissot, J., Ramadhani, W., Vergara, L., Rogers, W.: Participatory research approach for evaluating home environment for older adults with disabilities. Innov. Aging **6**, 524 (2022). https://doi.org/10.1093/geroni/igac059.1999
22. Wright, C.J., Zeeman, H., Whitty, J.A.: Design principles in housing for people with complex physical and cognitive disability: towards an integrated framework for practice. J. Housing Built. Environ. **32**, 339–360 (2017). https://doi.org/10.1007/s10901-016-9517-2
23. Costa, P., Laurìa, A., Chiesi, L.: Promoting autonomy through home adaptations. Appropriation of domestic spaces in Italy. Disabil. Soc. **36**, 1332–1355 (2021). https://doi.org/10.1080/09687599.2020.1783205
24. Bosia, D., Marchiano, G.: Flexible and inclusive housing: adaptation to the changing needs of inhabitants. Presented at the (2024). https://doi.org/10.54941/ahfe1005628
25. Colnar, S., Dimovski, V., Grah, B., Rogelj, V., Bogataj, D.: Gerontechnology: literature review and research Agenda. In: 2020 59th Annual Conference of the Society of Instrument and Control Engineers of Japan (SICE). pp. 391–396. IEEE (2020). https://doi.org/10.23919/SICE48898.2020.9240225
26. Ma, C., Guerra-Santin, O., Mohammadi, M.: Smart home modification design strategies for ageing in place: a systematic review. J. Housing Built Environ. **37**, 625–651 (2022). https://doi.org/10.1007/s10901-021-09888-z
27. Kim, D.: Empowering older adults through smart technology: a new era in aging-in-place and home health care. Innov. Aging **8**, 618 (2024). https://doi.org/10.1093/geroni/igae098.2024
28. Nielsen Norman Group: 28 Tips for Creating Great Qualitative Surveys. Accessed on 02 July 2025 https://www.nngroup.com/articles/qualitative-surveys/.
29. Mondada, L.: Ethics in action: anonymization as a participant's concern and a participant's practice. Hum. Stud. **37**, 179–209 (2014). https://doi.org/10.1007/s10746-013-9286-9
30. Wutich, A., Beresford, M., Bernard, H.R.: Sample sizes for 10 types of qualitative data analysis: an integrative review, empirical guidance, and next steps. Int. J. Qual. Methods (2024). https://doi.org/10.1177/16094069241296206
31. Zallio, M., Clarkson, P.J.: Inclusion, diversity, equity and accessibility in the built environment: a study of architectural design practice. Build. Environ. **206**, 108352 (2021). https://doi.org/10.1016/j.buildenv.2021.108352
32. Carlsson, G., Jonsson, O., Olander, S., Salén, M., Månsson Lexell, E., Slaug, B.: Exploration of a Web-based accessibility tool for public facilities. Facilities **41**, 66–84 (2023). https://doi.org/10.1108/F-10-2022-0132
33. González-Alonso, M.Y., González-Lozano, B.: Challenges in housing accessibility towards universal design. Architecture **4**, 917–929 (2024). https://doi.org/10.3390/architecture4040048
34. Mayordomo-Martínez, D., García-Mateos, G.: Evaluating accessibility solutions in collective residential buildings: field research in Southeast Spain. Buildings **14**, 1621 (2024). https://doi.org/10.3390/buildings14061621
35. Bernd, T., Van Der Pijl, D., De Witte, L.P.: Existing models and instruments for the selection of assistive technology in rehabilitation practice. Scand. J. Occup. Ther. **16**, 146–158 (2009). https://doi.org/10.1080/11038120802449362

36. Dubey, A.K., Gulabani, K., Mewara, H.S., Trivedi, P.: Challenges in design & deployment of assistive technology. In: 2014 International Conference on Signal Propagation and Computer Technology (ICSPCT 2014). pp. 466–469. IEEE (2014). https://doi.org/10.1109/ICSPCT.2014.6884992
37. Shi, Y., Gao, T., Jiao, X., Cao, N.: Understanding design collaboration between designers and artificial intelligence: a systematic literature review. Proc. ACM Hum. Comput. Interact. **7**, 1–35 (2023). https://doi.org/10.1145/3610217
38. Petráková, L., Šimkovič, V.: Architectural alchemy: leveraging Artificial Intelligence for inspired design – a comprehensive study of creativity, control, and collaboration. Archit. Pap. Fac. Archit. Design STU. **28**, 3–14 (2023). https://doi.org/10.2478/alfa-2023-0020
39. Na, S., Heo, S., Han, S., Shin, Y., Roh, Y.: Acceptance model of Artificial Intelligence (AI)-based technologies in construction firms: applying the technology acceptance model (TAM) in combination with the technology–organisation–environment (TOE) framework. Buildings **12**, 90 (2022). https://doi.org/10.3390/buildings12020090
40. Matter, M.N., Gado, N.G.: Artificial Intelligence in architecture: integration into architectural design process. Eng. Res. J. **181**, 1–16 (2024). https://doi.org/10.21608/erj.2024.344313
41. Spoladore, D., Arlati, S., Sacco, M.: Semantic and virtual reality-enhanced configuration of domestic environments: the smart home simulator. Mob. Inf. Syst. **2017**, 1–15 (2017). https://doi.org/10.1155/2017/3185481
42. Spoladore, D., Sacco, M.: Semantic and Dweller-based decision support system for the reconfiguration of domestic environments: RecAAL. Electronics (Basel). **7**, 179 (2018). https://doi.org/10.3390/electronics7090179
43. Shanti, Z., Al-Tarazi, D.: Virtual reality technology in architectural theory learning: an experiment on the module of history of architecture. Sustainability. **15**, 16394 (2023). https://doi.org/10.3390/su152316394
44. Xie, B.: The revolutionary role of virtual reality technology (VR) in architectural design review. Educ. Reform Dev. **7**, 218–224 (2025). https://doi.org/10.26689/erd.v7i1.9595
45. Hollebeek, L.D., Clark, M.K., Andreassen, T.W., Sigurdsson, V., Smith, D.: Virtual reality through the customer journey: framework and propositions. J. Retail. Consum. Serv. **55**, 102056 (2020). https://doi.org/10.1016/j.jretconser.2020.102056
46. Socci, M., Principi, A., Lamura, G.: Ageing policies-access to services in different Member States Annex IV-Country study on Italy EN ANNEX. (2021)

Collaborative Healthcare Networks: Design

Collaborative Processes for the Deployment of Rural Medical Homes: Simulation Study

Marius Huguet[1](✉), Xavier Boucher[2], Vincent Augusto[2], Nour Mezni[1], and Chloé Gouttefangeas[3]

[1] Center for Biomedical Engineering (I4S Department), Mines Saint-Etienne, 42023 Saint-Etienne, France
{Marius.Huguet,Nourelhouda.Mezni}@emse.fr

[2] Mines Saint-Etienne, Univ Clermont Auvergne, INP Clermont Auvergne, CNRS, UMR 6158 LIMOS, 42023 Saint-Etienne, France
{Boucher,Augusto}@emse.fr

[3] Altermedis, 6 Rue Huber Dagnaud, 43130 Retournac, France

Abstract. To improve access to primary care in underserved areas, policies have promoted multidisciplinary medical homes (e.g., family health groups, patient-centered medical homes). Through the development of medical homes, the expected improvements in accessibility concern both the likelihood of accessing primary care and the frequency of healthcare utilization. This study analyzes the impact of collaborative organizational models within territorial medical home networks, on various performance dimensions and using a simulation-based approach. The goal is to develop a decision-aid tool to assist local managers in optimizing organizational design. We assess different collaboration scenarios, including intra-home teamwork among healthcare professionals and inter-home cooperation. Our findings highlight that simply establishing medical homes is not enough—effective collaboration frameworks are essential to maximizing efficiency and improving primary care accessibility.

Keywords: Primary Care · Discrete-Event Simulation · Medical Home · Collaboration

1 Introduction

Health inequalities and access to care are major public health concerns. Access to healthcare is a multidimensional concept that includes a willingness-to-pay component, as well as a non-financial component related to the availability of healthcare services within a reasonable distance from patients' homes and accessibility via transportation. There is extensive evidence of disparities in health status among different social groups in all countries, regardless of whether they are low-, middle-, or high-income [1]. Significant inequalities in healthcare access have also been highlighted in most OECD countries, strongly influenced by spatial variations in healthcare service availability for different social groups [2]. These inequalities have substantial social and economic costs for individuals and societies and are the target of numerous public policies.

Published by Springer Nature Switzerland AG 2026
L. M. Camarinha-Matos et al. (Eds.): PRO-VE 2025, IFIP AICT 770, pp. 363–378, 2026.
https://doi.org/10.1007/978-3-032-05673-3_22

Access to primary care has been identified as a key lever for reducing socio-economic and spatial health inequalities. An analysis of the 2016 Commonwealth Fund International Health Policy Survey of Adults, conducted in 11 countries (Australia, Canada, France, Germany, Norway, the Netherlands, New Zealand, Sweden, Switzerland, the United Kingdom, and the United States), highlights that low-income individuals are more likely to face multiple barriers to accessing care, particularly before reaching primary care facilities [3].

In France, the Ministry of Health and Prevention announced in June 2023 a €50 million action plan to improve access to primary care in underserved areas [4]. To attract new healthcare professionals to these regions and create multidisciplinary care teams around patients, the plan aims to establish 4,000 multidisciplinary medical homes (i.e., maison de santé pluridisciplinaire in French) by 2027. In other OECD countries, similar forms of organization (e.g., medical home in the US, family health groups in Canada, patient-centered medical home in the UK) have emerged since the 2000s, in response to the significant rise in chronic diseases and a medical demographic crisis [5].

Through the development of medical homes, the expected improvements in accessibility concern both the likelihood of accessing primary care and the frequency of healthcare utilization, which has been identified as a major component of primary care access inequalities [6]. These structures also aim to strengthen healthcare provision in medically underserved areas, attracting young doctors while promoting collaboration between different healthcare professionals.

While this territorial model appears interesting to address health inequalities and for the overall improvement of healthcare delivery, the deployment of medical homes suffers of organizational difficulties, notably due to the complexity to define the efficient and well-balanced organizational modes which could both guarantee a high healthcare efficiency for the local population and a consistent quality of life and profession for the healthcare practitioners. This complexity is linked on the once side to the flexibility of the model where the healthcare offer can include many variations, depending on the competencies of professionals involved and the way to organize their collaboration and on the other side to the lack of organization management skill for the decision-makers of the medical homes who are generally doctors. To answer these challenges, this paper intends to analyze the impact of flexible organizational modes within medical home territorial networks on different dimensions of the performance, using a simulation-based approach which could later provide a decision-aid solution to help the local managers for this organizational design. We investigate more precisely the following issues:

- The opportunity to increase internal collaboration among professionals at the level of single medical homes.
- The opportunity to implement local networks of medical homes by the implementation of network collaboration mechanisms.
- The recommendations to be proposed for a generic model of medical homes
- The potential of using simulation and digital twin technologies as a decision-aid approach in such a context

The study starts in Sect. 2 by a state of the art, before highlighting in Sect. 3 the case study developed together with an overview of the simulation-based methodology proposed. The simulation model is presented in Sect. 4 and the outputs of the simulation experiments are developed in Sect. 5. The conclusion highlights the final recommendations from this work.

2 State of the Art

2.1 Medical Homes and Collaboration

In the scientific literature, studies show that medical homes have been an effective lever for attracting young doctors to areas they previously avoided [7]. Indeed, regions facing medical desertification issues with medical homes experience a better evolution in the density of private general practitioners compared to those without medical homes.

The establishment of medical homes in France has also had a significant impact on doctors' remuneration [8, 9]. An increase in the active patient base of general practitioners has been observed, without affecting the total number of consultations performed. In other words, the number of procedures per patient is lower in medical homes, made possible by the multidisciplinary approach and collaboration between healthcare professionals. Notably, this result does not indicate a decline in the quality of care. In fact, doctors in medical homes receive, on average, 9% more in performance-based public health incentives (i.e., Rémunération sur Objectif de Santé Public (ROSP) in French). This increase in productivity makes medical homes more appealing to young doctors, especially as many general practitioners express concerns about excessive workload and its impact on their long-term commitment to the profession [10].

Beyond improving access to care, studies have also highlighted the impact of medical homes on other aspects of the healthcare system. Research has shown a decrease in emergency room visits and, to a lesser extent, a reduction in hospital admissions [11, 12].

However, a qualitative study pointed out that while medical homes demonstrate real momentum, their organizational model is still evolving [13]. Specifically, regarding two key objectives—internal coordination and cooperation—findings indicate a low level of innovative practices that support interdisciplinary and interprofessional collaboration. Without further development in this area, there is a risk that these centers may remain mere groupings of professionals rather than fully integrated healthcare organizations.

2.2 Simulation and Digital Twins for Healthcare Organisation and Processes

In recent years, recommendations have been made to encourage greater use of modeling and simulation methods for complex systems to support public health decision-making [14]. While randomized clinical trials are relatively easy to conduct for interventions at the individual level, it is often impossible to randomize a population-level intervention, such as an innovation involving organizational changes in healthcare systems.

The use of methods such as discrete event simulation has significantly expanded to provide a methodological framework for the prior evaluation of organizational scenarios. For example, numerous studies have used discrete event simulation models to assess the performance of different telemedicine adoption scenarios—one of the major organizational changes following the COVID-19 pandemic [15, 16]. More broadly, modeling and simulation methods are widely used to optimize patient care pathways, offering retrospective organizational diagnostics and simulating/evaluating alternative organizational structures [17–19].

In the context of primary care, a hybrid model combining agent-based modeling with discrete-event simulation was developed to analyze the primary care system in Germany [20]. This model examined the effects of demographic shifts, such as an aging population, alongside a decline in the number of physicians. By doing so, it provided insights into patient access to care and physician utilization rates beyond the conventional physician-to-patient ratio.

Similarly, a discrete-event simulation model was designed to assess the impact of patient triage to primary care in the United Kingdom [21]. This model simulated a scenario in which all patients were efficiently redirected to appropriate primary care facilities under an unlimited capacity assumption. The study evaluated the potential reduction in emergency department visits as a result of the triage system.

A comparable study in Portugal used a discrete-event simulation model to assess the transition of traditional primary health care centers (PHCCs) into family health units (FHUs) [22]. The analysis focused on key performance indicators such as waiting times, costs, and consultation volumes. More recently, the development of digital twins—virtual representations of physical systems in real time—has become a key focus of health research [23]. Organizational digital twins are designed to model, simulate, and manage healthcare delivery processes [24–27]. Compared to traditional modeling and simulation methods, digital twins are dynamically updated in near real-time to track the evolution of actual systems. As an illustration, this methodology is currently being developed to model emergency medical call centers organization as well as patient flow in emergency departments, helping to identify system bottlenecks and analyze resource planning constraints [28, 29].

3 Case Study and Research Methodology

3.1 Case Study: Territorial Deployment of Rural Medical Homes

The case study developed below directly addresses the context of territorial healthcare desertification identified in the literature. The context concerns the rural department of Haute-Loire in France which typically suffers of a weak density of general practitioners and thus a bad distribution of primary care offer. Medical homes have started to develop within the department inducing a new attractiveness for the local installation of healthcare practitioners. The French economic model of medical homes generates two levels of collaboration: the collaboration among professionals at the level of each medical home, and the potential collaboration among several distinct medical homes.

A rural medical home is an economic entity, which gathers several types of healthcare professionals who can collaborate to try and ensure a better efficiency in overall healthcare delivery: doctors, nurses, medical assistants, etc. Economically, the medical homes benefit from a specific and collective funding help from Regional Healthcare Institutions (depending of the French Healthcare Ministry) while all professionals act as liberal actors. The efficiency of the healthcare offer strongly depends on their ability to coordinate their various competencies. Such medical homes generally define a collective healthcare project and ambition which can contribute to long term missions like prevention, healthcare education and social actions. Thus, the first organizational question to be addressed is the delimitation of the internal healthcare competences within a medical home, together with the pertinent collaboration level among them.

At a second level of collaboration, local medical home can also be organized in collaborative networks of medical homes, enhancing the potential of collaboration mechanisms to improve the overall efficiency of the territorial healthcare system. The case study addressed in the paper is developed in collaboration with Altermedis structure, which gathers 3 medical homes, situated with a good geographical proximity each in a distinct rural village of the same department. This paper addresses the following collaborative issues for the Altermedis case study:

- At internal level of single medical homes, the goal is to assess alternative opportunities to integrate new healthcare professionals, complementary to the medical doctors. The French healthcare system proposes currently two types of profiles, 'Medical assistant' and 'Asalée nurses', each with different skills who can take in charge part of the healthcare tasks generally executed by the doctors. Additionally, another opportunity is the recent deployment of teleconsultation which is also a pertinent lever to try and increase healthcare efficiency. The study aims at analyzing the impacts of these various organizational options within each single medical home.
- At the inter-organizational level, among the 3 medical homes of the network, the objective of the study is to analyze pertinent solutions to manage emergency patient flows. Normal patient flows are characterized by anticipatory schedules, when emergency flows are characterized by no anticipation, thus inducing perturbations in the healthcare delivery to normal flows. The networked organization bring the added-value to make possible a mutualization of patient flows among the 3 medical homes, with the opportunity to position dedicated doctors to manage the emergency flow, with a necessity of local travels among the various medical homes. The impact could be positive, allowing to reduce drastically the perturbation of the normal patient flows, thus increasing the overall healthcare efficiency.

3.2 Simulation Based Research Methodology.

An applied research methodology has been structured to study the potential of collaboration in these healthcare networks. The research protocol is based on the use of organizational simulation, in order to virtualize and assess the organizational mechanisms under study. The research protocol is structured according the following steps (Fig. 1).

Conceptual modelling serves as the initial step toward organizational modelling. It involves capturing, structuring, and formally representing key knowledge about healthcare processes in an overarching conceptual model. This model provides a high-level view that can be progressively refined in subsequent phases.

During this first step, organizational issues and challenges—particularly those faced by professionals such as doctors in Medical Homes—are also identified and documented. Based on the conceptual model, the process advances to detailed organizational modelling, which includes two key activities: detailed data collection and model building and validation.

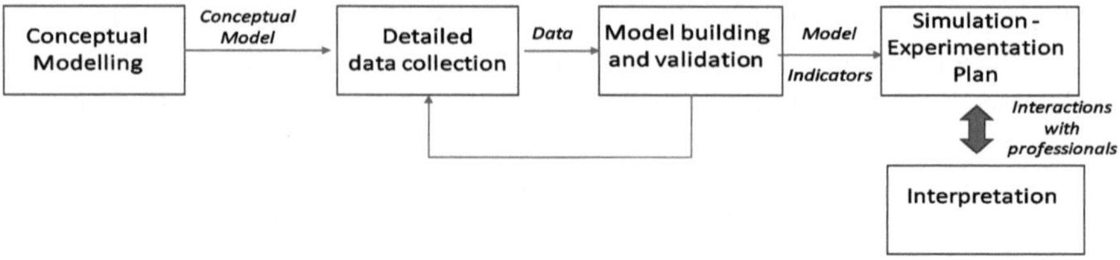

Fig. 1. Research protocol.

A detailed model is then constructed using an event-driven simulation platform, enabling the generation of relevant organizational indicators to address the previously identified challenges. These two steps—model building and validation—are iterative and carried out in close collaboration with healthcare professionals.

The fourth step involves developing robust experimentation plans through simulation, aimed at evaluating the indicators needed for a comparative analysis of the collaborative organizational mechanisms under study.

Finally, in the last step, results are interpreted in conjunction with healthcare professionals to generate well-informed and actionable recommendations for future improvements.

In the following sections, key results of these various steps are presented synthetically including elements of the conceptual model, simulation-oriented data, simulation model, indicators, experimentations with their outputs then interpretations.

4 Simulation Model

4.1 Conceptual Model

Each medical home is an independent entity, operating autonomously, without interconnection or overlap in patient flows between them. This fundamental assumption allows us to treat each facility as a distinct system, with its own resources and internal processes. To effectively model these centers, it is essential to precisely define the patient care pathway within each one.

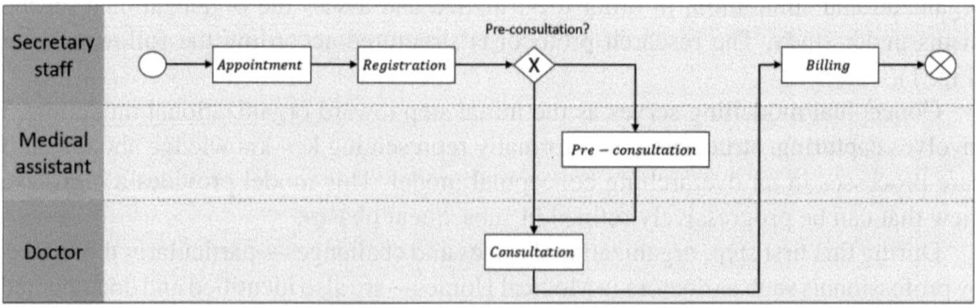

Fig. 2. Conceptual model of the care pathway of a patient at a medical home.

The patient care pathway generally begins with scheduling an appointment. The patient can book in advance either through the Doctolib platform or by directly contacting the medical secretary by phone. Upon arrival at the medical home, the patient is welcomed by the secretary, who records their personal information. In the absence of a medical secretary, the doctor themselves handles the registration and administrative tasks.

Then, several types of consultations are available: a standard consultation with a doctor, a dual consultation with a medical assistant, a dual consultation with an Asalée nurse, and teleconsultation. The choice of consultation type depends on the patient's preferences and the availability of healthcare professionals. In a standard consultation, the patient is seen solely by the doctor. In dual consultations, the patient first undergoes a pre-consultation with the medical assistant (or the Asalée nurse), who performs preliminary tasks such as measuring vital signs (heart rate, blood pressure, temperature, etc.). This process helps optimize the doctor's time, making their intervention shorter than in a standard consultation. Teleconsultation, on the other hand, is conducted remotely via the platform Doctolib. Finally, after the consultation, the patient returns to the reception to settle the payment and administrative tasks with the secretary staff.

Patients visit doctors for various reasons, each leading to a specific care pathway. Each pathway may include particular medical procedures and additional tasks, depending on the patient's needs. We have identified and distinguished eight distinct care pathways, which we define as follows: (1) general medicine consultation; (2) Pediatric consultation; (3) Gynecology consultation; (4) Prescription renewal; (5) Home visit; (6) Teleconsultation; (7) Emergencies; (8) Other. In our model, all pathways are handled similarly, but the consultation duration and the resources vary depending on the reason for the visit.

4.2 Data

In this study, we used data from the Doctolib platform. This is an online platform commonly used in France for booking medical appointments. It allows patients to find doctors and other healthcare professionals, check their availability, and book consultations directly through the platform. This solution is widely used in medical homes and medical practices. The platform also offers teleconsultation tools, providing greater flexibility and improved accessibility for patients. Additionally, Doctolib centralizes medical information, making it easier to track consultation history and treatments, thereby enhancing medical follow-up and care coordination.

As part of this project, we had access to the Doctolib accounts of three medical homes, which allowed us to obtain the following information:

- The daily number of consultations in each medical home. We extracted this data from Doctolib for the period from 02/01/2024 to 06/30/2024.
- The distribution of consultation reasons. For each consultation, the doctor records the reason on the Doctolib platform. We can therefore extract the number of consultations for each reason. We decided to group these reasons into eight categories: general medicine, pediatrics, gynecology, prescription renewal, home visits, teleconsultation, emergencies, and others.

Additionally, after several meetings and discussions with healthcare professionals from the three medical homes, we gathered valuable information, such as the duration of consultations for each care pathway, doctors' schedules, and the time required for tasks like reception and billing.

4.3 Discrete-Event Simulation (DES) Model

We implemented the conceptual model presented in Figure 2 using a DES approach. Figure 3 depicts the DES model for a single medical home, considering the four types of consultation (e.g., standard consultation with a doctor, a dual consultation with a medical assistant, a dual consultation with an Asalée nurse, and teleconsultation). As each medical home is an independent entity, the full model includes three independent sub-models for each medical home.

Table 1 summarizes the calibration of the parameters of the DES model. We calibrated the agent-generating process based on the daily number of consultations performed in each medical home. We took into account the clear daily seasonal effect visible in Fig. 4, and thus considered a separate generating process for each day of the week, and each medical home. We assumed a Poisson distributed generating process, and we calibrated the distribution based on the data extracted from Doctolib. Each agent is generated along with a reason for consultation, drawn from the distribution described in Table 1. Consultation durations are assumed to be drawn from triangular distributions, which were calibrated in collaboration with experts from the three medical homes, and differentiated for each consultation reason. The model was simulated over 6 months, to cope with the data extracted from the Doctolib platform as described in Sect. 4.2.

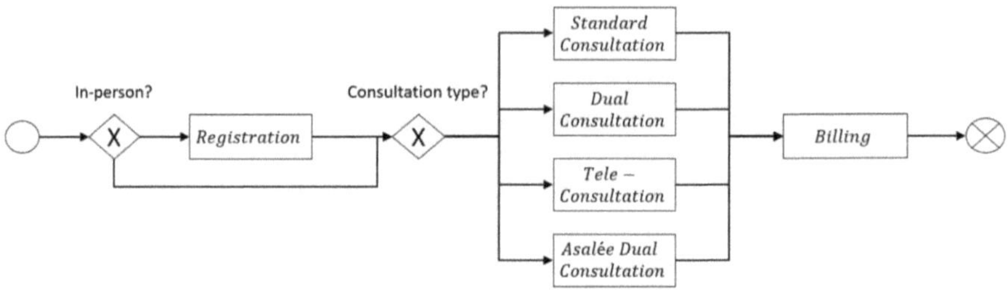

Fig. 3. Overview of a DES model for a single medical home, considering the four types of consultation.

To evaluate the results from the simulation model, two categories of key performance indicators (KPI) have been established to measure the impact of care organization strategies on patient management. These indicators include: patient satisfaction, which assesses the quality of care and waiting times; and medical staff satisfaction, which reflects the well-being and working conditions of healthcare providers. The following KPIs are considered:

- Waiting time from admission to consultation with a doctor (in minutes)
- Total number of patients treated

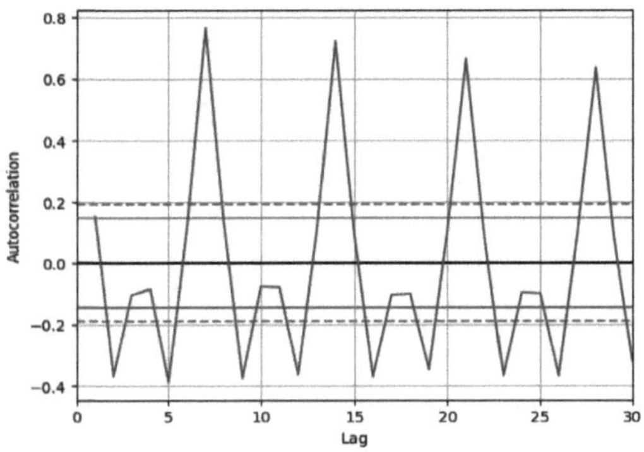

Fig. 4. Autocorrelation function of daily number of consultations.

- Workload, measured by resource utilization
- Surplus number of patients, occurring when the combined load of scheduled and unscheduled patients exceeds capacity, resulting in additional working hours or patients left without being seen
- Average number of overtime hours

We conducted 4 experiments and an extra validation experiment (i.e., base scenario) (Table 2). In the base configuration, one Asalee nurse is working 1.5 working day in

Table 1. Calibration of the parameters.

Parameters	MH1	MH2	MH3	Source
Agent generating process (Poisson distribution with parameter λ):				
- Monday	$\lambda = 84.0$	$\lambda = 35.2$	$\lambda = 17.7$	Data Doctolib
- Tuesday	$\lambda = 72.3$	$\lambda = 38.0$	$\lambda = 19.2$	
- Wednesday	$\lambda = 58.8$	$\lambda = 19.8$	$\lambda = 19.0$	
- Thursday	$\lambda = 54.9$	$\lambda = 32.1$	$\lambda = 21.4$	
- Friday	$\lambda = 63.1$	$\lambda = 35.2$	$\lambda = 17.1$	
- Saturday	$\lambda = 15.8$	$\lambda = 13.5$	$\lambda = 6.4$	
- Sunday	$\lambda = 7.8$	$\lambda = 8.3$	$\lambda = 4.0$	
Consultation reason (%):				
- General medicine	47.1	53.6	76.4	Data Doctolib
- Paediatrics	8.92	9.4	1.8	
- Gynaecology	1.15	0.8	0.28	
- Prescription renewal	7.36	3.9	0.76	
- Home visit	3.71	7.45	3.9	
- Teleconsultation	1.22	1.7	0.36	

(*continued*)

Table 1. (*continued*)

Parameters	MH1	MH2	MH3	Source
- Emergency	28.19	22.35	16.4	
- Other	2.35	0.8	0.1	
Consultation duration (Triangular(min,mode,max) in minutes):				
- General medicine	T(15,20,25)			Meeting with experts
- Paediatrics	T(20,25,30)			
- Gynaecology	T(20,22,30)			
- Prescription renewal	T(15,20,25)			
- Home visit	T(30,35,40)			
- Teleconsultation	T(10,15,20)			
- Emergency	T(20,25,30)			
- Other	T(20,22,25)			
Other activities duration (Triangular(min,mode,max) in minutes):				
- Registration	T(2,3,5)			Meeting with experts
- Billing	T(2,3,5)			
- Pre-consultation	T(6,8,10)			

Table 2. Description of the experiments.

Description	Base scenario	Exp. 1	Exp. 2	Exp. 3	Exp. 4
Simulation features					
- Replication count	25	25	25	25	25
- Replication length	6 months	6 months	6 months	6 months	6 months
Parameters variation					
- Asalee nurse for dual consultation	No	Yes	Yes	No	No
- Schedule Asalee nurse	-	1.5 days per week	3 days per week	-	-

(*continued*)

Table 2. *(continued)*

Description	Base scenario	Exp. 1	Exp. 2	Exp. 3	Exp. 4
- # of doctors dedicated to emergency consultations	0	0	0	1	2

Note: Experiment (Exp.); number of (#).

medical home n°1, and is having independent consultation on her side. In experiment 1, we explore the performance of also allowing the Asalee nurse to work in close collaboration with doctors, by having duo-consultation with them. Similarly, the same logic is experimented in experiment 2, where the availability of the Asalee nurse is extended to three full working day at medical home n°1. In experiment 1 and 2, we also model the independent flow of consultation the Asalee nurse is having on her own, in order to take into account its impact on her availability for duo-consultations.

The management of emergency consultations is often cited by doctors as one of the main causes of schedule disruption. Emergency appointments interfere with daily planning, creating a workload overload and overtime. To investigate potential organizational improvements, two additional experiments are being tested. In experiment 3, one doctor is dedicated to handling emergency consultations and travels between medical homes, thus allowing other doctors to focus on planned consultations.

Similarly, in scenario 4, two doctors are dedicated to the unscheduled flow.

4.4 Outputs: Collaborative Mechanisms for Rural Medical Homes

Table 3 summarizes the results of experiments 1 and 2, related to the organization of medical home 1 (MH1), comparing them to the baseline scenario. Overall, there is only a slight difference in the KPIs among the three evaluated scenarios. In the first scenario, the Asalée nurse handled on average 164 duo consultations, and 550 in the second scenario, over a six-month period. Although these numbers are not very high, this can be explained by the fact that the nurse already has her own consultations to manage. Additionally, duo consultations are relatively long, which limits the number of patients she can take care of. Based on these results, there is no significant difference in indicators such as the number of patients handled, the average waiting time, the number of surplus patients, and the number of overtime hours. However, a decrease in the physicians' utilization rate is observed. In summary, while the use of the Asalée nurse does not allow for the treatment of a significantly higher number of patients, it does help to reduce the workload of physicians.

Table 4 presents the results of Experiments 3 and 4 related to the implementation of a specific process for emergencies. Unlike experiments 1 and 2, experiments 3 and 4 assess forms of inter-medical homes cooperation. In experiment 3, the objective is to ensure that a doctor is always available to handle emergencies by moving between different sites. However, this responsibility will not fall on a single doctor but will instead be shared among the seven doctors from the medical homes, who will take shifts each day. Thus, the doctor in charge of emergencies on a given day will be responsible for treating all urgent patients across all sites, requiring travel which are taken into account in the workload computation.

Table 3. Results of experiments 1 and 2.

Metrics	Base scenario	Exp. 1 MH1	Exp. 2 MN1
Resources:			
- Number of overtime hours	640.1	669.72	657.64
	-51.3	-37.03	-33.08
- Average physician workload (hours)	2349.3 (20.2)	2346.4 (30.5)	2277.1 (24.8)
- Asalée nurse workload (hours)	-	85.8	330.4 (4.3)
		-6.4	
Patients:			
- Number of patients treated	8045.6 (61.4)	8062.76 (83.31)	8054.92 (70.76)
- Number of surplus patients	190.2 (36.4)	194.38	204.24
		-33.83	-32.87
- Average waiting time (minutes)	8.5	9.15	9.5
	-0.46	-0.38	-0.31
- Number of duo consultations with Asalée	-	164.72	550.76
		-5.37	-5.34

Analyzing the simulation results for this scenario, the first observation is that the surplus indicator for unscheduled consultation is very high. The doctor manages to treat an average of 1603.9 emergency cases, but an average of 645.8 cases remain as surplus, representing 29% of the total demand. This shows that the initial assumption about handling the surplus is no longer valid. In fact, the number of patients in surplus is too high for a single doctor to handle through overtime. The main conclusion is that a single doctor cannot manage the emergency flow. The dedicated doctor's average workload is 1239 h, and the average waiting time for an emergency consultation, including travel, reaches 100.2 min.

In experiment 4, we continue to focus on emergency flow management, this time by mobilizing two emergency doctors. This experiment builds upon experiment 3, which revealed that a single doctor cannot efficiently handle all emergency consultations. We therefore explored the possibility of improving the process for unscheduled consultations by distributing this responsibility between two doctors, with a rotating schedule among the seven available doctors.

In this experiment, an average of 2238.8 patients are treated, compared to 2168.6 in the baseline scenario, with a negligible average overflow of 8.44 patients. This slight increase in the number of emergency patients treated is accompanied by a slight decrease in the number of scheduled patients treated, leading to a slight decline in the total number of patients handled. This indicates that the emergency flow is fully absorbed but slightly affects the overall patient flow. In this scenario, the average workload of the dedicated physicians for unscheduled consultations is 1558 h, and the average waiting time decreases significantly compared to the previous scenario, reaching approximately 28.3 min.

Table 4. Results of experiments 3 and 4

Metric	Base scenario			Experiment 3			Experiment 4		
	MH1	MH2	MH3	MH1	MH2	MH3	MH1	MH2	MH3
Resources:									
- Number of overtime hours	640.1 (51.3)	27.1 (3.4)	4.5 (1.8)	296.8 (28.8)	25.72 (3.41)	0.08 (0.2)	310.3 (16.4)	29.1 (4.1)	0.04 (0.2)
- Average physician workload (hours)	2349.3 (20.2)	1111.1 (14.4)	753.5 (11.1)	1796.8 (25.4)	918.2 (13.1)	264.2 (10.3)	1696.8 (20.9)	905.7 (16.2)	188.9 (6.1)
Patients:									
- Number of scheduled patients treated	6745.2 (70.2)	2849.8 (52.9)	1464.2 (24.1)	6642.5 (71.1)	2949.2 (51.2)	637.5 (18.4)	6405.8 (59.1)	2904.6 (60.9)	453.7 (20.2)
- Number of unscheduled patients treated	1319.4 (32.5)	560.8 (18.8)	288.3 (14.8)	799.2 (20.7)	485.5 (18.4)	319.2 (15.8)	1118.3 (39.8)	671.4 (28.9)	449.1 (20.1)
- Number of surplus patients	190.2 (36.4)	1272.1 (28.1)	151.9 (20.8)	244.1 (42.6)	37.4 (10.1)	951.6 (33.1)	543.3 (40.8)	78.4 (12.2)	1135.5 (37.2)
- Average waiting time (minutes)	8.5	10.1	0.2	19.1	10.1	0.01	41.5	20.1	0.01
Specific process for emergencies:									
- Average waiting time (minutes)	-			100.2 (0.7)			28.3 (1.12)		
- Number of surplus patients	-			645.8 (28.9)			8.44 (4.1)		
- Average workload of the dedicated physician	-			1239.4 (18.4)			1558.3 (39.1)		
Total number of scheduled patients	11059.4 (82.1)			10229.2 (93.5)			9764.2 (93.1)		
Total number of unscheduled patients	2168.6 (40.4)			1603.9 (12.3)			2238.8 (50.2)		

Note: The average over replication runs is indicated for each key performance indicator, with standard deviation in parentheses. Medical Home (MH).

A notable improvement in the efficiency of the organizational model concerns the number of overtime hours worked, specifically for medical home No. 1, which reduces the time doctors work beyond theoretical hours by half. With this reallocation of resources, we observe a trade-off between absorbing the urgent patient flow and conducting scheduled consultations. Indeed, there is a slight decline in performance for scheduled consultations, with an increase in overflow and a decrease in the total number of patients treated.

5 Conclusions and Perspectives

This study has explored the organizational dynamics of rural medical homes through a simulation-based approach, aiming to provide local healthcare managers with actionable insights for improving service delivery and resource allocation. Our analysis has demonstrated that while the establishment of medical homes creates a structural opportunity for enhanced access to care, the real benefits in terms of efficiency, patient satisfaction, and workload balance rely heavily on the design of collaboration mechanisms — both internally among professionals and externally between medical homes.

At the internal level, the integration of complementary healthcare roles, such as Asalée nurses and medical assistants, was shown to relieve doctors' workloads without significantly expanding the number of patients treated. Although the introduction of duo consultations did not lead to major improvements in patient flow, it did create a more sustainable distribution of tasks, potentially enhancing job satisfaction and reducing burnout among physicians. At the inter-organizational level, the results highlight the clear potential of networked collaboration, particularly for handling emergency consultations, which often disrupt scheduled care. Scenarios involving dedicated doctors for emergency flows demonstrated a significant reduction in overtime hours worked when at least two physicians shared this role, although this required trade-offs in scheduled patient handling.

From a broader perspective, the study underscores the value of discrete-event simulation technologies as decision-support tools in healthcare planning. These approaches enable managers to preemptively assess the operational impact of organizational changes in a virtual environment, making them highly relevant for complex and evolving care ecosystems like rural medical homes. In terms of generalizability, the consultation time durations used in the model were calibrated based on expert opinions.

As such, these values may be specific to the case study examined and should be refined before applying the model to other providers or regions.

Future research should focus on expanding this simulation framework to include socio-demographic factors, patient outcomes, and financial performance, further supporting data-driven decision-making for policymakers and healthcare providers. Additionally, incorporating real-time data through digital twin systems offers promising avenues for adaptive, ongoing optimization of primary care delivery.

Acknowledgements. This research and publication are supported by the ERASMUS + EU Project CODEMO, CoCreative Decision Makers for 5.0 Organisations, Project Nr. 101104819, Co-funded by the European Commission.

References

1. Beckfield, J., Olafsdottir, S.: Health inequalities in global context. Am. Behav. Sci. **57**(8), 1014–1039 (2013). https://doi.org/10.1177/0002764213487343
2. Doorslaer, E., Van Masseria., C.: OECD health equity research. inequalities in access to medical care by income. Can. Med. Assoc. J. **174**(2), 177–183 (2006). https://doi.org/10.1503/cmaj.050584
3. Corscadden, L., Levesque, J.F., Lewis, V., Strumpf, E., Breton, M., Russell, G.: Factors associated with multiple barriers to access to primary care: An international analysis. Int. J. Equity Health (2018). https://doi.org/10.1186/s12939-018-0740-1
4. Ministère de la Santé et de la Prévention. Plan d'action 4 000 Maisons de Santé Pluriprofessionnelles (2023). https://Sante.Gouv.Fr/IMG/Pdf/Dp_msp.Pdf. [Accessed Feb 2025]
5. Arend, J., Tsang-Quinn, J., Levine, C., Thomas, D.: The patient-centered medical home: history, components, and review of the evidence. Mt. Sinai J. Med. J. Transl. Personalized Med. **79**(4), 433–450 (2012). https://doi.org/10.1002/msj.21326
6. Lueckmann, S.L., Hoebel, J., Roick, J., et al.: Socioeconomic inequalities in primary-care and specialist physician visits: a systematic review. Int J Equity Health. (2021). https://doi.org/10.1186/s12939-020-01375-1
7. Chevillard, G., Mousquès, J.: Les maisons de santé attirent-elles les jeunes médecins généralistes dans les zones sous-dotées en offre de soins ? Questions d'économie de la santé, IRDES (2020)
8. Cassou, M., Mousquès, J., Franc, C.: Exercer en maison de santé pluriprofessionnelle a un effet positif sur les revenus des médecins généralistes. Questions d'économie de la santé, IRDES (2021)
9. Loussouarn, C., Franc, C., Videau, Y., Mousquès, J.: The impact of a French experiment on doctor-nurse cooperation on general practitioner activity. Rev. Econ. Polit. **129**(4), 489–524 (2019)
10. Croxson, C.H., Ashdown, H.F., Hobbs, F.R.: GPs' perceptions of workload in England: a qualitative interview study. Br. J. Gen. Pract. **67**(655), e138–e147 (2017). https://doi.org/10.3399/bjgp17X688849
11. Jackson, G.L., Powers, B.J., Chatterjee, R., et al.: The patient-centered medical home. Ann. Intern. Med. **158**(3), 169–178 (2013). https://doi.org/10.7326/0003-4819-158-3-201302050-00579
12. Reid, R.J., Coleman, K., Johnson, E.A., et al.: The group health medical home at year two: cost savings, higher patient satisfaction, and less burnout for providers. Health Aff. **29**(5), 835–843 (2010). https://doi.org/10.1377/hlthaff.2010.0158
13. Sebai, J., Yatim, F.: Les maisons de santé pluriprofessionnelles en France : une dynamique réelle mais un modèle organisationnel à construire. Revue française d'administration publique. **164**(4), 887–902 (2018). https://doi.org/10.3917/rfap.164.0887
14. Rutter, H., Savona, N., Glonti, K., et al.: The need for a complex systems model of evidence for public health. Lancet. **390**(10112), 2602–2604 (2017). https://doi.org/10.1016/S0140-6736(17)31267-9
15. Huguet, M., Sarazin, M., Perrier, L., Augusto, V.: How we can reap the full benefit of teleconsultations: economic evaluation combined with a performance evaluation through a discrete-event simulation. J. Med. Internet Res. (2022). https://doi.org/10.2196/32002
16. Qiao, Y., Ran, L., Li, J.: Optimization of teleconsultation using discrete-event simulation from a data-driven perspective. Telemedicine e-Health. **26**(1), 114–125 (2020). https://doi.org/10.1089/tmj.2018.0229
17. Boyle, L.M., Marshall, A.H., Mackay, M.: A framework for developing generalisable discrete event simulation models of hospital emergency departments. Eur. J. Oper. Res. **302**(1), 337–347 (2022). https://doi.org/10.1016/j.ejor.2021.12.033

18. Doudareva, E., Carter, M.: Discrete event simulation for emergency department modelling: a systematic review of validation methods. Oper. Res. Health Care **33**, 100340 (2022). https://doi.org/10.1016/j.orhc.2022.100340
19. Le Lay, J., Augusto, V., Alfonso-Lizarazo, E., et al.: COVID-19 bed management using a two-step process mining and discrete-event simulation approach. IEEE Trans. Autom. Sci. Eng. **21**(3), 3080–3091 (2024). https://doi.org/10.1109/TASE.2023.3274847
20. Comis, M., Cleophas, C., Büsing, C.: Patients, primary care, and policy: agent-based simulation modeling for health care decision support. Health Care Manag. Sci. **24**(4), 799–826 (2021). https://doi.org/10.1007/s10729-021-09556-2
21. Pilbery, R., Smith, M., Green, J., Chalk, D., O'Keeffe, C.A.: Modelling NHS England 111 demand for primary care services: a discrete event simulation. BMJ Open **13**(9), e076203 (2023). https://doi.org/10.1136/bmjopen-2023-076203
22. Fialho, A.S., Oliveira, M.D., Sá, A.B.: Using discrete event simulation to compare the performance of family health unit and primary health care centre organizational models in Portugal. BMC Health Serv. Res. **11**(1), 274 (2011). https://doi.org/10.1186/1472-6963-11-274
23. Katsoulakis E, Wang Q, Wu H, et al. Digital twins for health: a scoping review. *NPJ Digit Med*. 2024;7(1). https://doi.org/10.1038/s41746-024-01073-0
24. Elkefi, S., Asan, O.: Digital twins for managing health care systems: rapid literature review. J. Med. Internet Res. **24**(8), e37641 (2022). https://doi.org/10.2196/37641
25. Sun, T., He, X., Li, Z.: Digital twin in healthcare: recent updates and challenges. Digit Health (2023). https://doi.org/10.1177/20552076221149651
26. Mohamed, N., Al-Jaroodi, J., Jawhar, I., Kesserwan, N.: Leveraging digital twins for healthcare systems engineering. IEEE Access **11**, 69841–69853 (2023). https://doi.org/10.1109/ACCESS.2023.3292119
27. Venkatesh, K.P., Raza, M.M., Kvedar, J.C.: Health digital twins as tools for precision medicine: considerations for computation, implementation, and regulation. NPJ Digit. Med. **5**(1), 150 (2022). https://doi.org/10.1038/s41746-022-00694-7
28. Karakra, A., Fontanili, F., Lamine, E., Lamothe, J.: A discrete event simulation-based methodology for building a digital twin of patient pathways in the hospital for near real-time monitoring and predictive simulation. Digital Twin. **2**, 1 (2022). https://doi.org/10.12688/digitaltwin.17454.1
29. Penverne, Y., Martinez, C., Cellier, N., et al.: A simulation based digital twin approach to assessing the organization of response to emergency calls. NPJ Digit. Med. **7**(1), 385 (2024). https://doi.org/10.1038/s41746-024-01392-2

Interoperable Tools for Deploying Patient Deterioration Collaborative Monitoring During Hospitalization

Joan Lario[1,2](✉), Miguel Ángel Mateo[1], Llanos Cuenca[1], and Angel Ortiz[1]

[1] Research Centre on Production Management and Engineering (CIGIP), Universitat Politècnica de València, Camino de Vera S/N, 46022 València, Spain
jlario@cigip.upv.es

[2] Department of Business Organization, Universitat Politècnica de València, València, Spain

Abstract. This paper presents a framework for interoperable hospital monitoring systems aimed at the early detection of patient deterioration during hospitalization. By integrating IoT-enabled sensors with containerized microservices, the system continuously monitors vital signs in real time. The proposed architecture enhances healthcare efficiency by automating data acquisition, processing, and alert generation, supporting evidence-based clinical decisions, and reducing reliance on manual monitoring. This approach is particularly beneficial in scenarios with limited staff availability, such as weekends or outlier admissions, and in managing infectious diseases cases, where timely monitoring and response are critical. The hospital deployment of patient monitoring deterioration solutions requires a collaborative network to design, develop and integrate the solutions. The framework incorporates scalable and low-cost hardware that uses open-source platforms like Node-RED and Docker for interoperability across devices, platforms, servers, and databases. By enabling predictive analytics, the solution improves patient outcomes, optimizes hospital resource use, and supports the transition toward smart healthcare systems. The design is proposed for medium-sized hospitals to ensure broad adoption and long-term sustainability.

Keywords: healthcare · monitoring · hospital · IoT · interoperability · data · sensor

1 Introduction

The Spanish National Health System (NHS) treats an average of 4 million patients yearly at its 310 acute care hospitals. The healthcare network has 93.199 doctors and 171.963 nurses dedicated to caring for the acute care hospital network [1]. The annual Spanish public healthcare expenditure is more than 94 billion of euros, representing 7.8% of the Gross Domestic Product (GDP). Compared with the average healthcare expenditure in the European Union, which stands at 3.562 euros per capita, Spain is located eighth in total expenditure as a percentage of GDP per capita [1]. If healthcare expenditure is

Published by Springer Nature Switzerland AG 2026
L. M. Camarinha-Matos et al. (Eds.): PRO-VE 2025, IFIP AICT 770, pp. 379–393, 2026.
https://doi.org/10.1007/978-3-032-05673-3_23

evaluated based on functional classification, it can be seen that the largest percentage is covered by hospital and specialised services, with an annual amount exceeding 55 billion euros [1]. This represented more than 60% of the total consolidated expenditure in 2022 (Fig. 1), hence the importance of its efficiency and cost reduction through operational management tools. Hospital services encompass healthcare provided in hospitals or specialised centres, including hospitalisation, diagnosis, treatment, surgery, consultations, and emergencies. According to the latest data from the Active Population Survey (EPA) conducted by the National Statistics Institute, more than 200.000 medical professionals work in the public sector, of which 171.963 (77.7%) work in hospitals [2]. Staff compensation is the most significant percentage of healthcare expenditure (Fig. 2), accounting for over 40% of the total cost [1]. Therefore, a reduction in the costs of medical and nursing staff will also lead to a significant reduction in total hospital costs and, consequently, in healthcare expenditures. Over the last five years (2017–2021), Spanish healthcare spending has grown at an annual rate of 5.8%, reaching 2.789 € per capita in 2021.

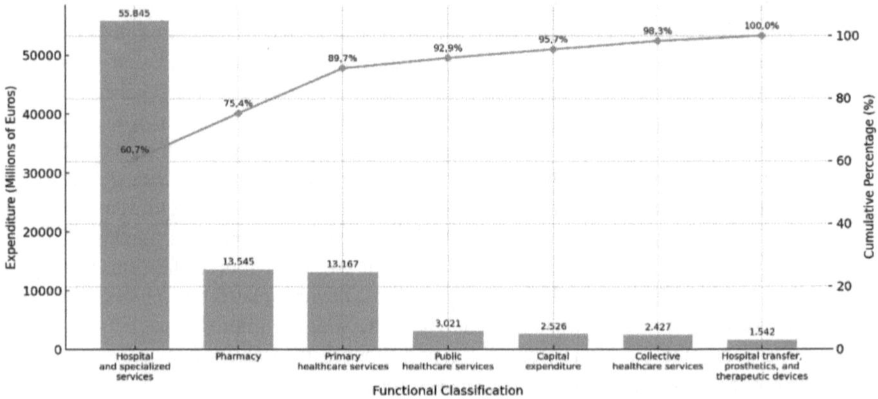

Fig. 1. Consolidated public healthcare expenditure by functional classification (millions €) (Adapted from: Informe Anual del Sistema Nacional de Salud 2023, Min. Sanidad Gobierno de España).

Developing digital solutions for patient monitoring during hospitalisation may decrease the workload assigned to medical personnel and the related cost associated. The patient-centred monitoring solutions based on non-invasive sensors and algorithms for early warning systems can create a safe, dynamic, and real-time decision-making for a collaborative working environment between humans and IoT systems [3, 4]. A deterioration in a patient's health during hospitalisation can increase hospital stays and even lead to admission to intensive care units (ICUs). ICU admission presents a higher mortality rate (6.6%) compared with other services, and the average ICU stay is 5.1 days, increasing the total patient hospitalisation and the consumption of physical and human resources and their cost [5]. Both consequences increase healthcare costs. The hospital mortality rate currently stands at 5.3%, but this can vary significantly during the week or on weekends/holidays, increasing the personal workload and even introducing deficiencies and/or lack of quality in the provided services, as will be analysed in more detail in the following subsection. On the other hand, assessing the tangible effect on healthcare resource burden following the acute infection episode holds paramount significance, given its implications for the resources that healthcare systems must allocate [6].

The National Health System (NHS) has launched the Digital Transformation Plan for Primary and Community Care as a strategic initiative coordinated by the Ministry of Health in collaboration with the autonomous communities [7]. This plan is part of the Digital Health Strategy 2021–2026. The collaborative effort seeks to modernize primary care, improve the efficiency of healthcare management, and deliver high-quality digital services to citizens. One of the work lines focuses on patient telemonitoring, aiming to establish a unified conceptual framework and standardized methodology. This includes defining both the technical and functional requirements of the telemonitoring platform and its components [7].

1.1 Hospital Care

In 2022, the NHS network had 751 hospitals, with 126.000 beds installed and 114.641 beds in operation (Table 1). Based on their healthcare purpose, hospitals within the Spanish NHS are divided into 69% acute care hospitals and 31% long-stay hospitals, with slight variations over the last decade [2]. The distribution of hospitals based on the number of available beds is summarized in Table 1, where 70% of them have fewer than 200 beds installed [2].

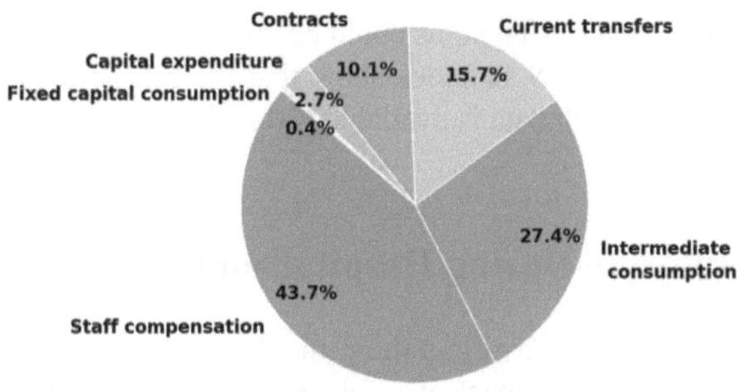

Fig. 2. Consolidated public health expenditure by economic classification (millions of euros) (Adapted from: Informe Anual del Sistema Nacional de Salud 2023, Min. Sanidad del Gobierno de España).

When analysing hospitalisation volume based on hospital size, medium-sized hospitals (200 to 1.000 beds) have the highest volume of hospitalisations, accounting for 64% of the total. This means they receive more than 2.3 million patients annually, of which 72% were urgent and 28% were scheduled. This percentage of urgent hospitalizations highlights the likelihood of complications during admission, affecting the quality of care, treatment and its results during admission.

The average cost per discharge is estimated at 5.158 € per patient for 2022 [5]. Hence, it is important to implement improvements in its operational management through digital

Table 1. Total number of hospitals by size 2022 (number of installed beds). (Adapted from: Informe Anual del Sistema Nacional de Salud 2023, Ministerio de Sanidad del Gobierno de España).

Hospitals by size	Number of hospitals	Number of hospital discharges by hospital size
Hospitals with fewer than 200 beds	534 (71%)	581.998 (16%)
Hospitals with between 200 and 500 beds	141 (19%)	1.160.043 (32%)
Hospitals with between 501 and 1.000 beds	58 (8%)	1.177.401 (32%)
Hospitals with more than 1.000 beds	18 (2%)	743.981 (20%)
Total	751	3.663.423

solutions that allow patient monitoring to prevent deterioration, improve healthcare, and reduce average hospital stays, with the consequent most efficient use possible of medical and physical personnel resources. Linking these solutions to the scalability needs of medium-sized hospitals is essential to ensure their effective adoption and long-term sustainability. It should be noted that the average hospital stay depends on the pathology suffered, which is, on average, 7.8 days. Therefore, the annual turnover rate in NHS hospitals is 34.9 patients per bed, a 2.2% reduction over 10 years [2]. Another indicator related to monitoring patients' vital signs could be the rate of readmissions to acute care hospitals. Current Spanish NHS statistics show that the rate of readmissions stood at 8.4% in the last year for which data is available (2022), with a slight upward trend over the last decade [1].

2 Patient Monitoring During Hospitalization

It is essential to systematically assess patient incidents during hospitalization, particularly in failure to rescue, the impact of weekend admissions, and outlier admissions. Identifying and documenting changes in a patient's condition, potential causes, and severity is critical for timely intervention. Medical and nursing staff play a vital role in continuously monitoring patients' clinical status to recognize early signs of deterioration. Establishing clear digital records of these incidents facilitates appropriate clinical responses, enhances patient safety, supports accountability, and improves outcomes through more informed decision-making and resource allocation. This will require capturing, transmitting, and evaluating the patient's health status in real time. Monitoring systems will enable this.

Recent developments in electronic devices, Internet of Things (IOT) and software enable the creation of interoperable solutions for healthcare vital sign monitoring, with the consequent increase in the quality of healthcare services and greater speed in detecting incidents in the evolution of the patient's health status [8]. By capturing data from

Table 2. Physiological parameters to monitor patient deterioration (Adapted from:[9]).

Vital parameter	Value (Severity Level)
Body temperature (^{0}C)	≤35 (High); 35,1–36 (Low); 36,1–38, 0 (Normal); 38,1–39,0 (Low); 39,1–40 (Medium); ≥40 (High)
Oxygen saturation (%)	≤91 (High); 92–93(Medium); 94–95 (Low); ≥96 (Normal)
Systolic blood pressure (mmHg)	≤90 (High); 91–100 (Low); 101–140 (Normal); 141–180 (Low); 181–200 (Medium); ≥211 (High)
Heart rate (BPM)	≤40 (High); 41–50 (Low); 51–90 (Normal); 91–110 (Low); 111–149 (Medium); ≥150 (High)
Respiratory rate (BPM)	≤8 (High); 9–11(Low); 12–20 (Normal); 21–24 (Low); 25–30 (Medium); ≥30 (High)

different sensors or devices, the patient's health condition can be captured, transmitted and evaluated under real-time conditions. The vital sign monitoring systems have the potential to detect adverse events which can lead to unplanned care escalation, demanding a reassignment of medical and nursing staff as well as medical equipment and physical resources. IoT devices have the potential to inform healthcare providers of the potential for the development of medical complications during hospitalisation.

Patient monitoring data can be considered a critical resource for enhancing personalized healthcare, enabling improved patient care and clinical evaluation. Key enablers include automated data collection and interoperable tools. Addressing future healthcare challenges will rely on digital-intensive solutions that facilitate efficient data access, sharing, and analysis. These technologies aim to integrate patients and diverse healthcare professionals into cohesive, data-driven care ecosystems thanks to the development of these solutions in a collaborative network. Collaborative networks involving administration, healthcare professionals, technological providers, and research centers, among other stakeholders involved, are expected to develop and integrate patient deterioration services [4, 10].

2.1 Manual Monitoring

Manual vital sign monitoring relies on health personnel to record the vital signs [11]. These health records are usually done in paper form, and present the drawback of requiring time to search, retrieve, update patient information records and calculate warning indicators, with the consequent consumption of medical and nursing personnel resources and the reduction of their available quantity. The patients hospitalised in different clinical areas can suffer adverse events during their stay, the early detection of these changes may avoid the adverse clinical events. Nursing staff monitor the patient's status by recording the vital signs on a daily basis to identify, through warning score indicators, the patient´s risk of deterioration. These vital-sign measurements are typically recorded every 6, or 12, or 24 hours (Table 2). It can be considered that the manual monitoring of patients' vital signs is a labour-intensive task that requires specialised medical staff to carry out, decreasing their availability to perform other healthcare activities [12]. Table 2 summarises physiological parameters to monitor patient deterioration and evaluate the severity of the medical conditions. Apart from the classification of several parameters, the variable of time is also an important parameter to consider in order to evaluate the patient's deterioration. Under this scope, the implementation digital solutions for monitoring patient's can enhance the evaluation due to the inclusion of time series. Implementing time series analysis into digital solutions or devices can enhance the critical role in evaluating and monitoring hospitalised patients. Assessing the dynamic progression of vital signs and clinical parameters. It enables early detection of physiological deterioration, supports evidence-based decision-making, and facilitates real-time response to acute changes or changes produced over the inspection timeframe.

2.2 Failure to Rescue in Hospital Care

Failure to Rescue in hospital care can be defined as a death that occurs after a patient suffers a complication during their hospitalization that was not present at the time of admission. If the patient's deterioration goes unnoticed for several hours, it can result in higher hospitalisation lengths, acuity care and admission costs [13]. The study carried out by J. Vicent et al. (2018) highlighted an elevated patient mortality when vital sign monitoring was performed on timeframes 24-16 h than 16-8 h or 8-0h, before triggering medical emergency teams (MET) [14]. After 24 h of MET event, forty per cent of patients are transferred to a High Dependency Unit (HDU) or Intensive Care Unit (ICU), with the consequent decrease in the availability of their significantly high-cost medical resources. Davis et al. (2002) analysed the failure to rescue during hospital admission, where 2% resulted in patient death. Ghaferi et al. (2009) categorised the factors that impact the failure to rescue, focusing on the prompt recognition of the vital sign deterioration and the clinical response to manage the treatment [15]. The development of devices and the integration of interoperable tools will allow the development of digital patient deterioration monitoring solutions during hospitalization. Automating data acquisition and evaluating vital signs will enhance prompt response after patient deterioration.

2.3 Impact of Weekends or Holidays on Services

The differential allocation of hospital resources on weekends directly impacts mortality, compared to regular, daily patient care during the week. This fact has been studied by several researchers, where the norm is that patients hospitalized on weekends or holidays receive poorer medical care, with longer wait times for tests or interventions [16]. This leads to a 16% increase in mortality due to the well-known weekend phenomenon [17, 18]. This increase in mortality is caused by several factors, such as delayed diagnostic and therapeutic testing, the use of hospitalisations on holidays or weekends, and a reduction in the number of professionals (physicians, nurses, or non-medical staff), with the resulting problem of excessive workload for performing tests and measurements of vital signs, with its influence on the healthcare of patients and their medical treatment [19]. The reduction in healthcare resources on weekends is more likely to cause adverse events related to patient health, leading to an increase in the average length of stay, lower availability of specific resources for other treatments and, consequently, an increase in hospitalization costs [20, 21]. This inequality necessitates the search for technological solutions that allow the healthcare system to be agile, flexible, and innovative to improve the service provided during hospitalisation.

2.4 Outlier Admissions

An outlier patient is an admission not assigned to a unit that corresponds to the medical service that treats their condition. These admissions in other ward may be affected by the distribution of beds in the departments, seasonal variations, or epidemiological effects. This type of admission disrupts the normal functioning of medical services or nursing units, as they have to deal with new treatment guidelines from other specialities or lack the skills or training for daily work.

The study by Cabrera et al. (2019) highlights the increase in the average stay, with the consequent decrease in the availability of medical personnel resources and physical equipment as well as the mortality rate of outlier admissions compared to non-outlier admissions. This study evaluated more than 11.000 admissions and found that the average stay for outlier admissions was 13% longer, with a mean stay of 8.11 days [22]. These patients, who are placed in other hospital units or services, increase the workload of nurses or other healthcare professionals, increasing travel time, delaying diagnostic testing, and changing visiting hours. Integrating medical devices, supported with interoperable tools for scalability in medium-sized hospitals, may help mitigate these challenges by enabling automated monitoring of vital signs, which is especially beneficial when patients are located in units not specialised in their condition. This approach, enhanced with clinical decision-support algorithms and automated communication of patient deterioration, facilitates timely interventions and reduces the dependency on physical presence for status updates. Together, these technologies can alleviate the additional workload imposed on healthcare staff by outlier admissions, promoting more efficient and safer patient management across inappropriate ward.

3 IoT Patient Deterioration Monitoring

Thanks to the Internet of Things (IoT), the field of healthcare is making significant advancements in gathering and processing high-quality data [23]. The development of this remote patient monitoring can measure health conditions such as body temperature, heart rate, oxygen saturation, respiratory rate and blood pressure. The interoperability of remote patient monitoring systems enables the deployment of digital solutions in public hospitals for improving patient care. This digital solution for patient monitoring based on data collection present major challenges, including data privacy and information exchange related to medical regulations.

This paper aims to serve as a reference and guide for designing and deploying automation and supervision systems within the context of Industry 4.0. it focuses on implementing vital signs sensors to monitor patient deterioration and proposes an interoperable architecture that facilitates the integration of various sensor-based data collection devices to improve healthcare delivery.

3.1 Hospital Health Monitoring Framework

The proposed framework aims to improve the interoperability of different sensors, tools, and algorithms to deploy a solution for monitoring patient deterioration during hospitalization. This tool is designed to improve nursing performance by facilitating the capture of vital signs in real time, data processing for decision-making, and an alert system to notify healthcare professionals during patient deterioration. The aim is to improve healthcare information's widespread interoperability, boosting patient health-related data analytics.

The proposed architecture aims to integrate sensors with IoT devices in medium- to large-scale hospitals that can measure patient vital signs and perform analytics to improve personalised care (Fig. 3). By deploying microservices that integrate different sensors responsible for capturing vital signs, and their interoperability with different tools, platforms, or operating systems, healthcare can be tailored to the patient's needs. The development of these solutions requires a multidisciplinary team of different branches of science, from computer science, electronics, telecommunications, and manufacturing engineering to medical professionals, to address the complex challenges of developing a patient monitoring solution.

Figure 3 illustrates the proposed architecture of an inpatient monitoring system. This system integrates sensors and devices with a central server, enabling real-time health monitoring and the early detection of clinical deterioration. Leveraging Internet of Things (IoT) principles ensures the system is interoperable, scalable and reliable within the hospital infrastructure. Various physiological sensors, including temperature, pulse and oximetry sensors, continuously monitor patients' vital signs. These sensors transmit the data to a local device in the room via the relevant communication protocols. If the device is within close range and low power consumption is a consideration, Bluetooth is used. If a longer range is required, Wi-Fi can be used, or wired communication (LAN) can be used as an alternative for severe cases where continuous data flow must be guaranteed in case of wireless interruptions.

The room device acts as an edge unit capable of initial data management and protocol translation. Supporting a wide range of devices, including Intel Edison, Arduino, Raspberry Pi and NVIDIA Jetson, it allows flexibility in hardware selection based on performance and cost requirements. These platforms can run services in Docker containers, providing an isolated, modular environment for system components.

Node-RED is used as a visual programming tool to facilitate sensor integration, workflow automation, and communication with external systems. Data from the room devices is transmitted to a centralised server via standard protocols such as HTTP and MQTT. The server orchestrates the entire monitoring workflow. It collects and processes incoming data via Node-RED and Apache Kafka, enabling the handling of various data streams. The server also hosts analytical models, typically developed in Python, which calculate clinical risks based on trends in patients' vital signs. This architecture provides a global view of how acquisition nodes operate, connected to a gateway or central server with greater processing capacity. This improves interoperability and information sharing within the hospital infrastructure. The data acquired with the several sensors can be recorded temporarily in an array or recorded in a database; this information can be

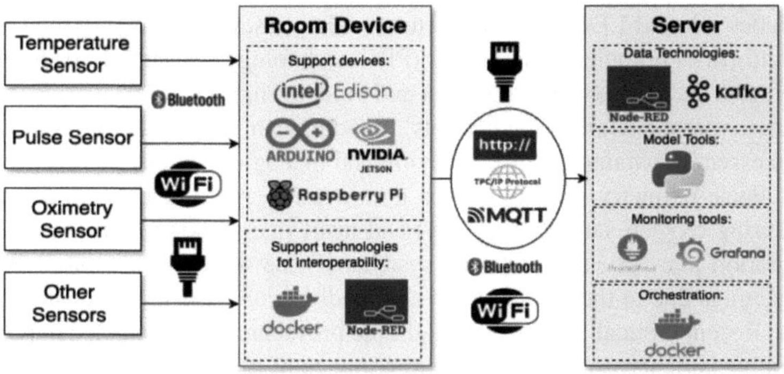

Fig. 3. Interoperable patient deterioration monitoring framework.

employed to calculate the early warning system indicators, and the dashboard to monitor the patient's condition during their hospitalisation period.

3.2 Sensor Data Sources

Current electronic sensors or devices to measure some vital signs lack interoperability and require the development of an architecture for communication, data exchange, evaluation and implementation of algorithms for decision-making. The integration of microservices on the patient's monitoring solutions enables the deployment of low-power, compact and cost-effective systems which can acquire the patient´s vital parameters. The integration of non-invasive sensors to measure heart rate, SpO2, and body temperature can be employed to reduce the workload of health professionals [24].

Temperature sensor. Body temperature measurement is essential to monitor the patient's status during hospitalisation. Several types of sensors can be employed to acquire the body temperature. The precision analogue sensor offers a linear voltage output proportional to temperature in °C [25]. The infrared-based non-contact sensor (MLX90615) provides high-resolution (0.02 °C) and accurate temperature readings via two thermopile detectors and an onboard signal processor [26]. The digital sensor (DS18B20) can measure the temperature across a —55 °C to 125 °C range [27]. These sensors enable reliable, low-power temperature acquisition, with data processed by a microcontroller that digitises outputs for further storage and analysis.

Pulse Sensor. Heart rate monitoring is used to evaluate the patient's health conditions and to detect cardiovascular conditions early. The optoelectronic pulse sensors are employed to measure heartbeats non-invasively and continuously. These sensors emit infrared (IR) light through tissue, typically the fingertip or wrist, and detect variations in blood volume with each heartbeat, based on the intensity of reflected or transmitted light. The sensors utilise IR LEDs and photodiodes to detect blood flow. As blood volume increases, more light is absorbed, altering the photodiode's resistance and generating voltage changes. These are processed by comparators or amplifiers like the LM358 and MCP6001 to derive beats per minute (BPM) [25, 26]. Commercial pulse sensors, such as those integrating APDS-9008 and MAX30102 components, offer compact designs and compatibility with wearable systems via I2C communication [26]. The MAX30102 also includes internal LEDs, photodetectors, and optics, making it suitable for mobile health platforms. Photoplethysmography (PPG) technology also applies to physiological measurements such as oxygen saturation and volume changes.

Oximetry sensor. Monitoring patients' blood oxygen saturation during hospitalisation is an essential parameter for identifying and managing various medical conditions [28–30]. Pulse oximetry sensors offer a non-invasive, rapid, and continuous method for measuring oxygen saturation (SpO_2) and heart rate, making them highly suitable for integration into patient monitoring systems. These sensors are commonly used in clinical settings due to their ease of use and feedback on patient oxygenation status in real time. Recent clinical findings highlight the prevalence of undetected hypoxemia in postoperative patients, emphasising the importance of continuous SpO_2 monitoring to support timely medical intervention and improved patient outcomes [31].

3.3 Room Devices

The room device will be employed to connect the different sensors to measure the vital signs, and the deployment of the microservices will enable the interoperability between the database, algorithms and operating systems. The integration of technologies like Node-RED and Docker within the microcontroller-based devices allows for efficient data transmission over local networks or the internet, enhancing interoperability and data sharing across the hospital infrastructure. Devices such as the Raspberry Pi, Arduino, Jetson Nano or Intel EDISON support the deployment of microservices using commercially available solutions, including containerization through Docker and visual data orchestration via Node-RED [12, 24, 25, 30]. This module gathers data measured from different sensors installed and enables communication with other solutions through IoT.

3.4 Containerization Technologies

The integration of virtualisation technologies such as Docker containers enables efficient resource utilisation; SO, sensor and database interoperability for advanced implementation with low management cost. Containers provide portability, efficient deployment, scalability, and minimal overhead [32, 33]. These executable packages operate in isolation from other systems on host machines [34]. Docker Containers enable a lightweight, portable solution for executing applications or solutions in isolated environments for patient vital sign monitoring. The security of applications deployed on fog nodes is enhanced by containerizing the data and resources. Docker can be utilized for data processing and to maintain cross-platform compatibility, ensuring the system functions reliably across various devices and operating systems. They enhance interoperability for systems and services while improving deployment, scalability, and redundancy capabilities [33, 35]. In health monitoring systems, containers facilitate the use of microservices, and they are also widely adopted in IoT architectures and Fog/Cloud computing. The Docker technology has been employed in the current framework to containerise the solution, allowing it to run on most devices and operating systems.

3.5 Microservices

Integrating microservices that enable interoperability between sensors, algorithms, and digital platforms improves the healthcare information system, enhancing data exchange between stakeholders and decision-making, which improves hospital management. The Node-RED event-driven application offers several key advantages: it is compatible with software containers, it can run on most lightweight devices, it supports the collaborative development of event-driven applications, and it facilitates the seamless import and export of workflows [36]. The aim of the event-driven solution is to integrate sensors and microservices to improve data exchange, analytics and decision-making for deploying solutions based on patient monitoring to more personalise care. The deployment of microservices enables the creation of general pipelines between sensors, devices, the databases and algorithms for processing the vital signs to support the patient monitoring.

To improve the remote patient´s monitoring, the data acquired from the sensor through the microcontroller needs to be transmitted to the central station for storage or evaluation. By using several communications protocols, the collected data is transmitted to the central station, where the microservices are deployed for implementing health care indicators and communication to medical staff. The communication between sensors that gather patient vital signs, installed on-premise in the hospital room, and the cloud or server infrastructure is achieved through an open-source Node-RED low-code platform. Node-RED supports a wide range of communication protocols, enabling seamless data exchange with various types of devices or sensors, including PLCs through industrial protocols such as OPC, Modbus TCP, PROFINET, MQTT, and others [33, 37]. Additionally, Node-RED can integrate with both SQL and NoSQL databases to query, retrieve, or store data [34, 37]. It also has the capability to interact with medical databases for enhanced functionality and interoperability.

3.6 Monitoring Services and Indicators

Integrating information and decision-making systems can reduce the average stay by improving the use of healthcare resources and developing clinical practice. The objective is to develop a framework that identifies complex events (patient health deterioration), extracts meaningful insights by executing spatial-temporal data mining algorithms, and deploys early warning systems. Additionally, the system will incorporate components for data visualisation and automated alert generation to improve patient care and the operational performance of health professionals.

The early warning indicator acquires several vital signs (heart rate, blood oxygen saturation (SpO_2), respiratory rate, cuffless systolic and diastolic blood pressure (SBP and DBP), body temperature, stroke volume (SV), cardiac output, and systemic vascular resistance (SVR)) to track a patient´s progression over the hospitalisation period [9]. These types of indicators will be developed and implemented in the proposed patient deterioration monitoring thanks to the deployment of Docker and event-driven technologies. Healthcare innovation demands cross-sector knowledge integration, requiring diverse actors to work within a collaborative network to address technological and compliance challenges for patient monitoring deterioration tools [38–40]. For vital sign monitoring, a threshold level for each vital sign will be created. When the parameter reaches a value, it will set an alarm, and the nursing staff has to perform a specific evaluation or intervention [9]. This characteristic will allow the solution to evaluate and quantify the abnormal events to avoid errors in reading that may lead to alarm fatigue. The warning system based on vital signal monitoring should be created to recognise the evolution of patient health and timely detect and trigger the clinical response when a deterioration has occurred [30]. Once the hospitalised patient has developed deterioration, a warning should be generated to trigger an immediate response by the medical staff. This monitoring solution will address several compliance requirements to collect and analyse patient data, requiring service providers and public institutions' participation and collaborative effort [38, 41, 42].

4 Conclusions

This study presents an interoperable, IoT-based framework for real-time monitoring of hospitalised patients to detect early signs of clinical deterioration. The proposed system enables efficient, scalable deployment within hospital infrastructures—particularly in medium-sized facilities, by integrating low-cost sensors, microcontroller platforms, and containerised microservices. The architecture supports real-time data acquisition, transmission, and processing of vital signs, allowing medical staff to make timely, informed decisions. This approach has the potential to reduce failure-to-rescue events, ICU admissions, and extended hospital stays, especially in high-risk situations such as weekend or outlier admissions. The system also reduces the burden on healthcare professionals by automating data collection and alert generation, enhancing care quality and operational efficiency.

Additionally, using open-source platforms like Node-RED and Docker improves system interoperability, scalability, and ease of integration with existing hospital systems. Future work will focus on validating this framework in clinical settings and enhancing predictive analytics capabilities. The proposed solution represents a significant step toward data-driven, proactive hospital care in the context of innovative healthcare systems.

References

1. Ministerio de Sanidad Informe Anual Del Sistema Nacional de Salud 2022. Departamento de Salud pp. 218–236 (2023)
2. Sanidad, M.D.E.: Sistema nacional de Salud, 2023. (2024)
3. Gomes, J.F., Iivari, M., Koivumäki, T., Immonen, M., Jansson, M., Pikkarainen, M., Rasmus, K., Xu, Y.: Care Pathway as the Basis for Collaborative Business Model Innovation in Healthcare; Springer International Publishing, Vol. 662 IFIP, (2022). ISBN 9783031148439
4. Dias, C., Escoval, A.: The open nature of innovation in the hospital sector: the role of external collaboration networks. Health Policy Technol. **1**, 181–186 (2012). https://doi.org/10.1016/j.hlpt.2012.10.002
5. Ministerio de Sanidad Registro de Actividad Sanitaria Especializada (RAE-CMBD): Actividad y Resultados de La Hospitalización En El SNS. Año (2020)
6. Valdivieso-Martinez, B., et al.: Impact of long SARS-CoV-2 omicron infection on the health care burden: comparative case-control study between omicron and pre-omicron waves. JMIR Public Health Surveill. **10**, e53580 (2024). https://doi.org/10.2196/53580

7. Secretaria General de Salud Digital, I. e I. para el S. Estrategia de Salud Digital. Sistema Nacional de Salud. Ministerio de Sanidad. Gobierno de España (2021)
8. Vitabile, S., et al.: Medical data processing and analysis for remote health and activities monitoring. Springer Int. Publ. (2019)
9. Eisenkraft, A., et al.: Developing a real-time detection tool and an early warning score using a continuous wearable multi-parameter monitor. Front. Physiol. **14**, 1–11 (2023). https://doi.org/10.3389/fphys.2023.1138647
10. Morley, J., Murphy, L., Mishra, A., Joshi, I., Karpathakis, K.: Governing data and Artificial Intelligence for health care: developing an international understanding. JMIR Form. Res. **6**, 1–13 (2022). https://doi.org/10.2196/31623
11. Ramalingam, M., Puviarasi, R., Chinnavan, E., Foong, H.K.: Self-monitoring framework for patients in IoT-based healthcare system. Int. J. Innovative Technol. Exploring Eng. **8**, 3641–3645 (2019). https://doi.org/10.35940/ijitee.L3813.1081219
12. Nayyar, A., Puri, V., Nguyen, N.G.: BioSenHealth 1.0: a novel internet of medical things (IoMT)-based patient health monitoring system. Springer Singapore (2019). Vol. 55; ISBN 9789811323249
13. Seitz-Rasmussen, H.E.S., Føns-Sønderskov, M., Kodal, A.M., Bestle, M.H.: Improving patient outcomes following vital sign monitoring protocol failure: a retrospective cohort study. Health Sci. Rep. **7**, 1–7 (2024). https://doi.org/10.1002/hsr2.1754
14. New Zealand Nurses Organization Failure to Rescue: A New Zealand Nursing Perspective. **2012**, 1–10 (2012)
15. Hastings-Tolsma, M., Nolte, A.G.W.: Reconceptualising failure to rescue in midwifery: a concept analysis. Midwifery **30**, 585–594 (2014). https://doi.org/10.1016/j.midw.2014.02.005
16. Zambrana-García, J.L., Granados, C.J., Zambrana-Luque, J.L.: Mortalidad y Atención a Pacientes Hospitalizados Durante Los Fines de Semana. Rev. Calid. Asist. **32**, 248–254 (2017). https://doi.org/10.1016/j.cali.2017.07.001
17. Zambrana García, J.L.: Alternativas al exceso de mortalidad hospitalaria prematura en fines de semana. Med. Clin. (Barc.) **127**, 77 (2006). https://doi.org/10.1157/13090000
18. Aylin, P., Yunus, A., Bottle, A., Majeed, A., Bell, D.: Weekend mortality for emergency admissions. a large, multicentre study. Qual Saf Health Care **19**, 213–217 (2010)https://doi.org/10.1136/qshc.2008.028639
19. Aldridge, C., et al.: Weekend specialist intensity and admission mortality in acute hospital trusts in england: a cross-sectional study. Lancet **388**, 178–186 (2016). https://doi.org/10.1016/S0140-6736(16)30442-1
20. Barba, R., Losa, J.E., Velasco, M., Zapatero, A.: Mortality among patients admitted to hospitals on weekends [1]. Med. Clin. (Barc.) **125**, 794 (2005). https://doi.org/10.1016/s0025-7753(05)72192-8
21. Pauls, L.A., Johnson-Paben, R., McGready, J., Murphy, J.D., Pronovost, P.J., Wu, C.L.: The weekend effect in hospitalized patients: a meta-analysis. J. Hosp. Med. **12**, 760–766 (2017). https://doi.org/10.12788/jhm.2815
22. Cabrera Torres, E., García Iglesias, M.A., Santos Jiménez, M.T., González Hierro, M., Diego Domínguez, M.L.: Los Ingresos Ectópicos y Su Relación Con La Aparición de Complicaciones y Estancias Prolongadas. Gac. Sanit. **33**, 32–37 (2019). https://doi.org/10.1016/j.gaceta.2017.07.012
23. Afifi, S., Emad, A., Taha, R., Baig, M.: An efficient IoT-based mobile application for continuous monitoring of patients. 2023 IEEE EMBS Special Topic Conference on Data Science and Engineering in Healthcare, Medicine and Biology, IEEECONF **2023**, 165–166 (2023). https://doi.org/10.1109/IEEECONF58974.2023.10404207
24. Basu, S., Ghosh, M., Barman (Mandal), S.: Raspberry PI 3B+ based smart remote health monitoring system using IoT platform. Springer Singapore, (2020) Vol. 602, ISBN 9789811508288

25. Krishnan, D.S.R., Gupta, S.C., Choudhury, T.: An IoT based patient health monitoring system. Proceedings on 2018 International Conference on Advances in Computing and Communication Engineering, ICACCE 2018, pp. 1–7 (2018). https://doi.org/10.1109/ICACCE.2018.8441708
26. Wu, T., Wu, F., Redoute, J.M., Yuce, M.R.: An autonomous wireless body area network implementation towards IoT connected healthcare applications. IEEE Access **5**, 11413–11422 (2017). https://doi.org/10.1109/ACCESS.2017.2716344
27. Mararif, M.R., Priyanto, A., Setiawan, C.B., Winar Cahyo, P.: The design of cost efficient health monitoring system based on internet of things and big data. 9th International Conference on Information and Communication Technology Convergence: ICT Convergence Powered by Smart Intelligence, ICTC 2018, pp. 52–57 (2018)https://doi.org/10.1109/ICTC.2018.8539374
28. Vincent, J.L., et al.: Improving detection of patient deterioration in the general hospital ward environment. Eur. J. Anaesthesiol. **35**, 325–333 (2018). https://doi.org/10.1097/EJA.0000000000000798
29. Rangasamy, S., Rajamohan, K., Basu, D., Menezes, K.J., Chongder, A.: Revolutionizing healthcare with IoT: connecting the dots for better patient outcomes. AI and IoT Technology and Applications for Smart Healthcare Systems pp. 204–223 (2024) https://doi.org/10.1201/9781032686745-13
30. Senbagavalli, M., Singh, S.K.: Improving patient health in smart healthcare monitoring systems using IoT. 2022 International Conference on Futuristic Technologies, INCOFT 2022 **2022**, 1–7 (2022). https://doi.org/10.1109/INCOFT55651.2022.10094409
31. Yaakob, N., Almashor, M., Muhammed Ahmed, A.F.: Cost effective IoT-based remote healthcare monitoring system for developing countries. Proceedings - 5th IEEE International Conference on Smart Internet of Things, SmartIoT 2021 **2021**, 13–20 (2021). https://doi.org/10.1109/SmartIoT52359.2021.00012
32. Kousiouris, G., Kyriazis, D.: Enabling containerized, parametric and distributed database deployment and benchmarking as a service. ICPE 2021 - Companion of the ACM/SPEC Inter Confer on Performance Engineering, pp. 77–80 (2021). https://doi.org/10.1145/3447545.3451188
33. Soderi, M., Kamath, V., Morgan, J., Breslin, J.G.: Advanced Analytics as a Service in Smart Factories. SAMI 2022 - IEEE 20th Jubilee World Symposium on Applied Machine Intelligence and Informatics, Proceedings pp. 425–430 (2022). https://doi.org/10.1109/SAMI54271.2022.9780768
34. Tansangworn, N.: Development of IoT edge hub for wireless sensor networks based on docker container. Proceedings - 2020 IEEE International Conference on Smart Internet of Things, SmartIoT 2020, pp. 356–357 (2020). https://doi.org/10.1109/SmartIoT49966.2020.00068
35. Pérez, A., Moltó, G., Caballer, M., Calatrava, A.: Serverless computing for container-based architectures. Futur. Gener. Comput. Syst. **83**, 50–59 (2018). https://doi.org/10.1016/j.future.2018.01.022
36. Rosa-Bilbao, J., Boubeta-Puig, J., Rutle, A.: EDALoCo: enhancing the accessibility of blockchains through a low-code approach to the development of event-driven applications for smart contract management. Comput. Stand. Interfaces **84**, 103676 (2023). https://doi.org/10.1016/j.csi.2022.103676
37. Folgado, F.J., Calderón, D., González, I., Calderón, A.J.: Review of Industry 4.0 from the perspective of automation and supervision systems: definitions, architectures and recent trends. Electronics (Switzerland) (2024). https://doi.org/10.3390/electronics13040782
38. Lario, J.; Mateos, J.; Poler, R., Ortiz, Á.: Collaborative network for the development of non-destructive inspection technologies: elicitation requirements in an industrial environment. Springer Nature Switzerland (2023). Vol. 688 AICT, ISBN 9783031426216

39. Pessot, E., De Togni, G.: A framework for the collaborative evaluation of service outsourcing contracts in pharmaceutical logistics. Springer Int. Publ. (2020). Vol. 598, ISBN 9783030624118
40. Camarinha-Matos, L.M., Afsarmanesh, H.: The evolution path to collaborative networks 4.0. Springer Int. Publ. Vol. 600 (2021). https://doi.org/10.1007/978-3-030-81701-5_7
41. Kraus, S., Schiavone, F., Pluzhnikova, A., Invernizzi, A.C.: Digital transformation in healthcare: analyzing the current state-of-research. J. Bus. Res. **123**, 557–567 (2021). https://doi.org/10.1016/j.jbusres.2020.10.030
42. Petersen, S.A., Evjen, T.Å., Hosseini Raviz, S.R., Krogstie, J.: Leveraging on enterprise building information models in health care services: the case of St. Olav University Hospital. IFIP Adv. Inf. Commun. Technol. 598, 644–653 (2020). https://doi.org/10.1007/978-3-030-62412-5_53

Design of a Sustainable Food Waste Management System for Collaborative Healthcare Facilities

Safa Chabouh[1](✉), Imen Bouajila[2], Ghassen Abid[2], Helmi Ben Amara[3], and Sondes Hammami[1,4]

[1] LR11ES20 Analysis, Conception and Control of Systems Laboratory, Tunis El Manar University, National Engineering School of Tunis, 1002 Tunis, Tunisia
safa.chabouh@enit.utm.tn
[2] National Engineering School of Tunis, Tunis, Tunisia
[3] Bi'nergy, Tunis, Tunisia
[4] Carthage University, National Engineering School of Carthage, Ariana, Tunisia

Abstract. Healthcare institutions generate significant amounts of food waste, which poses both environmental and operational challenges. This work proposes a shared food waste valorization system for two nearby hospitals. Based on the estimated annual volume of food waste from one hospital, we extrapolate to a joint system serving both facilities. The objective is to assess the amount of energy that can be generated through anaerobic digestion and to size the digestive equipment accordingly. Our approach supports the transition toward greener hospital infrastructure and promotes resource sharing between healthcare entities. The system is designed to be adaptable and scalable, forming the basis for a collaborative and circular healthcare network. This contribution aligns with the goals of Healthcare 4.0 and 5.0 by integrating sustainability, digital modeling, and decision-support elements in the configuration of health infrastructure.

Keyword: Circular Economy · Food waste. Sustainability · Hospitals · Collaboration

1 Introduction

According to the FAO, food waste (FW) refers to the reduction in quantity or quality of edible food intended for human consumption throughout the supply chain, including at the consumption level such as food services and household [1]. A distinction should be made between food losses, which happen earlier in the supply chain due to factors like climate, disease, or poor infrastructure [2], and FW, which occurs at the retail and consumption stages through the discarding of still-edible items. This paper focuses on FW. FW poses serious environmental, economic, and social challenges—contributing to environmental degradation, financial losses across the supply chain, and deepening social inequalities in access to food. Ecologically, wasting 1.3 billion tons of food annually

Published by Springer Nature Switzerland AG 2026
L. M. Camarinha-Matos et al. (Eds.): PRO-VE 2025, IFIP AICT 770, pp. 394–410, 2026.
https://doi.org/10.1007/978-3-032-05673-3_24

means also wasting the resources used to produce it—such as water, land, and energy [1]. For instance, agriculture uses about 70% of the world's freshwater, a large portion of which is lost with FW [3]. Additionally, rotting food in landfills produces methane, contributing to 8% of global greenhouse gas emissions [3]. It also drives biodiversity loss and ecosystem degradation through deforestation, overuse of soil, and pollution [4]. Economically, FW costs about $940 billion per year worldwide [5]. Socially, food waste worsens hunger and food insecurity. While 811 million people go hungry globally, enormous quantities of edible food are thrown away [6]. This waste also burdens local waste management systems, raising municipal costs and reducing funds available for essential public services. Addressing FW could improve food equity, social welfare, and resource efficiency. According to the United Nations Environment Programme (UNEP) Food Waste Index Report [7], the vast majority of research on FW has focused on the household sector, leaving significant gaps in understanding the issue of FW in other critical sectors such as food service.

This paper addresses FW in food services especially public hospitals where the complexity of operations—including the need to serve nutritionally balanced meals tailored to diverse patient needs—leads to significant waste. In fact, hospital food services have been identified as some of the largest contributors to food waste within the foodservice sector [8]. We are particularly interested FW in public hospitals in Tunisia. in Moreover, this study aims to develop a sustainable hospital FW (HFW) management system to reduce FW impacts.

In Tunisia, FW is a growing challenge affecting the environment and the economy. Around 20% of food produced nationally is wasted, largely due to inefficiencies in production, distribution, and consumption, particularly in urban areas and the service sector [9]. Sources of food waste in Tunisia span multiple sectors. In the urban sector, Greater Tunis generates significant amounts of kitchen waste due to its dense population and concentration of institutions such as hospitals, schools, and universities. However, the lack of accurate quantification and the mixing of household organic waste with other residues—subsequently sent to landfills without pre-treatment—pose challenges to effective waste management [10].

To effectively address FW, two main strategies are essential: reduction and valorization. Waste reduction can be achieved by re-dimensioning food portions in settings like restaurants, hotels, and cafeterias, particularly within the hospitality sector where oversized servings often lead to high waste levels. Alternatives such as offering smaller portions or allowing consumers to choose quantities, and reducing buffet-style service, can significantly cut down on waste while optimizing costs and enhancing customer satisfaction [3]. Simultaneously, both strategies contribute to building a more sustainable and resource-efficient food system [11].

FW valorisation aligned with circular economy principles, treats waste as a resource. It includes converting food scraps into animal feed, compost, biogas, or new products such as plant-based ingredients, cosmetics, and pharmaceuticals—promoting sustainable agriculture, energy production, and efficient use of resources like water and land [12]. A key strategy within this framework is anaerobic digestion, a biological process that transforms organic waste into renewable energy in the form of biogas.

In the following section, we begin by reviewing several studies on the valorization of hospital waste especially FW. Next, we examine research focused on collaborative management of hospital FW. Finally, we highlight the existing research gaps and present our contribution.

2 Literature Review

The issue of HFW is drawing growing interest from researchers. Especially, the UNEP Food Waste Index Report [7] highlighted a focus on the household sector and identified significant gaps in understanding the issue of FW in food service sector suh as public hospitals. This report showed also that only nine high-income nations representing only 32% of the global population —Australia, Austria, China, Denmark, Estonia, Germany, Sweden, the United Kingdom, and the United States—have developed high-confidence estimates of FW in the food service sector. This underscores the urgent need for broader, globally representative data on FW in Food service operations. This lack of data touches particularly hospital food services which have been identified as some of the largest contributors to FW within the foodservice sector [8]. Numerous studies on Hospital FW (HFW) were conducted primarily in Europe and North America [13] emphasising the volume of food wasted in hospitals along with its significant economic and environmental implications. However, there is a still a lack of research studies on the HFW within the Eastern Mediterranean Region (EMR), including Tunisia [13]. This paper contributes to literature on HFW by providing data and estimates on Tunisian HFW. In Tunisia and across the broader EMR, the literature on HFW quantification and valorization in hospitals is almost non-existent [13]. No published research specifically quantifies food waste generated by hospitals or assesses how it could be leveraged for energy or materials recovery. This absence is particularly critical given the UNEP report's findings, which stress the underrepresentation of non-household sectors in global food waste assessments and the particularly high levels of HFW.

The second contribution of this paper lies in the developement of a HFW valorization system. Recent studies have investigated various technological pathways for valorizing food and organic waste from hospitals, albeit mostly at small scales or in different contexts. Esteban-Lustres et al. [14] demonstrated that waste composition depends on meal type, enabling targeted valorization strategies. This study emphasized how HFW can be transformed into value-added products through environmentally friendly methods. However it did not address energy recovery or large-scale applications.

Rahman and Melville [15] explored anaerobic digestion of non-hazardous medical waste, including HFW in Bangladesh generating biogas sufficient to meet local cooking energy demands and electricity needs while producing biofertilizer. Meanwhile, Hathi et al. [16] focused on transforming food waste from a university canteen into biodegradable plastics through microbial fermentation, addressing the environmental burden of conventional plastics. Although innovative, these studies were limited to pilot projects and did not specifically consider hospital networks or integrated energy recovery planning.

Beyond the quantification and valorization of HFW itself, several researchers emphasized system-level strategies and collaborative optimization for managing the wastes of the healthcare sector. Ghasemi et al. [17] proposed a bi-objective MILP model for the COVID-19 context, optimizing facility locations and waste flows across multiple disposal technologies, including those with energy recovery. Chauhan and Singh [18] applied ARIMA models to forecast healthcare waste volumes to inform more efficient collection and disposal operations, and Govindan et al. [19] incorporated complex logistics elements—such as green vehicle routing and fuel-consumption-dependent costs—into a fuzzy goal programming model for medical waste management. While these studies highlight the benefits of proactive and collaborative planning, they generally treated healthcare waste as an aggregate stream, without isolating HFW or evaluating its valorization potential.

Overall, existing studies have largely concentrated on (i) isolated valorization technologies tested in pilot settings, (ii) integrated waste management models that do not differentiate food waste, or (iii) foodservice waste quantification efforts confined to high-income countries. To our knowledge, there are no studies that quantify food waste generated by a hospital network in Tunisia, estimate its thermal and electrical energy potential, or propose appropriately sized valorization infrastructure.

To address this gap, this study investigates two nearby hospitals in Tunisia, developing a specific methodology to quantify HFW from patient meal trays. We then extrapolate these findings to estimate total food waste across the network, calculate potential energy recovery (thermal and electrical), and recommend suitable valorization technologies and their sizing. This work thus contributes to filling critical data and methodological gaps, supporting the advancement of sustainable, circular approaches to hospital food waste management in an underexplored regional context.

3 Methodology

In this paper, we are interested in a circular economy system of FW generated by two hospitals aiming, for a sustainable management system. The key principle of the circular economy is "closing the loop," meaning that resources are continually reused and recycled, reducing reliance on raw materials and minimizing waste. FW valorization exemplifies this idea by turning organic waste, often seen as a problem, into useful products. In the case of anaerobic digestion, FW is converted into biogas (a renewable energy source) and digestate (which can be used as fertilizer). These outputs contribute to resource recovery, reduce the need for virgin materials, and enhance sustainability by offering an alternative to traditional waste disposal methods [20].

Figure 1 presents a framework for an example of hospital FW valorization system. The hospital or a group of hospitals generates a quantity of food waste "FW" (Q). This FW is then introduced to anaerobic digester to produce biogas and digestate. Through anaerobic digestion, FW is transformed into biogas, which can be used to generate electricity, heat, or even fuel for vehicles. This not only helps reduce reliance on fossil fuels but also provides a clean, renewable energy source. The biogas produced can be fed into the energy grid or utilized within the community, thus promoting energy efficiency and self-sufficiency [21]. In our case, the generated electricity and thermic energy will be returned to the hospitals. On the other hand, the digestate produced during the anaerobic digestion process is rich in nutrients and can be repurposed as an organic fertilizer.

This latter can be used not only for the hospitals' gardens but also into the agricultural system, reducing the need for synthetic fertilizers that require intensive resource use and can harm the environment [22].

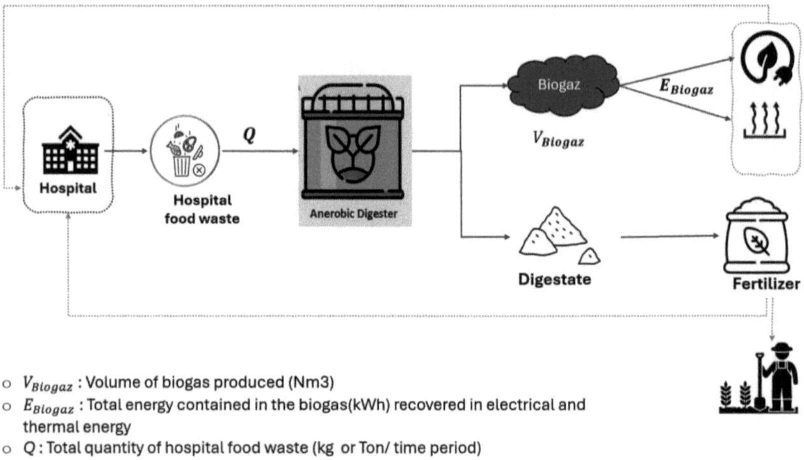

Fig. 1. A Framework for hospital FW valorization system

This study addresses a strategic-level issue focused on evaluating food waste generated by a group of two comparable hospitals. The objective is to evaluate food waste of hospitals and determine the appropriate type and size of valorization equipment for these hospitals. The study begins by analyzing the waste generation process at one hospital. After estimating the volume and selecting suitable equipment for this hospital, the findings are then extended to the entire group.

To carry out this study, a multi-step approach has been developed as illustrated in Fig. 2. This methodology was defined based on a real case study: a Tunisian public hospital.

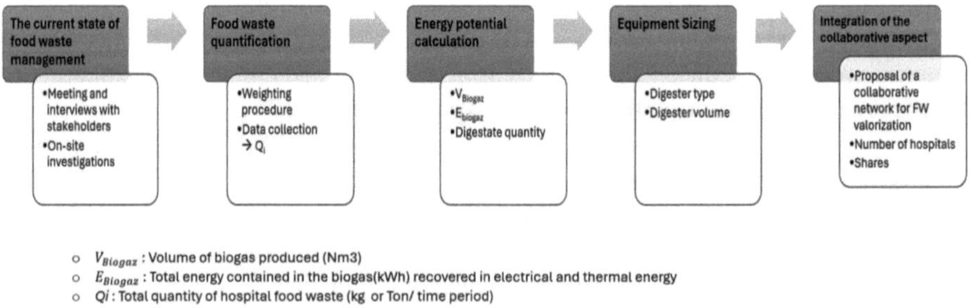

Fig. 2. Methodology of the study

The first step aims to understand the existing food waste system and identify the types of data that need to be gathered as well as issues related the food waste management process. Based on these outputs, data are collected and are used as inputs to determine the energy potential and digestor sizing for a sustainable food waste management system. These former steps were conducted with the assistance of an expert in the field of biogas generation, which is a Tunisian company specialized in standardized exhaustors, cogenerators and methanization solutions[1]. After understanding and setting the route for designing a FW management system, we propose in the fifth step the integration of the collaborative aspect between a network of nearby hospitals. The detail of each step is presented in the following subsections.

3.1 The Current State of Food Waste Management

This phase aims at studying the food waste generation, quantification and management processes at the hospital. For this purpose, several interviews were held with relevant stakeholders such as the hospital executives, the kitchen staff and meals distribution workers to understand the current food waste management practices. To consolidate this information and delve into the real challenges faced by the institution as well as the issues encountered, on-site investigations were conducted. These observations allowed us to gather essential information about the internal organization and establish a preliminary diagnosis of the issues related to waste management. The process is illustrated in Fig. 3.

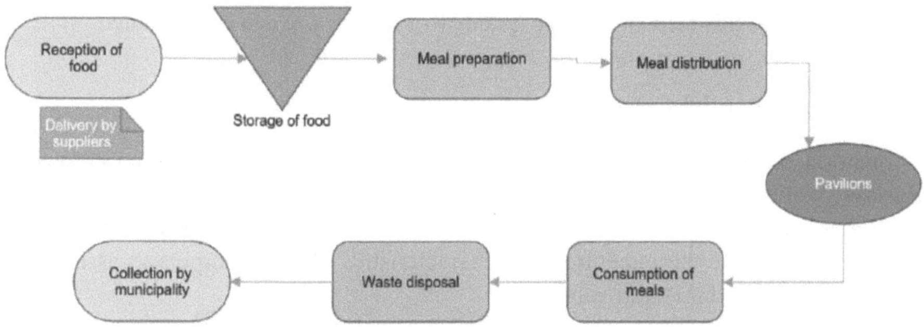

Fig. 3. Existing food preparation and waste management process

Based on this investigation step, two major issues are highlighted:

i) The absence of a dedicated and appropriate food waste management system. For instance, there is no procedure to adequately separate food waste from other wastes—it is discarded in the same trash cans as paper, cardboard, plastic, and other waste materials, rather than being sorted for potential reuse or recycling.
ii) The significant absence of systematic quantification of the discarded food quantities.

These issues underscore the urgent need to accurately measure the extent of waste generated by the catering, which lead us to the third step "food waste quantification".

---

[1] https://www.binergy.com.tn/en/.

3.2 Food Waste Quantification

To obtain a representative estimate with the collaboration of hospital executives, as well as kitchen and meal distribution staff, four pilot pavilions were selected to undergo the quantification process. The aim was to focus our efforts on specific areas while ensuring that the results could be extrapolated to the whole institution. The objective was to quantify food waste and identify its main sources, providing a basis for future waste reduction/valorization strategies.

To assess the amount of food waste generated by patients, a circular weighing system was introduced in the hospital over two weeks. This latter involved measuring the quantity of food served and the amount consumed. The procedure consisted of weighing: i) the meals before distribution to patients using an electronic scale to determine the initial quantity served, then ii) the plate leftovers after consumption to measure the amount of uneaten food.

We conducted two weighing sessions in each pavillon. To ensure accuracy, a meal distribution worker was trained on the weighing procedure by providing clear instructions on how to weigh the trays before and after meal distribution. Furthermore,

we outlined how to record the measurements properly. By standardizing the process, the risk of discrepancies in data collection was minimized.

Each day, we focused on a specific department, allowing for a detailed and comparative observation of food waste across the different hospital services.

At the end of this step an average quantity of food waste can be estimated.

3.3 Energy Potential Calculation

As mentioned earlier, food waste is processed through equipment called an **anaerobic digester**, which produces two main types of outputs: **biogas** and **digestate**. The biogas undergoes further treatment to generate both electrical and thermal energy. In this subsection, we evaluate the quantities and characteristics of these outputs to assess their energy potential and material value.

Recovered Electric and Thermic Energy

To determine the energy potential generated from biogas, it is necessary to calculate the volume of biogas (V_{biogas}) produced by the anaerobic digestion of food waste. It is calculated using equation (1) [23].

$$V_{biogas} = Q \times DM \times OM \times BMP \quad (1)$$

where:

- Q : Total quantity of food waste (Kg)
- DM refers to Dry Matter and represents the fraction of waste that does not contain water. It is expressed as a percentage of the total quantity (Q) of the waste. Dry matter is crucial in assessing organic waste since it helps determine the proportion of material that can be processed for energy recovery, such as anaerobic digestion [23].

- OM refers Organic Matter which is the fraction of the dry matter composed of biodegradable compounds (carbohydrates, lipids, proteins, etc.). It is expressed as a percentage of dry matter (DM). This parameter is essential because only organic matter can be broken down by microorganisms to produce biogas in anaerobic digestion processes [24].
- BMP refers to Biochemical methane potential or methanogenic potential of the waste (Nm3 of biogas per kg). It is a laboratory test that measures the maximum amount **of methane** (CH_4) of biogas that can be produced from the anaerobic degradation per unit of organic matter during anaerobic digestion under controlled conditions. It is a key indicator for evaluating the energy potential of waste in anaerobic digestion [25].

Once the biogas volume is determined, the energy contained in biogas E_{biogas} can be calculated (equation 2 [23]) using its calorific value (CV). This latter refers to the amount of energy released when a specific volume of biogas is combusted and represents the methane content (in %) of the biogas. It depends mainly on the methane (CH_4) content in the waste, since methane is the primary energy carrier in biogas. It is influenced by the type and composition of the food waste, digestion conditions, and retention time [26].

Then, the recovered electric and thermic energies produced can be calculated. They are denoted respectively E_{elec} and E_{th} and given by equations (3) [27] and (4) [28]. E_{elec} and E_{th} depend respectively on the electrical efficiency η_{elec} and thermic efficiency η_{th} of the engine/generator.

$$E_{\text{biogas}} = V_{\text{biogas}} \times CV \tag{2}$$

$$E_{\text{elec}} = E_{\text{biogas}} \times \eta_{\text{elec}} \tag{3}$$

$$E_{\text{th}} = E_{\text{biogas}} \times \eta_{\text{th}} \tag{4}$$

Calculation of the Annual Digestate Quantity

Finally, to estimate the annual quantity of digestate produced, we use the following formula (equation (5) [29]:

$$Q_{\text{digestate}} = Q \times (1 - (DM \times OM)) \tag{5}$$

3.4 Equipment Sizing

Digesters, also known as anaerobic digestion reactors or biodigesters, are systems designed for the biological degradation of organic matter in the absence of oxygen (anaerobic conditions), during which biogas is produced. Various types of digesters exist, each adapted to specific operating conditions and substrate types. Anaerobic digesters are also classified based on the total solids content of the organic substrate into wet and dry digesters. The quality and type of feedstock (e.g., food waste, agricultural waste; industrial organic waste …) greatly influence biogas yield, digestion performance, and digestate quality. Given that food waste is rich in moisture, wet digestion remains a preferred choice for maximizing decomposition efficiency. The continuously stirred anaerobic digester as a wet digestor is often preferred because of its effectiveness in processing materials with high moisture content [30]. The continuous mixing process ensures uniform breakdown of organic matter, leading to consistent biogas production. Additionally, the wet digestion system accelerates microbial activity, reducing retention time and maximizing energy recovery. It enables both the production of biogas and the generation of high-quality digestate. However, this method requires a significant amount of water and energy for mixing and heating, which may increase operational costs.

To size the wet anaerobic digestor, the digestor volume should be estimated based on the hydraulic retention time (HRT) and the daily volume of food waste (Daily volume) (see Eq. (6) [31]). This latter can be calculated using Eq. (7) [32].

$$\text{Digester Volume}\left(\text{m}^3\right) = \text{Daily Volume} \times \text{HRT (days)} \tag{6}$$

$$\textit{Daily volume}\left(\text{m}^3\text{per day}\right) = \frac{\textit{Daily Mass}\ (\text{Kg per day})}{\textit{Density}\ \left(\text{Kg per m}^3\right)} \tag{7}$$

3.5 Integration of the Collaborative Aspect

After understanding how to design a hospital food waste management system. We extend this framework to integrate the collaborative aspect between health care facilities.

Figure 4 Presents a framework for shared food waste valorisation system between a network of health care facilities. Let us consider a set of nearby hospitals which could be located within a specific region and are geographically close to each other's. Each one of them generates a quantity of food waste (Q_i). These hospitals collaborate to valorise the overall food waste quantity ($Q = \sum Q_i$). To do so, the wastes from different facilities are transported and collected in a hospital that is approximately at the centroid of the group where a common anaerobic digester located within that hospital will be used to produce biogas and digestate from the total collected waste. The generated electrical and thermic energies will be distributed among the hospitals according to a rate equal to $Q_i / \sum Q_i$ to each hospital i. On the other hand, the digestate produced during the anaerobic digestion process is rich in nutrients and can be repurposed as an organic fertilizer.

To illustrate this approach, a real case study was conducted involving two nearby public hospitals in the Ariana governorate of Tunisia: Abderrahmen Mami Hospital and Mahmoud el Materi Hospital, located less than 0.5 km apart. The total amount of food waste generated by El Materi Hospital will be assessed through a specific field study. Once this assessment is completed, the previously described method will be applied to recalculate the volumes of the various by-products—namely energy and digestate—that can be produced, this time considering the combined amount of waste generated by both facilities. The digester sizing will then be adjusted based on this total quantity. The issue of digestate management and localization is beyond of the scope of this study and will be addressed in a subsequent study.

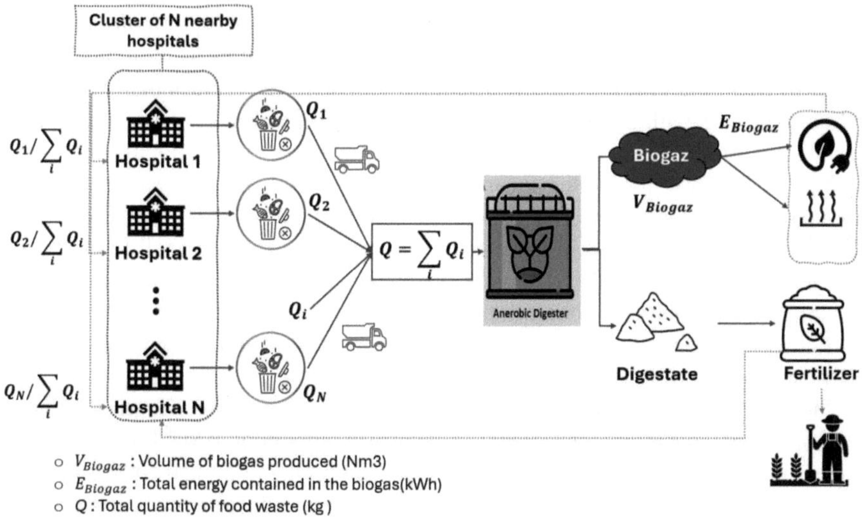

Fig. 4. Framework for a sustainable food waste management system for a collaborative health care network

4 Results and Discussion

This section presents the estimation of food waste generation at Mami Hospital, followed by the assessment of energy potential and the sizing of the anaerobic digester.

4.1 Food Waste Estimation at Abderrahmen Mami and Matri Hospitals

First FW estimation will be conducted at Abderrahmen Mami Hospital.Then the Matri's one will be estimated by extrapolating the first result.

The FW weighting step in 4 hospitalization departments in Abderrahmen Mami Hospital allowed to gather data regarding the average food waste percentage recorded over two measurement sessions (2 weeks in February 2025). First, we explore average percentage of FW and compare it to estimates in previous studies. Then we analyze FW distribution among not only weighting sessions (referred ad Week 1 and Week 2) but also studied hospital departments.

Average FW percentage at Abderrahmen Mami Hospital

Over two weeks, the average percentage of FW is 48,56%. 3 kg of waste per department per day is averagely generated. This implies a daily quantity of 36 kg of FW for all the departments and for 332 hospitalization bed. Hence, 108 g of FW is generated per patient (or hospitalization bed) per day. Several studies have analyzed food waste levels in hospitals across different regions. A study conducted in three Australian hospitals found an average daily plate waste of 227.7 kg, making up approximately 45% of total food waste [33]. This percentage aligns closely with the waste levels observed at Abderrahmen Mami Hospital. In the United Kingdom, the National Health Service (NHS) Trusts reported that 6,500 tonnes of unserved meals were discarded across all hospitals in the 2020–2021 period [33]. While the NHS data focuses on unserved meals rather than total food waste, the issue of uneaten hospital meals is a common challenge, similar to what was observed at Abderrahmen Mami Hospital, particularly in Pavilion B, where patients with dietary restrictions receive additional meals from their families but still take hospital-provided meals, leading to increased waste. Finally, a review of hospitals in the Eastern Mediterranean Region (EMR), covering countries such as Iran, Saudi Arabia, and Qatar, reported an average food waste of 25.4% of total food served [13]. The lower waste levels in these hospitals could be attributed to different hospital management systems, meal distribution processes, and cultural attitudes toward food consumption. In contrast, Abderrahmen Mami Hospital exhibits considerably higher waste levels, suggesting potential inefficiencies in meal planning, portion control, or patient acceptance of hospital-provided meals.

These findings suggest that food waste in hospitals is a widespread issue. Compared to the provided benchmark, especially 25.4% waste reported in EMR hospitals, Abderrahmen Mami Hospital's waste levels are high, emphasizing a need for better patient meal customization, and waste reduction strategies. Beyond waste reduction strategies, given the high volume of FW that could be accumulated, the FW valorization prevails as considerable solution.

Average FW per weighting session

The first session exhibited an average waste percentage of 41.75% while the second one showed a higher percentage of 55.56%. This increase suggests a variation in food consumption patterns, potentially influenced by menu composition, patient intake, or meal distribution practices. The higher waste percentage in the second week at Abderrahmen Mami Hospital (55.56%) further indicates that external factors, such as menu variations or patient turnover, may contribute to fluctuations in waste levels.

The increasing food waste percentage from session 1 to session 2 suggests that waste levels at Abderrahmen Mami Hospital are dynamic and influenced by multiple factors:

- Some patients receive home-prepared meals from their families due to specific dietary needs (e.g., gluten-free diets), yet they still take the hospital meals, leading to significant plate waste.
- meal composition, patient intake, and hospital service conditions impact waste generation.

FW rate per hospitalization department

The data collected from Mami Hospital provides valuable insights into the extent of food waste generated across different hospital pavilions. Figure 5 Illustrated the FW rate per hospitalization department. The highest FW percentage was recorded in Pavilion B on February 12th (71.4%), where 2,332 kg of food was discarded out of 3,267 kg prepared.

- The lowest waste percentage occurred in Cardiovascular Surgery on February 13th (24.1%), where only 537 kg of food was wasted from a total of 2,230 kg
- A second peak in FW was observed on February 19th in Pavilion B (57.7%), suggesting a persistent issue in this service.

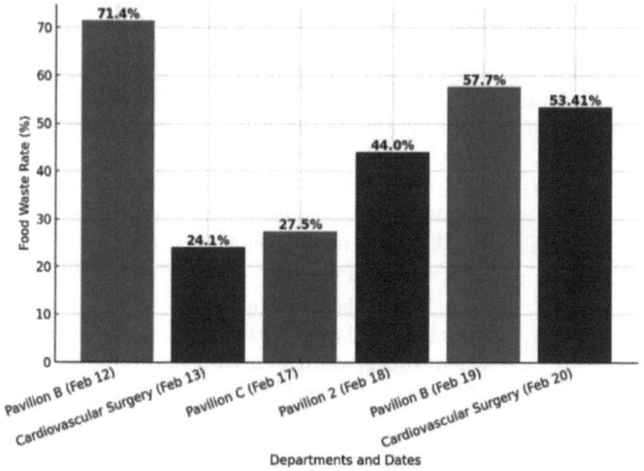

Fig. 5. FW rate per hospitalization department and per date

Pavilion B appears to be the most wasteful, with two instances of high food waste percentages exceeding 50%. This may indicate an issue related to portion sizing, patient dietary restrictions, or unappealing meals. Additionally, Pavilion B recorded the highest food waste percentage overall, which could also be attributed to lower patient appetite compared to other pavilions. Factors such as the health condition of patients, their ability to consume meals, and specific dietary preferences may play a role in this trend.

Moreover, some patients in Pavilion B follow specific dietary regimes, such as gluten-free diets. Their families often bring them customized meals that better suit their dietary needs. However, these patients still receive the standard hospital meals, leading to increased food waste as they may not consume both. This situation highlights the need for a more personalized meal distribution system to reduce waste while ensuring patients' dietary requirements are met.

Average FW at El Materi Hospital
A daily total quantity of 36 kg of FW and a daily quantity 108 g of FW is generated per patient (or hospitalization bed) are generated at Abderrahmen Mami hospital. Based on this result and given that Matri hospital hospitalization capacity is around 100 bed all departments combined, the daily total quantity of FW can be estimated to 11 kg per day.

4.2 Energy Potential Estimation and Digestor Sizing

Data and hypothesis
Hospital food waste consists mainly of meal leftovers, including starches (pasta, potatoes, couscous), proteins (chicken, meatballs), vegetables (peas, salad), and sauces. For these types of biowaste, we adopt data from anaerobic digestion studies of biowaste as presented in Table 1.

Table 1. Data, values and hypothesis

Data	Value / Hypothesis	Reference
Q: Total annual FW quantity in Kg/year	Over a full year,Abderahmen Mami hospital produces nearly 12096 kg of waste, equivalent to approximately 12 tons per year. Materi Hospital produces around 3643 kg of FW per year.	Subsection 4.1
Daily FW quantity	36 kg/day for Abderrahmen Mami hospital and 11 kg/day for El Materi hospital which results in a total daily quantity of 47 kg/day.	
% of Q	for DM estimation: 25–30%	ADEME (French Agency for Ecological Transition), Guide on Biowaste Methanization [34].
% of DM	for OM estimation: 80–95%	
BMP	Under optimal conditions, the BMP can be estimated at around 600 Nm3 of biogas per Kg of waste. This estimate assumes substrates that are rich in organic matter and well-controlled anaerobic digestion conditions, which maximize biogas production.	Expert
CV	CV typically around 6.5 kWh/Nm3. This value is specific to the type of waste used in this project.	Expert
η_{elec}	between 30% and 40%	[27]
η_{th}	between 40% and 50%	[28]
HRT	30 days	[31]
Density	In the absence of specific data for our case, we will use an estimated average density of 400 kg/m3.	The UK organization WRAP reports an average food waste density of 500 kg/m3, based on a survey of household waste [35]. • A study conducted in Taman Universiti, Skudai, Malaysia, found a bulk density of 300 kg/m3 for food waste [31].

5 Results

Using these data and formulas (2)–(7), the results show that a digester with a volume of approximately 2.7 m^3 would be required to valorize Abderrahmen Mami Hospital. On the other hand, a digester with a volume of 3.525 m^3 would be required to valorize both hospitals FW. Fig. 6. And 7 illustrate the FW valorisation unit size and energy production volumes for Abderrahmen Mami hospital only and both hospitals respectively.

Figure 6 Shows a complete system illustrating the transformation of food waste into energy. It begins with a digester of 2.7 m^3 into which 36 kg of food waste per day is introduced. This organic input undergoes anaerobic digestion, producing biogas and digestate. The biogas is then fed into a cogeneration unit, which converts it into 3624.19 kWh per year of electric energy 4756.75 kWh per year of thermic energy. Meanwhile, the remaining digestate (9192.96 kg/year) can be used as a nutrient-rich fertilizer. The produced thermal and electric energy represent 0.08% of the total energy consumed by the hospital if we consider an energy intensity of 13.70 MWh of electric energy per bed per year and 19,26 MWh of thermal energy per bed per year[2]. The[3] estimated gain is about 4000 TND per year for Abderrahmen Mami hospital. The developed FW valorization system considers the daily FW quantity of one hospital.

Figure 7 illustrates, in addition, the integration of the collaborative aspect between two hospitals where:

- the digester is located at the first hospital (Abderrahmen Mami) as it contributes to ≈70% of the total FW to be treated,
- the collected FW from the second one (Matri) (which is about 11 kg) is transported daily to the vaporization unit located at Hospital 1. Given the distance is about 0,450 km, the transportation cost can be considered too low and even negligeable. The distribution of energy between both hospitals I aligned with the contribution of each hospital in the total quantity of FW. Hence, around 70% of energy produced will be used by the first hospital and the remaining 30% will be distributed to the second hospital.

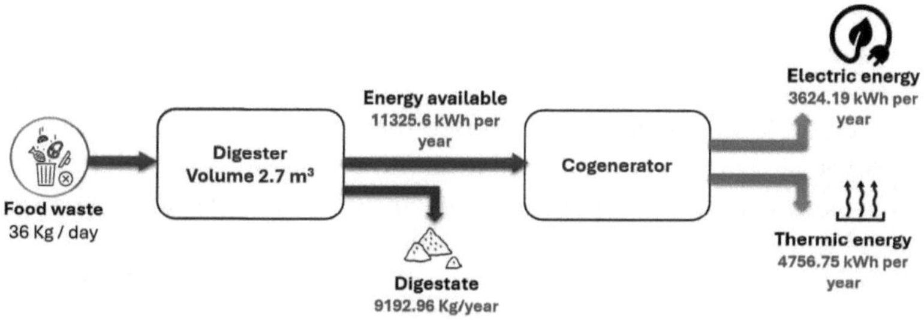

Fig. 6. FW valorisation unit size and energy production volumes for Abderrahmen Mami Hospital

All these results presented estimates based on a set of collected and estimated data. These results could be more refined based on more accurate data.

[2] https://energieplus-lesite.be/theories/consommation-energetique/statistiques-de-consommation/consommation-d-electricite-et-de-combustible-dans-la-sante/.

[3] https://lapresse.tn/2024/11/27/le-secteur-de-la-sante-a-lepreuve-du-climat-un-modele-hospitalier-moins-energivore-plus-durable/#:~:text=Ceci%20%C3%A9tant%2C%20%C2%ABce%20secteur%20repr%C3%A9sente,ramener%20ce%20taux%20%C3%A0%2050%25.

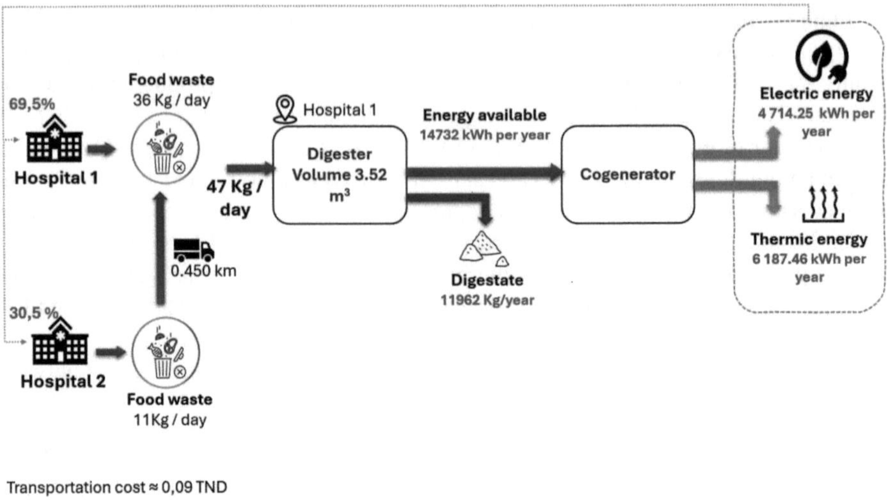

Fig. 7. Integration of the collaborative aspect between Abderrahmen Mami and El Materi Hospitals for FW valorization

6 Conclusion and Perspectives

This study has addressed the issue of FW in hospital settings, highlighting its environmental, economic, and operational implications. Through a detailed case study at Abderrahmen Mami Hospital, we quantified food waste generation and identified key contributing factors. The findings emphasized the need not only to reduce waste but also to valorize it through anaerobic digestion, with the aim of generating both thermic and electrical energy. The extension of this analysis to Mahmoud el Materi Hospital, based on the developed methodology, allowed for the dimensioning of a shared anaerobic digester that accounts for the combined waste volume from both hospitals. The results enable the calibration of a waste treatment system for a hospital and explore the feasibility of extending it to a neighbouring facility. This work contributes to setting the route for the design of a shared FW valorization system in Tunisia, through conducting the first steps of FW estimation, energy potential calculation and digester sizing. Several steps are to be conducted following this study such as conducting an in-depth evaluation on the actual value of mutualization, its concrete advantages and the efficiency of shared system. A comparative analysis between the results obtained for the non-collaborative and collaborative scenarios will be carried out based on more accurate data. Moreover, a benefit cost analysis based on real costing data from both hospitals will feed these discussions.

As a perspective, further work is required at the tactical and strategical levels. Future research should address the optimal location of the digestion facility, the logistics of transporting FW from each hospital to the central digester, and the effective distribution of the generated energy between the two sites. Moreover, the study of engagement with waste management authorities, agricultural users of digestate, or regulatory bodies that would be part of a full circular economy loop will contribute to drawing the hole picture of the shared hospital FW valorization system. These elements are essential for the implementation of an integrated, sustainable, and circular FW management.

References

1. FAO. Global food losses and food waste – Extent, causes and prevention. Rome (2011)
2. FAO. The State of Food and Agriculture 2019. Moving forward on food loss and waste reduction. Rome. Licence: CC BY-NC-SA 3.0 IGO (2019)
3. Mokrane, S., Buonocore, E., Capone, R., Franzese, P.P.: Exploring the global scientific literature on food waste and loss. Sustainability **15**(6), 4757 (2023)
4. Xue, L., Song, G., Liu, G.: Wasted food, wasted resources? A critical review of environmental impact analysis of food loss and waste generation and treatment. Environ. Sci. Technol. **58**(17), 7240–7255 (2024)
5. Kotykova, O., Babych, M.: Economic Impact of Food Loss and Waste. AGRIS on-line Pap. Econ. Inform. **11**(3), 55–71 (2019). https://doi.org/10.7160/aol.2019.110306
6. FAO, IFAD, UNICEF, WFP and WHO.: The state of food security and nutrition in the world 2022. Repurposing food and agricultural policies to make healthy diets more affordable. Rome, FAO (2022). https://doi.org/10.4060/cc0639en
7. United Nations Environment Programme: Food Waste Index Report 2021. Nairobi (2021)
8. Williams, P., Walton, K.: Plate waste in hospitals and strategies for change. e-SPEN, Eur. e-J. Clin. Nutrit. Metab. **6**(6), e235-e241 (2011)
9. RDD.: Le gaspillage alimentaire un véritable problème en tunisie (2021)
10. Chaher, N.E.H., et al.: Potential of sustainable concept for handling organic waste in Tunisia. Sustainability **12**(19), 8167 (2020)
11. Ellison, B., Muth, M.K.: The economics of food loss and waste. In: A Modern Guide to Food Economics (pp. 144–169). Edward Elgar Publishing (2022)
12. Sarangi, P.K., Pal, P., Singh, A.K., Sahoo, U.K., Prus, P.: Food waste to food security: Transition from bioresources to sustainability. Resources **13**(12), 164 (2024). https://doi.org/10.3390/resources13120164
13. Hoteit, M., et al.: A review on hospital food waste quantification, management and assessment strategies in the eastern Mediterranean region. J. Agric. Food Res. **15**, 100959 (2024)
14. Esteban-Lustres, R., Torres, M.D., Pazos, A., Enjamio, C., Piñeiro, B., Domínguez, H.: Preliminary evaluation of pressurized hot water extraction for the solubilization of valuable components from hospital kitchen wastes. Biomass Convers. Biorefinery **14**(4), 4621–4633 (2024)
15. Rahman, K.M., Melville, L.: An investigation into the conversion of non-hazardous medical wastes into biogas—A case study from the health and family planning sector in Bangladesh. Processes **11**(5), 1494 (2023)
16. Hathi, Z.J., et al.: Fermentative bioconversion of food waste into biopolymer poly (3-hydroxybutyrate-co-3-hydroxyvalerate) using Cupriavidus necator. Environ. Res. **215**, 114323 (2022)
17. Ghasemi, P., Goli, A., Goodarzian, F., Ehmke, J.F.: Simulation-based genetic algorithm for optimizing a municipal cooperative waste supply chain in a pandemic. Eng. Appl. Artif. Intell. **139**, 109478 (2025)
18. Chauhan, A., Singh, A.: An ARIMA model for the forecasting of healthcare waste generation in the Garhwal region of Uttarakhand, India. Int. J. Serv. Oper. Inf. **8**(4), 352–366 (2017)
19. Govindan, K., Nasr, A.K., Mostafazadeh, P., Mina, H.: Medical waste management during coronavirus disease 2019 (COVID-19) outbreak: a mathematical programming model. Comput. Ind. Eng. **162**, 107668 (2021)

20. Collard, F.: L'économie circulaire. Courrier Hebdomadaire du CRISP **24552456**(10), 5–72 (2020)
21. European Biogas Association (EBA). The role of biogas in the circular economy. Eur. Biogas Assoc. (2020). Accessed: 17 March 2025
22. International Renewable Energy Agency (IRENA): Biogas for electricity generation. Int. Renew. Energy Agency (2017). Accessed: 17 March 2025
23. Mata-Alvarez, J., Dosta, J., Macé, S., Astals, S.: Codigestion of solid wastes: a review of its uses and perspectives including modeling. Crit. Rev. Biotechnol. **31**(2), 99–111 (2011)
24. Angelidaki, I., et al.: Defining the biomethane potential (BMP) of solid organic wastes and energy crops: a proposed protocol for batch assays. Water Sci. Technol. **59**(5), 927–934 (2009)
25. Raposo, F., Banks, C.J., Siegert, I., Heaven, S., Borja, R.: Influence of inoculum to substrate ratio on the biochemical methane potential of maize in batch tests. Process Biochem. **41**(6), 1444–1450 (2006)
26. Chynoweth, D.P., Owens, J.M., Legrand, R.: Renewable methane from anaerobic digestion of biomass. Renew. Energy **22**(1–3), 1–8 (2001)
27. Bello, O.S., Mollah., M.F.: Biogas production and utilization for renewable energy in developing countries: a review. Renew. Sustain. Energy Rev. **104**, 328–338 (2019)
28. Morgan, H.M., Jr., et al.: A techno-economic evaluation of anaerobic biogas producing systems in developing countries. Biores. Technol. **250**, 910–921 (2018)
29. Inayat, A., et al.: Sustainable energy production from waste: a review of hybrid approaches combining anaerobic digestion and gasification. Int. J. Energy Res. **2025**(1), 6644084 (2025)
30. Liu, Y., Wachemo, A.C., Yuan, H., Li, X.: Anaerobic digestion performance and microbial community structure of corn stover in three-stage continuously stirred tank reactors. Biores. Technol. **287**, 121339 (2019)
31. Foday, E.H., Jr., et al.: Municipal solid waste characteristics in Taman Universiti, Skudai, Johore Malaysia. J. Adv. Res. Des. **38**(1), 13–20 (2017)
32. Feng, Y., Liu., Z.: Food waste management: a review of the present and future perspectives. Renew. Sustain. Energy Rev. **91**, 390–397 (2018)
33. National Health Service (NHS) Trusts: Annual report on food waste in NHS facilities (2020–2021). PMC (2021). Accessed: 17 March 2025
34. ADEME. Guide de la méthanisation des biodéchets. (2020). https://www.ademe.fr
35. WRAP. Household food and drink waste in the UK (2009)

Collaborative Healthcare Networks: Decision Systems

Generative Responsiveness in Assistive Care Ecosystem - GRACE

Thais A. Baldissera[1,3](✉), Cristiano De Faveri[2], and Luis M. Camarinha-Matos[3]

[1] Instituto Federal Farroupilha, Júlio de Castilhos, Rio Grande do Sul, Brazil
[2] NOVA School of Science and Technology, NOVA University Lisbon, Campus de Caparica, 2829-516 Caparica, Portugal
c.faveri@alumni.fct.unl.pt
[3] NOVA School of Science and Technology, UNINOVA-CTS and LASI, NOVA University Lisbon, Campus de Caparica, 2829-516 Caparica, Portugal
{t.baldissera,lcm}@fct.unl.pt

Abstract. The growing aging population presents significant challenges for delivering personalized, adaptive, and sustainable elderly care. Traditional care models often fall short in addressing the complex and dynamic needs of seniors, thus underscoring the need for integrated ecosystems that leverage both technological advancements and human capacities. This work introduces Generative Responsiveness in Assistive Care Ecosystem (GRACE), a human-AI collaborative framework currently under development. GRACE aims to support elderly individuals through continuous health monitoring, predictive analytics, emotional support, and dynamic service composition and evolution. Building on prior research, including the Elderly Care Ecosystem (ECE) concept and methodologies for service composition (SCoPE) and evolution (SEvol), GRACE is designed to facilitate the co-creation of evolving care solutions. The approach aims to integrate human stakeholders - seniors, families, caregivers, and healthcare providers - with AI agents in a hybrid network architecture. The framework comprises three distinct layers - Sensing and Acting, Cognitive and Analytics, and Interaction - fostering synergistic collaboration between human actors and AI. This paper outlines GRACE's conceptual foundations, presents its initial functional design, and illustrates human-AI collaboration scenarios. It also discusses anticipated organizational, technological, and ethical challenges in real-world deployment and concludes by identifying key research directions for scaling, refining, and assessing the long-term impact of such AI-driven collaborative ecosystems in elderly care.

Keywords: Elderly Care Ecosystem · Human-AI Collaboration · Hybrid Collaborative Networks

1 Introduction

Ongoing demographic shifts clearly indicate that people are living longer, and when combined with declining fertility rates, this results in an increasingly aging population. While greater life expectancy is a positive development, it also creates significant and

Published by Springer Nature Switzerland AG 2026
L. M. Camarinha-Matos et al. (Eds.): PRO-VE 2025, IFIP AICT 770, pp. 413–427, 2026.
https://doi.org/10.1007/978-3-032-05673-3_25

intricate challenges for healthcare and social support systems [1]. Current approaches to implement elderly care platforms are frequently characterized by a predominantly techno-centric orientation, often overlooking the holistic and deeply personal nature of care [2]. Furthermore, these systems typically operate with a high degree of service-provider isolation, leading to fragmented care delivery that fails to adequately address the nuanced, dynamic, and highly individualized needs of seniors throughout their life stages. This limitation is particularly acute in accommodating the fluctuating physical, cognitive, and psychosocial requirements that accompany advanced age.

A typical example of a service in this domain is a medication reminder application that delivers fixed-time alerts prompting elderly users to take their prescribed medication. While such a solution may be adequate for highly autonomous individuals, it frequently fails in contexts involving cognitive decline, sensory impairments, or limited caregiver involvement. These systems typically lack mechanisms to verify whether the medication was actually taken or to adjust to changes in user's health status, resulting in reduced efficacy and potential health risks. Additionally, an individual may require multiple care services simultaneously, highlighting the need for integrated service packages, eventually involving collaboration among various service providers.

In fact, fragmented service often fails to meet the diverse, evolving, and highly personalized needs of seniors across different stages of later life. Consequently, there's a growing demand for innovative care ecosystems. These are not just about advanced technology; they should be fundamentally human-centered, offering flexibility and the adaptability to respond to the changing requirements of an aging population.

When integrated into a broader collaborative ecosystem - encompassing several other services such as wearable health monitoring devices, voice-based assistants, and dynamic electronic health records and involving family caregivers, healthcare professionals, and other service providers, – care delivery must follow a personalized and evolutionary approach, supported by a coordinated alliance of service providers.

Through real-time data exchange and human-AI interaction, a care ecosystem support platform can dynamically adjust medication schedules, modify alert modalities, enable contextual supervision, and facilitate social engagement. By adopting an integrated and collaborative perspective, elderly care becomes more effective, user-centred, and capable of evolving over time in alignment with each individual's changing needs and health trajectory.

As such, collaborative networks, and particularly collaborative care ecosystems, are increasingly recognized as a promising and potentially transformative organizational paradigm in the domain of elderly care. These ecosystems extend beyond the direct care recipients to include their families, social support circles, professional caregivers, interdisciplinary healthcare providers (e.g., physicians, nurses, therapists), relevant commercial enterprises (e.g., technology developers, service providers), and, increasingly, AI agents. The integration of these diverse actors within a unified network structure is not merely a logistical convenience but a fundamental necessity for leveraging a broader spectrum of resources, expertise, and perspectives essential to delivering comprehensive, personalized, and adaptive care.

In alignment with this approach, this paper presents an ongoing research initiative titled GRACE (Generative Responsiveness in Assistive Care Ecosystem), which proposes a human–AI collaborative framework designed to enhance elderly care through the integration of generative AI technologies. The term "Generative" denotes the use of generative AI as a core technological element, while "Responsiveness" emphasizes the envisioned system's capacity to dynamically adapt to the evolving needs of senior adults. "Assistive" highlights the focus on active support for caregiving tasks, and "Care Ecosystem" underscores the collaborative, adaptive, and human-centered orientation of the proposed framework.

GRACE is designed to enable real-time health monitoring, predictive analytics, emotional support, and personalized service integration and orchestration by interconnecting human and AI agents within a flexible and evolving care environment. Its conceptual foundation draws on existing models such as the Elderly Care Ecosystem (ECE) [3], the Service Composition and Personalization Environment (SCoPE) [4], and the Service Evolution Environment (SEvol) [5].

The remainder of this paper is organized as follows: Sect. 2 presents a brief Human-AI background; Sect. 3 details the applications and considerations of AI tools and systems in elderly care; Sect. 4 introduces the GRACE framework and discusses the Elderly Care Ecosystem in a context of human-AI interaction; Sect. 5 concludes the paper outlining directions for future research.

2 Human-AI Collaboration Background

Ongoing discussions about the impact of AI on the human society, often consider three main perspectives [6]:

(1) ***technology-centric view***, which asserts that AI will soon surpass humans in virtually all domains, posing a major risk through the rise of superintelligence;
(2) ***human-centric view***, which argues that humans will always retain superiority over AI in social and societal domains, warning that the greatest danger lies in neglecting the inherently social nature of humanity when designing technology; and
(3) ***collective intelligence-centric view***, which emphasizes that true intelligence arises from the collaboration between human and AI agents, also highlighting that poorly designed technologies may generate systemic, collective problems that are difficult to anticipate and control.

From a ***technology-centric perspective***, AI is seen as a transformative force capable of surpassing human limitations in elderly care. Systems leveraging AI can continuously monitor health parameters, predict risks, and autonomously manage care routines with precision and consistency [7, 8]. Proponents of this view argue that minimizing human intervention increases efficiency, reduces errors, and ensures 24/7 support for elderly individuals [9]. In collaborative networks, AI agents could optimize resource allocation across multiple care providers, enhancing service quality while reducing operational burden [2].

Conversely, the ***human-centric perspective*** emphasizes that human qualities such as empathy, ethical judgment, and social interaction are irreplaceable in elderly care [10,

11]. While AI can assist by providing information and automating tasks, human caregivers must remain at the core of care delivery, especially to address the emotional and social needs of seniors. Collaborative networks, in this view, could use AI to empower human actors—such as family members, professional caregivers, and community volunteers—rather than replace them. Maintaining a human-centered approach ensures that technology enhances dignity, respect, and personal connection in elderly support systems [11].

Finally, the ***collective intelligence-centric perspective*** suggests that more effective solutions can result from the synergistic collaboration between humans and AI agents [2, 12, 13]. Under this approach, AI and humans work together within dynamic, adaptive networks where each contributes their strengths: humans offer empathy, intuition, and ethical oversight, while AI brings analytical capacity, memory, and predictive power. In the case of elderly care, this perspective also highlights the importance of governance models and trust-building mechanisms to manage the complexity of human-AI collaboration at scale.

Collective intelligence-centric perspective aligns closely with the growing body of research on Human-AI Collaboration (HAIC), which frames AI not as a replacement for human labor or decision-making, but rather as a partner or teammate in a collaborative relationship aimed at achieving shared goals [14]. HAIC shifts from traditional human-machine interaction - often focused on control and task efficiency - toward a more integrated model of joint decision-making, mutual learning, and adaptive behaviour.

Preliminary evidence of potential HAIC's effectiveness has emerged across diverse sectors, including healthcare, where studies have focused on image analysis and diagnostic support (e.g., [7, 8, 15, 16]), mental health, where HAIC is evaluated through bias and empathy-related metrics [11, 17], and radiology, with emphasis on both quantitative accuracy and qualitative user feedback [9, 18]. In the finance domain, human-AI collaboration has been applied to fraud detection and prediction modeling, using techniques such as genetic algorithms and evidential reasoning [19–21]. Another example can be found in the support of collaborative energy ecosystems [12]. In the manufacturing sector, examples include process optimization and safety monitoring via recurrent and neural networks [22, 23]. HAIC has also been explored in education, where it informs pedagogical approaches and academic integrity discussions [24, 25], and in design and art, enhancing creativity and human-AI co-creation through generative [13, 26, 27]. Other studies examine cases of adaptive teaming [28], public sector use [29], and LLM-based multimodal interactions [30], reflecting the broad and growing scope of human-AI collaboration. Another study [31] discusses effective strategies for the introduction of HAIC in organizations.

3 AI Tools and Systems in Elderly Care

Recent advancements in AI have led to the development of a wide range of tools and systems with the potential to transform elderly care. These technologies can assist in health monitoring, cognitive support, social interaction, and daily living assistance, contributing to greater independence, safety, and quality of life for elderly people.

An overview of some representative applications relevant to this context is provided in Table 1.

Table 1. Examples of AI application in elderly care

Case 1: AI-Powered Monitoring Systems **Examples:** Wearable devices and smart home sensors integrated with machine learning (e.g., fall detection, heart rate variability, sleep tracking). **Applicability:** Early detection of health issues, emergency response, and tracking of chronic conditions. **Reference:** [6, 25] highlight how AI in image and signal analysis enhances diagnostic accuracy; this can be adapted for elderly care by tracking subtle physiological changes. **Examples of commercial tools:** CarePredict, Ally Cares. **Benefits:** Improved response time and preventative care. **Risks:** Privacy concerns, false alarms, and user acceptance challenges.	Case 2: Conversational Agents & Virtual Companions **Examples:** Large Language Models (LLMs) used in chatbots and voice assistants (e.g., Alexa, ElliQ). **Applicability:** Companionship, reminders for medication, mental health support. **Reference:** [8, 23] show the growing capacity of AI to understand and respond empathetically, which is important for reducing loneliness and enhancing cognitive engagement. **Examples of commercial tools:** Joy, ElliQ. **Benefits:** Increased emotional well-being, cognitive stimulation. **Risks:** Over-reliance on AI, loss of human contact, ethical concerns about anthropomorphization
Case 3: AI-Based Decision Support for Caregivers **Examples:** Predictive analytics platforms for care planning and risk assessment. **Applicability:** Helps caregivers identify patterns, prioritize interventions, and reduce caregiver burden. **Reference:** [13, 32] explore collaborative systems and frameworks that can be extended to elderly care teams **Examples of commercial tools:** NurseMagic™, Cera Care. **Benefits:** Data-driven insights, personalized care plans. **Risks:** Data bias, inadequate contextual understanding, ethical responsibility in decision-making.	Case 4: Cognitive and Emotional Monitoring **Examples:** Systems that use Natural Language Processing and facial recognition to detect signs of depression, confusion, or distress. **Applicability:** Mental health assessment and personalized interventions. **Reference:** [15, 17] stress the importance of qualitative feedback in mental health AI applications. **Examples of commercial tools:** Hyodol AI Companion Doll **Benefits:** Early identification of cognitive decline or emotional distress. **Risks:** Emotional privacy concerns, false positives, over-diagnosis.

These cases illustrate the evolving landscape of AI application in elderly care, emphasizing collaborative interactions between humans and AI to enhance the well-being of older adults and support caregivers effectively.

4 Human-AI Collaboration in Elderly Care: The GRACE Framework

The growing challenges of elderly care require systems that are not only intelligent but also adaptive, personalized, and deeply human-centered. In this context, the GRACE system is being designed as a dynamic, human-AI collaborative ecosystem support platform, aiming to support evolving and personalized care throughout the aging process. Grounded in the principles of Collaborative Networks [33], GRACE brings together multiple stakeholders—elderly individuals, family members, caregivers, healthcare professionals, service providers, and AI agents—into a seamlessly coordinated care environment.

The platform relies on a multi-layered architecture consisting of five main levels: (i) Sensing and Actuator Layer: Responsible for real-time data acquisition through sensors, wearable devices, and smart environments; (ii) Cognitive and Analytics Layer: Hosting generative AI modules that perform data interpretation, predictive analytics, and personalized service orchestration; (iii) Interaction Layer: Facilitating communication and coordination among humans and AI agents; (iv) Service Composition and Evolution (cross-cutting layer): Using the SCoPE and SEVol method; and (v) Ethics and Governance Layer (cross-cutting): Ensures ethical integrity and user autonomy.

4.1 Service Composition Through the SCoPE Approach

To operationalize the vision of adaptability and personalization, GRACE adopts the Service Composition and Personalization Environment (**SCoPE**) [4], an approach previously developed within the broader framework of collaborative networks for elderly care. It is supported by concepts from the Elderly Care Ecosystem (ECE), which serves as the foundational model for personalization and dynamic service adaptation.

Central to this method is a customer profile model, which captures essential characteristics of each elderly individual. This model supports the matching between structured taxonomies of care needs and available `{service, provider}` pairs. The matching process yields a service adherence index, facilitating the identification and prioritization of the most relevant and appropriate services for each user [4].

The personalization process consists of the following steps:

- **Scope Filtering**: Preliminary selection of services based on a taxonomy of current care needs, filtering out irrelevant `{service, provider}` combinations.
- **Service Adherence Calculation**: A quantitative evaluation based on a multidimensional matrix that assesses how well each service aligns with the specific needs and preferences of the individual.
- **Service Composition and Ranking**: Construction of service bundles and final ranking of solutions, prioritizing those that offer the highest level of relevance, feasibility, and personalization.

This methodology enables continuous refinement of care delivery, ensuring that each service composition remains contextually aligned with the user's evolving profile. An important role for AI in this area is to facilitate the elicitation of the customer profile.

4.2 Service Evolution Through the SEvol Approach

The Service Evolution Environment (**SEvol**) [34] is a method for building an adaptive and evolutionary system based on the MAPE-K methodology [35], designed to support the evolution of solutions that cope with the elderly's evolving life stages. SEvol is adopted as a base for service evolution in GRACE.

Considering the elderly care ecosystems, the proposed SEvol applies the MAPE-K loop to analyze each new context change in collaboration with relevant stakeholders and adapt the service accordingly. Specifically, SEvol supports solution evolution to address the challenges arising from the elderly's evolving life stages by continuously adapting the service to fit the changing context.

Following the MAPE-K model, the SEvol method is implemented as a control loop composed of four main stages: (i) *Monitoring* events in the surrounding physical and social context, which includes both context changes and message exchanges between stakeholders; (ii) *Analyzing* the monitored data against solution requirements to identify the need for adaptation; (iii) *Planning* an evolution strategy that reconciles the current solution with the new customer context; and (iv) *Executing* the evolution strategy while minimizing disruptions caused by the implemented changes.

Through this adaptive process, SEvol enables the evolutionary development of elderly care services, ensuring their continued relevance and responsiveness to the dynamic needs of elderly individuals across different life stages. As a future extension, Machine Learning techniques can be used to detect behavioural patterns and reduce the adaptation space to make more efficient decisions in dynamic care environments.

4.3 Proposed Architecture and Development Roadmap for GRACE

GRACE aims to support a Hybrid Collaborative Network (HCN) a form of collaborative ecosystem in which humans (elderly individuals, caregivers, family members, healthcare professionals) and AI agents work together in an integrated and coordinated manner to achieve shared goals—in this case, supporting independent and dignified aging. In this model, AI does not replace humans but rather augments their capabilities, enhancing health monitoring, data analysis, and the delivery of personalized care support. The network combines human intelligence (empathy, ethical judgment, creativity) with AI (rapid analysis, pattern prediction, task automation), forming a synergistic collaboration.

To enable human-AI collaborative care, we propose a modular architecture for the GRACE system, designed to integrate real-time sensing, contextual reasoning, and human-centric decision support. The architecture is composed of three interdependent layers and two cross-cutting components:

- **Sensing and Actuator Layer:** Responsible for the continuous acquisition of multimodal data (e.g., biometric, environmental, and behavioral) from IoT-enabled devices, wearable sensors, and voice interfaces. This layer relies on edge computing capabilities to enable low-latency processing and privacy-preserving inference.

- **Cognitive and Analytics Layer:** This layer contains the system's inferential core, incorporating machine learning algorithms, large language models (LLMs), and probabilistic reasoning mechanisms to extract actionable insights. Contextual embeddings and knowledge graphs enable temporal and semantic coherence in care-related decisions.
- **Interaction Layer:** Facilitates transparent and adaptive user engagement via multimodal interfaces (text, speech, visual). It serves as a communication bridge between the AI agents and various stakeholders (e.g., elderly, caregivers, family members).
- **Service Composition and Evolution Layer (cross-cutting):** Supports the dynamic assembly and personalization of care workflows using the SCoPE and SEVol method. It leverages agent-based models and rule-based planning to align interventions with user preferences, contextual data, and caregiver feedback.
- **Ethics and Governance Layer (cross-cutting):** Embeds regulatory compliance, fairness auditing, consent management, and value-sensitive design principles across all system layers. This ensures ethical integrity and respect for autonomy in all forms of interaction.

A graphical representation of the architectural model is sketched in Fig. 1, illustrating the interconnections and data flows between components.

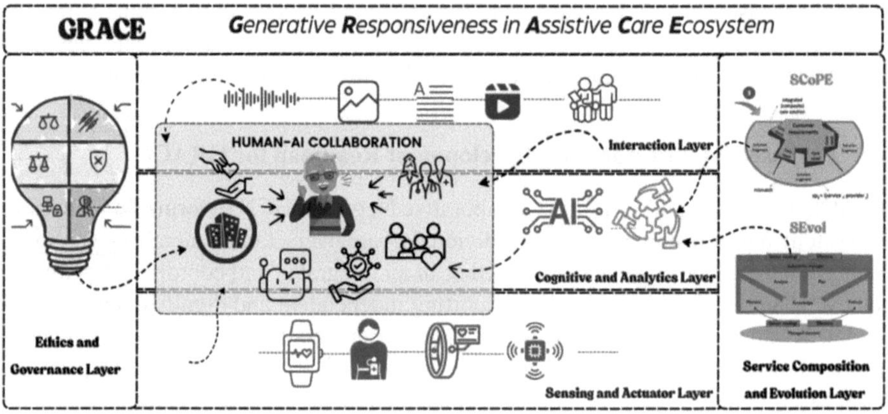

Fig. 1. GRACE components

A defining feature of the GRACE system is its operationalization of hybrid collaborative intelligence through interactions between human and AI agents. These interactions are not limited to isolated tasks but are embedded throughout the care process, enabling dynamic adaptation, informed decision-making, and co-creation of services across the care lifecycle.

The implementation plan comprises three major phases, following an iterative, human-centered design methodology [10]:

- Phase I – Foundational Prototyping, which focuses on developing minimal viable modules for key functionalities, including real-time health anomaly detection, Natural Language Processing-based [36] emotional inference, and caregiver interaction interfaces. This phase also involves establishing secure data pipelines and simulating edge-cloud integration scenarios.

Fig. 2 illustrates key components of the GRACE system designed to support remote elderly care through empathetic interaction and real-time health monitoring. Fig. 2 (a) depicts a video call session with "Mrs. Ellen Schmidt," showcasing an integrated chat interface within the communication screen. The dialogue contains emotional cues—such as reminiscing about past experiences and planning upcoming activities—demonstrating the system's capability for contextual understanding. The use of emoticons and color-coded speech bubbles enhances the communication experience by signaling tone and sentiment, reflecting an empathy-aware interface designed to foster meaningful caregiver–patient interactions. This module leverages Natural Language Processing (NLP) to infer emotional states and adjust the interaction style accordingly.

Fig. 2(b) presents the Health Monitoring Dashboard, which displays real-time alerts for physiological anomalies detected in Mrs. Schmidt's biometric data. Alerts include instances such as high blood pressure, elevated body temperature, and abnormal oxygen saturation levels. Each alert is visualized using intuitive iconography and a color-coded risk scale, allowing caregivers to quickly assess the severity of each event. Mrs. Schmidt's

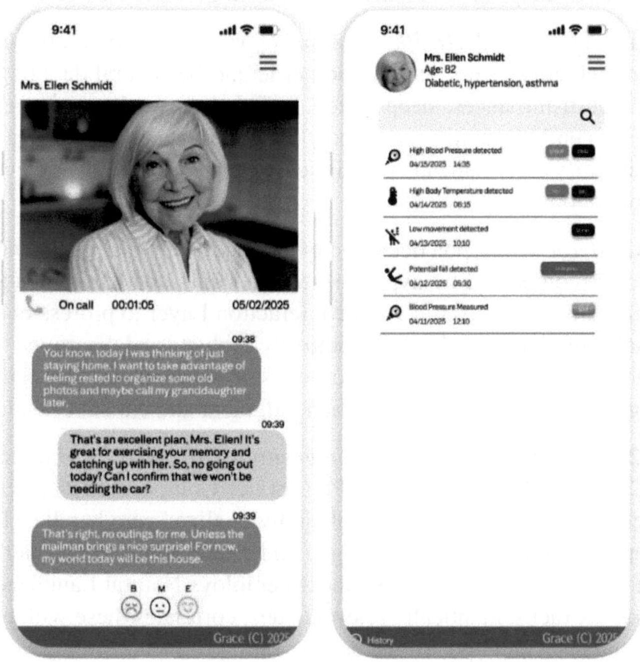

(a) (b)

Fig. 2. Examples of GRACE components

underlying health conditions—diabetes, hypertension, and asthma—are clearly indicated at the top of the interface, enabling personalized and context-aware decision-making. This dashboard exemplifies the system's real-time health anomaly detection capabilities and its integration with secure data pipelines and edge-cloud architecture for continuous monitoring.

- Phase II – System Integration and Service Orchestration, extending the SCoPE method and validating care bundling logic using both synthetic and real user profiles. It also involves deploying the interaction and orchestration layers in controlled test environments to support multi-agent coordination.
- Phase III – Pilot Deployment and Refinement, consisting of pilot case studies in residential care settings and living labs, with the aim of collecting multi-stakeholder feedback to iteratively refine system usability, personalization, and overall performance.

4.4 GRACE Illustrative Scenarios

To illustrate the proposed conceptual model underpinning the GRACE system (Fig. 1), the following examples exemplify key modalities of human–AI collaboration within the hybrid care architecture, demonstrating how artificial and human agents collaboratively deliver personalized, adaptive, and ethical services in geriatric care contexts:

- **Scenario 1 -** ***AI-Assisted Health Monitoring with Human Oversight*****:** Wearable devices and ambient sensors acquire biometric and behavioral data (e.g., heart rate variability, gait disturbances, sleep patterns). This information is processed in real-time by the system's Cognitive and Analytics Layer, underpinned by generative AI models, to identify early indicators of clinical deterioration, such as elevated fall risk or respiratory anomalies.

Human–AI Interaction: Upon detection of a potential anomaly, AI generates a contextualized alert accompanied by hypothesized etiologies and recommended interventions. This information is delivered via the Interaction Layer to professional caregivers and/or informal care partners, who collaboratively evaluate and determine the appropriate course of action (e.g., scheduling a clinical consultation or modifying daily activities), integrating algorithmic inference with human judgment and ethical considerations.

- **Scenario 2 -** ***Personalized Service Composition Informed by Human Feedback*****:** The GRACE system leverages the SCoPE (Service Composition via Preference Elicitation) method to dynamically assemble individualized care bundles. For instance, if a user reports symptoms such as fatigue and reduced appetite during voice-based interaction with a virtual companion, the AI employs Natural Language Processing techniques to extract semantically relevant cues, correlates these with physiological and contextual data, and updates the user's health profile accordingly.

Human–AI Interaction: Based on this multimodal assessment, the system proposes a revised care plan - potentially involving nutritional interventions, psychosocial monitoring, or home-based services - which is then subjected to human validation. Caregivers or family members may contextualize or personalize these suggestions (e.g., opting for home-delivered meals instead of clinic visits), resulting in an adaptive and co-designed workflow responsive to both explicit user input and implicit behavioral signals.

- **Scenario 3 - *Emotional Support via Empathic Agents and Social Mediation:*** Conversational agents powered by large language models (LLMs), such as ChatGPT-like systems, deliver cognitive stimulation, companionship, and behavioral reminders. These agents are fine-tuned to detect affective states (e.g., sadness, anxiety) based on vocal prosody, lexical content, and interaction frequency.

Human–AI Interaction: When emotional distress is inferred, the agent activates a graduated escalation protocol—offering calming strategies, empathetic dialogue, or suggesting virtual contact with a family member. If symptoms persist, the system alerts a designated human caregiver or social worker for direct intervention. This approach combines algorithmic empathy with human emotional intelligence, promoting psychosocial well-being.

- **Scenario 4 - *Co-Evolution of Services via Human Feedback Loops*:** All interactions - decisions made, services accepted or declined, and satisfaction feedback - are systematically logged and analyzed to inform continuous learning within the AI models.

Human–AI Interaction: For example, if several users express dissatisfaction with a specific telehealth interface, the system aggregates this qualitative feedback and flags it for redesign by service developers. Such feedback loops facilitate iterative refinement of care services, integrating lived experience with machine learning optimization, thus enabling the progressive alignment of system behavior with user values and usability standards.

These illustrative scenarios substantiate the core tenet of GRACE as a co-active socio-technical system, wherein human and AI agents operate as synergistic partners. By integrating algorithmic capabilities in reasoning and pattern recognition with human ethical reasoning, affective understanding, and contextual awareness, GRACE is expected to operationalize a resilient, ethical, and human-centered paradigm for AI-enabled aging-in-place ecosystem.

4.5 Current Status and Development Methodology

At its current stage, GRACE is in an advanced conceptual and early prototyping phase. Foundational modules—such as health anomaly detection and the integration layer for multimodal data aggregation—have been designed and partially implemented. Initial validation took place in controlled laboratory settings using synthetic user profiles and scenarios to assess interoperability and response consistency.

Building on these foundations, GRACE adopts a human-centered, iterative development approach comprising four phases. First, requirements elicitation involves interviews and workshops with older adults, families, and professionals to define functional and ethical criteria, with attention to cognitive and sensory limitations. Next, interactive prototypes are developed and refined through stakeholder feedback. Subsequently, controlled pilots in living labs and care facilities evaluate usability and initial impact. Finally, longitudinal studies monitor health and well-being outcomes over extended periods.

To ensure ethical integrity throughout, the project implements robust consent management, comprehensive data protection measures, and active stakeholder participation in governance processes. Furthermore, collaboration is coordinated through a consortium of healthcare providers, technology partners, and social institutions to align efforts and evolve the system collectively.

5 Conclusions and Future Work

The GRACE system presents a novel approach to elderly care by leveraging hybrid collaborative networks that bring together human empathy and AI-driven intelligence. Through a multi-layered architecture encompassing sensing, analytics, and interaction, the system is aimed at delivering personalized and evolving care services that respond to the changing needs of elderly individuals while involving caregivers, families, and service providers in an integrated support ecosystem.

Preliminary estimates suggest that GRACE effectively improves care quality by enabling monitoring, early intervention through predictive analytics, and coordinated service delivery. By fostering collaboration among all stakeholders, the system empowers human decision-making with AI insights, enhancing both safety and autonomy for the elderly. Importantly, user case studies indicate that trust in the system improves when decisions are transparent, communication is consistent, and human actors remain in control [37].

Although GRACE may represent a significant advancement in designing collaborative networks for elderly care, its successful implementation requires addressing several organizational, technological, and ethical challenges. Organizationally, coordinating diverse stakeholders - such as elderly individuals, family members, caregivers, and service providers - with differing expectations and evolving roles demands flexible and shared frameworks. Technologically, ensuring interoperability among heterogeneous systems, scalability to large populations, and transparency in AI-driven decisions are critical for effective service delivery. Ethically, GRACE must guarantee data privacy, comply with regulations, and uphold human-centered values by fostering trust through explainability, user consent, and human oversight. Overcoming these challenges is essential for GRACE to truly augment human capabilities and promote sustainable, trustworthy human-AI collaboration in elderly care ecosystems.

In terms of adoption and scalability, the project adopts a progressive and evidence-driven deployment strategy, initially launching small-scale pilot implementations to validate core functionalities and gather practical insights. These pilots will serve as controlled environments to assess the interoperability of the platform, identify unforeseen challenges, and fine-tune system configurations before broader dissemination.

This incremental approach enables the flexible introduction of new services and functionalities within the elderly care ecosystem as needs evolve and technological capabilities mature. By proceeding step by step, the project mitigates the risks commonly associated with large-scale rollouts, such as user resistance, inadequate support structures, or insufficient infrastructure readiness. Additionally, strategies for user training, caregiver empowerment, and community engagement are envisioned to foster acceptance and build trust in AI-supported care processes.

Future work will prioritize the following research directions:

- ***Scalability and real-world deployment***: Expanding GRACE implementation across diverse settings to test its robustness and interoperability in complex care environments.
- ***Enhanced transparency***: Investigating mechanisms for improving AI explainability, especially in decision-making processes that impact health and well-being.
- ***Contextual personalization***: Extending system capabilities to incorporate a wider range of contextual data (e.g., lifestyle habits, environmental conditions) for more granular personalization.
- ***Advanced predictive capabilities***: Integrating more sophisticated models for early detection of risks, including mental health conditions and emergency scenarios.
- ***Long-term impact evaluation***: Conducting longitudinal studies to assess the social, emotional, and health outcomes of hybrid human-AI collaborative systems in elderly care.

By addressing the outlined challenges and continuously advancing adaptive, ethical, and user-centered solutions, we aim to contribute to a future in which aging is supported with dignity, autonomy, and collective intelligence.

Acknowledgments. This work is supported in part by the Portuguese Foundation for Science and Technology through the projects CTS/00066.

References

1. OECD - Organisation for Economic Co-operation and Development, Health at a Glance 2023. OECD Indicators (2023). https://doi.org/10.1787/7a7afb35-en
2. Baldissera, T.A., De Faveri, C., Oliveira, M.A., Camarinha-Matos, L.M.: Collaborative communication and monitoring ecosystem for elderly care. In: Working Conference on Virtual Enterprises, pp. 34–49, Springer (2024). https://doi.org/10.1007/978-3-031-71743-7_3
3. Baldissera, T.A., Camarinha-Matos, L.M., De Faveri, C.: Designing elderly care ecosystem in collaborative networks environment. In: 2017 International Conference on Computing Networking and Informatics (ICCNI), pp. 1–9 (2017). https://doi.org/10.1109/ICCNI.2017.8123818
4. Baldissera, T.A., Camarinha-Matos, L.M.: SCoPE: Service composition and personalization environment. Appl. Sci. (Switzerland) **8**(11) (2018). https://doi.org/10.3390/app8112297
5. Baldissera, T.A., Camarinha-Matos, L.M.: Evolutionary and adaptive elderly care ecosystem. In: Lecture Notes in Computer Science (including subseries Lecture NoteArtificial Intelligence and Lecture Notes in Bioinformatics) (2019). https://doi.org/10.1007/978-3-030-24308-1_24
6. Peeters, M.M.M., et al.: Hybrid collective intelligence in a human–AI society. AI Soc. **36**(1) (2021). https://doi.org/10.1007/s00146-020-01005-y
7. van Leeuwen, K.G., de Rooij, M., Schalekamp, S., van Ginneken, B., Rutten, M.J.C.M.: How does artificial intelligence in radiology improve efficiency and health outcomes? (2022). https://doi.org/10.1007/s00247-021-05114-8
8. Vollmuth, P., et al.: Artificial intelligence (AI)-based decision support improves reproducibility of tumor response assessment in neuro-oncology: an international multi-reader study. Neuro Oncol. **25**(3) (2023). https://doi.org/10.1093/neuonc/noac189
9. Reddy, S., et al.: Evaluation framework to guide implementation of AI systems into healthcare settings (2021). https://doi.org/10.1136/bmjhci-2021-100444

10. Harte, R., et al.: A human-centered design methodology to enhance the usability, human factors, and user experience of connected health systems: a three-phase methodology. JMIR Hum Factors **4**(1) (2017). https://doi.org/10.2196/humanfactors.5443
11. Sharma, A., Lin, I.W., Miner, A.S., Atkins, D.C., Althoff, T.: Human–AI collaboration enables more empathic conversations in text-based peer-to-peer mental health support. Nat. Mach. Intel. **5**(1) (2023). https://doi.org/10.1038/s42256-022-00593-2
12. Adu-Kankam, K.O., Camarinha-Matos, L.M., Obeng, E.: Hybrid collaborative networks in energy ecosystems. In: Camarinha-Matos, L.M., Ortiz, A., Boucher, X., Barthe-Delanoë, A.-M. (eds.) Navigating unpredictability: collaborative networks in non-linear worlds, pp. 3–21. Springer Nature Switzerland, Cham (2024). https://doi.org/10.1007/978-3-031-71739-0_1
13. Rezwana, J., Lou Maher, M.: Designing Creative AI Partners with COFI: A Framework for Modeling Interaction in Human-AI Co-Creative Systems. ACM Trans. Comp.-Human Interact. **30**(5) (2023). https://doi.org/10.1145/3519026
14. Fragiadakis, G., Diou, C., Kousiouris, G., Nikolaidou, M.: Evaluating human-ai collaboration: A review and methodological framework. arXiv preprint arXiv:2407.19098 (2024). https://doi.org/10.48550/arXiv.2407.19098
15. Farič, N., et al.: Early experiences of integrating an artificial intelligence-based diagnostic decision support system into radiology settings: a qualitative study. J. American Medical Info. Asso. **31**(1) (2024). https://doi.org/10.3233/SHTI230787
16. Aleid, A., et al.: Artificial intelligence approach for early detection of brain tumors using MRI images. Applied Sciences (Switzerland) **13**(6) (2023). https://doi.org/10.3390/app13063808
17. Calisto, F.M., Santiago, C., Nunes, N., Nascimento, J.C.: BreastScreening-AI: evaluating medical intelligent agents for human-AI interactions. Artif. Intel. Med. **127** (2022). https://doi.org/10.1016/j.artmed.2022.102285
18. Al-Fatlawi, A., Al-Khazaali, A.A.T., Hasan, S.H.: AI-based model for fraud detection in bank systems. Fusion: Practice and Applications **14**(1) (2024). https://doi.org/10.54216/FPA.140102
19. Sachan, S., Almaghrabi, F., Yang, J.B., Xu, D.L.: Human-AI collaboration to mitigate decision noise in financial underwriting: a study on FinTech innovation in a lending firm. Int. Rev. Fin. Anal. **93** (2024). https://doi.org/10.1016/j.irfa.2024.103149
20. Chakravorti, T., et al.: Artificial prediction markets present a novel opportunity for human-AI collaboration. In: Proceedings of the International Joint Conference on Autonomous Agents and Multiagent Systems. AAMAS (2023). https://doi.org/10.48550/arXiv.2211.16590
21. Sankaran, G., Palomino, M.A., Knahl, M., Siestrup, G.: A modeling approach for measuring the performance of a human-AI collaborative process. Appl. Sci. (Switzerland) **12**(22) (2022). https://doi.org/10.3390/app122211642
22. Massaro, A.: Multi-level decision support system in production and safety management. Knowledge **2**(4) (2022). https://doi.org/10.3390/knowledge2040039
23. Oravec, J.A.: Artificial intelligence implications for academic cheating: expanding the dimensions of responsible Human-AI collaboration with ChatGPT and bard. J. Interact. Learn. Res. **34**(2) (2023). Accessed: 06 May 2025. https://api.semanticscholar.org/CorpusID:260810272
24. Nikolopoulou, K.: Generative artificial intelligence in higher education: Exploring ways of harnessing pedagogical practices with the assistance of ChatGPT. Int. J. Changes in Educ. **1**(2), 103–111 (2024). https://doi.org/10.47852/bonviewIJCE42022489
25. El-Zanfaly, D., Huang, Y., Dong, Y.: Sand playground: designing human-AI physical interface for co-creation in motion. ACM Int. Conf. Proc. Series (2022). https://doi.org/10.1145/3527927.3532791
26. Arias-Rosales, A.: The perceived value of human-AI collaboration in early shape exploration: an exploratory assessment. PLoS One **17**(9) (2022). https://doi.org/10.1371/journal.pone.0274496

27. Hauptman, A.I., Schelble, B.G., McNeese, N.J., Madathil, K.C.: Adapt and overcome: perceptions of adaptive autonomous agents for human-AI teaming. Comput. Human Behav. **138** (2023). https://doi.org/10.1016/j.chb.2022.107451
28. Alon-Barkat, S., Busuioc, M.: Human-AI interactions in public sector decision making: 'Automation Bias' and 'Selective Adherence' to Algorithmic Advice. J. Pub. Administr. Res. Theory **33**(1) (2023). https://doi.org/10.1093/jopart/muac007
29. Zhao, L., et al.: Chatspot: Bootstrapping multimodal llms via precise referring instruction tuning. arXiv preprint arXiv:2307.09474 (2023). https://doi.org/10.24963/ijcai.2024/193
30. Zheng, Q., Gou, J., Camarinha-Matos, L.M., Zhang, J.Z., Zhang, X.: Digital capability requirements and improvement strategies: organizational socialization of AI teammates. Inf. Process. Manag. **60**(6), 103504 (2023). https://doi.org/10.1016/j.ipm.2023.103504
31. Dziorny, A.C., et al.: Clinical decision support in the PICU: implications for design and evaluation. Pediatric Critical Care Medicine **23**(8) (2022). https://doi.org/10.1097/PCC.0000000000002973
32. Camarinha-Matos, L.M., Afsarmanesh, H.: Collaborative networks: a new scientific discipline. J. Intel. Manuf. **16**(4–5) (2005). https://doi.org/10.1007/s10845-005-1656-3
33. Baldissera, T.A., Camarinha-Matos, L.M.: Evaluating the Applicability and Utility of an Elderly Care Ecosystem. In: Collaborative Networks and Digital Transformation: 20th IFIP WG 5.5 Working Conference on Virtual Enterprises, PRO-VE 2019, Turin, Italy, September 23–25, 2019, Proceedings 20, pp. 365–378. Springer (2019). https://doi.org/10.1007/978-3-030-28464-0_32
34. Arcaini, P., Riccobene, E., Scandurra, P.: Modeling and analyzing MAPE-K feedback loops for self-adaptation. In: 2015 IEEE/ACM 10th International Symposium on Software Engineering for Adaptive and Self-Managing Systems, pp. 13–23. IEEE (2015). https://doi.org/10.1109/SEAMS.2015.10
35. Klabunde, R.: Daniel Jurafsky/James H. Martin: Speech and Language Processing. An Introduction to Natural Language Processing, Computational Linguistics, and Speech Recognition. Zeitschrift fur Sprachwissenschaft **21**(1) (2002). https://doi.org/10.1515/zfsw.2002.21.1.134
36. Binns, R., Van Kleek, M., Veale, M., Lyngs, U., Zhao, J., Shadbolt, N.: It's Reducing a Human Being to a Percentage' Perceptions of Justice in Algorithmic Decisions. In: Proceedings of the 2018 Chi conference on human factors in computing systems, pp. 1–14 (2018). https://doi.org/10.1145/3173574.317395

Territorial Collaboration and Personalisation to Improve Healthcare Pathways: The Case Study of Hip or Knee Arthroplasty

Ahmed Bakali El Kassimi[1,2(✉)], Marianne Sarazin[1,2], Xavier Boucher[1], Ghada Ben Meriem[1], and Pierre Luc Fresard[2]

[1] Mines Saint-Etienne, Univ Clermont Auvergne, INP Clermont Auvergne, CNRS, UMR 6158 LIMOS, 42023 Saint-Étienne, France
{ahmed.bakali,boucher}@emse.fr, m1sarazin@mutualite-loire.com
[2] Équipe De Recherche, Clinique Médico-Chirurgicale Mutualiste, Aésio Santé, 42100 Saint-Étienne, France
pfresard@mutualite-loire.com

Abstract. With increasing economic constraints and the scarcity of human resources in the territories, care pathways' coordination is becoming increasingly complicated, with a risk of the "loss of chance" for patients. This study proposes a discrete-event simulation (DES) model to evaluate the allocation of care resources (hospital and non-hospital) at regional level, in order to ensure the organization of a care pathway, whatever the patient's clinical or environmental conditions. To this end, the study is based on the treatment of patients undergoing hip or knee replacement surgery. The model aims to identify existing regional disparities and improve care coordination during the post-operative phase. By integrating key performance indicators such as waiting times, resource utilization rates and associated costs, the DES model supports evidence-based recommendations for optimizing resource allocation at discharge. This tool serves as a decision-support system to assess the impact of alternative care strategies, address issues related to inequalities in access to healthcare and improve clinical outcomes during the recovery phase.

Keywords: Postoperative care · Hip & Knee arthroplasty · Territorial approach

1 Introduction

In France, population ageing is accompanied by a steady rise in comorbidities such as osteoarthritis, particularly affecting the hip and knee. This has led to a growing demand for joint replacement surgeries, including total hip and knee arthroplasties. Health systems are therefore facing a major challenge: adapting the provision of care to meet this increasing demand, in a context marked by significant resource shortages, especially in certain regions. The postoperative phase, which involves both hospital-based services and community care (rehabilitation centers, physiotherapists, nurses, and surgeons), particularly exemplifies this strain.

Published by Springer Nature Switzerland AG 2026
L. M. Camarinha-Matos et al. (Eds.): PRO-VE 2025, IFIP AICT 770, pp. 428–445, 2026.
https://doi.org/10.1007/978-3-032-05673-3_26

The uneven distribution of required resources creates logistical obstacles that may compromise the quality of care. These include treatment delays, prolonged hospital stays, and multiple transfers for patients, all of which can undermine the effectiveness of postoperative protocols and adversely affect clinical outcomes. As a result, there is a pressing need to implement a more personalized and better coordinated approach to ensure optimal care tailored to the specific needs of each patient.

In this context, the modeling and simulation of postoperative care pathways emerge as powerful tools to support decision-makers in evaluating current organizational structures and designing alternative strategies. These approaches enable the representation of patient flows, the analysis of resource utilization, and the incorporation of uncertainties inherent to this stage of care. They offer a valuable forward-looking perspective for optimizing the territorial organization of care delivery at both local and national levels. After a literature review on the improvement of coordination and collaboration at territorial level for healthcare pathways (Sect. 2), the paper outlines the methodological approach adopted for the study (Sect. 3), and provides an in-depth description of the simulation model's development and validation (Sect. 4). Section 5 focuses on a French territorial case study related to postoperative care for hip and knee replacements.

2 Literature Review

2.1 The Need for Territorial Coordination and Collaboration for Hip and Knee Arthroplasty Care in the Postoperative Phase in France

In response to territorial disparities and inequalities in access to healthcare in France, several measures have been implemented to address these challenges and promote a fairer distribution and organization of healthcare resources, as reported in the Information Report No. 137 of the French Senate (rapport d'information n° 137 du Sénat) [1]. For example, the "contrat de stabilisation et de coordination" (COSCOM) encourages physicians to engage in care-coordination initiatives [2]. In this context, territorial coordination of postoperative care for hip and knee arthroplasty appears as a key component in addressing the growing demand for such procedures, meeting patient needs at the regional level, and enabling the personalization of postoperative care pathways. Various studies and reports have highlighted disparities in access to key resources during this phase. The 2024 Report on the Demography of Physiotherapists (rapport de la démographie des kinésithérapeutes) notes that although the overall density of physiotherapists has increased across France, the supply remains inadequate in high-demand areas such as Normandie, Centre-Val de Loire, and Île-de-France [3]. Similarly, a 2021 study by the DREES identified geographic disparities in access to medico-social structures, particularly in services providing home assistance and support for the elderly [4].

A more recent study published in 2023 by the DREES, adopting a territorial perspective, emphasized the uneven geographic accessibility of both medico-social services and healthcare services for supporting older adults, including professionals working in medical and rehabilitation care centers. It highlights that access to these services remains heterogeneous across metropolitan France and emphasizes the strong complementarity between institutional and home-based care. It also points to significant territorial variations in specialization, as territorial organization tends to favor either institutional facilities or home-based care, depending on the nature of locally available resources [5].

2.2 Initiatives to Improve Coordination and Existing Barriers

Several initiatives have sought to improve coordination as a response to healthcare access issues and territorial disparities. These include the development of protocols, pilot programs, and strategic approaches aiming to enhance coordination across regions. One such initiative is the creation of Territorial Professional Health Communities (Communautés professionnelles territoriales de santé, CPTS), established by the law of 26 January 2016 on the modernization of the healthcare system. These CPTS bring together healthcare professionals from a given area who voluntarily organize to work collectively for a defined population. One of their objectives is to implement care pathways that address the specific needs of the territory and support better structuring and coordination among professionals [6, 7]. The Paerpa program, launched in 2014 in nine pilot territories and expanded nationwide in 2016, aims to improve the care of older adults at risk of losing autonomy and to preserve their independence by reinforcing coordination among healthcare, social, and medico-social stakeholders within a given territory [8]. While this initiative targets the elderly in general, regardless of their care setting, other programs more specifically support hospital-based care transitions, such as hip or knee arthroplasty, particularly during the hospital-to-home phase. For example, the PRADO program, launched by the French National Health Insurance in 2010, aims to facilitate patients' return home after hospitalization by anticipating and coordinating their needs within their area of residence [9]. The enhanced recovery after surgery programs (ERAS) have also been widely implemented in this context, placing significant emphasis on care coordination and its impact on outcomes. Malléjac et al. studied the impact of ERAS programs on length of stay, discharge patterns, and 90-day readmission rates by comparing outcomes between two groups of private clinics, those with and without ERAS accreditation. Their findings showed that patients in ERAS-accredited clinics had an average reduction of 0.3 days in length of stay and a 15% higher likelihood of returning home, without an increase in 90-day readmission risk [10]. Despite the effectiveness of these initiatives in improving postoperative care coordination, their implementation and broader deployment still face several obstacles. These challenges limit both the expansion of such programs and the ability to assess their impact across all regions. For instance, the IGAS Report No. 2021-092R on the pilot program for direct access to physical therapy services [11] reveals that fewer than 5% of physical therapists are involved in coordinated care structures. According to data from the French National Health Insurance Fund (CNAM), around 4,000 physical therapists currently practice within multidisciplinary health centers, health centers, or territorial professional healthcare communities (CPTS). ERAS programs face similar limitations. One major issue is the absence of financial incentives that are proportionate to the resources invested by healthcare institutions. This was highlighted in a study conducted by Aaech et al. [12] at the University Hospital of Tours in France, which analyzed outcomes over a two-month period in 2019. The study, covering 17 relevant DRGs (Diagnosis-Related

Group) and 263 hospital stays, reported disappointing results considering the substantial human resource costs involved, based on the evaluation criteria set by the French National Health Authority (HAS) [13].

2.3 Scientific Literature on Territorial Care Pathway Management Approaches

Scientific literature on territorial healthcare management has increasingly attracted attention in the context of public health crises, particularly during the COVID-19 pandemic. Many studies have applied statistical and optimization models to manage healthcare resources and coordinate care across regions during periods of intense demand. A major focus has been the management and sharing of hospital capacities, such as beds and healthcare staff. For example, Parker et al. (2024) proposed robust optimization models to manage hospital capacity surges by efficiently allocating beds and transferring patients across facilities. Their simulations showed that transferring only 32 patients over a 63-day period, approximately one transfer every two days, could have reduced the need for additional capacity by nearly 90% [14]. Other studies have adopted more qualitative perspectives. Larson et al. introduced a dynamic approach to hospital surge management that goes beyond simply adding resources. Their framework includes strategies such as preserving existing capacity, smoothing demand, and adapting to the specific characteristics of surges. Based on the analysis of five hospitals facing COVID-19-related stress, the study identified key practices that enhanced responsiveness and adaptability [15].

In addition to crisis management, some studies have focused on reducing territorial disparities. Delgado et al. developed an equity-based optimization model for locating healthcare facilities, including hospital beds and COVID-19 vaccination centers. Their model balances accessibility, demand, and spatial justice. By incorporating the Gini index into a nonlinear programming framework, the authors demonstrate that maximizing coverage does not ensure equity without an appropriate distribution of resources [16].

Besides optimization and qualitative frameworks, simulation has also proven useful for developing strategic responses to territorial healthcare challenges. Several literature reviews have emphasized the relevance of simulation models in health decision-making contexts [17, 18]. One notable example is the discrete-event simulation model by Rutherford et al., which was developed for eight intensive care units in British Columbia. The model supports capacity planning during both COVID-19 and seasonal flu surges by helping decision-makers balance patient access and cost-efficiency, and by offering strategies to avoid large-scale public health interventions. Despite the richness of this literature, we found no studies applying discrete-event simulation to the territorial management of postoperative care pathways for patients undergoing hip or knee arthroplasty. We believe that addressing this gap could provide valuable insights for policymakers, especially as care trends continue to shift toward home-based recovery and short-stay pathways. These evolving practices are documented in recent national reports, such as that by DREES [19], and are central to the strategies explored in our study.

3 Methodology

3.1 Problem Definition and Overview of the Methodology

The challenge of this study is to propose a model capable of optimizing quality and efficiency of patients care pathways, through a higher coordination among territorial care resources taking into account patients environmental and clinical conditions. To tackle this problem we address two main questions:

- How can we assess a territory's capacity to deliver care that meets the specific needs of its population?
- What personalized strategies can be implemented to account for both available resources and individual patient needs, while ensuring compliance with the required care protocol?

The methodological approach developed in the paper, uses patient pathway simulation to develop the expected decision aid. Methodologically the approach is based on three main phases: (1) the elaboration of generic model, addressing a dedicated healthcare disease, and replicable in distinct territories to represent their specificities and (2) the specialisation of this generic model with data extracted from a specific territorial case study, (3) the deployment of an experimental simulation plan on the specialized simulation model so as to generate applicable organizational recommendations (Fig. 1).

Fig. 1. Methodology phases

For the elaboration of the generic model (Phase 1), it is important to take into account the expertise of professionals on the care pathway under study. Thus, the simulation model created will be applied to a defined care area, where various care pathways and scenarios can be tested. These scenarios will represent alternative ways to take in charge the patients, depending on alternative coordination modes of territorial healthcare resources with the ambition both (i) to allow a high personalisation which could consider the characteristics of the patients and (ii) to assess territorial healthcare capacities as a decision-making tool.

In this study, the generic construction of the model is based on the example of the post-operative care pathway for patients undergoing hip or knee arthroplasty (THA or TKA). The care pathway must follow a strict clinical protocol, the implementation of which is then adapted to the patient's individual characteristics (such as co-morbidities and frailty), their living environment (residence, social conditions, etc.) and the resources available. To this end, this work draws on the expertise of orthopaedic surgeons, who are responsible for specialist follow-up, nurses, who manage immediate post-operative care (wound care, pain management, etc.), and physiotherapists, who provide orthopaedic rehabilitation. All those professionals belong to the staff of the "Clinique mutualiste de saint Etienne" that serve as an experimental ground.

In this context, several types of care pathways can be configured immediately after surgery:

- In a rehabilitation centre, either on a full-care basis (full hospitalisation: FH) or on a partial-care basis (PH) (the patient comes only during the day and not every day depending on the protocol)
- at home with the services of a private physiotherapist and nurse

The different stages of professional involvement and the organizational structure of the care pathway are illustrated in Figure below (Fig. 2).

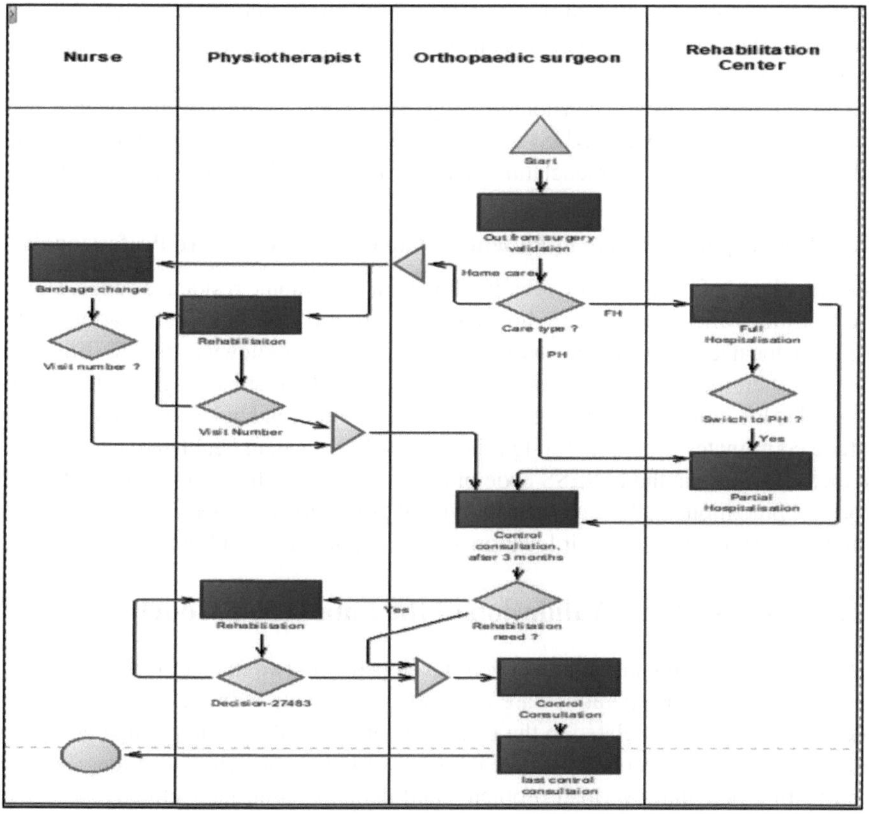

Fig. 2. Postoperative clinical pathway of Hip and Knee replacement

3.2 Basic Data Sources and Pathway Description

Several data sources have been used to describe THA and TKA patient pathways and the activity of healthcare professionals in a given area.

3.2.1 Patient and Pathway Description

Data was extracted from the French national health insurance database (SNDS). The patients included were those who had at least one hospital stay in 2018 involving a surgical procedure for hip or knee prosthesis implantation (THA or TKA). All the data linked to those patients were then considered characterising their post operative care pathways until 2020.

To categorize patients, the severity of the "Groupe Homogène de Malades" (GHM) from 1 to 4 was considered . GHM is the French patients 'stays classification for acute care as knee or hip surgery . Severity depends on patients comorbidities that are potentially involved in post operative rehabilitation pathway orientation.

The discharge modality at the end of an acute hospital stay determines the patient's subsequent care pathway and was used to know either the patients went to a rehabilitation centre or went back home .

Rehabilitation centres was assessed using the "Groupes Médico-Économiques" (GME), a classification system that considers both clinical complexity, resource consumption and financial value. This system estimates patient health status and the intensity of care required in this study.

Out-centre pathway was considered using independent healthcare professional insurance reimbursement code (SNDS) and their weighting linked to a special care. These codes are based on the "Nomenclature Générale des Actes Professionnels (NGAP)".

3.2.2 Geographic Location of Patients, Centers, and Healthcare Professionals

Patients' places of residence are identified by their geographic residence codes. Healthcare facilities, whether acute care hospitals (MCO) or post-acute rehabilitation centers (IRF), are located using a unique national facility identifier known as the FINESS code. This identifier, includes geographic information, with the first two digits indicating the geographic location corresponding to a French department and linked with longitude and latitude coordinates available through the SNDS. Independent healthcare professionals are located either via the FINESS code of the center where they practice or, in the case of private practitioners, through their individual professional registration number which contain information above their location corresponding also to a French department.

4 Development and Validation of the Simulation Model

The discrete-event simulation model was developed with two main objectives. The first is to replicate the postoperative care pathways of patients within a given territory in order to identify issues related to the management of healthcare supply and demand in the studied area. The second objective is to test various organizational strategies aimed at mitigating potential overload problems and demonstrating their effectiveness. This section presents the key assumptions underlying the model and details the modeling parameters and techniques employed.

In this part all conditions that contributed to the model construction will be described. As available data were not so closed to reality, assumptions were made on data according to professional expertise and literature. Then, performance indicators were selected in order to evaluate patients care pathway constraints.

4.1 Assumptions on Processing Data

Assumptions concern both resource capacity, geographic distributions, care consumption, patients flow and rehabilitation care modalities.

- Resource capacity: a daily resource capacity has been taken into account for both rehabilitation centers and independent professionals corresponding: for rehabilitation centers, to the daily average of patients present per day in 2018 and for independent healthcare professionals, to the average number of consultations carried out per day at an area level.
- Geographic professionals and patients distribution: in order to specify the geographical granularity of physiotherapists and nurses in a given area of the French department, their department number was multiplied by the percentage of inhabitants present in this geographical area and calculated on the basis of the population density of the department as a whole, considering an homogeneous distribution of professionals across this department. Using patients geographic codes, the percentage of patients associated with each geographic area was integrated into the simulation model to reflect spatial disparities and support the design of care strategies adapted to patient location.
- Care consumption: rehabilitation centers consumption was characterized by the average length of stay (LOS), and number of stay, physiotherapists and nurses consumption by the average number of procedures performed, according to triangular law as seen in Table 1.
- Patient Arrival Flow: patient arrivals follow was considered a Poisson distribution, with the daily mean varying by month, as illustrated in Fig. 3.

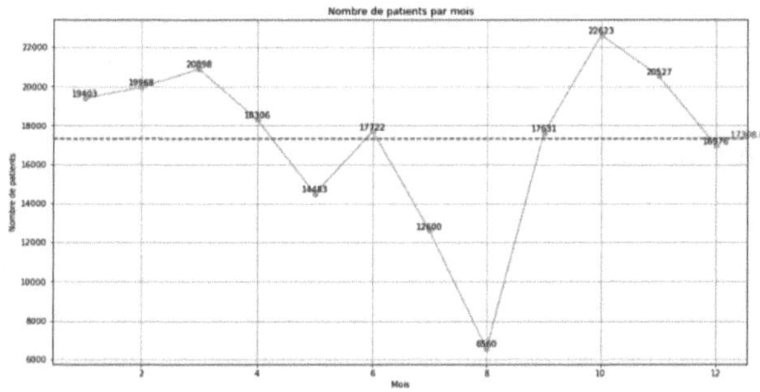

Fig. 3. Monthly evolution of the number of patients in 2018 at the national level

- Rehabilitation Care Modalities: The distribution of rehabilitation modes for patients undergoing THA and TKA is presented in the Table 2. Given the low variability in discharge modes, it was decided to consider the average annual distribution of discharge modes.

Table 1. Parameters of triangular distributions by care pathway

Item	surgery	Triangular distribution
LOS FH	TKA THA	triangular(3, 4, 4.5) triangular(2.5, 3, 3.5)
LOS FH + PH	TKA THA	triangular(2.5, 3, 3.5) triangular(1.5, 2, 2.5)
Number of stay PH	TKA THA	triangular(20, 25, 30) triangular(15, 20, 25)
Number of stay FH + PH	TKA THA	triangular(15, 20, 25) triangular(10, 15, 20)
Physiotherapist number of procedure	TKA THA	triangular(20, 25, 30) triangular(15, 20, 25)
Nurse number of procedure	THA + TKA	triangular(9, 10, 12)

Table 2. Distribution of rehabilitation modes for THA & TKA, Île-de-France, 2018.

Mode	THA(%)	TKA(%)
Home	71	34
FH	26	49
PH	1	9
FH + PH	2	8

4.2 Performance Indicators

Performance indicators are used to assess the state of a situation. In this context, they were chosen with healthcare professionals for their ability to identify situations usually encountered in the day-to-day management of care pathways, and which can be a source of "loss of chance" for patients. They include : the organization of rehabilitation, which is often complicated by a lack of capacity, particularly for independent physiotherapists, and can therefore delay treatment (resource Occupancy Rate for rehabilitation centers and independent professionals, time to Care Initiation); the distance involved in treatment (Average Travel Distance), which can be a source of poor patient compliance with the protocol; and the total cost of treatment (Cost of Care), which is a national concern in France, forcing professionals to make changes in their way to organize pathways . Those performance indicators are described below:

- **Resource Occupancy Rate for rehabilitation centers and independent professionals:** The daily occupancy rate of each resource is calculated using the following formula: Occupancy Rate = (Number of occupied slots per day / Total daily capacity)

$\times$ 100. An annual and monthly average of these rates is then computed in order to identify potential overloads throughout the year.
- **Average Travel Distance:** This indicator assesses the geographic accessibility of care within the patient's residential area. It represents the total distance in kilometers between the patient's home and the care location (either a private practitioner or rehabilitation center). The simulation provides an annual average travel distance for the year 2018.
- **Time to Care Initiation:** Time to care initiation is defined as the average number of days between the surgical intervention and the start of postoperative care, for each care pathway category. This indicator reflects the territory's capacity to mobilize resources in a timely manner to meet patient needs
- **Cost of Care:** The total cost per patient is calculated by combining treatment (hospitalizations and consultations) -related expenses and transportation costs. Note: All indicators are computed after a one-month warm-up period, which allows the model to reach a stable state that accurately reflects the real-world functioning of the system.

4.3 Model Validation

To assess the validity of the simulation model, several complementary validation techniques were applied. Event trace animation and monitoring were used to empirically verify the execution of simulated processes and their alignment with the logic of the actual care delivery system. This validation was further reinforced through expert feedback and by comparing the simulated indicators with real data from 2018 (Table 3).

Table 3. Validation of simulated results against actual 2018 data

KPI	Real (μ0)	Simulated	IC à 95% [BI, BS]	|BI - μ0|	|BS-μ0|	ε = Max(|BI -μ0|, *|BS - μ0\|)/μ0
LOS FH	39 days	38 days	[36, 40]	3	1	8%
LOS PH	56 days	58 days	[55, 61]	1	5	9%

The number of replications was set to 31, based on the average length of stay in rehabilitation care (IRF) as the reference indicator. The objective was to achieve a precision of ±2 days within a 95% confidence interval. Table 1.7 presents the results of this comparison, which show that the differences between the simulated values and historical data remain within acceptable margins, thereby confirming the validity of the model.

5 Territorial Case Study and Analysis

In order to assess the relevance of the simulation model to diagnose system inefficiencies and design strategies adapted to the postoperative care needs of patients undergoing hip or knee arthroplasty and after their hospital stay and potentially other care pathways, the model was tested in a specific territory. Several scenarios were considered corresponding to situations that could be encountered in a real context. Three experimental strategies were considered:

- Fixed resource capacities and patient flows, but with post-operative discharge fluctuation;
- Fixed patient flow, with variable resource allocation via flexibility on existing resource capacity or new resource deployment;
- Variable volume of patients flows;

5.1 Case Study

The Île-de-France region was selected as a study area. This region is particularly suitable due to its high population density and concentration of healthcare resources, which are unevenly distributed and predominantly located in metropolitan areas. This spatial imbalance makes it an ideal setting for testing the model's ability to support territorial healthcare planning. The following daily capacities were used as reference values in the simulation for this territory: full inpatient rehabilitation (FH): 717 slots/day, day hospitalization (PH): 285 slots/day, physiotherapy: 1,336 sessions/day, and nursing care: 1,184 sessions/day.

5.2 Experimentation of Strategies

A sensitivity analysis of the input parameters that are likely to vary the output data would improve the robustness of the model under variable conditions, and could focus on possible areas for improvement. The current study only focuses on the variation in the resource capacities parameter, which has the greatest impact. The rest of the sensitivity analyses will be developed in the future.

5.2.1 Strategy 1: Fixed Resources, Discharge Variability After Surgery

This first group of scenarios evaluates the impact of a strategy that maintains a constant overall care capacity while altering the distribution of discharge destinations, with an emphasis on promoting discharge to home rather than to inpatient rehabilitation. This approach, suggested by physicians, aims to improve access to care in regions with limited availability of rehabilitation centers. It is supported by recent studies showing that home-based care provides clinical outcomes comparable to those of inpatient rehabilitation, while also contributing to reduced healthcare costs. The real-world situation (Scenario 1.1) is compared to two alternative scenarios (Scenarios 1.2 and 1.3), in which the discharge distribution is progressively adjusted as shown below (Table 4).

Table 4. Distribution of discharge modes by scenario

THA			
Discharge mode	Scenario 1.1	Scenario 1.2	Scenario 1.3
% Home	71%	80%	75%
% FH	26%	17%	10%
% PH	1%	1%	7%

(continued)

Table 4. (*continued*)

THA			
Discharge mode	Scenario 1.1	Scenario 1.2	Scenario 1.3
% FH + PH	2%	2%	8%
TKA			
	Scenario 1.1	Scenario 1.2	Scenario 1.3
% Home	34%	50%	45%
% FH	49%	33%	25%
% PH	9%	9%	17%
% FH + PH	8%	8%	13%

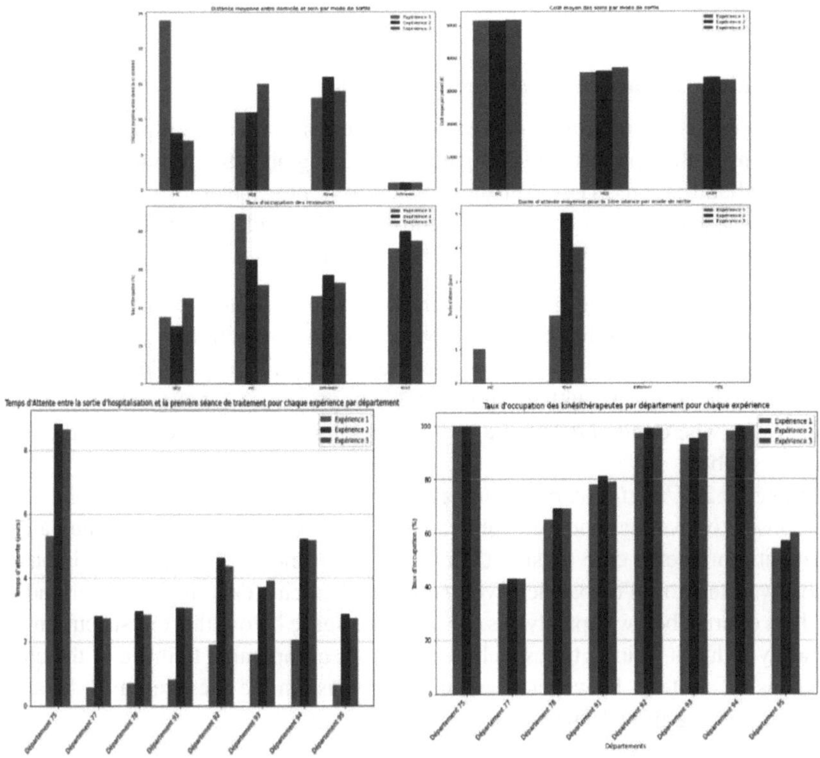

Fig. 4. Comparison of performance indicators across the three experiments

Based on the results illustrated in figures above, Scenario 1.3 proves to be the most effective strategy, achieving a favorable balance between cost-efficiency, improved accessibility, optimized resource utilization, and reduced waiting times. Inpatient rehabilitation (FH) remains the most costly pathway across all scenarios. However, shifting patients toward home-based care and day hospitalization (PH) reduces overall costs, even when accounting for slightly higher transportation expenses. As shown in the figure, geographical access improves significantly in Scenarios 1.2 and 1.3, with travel distances notably reduced. Although PH involves slightly longer trips in Scenario 1.3, they remain under 15 kilometers and within acceptable limits. Scenario 1.3 also leads to better use of physiotherapy resources (with occupancy reaching 80%) and alleviates the overload observed in inpatient rehabilitation units under Scenario 1.1. Waiting times, particularly in HC, are reduced in alternative scenarios, though delays in accessing physiotherapy persist (Fig. 4).

The analysis of waiting times by administrative department highlights significant territorial disparities. In Department 75 (Paris), for example, waiting times exceed one week, a threshold generally considered clinically unacceptable. This imbalance is largely driven by extremely high resource occupancy rates in certain departments, as illustrated in the figure below. This suggests that a more balanced redistribution of resources may be needed to improve access to care and reduce waiting times, particularly in high-demand areas such as Paris.

5.2.2 Strategy 2: Variable Resource Allocation

This group of scenarios examines two complementary strategies designed to improve access to physiotherapy while pursuing the overarching objective of reducing reliance on inpatient rehabilitation (FH). Given the critical role of physiotherapy in the postoperative care pathway, and the significant delays currently observed, especially in high-demand areas, optimizing the use of this resource is essential.

- *Strategy 2.1: Increasing resource capacity:* The first strategy consists in expanding physiotherapy availability by adding five additional appointments per day per department. As shown in the figure below, this measure significantly reduces waiting times across all departments, with the most notable improvement observed in Paris (Department 75), where initial delays exceeded one week, a threshold considered clinically unacceptable.
- *Strategy 2.2: Utilizing capacity in neighbouring departments:* The second strategy proposes to leverage underutilized capacity in neighbouring departments, allowing patients to receive care outside their home department. This approach is based on observed territorial disparities, with some departments experiencing overload while others operate below capacity. As shown in the figure below, this redistribution significantly reduces waiting times, achieving results comparable to those of the capacity expansion strategy. However, it entails an increase in the average travel distance for patients, rising from 15 to 30 kms.

Both strategies demonstrate a clear potential to reduce waiting times. Increasing local capacity offers a direct solution but requires additional resources. By contrast, redistributing patients across departments makes more efficient use of existing capacity but introduces challenges related to accessibility. In the broader context of limiting dependence on inpatient rehabilitation, improving access to physiotherapy through either capacity expansion or coordinated regional planning appears to be a key factor in enhancing the overall performance of the care system (Figs. 5 and 6).

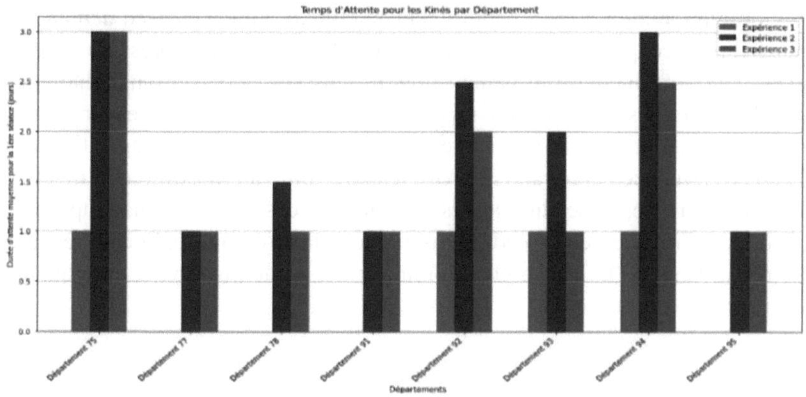

Fig. 5. Average waiting time for first sessions by department with increased resources (Strategy 2.1)

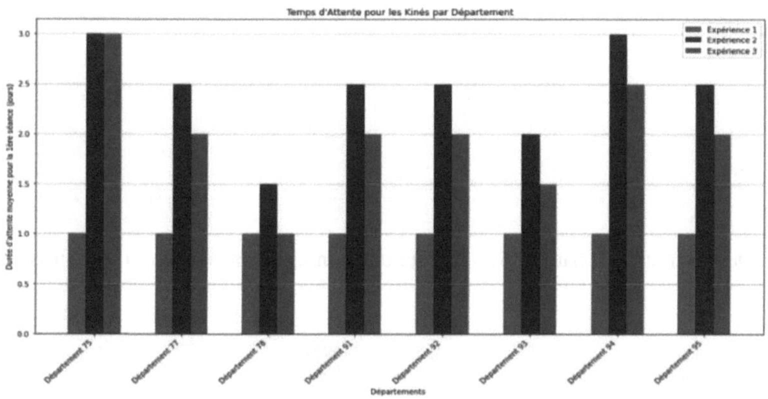

Fig. 6. Average waiting time for first sessions by department when allowing patients to exit their home department (Strategy 2.2)

5.2.3 Strategy 3: Variable Patient Flow

In this third scenario, the daily patient flow was increased in order to evaluate the capacity of healthcare resources to absorb a rising demand. This adjustment reflects broader demographic trends, particularly population ageing, which is well documented in the literature. In France, the proportion of individuals aged 65 and over continues to grow steadily. This demographic shift is especially relevant to the target population of this study, as it leads to increased demand for procedures such as prosthetic surgery and associated postoperative care, which primarily concern older adults.

The objective of this scenario is to assess the impact of a 20% rise in patient flow on waiting times and resource utilization, within the context of the three previously defined scenarios. To simulate this change, the arrival distribution was modified by increasing the average number of patients per day. The resulting outcomes are presented in the figure below.

This simulation allows for a better understanding of how increased demand affects system performance, particularly with regard to delays in care and pressure on available resources. The 20% increase in patient flow reveals key organizational challenges. In Scenario 1, limited resources lead to unacceptable waiting times and resource overload, especially in inpatient rehabilitation. Scenarios 2 and 3, by redistributing patients toward DOM and HDJ, reduce delays and improve resource utilization. Although travel-related costs slightly increase, these alternatives remain more cost-effective than inpatient care. The results confirm the need to adapt discharge pathways and reallocate resources to address rising demand linked to population ageing, while preserving care quality and controlling costs (Figs. 7 and 8).

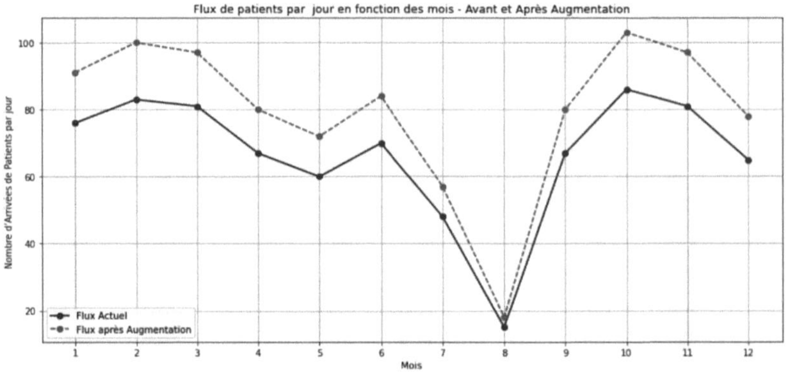

Fig. 7. Daily variation in patient arrivals over the months before and after the increase in flow

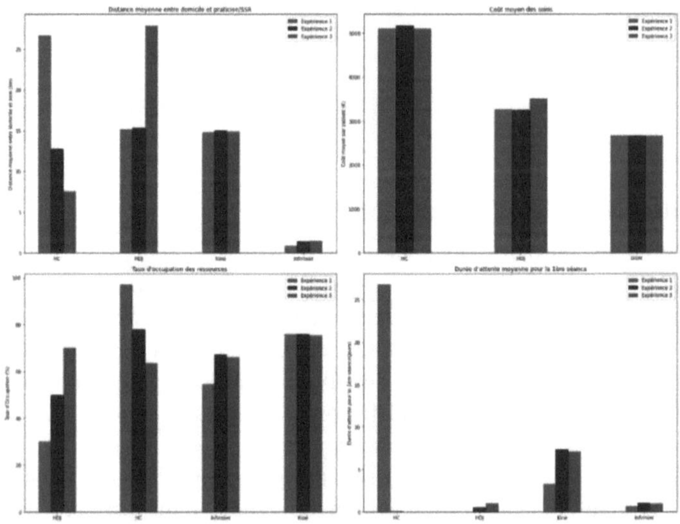

Fig. 8. Comparison of performance indicators for the three experiments after the flow increase

5.2.4 Discussion

The findings suggest that reorganizing care pathways, in particular by strengthening home-based care and improving the coordination of day hospitalization, can help alleviate hospital pressure while preserving, and in some cases improving, the quality and accessibility of care. The potential of a better collaboration among all territorial healthcare resources appears as an important driver towards a better management of overall healthcare systems.

Even if this approach remains highly quantitative, it is nonetheless closely linked to qualitative aspects, since the proposed indicators were developed by clinicians seeking to improve patients' care pathways. Indeed, in the context of THA and TKA, resumption of walking and daily activity (home return) as quickly as possible are factors that can limit post-operative vascular complications (embolisms, venous thrombosis, etc.) and muscle loss, which slows down rehabilitation. Matching management models to the rehabilitation process is therefore a very important factor for practitioners, who can be sure of being able to offer the most operational care pathway according to the care protocol. For the patient, this optimization strengthens adherence to treatment by favouring geographical proximity and the earliest possible home return, thereby limiting the number of hospital admissions.

This simulation tool therefore offers a clear added-value in the management of care pathways. Complementary with current management methods, which are still very time-consuming for practitioners and nurses and stressing for patients waiting for a care pathway solution, it can help to guide the organization by quickly proposing solutions that best suit the personalized context of the patients, specially their home geographical area and healthcare professionals working in the area.

6 Conclusion

The simulation model developed in this article has the innovative advantage of offering a pathway management approach that takes into account the resources of an area and the constraints of a care protocol. Its construction based on the specific case of THA and TKA and, the circumscribed territory of the Ile de France made it possible to consider the advantages and possible improvements of the model. This approach also made possible to consider the operational uses of interest to healthcare professionals and health decision-makers. The genericity of the model and decision-making approach are an important perspective. Further research steps are necessary to address this issue : notably to develop larger sensitivity analyses to test the robustness of the model to uncertainty on several parameters, but also to make possible its replicability to other fields and other pathologies requiring a structured modelling methodology to adapt the models to other contexts affected by the territorial organization of care pathways.

References

1. Sénat: Inégalités territoriales d'accès aux soins : aux grands maux, les grands remèdes. https://www.senat.fr/rap/r24-137/r24-137.html

2. Contrat_CDS_stabilisation.pdf. https://www.centre-val-de-loire.paps.sante.fr/system/files/2019-10/Contrat_CDS_stabilisation.pdf
3. Ordre des masseurs-kinésithérapeutes. Communiqué de presse – Rapport de la démographie des kinésithérapeutes 2024 : état des lieux et enjeux pour l'avenir de la kinésithérapie en France (2024). https://www.ordremk.fr/actualites/ordre/communique-de-presse-rapport-de-la-demographie-des-kinesitherapeutes-2024-etat-des-lieux-et-enjeux-pour-lavenir-de-la-kinesitherapie-en-france/
4. Direction de la recherche, des études, de l'évaluation et des statistiques. Des disparités territoriales d'accessibilité géographique aux structures médico-sociales destinées aux personnes âgées. https://drees.solidarites-sante.gouv.fr/communique-de-presse/des-disparites-territoriales-daccessibilite-geographique-aux-structures-medico
5. Direction de la recherche, des études, de l'évaluation et des statistiques. Accessibilité géographique à l'offre médico-sociale et sanitaire pour les personnes âgées : une approche territoriale. https://drees.solidarites-sante.gouv.fr/publications-communique-de-presse/etudes-et-resultats/accessibilite-geographique-loffre-medico
6. Ministère du Travail, de la Santé, des Solidarités et des Familles. CPTS : s'organiser sur un même territoire pour renforcer les soins aux patients. 14 Aug 2024. https://sante.gouv.fr/systeme-de-sante/structures-de-soins/cpts-s-organiser-sur-un-meme-territoire-pour-renforcer-les-soins-aux-patients/
7. Agences Régionales de Santé. Les communautés professionnelles territoriales de santé. https://www.ars.sante.fr/les-communautes-professionnelles-territoriales-de-sante
8. Ministère du Travail, de la Santé, des Solidarités et des Familles. Le dispositif Paerpa. https://sante.gouv.fr/systeme-de-sante/parcours-des-patients-et-des-usagers/le-parcours-sante-des-aines-paerpa/article/le-dispositif-paerpa
9. Ameli. Prado, le service de retour à domicile. https://www.ameli.fr/loire/medecin/exercice-liberal/services-patients/prado
10. Malléjac, N., Or, Z.: Évaluation d'impact d'une nouvelle organisation des soins à l'hôpital sur les parcours de soins. Rev. Epidemiol. Sante Publique **67**(Suppl 1), S86–S87 (2019). https://doi.org/10.1016/j.respe.2019.01.045
11. Bruant-Bisson, A., Laffon, P., Marty, M. : Expérimentation de l'accès direct aux actes de masso-kinésithérapie. 2021–092R (2021)
12. Aesch, B., Castel, S., Capsec, J., Fourquet, F., Rusch, E., Grammatico-Guillon, L.: La Réhabilitation améliorée après chirurgie (RAAC): analyse de l'impact au CHRU de Tours. France. Rev Epidemiol Sante Publique. **68**, 20 (2020). https://doi.org/10.1016/j.respe.2020.01.043
13. DGOS. Expérimentation d'un paiement à l'épisode de soins pour des prises en charge chirurgicales - EDS (2023). https://sante.gouv.fr/IMG/pdf/eds_faq_v2.pdf
14. Parker, F., Ganjkhanloo, F., Martínez, D.A., Ghobadi, K.: Optimal Hospital Capacity Management During Demand Surges. arXiv. 2024 Mar 29. https://doi.org/10.48550/arXiv.2403.15738
15. Larson, J.D., Lai, A.Y., DePuccio, M.J., Hilligoss, B.: Managing surges in demand: a grounded conceptual framework of surge management capability. Med. Care Res. Rev. **81**(3), 245–258 (2024). https://doi.org/10.1177/10775587241226485
16. Delgado, E.J., Cabezas, X., Martin-Barreiro, C., Leiva, V., Rojas, F.: An equity-based optimization model to solve the location problem for healthcare centers applied to hospital beds and COVID-19 vaccination. Mathematics. **10**(11), 1825 (2022). https://doi.org/10.3390/math10111825
17. Forbus, J.J., Berleant, D.: Discrete-event simulation in healthcare settings: a review. Modelling. **3**(4), 417–433 (2022). https://doi.org/10.3390/modelling3040027
18. Zhang, X.: Application of discrete event simulation in health care: a systematic review. BMC Health Serv. Res. **18**(1), 687 (2018). https://doi.org/10.1186/s12913-018-3456-4

19. Direction de la recherche, des études, de l'évaluation et des statistiques. Les établissements de santé en 2022 - Édition 2024. https://drees.solidarites-sante.gouv.fr/publications-communique-de-presse/panoramas-de-la-drees/240718_Panorama_EtablissementsSante2024

Towards a Data-Driven Decision Support System for Enhanced Healthcare Collaboration

Safa Bhar Layeb[1(✉)], Leah Rifi[2], Audrey Fertier[1], Sébastien Rebière[1], Nicolas Salatgé[1], Olivier Oger[3], Philippe Olivier[3], and Franck Fontanili[1]

[1] Centre Génie Industriel, IMT Mines Albi, Université de Toulouse, 81000 Albi, France
safa.layeb@mines-albi.fr
[2] Univ. Grenoble Alpes, Grenoble INP, G-SCOP, 38000 Grenoble, France
[3] CHC Liège, Boulevard Patience et Beaujonc, 4000 Liège, Belgique

Abstract. Collaboration in healthcare is a complex and critical challenge, especially in environments where key resources, such as surgeons, are both scarce and costly. Operating rooms are high-stakes environments that demand precise coordination among multiple care units to ensure efficient and effective patient management. In this context, we used R-IOSUITE, a decision support system originally designed for crisis management, and now extended to model and manage collaboration across hospital units in surgical care pathways. R-IOSUITE is built upon a metamodel specifically designed to represent collaborative processes. Our research begins by adapting this metamodel to healthcare settings and the coordination of surgical patient pathways. One of the key features of the framework is its ability to infer, propose, and represent a shared, holistic planning approach across all stages of the surgical care process. The proposed framework is a POC (Proof of Concept) validated through a case study involving several hospital units. The results highlight the platform's adaptability to healthcare-specific contexts and its potential to improve both the supervision and coordination of surgical pathways. This work contributes to enabling effective collaboration in complex and resource-constrained healthcare environments.

Keywords: Operating Rooms Planning and Scheduling · Healthcare Collaboration · Shared Resources · Situation Awareness · Proof of Concept

1 Introduction

In healthcare facilities such as hospitals or private clinics, Operating Rooms (OR) represent both the most significant cost and revenue centres [1]. In addition, surgeons, and more broadly medical professionals, are among the most expensive human resources [2]. Given these economic constraints, optimizing resource utilization is crucial, and effective collaboration plays a key role in reducing costs while maintaining high standards of care.

OR Planning and scheduling problem is a challenging NP-hard problem with several variants that have been both widely recognized and thoroughly investigated in the

Published by Springer Nature Switzerland AG 2026
L. M. Camarinha-Matos et al. (Eds.): PRO-VE 2025, IFIP AICT 770, pp. 446–461, 2026.
https://doi.org/10.1007/978-3-032-05673-3_27

existing literature [3]. Numerous methods were deployed, including mathematical optimization (e.g. [4]), discrete-event simulation for the simulation of patient and resource flow (e.g. [5]), heuristics and metaheuristics for approximating solutions [6], and artificial intelligence methods (e.g., reinforcement learning [7]) for prediction or decision-making.

However, despite the extensive research conducted in this field, Few works has investigated taking into account shared resource planning between units [8] and the integration of a patient pathway view in a collaborative context [9]. By contrast, the focus of surgery optimisation is on the efficiency of intra-block operations. However, in order to achieve optimal coordination in the hospital as a whole, it is crucial to optimize end-to-end patient flow, from admission through to the care services. The issue is further complicated when it comes to addressing this problem in the context of a collaborative effort between multiple hospitals. Furthermore, the agility aspect is a poorly researched area because it is essential to adapt to unexpected situations and dynamic changes that have direct impacts on these complex processes.

To address these challenges, we propose a generic and context-aware decision support system (DSS). Since our objective is to develop a model that ensures interoperability across different clinical settings, we rely on a metamodel-based approach, selecting the COSIMMA metamodel [10]. This metamodel facilitates data structuration and collaboration analysis within the healthcare system. One of the key contributions of this study is a conceptualization layer that extends the concepts of the COSIMMA metamodel, designed to represent collaboration in various application domains, to the healthcare domain, and more specifically to the management of the patient pathways in hospitals.

As a study-case, we focused on *Groupe Santé CHC* (CHC), a Belgian healthcare group managing four different hospitals. Indeed, this work is being carried out in close collaboration between IMT Mines Albi, France, and CHC Liège in Belgium. Essentially, it is a shared laboratory, bringing together a team of academics and engineers from the Industrial Engineering Centre and a team of healthcare professionals from CHC [11, 12]. The aim is to develop digital twins of the operating blocks at all four CHC sites, particularly MontLégia and Waremme, to enable more effective planning of operating blocks and optimisation of hospital resource utilisation.

The remainder of this paper is organized as follows. Section 2 details the investigated case of the collaborative healthcare network. Section 3 introduces R-IOSUITE. Section 4 details the methodology, implementation, and potential impact of the proposed DSS, highlighting its ability to enhance resource management and improve operational efficiency in multi-site clinical environments. Section 5 drives conclusions and draws avenues for future research.

2 Case Study

In this section, we present the surgical patient pathway that we investigate. In the context of the shared laboratory with CHC Liège, the case study is driven by realistic data, ensuring a strong empirical foundation. First, we describe each of the steps (task, duration and resources required). Second, we provide our simplifying assumptions with their justifications. Third, we describe our case-study operating schedule.

We make the difference between the surgical suite, which is the entire surgical service, and the operating room, which is the room where the surgery is actually performed.

In the surgical suite, one can usually find areas dedicated to the patient (transfer area, operating rooms, post-anesthesia care unit (PACU)…), areas dedicated to the staff (break room, offices, lockers, bathrooms…), as well as storage rooms for drugs and material resources. An operating schedule is a schedule describing the date, time, resources and patient information of each scheduled surgery case.

2.1 Collaborative Partner Overview

The *Groupe santé CHC*, a major healthcare player in the province of Liège (Belgium), comprises hospitals, medical centers, retirement homes, specialized care facilities and operational services. It has more than 1,800 beds and employs almost 5,900 people, catering for a local patient base and increasingly for those from further afield, thanks to the diversity of its services. In this study we focus on two hospitals of this group: the *Clinique CHC MontLégia* and the *Clinique CHC Hermalle.*

The *Clinique CHC MontLégia* opened in 2020. It offers comprehensive medical services (hospitalization, consultations, medical examinations) with state-of-the-art equipment, employing over 2,000 professionals. The *Clinique CHC Hermalle* is a general hospital known for its proximity care which employs over 400 professionals. Both hospitals have surgical suites; ML is equipped with more than 20 operating rooms, while HM has 5. MontLégia (ML) is a large, centralized hospital offering a full spectrum of advanced medical care, while Hermalle (HM) serves as a smaller, community-focused facility specializing in palliative care.

Table 1 details the bed distribution for both hospitals, specifying total capacity, acute care beds (used for short-term treatment), inpatient beds (for patients staying overnight), and outpatient beds (for same-day treatments). It also highlights the number of inpatient beds specifically allocated for surgical care. ML has nearly seven times more total beds and four times more outpatient beds than HM. Notably, HM does not perform inpatient surgery, whereas almost 30% of ML's beds are dedicated to it.

Table 1. Number of beds per hospital

Number of beds	*Clinique CHC MontLégia (ML)*	*Clinique CHC Hermalle (HM)*
Total bed capacity	720	110
Total acute beds	694	110
Total inpatient beds	600 (198 for surgery)	78 (0 for surgery)
Total outpatient beds	120	38

In this article, we study the possibility of transferring patients from ML to HM in case of overtime detected in the provisional schedule.

2.2 Patient Pathway Description

We study a linear **8-step patient pathway** (Fig. 1). The process starts when the patient enters the surgical suite and ends when he/she exits it. Thus, it fully takes place in the surgical suite. In the figure, each block corresponds to a pathway step. Yellow steps are in the transfer area. Blue steps are in the operating room. Green steps are in the PACU. When the patient exits the OR, a bio-cleaning agent is responsible for cleaning the OR for the next surgery. Below the name of each step is a list of the resources required for the tasks to be performed.

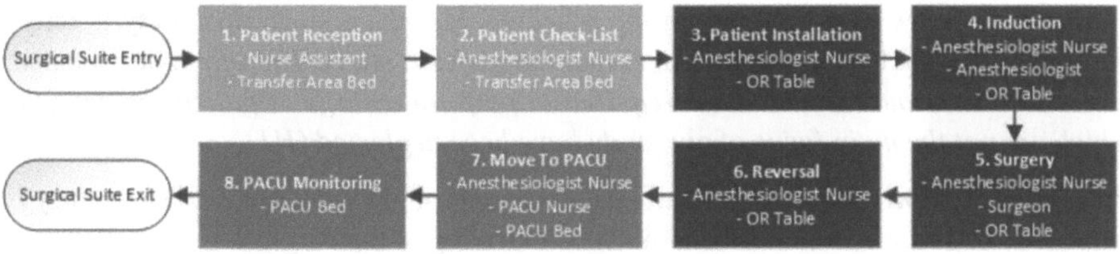

Fig. 1. Process flow of the surgical patient pathway.

The patient pathway displayed in Fig. 1 involves:

- 5 types of **human resources**: nurse assistant, nurse anesthesiologist, surgeon, anesthesiologist and PACU nurse.
- 3 types of **material resources**: the transfer area bed, the operating room table, and the PACU bed.
- 3 **locations**: the transfer area, the operating room, and the PACU.

We now provide a brief description of each of these steps. We regularly refer to hypothesis *H(i)*. These are explained and justified in the following section. The steps are the following:

1. **Patient Reception.** The nurse assistant welcomes the patient at the suite entry and moves him/she to the transfer area. The patient is already lying down on the transfer area bed (see H1 and H2). The nurse assistant checks the identity of the patient.
2. **Patient Check-list.** The anesthesiologist nurse meets the patient and performs the patient check-list to ensure that the surgery can occur (see H3 and H1).
3. **Patient installation.** The anesthesiologist nurse moves the patient from the transfer area to the operating room (see H4, H5 and H6). He/she moves the patient from the transfer area bed to the OR table and prepares him/her for both the induction and the surgery.
4. **Induction**. The anesthesiologist nurse and the anesthesiologist perform and maintain the general anesthesia (see H7). The anesthesiologist leaves the OR at the end of this step (see H5).
5. **Surgery**. The surgeon performs the surgical act (see H8). The surgeon leaves the OR at the end of this step (see H5).
6. **Reversal**. The anesthesiologist nurse performs the reversal (i.e. wound dressing) (see H9).

7. **Move to PACU**. The anesthesiologist nurse and the PACU nurse move the patient from the OR to the PACU. Then, they move the patient from the OR table to the PACU bed while discussing the state of the patient.
8. **PACU monitoring**. The patient slowly wakes up from the general anesthesia (see H10, H11 and H12).

2.3 Simplifying Assumptions

The only resources that are limitant in this study are the OR (and therefore their tables), the surgeons (who can perform surgery in several OR), and the anesthesiologist (who can perform induction in several OR). The other resources mobilized are not limitant and have thus low to no impact on the schedule. However, since this study is only a building block we have decided to add them to the case study. *Therefore, many human and material resources which are required to perform a surgical patient pathway but which are not the main focus of our study have been neglected (H1).*

Patient Reception (step #1). Usually patients are brought to the surgical suite entry by either one or several stretcher-bearers. When arriving at the surgical suite, patients are either on their hospital room bed or already on a transfer bed. In the first case, they are moved to the transfer area bed upon their arrival. Since we are focusing on the process and resources within the surgical suite, *we do not take into account the stretcher-bearers (see H1), and we consider that the patients start the process on their transfer area bed (H2).*

Patient Check-list (step #2). If during the patient the staff declares that the patient is unfit for surgery, they can stop the process and send him/her back to his initial service. This can happen for instance during the patient reception if the patient does not have his/her file, during the patient check-list if the patient ate before the surgery, or during the patient installation if the patient has an unplanned rash on the body. For simplification, *we consider that each scheduled patient will follow their full surgical patient pathway (H3).*

The surgical team (meaning the staff going in the OR with the patient) is composed of at least one surgeon, one anesthesiologist and one or several nurses (instrumentist, surgical assistant, circulating nurse, and anesthesiologist nurse) depending on the anesthesia and surgery type. Since our study focus is mainly of the surgeons, *we only model the anesthesiologist nurse among all the room nurses (see H1).*

Patient installation (step #3). Who enters and stays with the patient in the operating room can vary from one case to the other. For instance, a surgeon (respectively an anesthesiologist) can be performing a surgery (respectively an induction) on another patient when a new one enters the OR. On top of that, the nurses are usually allowed to perform the installation and the reversal tasks without the presence of any doctor in the OR (if he/she is in the hospital). Therefore, *we make the hypothesis that the nurse anesthesiologist is present with the patient from OR entry to OR exit (H4), that the anesthesiologist is only present during the induction (step #4) (H5), and that the surgeon is only present during the surgery (step #5) (H6).*

Induction (step #4). The induction phase in a patient pathway can vary because of the anesthesia type (general anesthesia, loco-regional anesthesia, local anesthesia, sedation, no anesthesia, etc.), the staff performing and monitoring the anesthesia (anesthesiologist, nurse anesthesiologist, non-specialized nurse, etc.) and the place where the anesthesia is performed (PACU, OR, anesthesia area, etc.). For this first study, *we make the hypothesis that all patients receive a general anesthesia, and that it is performed by both the anesthesiologist and the nurse anesthesiologist in the OR (H7).*

Surgery (step #5). Depending on the sources, there are around a dozen surgical specialties and hundreds of surgery types. In this first study case, we study the operating schedule of 3 orthopedic OR. For ease of modeling, *we only model 5 types of surgery: total hip replacement (posterior approach), total hip replacement (anterior approach), total knee replacement, hip fracture and rotator cuff suture (H8).*

Reversal (step #6). This step can be performed by the surgeon, the circulating nurse and the instrumentalist nurses (either together or on their own). Since in our model the surgeon has already exited the OR at this step, and that we only consider the anesthesiologist nurse, *we make the hypothesis that the anesthesiology nurse is the only one present with the patient during the reversal step (H9).*

Move to PACU (step #7). No additional comment for this step.

PACU Monitoring (step #8). During this step, the PACU nurse checks the patient's state several times until he/she fully wakes up. However since, the PACU nurse is responsible for all the patients in the PACU, *we do not consider that the PACU nurse is a resource required for this step to be fulfilled (H10).*

Sometimes, the surgeon does a brief report to the patient regarding how the surgery went. Modeling this discussion is complicated since it could prevent the modeling surgeon from starting a surgery in time. In real-life, the doctor intuitively chooses a time that will not disrupt the rest of the schedule. Therefore, *we consider that the surgeon does not contact the patient during the PACU monitoring step (H11).*

Once the patient is awake, the nurse calls the stretcher-bearers for the patient to be moved back to either a surgical or medical service (for inpatients) or to the ambulatory service (for outpatients). *We do not model the stretcher-bearer's patient exit of the PACU (H12).*

Steps Durations. *The duration of each step is assumed to be known in advance, following a deterministic modeling approach (H13).* To inform these durations, we conducted real-life observations of patient pathways, interviewed staff members, and extracted the surgical suite's operating schedule from the ML software system. *For surgical procedures, we used the average duration of each surgery type performed at ML (H14). For all other steps, we determined durations based on our observations and interviews (H15).*

The specific durations used are: patient reception (5 min), patient check-list (15 min), patient installation (15 min), induction (15 min), reversal (15 min), move to PACU (5 min), PACU monitoring (120 min), total hip replacement (posterior approach) (95 min), total hip replacement (anterior approach) (95 min), total knee replacement (180 min), hip fracture (40 min), and rotator cuff suture (50 min).

2.4 Operating Schedule Description

In this specific article, we study the operating schedule execution of 6 orthopedic OR spread between two of these hospitals: *Clinique CHC Montlégia* (ML), *Clinique CHC Hermalle* (HM).

OR#1, #2 and #3 are in ML. OR#4, 5 and 6 are in HM. OR#1, 2 and 4 are open 10 h per day. OR#3, 5 and 6 are open 8 h per day. Therefore, ML surgical suite is open 28 h while HM surgical suite is open 26 h.

In Table 2 (respectively Table 3), we describe for each day of the week how many of each surgery type need to be scheduled in the ML (respectively HM) surgical suite. The surgical cases are not linked to a surgeon or to an OR yet.

Table 2. Initial number of each surgery type scheduled in ML surgical suite.

Weekday	# THP (posterior approach)	# THP (anterior approach)	# TKR	# Hip fracture	# Rotator cuff suture
Monday	5	1	4	1	2
Tuesday	5	0	2	3	2
Wednesday	1	2	6	2	1
Thursday	5	2	1	1	2
Friday	1	0	5	3	2

Table 3. Initial number of each surgery type scheduled in HM surgical suite.

Weekday	*# THP (posterior approach)*	*# THP (anterior approach)*	# TKR	*# Hip fracture*	*# Rotator cuff suture*
Monday	3	1	2	1	1
Tuesday	3	1	2	2	1
Wednesday	2	1	3	1	1
Thursday	2	2	2	1	1
Friday	2	0	3	3	2

We consider that the strategy adopted by both surgical suites is open scheduling, meaning that several surgeons can perform surgeries in the same room the same day (i.e. the OR shifts are not dedicated to one surgeon like on the block scheduling strategy).

3 R-IOSUITE: A Decision Support System to Support Collaborations

R-IOSUITE is an open source decision-support tool. This TRL 7 research prototype is historically dedicated to crisis management. It encompasses [10]:

1. The interpretation of data (from open data, sensors, social networks, etc.) to instantiate a model of the crisis situation, describing the context, the parties involved, their know-how, and the risks and incidents to be dealt with;
2. The deduction of a response schema to support the collaboration of stakeholders in the response chosen by those in charge of the response;
3. The orchestration of tasks between stakeholders; in parallel with the monitoring of the crisis situation (by continuing to interpret data on the fly);
4. The detection of deviations from the planned situation and the proposition of adaptations (in the form of a new response plan).

R-IOSUITE is available at *r-iosuite.com*. As displayed in Fig. 2, it consists of 16 specialized applications dedicated to case study governance (R-IOGA), visualization (R-IOPLAY), modelization (R-IODA, R-IOTE), meta-modelization (R-IOME), process simulation (R-IOSEPE), data simulation (R-IOSEMIT), data listening (R-IOSE), interpretation rules (R-IORED), strategies of collaboration (R-IODED) and orchestration (R-IOWA). Since 2012 it has been demonstrated in 15 case studies, among them 14 dedicated to crisis management.

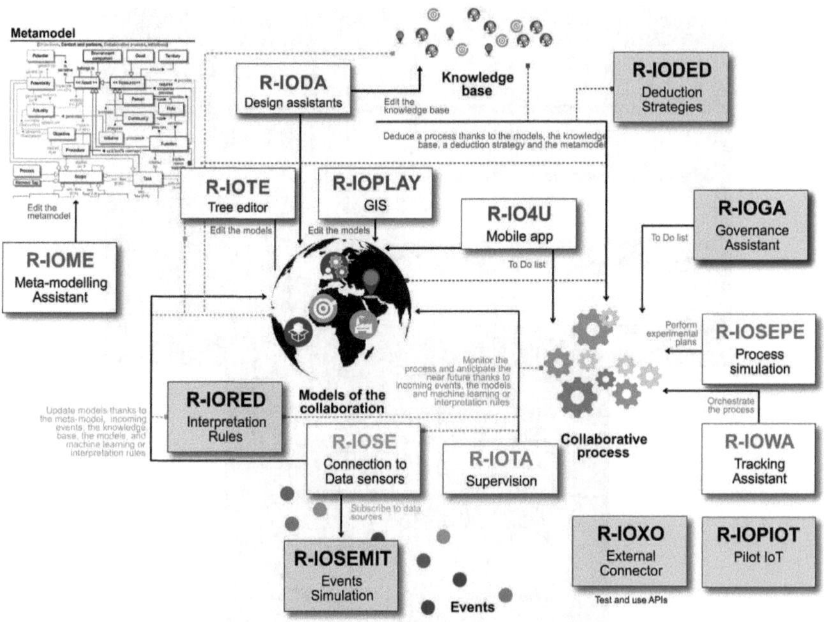

Fig. 2. R-IOSUITE's architecture big picture available at r-iosuite.com

The interoperability between all applications is ensured by the use of a common conceptualization: a metamodel [13]. R-IOSUITE's metamodel is the COSIMMA metamodel dedicated to collaboration. It includes the conceptualization of: the context of the collaboration, the stakeholders, what they can do and share, and their common objectives. R-IOSUITE can be used to model and manage a supply chain [14], as well as to support a city's response to a flood [15]. It enables a flexible, holistic, and rational approach to managing collaborative processes, regardless of the application domain.

This study tailored metamodels of R-IOSUITE and explored how it can be used to manage collaboration between departments within the same hospital, focusing on patient pathways. The aim is to take advantage of R-IOSUITE's flexibility, holistic perspective and rational decision-making capabilities, while ensuring that it is adapted to the specific vocabulary and context of hospital managers.

4 Experimentation

Our goal is to study how patients can be moved from one surgical suite to another in order to smooth the workload, satisfy all the patient demand, respect the constraint on staff and operating room shift times, and integrate non-elective surgeries to the schedule.

All the case studies released in 2025 on R-IOSUITE are displayed in Figs. 3 and 4. This paper includes the development of a new case study which can be loaded with the "load external project" button at the bottom of the web page.

Fig. 3. On the left, a view of all the case studies already available in R-IOGA (the governance assistant app of R-IOSUITE). On the right, a view of the steps and modals required to load a project.

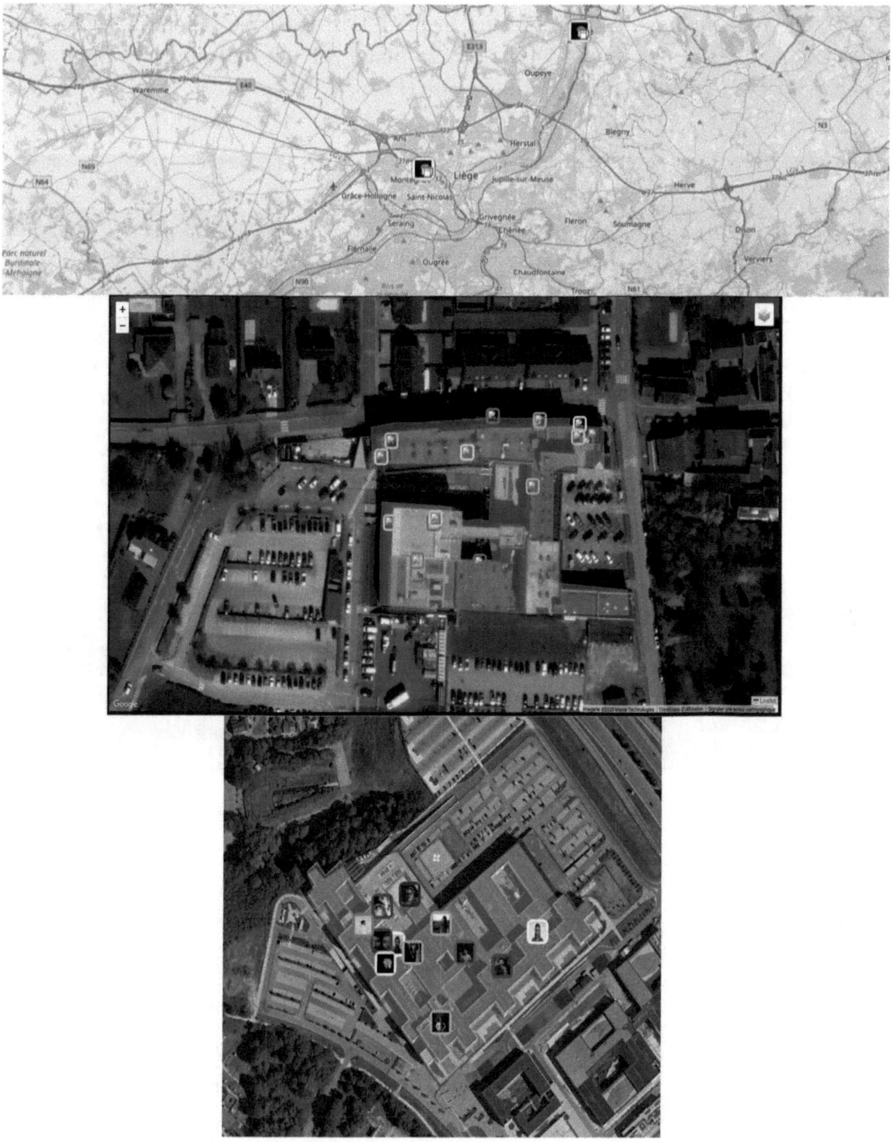

Fig. 4. Map view of the case study context in R-IOTA (the tracking assistant app of R-IOSUITE), as displayed through its Geographic Information System. At the top, the standard map view; at the bottom left, the satellite view of *Clinique CHC Hermalle*; and at the bottom right, the satellite view of *Clinique CHC MontLégia*.

During the design phase, we have integrated the resources into the original R-IOSUITE knowledge graph for the Hermalle site as shown in Fig. 5. The 'REFERENCES' label marks knowledge common to the entire CHC Liège sites, while the 'ACTIVE' label identifies information specific to a particular site, i.e. the Hermalle site, at a given point in time. Accessible via the R-IOTE app.. We report in Table 4 the resources features deployed during the design phase. Figure 6 displays a visualization of the available resources at the Hermalle site (Fig. 7).

Fig. 5. R-IOSUITE Knowledge Graph Visualization: Hermalle Site Resources

Table 4. Design features

Resource Type	Number	Limiting resources?
Transfer area Bed	13 per hospital	Not a limiting resource
PACU bed	13 per hospital	Not a limiting resource
Operating rooms	3 per hospital	Can be a limiting resource
Orthopedic Surgeon	3 per hospital	Not a limiting resource
Anesthesiologist	3 per hospital	Not a limiting resource
Anesthesiologist Nurse	3 per hospital	Can be a limiting resource
PACU Nurse	13 per hospital	Not a limiting resource
Nurse Assistant	13 per hospital	Not a limiting resource
Bio-cleaning Agent	3 per hospital	Not a limiting resource

Priorities to be scheduled the 5/29:

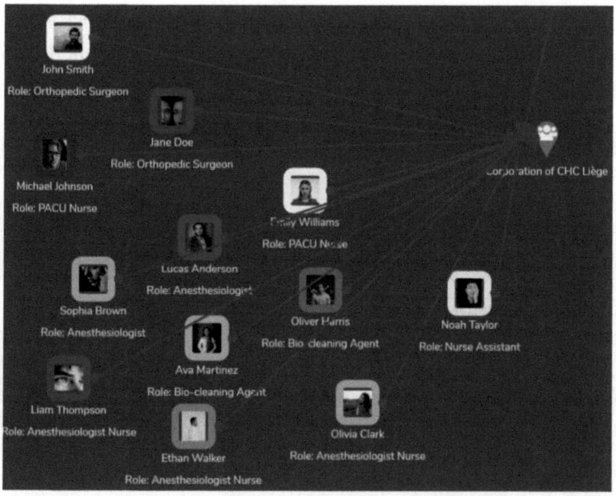

Fig. 6. A view of the available resources at the Hermalle site. Accessible via the R-IODA app.

- Liam Nan (PTH);
- Luke Perfo (PTH);
- Carol Dole (HIP);
- Greg Ringer (SHOULDER);
- Hannah Carrer (HIP);
- Jenny Zole (HIP);
- Julie Silva (Shoulder)

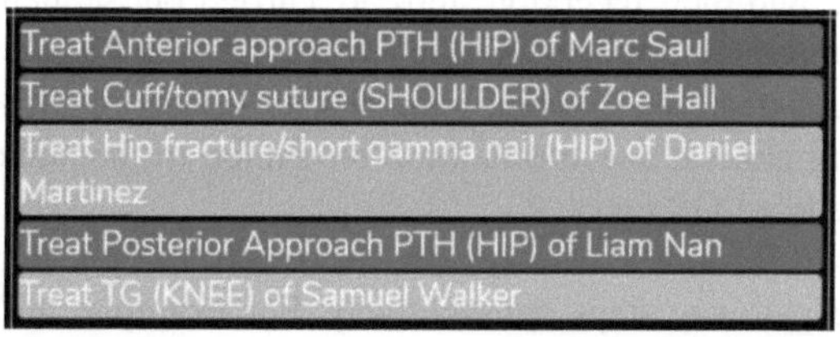

Fig. 7. Visualization of the patients to be scheduled for surgery at the Hermale site on Thursday, 5/29. Accessible via the R-IOCAL app. On the left, a request is made to generate the complete, cross-department surgical pathway planning.

We input our requirements into R-IOSUITE, asking it to generate an operating schedule that satisfies all constraints. These inputs included the number and types of surgeries to be scheduled each day across the two surgical suites defined in the design phase. At this stage, R-IOSUITE is already aware of the patient pathway steps and the available resources. It is worth noting that if too many surgeries are scheduled for a single day, R-IOSUITE automatically reschedules some for the following days. Figure 8 shows a provisional schedule proposed by R-IOSUITE for one operating room (OR) at HM on June 29th. Each patient pathway is represented by a different color (in order: light green, blue, purple, dark green, and yellow), and each surgery is performed by a different surgeon. The steps illustrated correspond to those previously defined in Sect. 2.

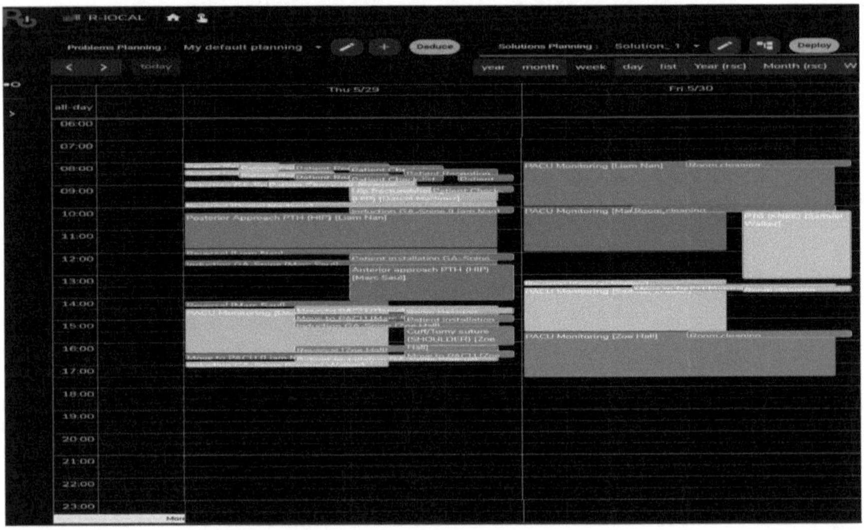

Fig. 8. Visualization of one of the schedules proposed by R-IOSUITE for the 13 surgeries requested on Thursday, 5/29. Accessible via the R-IOCAL app.

Several observations can be made regarding the model's limit:

1. **Simultaneous Patient Reception.** All patients are summoned to the surgical suite at the same time, and their reception steps are carried out sequentially by the nurse assistant. This approach could be viable in hospitals that accept keeping patients waiting in the transfer area to reduce the risk of downstream delays. In practice, patients receiving general anesthesia are often called to the suite one to two hours before their scheduled OR entry.
2. **Discontinuities in Patient Pathways.** In the current design, R-IOSUITE does not always schedule pathway steps consecutively. For example, the "move to PACU" step for the light green patient occurs around 2:30 PM, whereas their reversal step ends around 10:00 AM. While such delays may occur in real situations due to PACU overcrowding, this is unlikely here, as the light green patient is the first case of the day.
3. **Room Cleaning Not Modeled Accurately.** Room cleaning steps are not consistently placed. For instance, there is no cleaning scheduled between the blue and pink patients, which does not align with standard OR protocols.
4. **PACU Capacity Misrepresented.** The way PACU monitoring is scheduled suggests that only one patient can occupy the PACU at a time. This is incorrect, as the PACU is typically designed to accommodate multiple patients simultaneously.

This provisional schedule exceeds the timeframe of a single day. Although there are clear areas for improvement in how patient pathways are modeled, this scenario presents a valuable opportunity to explore how R-IOSUITE might assist in balancing overloaded and underloaded schedules across surgical suites. Therefore, based on inter-site collaboration, R-IOSUITE proposes to open an OR in ML to accept patients that do not fit in the initial schedule. Purple and blue patients are moved to ML while light green, dark green and yellow ones are kept in HM (Fig. 9).

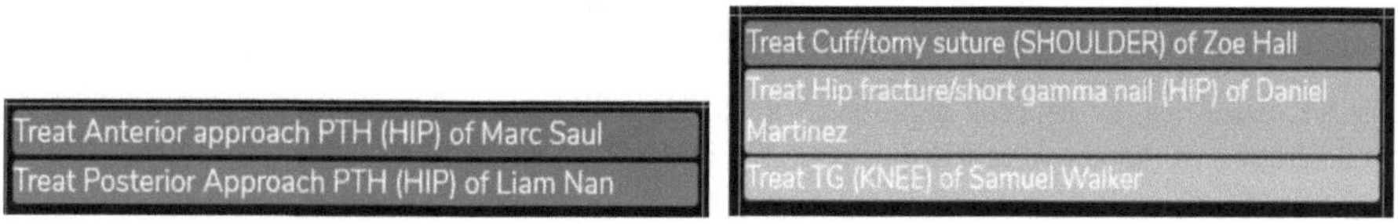

Fig. 9. Balancing Surgical Schedules: R-IOSUITE's Inter-Site OR Reallocation

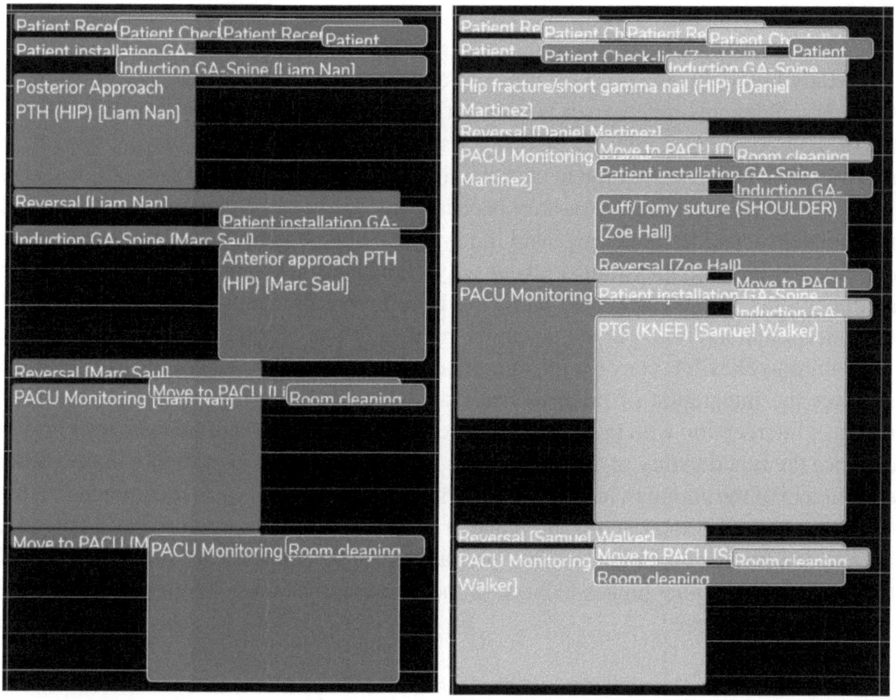

Fig. 10. On the left, the new schedule for the Montgélia site from 8 AM to 5:10 PM. On the right, the new schedule for the Hermalle site from 8 am to 5.40 pm. Available at the R-IOCAL app.

Figures 10 and 11 collectively illustrate R-IOSUITE's capability in optimizing surgical schedules through inter-site collaboration. Figure 10 presents the newly distributed surgical schedules for both the Montgélia (left, 8 AM - 5:10 PM) and Hermalle (right, 8 AM - 5:40 PM) sites, demonstrating how patients are reallocated to balance loads. Complementing this, Fig. 11 visualizes the underlying process orchestration for the Hermalle

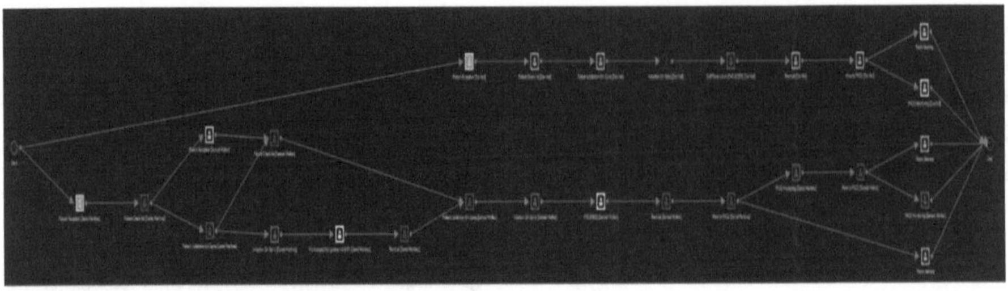

Fig. 11. View of the process deployed for the Hermalle site at 8 a.m. on 5/29. It enables the orchestration of the above schedule. Available in the R-IOWA app.

site's schedule at 8 AM on May 29th, showcasing how the system efficiently manages and deploys the complex activities to implement these revised plans.

5 Conclusion and Perspectives

This study highlights the need for efficient collaboration tools in healthcare, especially where resources are limited, such as in operating rooms. We have demonstrated the potential of repurposing R-IOSUITE, an open crisis management decision support system, to make a substantial contribution to coordination across hospital units across surgical care pathways. CKey areas of success have been identified in the effective transposition of the metamodel to healthcare settings and the system's ability to infer and propose typical, end-to-end planning. Flexibility and capacity of the platform to increase the control and administration of such advanced pathways have been sufficiently proven by our Proof of Concept that has been piloted through a multi-unit real-world case study in Belgium.

Future work will focus on a select number of primary areas. The proposed approach involves the integration of predictive analytics for operating time and real-time HL7 message interception with the existing framework. The objective of this integration is to enhance the functionality of the framework. The result of this integration will be further enrichment of the digital twin modelling of operating rooms. It is also recommended that the integration of patient geolocation and crisis management be explored as a potential avenue for future research. Another crucial step is to consider the generalisation of this framework to other higher-technology healthcare procedures, extending beyond the scope of surgical care.

Acknowledgement. The authors would like to thank Guillaume Dessevre, Mohamed Maazoune, and Frederick Benaben from the CGI for their valuable input and contributions to this work.

References

1. Gür, Ş, Eren, T.: Application of operational research techniques in operating room scheduling problems: literature overview. J. Healthc. Eng. **2018**(1), 5341394 (2018)
2. Childers, C.P., Maggard-Gibbons, M.: Understanding costs of care in the operating room. JAMA Surg. **153**(4), e176233–e176233 (2018)

3. Zhu, S., Fan, W., Yang, S., Pei, J., Pardalos, P.M.: Operating room planning and surgical case scheduling: a review of literature. J. Comb. Optim. **37**, 757–805 (2019)
4. Sefraoui, K., Maliki, F., Omrane, N.A., Layeb, S.B., Souier, M.: On solving integrated operating room planning and scheduling problem. In: 2024 ASU International Conference in Emerging Technologies for Sustainability and Intelligent Systems (ICETSIS), pp. 929–933. IEEE (2024)
5. Rifi, L., Fontanili, F., Jeanney, M.: A tool-based approach to analyze operating room schedule execution: application to online management. Healthc. Sys. Challen. Opportunit. 179–193 (2022)
6. Wang, L., Demeulemeester, E., Vansteenkiste, N., Rademakers, F.E.: Operating room planning and scheduling for outpatients and inpatients: A review and future research. Operat. Res. Health Care **31**, 100323 (2021)
7. Bennour, K., Ghazouani, I., Bedhief, A.O., Layeb, S.B., Aissaoui, N.O.: Towards tailoring reinforcement learning to solve the online surgery-planning and scheduling problem. In: Proceedings of International Conference on Decision Aid and Artificial Intelligence (ICODAI 2024), Vol. 12, p. 170. Springer Nature (2025)
8. Sefraoui, K., Maliki, F., Omrane, N.A., Layeb, S.B., Souier, M.: Ressource planning and scheduling for operating room management: current state and challenges. In: 2023 International Conference on Decision Aid Sciences and Applications (DASA), pp. 480–484. IEEE (2023)
9. Roshanaei, V., Luong, C., Aleman, D.M., Urbach, D.R.: Collaborative operating room planning and scheduling. INFORMS J. Comput. **29**(3), 558–580 (2017)
10. Congès, A., Fertier, A., Salatgé, N., Rebière, S., Benaben, F.: R-IO SUITE: integration of LLM-based AI into a knowledge management and model-driven based platform dedicated to crisis management. Software and Systems Modeling, 1–26 (2024)
11. Maazoun, M., et al.: Optimizing operating room planning through duration prediction: application in a belgian clinic (optimisation de la planification opératoire par la prédiction des durées: Application dans une clinique en Belgique). The 3rd TIDS (Health Data Processing) Action at the 7th GdR MaDICS 2025 Symposium, pp. 1–4 (2025)
12. Ben Ayad, S., Oger, O., Olivier, P., Layeb, S.B., Fontanilli, F.: From HL7 Message Reception to PostgreSQL Database: A Case Study in a Belgian Clinic (De la réception des messages HL7 à une base de données PostgreSQL : étude de cas au sein d'une clinique en Belgique). The 3rd TIDS (Health Data Processing) Action at the 7th GdR MaDICS 2025 Symposium, pp. 1–4 (2025)
13. Chen, D., Doumeingts, G., Vernadat, F.: Architectures for enterprise integration and interoperability: Past, present and future. Comput. Ind. **59**(7), 647–659 (2008)
14. Fertier, A., et al.: Managing events to improve situation awareness and resilience in a supply chain. Comput. Ind. **132**, 103488 (2021)
15. Fertier, A., Barthe-Delanoë, A.M., Montarnal, A., Truptil, S., Bénaben, F.: A new emergency decision support system: The automatic interpretation and contextualisation of events to model a crisis situation in real-time. Decis. Support Syst. **133**, 113260 (2020)

AI and Simulation-Supported Decision-Making in Collaborative VUCA Environments

Clarifying the Concept of Meta-Models for Collaborative Decision-Making in Engineering Complex Systems

Mubeen Ur Rehman(✉), Alessandro Bertoni, and Johan Wall

Blekinge Institute of Technology, 37179 Karlskrona, Sweden
{mubeenur.rehman,alessandro.bertoni,johan.wall}@bth.se

Abstract. The interchangeable usage of the term "meta-model" has caused confusion and ambiguity in research community, blurring their distinctions and applications in the context of collaborative decision-making, with a special focus on complex engineering systems. The definitions of the term found within the targeted application area are mapped and compared. The findings reveal two major interpretations of the term meta-model. One is a framework or blueprint for ensuring consistency and standardization among models, and the other is for approximating complex simulation models, providing computational efficiency. Meta-models, in both of their interpretations, serve different purposes, functions, and the scope of application. The two interpretations have a non-exclusive nature, meaning that both interpretations can be complementary rather than mutually exclusive. The goal of the study is semantic clarification to enhance comprehension and facilitate appropriate utilization of the definition within the realm of collaborative decision-making in complex engineering systems.

Keywords: meta model · collaborative-decision-making · systems-engineering

1 Introduction

During the process of designing complex systems, several crucial decisions are made based on information that is often fragmented or immature [1]. Complex simulation models are often used to understand and eventually predict the behavior of a system that has yet to be designed, aiming to support more informed decision-making [2]. The development of "meta-models" is often referred to in engineering literature as a solution to address the complexity of integrating the results of multi-disciplinary simulations. The word "meta" originated from ancient Greek and was used as a prefix meaning "beyond," "after," or "about." When combined with a term, it generates a concept that operates at a higher level of abstraction than the original concept. These terms represent some implications like "super," "fundamental," and "specification" from an abstract perspective. Such a definition has generated different interpretations in the engineering community about the essence of a meta-model. For instance, while [3], refer to a meta-model as a framework or representation that captures the relationships and interactions

Published by Springer Nature Switzerland AG 2026
L. M. Camarinha-Matos et al. (Eds.): PRO-VE 2025, IFIP AICT 770, pp. 465–481, 2026.
https://doi.org/10.1007/978-3-032-05673-3_28

between different levels of models within a complex system, [4] use the term "meta-model" as a synonym of surrogate model, that is, a model of a possibly unknown model in the context of data-driven approach, built from a training data set, related some input parameters to some quantities of interest, approximating the mapping between the input parameters and the quantities of interest. In engineering design, what a meta-model is and how it is to be interpreted may encounter misunderstandings since a common agreement regarding its definition is often not achieved.

Multi-disciplinary design teams often operate with different interpretations of the term meta-model. For instance, an architectural team may develop a conceptual meta-model based on OMG based semantics, defining system components, behaviours, and constraints [5], while the simulation team concurrently constructs a surrogate meta-model using ML or regression techniques [6]. Such semantic misalignment often results in practical difficulties as it creates problems in integration, traceability across abstraction layers is lost, and model transformation becomes a manual and error-prone task [7]. These integration breakdowns [8] in collaborative model-based design literature, it illustrates the need for clearer semantic clarification to support semantic interoperability in collaborative engineering settings [9].

Focusing on the utilization of the term "meta-model" when engineering complex systems, this paper explores the various interpretations of the concept of "meta-model" and applications of meta-modeling solutions, with the intent to improve the consistency and collaboration within the research community by mapping meta-model application areas, views, and scope. The paper aims to answer the questions:

- How is the term "meta-model" defined and interpreted across various disciplines in the context of collaborative decision making for complex engineering systems?
- What are the different application areas, views, and scopes among the different interpretations?

The paper is based on the scoping review, research approach used in the paper is described in detail in Sect. 2. The results of the review, its analysis, and classification are presented in Sect. 3. Section 4 discusses the variation in interpretation of the term meta-model. Finally, Sect. 5 draws the final conclusions remarking how ensuring consistency in interpretation is crucial for standardization and integration across multi-disciplinary collaborative environments.

2 Research Approach

The research methodology utilizes a scoping literature review to investigate the heterogeneous interpretations of meta-models across various domains of complex engineering systems. A scoping review, according to [10] is a form of knowledge synthesis that addresses an exploratory research question aimed at mapping key concepts, types of evidence, and gaps in research by systematically searching, selecting, and synthesizing existing knowledge. For the identification of relevant keywords and their synonyms, brainstorming sessions were held, which were then structured into a comprehensive search string, shown in Table 1.

Upon selection of the initial set of keywords, an iterative process was followed to craft a comprehensive search string that would yield the maximum number of relevant research articles. The search string was iteratively reviewed during two refinement sessions with the collaboration of three researchers in the field of systems engineering and product development. During these sessions, keywords were systematically identified based on the research question. Synonyms, related terms, and alternative phrasings of the keywords were identified and listed. The keywords focused on the concept of meta-modeling, product service systems, systems-of-systems, and digital twins, including all the possible identified synonyms. The keyword 'digital twin' was included in the search string because it was identified as a key emerging concept in the modeling and simulation of complex systems, particularly in the context of systems engineering and system-of-systems, when discussing the use of virtual models as boundary objects and the interoperability and interface of several different models. The search string utilized in the search is shown in Table 1. The search string presented in Table 1 is divided into four distinct parts based on the keywords used. To replicate the search, these parts can be combined accordingly.

To assess the robustness of the search string, the results were evaluated by comparing them against a known set of relevant papers, ensuring that the search string was encompassing. [11] refers to these selected papers as a "quasi-gold standard" (QGS) [5, 6], which represents a subset of the hypothetical gold standard, which is a subset of all relevant papers on the topic.

The SCOPUS database was selected as the primary platform for the search, mainly due to its extensive coverage and the multiple examples of utilization in the engineering design community. The search was also complemented by accessing other databases during the snowballing process (i.e., Google Scholar, IEEE, and Web of Science).

Table 1. SCOPUS search string used in the review

Meta-model	TITLE-ABS-KEY ("Meta-model" OR "Metamodeling" OR "meta-data model" OR "model emulation" OR "metamodel" OR "meta-model" OR "Model* communication" OR "Model* architecture") **AND**
System of Systems	(TITLE-ABS-KEY ("System-of-systems" OR "System of systems" OR "System-of-Systems" OR "complex systems" OR "system integration" OR "Systems of Systems") **OR**
Digital Twin	TITLE-ABS-KEY ("digital twin" OR "cyber twin" OR "digital model" OR "virtual twin" OR "digital shadow" OR "digital thread" OR "digital counterpart") **OR**
Product Service Systems/Systems Engineering	TITLE-ABS-KEY ("Systems engineering" OR "Product service-systems" OR pss* OR "Smart Product service-systems" OR "Smart PSS" OR " product-service bundle" OR "integrated product service" OR "industrial product service" OR "product service offer"))

A total of 1536 papers matched the initial screening process, which was then refined utilizing the process described in the following subsection.

2.1 Literature Selection

The literature selection process followed exclusion criteria to ensure the chosen studies' relevance, reliability, and objectivity. The systematic review followed the steps shown in Fig. 1, where the corresponding number of papers resulting from each step is also indicated in the middle of each box.

The exclusion of papers was carried out using several criteria, depicted in Figure 1 as F1, F2, and F3. In detail, upon compiling the initial list of 1536 papers, a filtering process, F1, was applied during step 3. The F1 filter consisted of three key components. At first, it limited the selection to papers written in English. Secondly, it excluded document types such as books, chapters, reviews, and editorials, effectively narrowing the scope to peer-reviewed journal articles and conference papers. Thirdly, the filter restricted the selection to papers within the domains of Engineering, Computer Science, and Mathematics, as the focus was on the modeling of complex engineering systems. This initial filtering process reduced the number of papers by approximately one-fifth, bringing the total down to 1,215 papers.

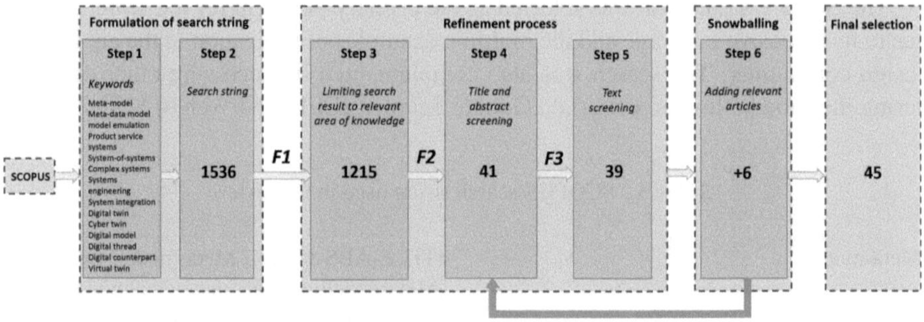

Fig. 1. Process flow of refining research papers

In step 4, titles and abstracts were screened using F2, and papers not related to meta-modeling, model-based solutions, theories of modeling, complex systems, simulations, and optimization were excluded because they did not cover both the theoretical foundations and practical applications of meta-models. Although "optimization" was not listed in the keywords, however, it was included in the filtration process due to the linkage between optimization techniques and the use of meta-models as surrogates. It also allowed the inclusion of papers from themes such as design space exploration, multi-objective trade-offs, sensitivity analysis, and uncertainty quantification, which are inherently optimization-driven works.

Finally, in step 5, using F3, the full text of each paper was examined, ensuring that the body of the text provided a clear definition of meta-models and their contextual application. Two additional papers were excluded at this stage for not meeting the criteria, leaving a final selection of 39 papers. Table 2 summarizes the filtering process, describing the exclusion criteria.

During step 6, further papers were added using snowballing or citation chasing. As an iterative process, the selected literature underwent abstract and text screening, resulting in the inclusion of 6 additional papers. The filtration process rendered 45 papers aligning with the research objectives.

A set of classification criteria was defined to analyse the selected literature. Scopus provided an initial subject-based filtering of papers, focusing on computer science, mathematics, and engineering (Filter F1). However, since Scopus classifies papers by the journal's subject area rather than actual content, a deeper analysis requires manual classification based on paper content and specific criteria.

Table 3 outlines the criteria used to classify papers by subject and application area. Subject area classification focused on engineering, computer science, and mathematics, as these bests represent the study of complex engineering systems. Fields like material science or social science were excluded due to their limited focus on integrated system-level modeling.

Classifying papers by subject area helped reveal how meta-models are applied across disciplines and highlighted trends in their interpretation and use. Each meta-model was mapped to its subject and application area to explore cross-domain relationships and usage contexts. Classification aimed to examine whether the interpretation of the meta-model changes depending on its application, if a consistent understanding of meta-models persists across different application areas, or if notable variations exist. The goal was to uncover trends and extract meaningful insights. The application area of computational engineering involves methods and techniques for modeling, predicting, and optimizing complex systems using computational methods. These methods included kriging, regression techniques, reinforcement learning, machine learning, etc. In the case of systems engineering for complex systems, the focus was on designing, integrating, and managing these intricate systems. For transportation engineering, the emphasis was on optimizing transport networks such as water distribution systems, railway lines, and fleet management. In the manufacturing domain, papers were classified if they addressed manufacturing processes or dealt with the automation of production in complex systems. All classifications, whether by application or subject area, provided objectivity and deeper insights into trends and the use of meta-models across different fields.

Table 2. Classification Criteria based on application and subject areas

Subject Area	**Criteria**
Engineering	Focusing on designing, simulating, or optimizing engineering processes.
Computer Science	Involves developing or utilizing algorithms, data-driven solutions, and software tools.
Mathematics	Utilizing mathematical algorithms and numerical methods.
Application Area	**Criteria**
Computational Engineering	Involving methods for modeling, prediction, and optimization using computational methods.
Systems Engineering	Focusing on designing, integrating, and managing complex systems.
Transportation Engineering	Focusing on optimizing transport networks and integrating smart technologies.

(continued)

Table 2. (*continued*)

Subject Area	Criteria
Manufacturing	Involving manufacturing processes, automation, and production optimization.
Civil and Environmental Engineering	Focusing on water distribution systems, sustainable infrastructure management, and construction.

3 Results

Figure 2 describes the extended use of meta-models across various application areas. Systems engineering constituted the largest portion, representing 18 papers. The application area under systems engineering is focused on the design [13], integration [8] and management of complex systems [14]. 17 papers were related to computational engineering, which involved methods for modeling, prediction, and optimization using various computational methods [15]. Four papers fell under manufacturing engineering, focused on manufacturing processes, automation, production optimization, and integration of advanced manufacturing technologies, i.e., Industry 4.0.

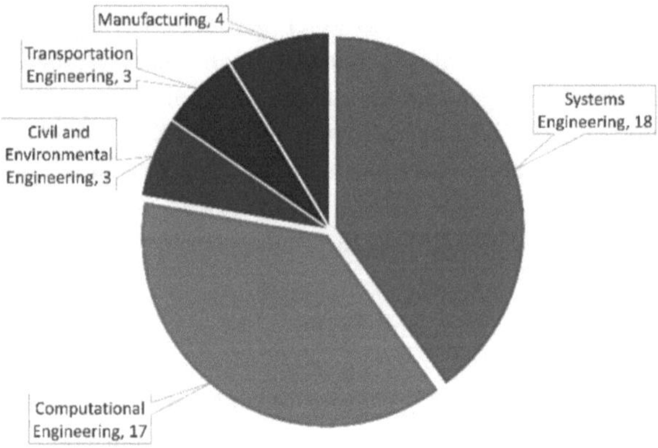

Fig. 2. Application areas of Meta-model

Civil and environmental engineering accounted for three papers, which included topics such as water distribution systems, sustainable infrastructure management, and construction. Similarly, transportation engineering contributed three papers, focused on the optimization of transport networks and the integration of smart technologies.

Table 3. Mapping the focus of the definitions of Meta-model in the literature

Ref.	Surrogate	Framework	Abstraction	Knowledge	Integration
[16] Lin et al.		o			
[17] Toffol et al.		o		o	o
[18] Zhou et al.	o				
[19] Broad et al.	o				
[20] Shirvani et al.		o			o
[21] Cha et al.			o		
[22] Ge et al.			o		o
[23] Goppert et al.		o			o
[5] Medini et al.		o			
[9] Bakirtzis et al.		o			
[24] Lyazidi et al.		o		o	o
[25] Haimes et al.		o			o
[26] Ghorbani et al.		o	o		
[27] Raune et al.	o		o		
[28] Longo et al.	o				
[29] Ribeiro et al.		o			
[7] Belkadi et al.		o		o	o
[30] Mostafavi et al.	o				
[13] Mcharek et al.		o	o	o	o
[3] Mhenni et al.			o	o	o
[31] Tekinerdogan		o	o		o
[32] Woitsch et al.		o			o
[33] Can et al.	o				
[34] Piriou et al.		o		o	o
[35] Cao et al.				o	o
[36] Zerwas et al.		o		o	o
[37] Zhao et al.	o				
[38] Wang et al.		o	o	o	o
[39] Kieu et al.	o	o			
[40] Messac et al.	o				
[41] Zhu et al.	o				
[42] Torregrosa et al.	o				
[43] Chabanet et al.	o				

(*continued*)

Table 3. (*continued*)

Ref.	Surrogate	Framework	Abstraction	Knowledge	Integration
[44] Lee et al.	o	o			o
[6] Khosravi et al.	o				
[45] Knudde et al.	o				
[46] Yonglin et al.		o	o		
[47] Coelho et al.	o				
[48] Touhami et al.	o				
[49] Kaseb et al.	o				
[4] Aucejo et al.	o				
[50] Jensen et al.	o				
[51] Dammak et al.	o				
[52] Pardis et al.	o				
[53] Ferraz et al.	o				

Table 4 maps out the focus of the meta-model definition across the selected literature. Each row corresponds to a specific reference, while each column represents a thematic focus identified during the review. The table cross-references each definition against these themes to illustrate the variety and overlap in how meta-models are conceptualized. Surrogate refers to the use of meta-models as simplified or approximate representations of complex systems. These models serve as stand-ins for detailed simulations, enabling faster analysis or decision-making. A framework captures the interpretation of meta-models as structural or conceptual blueprints that guide the organization, development, or integration of other models. Abstraction involves the use of meta-models to represent high-level concepts by filtering out unnecessary detail. This supports clearer communication and a broader understanding of the system being modeled. Knowledge reflects the role of meta-models in representing and preserving domain knowledge, ensuring consistency and traceability of information across different stages of collaborative design and decision-making. Integration focus involves using meta-models as mechanisms for integrating heterogeneous models, tools, or data sources to support interoperability and collaboration by aligning different models under a unified structure or ontology.

4 Variation of Interpretation of the Term "Meta-Model"

The definitions extracted from the papers showed that the meta-model concept is currently used in different contexts and can be broadly categorized into two main interpretations. If the meta-model is a higher-level structure that defines rules, relationships, and syntax for constructing other models or defines how other models are modelled or understood, it is classified as a framework or blueprint. The analysis shows that this interpretation is particularly prevalent in the application area of systems engineering. Here, the meta-model provides a framework that enables consistency, integration, and management of complex systems or models.

In the other interpretation, the meta-model is used as a simplified or approximate model to approximate more complex and computationally expensive models, which are often difficult to compute as they require extensive computational resources. The following subsections analyse the definition in detail.

4.1 Definition of Meta-Model in Systems Engineering: Blueprint or Framework

This section addresses the research question posited in Sect. 1, leveraging the quantitative analysis findings alongside the groundwork laid out in Sect. 3. Based on the common aspects of the definition in the literature within the context of systems engineering, a meta-model definition can be derived as:

> "a higher-level model [21], which defines the concepts [9, 18, 37] relationships [7, 10, 19, 20] and rules [31] used to create other models."

The functions of the meta-model are (1) to serve as a blueprint or framework [12, 21, 23, 54] for building specific models within a domain or system; (2) to provide an abstract representation [9, 13] of the elements and their relationships that can exist in the actual models; (3) to define the syntax in the form of language [5] and rules that govern how models should be constructed, interpreted, and connected within the system and with external systems; (4) to ensure consistency [23, 26] and coherence among various models within a system, by capturing the essential concepts and their interconnections.

In systems engineering, a meta-model acts as a model of the model [13, 19] by guiding the design and construction of specific models that adhere to its defined structure and framework. It allows for uniformity and understanding across different model instances and supports the creation of complex and interconnected systems with clear rules and constraints. It is an enabler of system modeling. Meta-model can be of a multi-layered architecture based on the layer of abstraction. The highest level of meta-model can be classified as a meta-model that captures the real-world concepts [31].

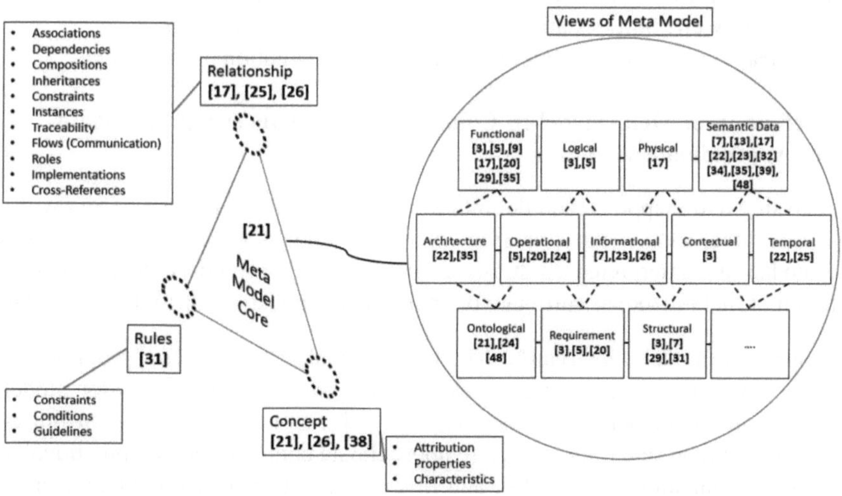

Fig. 3. Visual representation of the Meta-model as a framework or blueprint

Figure 3 provides a visual representation of the meta-model's definition derived from the literature analysis. The figure illustrates the structure of the meta-model. On the left, the triangle represents the core of the meta-model, signifying the three foundational pillars that support it. On the right, a different perspective of the meta-model is presented. The dotted lines within the circle illustrate the connections between different viewpoints, showing how two perspectives can be linked to offer complementary insights into the same complex system. Each square within the large circle represents a specific view, with the numbers indicating the reference for each paper. The visualization emphasizes the meta-model's capacity to be viewed from multiple angles, allowing for comprehensive analysis and interpretation of the modeled system. Its versatility supports the differing roles and objectives of various stakeholders.

The meta-model core defines the structure of a meta-model by integrating three foundational elements: concepts, relationships, and rules. Concepts represent abstract entities or elements within a system and are defined through attributes, properties, and characteristics. Relationships describe how concepts interact or depend on one another, often represented through associations or other connection types. Rules serve as constraints or guidelines that govern the structure and behavior of concepts and relationships, ensuring consistency and interoperability in modeling.

Additionally, meta-models can be viewed from different perspectives, known as "views," which highlight specific aspects of the system. These include:

- **Architecture view:** Represents system structure and relationships.
- **Contextual view:** Shows interactions with external entities.
- **Functional view:** Focuses on system functions and behavior.
- **Informational view:** Deals with data flow and consistency.
- **Logical view:** Emphasizes technical concepts and logical connections.
- **Ontological view:** Integrates ontology to define concepts and their interrelations.
- **Operational view:** Describes tasks and system behavior over time.
- **Physical view:** Connects abstract models to physical characteristics.
- **Requirement view:** Structure user needs and system requirements.
- **Semantic data view:** Focuses on the meaning and relationships of data.
- **Structural view:** Shows static organization of model components.
- **Temporal view:** Manages time-based aspects and evolution of the model.

4.2 Definition of Meta-Model in Computational Engineering: Surrogate or Approximate Models

By analysing and mapping each definition of meta-model used in the papers with the application area, another interpretation emerged in computational engineering, where meta-models are interpreted as surrogate or approximate models. Synthesizing the definition of meta-model as surrogate or approximate models leads to the following:

> "A Surrogate model, which can be called with several names such as approximation model [25, 47], response surface model [40, 44], emulator [39], regression model [27], prediction model [44], substitute model [43] along with others, constitutes a simplified representation utilized to approximate complex and computationally intensive simulation models [39], and it is designed to replicate the behavior of

complex systems, providing an efficient and time-saving way for predicting system behavior with notably reduced computational resources [42]."

In computational engineering, the surrogate model acts as 'model of the model' through the simplified representation of the input/output relationship (or 'response function') derived from the underlying simulation model [27]. It means that the surrogate model acts as a substitute for actual high-fidelity models to predict the output of the complex system and thereby simulate the sought behavior. Utilizing a surrogate model enables, for example, design optimization by helping explore a large design space efficiently [33, 41]. The surrogates encapsulate the core relationships between input variables and resultant outputs [31, 41, 44], thereby curbing the temporal and resource-intensive nature of recurrent simulations. The computational efficiency makes surrogate models especially valuable in scenarios requiring optimization [55], sensitivity analysis [50], and uncertainty quantification [6], where numerous iterations of a complex model are necessary. The primary objective of the surrogate model is to achieve a balanced trade-off between accuracy and efficiency, enabling the exploration of the design space without the burden of extensive computational demands.

4.3 Clarifying Differences Based on Key Aspects

Meta-models, in both of their interpretations, serve different purposes and functions. The meta-model as a framework captures the high-level blueprint or the schema by defining concepts related to different relationships guided by overall rules and guidelines. It sets the rules for creating other models. It describes the syntax and semantics of the model to ensure consistency, validity, and interoperability across models.

On the other hand, a meta-model as a surrogate simulates the behavior of complex, high-fidelity computational models. Its purpose is to remove the intricacies by modeling the mathematical relationship between input and output parameters. The function it serves is the reduction of time and resources through mimicking the behavior of the same complex system as accurately as needed. However, it does sacrifice accuracy for computational gain [33].

Another major difference lies in the scope of application. The meta-model as schema ensures the consistency, coherence, and standardization through guiding the development of models through a set of rules and constraints and following a set of regulated ontologies. It identifies missing elements, potential inconsistencies, or areas of improvement in the design of complex systems [21].Whereas in surrogates, the application becomes paramount, especially when the models are too complex, and the design space is too big to compute. In such a case, the bottleneck is the time and computational resources, as optimizing multiple design parameters in large and complex models could be both time-consuming and computationally resource intensive.

The level of abstraction also differs between the two interpretations. One focuses on providing high-level blueprints essential for constructing models within a specific domain, while the meta-model, as a surrogate, tends to be more concrete as it deals with quantitative approximations of the complex system behavior [17, 33]. This divergence leads to differing levels of abstraction: meta-models as frameworks operate at a higher level of abstraction compared to surrogate or approximate models. But this does not mean that both interpretations are mutually exclusive. They can be complementary and are often used simultaneously.

In collaborative decision making for complex systems, both high-level frameworks and detailed surrogates may be necessary. The framework provides the overall structure and ensures consistency across different modeling domains, while surrogate meta-models can be employed for specific, computationally intensive tasks. For instance, behind a specific view of a meta-model, surrogate models may operate to deliver detailed results. The view offers the overarching framework, while the underlying surrogates provide the necessary detailed outcomes. This reflects the concept of differing levels of abstraction, where meta-models function at various layers, each playing a crucial role in the modeling process. As such, meta-models act as models of models, suggesting that multiple layers can coexist, each contributing to the system at different levels of abstraction.

Table 4. Differences between the two interpretations of the Meta-model

Key Aspects	Meta-model as a framework	Meta-model as a surrogate or approximate model
Purpose and Function	Provides a high-level blueprint defining concepts, relationships, and rules for constructing models within a domain. It offers an abstract representation of system elements and their connections.	Simulates the behavior of a complex, computationally intensive model, offering a faster and more efficient way to estimate outcomes without extensive computations.
Scope and Application	Ensure consistency, coherence, and standardization in model creation, guiding the design and development of various models to maintain a uniform structure within a system.	Used when the original model is resource-intensive or time-consuming. It approximates the complex model's behavior to facilitate optimization, sensitivity analysis, or uncertainty quantification.
Level of Abstraction	Operates at a higher level of abstraction, capturing fundamental relationships and concepts common across multiple models, without directly replicating specific model behaviors.	Operates at a lower level of abstraction, focusing on mimicking the input-output relationships of a complex model as accurately as needed. It simplifies the computational process while retaining essential characteristics of the original model to ensure reliable approximations.
Interpretation of Results	Offers guidance for creating models and ensuring interoperability, rather than direct approximations of complex model outputs.	Provides approximate predictions of the complex model's outputs, enabling quick assessments without needing to run the full model.

Another distinction lies in interpreting the results. Meta-model as a framework offers guidance for creating models and ensures interoperability. To achieve semantic interoperability in a collaborative context, formalized mappings or transformational mechanisms may be used. For example, meta-models as a framework can be annotated with semantics that describe how their components relate to surrogate model parameters [56]. Transformational tools such as Atlas Transformational Language (ATL) and Query/View/Transformation (QVT) [57] can be used to map (semi-) automatically generate inputs for surrogate models. Another approach to enhance interoperability is to adopt a view-based modeling approach, where each stakeholder interacts with tailored model views.

The interpretation of the results revolves around identifying patterns, validating assumptions, and establishing shared vocabulary for communication among stakeholders [21]. For a meta-model as a surrogate, the interpretation of results is based on the evaluation of the accuracy and reliability of the surrogate model in predicting the output of the original high-fidelity simulation model [3, 33]. The results are also used to guide the decision-making, optimization of design, and identification of improvements to the system being modelled [43].

5 Conclusions

The review offers a summary of the interpretation of the meta-models relevant to the domain of collaborative decision making for complex systems. When viewed as a framework, meta-models provide high-level blueprints focusing on standardization and coherence in model creation, ensuring that models within a system or domain share common concepts, relationships, and rules for constructing models within a specific domain. When meta-models are interpreted as surrogates or approximate models, they function as efficient, lower abstracted models to replicate the behavior of complex systems. This interpretation is used in computationally intensive tasks such as optimization and uncertainty quantification, where quick, approximate predictions are necessary to save time and resources.

Meta-models, in both of their interpretations, serve different purposes, functions, and the scope of application. The study also highlights the non-exclusive nature of these interpretations, which means that both interpretations can be complementary rather than mutually exclusive. In complex engineering systems, the integration of both high-level frameworks and detailed surrogate models is often required. The framework ensures that the overall structure and design principles are maintained across different modeling domains, while surrogate models provide the computational efficiency needed for specific, resource-intensive tasks. This allows for a more comprehensive modeling process, where different levels of abstraction coexist and contribute to a holistic understanding of the system. Thus, the concept of meta-models as models of models is reinforced, suggesting that multiple layers of meta-models can operate simultaneously, each playing a distinct yet interconnected role in the design and analysis of complex systems.

In a collaborative context, semantic interoperability can be achieved through formalized mappings or transformational mechanisms. Meta-models as a framework can be annotated with semantics that describe how their components relate to surrogate model parameters. Similarly, transformational tools such as ATL and QVT could be used to (semi-)automatically generate inputs for surrogate models. Another approach to enhance interoperability could be to adopt a view-based modeling approach, where each stakeholder interacts with tailored model views.

Overall, the review intends to serve as a valuable reference for the research community navigating the diverse definitions and applications of meta-models for collaborative decision-making in complex engineering. Through a scoping review, the study provides not only a classification of how meta-models are used but also a semantic clarification that has been used inconsistently across disciplines. By identifying terminological inconsistencies, it aims to support more effective communication in a collaborative environment, especially in those settings where a lack of common consensus and understanding leads to challenges such as hindered collaboration and integration issues. The authors believe that the review will also contribute to clearer communication within the field of complex engineering systems, providing insights into the versatile applications of meta-models across disciplines. Additionally, the identification of overlaps, gaps, and conceptual misalignment in literature, the study provides a theoretical grounding of meta-models in collaborative, early-stage engineering design.

References

1. Ullman, D.G.: The Mechanical Design Process, 3rd edition. Boston, Mau, McGraw-Hill [2003] ©2003 (2003). https://search.library.wisc.edu/catalog/9910037687002121
2. Robinson, S.: Simulation: The Practice of Model Development and Use, 2nd edition (2014)
3. Mhenni, F., et al.: Heterogeneous models integration for safety critical mechatronic systems and related digital twin definition: application to a collaborative workplace for aircraft assembly. Appl. Sci. Switz. **12**(6) (2022). https://doi.org/10.3390/app12062787
4. Aucejo, M.: A data-driven metamodel-based approach for point force localization. Mech. Syst. Signal Process **171** (2022). https://doi.org/10.1016/j.ymssp.2022.108881
5. Medini, K., Boucher, X.: Specifying a modelling language for PSS engineering – a development method and an operational tool. Comput. Ind. **108**, 89–103 (2019). https://doi.org/10.1016/j.compind.2019.02.014
6. Khosravi, A., Nahavandi, S., Creighton, D.: A prediction interval-based approach to determine optimal structures of neural network metamodels. Expert Syst. Appl. **37**(3), 2377–2387 (2010). https://doi.org/10.1016/j.eswa.2009.07.059
7. Belkadi, F., Dremont, N., Notin, A., Troussier, N., Messadia, M.: A meta-modelling framework for knowledge consistency in collaborative design. Annu. Rev. Control. **36**(2), 346–358 (2012). https://doi.org/10.1016/j.arcontrol.2012.09.016
8. Moser, T., Biffl, S.: Semantic integration of software and systems engineering environments. IEEE Trans. Syst. Man Cybern. Part C Appl. Rev. **42**(1), 38–50 (2012). https://doi.org/10.1109/TSMCC.2011.2136377
9. Bakirtzis, G., Sherburne, T., Adams, S., Horowitz, B.M., Beling, P.A., Fleming, C.H.: An ontological metamodel for cyber-physical system safety, security, and resilience coengineering. Softw. Syst. Model. **21**(1), 113–137 (2022). https://doi.org/10.1007/s10270-021-00892-z
10. Colquhoun, H.L., et al.: Scoping reviews: time for clarity in definition, methods, and reporting. J. Clin. Epidemiol. **67**(12), 1291–1294 (2014). https://doi.org/10.1016/j.jclinepi.2014.03.013
11. Vi Tran, H.K., Börstler, J., Bin Ali, N., Unterkalmsteiner, M.: How good are my search strings? Reflections on using an existing review as a quasi-gold standard. E-Inform. Softw. Eng. J. **16**(1), 220103 (2022). https://doi.org/10.37190/e-Inf220103

12. Zhang, H., Babar, M.A., Tell, P.: Identifying relevant studies in software engineering. Inf. Softw. Technol. **53**(6), 625–637 (2011). https://doi.org/10.1016/j.infsof.2010.12.010
13. Mcharek, M., Hammadi, M., Azib, T., Larouci, C., Choley, J.Y.: Collaborative design process and product knowledge methodology for mechatronic systems. Comput. Ind. **105**, 213–228 (2019). https://doi.org/10.1016/j.compind.2018.12.008
14. Locatelli, G., Mancini, M., Romano, E.: Systems Engineering to improve the governance in complex project environments. Int. J. Proj. Manag. **32**(8), 1395–1410 (2014). https://doi.org/10.1016/j.ijproman.2013.10.007
15. Krzywanski, J., Sosnowski, M., Grabowska, K., Zylka, A., Lasek, L., Kijo-Kleczkowska, A.: Advanced computational methods for modeling, prediction and optimization—a review. Materials **17**(14), 3521 (2024). https://doi.org/10.3390/ma17143521
16. Lin, T., Chai, X., Li, B.: Top-level modeling theory of multi-discipline virtual prototype. J. Syst. Eng. Electron. **23**(3), 425–437 (2012). https://doi.org/10.1109/JSEE.2012.00054
17. Toffol, F., Ricci, S.: A Meta-Model for composite wingbox sizing in aircraft conceptual design. Compos. Struct. **306** (2023). https://doi.org/10.1016/j.compstruct.2022.116557
18. Zhou, Q., Shao, X., Jiang, P., Zhou, H., Shu, L.: An adaptive global variable fidelity metamodeling strategy using a support vector regression based scaling function. Simul. Model. Pract. Theory **59**, 18–35 (2015). https://doi.org/10.1016/j.simpat.2015.08.002
19. Broad, D.R., Maier, H.R., Dandy, G.C., Asce, M.: Optimal Operation of Complex Water Distribution Systems Using Metamodels. https://doi.org/10.1061/ASCEWR.1943-5452.0000052
20. Shirvani, F., Beydoun, G., Perez, P., Scott, W., Campbell, P.: An architecture framework approach for complex transport projects. Inf. Syst. Front. **23**(3), 575–595 (2021). https://doi.org/10.1007/s10796-019-09978-y
21. Cha, S., Vogel-Heuser, B., Fischer, J.: Analysis of metamodels for model-based production automation system engineering. IET Collab. Intell. Manuf. **2**(2), 45–55 (2020). https://doi.org/10.1049/iet-cim.2020.0013
22. Ge, B., Hipel, K.W., Yang, K., Chen, Y.: A novel executable modeling approach for system-of-systems architecture. IEEE Syst. J. **8**(1), 4–13 (2014). https://doi.org/10.1109/JSYST.2013.2270573
23. Göppert, A., Grahn, L., Rachner, J., Grunert, D., Hort, S., Schmitt, R.H.: Pipeline for ontology-based modeling and automated deployment of digital twins for planning and control of manufacturing systems. J. Intell. Manuf. **34**(5), 2133–2152 (2023). https://doi.org/10.1007/s10845-021-01860-6
24. Lyazidi, A., Mouline, S.: A metamodel-driven definition and implementation of ONDAR: a home automation ontology (2018)
25. Andrijcic, E., Haimes, Y.Y.: Metamodeling of interdependent systems: application to bridge infrastructure management. J. Infrastruct. Syst. **23**(2) (2017). https://doi.org/10.1061/(asce)is.1943-555x.0000322
26. Ghorbani, A., Dijkema, G.P.J., Bots, P., Alderwereld, H., Dignum, V.: Model-driven agent-based simulation: Procedural semantics of a MAIA model. Simul. Model. Pract. Theory **49**, 27–40 (2014). https://doi.org/10.1016/j.simpat.2014.07.009
27. Ruane, P., Walsh, P., Cosgrove, J.: Development of a digital model and metamodel to improve the performance of an automated manufacturing line. J. Manuf. Syst. **65**, 538–549 (2022). https://doi.org/10.1016/j.jmsy.2022.10.011
28. Longo, F., Huerta, A., Nicoletti, L.: Performance analysis of a Southern Mediterranean seaport via discrete-event simulation. Strojniski VestnikJournal Mech. Eng. **59**(9), 517–525 (2013). https://doi.org/10.5545/sv-jme.2013.963
29. Ribeiro, L., Gomes, L.: Describing structure and complex interactions in multi-agent-based industrial cyber-physical systems. IEEE Access **9**, 153126–153141 (2021). https://doi.org/10.1109/ACCESS.2021.3127344

30. Mostafavi, A., et al.: Agent-Based Simulation Model for Assessment of Financing Scenarios in Highway Transportation Infrastructure Systems. J. Comput. Civ. Eng. **30**(2) (2016). https://doi.org/10.1061/(asce)cp.1943-5487.0000482
31. Tekinerdogan, B.: On the Notion of Digital Twins: A Modeling Perspective. Systems **11**(1) (2023). https://doi.org/10.3390/systems11010015
32. Woitsch, R., Sumereder, A., Falcioni, D.: Model-based data integration along the product & service life cycle supported by digital twinning. Comput. Ind. **140** (2022). https://doi.org/10.1016/j.compind.2022.103648
33. Can, B., Heavey, C.: A comparison of genetic programming and artificial neural networks in metamodeling of discrete-event simulation models. Comput. Oper. Res. **39**(2), 424–436 (2012). https://doi.org/10.1016/j.cor.2011.05.004
34. Piriou, P.Y., Faure, J.M., Deleuze, G.: A meta-model to support the integration of dependability concerns into systems engineering processes: an example from power production. IEEE Syst. J. **10**(1), 15–24 (2016). https://doi.org/10.1109/JSYST.2014.2328663
35. Cao, Y., Liu, Y., Paredis, C.J.J.: System-level model integration of design and simulation for mechatronic systems based on SysML. Mechatronics **21**(6), 1063–1075 (2011). https://doi.org/10.1016/j.mechatronics.2011.05.003
36. Zerwas, T., et al.: Customer-centric and function-oriented development of mechatronic systems. Forsch. Im IngenieurwesenEngineering Res. **87**(1), 507–519 (2023). https://doi.org/10.1007/s10010-023-00658-7
37. Zhao, D., Xue, D.: A multi-surrogate approximation method for metamodeling. Eng. Comput. **27**(2), 139–153 (2011). https://doi.org/10.1007/s00366-009-0173-y
38. Wang, C.B., Chen, T.Y., Chen, Y.M., Chu, H.C.: Design of a Meta Model for integrating enterprise systems. Comput. Ind. **56**(3), 305–322 (2005). https://doi.org/10.1016/j.compind.2004.10.003
39. Kieu, M., Nguyen, H., Ward, J.A., Malleson, N.: Towards real-time predictions using emulators of agent-based models. J. Simul. (2022). https://doi.org/10.1080/17477778.2022.2080008
40. Messac, A., Mullur, A.A.: A computationally efficient metamodeling approach for expensive multiobjective optimization. Optim. Eng. **9**(1), 37–67 (2008). https://doi.org/10.1007/s11081-007-9008-0
41. Zhu, P., Pan, F., Chen, W., Zhang, S.: Use of support vector regression in structural optimization: Application to vehicle crashworthiness design. Math. Comput. Simul **86**, 21–31 (2012). https://doi.org/10.1016/j.matcom.2011.11.008
42. Torregrosa, S., Champaney, V., Ammar, A., Herbert, V., Chinesta, F.: Surrogate parametric metamodel based on Optimal Transport. Math. Comput. Simul **194**, 36–63 (2022). https://doi.org/10.1016/j.matcom.2021.11.010
43. Chabanet, S., Bril El-Haouzi, H., Thomas, P.: Coupling digital simulation and machine learning metamodel through an active learning approach in Industry 4.0 context. Comput. Ind. **133** (2021). https://doi.org/10.1016/j.compind.2021.103529
44. Lee, M., et al.: Metamodel-based multidisciplinary design optimization of a deep-sea manganese nodules test miner. J. Appl. Math. **2012** (2012). https://doi.org/10.1155/2012/326954
45. Knudde, N., Dutordoir, V., Herten, J.V.D., Couckuyt, I., Dhaene, T.: Hierarchical gaussian process models for improved metamodeling. ACM Trans. Model. Comput. Simul. **30**(4) (2020). https://doi.org/10.1145/3384470
46. Yonglin, L., Zhi, Z., Qun, L.: An ontological metamodeling framework for semantic simulation model engineering. J. Syst. Eng. Electron. **31**(3), 527–538 (2020). https://doi.org/10.23919/JSEE.2020.000032

47. Filomeno Coelho, R.: Metamodels for mixed variables based on moving least squares: application to the structural analysis of a rigid frame. Optim. Eng. **15**(2), 311–329 (2014). https://doi.org/10.1007/s11081-013-9216-8
48. Sabuncuoglu, I., Touhami, S.: Simulation metamodelling with neural networks: an experimental investigation. Int. J. Prod. Res. **40**(11), 2483–2505 (2002). https://doi.org/10.1080/00207540210135596
49. Kaseb, Z., Montazeri, H.: Data-driven optimization of building-integrated ducted openings for wind energy harvesting: Sensitivity analysis of metamodels. Energy **258** (2022). https://doi.org/10.1016/j.energy.2022.124814
50. Jensen, H.A., Jerez, D.J., Valdebenito, M.; An adaptive scheme for reliability-based global design optimization: a markov chain monte carlo approach. Mech. Syst. Signal Process. **143** (2020). https://doi.org/10.1016/j.ymssp.2020.106836
51. Dammak, K., Baklouti, A., El Hami, A.: Optimal reliable design of brake disk using a Kriging surrogate model. Mech. Adv. Mater. Struct. **29**(28), 7569–7578 (2022). https://doi.org/10.1080/15376494.2021.2002983
52. Pourmohammadi, P., Saif, A.: Robust metamodel-based simulation-optimization approaches for designing hybrid renewable energy systems. Appl. Energy **341** (2023). https://doi.org/10.1016/j.apenergy.2023.121132
53. Ferraz, F.M.B., et al.: Metamodelling the hot deformation behaviour of titanium alloys using a mean-field approach. Mater. Today Commun. **35** (2023). https://doi.org/10.1016/j.mtcomm.2023.106148
54. Rodrigues Da Silva, A.: Model-driven engineering: a survey supported by the unified conceptual model. Comput. Lang. Syst. Struct. **43**, 139–155 (2015). https://doi.org/10.1016/j.cl.2015.06.001
55. Becker, J., Beverungen, D., Knackstedt, R.: LNBIP 42 - A Method for Selectively Designing Modeling Languages for Product-Service Systems (2012)
56. Towards automatic model synchronization from model transformations | Proceedings of the 22nd IEEE/ACM International Conference on Automated Software Engineering. Accessed: 07 Jul. 2025. https://doi.org/10.1145/1321631.1321657
57. Kleppe, A.G., Warmer, J.B., Bast, W.: MDA explained: the model driven architecture; practice and promise, 5. print. in Addison-Wesley object technology series. Addison-Wesley, Boston Munich (2007)

An Intelligent Collaborative Decision Support System for Climate Disaster Management

Pedro S. Zanchett[1(✉)], Gustavo R. Lemos[1], and Ricardo J. Rabelo[2]

[1] Leonardo da Vinci University Center (UNIASSELVI), Indaial, (SC), Brazil
pedrozanchett@uniasselvi.com.br
[2] UFSC – Federal University of Santa Catarina, Florianópolis, (SC), Brazil
ricardo.rabelo@ufsc.br

Abstract. Natural disasters (NDs) are becoming increasingly frequent, often causing severe disruptions in urban areas. Managing these events throughout their life cycle requires addressing their unique characteristics, varying intensities, and unpredictable progression. This involves complex analyses, planning, coordination, and monitoring based on extensive information and the collaboration of multiple actors, including civil defense teams, hospitals, armed forces, and firefighters. Collaborative Decision Support Systems (CDSS) can aid in managing such complexity and supporting group decision-making. However, actors remain responsible for interpreting data and making final decisions before many possible alternatives, which are prone to errors and delays due to the high volume of information and the stressful conditions typical of disaster scenarios. To address this challenge, the paper proposes integrating Generative AI (GAI) into CDSS to enhance human decision-making during certain phases of disaster management. A software prototype focused on wildfire-related climate disasters has been developed to demonstrate the approach's potential. The paper concludes with preliminary results and suggests directions for future research.

Keyword: natural disaster · collaborative decision support system · generative AI

1 Introduction

Natural disasters (ND) are increasingly happening, bringing many social, economic, and environmental consequences in the short and long term to cities, infrastructures, and natural resources, affecting logistics and supply chains [1–3]. The need for more comprehensive policies and solutions for better ND management has been emphasized and coordinated by some international organizations, namely United Nations, via the *Senday Framework*, aiming at preventing the creation of new risks, reducing existing risks, and increasing resilience to disasters [4].

Handling an ND requires coordination, collaboration and management, resources efficiency, effectiveness, and environmental care [5]. However, managing an ND is

Published by Springer Nature Switzerland AG 2026
L. M. Camarinha-Matos et al. (Eds.): PRO-VE 2025, IFIP AICT 770, pp. 482–499, 2026.
https://doi.org/10.1007/978-3-032-05673-3_29

highly complex due to its inherently dynamics, real-time changes, and often unpredictable nature. These events evolve rapidly and in unforeseen ways, requiring continuous coordination and discussions among multiple actors – such as civil defense, police, paramedics, armed forces, and firefighters, throughout the different stages of an ND. Effective response demands constant information exchange, collaborative analysis, and decision-making based on the evolving situation, including impacts on people, infrastructure, and affected areas [6]. This complexity is further compounded by challenges in information management. Data is often fragmented, outdated, or difficult to access, particularly because actors are physically dispersed across impacted regions, making real-time collaboration and coordinated decision-making especially difficult [6, 7].

Tools like *WhatsApp, Zoom, Google Meet,* and *Microsoft Teams* are commonly used to support communication and quick messaging, but they lack integrated data management and synthesis capabilities [6, 8, 9]. Collaborative and groupware platforms facilitate the exchange of data and viewpoints in some coordinated manner [10]. The challenge lies in the overwhelming volume of data. Decision-makers must correlate multiple and disparate data sources, evaluate scenarios, consult historical records, adhere to several action protocols (legal, technical, and health-related), and coordinate with other actors, often under high-stress conditions. This complexity can lead to errors, delays, and less effective decisions [9, 11, 12].

Collaborative (or Group) Decision Support Systems (CDSS) represent a powerful approach to face those issues, providing platforms designed to assist multiple actors in conducting more complex analyses and facilitating collective discussions, consensus, understanding sharing, collective intelligence, more effective coordination, and more reliable decision-making [9, 13–15].

Although this assistance, CDSS' capabilities are constrained by limited intelligence. They typically generate recommendations and solutions based on predefined, static knowledge bases [16–19], including that the interpretation and reasoning upon data and decision scenarios are primarily carried out by humans [11, 20].

In order to deal with this limitation, this paper showcases a CDSS that integrates Generative AI (GAI) to enhance decision-making tasks during some phases of an ND without solely depending on direct user inputs or manual intervention.

GAI has emerged as a powerful approach for automating processes and generating insights, solutions, or suggestions by intelligently analyzing data from diverse sources [21]. This integration fosters hybrid collaborative intelligence and greater transparency, facilitating human interaction, cognitive processes, and interoperability [22, 23]. It also helps alleviate cognitive overload and reduce heuristic biases by delivering data-driven support and predictive insights rooted in systems' reasoning [37].

How can GAI enhance collaborative decision-making? To illustrate its potential, a software prototype has been developed using the *ChatGPT 4.1* Generative AI tool[1]. The prototype is designed to support a civil defense team in a southern Brazilian city in managing a hypothetical climate-related *wildfire* scenario once it is on its way.

This paper is structured as follows: Sect. 1 introduced the problem and outlined the paper's objective. Section 2 gives an overview of the complexity of managing an ND. Section 3 summarizes the research methodology and provides a brief literature review.

---

[1] https://openai.com/index/gpt-4-1/.

Section 4 presents an overview of the intelligent CDSS developed. Section 5 focuses on the prototype itself. Finally, Sect. 6 offers preliminary conclusions and outlines directions for future work.

2 Natural Disasters Management

A natural disaster (ND) can be defined as"*the negative impact following an actual occurrence of natural hazard in the event that it significantly harms a community*" [1].

ND can be classified into two main categories: natural (such as geological, climatological, and biological disasters) and technological events (including radioactive hazards, warfare events, and the transportation of hazardous materials). Each category contains various subtypes; for instance, the climatological category includes events like droughts and wildfires [25].

Handling an ND requires specific and multi-criteria analyses regarding the different types of events, their usual uniqueness, also considering their geographical extent, severity, criticality of the affected areas, and impacted people [8, 11].

In general, managing DN involves four main phases [5]: Mitigation, Preparedness, Response, and Recovery. Other authors group them into different clusters with a notion of life cycle, as pre-disaster (prevention and mitigation), during the disaster (preparedness and response), and post-disaster (recovery and restoration) [6]. This includes identifying and managing numerous independent, distributed, and role-specific actors to involve (such as civil defense units, hospitals, paramedics, armed forces, firefighters, and food and water suppliers) and that used to work (as) in different and coordinated teams, assessing available and needed resources, and determining appropriate measures for each stage [11].

Some actions demand highly complex reasoning, in addition to tasks such as planning, coordination, and monitoring – all carried out within varying governance models and data access privileges. This complexity increases due to the inherently unpredictable evolution of each ND, and that one ND can trigger or coincide with another, creating interconnected events [8, 11].

3 Research Methodology and Basic Literature Assessment

3.1 Research Methodology

This study was conducted using the *Action Research* methodology [24], which focuses on generating practical change while simultaneously producing new knowledge. Particularly suitable for exploratory research, this approach enables the development of innovative solutions to real-world problems through iterative refinement cycles. It is typically applied to specific, context-dependent situations where improvements or new insights are sought. This paper marks the conclusion of the first cycle of such a process.

The research began with an analysis of decision-making protocols, the governance model, and the key stakeholders involved in wildfire response within a specific civil defense organization. Subsequently, an initial literature review was conducted, examining scientific publications on CDSS applications that incorporate AI or GAI to support human decision-making in ND management. The goal was twofold: to identify existing knowledge gaps in relation to the needs of the selected civil defense unit, and to incorporate relevant findings into the proposed model and prototype system. A software prototype was then developed and preliminary evaluated experimentally.

3.2 Basic Literature Assessment

The literature review revealed various applications of AI in the context of ND management. Examples include the use of fuzzy logic to structure decision-making protocols and associated knowledge [26], the application of ontologies [27], and the deployment of machine learning techniques for optimizing resource allocation and predicting disaster events [26]. Other studies have leveraged AI to process data from Big Data and Internet of Things (IoT) sources, enhancing the relevance and accessibility of information for further collaborative analyses [28–32].

Beyond collaborative DSS for disaster management, studies such as [33] focus on how AI-assisted platforms can consolidate scattered information to generate a Common Operational Picture (COP), ensuring that all involved teams share a unified view of events and resources. Similarly, [34] investigates the use of AI to optimize communication flows and the dynamic allocation of tasks in response to disasters, thereby facilitating interaction and mutual support among different agencies.

In [27], a theoretical framework is proposed that integrates GAI into a DSS to assist a single decision-maker during various stages of flood management in a Chinese city. Studies such as [35] and [36] highlight AI's features in group decision-making and negotiation processes. They emphasize AI's potential in learning from data, recognizing patterns, automating tasks, optimizing planning, adapting responses to users, predicting events, and improving transparency.

In [37] a list of 13 criteria to evaluate a collaborative decision-making system using GAI is provided, together with a comprehensive study comparing human interactions with and without GAI. They revealed many benefits using GAI but pointing out the potential dependency on GAI that can lead to the waste of human decision-making skills and the continuation of biases inherent in the algorithms and data used by GAI systems. In [37] is made a study on collaborative learning using GAI, analyzing the impact of having an intermediate tutor ('human under the loop') and without tutors ('human in the loop'), which might be useful in teaching decision-makers.

A significant advancement in this area is the growing integration of Large Language Models (LLM) with Retrieval-Augmented Generation (RAG) techniques. The RAG approach, highlighted by [38], enables LLM to retrieve relevant information from external and domain-specific knowledge bases (such as protocol documents, historical incident data, or real-time reports) before generating their responses. This capability is particularly valuable in disaster management, as it mitigates the risk of hallucinations and ensures that the GAI outputs are factual, contextualized, and aligned with critical operational data, providing a higher level of reliability for high-stakes decision-making.

Studies such as [34] and [39] have employed LLM and RAG for tasks including automatic summarization of field reports, real-time translation of emergency documents, and generating responses to complex queries about crisis procedures based on operational manuals. These works underscore the GAI potential, not only as a language processing tool, but also as a proactive element in collaborative information management, contributing to faster and more accurate situational understanding and the development of more effective response strategies. Other studies have applied GAI but for supporting mono decision making.

In summary, despite recent advances in the application of GAI and LLMs to specific aspects of disaster management and group decision-making, no studies were found in the literature that report on the implementation of CDSS integrating GAI for natural disaster management. This work aims to address this gap by doing an initial investigation on how GAI can help decision-makers using a CDSS in the response and management of natural disasters.

4 The Intelligent CDSS for Natural Disasters

4.1 The Developed CDSS as a Derivation from a Reference Architecture

The CDSS was developed as a derivation from the *RADIAN* open reference architecture [6], which serves as a foundational framework for creating customized DSS aimed at managing various types of NDs throughout their life cycles. *RADIAN* supports a range of functions, including planning, management, supervision, data collection and integration, monitoring, and multi-actor collaborative decision-making.

The prototype specifically addresses a hypothetical *wildfire* scenario to be managed by the civil defense agency of Florianópolis, Brazil. This agency follows a set of predefined action protocols (like high-level workflows) that must be executed in a coordinated manner involving predefined types of actors. These participants are assigned based on legal responsibilities and the nature of the ND, while also complying with technical, sanitation, safety, and operational guidelines.

Each ND is unique in terms of intensity, geographical scope, and impacted areas. As such, when an ND occurs, the civil defense must assess its characteristics and activate the appropriate action protocol. Because these protocols are designed to be generic, they require continuous instantiation, meaning that specific actors must be assigned, resources allocated, and concrete actions defined (*what to do, when,* and *where*) as the situation evolves. This process continues iteratively based on feedback from implemented actions until the civil defense considers the ND as finished.

RADIAN comprises 39 high-level functionalities, organized into various modules across three main architectural components. During the derivation process, CDSS developers are expected to identify which of these functionalities are relevant for their specific application. Each functionality can be implemented using different technologies, including multiple software systems, provided they collectively adhere to the globally coherent logic and behavioral expectations defined by *RADIAN*.

For the development of the prototype, a subset of these functionalities has been selected. Figure 1 shows the *RADIAN* reference architecture, with the chosen functionalities highlighted in yellow dashed lines. Given that the main objective of this paper is to illustrate how GAI can enhance collaborative decision-making during a ND (in this case, within the *response* phase), these selected functionalities were implemented in a simplified form.

Due to the critical nature of civil defense systems and the legal restrictions to integrate prototypes directly into the real operational infrastructure, it was developed to run in a controlled, standalone environment. It uses randomly generated data from specific services to simulate real scenarios.

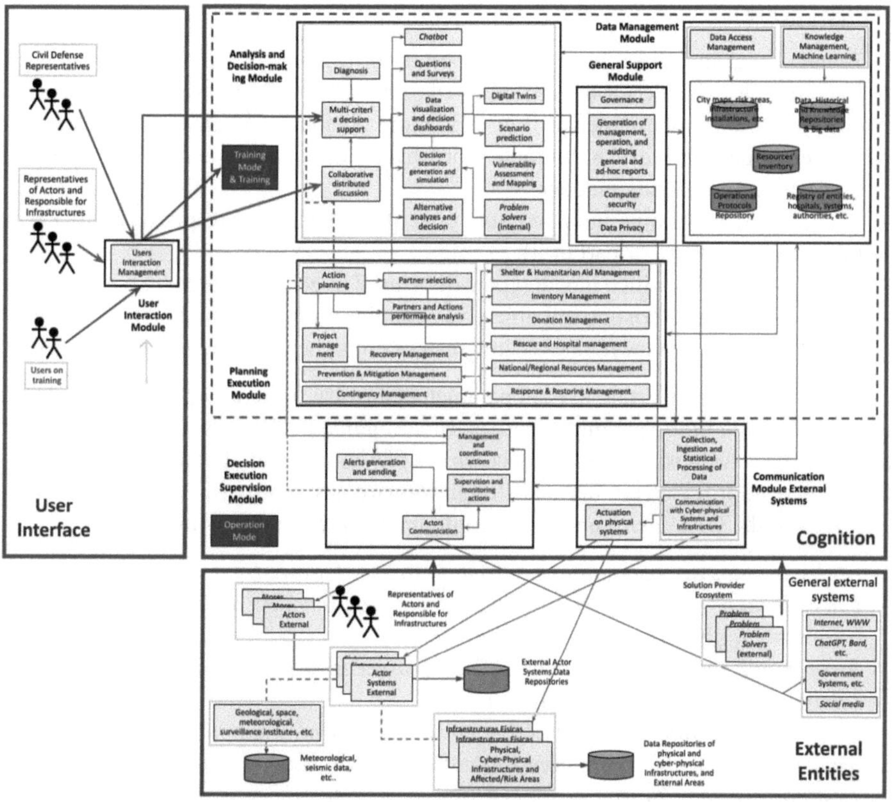

Fig. 1. The *RADIAN* architecture and the selected functionalities (Source: The Authors)

4.2 The Used Generative AI Tool

Despite being a prototype devised for a hypothetical case, it effectively incorporates GAI and follows the official action protocols used by the Florianópolis civil defense.

The *OpenAI ChatGPT 4.1*[2] tool has been used for this experiment. It was chosen due to its technical maturity, which involves aspects such as the high level of input natural language expression and results, processing speed, integration flexibility, API robustness, and extensive documentation. However, the system's architecture was designed agnostically, allowing the use of other generative models, such as *Google Gemini* or *Meta Llama*, in a relatively quick and simple way, due to the adoption of integration patterns via *RESTful* API and the abstraction of the developed code.

[2] https://openai.com/index/gpt-4-1/.

ChatGPT 4.1's API offers a suite of cloud-based services that operate on an input-output model: a prompt is submitted, and a response is generated based on predefined parameters. The API supports both simple, single-prompt interactions and more complex, context-aware exchanges – like a chat – facilitated by the *OpenAI* client library. Several configurable parameters are available, with the most relevant ones for this work outlined below:

- *Temperature*: it defines the level of creativity or randomness in the AI's responses. For example, a value set to zero means that the GAI will provide always the same answer. Lower values (such as 0.2) yield more objective and predictable responses. Higher values (such as 0.8) promote more diverse and more 'creative' responses, but this can generate hallucinations.
- *Max tokens*: it delimits the maximum size of the generated response, in tokens (a token can be a word or part of it);
- *Model*: it specifies which model type will be used to generate responses. Each model has specific characteristics and objectives, ranging from faster and more economical options to more advanced ones, with greater comprehension and reasoning capacity.

The 'most correct' value to each parameter can vary from prompt to prompt. In the case of the *temperature* parameter and, considering that a ND is a very critical event (in our example – see next section – the *wildfire* is of highest level of severity), it was set to zero in way to provide very fast and straightforward answers.

Overall, the GAI environment was configured using the following prompts:

- *All listed rules are inviolable and must be strictly followed;*
- *Check if there is a useful contribution, correction or other action to suggest before answering a question. Otherwise, answer 'null';*
- *Answer in a formal, structured, clear and direct way, using textual format, without symbols, emojis or greeting expressions;*
- *Be aware you are in an interactive environment with multiple and heterogeneous users. Interact with this environment only when you have relevant contributions;*
- *Don't answer questions about other users or people;*
- *Always check the veracity and coherence of the information, and the terminology adequacy to this context;*
- *Execute your actions using the following functions: < list of functions >.*
- *Call a function only when necessary.*

The prompts' design and the parameters' configuration have tried to follow the core principles and guidelines of prompt engineering [40].

The interactions between the users/system prototype and GAI are divided into two distinct categories: one in which the AI acts as a team member, and another in which it functions as a tool, without direct user intervention. When used as a teammate, the instructions provided do not allow the AI to perform sensitive actions. Conversely, when used as a tool, the prompts are encapsulated within fixed templates containing only controlled entry points, which can be indirectly modified by the user.

5 Implemented Prototype

The prototype was developed by combining four action protocols from the target civil defense agency in a simplified form, aiming to demonstrate the application of GAI in helping the involved actors in the wildfire in collaborative decision-making.

These protocols encompass activities such as weather forecasting, environmental monitoring, mobilization of resources, and alert communication. They require collaboration among various actors, who must access data from multiple sources and stakeholders, and make decisions through iterative analyses cycles. These decisions should account for the dynamic nature of wildfire's behavior throughout its life cycle respecting the governance model in place.

The figures below present examples of the graphical user interfaces (GUIs) designed to showcase how GAI has been integrated into the system.

A general scenario was devised, covering the following main steps: opening and ND characterization; actors' search and selection; governance setting up; ND severity analysis and affected areas; and alert message definition and communication.

Initially, the civil defense team accesses the CDSS and inputs the type of natural disaster ("wildfire") along with the mobilization level ("L3" on a scale from 0 to 3), indicating the highest severity level based on the agency's classification system (see Fig. 2). Once these fields are completed, the system performs two actions. First, it automatically retrieves and displays the relevant PDF documentation (Fig. 2A) (in other civil defense systems, this information might instead be presented through online dashboards). Second, the system queries the database for records of past similar events (Fig. 2D), providing historical data that may help inform the current response.

In parallel, a new OpenAI API client is instantiated, making a *http* request through the *client.responses.create* function, in which the model (gpt-4.1) is specified, and the instructions are provided: "*identify the institutions that should participate in a new occurrence that is being registered, analyze the situation and indicate which institutions are relevant to the occurrence based on the information and documents provided. Return only a list with the IDs of the selected institutions at the end*.".

For this prompt, the temperature is set to zero to ensure a fast and concise response, and the maximum token limit is set to 200, considering the civil defense may not initially know how many organizations will be needed to manage such a high-severity wildfire. After this, a prompt is issued in the following format: input parameters include the occurrence type <*wildfire*> and mobilization level <*L3*>, while the expected output is a *list of organizations*.

The selection of the 'temperature' parameter for prompts was guided by the need to control randomness and GAI creativity. Setting the temperature to zero ensures direct and consistent responses, which is critical in disaster scenarios. In contrast, a value of 0.4 was used for summarization tasks (as used later), aiming to strike a balance between objectivity and a more engaging tone, in line with findings from the literature on fine-tuning creativity in large language models.

All relevant actors and their profiles are pre-registered in a local database, along with historical documents from the civil defense containing general information on natural disasters. The system returns and displays a list of organizations best suited for the situation (Fig. 2B). Continuing within the same prompt thread, the system then

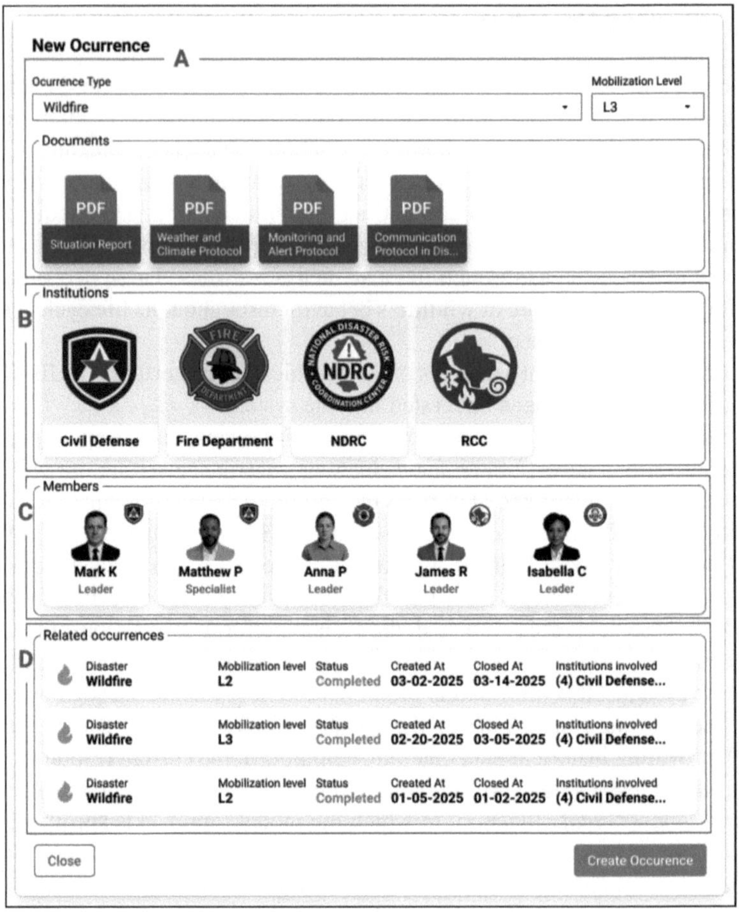

Fig. 2. Opening a new occurrence (Source: The Authors)

performs another query to identify the individuals who will compose the response team for managing the disaster (Fig. 2C).

Figure 3 presents the main GUI used to manage the wildfire event. At the top section (Fig. 3A), key information about the incident is displayed, namely: occurrence ID (*OC2056*), type of event (*wildfire*), mobilization level (*L3*), status (*in progress*), and the level of GAI interaction (*high-level*). The GAI interaction level indicates the degree of autonomy granted to the AI in performing tasks. While it can be manually adjusted, it can be set automatically based on the amount of relevant historical data available.

At the *low* setting, the GAI can produce responses using minimal available data but is restricted from taking any autonomous actions. When set to *medium*, it offers more refined insights and may perform limited actions on its own when appropriate. At the *high* level, the GAI generates detailed and accurate outputs and is authorized to carry out a wider range of more complex tasks independently.

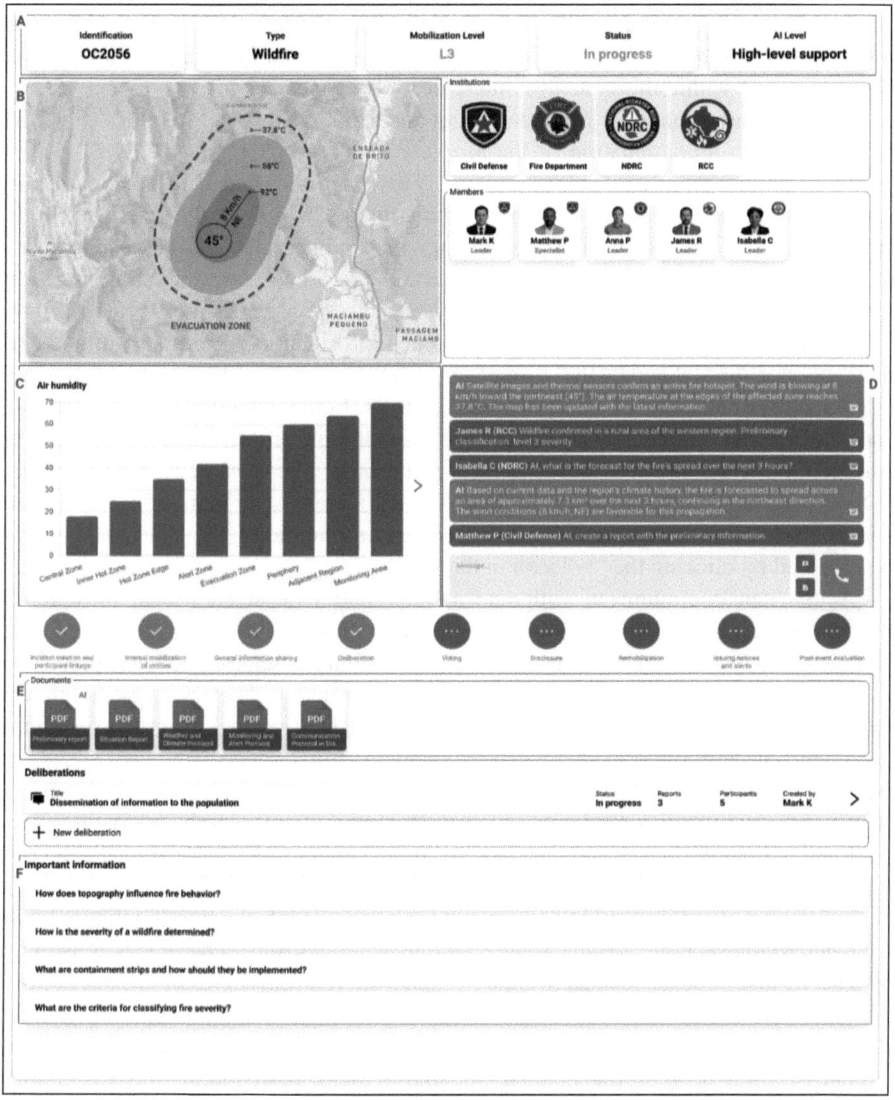

Fig. 3. Occurrence treatment (Source: The Authors)

Each civil defense agency can define its own standards for the type of information related to a specific ND that should be made available to users. The integrated GAI can produce not only textual descriptions but also visual elements such as maps and charts. Furthermore, when designing the GUI for a specific CDSS, the civil defense – typically the IT team responsible for deriving the system from the *RADIAN* architecture – can determine when and how this information is generated and presented.

The GAI operates in two modes: *reactive* and *autonomous*. In the reactive mode, it responds to user requests, supporting more detailed and collaborative analyses as needed. In the autonomous mode, GAI proactively generates and displays information it deems relevant based on the current context and situation. Both modes can function simultaneously within the same user interface.

An informative map was generated using data from sensors and satellites (Fig. 3B), created through a combination of the *Mapbox* tool[3] and OpenAI's *DALL·E*[4], which produces images from descriptive prompts. This map is designed to be dynamically updated with weather-related data in a *reactive* mode, as previously described. In the current example, it displays wind direction (45° NE), wind speed (8 km/h), and temperatures in affected areas (92 °C, 58 °C, and 37.8 °C), providing critical input for assessing fire intensity and determining evacuation zones and response measures.

Actors can request additional maps or related information via prompts, in line with their access rights defined by the system's governance model and based on what they see as relevant for collaborative analysis of the disaster. In the *autonomous* mode, the GAI can also generate supplementary visuals such as maps and graphs based on the evolving situation. For example, in response to a general prompt like "*generate graphics related to the current wildfire*", the system produced visualizations of air humidity, temperature, rainfall, air quality, and more (Fig. 3C shows only air humidity; the other graphics can be accessed by clicking the ">" icon in the GUI).

Actors can communicate with one another and request additional information through a chat feature (Fig. 3D). The green and gray circles below sections C and D indicate the current phase of the civil defense within the selected action protocol.

The document panel (Fig. 3E) is designed to offer involved actors access to relevant materials that support their collaborative analysis and decision-making processes. These documents are initially provided when the incident is first opened (see Fig. 2) and can be further complemented or updated autonomously by the GAI throughout the various stages of the natural disaster, based on what the GAI determines to be pertinent.

Finally, both the actors and the GAI can share general links, regulations, and other relevant resources (Fig. 3F) that they consider important for managing the incident. The general prompt used by the GAI to generate this type of information (configured with the *temperature* set to *0.2 to have some creativity without losing accuracy*) is constituted by a set of instructions, such as (roughly): '*generate relevant topics to this <wildfire> occurrence considering actors <x, y, z, ...>*', '*relevant topics refer to information about decision criteria, safety, operational protocols*', '*bring this information in JSON format structured in the form of title, content and source*', and '*search in the Internet and not only in the posted documents*'.

During the analysis of a natural disaster, numerous specific decisions must be made. One critical but often underlooked issue is the preparation and dissemination of alert messages to various stakeholders through different channels and formats. Because these alerts may contain sensitive information that could trigger panic or misunderstandings, the method, frequency, and wording of these messages are crucial and can significantly influence the affected population. While the final wording is typically up to the civil defense's press relations officer, the key actors involved in the response should agree on these aspects in advance.

[3] https://www.mapbox.com/.

[4] https://openai.com/index/dall-e-3/.

Given the various options for messages and styles, the CDSS enables different stakeholders to propose communications (Fig. 4A). In this instance, three messages were drafted by the public information/relations officer (PIO), while one was generated by the GAI using prompts based on the available documents. These messages target general bulletins, radio, TV, and government audiences. Stakeholders can engage in brainstorming discussions through a chat feature and cast votes (Fig. 4B). For example, the communication intended for the government has already received approval (*situation approved*) (Fig. 4A). The bulletin message, meanwhile, underwent refinement by GAI, which offered suggestions for improvement. This revised version was first approved by *Ms. Isabella* and *Mr. Mark*, and ultimately endorsed by *Mr. Mathew*, who holds the final authority according to the governance model. The remaining two messages are still awaiting final approval.

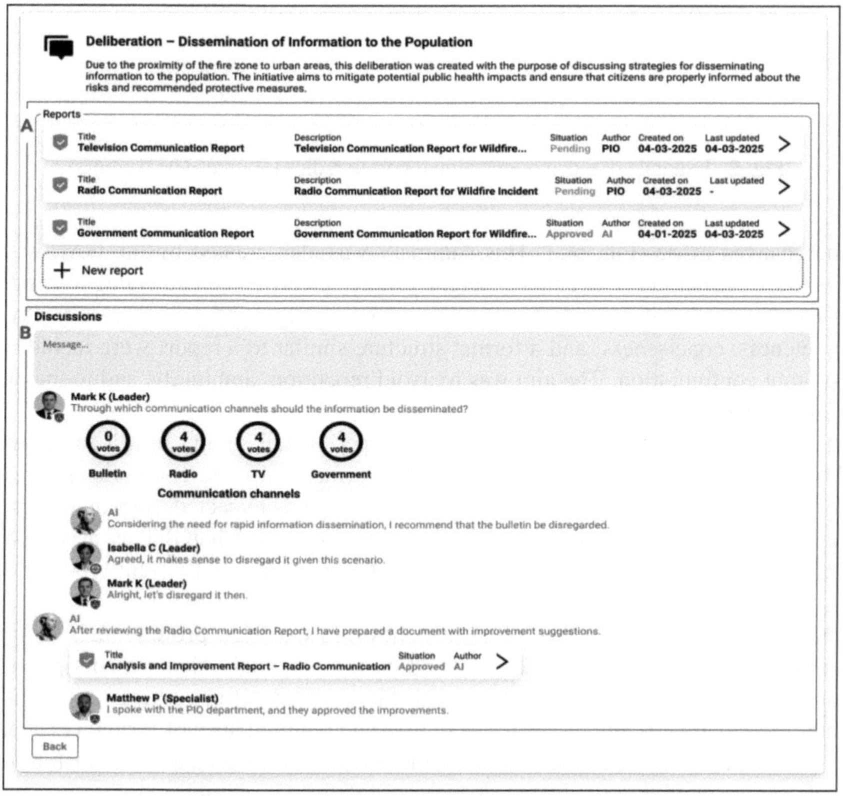

Fig. 4. Deliberation space (Source: The Authors)

Actors can refine pending messages and create multiple versions (Fig. 5A). The content of each message is displayed in the interface (Fig. 5B), where participants can evaluate and decide whether to approve the proposed version (Fig. 5C).

Lastly, a comparative analysis of the reports generated is conducted, including for auditing purposes. Both versions are displayed (Figs. 6A and B) along with a summary

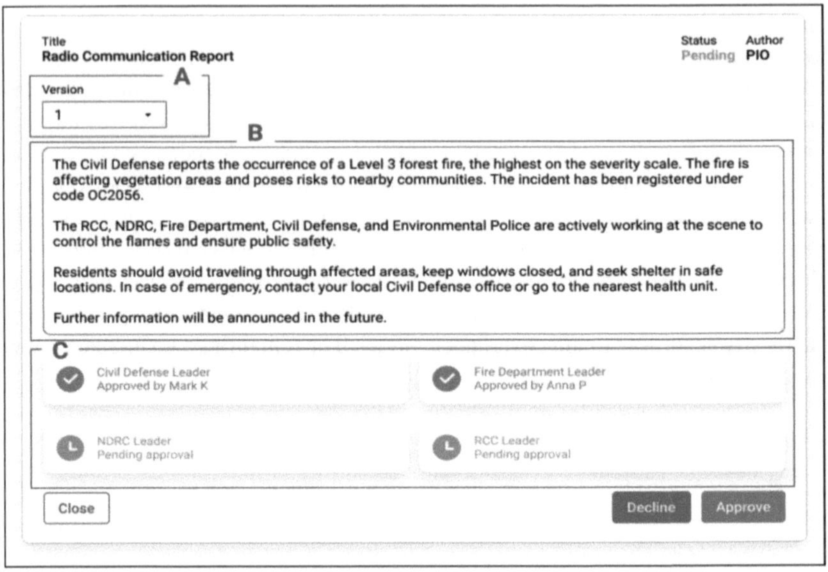

Fig. 5. Example of a communication report to radios (Source: The Authors)

of the changes made (Fig. 6C). This summary was also created by the GAI, with a *temperature* setting of *0.4* to enable a slightly more "creative" and engaging tone rather than just listing specific word changes. To ensure clarity, aspects such as objectivity, completeness, conciseness, and a formal structure similar to a report were included in the prompt configuration. The aim was to avoid repetition, ambiguity, and to maintain fidelity to the original content.

The prototype was tested in a controlled experimental setting in a local network looking at a hypothetical wildfire scenario. No formal and more comprehensive evaluation could be carried out. Functionally, it performed as expected, displaying results effectively through the implemented GUI, interacting with ChatGPT as needed, and processing its responses appropriately and quickly considering different types of data and sources.

After the prototype has been informally shown to some few professionals from the addressed civil defense agency, they agreed on the potential enhancements provided by the GAI in the messages exchange with the selected actors, giving more clarity, readability, and appropriateness in terms of tone and required level of formality for each type of communication without exceeding the standards established by the institutions. All this can be configured, adapted to each civil defense's culture, working protocols, and needs. The model showed being capable of quickly refining messages in a clear and adaptable manner, highlighting all modifications made to the text so they can be validated and refined by the actors.

A direct comparison with other studies was not possible to be made as no existing research implementing CDSS for ND with GAI integration was found in the literature.

Although the system is restricted to specific, duly registered and validated users, security measures have been implemented to ensure that prompts are executed as intended,

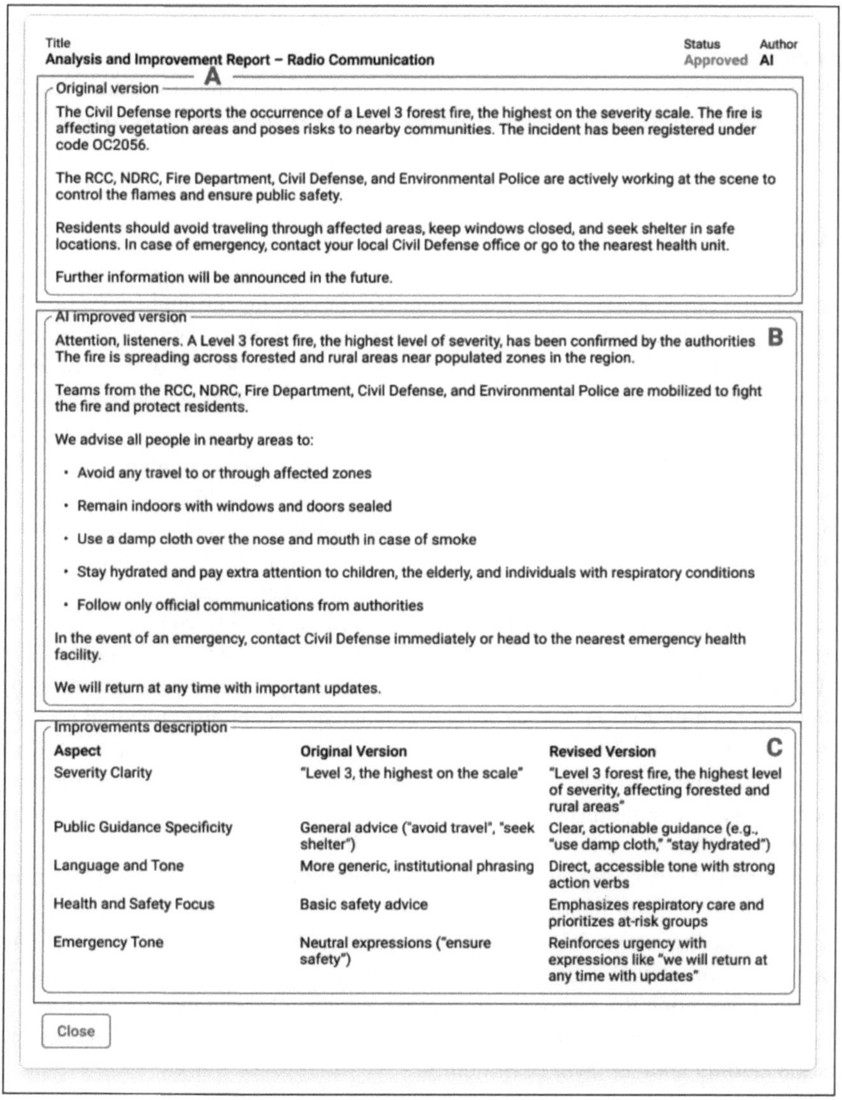

Fig. 6. Report with suggested improvements (Source: The Authors)

mitigating the risk of prompt injection. Among these measures are the separation of instructions and user-provided data using clear delimiters: system-level instructions are designated as 'system' while user inputs are defined as 'user'.

To address potential hallucinations, the system performs cross-validation against official documents and protocols provided by Civil Defense. It also allows for human operator oversight and review, supported by activity logs. In case of inaccurate responses, the system returns standardized messages requesting input adjustments or additional information. These templates are subsequently completed and executed by authorized operators, either during incident initiation or in real time, depending on the situational requirements.

From an implementation standpoint, integrating the CDSS functionalities with ChatGPT 4.1 turned out to be less challenging than initially expected thanks to its relatively user-friendly API.

6 Conclusions

This study has introduced findings from initial trials exploring the application of generative AI (GAI) to support civil defense decision-makers during collaborative discussions in the context of natural disasters (ND). A software prototype was developed to illustrate this concept, using a wildfire scenario involving a civil defense organization from Florianopolis, a medium-sized city in southern Brazil.

The experimental outcomes, which incorporated the OpenAI ChatGPT 4.1 tool into the system, highlighted some benefits. These included facilitating access to best practices, generating insights, addressing more complex queries that emerge during collaborative discussions, and adapting swiftly to the evolving circumstances of a ND. Furthermore, the system enabled the involvement of selected actors more efficiently and effectively. Overall, this approach showed good potential to enhance collaborative decision-making, also fostering greater transparency throughout the process.

The choice for Large Language Models (LLM) is justified by its ability to operate in highly complex scenarios using natural language, enabling contextual reasoning, adaptability, and scalability in subjective and uncertain environments, such as ND management. This approach seemed more effective than traditional methods primarily due to its capacity to handle unstructured inputs and generate natural language responses that support collaborative interactions among multiple actors.

Although GAI can offer significant benefits, it should be regarded as a supplementary tool. Plenty of information about an ND is not stored as data, and many decisions should take local contexts into account in managing the various phases of ND. Additionally, decision-makers must be highly skilled in crafting effective prompts for GAI tools and interpreting the responses in context, especially given the known issues such as hallucinations. Prompts can sometimes become excessively lengthy depending on the situation, adding another layer of difficulty.

This first prototype now serves as a foundation for future enhancements, allowing support for additional scenarios and situations. Moving forward, the research aims to incorporate voice-based interactions for more seamless human-system interactions; explore machine learning mechanisms to enable the CDSS to learn from past decisions and enrich existing action protocols; implement adaptive governance controls to respond to evolving ND, allowing dynamic partnerships, *ad-hoc* decisions, and access to new data; and implementing more complex collaborative scenarios involving multiple rounds of discussions and analyses of "what-if" scenarios.

References

1. United Nations Office for Disaster Risk Reduction. Global assessment report on disaster risk reduction: Our world at risk: Transforming governance for a resilient future. https://www.undrr.org/gar2022-our-world-risk
2. Munich, R: Natural catastrophe report 2024: analysis, assessments, positions (2024). https://www.munichre.com/en/solutions/analytics/natcatservice.html
3. Our World in Data: Global mortality rates from disasters, 1900–2020 (2025). https://www.ourworldindata.org
4. United Nations Office for Disaster Risk Reduction. Sendai Framework for Disaster Risk Reduction 2015–2030. www.undrr.org
5. Federal Emergency Management Agency (FEMA). Principles of disaster management and response efficiency. www.fema.gov. Acesso em: 11 Jul 2025
6. Zanchett, P.S., Rabelo, R.J.: Towards a reference architecture for collaborative decision support systems for natural disasters management. In: Proceedings PRO-VE'2024 – 25th IFIP Working Conference on Virtual Enterprises and Collaborative Networks, pp. 207–223. Springer (2024). https://doi.org/10.1007/978-3-031-71739-0_14
7. Gilligan, J.M.: Participatory simulations of urban flooding for learning and decision support. In: Winter Simulation Conference (WSC), pp. 3174–3175 (2015). IEEE Press
8. Bly, J., Francescutti, L.H., Weiss, D.: Disaster management: a state-of-the-art review. In: Natural Hazards, Intech Open (2021)
9. Bassano, C., et al.: An experience-based decision support system for supporting governance in enterprise. In: Applied Human Factors and Ergonomics and the Affiliated Conferences, AHFE 2015. Proceedings Procedia Manufacturing, pp. 3559–3566 (2015). https://doi.org/10.1016/j.promfg.2015.07.709
10. Tavares, J.F., da Silva Gonçalves, L., Gonçalves, P., Borges, M.R.S.: A systematic review on the use of groupware technologies in emergency management. In: Information Technology in Disaster Risk Reduction, vol. 550. Springer (2019). https://doi.org/10.1007/978-3-030-32169-7_3
11. Comes, T., Mayag, B., Negre, E.: Decision support for disaster risk management: Integrating vulnerabilities into early-warning systems. Information Systems for Crisis Response and Management in Mediterranean Countries, pp. 178–191 (2014)
12. Warner, J., Dewulf, A.: Disaster risk and decision-making. Oxford Research Encyclopedia of Natural Hazard Science (2023). https://doi.org/10.1093/acrefore/9780199389407.013.419
13. Filip, F.G., Zamfirescu, C.B., Ciurea, C.: Collaborative decision-making: concepts, methods, and supporting information and communication technologies. In: International Conference on Production Research, Springer, pp. 90–106 (2021)
14. Drissen-Silva, M.V., Rabelo, R.J.: A collaborative decision support framework for managing the evolution of virtual enterprises. Int. J. Prod. Res. **47**(17), 4833–4854 (2009). https://doi.org/10.1080/00207540902847389
15. Inan, I., Beydoun, G., Pradhan, B.: Developing a decision support system for Disaster Management: case study of an Indonesia volcano eruption. Int. J. Disaster Risk Reduct. **31**, 711–721 (2018)
16. Asimakopoulou, E., et al.: PERMS: an efficient rescue route planning system in disasters. Appl. Soft Comput. **111**, 107667 (2021)
17. Konate, J., Gueye, A., Zaraté, P., Camilleri, G.: Collaborative decision-making: a proposal of a semi-automatic facilitation based on an ontology. Int. J. Inform. Technol. Decis. Mak. 447–470 (2022). https://doi.org/10.1142/S0219622022500420
18. Liu, S., Zaraté, P.: Knowledge based decision support systems: a survey on technologies and application domains. Int. J. Decis. Support Syst. Technol. **6**(3), 21–44 (2014)

19. Nunes, I., Jannach, D.: A systematic review and taxonomy of explanations in decision support and recommender systems. User Model. User-Adap. Inter. **27**(4–5), 393–444 (2017)
20. Power, D.J.: Decision support systems: concepts and resources for managers, p. 69. Faculty Book Gallery (2002). ISBN 1-56720-497-X HD30.213. https://scholarworks.uni.edu/facbook/67
21. Sengar, S.S., Hasan, A.B., Kumar, S.: Generative artificial intelligence: a systematic review and applications. Multimed. Tools Appl. (2024). https://doi.org/10.1007/s11042-024-20016-1
22. Mailliez, M.; Chevroton, H.; Briand, C.; Truillet, P.; Lemercier, C. (2023). Stepping stone to smarter supervision systems: a human-centered multidisciplinary framework, Academic Press, 89–118
23. Paramesha, M., Rane, N., Rane, J.: Enhancing Resilience through Generative Artificial Intelligence such as ChatGPT (2024). https://doi.org/10.2139/ssrn.4832533
24. Oosthuizen, M.J.H.: Action research, topics in australasian library and information studies, research methods for students, academics and professionals. In: Williamson, K., et al. (eds.), pp. 159–175 (2002), https://doi.org/10.1016/B978-1-876938-42-0.50017-4
25. World Meteorological Organization. State of the climate in 2023 (2023). https://public.wmo.int/en/resources/state-of-the-climate
26. Mohammadian, M., Yamin, M.: Intelligent decision making and analysis using fuzzy cognitive maps for disaster recovery planning. Int. J. Inf. Technol. **9**, 225–238 (2017)
27. Shah, N., et al.: The rising role of big data analytics and IoT in disaster management: recent advances, taxonomy and prospects. IEEE Access **7**, 54595–54614 (2019)
28. Turban, E.; Aronson, J. E.; Liang, T. P. (2018). Decision support systems and intelligent systems. Pearson Education
29. Bessis, N., Dobre, C. (eds.): Big Data and Internet of Things: A Roadmap for Smart Environments. SCI, vol. 546. Springer, Cham (2014)
30. Li, J., Wang, X.: Intelligent decision support systems for emergency management. J. Risk Uncertainty Eng. Syst. **6**(2), 04020015 (2020)
31. Papadopoulos, T., Gunasekaran, A.: Big data and analytics in disaster management. Ann. Oper. Res. **283**(1–2), 1–4 (2019)
32. Yin, J., Xu, S.: A framework for intelligent decision support systems in disaster management. Int. J. Disaster Risk Reduct. **52**, 101936 (2021)
33. Smith, J., Johnson, K., Williams, L.: AI-driven common operational picture for multi-agency disaster response. J. Crisis Emergency Manage. **15**(2), 123–138 (2023)
34. Jones, A., Chen, B.: Intelligent task allocation and communication optimization in emergency operations. Int. J. Disaster Risk Reduct. **98**, 104123 (2024)
35. Siemon, D., Kaya, M.-F., Elshan, E.: Artificial Intelligence in Group Decision and Negotiation. Springer (2025)
36. Ghaffarian, S., Taghikhah, F.R., Maier, H.R.: Explainable artificial intelligence in disaster risk management: achievements and prospective futures. Int. J. Disaster Risk Reduct. **98**, 104123 (2023). https://doi.org/10.1016/j.ijdrr.2023.104123
37. Tan, S.C., Chen, W., Chua, B.L.: Leveraging generative artificial intelligence based on large language models for collaborative learning. Learn.: Res. Pract. **9**(2), 125–134 (2023). https://doi.org/10.1080/23735082.2023.2258895
38. Brown, S., Davis, M.: Retrieval-augmented generation for reliable language model responses in critical domains. In: Proceedings of the 2023 Conference on AI Systems, pp. 456–465 (2023)

39. Garcia, P., Lee, H.: Real-time document summarization for emergency managers using large language models with RAG. In: Proceedings of the 20th International Conference on Information Systems for Crisis Response and Management (ISCRAM 2023) (2023)
40. Sahoo, P., Singh, A.K., Saha, S., Jain, V., Mondal, S., Chadha, A.: A systematic survey of prompt engineering in large language models: Techniques and applications (2024). arXiv preprint arXiv:2402.07927

Leveraging AI Data Analytics Methodology for Social Sustainability of Working Environments: An Integrated Framework

Diletta Tosetto[1](✉), Andrea Zangiacomi[2], David F. Nettleton[3], Giulia Perin[1], and Rosanna Fornasiero[1]

[1] CNR-IEIIT, National Research Council, Padua, Italy
{dilettatosetto,giuliaperin,rosanna.fornasiero}@cnr.it
[2] CNR-STIIMA, National Research Council, Milan, Italy
andrea.zangiacomi@stiima.cnr.it
[3] IRIS Technology Solutions, Barcelona, Spain
david.nettleton@iris-eng.com

Abstract. This study presents an AI-enhanced framework to evaluate the social sustainability of working environments in European industrial systems. Focusing on four key dimensions (Gender Gap, Employment by Skill, Safety at Work, and Digital Skill Gap) the framework leverages machine learning techniques (clustering and decision trees) to classify and compare countries' social sustainability profiles over time. Results highlight significant disparities across European nations and temporal improvements in some indicators, reflecting increased policy attention. The integrated human–AI approach supports transparent, data-driven decision-making for policymakers and collaborative networks, contributing to harmonized, socially sustainable industrial development across the EU.

Keywords: social sustainability · AI-based analysis · industrial context · data-driven decision-making

1 Introduction

In an era of increasing global uncertainty, pressing sustainability challenges – social, economic, and environmental – are making improved decision-making processes at national and sectoral levels essential, supported by appropriate indicators [1].

While economic and environmental aspects have been widely studied [2], social sustainability remains an underexplored yet essential dimension [3]. Social challenges related to industrial activities, like employment disparities, gender gaps, and skills shortages, can impact the supply chain ability to adapt and respond to crises [4]. Moreover, measuring and monitoring these issues is essential for anticipating risks and guiding effective policy-making, especially in light of the implementation of Industry 5.0 paradigm [5].

Published by Springer Nature Switzerland AG 2026
L. M. Camarinha-Matos et al. (Eds.): PRO-VE 2025, IFIP AICT 770, pp. 500–519, 2026.
https://doi.org/10.1007/978-3-032-05673-3_30

Achieving social sustainability within CNs requires coordination among diverse stakeholders and the ability to monitor complex social dynamics across organisational and national boundaries. However, the lack of shared performance indicators and real-time decision-support tools often limits the effectiveness of collaboration [6]. Despite increasing attention, there remains a lack of standardized indicators to assess how collaboration contributes to sustainability and resilience. To enhance decision-making processes, there is a growing need for integrated frameworks supported by digital tools, real-time data, and decision support functionalities [7].

Moreover, the human-AI hybrid collaboration could ensure that AI acts as an augmentation tool rather than a substitute: it can provide interpretable outputs that support, rather than replace, human judgment. In CNs, where coordination, negotiation, and value alignment among human actors are essential, such human-in-the-loop AI systems foster transparency, trust, and shared understanding. Overall, it is necessary to develop frameworks to assess and improve social sustainability. By translating complex socio-economic data into clear, actionable insights, it strengthens informed decision-making and facilitates more focused, effective interventions.

Main gaps emerging from research can be summarized as follows. Firstly, available studies mostly focused on the definition of social indicators for monitoring specific sectors such as, for example, agriculture [8] and energy [9]. Sets of indicators capable of covering various working contexts and industries still must be properly identified. Moreover, it is necessary to define the appropriate boundaries to quantify targets for the identified indicators [10]. A comprehensive view of the social sustainability of working environments across different countries with a set of indicators commonly accepted and systematized is also missing. Finally, there is the need to leverage the potential of AI-driven tools [11, 12] and methods to facilitate the interpretation of indicators going beyond a static view and enabling more informed decision-making.

This research addresses the need for a systematic approach to assessing social sustainability by developing an AI-enhanced monitoring framework focused on the social dimension of sustainability in industrial systems.

We reviewed literature with a particular focus on workforce-related aspects of industrial social sustainability to identify relevant indicators.

Data for the most important EU manufacturing countries were extracted from Eurostat and aggregated into four macro-areas: Gender Gap, Employment by Skill Level, Digital Skill Gap, and Safety at Work. By applying clustering algorithms and decision tree techniques, countries were grouped according to similarities in social sustainability conditions. The hybrid approach integrates human expertise in indicator selection and interpretation with machine learning techniques for pattern recognition and classification. This enables a data-driven classification of social sustainability profiles. This synergy offers transparent, scalable, and actionable insights to support policymakers and Collaborative Networks (CNs) in designing tailored interventions, ensuring alignment across the EU industrial base, and promoting a level playing field.

The AI-enhanced framework proposed in this study contributes to filling this gap, assist CNs and policymakers in promoting socially sustainable industrial development within the European Union.

This study offers an interdisciplinary contribution by applying established machine learning methods to the domain of industrial social sustainability. The goal is to extract policy-relevant insights and enhance decision-making capabilities across countries and time periods. The novelty of the work lies in bridging technical AI tools with societal and policy challenges, specifically offering a decision-support framework that goes beyond purely technical AI research and contributes to more informed and targeted policy interventions.

2 Literature Background

In the face of growing global disruptions, from pandemics to climate-related events and geopolitical tensions, ensuring socially sustainable and adaptive industrial systems has become a priority. While economic and environmental aspects of sustainability are well established in both practice and scholarship, the social dimension remains less developed, despite its centrality in shaping collaborative capacity and long-term sustainability [13].

The ability of an industry to function effectively under pressure and adapt to changing conditions is closely linked to the state of its workforce and the broader social context in which it operates. To operationalize social sustainability in industrial assessments, it is essential to identify indicators that reflect both vulnerabilities and strengths within the labour force [14].

Currently, the social dimension includes many different areas, looks at various levels of analysis, and uses multiple methods. Due to this complexity, there is no single agreed-upon way to evaluate social impacts across different scales and researchers commonly adopted a systematic approach to identify social impacts employing multiple indicators. Many studies have focused on the definition of frameworks for specific industrial sectors as, for example, the work proposed by Packer and Zanasi [15] where indicators for social sustainability assessment in bio-district are analysed. Similarly, in Pilane et al. [9] a review of social sustainability indicators and related framework adopted in agriculture is presented. Kumar and A [16] investigated the importance of social impact in the freight transport industry in emerging economies proposing a framework which considers four social sustainability dimensions. The work of Afshari et al. [10] critically reviewed 420 social indicators in the literature and proposed a set of categories according to the different phases of the energy supply chain, related stakeholders and level of decisions. Other research such as Bianchini et al. [17] proposed a framework validated in the luxury industry for the assessment of social indicators in broad categories, according to a circular economy perspective, analysing them in terms of strategic, tactical, and operational levels.

This research focuses on four key macro-areas that capture critical aspects of workforce sustainability: Gender Gap, Employment by Skill, Safety at Work, and Digital Skill Gap. These domains were selected based on their documented relevance in the literature and their potential impact on the social sustainability of industrial systems.

2.1 Gender Equality

Gender inequality remains a pervasive challenge that undermines the inclusiveness and robustness of labour markets. Research has shown that women are often concentrated in lower-paying, precarious, and informal employment, with limited access to senior positions and career advancement [18]. These structural disparities not only affect individual well-being and economic opportunity but also compromise organizational resilience, as diverse and inclusive workforces have been found to enhance adaptive capacity and innovation [19]. Particularly in global supply chains, gender-based inequalities persist in areas such as wage equity, access to decent work, and representation in decision-making roles [20]. Initiatives in the fashion industry, such as Chloé's Social Performance & Leverage (SP&L) tool, aim to systematically assess and improve gender equity, highlighting its importance as a core resilience factor [21]. Moreover, integrating gender indicators into sustainability assessments aligns with Sustainable Development Goal 5 and supports organizational compliance with ESG frameworks that emphasize the importance of social sustainability dimensions, including diversity and inclusion [22].

2.2 Employment by Skill

The alignment between workers' qualifications and labour market demands is essential for ensuring a responsive and resilient industrial base. Skills mismatches (both overqualification and underqualification) can hinder organizational productivity, constrain career mobility, and exacerbate inequality in access to employment [23]. Several studies have emphasized the importance of linking educational attainment to occupational outcomes to better understand structural vulnerabilities in the workforce [24]. The integration of workers across different skill levels is critical for labour market resilience and inclusiveness. Recent evidence shows that the decline in middle-skill employment is less a result of displacement and more due to fewer younger workers entering these roles, often transitioning instead into low-skill occupations despite having middle-level qualifications [25]. This misalignment reflects inefficiencies in how educational backgrounds are matched to labour market needs, with potential consequences for productivity, social mobility, and economic stability [26].

2.3 Safety at Work

Occupational safety and health are fundamental components of decent work and a resilient labour system. Unsafe working conditions, manifested through high rates of fatal and non-fatal accidents, can severely disrupt organizational performance, reduce workforce availability, and damage firm reputation, particularly in supply chain–intensive industries [27]. The ability to prevent and manage workplace incidents is increasingly recognized as a core dimension of social sustainability, directly affecting not only individual well-being but also the broader capacity of firms and industries to respond to shocks and maintain continuity. International frameworks, such as the ILO's conventions on occupational safety and the EU's Vision Zero strategy, emphasize the role of systematic accident monitoring as key for evaluating working conditions and identifying vulnerable sectors. The use of comparable indicators across countries enables early detection of systemic risks and informs policies aimed at improving labour protections in alignment with SDG 8 on decent work and economic growth [28].

2.4 Digital Skill Gap

As digital transformation accelerates across industries, the availability of a workforce equipped with relevant digital competencies has become a key enabler of organizational adaptability and long-term resilience. Digital skills (ranging from basic ICT literacy to advanced data analytics and automation proficiency) are increasingly required across all sectors, making their diffusion a critical element of social sustainability and economic competitiveness [29]. The digital skill gap has emerged as a central challenge for both organizational competitiveness and inclusive economic participation. Lack of digital skills can limit workers' access to job opportunities, while also reducing firms' ability to implement technological innovations that drive efficiency and resilience [30, 31]. Recent data show that only 54% of individuals in the EU possess at least basic digital skills, with considerable variation by age, gender, and educational background [32]. These disparities highlight systemic barriers that must be addressed to ensure equitable access to digital work and avoid the creation of "digital divides" in the labour market. From a supply chain perspective, digitally skilled workers are essential for managing disruptions, enabling real-time analytics, and supporting the deployment of Industry 4.0 technologies [33, 34].

These indicators, drawn from established literature and institutional data sources, offer insight into both vulnerabilities and capabilities within the labour force. When processed through AI-enabled clustering techniques, they support the diagnosis of systemic weaknesses and the design of targeted interventions within collaborative human-AI industrial networks.

3 Proposing a Framework for Social Sustainability

Social sustainability is a core pillar of sustainable development, broadly concerned with enhancing human well-being, promoting equity, and ensuring the long-term viability of communities and societies [35, 36]. It is a multidimensional and context-dependent construct that encompasses both individual and collective dimensions of human and social capital. Key elements include access to basic services, health and safety, human rights, community development, and inclusive governance [37, 38].

Within this broad framework, this study specifically focuses on the social sustainability of the workforce, a critical yet often under-monitored dimension of sustainability in industrial systems. We define workforce social sustainability as the set of practices and conditions that ensure fair, safe, and inclusive working environments, while protecting labour rights, supporting worker well-being, and enabling long-term participation in the labour market [36, 39].

It includes, but is not limited to:

- Equitable access to employment and opportunities [37];
- Worker health, safety, and security [40, 41];
- Fair remuneration, non-discrimination, and inclusion [39, 42, 43];
- Participation in workplace decision-making [44];
- Ethical and regulatory compliance [38].

Given its dynamic and context-sensitive nature, social sustainability remains difficult to standardise and measure [37]. Nevertheless, it is increasingly acknowledged as central to the governance of global supply chains and to the development of adaptive and inclusive industrial systems [42, 45]. Our aim is to offer a more comprehensive and data-driven approach to assessing workforce social sustainability.

Building on this understanding, the present study proposes an AI-enhanced monitoring framework based on Eurostat indicators, designed to assess workforce-related social sustainability in European industrial workplaces and to support evidence-based policy and decision-making.

To evaluate social sustainability in industrial settings, we propose a framework built around four macro-areas that capture key dimensions of the social sustainability of the workforce. These are: Gender Gap, Employment by Skill, Digital Skill Gap, and Safety at Work. Each macro-area is operationalized through a set of indicators, selected based on relevance in literature and data availability across European countries from 2014 to 2023:

- Gender Gap highlights gender disparities in employment rates, pay, job precariousness, and access to senior positions.
- Employment by Skill examines how individuals with different educational backgrounds engage with the labour market, focusing on mismatches between qualifications and roles while linking economic activity with education.
- Safety at Work addresses workplace well-being by monitoring the incidence of occupational accidents, thereby providing insights into work-related risks and safety standards across countries.
- Digital Skill Gap measures the availability and employment of digitally skilled individuals, which is critical for enabling a technology-driven economy.

Table 1 presents the complete list of indicators within each macro-area, along with a short description and the main references from the literature.

To illustrate how this framework can be operationalized, we report a snapshot of selected indicators for the year 2022 across a sample of European countries. Table 2 below provide descriptive statistics for each macro-area. This yearly snapshot helps to compare the social sustainability performance between countries and identify gaps or strengths in each dimension.

Based on the presented data, some European countries stand out for their strong and balanced performance across the different dimensions of social sustainability, mainly due, especially for what concerns Nordic countries, to their related well-known welfare and labour policies that provide significant rights and protections to employees. These countries stand out for their strong social protection systems, high levels of unionization, and a work culture that prioritizes workers' well-being. Sweden and the Netherlands emerge as the most socially sustainable, consistently showing low rates of workplace accidents, strong gender equality outcomes (including low employment and pay gaps and high female leadership representation), high levels of individual digital skills, and inclusive labour markets for low-skilled workers. Ireland also performs well in terms of digital capabilities and gender inclusiveness, although its high level of over-qualification suggests inefficiencies in the alignment between education and employment. In contrast, countries like Italy, Romania, and Poland face recurring challenges: high gender

Table 1. Indicators by Macro-Area

Macro-Area	Indicator	Description	References
1. Gender Equality	**1.1 Gender Employment Gap**	Difference between employment rates of men and women aged 20–64.	[18–20, 22]
	1.2 Gender Pay Gap	Percentage difference in average gross hourly earnings between men and women.	
	1.3 Precarious Employment	Percentage of women in precarious employment.	
	1.4 Women in Senior Management	Percentage of women holding executive-level positions.	
2. Employment by Skill	**2.1 Employment Rate of Low-Skilled Persons**	Employment of low-skilled individuals (elementary education) as a proportion of the total population of low-skilled individuals (ages 20- 64).	[23, 24, 26]
	2.2 Overqualification	Employees who are overqualified for their positions.	
	2.3 Employment by Education (Medium/High Skill)	Employment of upper-secondary, post-secondary, and highly educated individuals among total employees.	
3. Safety at Work	**3.1 Fatal Accidents**	Number of fatal occupational accidents per 100.000 workers.	[27, 28]
	3.2 Non-fatal Accidents	Number of non-fatal occupational accidents per 100.000 workers.	
4. Digital Skill Gap	**4.1 Employment of ICT Educated Persons**	Employment of ICT educated persons/Total labour force with ICT education	[29–34]

(*continued*)

Table 1. *(continued)*

Macro-Area	Indicator	Description	References
	4.2 Employed ICT Specialists	ICT Specialist employed on total Employment	
	4.3 Individual Digital Skills	Individuals' level of digital skills (above basic digital skills)	

Table 2. Overview of Social Indicators (2022). ":" indicates that data is not available

Countries	Gender Equality (%)				Employment by Skill (%)			Safety at Work (per 100k workers)		Digital Skill Gap (%)		
	1.1	1.2	1.3	1.4	2.1	2.2	2.3	3.1	3.2	4.1	4.2	4.3
Czechia	14,9%	18,4%	0,2%	21,9%	55,1%	14,3%	95,6%	1,85	758,49	96,1%	4,3%	69,1%
Germany	7,7%	17,7%	0,3%	37,2%	53,5%	21,6%	88,4%	3,49	2799,69	89,2%	4,7%	59,7%
Ireland	11,4%	9,3%	1,3%	33,7%	65,1%	20,1%	85,4%	0,74	1483,98	97,7%	4,9%	52,2%
Spain	11,2%	9,2%	2,0%	35,7%	58,0%	14,3%	90,5%	1,70	612,48	96,6%	4,2%	58,9%
France	5,8%	12,8%	3,8%	45,2%	53,9%	28,4%	90,6%	0,97	794,05	94,1%	6,2%	72,9%
Italy	19,7%	3,8%	1,5%	42,6%	52,8%	22,3%	73,5%	2,03	1429,18	89,3%	4,1%	45,8%
Hungary	9,8%	17,5%	0,9%	10,4%	68,1%	15,2%	84,1%	0,31	1057,11	94,7%	6,9%	82,7%
Netherlands	7,9%	14,0%	0,7%	41,6%	69,7%	15,1%	65,2%	1,27	468,19	96,6%	4,3%	44,3%
Poland	12,9%	7,8%	2,2%	24,2%	47,2%	19,4%	96,4%	2,89	2573,17	91,8%	4,5%	56,0%
Portugal	5,8%	6,3%	1,0%	33,3%	44,9%	16,6%	87,2%	2,26	56,56	97,6%	2,6%	27,7%
Romania	18,6%	1,5%	:	17,7%	58,9%	36,0%	70,4%	2,03	2463,12	87,8%	4,4%	66,2%
Sweden	5,7%	10,4%	1,4%	35,2%	59,9%	13,6%	90,9%	0,76	851,31	91,2%	8,7%	66,4%

employment gaps, low individual digital skills, and, in the case of Romania and Hungary, very low female representation in leadership positions. France and Portugal, while scoring positively in some indicators (e.g., female employment or low-skilled worker inclusion), show high rates of workplace accidents, indicating structural weaknesses in occupational safety. Overall, this analysis highlights how social sustainability is a multidimensional phenomenon and stresses the importance of integrated policy efforts to reduce inequalities and foster inclusion across all the examined areas.

By aggregating indicators across these four macro-areas, this framework provides a comprehensive and dynamic tool to monitor and compare the social sustainability performance of national labour markets over time. This multidimensional approach is aligned with previous efforts to quantify and evaluate sustainability in social dimensions [e.g. 46–48].

4 Designing an AI-based Data Analytics Methodology for Social Sustainability: Preliminary Results

4.1 Indicator Selection and Normalization

All indicators were extracted from Eurostat, however, not all were used in their raw form. Some were processed after download, for instance, the indicator 2.3 (Employment by education – Medium and High skill) was derived by dividing the number of employees with upper secondary, post-secondary, and tertiary education (levels 3–8) by the total number of employees.

To enable the analysis, one representative indicator was selected for each macro-area. This selection was informed by a review of relevant literature and expert judgment, aiming to identify metrics that are both accessible at cross-country level and meaningful in capturing key aspects of social sustainability. The selected indicators are:

- Gender employment gap (for Gender Equality)
- Overqualification rate (for Employment by Skills)
- Non-fatal accidents (for Safety at Work)
- Employment of ICT educated persons (for Digital Skills Gap)

To facilitate cross-country comparison and build a synthetic view of each country's performance, the selected indicators were normalised.

This process reduces heterogeneity in units and scales while preserving the interpretability of the original variables. Each indicator was normalised using min-max scaling based on the full dataset spanning from 2014 to 2022. The normalisation formula is as follows:

$$x_{norm,i} = \frac{x_i - x_{min}}{x_{max} - x_{min}} \quad (1)$$

where x_i is the observed value for country i, x_{min} and x_{max} are the minimum and maximum values observed across all countries and years for that indicator, $x_{norm,i}$ is the resulting normalised value, scaled between 0 and 1.

4.2 Data Selection into Time Periods

Initially, different datasets were assembled and processed using clustering and decision tree algorithms, as well as various statistical analyses (principal component analysis, regression models, correlations, means, and standard deviations). The original plan was to compare individual years with a significant time gap (e.g., 2014 vs. 2022). However, we later opted to group the data into two multi-year periods: 2014–2018 and 2019–2022. By comparing these two periods, we can not only observe how countries evolved over time but also assess the consistency of their cluster membership and the changes in indicator dispersion over time, all within the same visual representation.

4.3 Data Analytics Background

Firstly, we clarify that in the current work, the AI we have applied consists of "machine learning" algorithms for data analytics, namely, unsupervised learning (clustering) and supervised learning (decision tree), which are linked as a data analytics pipeline. This approach is particularly valuable in contexts where no reliable a priori labeling exists for supervised learning, or where such labeling is difficult to obtain or lacks confidence.

The K-means [49] clustering algorithm is a widely used unsupervised machine learning algorithm which groups a set of data records into clusters, based on the similarity of the data points. The algorithm defines a number of centroids (or cluster centers) to iteratively assign data points to the nearest centroid. Then it recalculates the position of the centroids based on the assigned points. This is performed iteratively until a quality threshold is obtained (usually based on minimizing the intra-cluster distance and maximizing the inter-cluster distance).

In the current work, as well as having information value in itself, the clustering is used to supply the predictive labels (cluster ids) for the decision tree algorithm. This is useful when a pre-defined labelling does not exist for the data, which is the present case [11].

Cluster validation was performed using the elbow/knee method combined with entropy considerations. For both datasets (2014–2018 and 2019–2022), the optimal number of clusters was determined to be four. The elbow heuristic identifies the ideal number of clusters (k) by plotting the within-cluster sum of squares (WCSS) against k and locating the inflection point where the rate of decrease sharply diminishes. In our implementation, the Python parameter model.inertia_ was used in conjunction with the KneeLocator function to determine this point.

The decision tree algorithm [12, 50] used in the current work (from Python scikit-learn) represents an optimized version of the CART algorithm [51], and it is a supervised machine learning algorithm which is frequently applied for classification of variables. It constructs a model with a tree-like structure composed of nodes and branches, where each node represents a decision rule based on specific threshold for specific attributes selected by the algorithm as representative of the phenomenon under study. The decision tree progressively splits the data into subsets based on the outcome of the previous decision rule (True/False), defining the branches of the tree-like structure. This process goes on until a terminal node (leaf) is reached, completing the classification (e.g. class = 1).

A key part of a decision tree induction algorithm is the "information gain measure" which forms the basis of modern information theory developed by Shannon [52] and applied to the construction of decision tree by Hunt [53]. In the context of the partition of a training data set, the heuristic has a key dependence on an information gain calculation to evaluate which attribute to incorporate next, and where to incorporate it in the decision tree.

Let T be a set of training examples, each of the form $(x, y) = (x_1, x_2, x_3, ..., x_k, y)$ where $x_a \in vals(a)$ is the value of the ath attribute of example x and y is the corresponding class label. The information gain for an attribute a is defined in terms of entropy $H()$ as follows:

$$IG(T, a) = H(T) - \sum_{v\hat{I}vals(a)} \frac{|\{x\hat{I}T|x_a = v\}|}{|T|}.H(\{x\hat{I}T|x_a = v\}) \quad (2)$$

The mutual information is equal to the total entropy for an attribute if for each of the attribute values a unique classification can be made for the result attribute. In this case, the relative entropies subtracted from the total entropy are 0.

For the decision tree implementation, we used the DecisionTreeClassifier from the Python Scikit-Learn library. This classifier supports different criteria via the criterion parameter, such as ‘entropy’ (ID3 information gain metric) and ‘gini’ (CART metric). After testing, we selected the ‘entropy’ criterion because it yielded results more interpretable by domain experts. Feature importance is implicitly embedded in the information gain calculation, guiding the selection and positioning of features in the tree—features near the root represent more general attributes, while those deeper in the tree correspond to more specific splits.

Model accuracy was evaluated using Scikit-Learn’s accuracy score, which measures the proportion of correctly predicted labels on the test set. The training process was repeated for 5 iterations, with the model achieving the highest accuracy retained as the final model.

In the current work, the clustering and decision tree techniques provide a machine learning capability to the evaluation of the socio-economic indicators for each country and period, which help to interpret and evaluate the performance between countries and over time.

4.4 Clustering and Decision Tree

In this section, the results are presented of the application of the AI data analytics pipeline (clustering and decision tree) to the two datasets for the selected ranges 2014–2018 and 2019–2022.

Data 2014–2018. With reference to Fig. 1, it can be observed that countries such as Germany and Sweden exhibit relatively small dispersion over the years 2014–2018, whereas Italy and Portugal show a wider dispersion. A wider dispersion indicates greater variation in the indicator values during this period. Figure 1 also shows that Spain, Portugal, and France belong to the same cluster (cluster 0).

As described previously, the WCSS inertia metric was used to identify the optimal number of clusters. For the clustering in Fig. 1, the WCSS values for 1 to 10 clusters (rounded to two decimal places) were: [13.85, 7.64, 5.66, 4.47, 3.32, 2.69, 2.07, 1.63, 1.30, 1.00]. Using these values, the Python KneeLocator function identified 4 as the optimal number of clusters.

Looking at Table 3, the average values for each cluster reveal that cluster 2 has the most “favorable” indicators (low values for the first three indicators and high for the fourth). Cluster 0 is considered “less favorable”, as it has relatively high average values for indicators 2 and 3 and a relatively low average value for indicator 4. Cluster 1 demonstrates “mixed favorability”, with relatively high values for indicators 1 and 2 (not favorable) and a high value for indicator 4 (favorable). Finally, cluster 3 is classified as "less favorable", showing a relatively high average value for indicator 1 and a low value for indicator 4, despite relatively low values for indicators 2 and 3. This could suggest an overall evaluation of "mixed favorability," although the influence of indicators 1 and 4 may arguably place it closer to "less favorable".

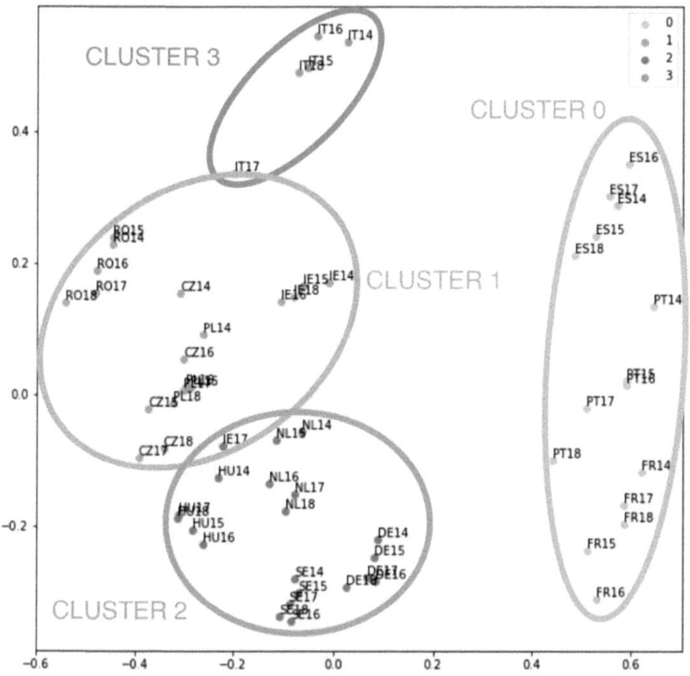

Fig. 1. Clustering of country data for 2014–2018. Standard two-letter ISO 3166–1 country codes represent European countries, with the two-digit number following each code indicating the year (e.g., "IE14" corresponds to Ireland in 2014). The color scheme represents cluster membership.

Data 2019–2022. With reference to Fig. 3, it can be seen that countries like the Netherlands and Sweden exhibit relatively small dispersion over the years 2019–2022, whereas Spain and Portugal show a wider dispersion. A wider dispersion indicates greater variation in the indicator values during this period. Interestingly, Ireland is assigned to two different clusters: cluster 0 for the years 2019–2020, and cluster 3 for 2021–2022. This suggests a significant change in its profile between these two periods.

The WCSS inertia metric was again employed to determine the optimal number of clusters. For the clustering shown in Fig. 3, the WCSS values for 1 to 10 clusters (rounded to two decimal places) were: [9.58, 5.70, 3.94, 2.74, 1.88, 1.31, 0.97, 0.75, 0.56, 0.44]. Based on these values, the Python KneeLocator function identified 4 as the optimal number of clusters.

Looking at Table 4, the average values for each cluster reveal that cluster 3 has the most "favorable" indicators (low values for the first three indicators and high for

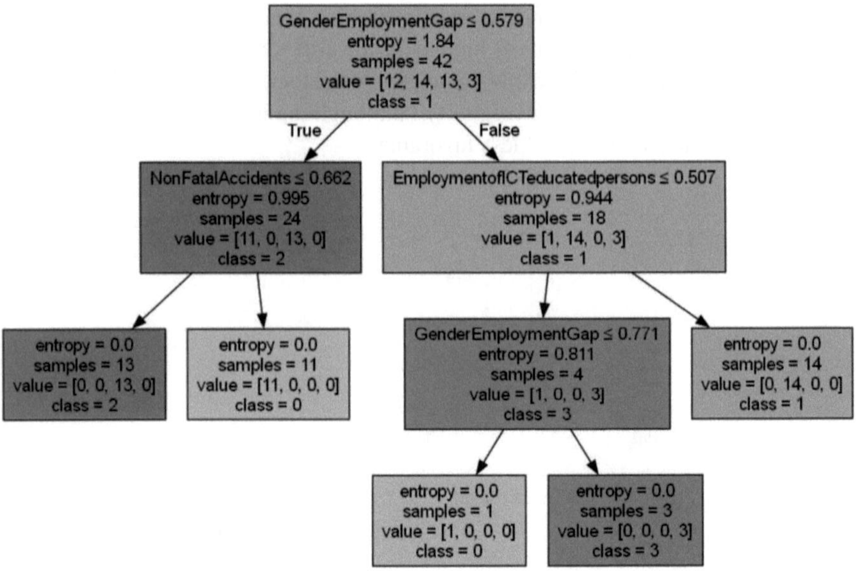

Fig. 2. Decision Tree of country data for 2014–2018

Table 3. Cluster data for 2014–2018

	Average values 2014-2018			
Cluster	**Gender Employment Gap**	**Overqualification**	**Non Fatal Accidents**	**Employment of ICT educated persons**
0	0,4	0,64	0,87	0,4
1	0,75	0,52	0,15	0,73
2	0,42	0,41	0,31	0,76
3	0,97	0,42	0,37	0,29
Overall Average	**0,57**	**0,51**	**0,4**	**0,62**

the fourth). Cluster 2 is "less favorable" as it has a relatively high average value for indicator 2 and a relatively low average value for indicator 4. Cluster 1 shows "mixed favorability", with a relatively high value for indicator 3 (unfavorable), relatively low values for indicators 1 and 2, and a high value for indicator 4 (favorable). Finally, cluster 0 also exhibits "mixed favorability", characterized by a relatively high average value for indicator 1 and a high value for indicator 4, despite relatively low values for indicators 2 and 3. This could result in an overall evaluation of "mixed favorability", although the weights of indicators 1 and 4 might arguably place it closer to "less favorable".

As mentioned earlier with respect to the clustering, Ireland (years 2021–2022) is now placed in cluster 3 due to its favorable values for indicators 3 and 4, whereas it belonged to cluster 0 (along with Romania, Czechia, and others, where it was grouped during all years 2014–2018) for 2019–2020. This reflects a significant improvement for Ireland. Additionally, Italy moved from a "less favorable" cluster in 2014–2018 to a "mixed favorability" cluster in 2019–2022.

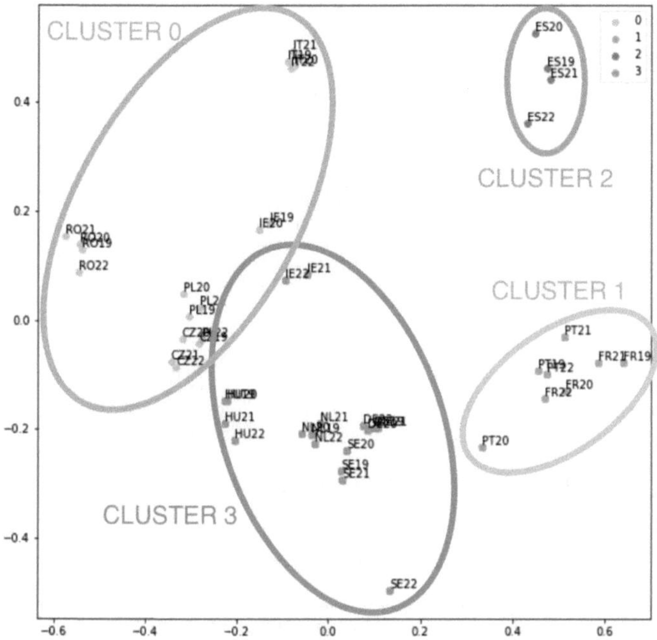

Fig. 3. Clustering of country data for 2019–2022. Standard two-letter ISO 3166–1 country codes represent European countries, with the two-digit number following each code indicating the year (e.g., "IE14" corresponds to Ireland in 2014). The color scheme represents cluster membership.

Comparison of data 2014–2018 vs 2019–2022. Comparing the two time periods in terms of clustering (Figs. 1 and 3), the overall groupings and country positions appear largely consistent. However, in the latter period (2019–2022), countries such as Italy, the Netherlands, and Romania exhibit reduced dispersion, indicating less variability in the indicator values over time.

This trend may be attributed to the fact that a decade ago, the concept of social sustainability was still emerging, and limited attention was given by industry and policymakers to systematically monitor these factors. In recent years, the growing interest in social sustainability has led many countries to adopt more robust policies and strategies, which have likely contributed to more stable and convergent indicator values.

Regarding the key indicators selected by the decision tree analysis (Figs. 2 and 4), the "Gender Employment Gap" remains the most prominent determinant, followed by "Non-Fatal Accidents." Notably, "Employment of ICT Educated Persons," which played a role in the 2014–2018 period, is not selected in the 2019–2022 period. This suggests a reduced criticality of this indicator, possibly due to improved performance and a narrower gap among countries.

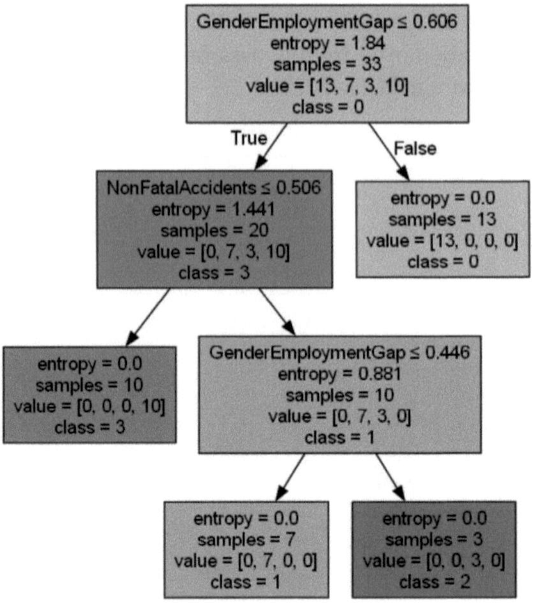

Fig. 4. Decision Tree of country data for 2019–2022

Table 4. Cluster data for 2019–2022

	Average values 2019-2022			
Cluster	**Gender Employment Gap**	**Overqualification**	**Non Fatal Accidents**	**Employment of ICT educated persons**
0	0,82	0,51	0,18	0,76
1	0,29	0,48	0,81	0,61
2	0,56	0,97	0,67	0,34
3	0,4	0,46	0,28	0,81
Overall Average	**0,55**	**0,52**	**0,36**	**0,72**

As described previously, decision tree precision was evaluated using Python's DecisionTreeClassifier with the 'entropy' criterion. The model was trained over 5 iterations, selecting the one with the highest accuracy. The best accuracy obtained for the 2014–2018 decision tree (Fig. 2) was 0.94, while for the 2019–2022 tree (Fig. 4) it reached 1.0.

Overall, a positive trend is observed when comparing the two periods, with general improvements across the analysed indicators (Tables 3 and 4). At the cluster level, the "most favorable" cluster (including Germany, Sweden, etc.) shows improvement across all indicators, with the exception of indicator 2 (overqualification).

Some clusters, such as Cluster 0 and Cluster 3 in 2014–2018, and Cluster 1 and Cluster 2 in 2019–2022, comprise countries with "weaker" performance across most indicators. Nevertheless, the cluster including France and Portugal (Cluster 0 in the first period, Cluster 1 in the second) shows marked improvement across all indicators, although indicators 3 and 4 still lag behind the average. The cluster that previously included Italy (Cluster 3 in 2014–2018) and later included Spain (Cluster 2 in 2019–2022) presents a mixed evolution, with improvements in indicators 1 and 4, but persistent challenges in indicators 2 and 3.

Finally, the "mixed favorability" cluster, comprising countries such as Czechia and Poland, experienced a slight decline in performance for indicators 1 and 3, with only marginal improvements in indicators 2 and 4.

4.5 Implications for Policy-Making

To illustrate the practical utility of this framework for decision-makers, consider the case of Ireland, which shifted from Cluster 0 in 2019–2020 to Cluster 3 in 2021–2022. This transition suggests an improvement in key social sustainability indicators, particularly in non-fatal workplace accidents and employment of ICT-educated individuals. A policymaker could use such insights to investigate which specific interventions (e.g., targeted labor safety programs or ICT education incentives) were implemented during this period, and consider replicating them in countries still lagging in those areas, such as Portugal or Spain.

Moreover, the persistent prominence of the Gender Employment Gap as the most influential variable across both periods (as identified by the decision tree analysis) highlights that addressing this gap remains a central challenge for achieving social sustainability. Policymakers in countries consistently associated with high values for this indicator (e.g., cluster 3 in 2014–2018 and cluster 0 in 2019–2022) may consider prioritizing gender-inclusive employment policies, such as expanding access to childcare services, introducing gender pay transparency measures, or supporting programs that foster women's participation in STEM and ICT sectors. Similarly, the consistently high levels of overqualification (indicator 2) observed in countries like Italy and Spain across both periods and multiple clusters may signal the need for labor market reforms or more effective skill-matching strategies.

By identifying clusters of countries with similar performance profiles and the key indicators driving divergence, the framework supports policymakers in tailoring interventions not only by country but also by typology, thereby enabling more targeted and potentially more effective policy responses.

5 Conclusions and Future Work

In a time of growing global uncertainty, addressing social, economic, and environmental sustainability challenges with the support of suitable indicators is crucial for better decision-making at national and sectoral levels. Social sustainability remains a less explored but vital, and monitoring and measuring social factors such as employment disparities or gender gaps are essential for risk anticipation and effective policymaking. This research proposes a systematic, AI-enhanced framework to assess social sustainability within industrial systems. Despite it represents a first attempt to understand how such hybrid approach can support policymakers and CNs in designing proper instruments and measures, preliminary results from this study reveal notable social sustainability disparities among European countries and underscore the important role of AI in improving the management of CNs. The set of indicators proposed aims to go beyond existing sector specific studies towards a thorough overview of the social sustainability of work environments in various countries, according to the future definition of a standardized and widely accepted set of indicators, capable of covering various working contexts and industries. In addition, the presented framework accomplishes the need to utilize AI-based tools and approaches to improve how indicators are understood, allowing for dynamic insights rather than a fixed view and helping to make better, more informed decisions. The adoption of clustering and decision tree techniques, as machine learning tools, enable indeed to analyze socio-economic indicators for various countries and time frames, facilitating a deeper understanding and comparison of their performance both geographically and temporally. Importantly, while the machine learning techniques used are standard, their integration into a policy-oriented framework represents the main contribution of this work. The strength of the approach lies in bridging AI-based analytics with social and policy domains, rather than in algorithmic innovation. In doing so, this study contributes to the growing field of research that leverages data science and AI for societal impact. Main limitations of the work consist in the definition of indicators at state level, and further developments will have to consider diversification options according to sectoral peculiarities and needs. Moreover, the robustness of the framework and clustering technique need to be tested with further base of data and including other countries, also from developing regions. From a data analytics point of view, future work could compare the DBSCAN clustering algorithm (Density-Based Spatial Clustering of Applications with Noise), which may better handle outliers, with the k-Means method. For supervised learning, SHAP (SHapley Additive exPlanations) could be benchmarked as an explainability technique against decision trees, as SHAP provides a model-agnostic approach to quantify the contribution of each feature to the prediction outcome.

References

1. Dizdaroglu, D.: The role of indicator-based sustainability assessment in policy and the decision-making process: a review and outlook. Sustainability **9**(6), 1018 (2017)
2. Luthin, A., Traverso, M., Crawford, R.H.: Circular life cycle sustainability assessment: an integrated framework. J. Ind. Ecol. **28**(1), 41–58 (2024)
3. Jabbarzadeh, A., Fahimnia, B., Sabouhi, F.: Resilient and sustainable supply chain design: sustainability analysis under disruption risks. Int. J. Prod. Res. **56**(17), 5945–5968 (2018)
4. Atanda, J.O.: Developing a social sustainability assessment framework. Sustain. Cities Soc. **44**, 237–252 (2019)
5. Silva, M.E., Pereira, M.M.O., Hendry, L.C.: Embracing change in tandem: resilience and sustainability together transforming supply chains. Int. J. Oper. Prod. Manag. **43**(1), 166–196 (2023)
6. Chalmeta, R., Barbeito-Caamaño, A.M.: Framework for using online social networks for sustainability awareness. Online Inf. Rev. **48**(2), 334–353 (2024)
7. Sadic, S., Demir, E., Crispim, J.: Towards a connected world: collaborative networks as a tool to accomplish the SDGs. J. Clean. Prod. **462**, 142726 (2024)

8. Pilane, P.M., Jordaan, H., Bahta, Y.T.: A Systematic Review of Social Sustainability Indicators for Water Use along the Agricultural Value Chain. Hydrology **11**(5), 72 (2024)
9. Afshari, H., Agnihotri, S., Searcy, C., Jaber, M.Y.: Social sustainability indicators: a comprehensive review with application in the energy sector. Sustain. Prod. Consum. **31**, 263–286 (2022)
10. Heide, M., Skrøder, N.K.P., Steffen, S.F., Hauschild, M., Ryberg, M.: Framework for selecting and setting boundaries for social sustainability indicators in a life cycle perspective. IOP Conf. Ser.: Earth Environ. Sci. **1196**(1), 012080 (2023)
11. Rokach, L., Maimon, O.: Clustering methods. In: Data Mining and Knowledge Discovery Handbook, pp. 321–352 (2005)
12. Suthaharan, S.: Decision Tree Learning. In: Suthaharan, S. (ed.) Machine Learning Models and Algorithms for Big Data Classification: Thinking with Examples for Effective Learning, pp. 237–269. Springer, Cham (2016)
13. Negri, M., Huaccho Huatuco, L., Stevenson, M.: Integrating sustainability and resilience in the supply chain: a systematic literature review and research agenda. Bus. Strateg. Environ. **30**(7), 2858–2886 (2021)
14. European Commission: 2020 Strategic Foresight Report: Charting the Course Towards a More Resilient Europe – Resilience Dashboards. Publications Office of the European Union, Luxembourg (2020). https://commission.europa.eu/strategy-and-policy/strategic-foresight/2020-strategic-foresight-report/resilience-dashboards_en
15. Packer, G., Zanasi, C.: Comparing social sustainability assessment indicators and tools for bio-districts: building an analytical framework. Front. Sustain. Food Syst. **7**, 1229505 (2023)
16. Kumar, A., Ramesh, A.: An MCDM framework for assessment of social sustainability indicators of the freight transport industry under uncertainty. A multi-company perspective. J. Enterp. Inf. Manag. **33**(5), 1023–1058 (2020)
17. Bianchini, A., Guarnieri, P., Rossi, J.: A framework to assess social indicators in a circular economy perspective. Sustainability **14**(13), 7970 (2022)
18. Silva, M.E., Fritz, M.M.C., Seuring, S., Matos, S.: Guest editorial: the social sustainability of global supply chains – a critical perspective on current practices and its transformative potential. Int. J. Phys. Distrib. Logist. Manag. **53**(1), 1–12 (2023)
19. Østergaard, C.R., Timmermans, B., Kristinsson, K.: Does a different view create something new? the effect of employee diversity on innovation. Res. Policy **40**(3), 500–509 (2011)
20. Barrientos, S., Gereffi, G., Rossi, A.: Economic and social upgrading in global production networks: a new paradigm for a changing world. Int. Labour Rev. **150**(3–4) (2011)
21. Vogue Business: Chloé Wants to Improve Fashion's Social Impacts. It's a Big Ask. Vogue Business (2021)
22. Eccles, R.G., Ioannou, I., Serafeim, G.: The impact of corporate sustainability on organizational processes and performance. Manag. Sci. **60**(11), 2835–2857 (2014)
23. McGuinness, S., Pouliakas, K., Redmond, P.: Skills mismatch: concepts, measurement and policy approaches. J. Econ. Surv. **32**(4), 985–1015 (2018)
24. Green, F., Henseke, G.: The changing graduate labour market: analysis using a new indicator of graduate jobs. IZA J. Labor Policy **5**(1), 1–25 (2016)
25. OECD: Employment Outlook 2020: Worker Security and the COVID-19 Crisis. OECD Publishing, Paris (2020)
26. Quintini, G.: Right for the Job: Over-Qualified or Under-Skilled? OECD Soc. Employ. Migr. Work. Pap. No. 120. OECD Publishing, Paris (2011)
27. Gimenez, C., Sierra, V., Rodon, J.: Sustainable operations: their impact on the triple bottom line. Int. J. Prod. Econ. **140**(1), 149–159 (2012)
28. ILO: Safety and Health at the Heart of the Future of Work: Building on 100 Years of Experience. ILO, Geneva (2023). https://www.ilo.org/global/topics/safety-and-health-at-work/lang-en/index.htm

29. Brynjolfsson, E., McAfee, A.: The Second Machine Age: Work, Progress, and Prosperity in a Time of Brilliant Technologies. W.W. Norton & Company, New York (2014)
30. Cedefop: Going Digital Means Skilling for Digital: Using Big Data to Track Emerging Digital Skill Needs. Publications Office of the European Union, Luxembourg (2020). https://www.cedefop.europa.eu/en/publications-and-resources/publications/9188
31. World Economic Forum: The Future of Jobs Report 2020. World Economic Forum, Geneva (2020). https://www.weforum.org/reports/the-future-of-jobs-report-2020
32. DESI: Digital Economy and Society Index. European Commission (2022)
33. Dubey, R., Bryde, D.J., Blome, C., Giannakis, M.: Facilitating artificial intelligence adoption in supply chains: an institutional theory perspective. J. Bus. Res. **128**, 961–972 (2021)
34. Ivanov, D., Dolgui, A., Sokolov, B.: The impact of digital technology and industry 4.0 on the ripple effect and supply chain risk analytics. Int. J. Prod. Res. **58**(3), 833–845 (2020)
35. Uttam, N., Dutta, P., Singh, A.: Influence of stakeholders on supply chain social sustainability: new insights from small suppliers in the Indian manufacturing sector. J. Clean. Prod. **444**, 141015 (2024)
36. Najjar, M., Yasin, M.M., Bell, M.Z., Bell, D.: Investigating social sustainability practices in global supply networks: a fuzzy-set qualitative comparative analysis. J. Clean. Prod. **447**, 141590 (2024)
37. Najjar, M., Small, M.H., Yasin, M.M.: Adopting and extending social sustainability practices across the supply chain. Compet. Forum **17**(1), 105–113 (2019)
38. Govindan, K., Shaw, M., Majumdar, A.: Social sustainability tensions in multi-tier supply chain: a systematic literature review towards conceptual framework development. J. Clean. Prod. **279**, 123075 (2021)
39. Amiri, S.E., Heikkilä, J., Moshtari, M.: Supplier relationship management approaches for diffusing social sustainability in supply chains: a systematic literature review. Int.. Procurem. Manage. **21**(5), 1–22 (2024)
40. Vaughan, Y.: Preventing modern slavery through corporate social responsibility disclosure: an analysis of the US hospitality and tourism industry. Cornell Hospitality Quart. **65**(1), 120–135 (2024)
41. Larimian, T., Sadeghi, A.: Measuring urban social sustainability: scale development and validation. Environ. Plann. B: Urban Analytic. City Sci. **48**(4), 621–637 (2021)
42. Silva, M.E., Fritz, M.M., Seuring, S., Matos, S.: Guest editorial: the social sustainability of global supply chains–a critical perspective on current practices and its transformative potential. Int. J. Phys. Distrib. Logist. Manag. **53**(1), 1–12 (2023)
43. Nath, V., Agrawal, R.: Agility and lean practices as antecedents of supply chain social sustainability. Int. J. Oper. Prod. Manag. **40**(10), 1589–1611 (2020)
44. Leal Filho, W., et al.: Barriers to institutional social sustainability. Sustain. Sci. **17**(6), 2615–2630 (2022)
45. Meehan, J., Pinnington, B.D.: Modern slavery in supply chains: insights through strategic ambiguity. Int. J. Oper. Prod. Manag. **41**(2), 77–101 (2021)
46. Badri Ahmadi, H., Kusi-Sarpong, S., Rezaei, J.: Assessing the social sustainability of supply chains using best worst method. Resour. Conserv. Recycl. **126**, 99–106 (2017)
47. Kumar, D., Garg, C.P.: Evaluating sustainable supply chain indicators using fuzzy AHP: case of indian automotive industry. Benchmarking Int. J. **24**, 1742–1766 (2017)
48. Narimissa, O., Kangarani-Farahani, A., Molla-Alizadeh-Zavardehi, S.: Evaluation of sustainable supply chain management performance: indicators. Sustain. Dev. **28**(1), 118–131 (2020)
49. Sinaga, K.P., Yang, M.S.: Unsupervised k-means clustering algorithm. IEEE Access **8**, 80716–80727 (2020)
50. Priyanka, K.D.: Decision tree classifier: a detailed survey. Int. J. Inf. Decis. Sci. **12**(3), 246–269 (2020)

51. Lamrini, B.: Contribution to decision tree induction with python: a review. IntechOpen (2020)
52. Shannon, C.E.: A mathematical theory of communication. Bell Syst. Tech. J. **27**(3), 379–423 (1948)
53. Hunt, E.B., Marin, J., Stone, P.J.: Experiments in Induction. Academic Press, New York (1966)

Author Index

Published by Springer Nature Switzerland AG 2026
L. M. Camarinha-Matos et al. (Eds.): PRO-VE 2025, IFIP AICT 770, pp. 521–523, 2026.
https://doi.org/10.1007/978-3-032-05673-3

MIX
Papier aus verantwortungsvollen Quellen
Paper from responsible sources
FSC® C105338

If you have any concerns about our products,
you can contact us on
ProductSafety@springernature.com

In case Publisher is established outside the EU,
the EU authorized representative is:
Springer Nature Customer Service Center GmbH
Europaplatz 3, 69115 Heidelberg, Germany

Printed by Libri Plureos GmbH
in Hamburg, Germany